Mac OS® X Leopard™
Bible

Updates

For updates to this book, please visit `www.wiley.com/go/leopard`.

Mac OS® X Leopard™ Bible

Samuel A. Litt,
Thomas Clancy, Jr.,
Warren Gottlieb,
Douglas Heyman,
Elizabeth Costa-Woods,
Seth B. Zuckerman

WILEY

Wiley Publishing, Inc.

Mac OS® X Leopard™ Bible

Published by
Wiley Publishing, Inc.
10475 Crosspoint Boulevard
Indianapolis, IN 46256
www.wiley.com

Copyright © 2008 by Wiley Publishing, Inc., Indianapolis, Indiana

Published simultaneously in Canada

ISBN: 978-0-470-04174-1

Manufactured in the United States of America

10 9 8 7 6 5 4 3 2 1

For general information on our other products and services or to obtain technical support, please contact our Customer Care Department within the U.S. at (800) 762-2974, outside the U.S. at (317) 572-3993 or fax (317) 572-4002.

Library of Congress Control Number: 2007926396

Trademarks: Wiley, the Wiley logo, and related trade dress are trademarks or registered trademarks of John Wiley & Sons, Inc. and/or its affiliates, in the United States and other countries, and may not be used without written permission. Mac OS and Leopard are trademarks or registered trademarks of Apple Computer, Inc. All other trademarks are the property of their respective owners. Wiley Publishing, Inc., is not associated with any product or vendor mentioned in this book.

Wiley also publishes its books in a variety of electronic formats. Some content that appears in print may not be available in electronic books.

About the Authors

Samuel A. Litt is an Apple Certified Technical Coordinator as well as a certified member of the Apple Consultants Network. He is a certified SonicWall security administrator, a Qlogic certified systems administrator, and is certified in Xsan and Avid Unity Storage Area Networks as well. He currently serves as the manager of Macintosh support for the Department of Information Technology and Telecommunications for the City of New York. His works published to date include the *Mac OS X Administration Basics Exam Cram Study Guide*, the *Mac OS X Bible* Panther and Leopard Editions, as well as several articles for Element K's *Mac Administrator Journal* and Quark's *X-RAY* magazine.

Elizabeth Costa-Woods has been working with Macs for over 10 years and is an Apple certified technical coordinator. She is currently a Macintosh systems administrator for the City of New York. Before working for the City, she worked for the City Volunteer Corp., Cause Effective, and the Nathan Cummings Foundation. Elizabeth currently lives in New Jersey with her husband and two children.

Thomas Clancy, Jr. is one of the four co-owners of Valiant Technology Inc., a consulting and support company in New York City, along with Douglas Heyman, Gene McMurray, and Georg J. Dauterman. Tom attended Queens College (CUNY) and received his bachelor's degree in European history and secondary education. Tom currently lives in Putnam County, New York (aka Ice Station Zebra) with his wife, Alice, and their two sons, Jack and Theodore. Tom would like to point out that he is not related to "the" Tom Clancy, although he is proud to be related to another Tom Clancy: his dad, a retired veteran of the FDNY (which is a more important job than "World Famous Author" no matter how you slice it, although the pay isn't as good, sadly).

Douglas Heyman is a longtime Mac user, having cut his teeth on the venerable System 6 on an SE with two 800K floppies and 1MB of memory. Early in his career, he worked as a writer and managing editor of numerous literary projects. Shifting his professional focus to one of his main loves, technology, he spent the next few years as in-house IT staff for a major New York advertising agency. He currently works as a founding partner and vice president of Valiant Technology, a New York-based technology solutions provider. Born and raised in New Jersey, he resides in Hoboken with his loving wife, Suzanne, and his wondrous son, Marcus.

Warren Gottlieb is a professional Mac IT consultant who has transformed a deeply rooted passion and hobby into his profession. He has worked with a number of the top Macintosh tech firms in New York City, and currently works with DeepTech, Inc., home to Manhattan's finest Mac specialists. Warren is pursuing his studies at the City University of New York's Hunter College. Despite many solitary Mac-hours, Warren most enjoys interacting with people, and loves to aid in their comfort and enjoyment of technology. Warren resides in Queens, New York, in a home where the ratio of Macs to humans is 3:1, and where AirTunes plays well into the early hours of the morning.

Seth B. Zuckerman is founder and president of Expert CC, LLC, a premier full-service Macintosh consulting firm based in sunny Long Beach, NY, servicing the Tri-State area. Expert CC's focus is the support and service of industries tasked with multimedia and digital arts content creation. Seth is an Apple certified technical coordinator as well as a certified SonicWall security administrator, holding Apple XSAN, Apple Desktop repair, and Apple Portable repair certifications.

For Mom & Dad

Sam

For Lewis, Vivi, and Java for bringing me to life.

Thanks very much!

To Jack and Ted Clancy.

You are my inspiration.

—Tom "Papa" Clancy Jr.

Credits

Acquisitions Editor
Ryan Spence

Project Editor
Martin V. Minner

Technical Editor
Nick Reilingh

Copy Editor
Scott Tullis

Editorial Manager
Robyn Siesky

Business Manager
Amy Knies

Sr. Marketing Manager
Sandy Smith

Vice President and Executive Group Publisher
Richard Swadley

Vice President and Executive Publisher
Bob Ipsen

Vice President and Publisher
Barry Pruett

Project Coordinator
Erin Smith

Graphics and Production Specialists
Stacie Brooks
Shawn Frazier
Jennifer Mayberry
Barbara Moore
Janet Seib
Erin Zeltner

Quality Control Technician
John Greenough

Proofreading
Broccoli Information Management

Indexing
Christine Spina Karpeles

Cover Design
Michael Trent

Cover Illustration
Joyce Haughey

Acknowledgments

Samuel A. Litt: First and foremost, I would like to thank my wife Jodi, and my daughters, Peri and Shana, for their love and devotion. I would like to thank Mom and Dad for their unwavering support. I would also like to thank my colleagues at the City of New York; Paul Cosgrave, Ronald Bergaman, Michael Lebow, Michael Bimonte, Christopher Ianniello, Marcos Merced, Arick Wierson, Jonathon Werbell and Kevin Sheekey as well as countless others for *thinking different* and providing a fertile and stimulating work environment and enabling me to do the job. I would like to thank Kevin Boland, Tommy Milanak, Gary Slobin, Ken Klein, Matt Rosencrans, and Jon Rubinstein for their friendship! Many, many thanks to my super smart and talented coauthors — Lisa, Warren, Tom, Doug, and Seth — without whose participation this project would be naught. A special thanks to the folks at Wiley; the Super Kim Spilker and the Mighty Marty Minner.

Elizabeth Costa-Woods: I'd like to thank my husband, Lewis Woods, for caring for our children while I chased my Mac dreams. It takes a BIG man to do what you've done and I will never forget it. I adore you. Vivianne and Tristan Woods, I am so proud to be your mother. The two of you will always be the biggest accomplishment of my life. To my parental units, you've taught me perfection and hard work and it's gotten me farther than I ever dreamed. I love you both very much. To my siblings, nephews, niece and godchildren, thank you for keeping me laughing. I love you all. To my girls, Rosie and Chantel, thank you for keeping it real and having my back.

Ed Abrahams, thank you for taking a chance on a girl perched atop a pile of coats; in one way or another, you have been the source of every job that I have ever had. Lauren Goldstein, you are an inspiration. I'll never forget you. To my sister, my friend, my advocate, Zanetta Addams-Pilgrim, thank you for your contributions to my career and my life. What would I do without you? To the board and staff of the Nathan Cummings Foundation, thank you for giving me the support and resources to discover my inner-tech. To Sam Litt, I'm your biggest fan. You will always be my mentor and friend.

Thomas Clancy, Jr.: I would like to thank my amazing wife Alice for all the support and the regular brownie donations to my writing sessions. I'd also like to thank my sons Jack and Ted for making my bad days disappear. I'd also like to acknowledge the daily contributions of every one of my team at Valiant: (in order of seniority) Doug Heyman, Gene McMurray, Georg Dauterman, Nick Nightingale, Stephen Zielinski, Andrew Yu, Eric deRuiter, and Andy Rodriguez. You all make going to work every day a joy, and your passion for technology keeps me going!

Douglas Heyman: I would like to thank my beautiful wife for putting up with me while I wrote this book, all of my family for being so supportive, the software developers who granted permission to reproduce their works, and the folks at Valiant Technology not directly represented here:

Gene McMurray, Georg Dauterman, Nick Nightingale, Andrew Yu, Nicole Carpino, Stephen Zielinski, and many more I've surely forgotten. A special thanks to Sam for continuously getting this book together.

Warren Gottlieb: To my twin sister Shari, who has been an unwavering force of support, kindness, and patience, as I tread old ground that is at times frustratingly familiar, yet new and different. From one published author to another, thank you for your immense help! Thank you Mom and Dad, for your unconditional love and attentiveness: Mom, for always making sure that I know, and for your emotional intelligence; Dad, for teaching me the fundamentals that lead to a new world of discovery — "Remember, no matter what happens, you can never break it." And to all those with whom I have had the pleasure of sharing that mantra. Thank you, also, to my friends — your level of support is both awesome and essential. I so very much appreciate those who in my absence pursue me, which is when I need them the most.

Seth B. Zuckerman: I would like to thank Jackie, Manny, Maddy, Maggie, and Minnie for their support throughout the growth of myself and my business. I would like to thank David Salav, Vincent DiSpigno, Ronald Ebner, Scott Schaeffer, Matthew Tannenbaum, and Sam Litt for their technical and industry guidance. I would like to thank Roy Morris for his insistence on my purchasing my first Macintosh computer. I would like to thank my friends, Kenneth Gerber, Michael Damelio, Andrew Sitzer, the Burton's, Anthony Chou, Mindie Schwartz, Sandra Zic, Kim Scharoff, Adam Lilling, Aly Davis, Randy Lerner, The Money Shots, and The Baby Batters. Other random thanks to Nick Manello, Birthright Israel, Irv Gordon, the Bubbamobile, Point Blank, Volvo, and anyone I have forgotten.

Contents at a Glance

Contents

Contents

Contents

Contents

Part II: At Work with Mac OS X   277

Chapter 8: Getting Help 279

Contents

Contents

Contents

Part III: Beyond the Basics of Mac OS X   605

Chapter 16: Printing and Faxing 607

Chapter 17: Managing System Preferences 623

Contents

Contents

According to popular legend, a Mac is so easy to use that you don't need to read books about it. Alas, if only that were true. The fact is that harnessing all the power of Mac OS X would take a substantial amount of time of exploring and tinkering, and not everyone has the time, the inclination, or the patience to devote to the mastery of an operating system. Save your time for having fun with games, surfing the Internet, or perhaps getting some work done. Benefit from the experience of others (in this case, we the authors)! Read this book so that you can leverage the full power of OS X without a lot of ambling around the desktop.

You might be under the impression that you don't need this book because of Apple's supplied Mac OS X Getting Started Guide and on-screen help. Though these are good sources of information, the *Mac OS X Leopard Bible* contains a great deal of information and how-to guidance that you won't find anywhere else.

Part I

Getting to Know Mac OS X

Chapter 1

Introduction and Installation of Mac OS X

From the moment you see Mac OS X, you know that it's different from any other computer operating system on the planet, including earlier iterations of Mac OS. Nothing else looks quite like it. Yet, use it a bit and you'll see that there is familiarity about its operation. Apple has made great efforts to ensure that Macintosh users as well as Windows users can leverage their previous OS skill sets. But what sets Mac OS X apart from its predecessors and its competition is the sum total of its parts.

This chapter provides an overview of the core technologies that comprise Mac OS X. Knowing the core technologies can help you master the overall operation of this world-class operating system. The chapter concludes by examining the system requirements of Mac OS X and its installation.

What Is Mac OS X?

Mac OS X is Apple's answer to the quest for a modern operating system. It combines the power and stability of Unix with the simplicity of Macintosh. In 1996, after continual failed attempts to develop its own next-generation operating system, Apple management looked outside the company and acquired NeXT Software, Inc. NeXT's OS at the time was called OpenStep. It had all the features that Apple desired in a modern OS: protected memory, preemptive multitasking, multithreading, and symmetric multiprocessing. With OpenStep as the foundation, Apple initially designated the code name Rhapsody for its new OS, but as the project matured, it was renamed to Mac OS X, keeping in line with the progression of Apple's existing system software monikers. Apple has enjoyed phenomenal success with Mac OS X, which has been adopted by over 5 million users, and Apple is now generally considered the largest vendor of Unix-based systems on the planet.

Mac OS 10.5 is another evolutionary step in the OS X product line. Apple claims it has more than 300 enhancements. One of the more significant enhancements, though most likely unperceivable to most users, is that the product is now a 64-bit Universal OS that is capable of running 32-bit software without recompilation. What does this mean in layman's terms? Mac OS X 10.5 can be installed on both Intel and PowerPC CPU-based Macs and will continue to run your existing Mac OS X application.

NOTE   Mac OS X is capable of addressing up to a whopping 16 exabytes of virtual memory. An exabyte is equivalent to 1,024 petabytes, and a petabyte is equivalent to 1,024 terabytes — that's a lot of memory.

Core Technologies of Mac OS X

The most important thing to know about Mac OS X is that it is based on open standards. This is because at the heart of OS X is Unix, which has played a major role in the development of the Internet. Because Unix is so Internet-centric, OS X can be integrated in virtually any computing environment. In fact, the X in Mac OS X represents the X in Unix. But fear not; although Mac OS X is a Unix operating system, its operation does not require the mastery of complex Unix command syntax. As Apple publicizes, the command line is there for those who would like to use it, but it isn't required for day-to-day operations. You can make as much or as little use of it as you want.

If OS X were compared to an automobile, you would see a similarity in that both are composed of many parts. All these parts have very distinct functions, and yet all make up a greater whole. Metaphorically speaking, the intention of Apple was to design a vehicle akin to a Formula 1 racing car. When the engineers at Apple set out to build OS X, they pulled together world-class technologies in an effort to build the most advanced consumer operating system the world has ever seen. The following sections take a closer look at these parts.

Darwin

The foundation of OS X is Darwin, which is an open source community/Apple joint effort. Though Darwin is a complete OS in and of itself, the primary objective of the Darwin project was to build an industrial-strength Unix-based operating system core that would provide greater stability and performance compared to all existing iterations of the Mac OS. Reviewing Darwin in detail is beyond the scope of this book. Instead, we review some of Darwin's more marketed features.

Mach microkernel

At the center of Darwin is the Mach microkernel based on FreeBSD 5.x, the foundation that provides basic services for all other parts of the operating system. Mach was developed at Carnegie-Mellon University, and its history is closely tied with BSD Unix (Berkeley Software Distribution). It is Mach that gives OS X the features of protected memory architecture, preemptive multitasking, and symmetric multiprocessing.

Protected memory

Protected memory isolates applications in their own individual memory workspaces. When an application crashes, the program can be terminated without having a negative effect on other running applications or requiring a restart of the computer.

Advance memory management

Advance memory management automatically manages physical RAM and virtual memory dynamically as needed. Virtual memory uses hard disk space in lieu of physical RAM. Information that would normally sit in RAM, but is not currently needed, is transferred to the hard disk to free up physical RAM for the demands of data/applications that need it. This alleviates out-of-memory conditions and eliminates the need, experienced by users of previous Macintosh desktop operating systems, of having to manually adjust memory allocations.

Preemptive multitasking

Mac OS X, like all Mac OS versions since System 7, allows more than one application to be open and operating at the same time. This capability is known as *multitasking.* Prior to OS X, the Mac OS employed a version of multitasking referred to as *cooperative multitasking.* In cooperative multitasking, applications sometimes seemed unresponsive because the system software could not efficiently manage the concurrent demands of multiple running programs. Mac OS X remedies this by implementing *preemptive* multitasking. Preemptive multitasking prioritizes processor tasks by order of importance. This more efficient method of managing processor tasks allows the computer to remain responsive, even during the most processor-intensive tasks.

Symmetric multiprocessing

Symmetric multiprocessing (SMP) provides support for multiprocessor Macintosh computer systems. This allows applications to take advantage of two or more processors by assigning applications to specific processors or by splitting parts of applications, known as *threads,* between multiple processors simultaneously. Mac OS X is further optimized to take advantage of SMP by employing a technique known as *optimized kernel resource locking.* Optimized kernel resource locking provides superior SMP performance by allowing multiple CPUs access to different portions of the kernel simultaneously. Mac OS 10.5 takes multiprocessing another step forward with its multicore processor competency, allowing it to harness the power of up to eight cores simultaneously, which is the maximum number of cores shipping inside of Macintosh computers at the time of this writing.

Graphics technologies in Mac OS X

When it comes to graphics, Mac OS X is one of the most powerful operating systems on the planet. To achieve this power, Mac OS X employs several standards-based technologies that are best-of-class. These technologies include Quartz, OpenGL, and QuickTime. Over the past couple of years, some of the greatest strides in hardware performance have come in the form of video hardware. Mac OS X 10.5 has been optimized to take advantage of this high performance video hardware. Designated as Core Image and Core Animation, this software optimization improves performance by reducing floating-point unit (FPU) CPU utilization by offloading it to the Graphic Processing Unit (GPU) of the video hardware. Not all video cards are Core Image/Animation capable, but it's safe to assume that if your Mac has shipped within the last two years, it will be either fully or partially compliant, because the technology is scaling and is dependent upon hardware capabilities. For a complete list of Core Image/Animation-compliant video cards, visit www.apple.com.

Quartz

Quartz is a powerful two-dimensional (2-D) graphics-rendering system. It has built-in support for the Portable Document Format (PDF), on-the-fly rendering, compositing, and anti-aliasing. It supports multiple font formats, including TrueType, PostScript Type 1, and OpenType. Quartz supports Apple's ColorSync color-management technology, allowing for consistent and accurate color in the print/graphics environment.

OpenGL

Open Graphics Library (OpenGL) started out as a technology initiative by Silicon Graphics, Inc., a manufacturer of high-end graphics workstations. It has since become an industry standard for three-dimensional (3-D) graphics rendering. It provides a standard graphics application programming interface (API) by which software and hardware manufacturers can build 3-D applications and hardware across multiple platforms on a common standard. OpenGL is very prevalent in gaming, computer-aided design (CAD), professional 3-D animation/modeling, and graphic design.

QuickTime

QuickTime is Apple's cross-platform multimedia authoring and distribution engine. It's both a file format and a suite of applications. QuickTime has been around since 1991 and has matured into a very powerful technology. It supports more than 50 media file formats encompassing audio, video, and still images. Some examples of these file formats include AIFF, AVI, JPEG, MIDI, MP3, MPEG-1, PICT, and TIFF. QuickTime has support for real-time video streaming, allowing viewers to tune in to live or prerecorded content on demand.

Aqua

Though Aqua is not a graphics technology in Mac OS X, it is its graphical user interface (GUI). Appearance-wise, it is a dramatic departure from OS 9's Platinum interface, although it retains certain common elements. This allows for greater familiarity for legacy Macintosh operators, thus making the transition to OS X a more intuitive experience.

Mac OS X's application environments

Application environments allow Mac OS X to run its modern OS-enabled applications while simultaneously supporting legacy Mac OS software. An application environment consists of various system resources, components, and services that allow an application to function. Mac OS X has five application environments: Cocoa, Carbon, Java, BSD, and Classic.

Cocoa

Cocoa applications are specifically developed for Mac OS X. Cocoa applications are incompatible with older Macintosh operating systems and, therefore, do not run on Mac OS 9. Cocoa applications take advantage of all of Mac OS X's modern OS features, such as advance memory management, preemptive multitasking, symmetric multiprocessing, and the Aqua interface. Apple evangelizes Cocoa for its modern object-oriented programming techniques and rapid application development tools, which make application development significantly faster and easier than for Carbon. Some examples of Cocoa applications are OS X's Mail and Preview applications as well as Netopia's Timbuktu for Mac OS X.

Carbon

The greatest advantage of the Carbon application environment is that developers can build applications that run in either Mac OS 9 or OS X. When running within OS X, Carbon applications take advantage of most of OS X's modern OS features, including the Aqua interface. In order for Carbon applications to run within Mac OS 9, the CarbonLib library must be present within the Extensions folder within the Mac OS 9 System folder. Ironically, some Carbon applications do not run under Mac OS 9. The most prominent is Microsoft's Office Version X for Mac.

Java

The Mac OS X Java environment is Java 2 Standard Edition-compliant. It can run both Java applications and applets. The key advantage of Java development is that Java applications can run on any platform that contains a cross-compatible Java Virtual Machine.

BSD

The BSD application environment usually deals with command-line executable shell scripts. A shell script is similar to an MS-DOS batch file in that they're both text files that contain a sequence of commands. Interestingly enough, shell scripts do not necessarily have to be executed from the command line. Shell scripts can be implemented within Cocoa applications, allowing them to be executed from the GUI.

Packages and bundles

A *package,* sometimes referred to as a *bundle,* is a single-icon, point-and-click representation of an application. Mac OS X's Carbon and Cocoa applications can be comprised of multiple subordinate files and resources. In the GUI, all of these subordinate pieces are neatly wrapped up into a representation of a single executable file for the end user. To view the contents of an application package, simply press and hold the Control key while highlighting the Carbon or Cocoa application icon. You're then provided the option to show the package's contents. For illustration purposes, Figure 1.1 depicts the contents of Safari for Mac OS X.

Frameworks

Mac OS X frameworks contain dynamically loading code shared by multiple applications. Frameworks alleviate the need for applications that contain common code to individually load that code for each instance of those applications running simultaneously.

FIGURE 1.1

When pondering packages remember the whole is greater than the sum of its parts.

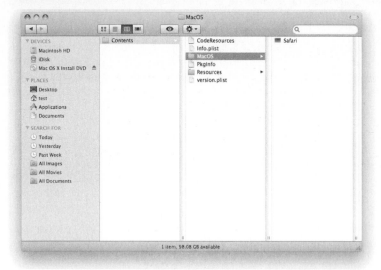

Installation Considerations for Mac OS X

Now that we have reviewed the core technologies of Mac OS X, let's focus on its installation process. Although Mac OS X has a very structured installation process, several variations of installation are available. The user's needs dictate the appropriate installation strategy. However, before any Mac OS X implementation can take place, it is necessary to evaluate the target computer to see whether it meets Apple's official hardware requirements.

Hardware requirements of OS 10.5

Apple's minimum hardware requirements for Mac OS X 10.5 is a factory-shipped Intel or PowerPC G4 867MHz processor with 512MB of RAM (1GB with Developers Tools), 9GB of available hard drive space (12GB with Developers Tools), a DVD drive, a built-in FireWire port, and an Apple-supplied video option. In addition, Boot Camp requires an Intel processor and will run either Windows XP Service Pack 2 or Windows Vista (BYOOS — bring your own OS). Photo Booth requires an iSight camera (built-in or external), USB video class (UVC) camera, or FireWire DV camcorder, and an Intel or PowerPC G5 processor. Backdrop effects require an Intel Core Duo or faster processor. Backdrop effects when using a DV camcorder require fixed focus, exposure, and white balance. iChat Video requires an iSight camera (built-in or external), a USB video class (UVC) camera or FireWire DV camcorder; and a 128-Kbps upstream and downstream Internet connection. Audio chats require a microphone and a 56-Kbps Internet connection. Front Row, Apple's entertainment media console, requires a Mac with built-in IR and an Apple Remote.

Leopard's revised DVD Player requires a 1.6GHz processor or faster for improved de-interlacing. As for third-party hardware, Apple states that OS X natively supports many third-party hardware devices, although some devices may require additional driver updates from their respective manufacturers to utilize a product's full feature set.

Preparing for the installation of OS X

After you've deemed that the target hardware meets OS X's minimum hardware requirements, you need to verify that the target computer's firmware is up to date. *Firmware* is programming that tells a computer's hardware how to behave. Starting with the original iMac, Macintosh computers have used a firmware-upgradeable hardware design. This design element on PowerPC Macs is a component of what is referred to as NewWorld Architecture. Intel Macs have an equivalent known as Extensible Firmware Interface (EFI). The Mac's firmware is contained in a programmable (flashable) read-only memory (PROM). This programmable firmware approach enables Apple to fix technical issues via patches and upgrades like any other software. As a result, this innovation allows Apple to achieve greater hardware stability and overall improved system performance via firmware updates. Using a utility referred to as a Flash-ROM updater, firmware can be upgraded (sometimes referred to as *revved*). The Mac OS 10.5 installer alerts you if your system's firmware is out of date. You can also determine your system's firmware by running Apple System Profiler. Apple's latest firmware may be included on the Mac OS X Install DVD. It can also be obtained either through Mac OS X's built-in Software Update mechanism or from www.info.apple.com/support/downloads.html.

> **NOTE** All PowerPC system firmware updaters released to date by Apple prior to the G5 are available via Mac OS 9 applications only. Updating a system's firmware using the Classic application environment in lieu of booting directly from Mac OS 9 is not recommended and Classic is no longer officially supported within Leopard.

Volume preparation for OS X

A Mac OS X startup volume can be formatted as an Extended (HFS+) or a Unix File System (UFS) volume. An HFS+-formatted volume's single biggest advantage is that it can be prepared as either *case preserving* or *case sensitive*. All Macintosh desktop operating systems to date have used file systems that have been dependent on case-preserving formatted volumes (this includes the old HFS format as well).

The opposite of the case-preserving format is the case-sensitive format. With the case-sensitive format, it is possible to have multiple files named identically in the same location/folder/directory. The only thing that would differentiate the files to the naked eye is the varied use of uppercase and lowercase characters. For example, you may have individual files named DOG, DoG, Dog, dOg, doG, dOG, and dog located in the same folder.

As mentioned previously, OS X also supports another format referred to as the Unix File System (UFS), although it isn't the preferred volume format because it doesn't support AirPort networking and is case sensitive. In addition, UFS volumes are not recognized by Mac OS 9 and their volume names cannot be customized after creation. Apple states that "a UFS format may be desired for developing Unix-based applications *within* OS X," and you should not choose this format unless you specifically need it.

Gathering setup information

Regardless of whether you're upgrading from Mac OS 9 or older versions of Mac OS X, if you want your computer to use the same Internet and network settings, before you install Mac OS X on it you need to make a note of your system's current preferences. Depending upon how you connect to the Internet, one or more of the following settings may need to be recorded. In Mac OS 9, the settings are located in the AppleTalk, File Sharing, TCP/IP, Remote Access, Modem, and Internet control panels. In Mac OS X, the settings are located in the Network and Sharing preference panes as well as in the Internet Connect application. In addition, you may need to get the settings for your e-mail account from your e-mail reader application.

Hard drive backup

To back up today's large hard drives, you need some type of storage device that can accommodate the capacity of your backup. These devices can include, but are not limited to, another internal IDE or SATA hard drive, a FireWire or USB hard drive, or a recordable optical or magnetic media drive. You *can* back up to a Finder-accessible volume by simply dragging and dropping the desired contents to another hard drive; however, before doing so, you need to be the owner of those contents and be sure to select ignore permissions from within the Get Info window of the intended destination volume. Another option to consider is Leopard's Time Machine backup utility, which is covered in greater detail in Chapter 21. Lastly, using a more advanced third-party backup utility, such as Retrospect from Dantz Development or BRU from Tolis Group, has the added benefit of superior logging and verification capabilities to ensure the successful outcome of a backup, in addition to the fact that both products support streaming tape media.

Preparing the destination volume

After you've backed up, you're ready to prepare your intended destination volume for Mac OS X installation. To do so, you need to use the Disk Utility application located on the Mac OS X Install DVD. Disk Utility is covered in Chapter 21.

If you're not installing on an Apple-branded hard disk, and third-party formatting software was used to prepare it, you need to investigate if the formatting software is Mac OS X-compatible. If not, you need to use formatting software that is compatible. Typically, an initialization is required, but some third-party formatting software can update and overwrite an existing driver without the need of an initialization.

A *driver* is a piece of software that enables an operating system to interface or control a hardware device. In general, the operation of driver software requires no action from the end user. All hard drives use driver software. It is imperative that the hard disk driver is compatible with the Mac OS version in use or problems will result.

Running the Mac OS X installer

After the destination volume is prepared, you're ready to run the Mac OS X Installer application, but before doing so, make sure to have your computer plugged in if you're installing on a portable system. You don't want your iBook or PowerBook going to sleep in the middle of an installation. At the time of this writing, the Mac OS 10.5 installer is contained on one DVD, though it's expected that CD media will be an available option by special request when Leopard is released. To install OS X, you're required to boot from the Mac OS X Install DVD. You can achieve this in the following four manners:

- Boot the Macintosh while holding down the C key.
- Use the Startup Manager. To activate the Startup Manager, hold down the Option key at startup. You're then presented with a graphical interface that enables you to select it as a startup disk.
- Select the Mac OS X Install DVD by using Mac OS X's Startup Disk Preference pane.
- You can boot from a Mac OS X Install DVD by inserting the DVD while booted from Mac OS X and locating and double-clicking the Install Mac OS X application, which requires the authorization of an administrator's account.

Figure 1.2 shows the Restart button in the Install Mac OS X window. When the computer starts from the Mac OS X Install DVD, the Installer program starts automatically and presents a series of screens that ask you to make certain choices as described in the following text.

FIGURE 1.2

The Restart button in the Install Mac OS X program restarts the computer with the Mac OS X Install DVD to begin installation.

Select Language

The Mac OS X installer supports installations for many languages. Select the appropriate language for the remainder of the installation process and click Continue.

Welcome

The Welcome screen acts as a prelude to the rest of the installation process. No action is required except for clicking Continue.

More Information

The Read Me screen presents the same contents that can be found in the Read Before You Install document on the Mac OS X Install DVD. Skipping this document is tempting, but the information provided may be important, so you should at least skim it. After reading the information, click Continue.

License

The License screen presents you with OS X's Software Licensing Agreement. The license agreement is filled with legalese, but you may want to look through it so that you know what you're agreeing to. For example, one provision states that you may only install the software on one computer at a time. You must click Continue, and a second confirmation screen appears in the form of a dialog sheet, requesting you to click Agree before you can continue with the installation process.

Make no mistake, Apple's legal department perceives that the License Agreement is important; they provide the convenience of a pop-up menu where you can choose to view it in a language other than English.

Select Destination

The Select Destination screen enables you to choose the destination volume for your Mac OS X installation. Click the Options button and a sheet appears, providing the choices to Upgrade Mac OS X, Archive and Install, and Erase and Install. Here's what those options mean:

- **Install Mac OS X/Upgrade Mac OS X:** Dependent upon whether a previous installation of Mac OS X exists, the first option appears as Install Mac OS X or Upgrade Mac OS X. Install Mac OS X installs Mac OS X for the first time on a specified volume, and Upgrade Mac OS X upgrades an existing installation of Mac OS X while preserving current applications, fonts, and preferences.

- **Archive and Install:** Moves existing System files to a folder named Previous System and then installs a fresh copy of Mac OS X. After a system folder has been designated as previous, it can no longer be used as a valid startup OS. Preserve Users and Network Settings is a suboption under Archive and Install, which facilitates the preservation of user accounts, home folders, and network settings.

- **Erase and Install:** Provides a clean slate. As with the Disk Utility, it erases your hard disk. The Erase and Install option also allows you to choose your disk format: MAC OS Extended (Journaled) or Mac OS Extended (Case-sensitive, Journaled). Journaling may help protect the data on your hard disk from unforeseen failures such as system freezing or power outages. As previously mentioned, *case sensitive* means that it matters whether or not letters are capitalized. For example, passwords in Mac OS X are case sensitive. In some instances, such as in the screen saver password window, the dialog box tells you if the Caps Lock key is pressed, alleviating the frustration of being sure you typed the correct password but having entered it unknowingly in all caps.

> **TIP** If there is a sole ATA/IDE hard drive in your Mac, and the Select a Destination screen does not display an available hard disk to install to, you need to verify that the intended target ATA/IDE drive is configured as a master drive on the bus.

After making your selections, click Continue.

Installation Types

The Installation Types screen provides two choices for installation types. The choices are Install and Customize. By default, the Mac OS X installer starts with the default install which is comprised of the packages Essential System Software, Print Drivers, Additional Fonts, Language Translations, and X11. Upon closer inspection of the Customize Install options, you'll see the mechanism for granularly controlling the selections of the packages that can be installed. Wise use of these selections can eliminate superfluous software from your Mac OS 10.5 install. After choosing your install type and making your selections, click the Install button.

Installing

The OS X installer now begins to verify the condition of your installation media and displays a drop-down dialog sheet providing a progress bar. You can skip this process by clicking the Skip button. When the disk has been verified or skipped, the installer commences the actual OS installation, which lasts about an hour, give or take, depending upon your installation type and selections. For the most part, this is an automated process that leaves you the time-honored task of progress-bar watching.

Finish Up

At this point, the installer performs several optimization and clean-up tasks to complete the installation process.

Stopping the Mac OS X Installer

Until you click the Install button to get the installation process under way, you can stop installation by choosing Installer ➪ Quit Installer. If you do this, the installer displays a dialog box that asks you to confirm that you really want to stop installation. Click the Restart button in this dialog box to have installation stop and your computer restart. When you hear your computer's startup chime, press and hold the Option key to select a valid startup disk other than the Mac OS X Install DVD. You can also eject the Mac OS X Install DVD by pressing the mouse button during restart.

Using the Setup Assistant

After the Mac OS X install process has been completed, the computer automatically reboots. Next, Mac OS X's Setup Assistant automatically launches and you hear some snazzy music as well as see some flashy graphics. You are also audibly prompted to choose if you would like to use Voice Over interface technology throughout the rest of the Setup Assistant process. When this is over, you are presented with the Setup Assistant's Welcome screen, which, depending upon your selections, guides you through the process of transferring user accounts from another system or volume, procuring an Apple ID for purchasing Apple products and services online, registering your OS software, setting up your first user account, and connecting to the Internet.

Welcome

The Welcome screen is where you select the country or region in which the Macintosh will be used. To see selections beyond the default countries, click the box adjacent to the Show All label, located under the selection widow. If you wait about 30 seconds, a modal dialogue sheet appears querying in easy-to-see large text if you require the use of Mac OS X's VoiceOver, Apple's Spoken Interface, to audibly guide you through the setup assistant process. After making your selection, click Continue.

Do You Already Have a Mac?

The Do You Already Have a Mac? screen allows for the migration of user and system data from another Mac, or from another volume on this Mac, or from a Time Machine backup. There is also a selection not to transfer anything. Transferring accounts from one system or volume to another does not affect the contents of the source. As a matter of fact, the transfer of accounts can be performed at any time, by running the Migration Assistant located in the Utilities folder inside of the Applications folder. When transferring an account from one volume or system to the next, the following things can be optionally migrated: Network settings, User accounts (including preferences and e-mail), Documents, and Applications. Apple notes that some applications may not transfer properly, thus requiring a reinstallation; and in order to play transferred songs purchased from the iTunes Music Store, you'll need to de-authorize your old system and authorize your new one. To transfer information from one Mac OS X system to another via FireWire, you'll obviously need a standard FireWire cable and your Mac must be capable of FireWire Target Disk mode.

Keyboard

Simply stated, this screen allows you to select the localized keyboard layout that is appropriate for the operation of your Macintosh specific to your geographic locality.

Select a Wireless Service

This screen assists with the facilitation of network connectivity. As the title implies, it has an obvious slant toward wireless connectivity and displays all visible wireless networks that can be perceived. To access a hidden wireless network click the Other Network option. Don't forget to specify your password (WPA/WEP) if your wireless network requires one. If you do not have a wireless network click Other Network for other options. Here is where you can configure your Mac to be directly attached to a cable or DSL modem as well as a local area network (LAN) via Ethernet. If none of these options suffice, click My computer does not connect to the Internet, and you are taken to the Personalize Your Settings screen. Later, revisit the Network preference pane within the System Preferences application to configure your Network settings.

Enter Your Apple ID

Eerily reminiscent of Microsoft's Passport, an Apple ID lets you make one-click purchases from the iTunes Music, iPhoto, and Apple Stores. If you already possess a .Mac membership, use that as your Apple ID; otherwise, have the Setup Assistant create one for you, or skip the process entirely. If you do elect to create an Apple ID, you are also provided with a 60-day trial membership to .Mac. .Mac is a combination of software and online tools that can enhance your "Internet experience" while using your Mac. After making your selections, click Continue. (For more details on .Mac, see Chapter 14.)

Registration Information

This is the product registration that is automatically sent to Apple when you connect the Mac to the Internet. You cannot leave anything blank except the e-mail address and the company or school. You can skip this screen by pressing ⌘+Q and then pressing the Skip button, which takes you directly to the Create Your Account screen and automatically configures your network settings for DHCP. Otherwise, after completing the Registration Information screen, click Continue. There is also a button for Shut Down, which can be used to shut down the Mac and allow it to be registered.

Personalize Your Settings

The Personalize Your Settings screen is where you select the keyboard layout that is appropriate for the country or region in which the Macintosh will be used. You can change the preference later, after you're into the computer. Make your language selection and click Continue. If you don't see your language, click the box adjacent to the Show All label, located under the selection widow.

Create Your Account

After you've submitted the necessary registration information, you need to set up your user account. Chapter 18 reviews user accounts in detail, but for now suffice it to say that the information you provide is necessary to perform administrative functions within Mac OS X. When creating your account, you'll need to specify both a Name and a Short Name. A Short Name is exactly what it sounds like—a short name. It alleviates the need for typing your whole name. You'll appreciate your short name when user authentication is requested by certain applications or during certain administrative functions within OS X.

A Short Name is automatically generated when you tab from the Name field to the Short Name field. But don't worry — it can be changed. A short name is all lowercase, has a maximum of eight characters, and cannot contain any spaces or the following characters: < > ' " * { } [ ] ( ) ^ ! \ # | & $? ~.

Make sure to pick a Short Name you like, because it can't be changed after the fact. After you've chosen your short name, you'll need to provide a password. Although OS X accepts more than eight characters for this field, it checks only the first eight. The last entry field allows you to provide yourself an optional password hint if desired. Finally, you need to select a picture that serves as an iconic representation of your user account. After making your selections, click Continue.

Select a Picture for This Account

This portion of the Setup Assistant allows you to take a snapshot for iconic representation of your user account if you're using an iSight camera or your Mac has one built-in. Otherwise, you can select one from a stock library within Mac OS X by selecting the Choose from the picture library option.

Select Time Zone

The Select Time Zone screen allows you to specify the time zone the computer will be operating in. Clicking your geographic location or typing the name of the closest city where the computer is located accomplishes this. After making your selection, click Continue.

Set the Date and Time

The Set the Date and Time screen lets you to set your computer's clock and calendar. When you're done, click Continue.

Don't Forget to Register

If by chance your registration information was not successfully sent to Apple or you opted to skip entering as discussed earlier, you'll be prompted with an additional screen stating Don't Forget to Register; just click the Done button at the bottom to move on.

Running Software Update

Finding that the installers provided by manufacturers of media in hand do not contain the most recent version of a product is not uncommon. Usually, software updates can be obtained via a manufacturer's Web site. Apple simplifies this process by automating the update process upon initial OS X startup. If by some chance this does not occur, the process can be manually activated via the Software Update preference panel. (This is reviewed in detail in Chapter 21.) Figure 1.3 shows OS X's Software Update preference panel, an excellent tool for obtaining the latest updates for Mac OS X.

As you can see, building an OS X box is not a difficult task. Taking the time to evaluate your installation considerations and applying the appropriate OS X installation strategy goes a long way toward ensuring a smooth migration from a previous Mac OS version.

FIGURE 1.3

No installation is complete without checking for product updates.

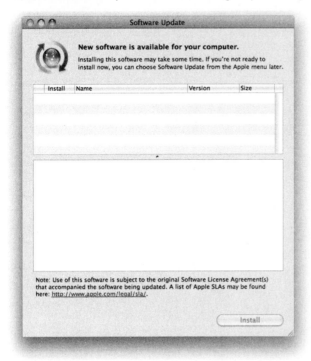

Summary

Mac OS X is a Unix operating system. It is built upon open standards, providing preemptive multitasking, symmetric multiprocessing, protected memory, and advanced memory management, as well as world-class graphics capabilities. Though it may be complex in design on the inside, on the surface, it retains its world-class usability and appearance that customers expect of the Mac OS.

Chapter 2

Exploring the GUI and Personalizing Your Workspace

This chapter will guide you through the Mac OS X environment. Not since the introduction of Mac OS X has the Mac graphical user interface (GUI, pronounced "gooey") seen such a dramatic change. With an updated Finder, new desktop pictures, and new screen savers, OS X just gets better with each version. Mac OS X consists of windows, menus, icons, and control elements. Apple calls this environment *Aqua*. It is an elegant, streamlined interface, rich in color and depth; nevertheless, it is possible to get lost as you explore the world of Aqua.

This chapter describes how to use the objects and controls in OS 10.5. You will learn how to open, close, and resize windows; select, move, and modify groups of icons; and delete files, use Apple's undo command, and create optical discs. This chapter discusses Exposé and introduces you to Spaces, Apple's new window management system. Most importantly, the Finder is explored in detail, and you learn how to use Finder-specific windows, menus, and control methods.

You will learn how to trick out your computer by customizing its appearance and behavior, modify the layout of Finder windows, change your desktop picture, set custom icons, and more. New features like Spaces make it easy to keep your workspace organized. With a little effort, your workspace will not only be functional, but stylish as well.

By the conclusion of this chapter, you will have a greater understanding of the basic elements of OS X as well as the terms and phrases used in following chapters. Before describing menus, windows, icons, and controls, this chapter explains how to begin a session in the Mac OS X environment, and concludes by explaining how you log out, restart, or shut down to end a Mac OS X session.

IN THIS CHAPTER

Starting up and logging in

Meeting your environment

Recognizing the desktop

Saving the screen

Finding out about the Finder

Setting appearance preferences

Working with folders, disks and other volumes

Looking at the Dock

Using Exposé, Dashboard, and Spaces

Sleeping, shutting down, restarting, or logging out

Starting Up and Logging In

Of course, when you first turn on your computer, it must go through a startup process. Startup begins with the Apple startup chime, a signal that the most basic hardware elements are operational. After the chime, the remaining hardware tests continue as the computer tests the hard drive for basic errors. After this, the remaining hardware elements activate as the full operating system software loads into RAM (random access memory) from a disk.

Starting up your computer

You start up a Macintosh by pressing either of the following:

- The power button on the computer
- The power button on most Apple flat-panel displays (on some older display models, the power button only turns the display on or off)

Once upon a time, the familiar Happy Mac icon appeared in the center of the screen while the Mac OS loaded. Mac OS 10.2 retired "Happy Mac," replacing it with a solid gray Apple logo. A spinning set of bars below the Apple logo indicates that the computer is busy loading core OS elements.

Next, a Mac OS X greeting appears, together with a gauge that measures startup progress. The spinning disk changes to an arrow-shaped pointer. This pointer tracks mouse movement, but clicking the mouse button has no effect at this time.

Logging in to Mac OS X

After the startup process has begun and OS X has loaded all of the basic system elements and completed activation of the kernel (background) operations, the login procedure begins. The *login procedure* is the process of identifying yourself to your computer. This is both a means of ensuring that your computer activates your particular environment (called your user account), and keeps unauthorized people from using the computer. The login procedure is mandatory but can be automated. In fact, Mac OS X is initially configured for automatic login and remains that way unless it is set for manual login. Upon completion of the login process, the appropriate user account is activated and the user can interact with the OS X environment.

What login accomplishes

The login procedure accomplishes two things:

- It proves that you are authorized to use the computer.
- It establishes which user you are, and this user identity determines what you can see and do on the computer.

Your user identity is especially important if you or an administrator has set up your computer for multiple users, such as members of a family or several workers in an office, because each user has personal preference settings and private storage areas. For example, you may prefer a different desktop theme, and you may not want other users to have access to the data you store on the computer or the application programs you use. As mentioned in the previous chapter, Mac OS X is truly a multi-user operating system. Because more than one user account can be set up on a particular computer, it's important to identify each user via a login. You can find information on setting up Mac OS X for multiple users in Chapter 18.

If you have left your computer configured for the default automatic login, you do not get the distinct honor of seeing the login screen. After the startup sequence, the computer just activates your user account, and all elements of your account are available. However, if your computer is configured for manual login, Mac OS X displays a login window, and you must provide a user account name and password before the startup process can continue. Instead of logging in, you may shut down or restart your computer by clicking the appropriate button in the window. The login window shows one of two screens. Each is covered under the following headings. Figure 2.1 shows examples of both types of login window.

FIGURE 2.1

When logging in to Mac OS X, you may have to type a valid account name and password (left) or you may be presented with a list of user accounts (right).

Logging in with a list of user accounts

If the login window shows a list of users, log in by following these steps:

1. **Select your account name.** Use the mouse to select your account from the list of users. The login window contents change to show your account only, along with a field for entering a password.

2. **Type your password.** Place the cursor in the Password field and enter your password; for privacy purposes, you can't see your password — the password appears as a series of dots.

Keep in mind that capitalization counts when entering the password; upper- and lower-case letters are not interchangeable. If you don't know the password for the selected user account, click the Go Back button to return to the initial login window and select a different user. If you don't know the password for any account, check with the person who configured your computer for multiple users.

3. **Press Return (or Enter) on the keyboard or use the mouse to click Log In.** The login window fades, and soon the Mac OS X desktop, menu bar, and Dock appear. (You can read more about the menu bar and the other objects in later sections of this chapter.)

Logging in without a list of user accounts

If the login window shows blank spaces for user account name and password, as shown earlier in Figure 2.1, follow these steps to log in:

1. **Type your user account name.** You can read the name you type. Capitalization matters only in the password field. If you don't know both your account name and password, check with the person who configured your computer for multiple users.

2. **Type your password.** Place the cursor in the Password field and enter your password; for privacy purposes, you can't see your password—the password appears as a series of dots. Keep in mind that capitalization counts when entering the password; upper- and lower-case letters are not interchangeable.

3. **Press Return (or Enter) on the keyboard or use the mouse to click Log In.** The login window fades, and soon the Mac OS X desktop, menu bar, and Dock appear. (You can read more about the menu bar and the other objects in later sections of this chapter.)

Why Is Security Important?

As you do more and more important work on your computer, such as banking, reviewing credit reports, submitting proposals to clients, trading stocks, or writing your first novel, your computer fills up with critically important and very sensitive information. In addition, most types of high-speed Internet connections keep your Mac available via the Internet 24 hours a day.

Through your DSL or cable modem or (heaven forbid) dial-up service, your Mac is open and available to countless computers around the world. Because of its basis in Unix (a fact that Apple marketing brings up at every turn), the security options you have with OS X are varied and powerful. That being said, Mac OS X is more open to misuse *because* of its Unix base. Unix has had over 30 years of evolution to enable the discovery of both loopholes and solutions to security.

Other users can turn the security options on or off, configure your computer for total remote control via the Internet, and guess your password more easily than you might imagine. As a result, your hot new Mac can become the new best friend of a hacker, who can steal or erase your documents as well as launch attacks that crash your machine or network. Unix is a powerful tool. Like a hammer or circular saw, Unix can build, but it can also destroy. The first line of defense against any type of unauthorized access is a tough password that you keep secret.

Dealing with login problems

If the login window shakes back and forth (like someone shaking his or her head no), either you entered an incorrect account name or password, or Mac OS X did not recognize the user account. The Password space clears so that you can retype the password. If you typed a user account name, it's a good idea to retype it; simply press the tab key to highlight the account name. If you selected a user account from a list, you can select a different account by clicking the Go Back button.

Meeting Your Environment

Once you complete the login process, you are ushered into the world of Mac OS X. Mac presents that world to you — complete with icons, folders, menus, and the desktop — through an application known as the Finder. The Finder, which is the core application at the heart of a user's interaction with the OS, is covered in greater detail later in this chapter. The following sections explore the various commonly seen elements throughout the operating system.

NOTE The Finder is not the same as Find. Find is a search function, designed to help users find documents, whereas the Finder is the system's main program that helps launch other applications (like TextEdit or Safari), and allows for exploration and viewing of drives, disks, and the folders they contain.

Investigating menus

The Macintosh OS uses menus to present lists of commands and attributes. You can issue a command or put an attribute into effect simply by choosing it from a menu using the mouse. Menus can take up a lot of space on the screen, so they remain hidden except for their titles. When you want to see a complete menu, click its title with the mouse, and voilà, you are presented with the content of the menu!

Choosing a command or attribute generally changes the state of an object. This object may be something you selected in advance, such as text that you want to make a different size. The object of a menu command may instead be an implicit part of the command, such as displaying a list of general preference settings when you choose the Preferences command from an available menu.

Although you always see menu titles in the menu bar at the top of the screen, menus can also appear outside the menu bar. For example, a pop-up menu may appear inside of a dialog box. You can see that these menus are available through the clever display of a distinctive arrow. In addition, the Mac OS can display contextual menus as a response to Control+clicking a particular object. The options and actions presented in the contextual menu are populated according to what the selected object is.

Using the menu bar

The menus in the menu bar at the top of the screen contain commands that are relevant to the application you are using at the time. The menus may also contain attributes that apply to objects that you utilize within the application. Menu titles appear in the menu bar, and you can use the mouse to display one menu at a time beneath its title. The menu bar is shown in Figure 2.2 as it initially appears in Mac OS X, with the application menu displayed.

FIGURE 2.2

The menu bar is a permanent fixture at the top of the screen. Note the application menu's title shows the name of the active application, in this case Finder.

To use the menu bar, position the mouse pointer over a menu title and click the mouse button once. The commands appear beneath the menu title so that you can see all of your options.

To choose a menu item, position the pointer over it to highlight it and click the mouse button. The menu item you choose flashes briefly and the menu fades away. The menu item's effect is then applied or a dialog window appears giving you more options.

Some menus have menus within them, aptly known as submenus. A distinctive black arrow pointing to the right indicates submenus. When your mouse navigates over a menu that contains a submenu, the pullout menu appears, displaying its options. See Figure 2.3.

When a command is not available or applicable to the current circumstances, it is dimmed out. A dimmed item's text is a faded, translucent gray, rather than the normal black solid text. In Figure 2.3, Import Image is an example of an unavailable command.

In Mac OS X, unlike previous Mac OS versions, an active menu stays open indefinitely until you make your selection. With a menu displayed, you can leave your finger off the mouse button and move the pointer up and down the menu, highlighting each menu item as the pointer passes over it. You can close a menu without choosing an item from it by clicking the mouse button when the pointer is on the menu's title or anywhere outside the menu.

While looking at any menu in the menu bar, you can activate a different menu by positioning the pointer over the other menu's title. You can click any menu item you see to choose it, or click outside any menu to stop looking at menus in the menu bar.

Why One Menu Bar?

The Mac OS has a permanent menu bar at the top of the screen for several reasons. One reason is that a menu bar at the top of the screen is an easy target to hit with the mouse. You can quickly slide the mouse pointer to the top of the screen, where it automatically stops at the menu bar. If the menu bar were at the top of a window in the middle of the screen (as in Microsoft Windows), you would have to take more time to position the pointer carefully over the menu bar.

The second reason is that having a permanent menu bar at the top of the screen gives you a reliable place for every application's commands. If each window on the screen had its own menu bar, you'd have to think about which one you wanted to use. Of course, Apple's method can also result in confusion because users must keep track of which application is active and responding to menu commands.

FIGURE 2.3

Pullout menus are a useful supplement to standard menus.

Understanding standard Mac OS X menus

In most Mac OS X applications, the left side of the menu bar includes several of the following standard menus:

- **Apple:** Located at the left end of the menu bar, the Apple menu has a miniature solid Apple logo for its title (unlike the six-color striped Apple menu logo in OS 9). Use this menu to get basic information about your Macintosh, update Apple software, modify System Preferences, or change Dock preferences. You can also use this menu to open a recently used application or document, or to force applications to quit. Additionally, the Apple menu has commands for putting the computer into sleep mode, restarting it, shutting it down, or logging out of your user account.

- **Application menu:** This menu is next to the Apple menu and is unique to the active application. It's the only menu that doesn't always display the actual name of the application; for example, when in Microsoft Word, the Application menu is titled *Word*. This menu includes commands that apply to the application as a whole. Use the application menu to get information about the current application, change preferences, get services from other applications (as described in Chapter 9), hide the current application or all others, or quit the application when you are done using it.

- **File:** Positioned next to the Application menu, the File menu contains commands that affect a whole document (or file), such as New, Open, Close, Save, and Print. Usually, applications that don't use documents don't have a File menu (video games, for example). More information on most of these commands is available in Chapter 5; the Print command is covered in Chapter 16.

- **Edit:** Located to the right of the File menu, the Edit menu contains commands that you can use to change a document's contents, such as Undo, Cut, Copy, Paste, and Select All. Read more about these commands in Chapter 5.

- **Window:** This menu item enables you to zoom (maximize) or minimize the active window, or bring all the listed windows in front of windows belonging to other applications. The Window menu lists other windows that belong to the same application and also may have additional commands for window manipulation.

- **Help:** This menu item gives you access to on-screen help. This menu is located immediately to the right of the last application-specific menu in the menu bar. In some cases, the application may have its own help menu, and the OS X Help menu may not be present. If this is true and you want to open the OS X Help, you can either switch to an Apple-made application such as the Finder or use ⌘+? . Chapter 8 has more information on the Help menu.

The right side of the menu bar is typically populated with system-specific menus like these:

- **Clock:** The Clock menu is on the right side of the menu bar and has a digital clock or an analog clock as its title. Click the clock to display the menu, which shows the current date, and enables you to switch between digital and a very small analog clock, and to open the Date & Time pane of the System Preferences application, which is covered in Chapter 17.

- **Sound:** The Sound menu usually appears next to the clock in the menu bar and enables you to adjust the computer's volume. This menu has a speaker icon as its title, and it subtly indicates the current sound level by an ever-increasing number of audio lines emitting from the speaker. A setting in the Sound pane of the System Preferences application determines whether the sound menu appears in the menu bar, as described in Chapter 17.

■ **AirPort:** The AirPort menu appears if your computer has an AirPort wireless networking card installed (all new Macs do). This menu's title icon shows four arcs (resembling a baseball field) that indicate the strength of the wireless network signal. You can use the AirPort menu to join a wireless network, create a wireless network, or turn the AirPort card off and on. With Mac OS X Apple has updated the AirPort menu. A padlock appears to the right of secure wireless networks. On the other hand, open networks simply display the network name without a padlock. It's a great way to quickly gauge the status of wireless networks. See Figure 2.4. Chapter 11 covers AirPort in much greater detail.

FIGURE 2.4

On the left side of the menu bar is the AirPort menu.

Each application may omit some of these menus and add its own menus on the left side, between the Edit menu and the Help menu. The menus on the right side of the menu bar may appear in a different order, and you can reorganize them according to your preference. In addition, the menu bar may have more icons with menus on the right side of the menu bar. For example, the menu bar may have an iChat icon, with a menu for setting your availability, viewing Buddy status, or switching between iChat or Jabber Buddies as discussed in Chapter 6.

Using pop-up menus

A *pop-up menu* appears within a dialog box or a control palette when you click the pop-up menu's title. The title may be a text label or an icon, and is marked with a pair of arrows pointing up and down to indicate that clicking it displays a pop-up menu. The menu may also be marked with a single arrow pointing to the right. As with the menus in the menu bar, you can display only one pop-up menu at a time. If a pop-up menu is open, it goes away automatically if you click the title of another pop-up menu. An example of a pop-up menu can be seen in Figure 2.5.

Using contextual menus

Searching through menus to find a particular command isn't much fun. Wouldn't it be better if all you saw were relevant commands? That's the beauty of contextual menus — they offer commands that make sense in a given context. You can display a contextual menu by pressing and holding the Control key while clicking an icon or right-clicking (if you use a multi-button mouse) a window or some selected text for which you want to choose a command or attribute. The contextual menu lists commands relevant to the item that you clicked. A contextual menu is shown in Figure 2.6.

FIGURE 2.5

An arrowhead marks a pop-up menu in the Print dialog box.

FIGURE 2.6

Pressing the Control key while clicking an item may display a contextual menu.

You can Control+click one item or a selection of several items. Control+clicking a selection of several items displays a contextual menu of commands that pertain to the whole group. Selecting several items is discussed later in this chapter.

TIP With a multi-button mouse or trackball, you can display contextual menus by simply pressing the right button. If your multi-button mouse or trackball does not already work this way, you can program it to simulate a Control+click whenever you press the right button. For instructions on programming a multi-button mouse or trackball, see the manufacturer's documentation. In 2005 Apple began shipping all of their systems with multi-button mice. Before purchasing a multi-button mouse, check with the manufacturer to ensure that Mac OS X supports the device.

Menu symbols

A variety of symbols may accompany a menu item. A triangle pointing to the right at the end of an item indicates that the menu has a submenu. An ellipsis (...) at the end of the item name indicates that choosing the item opens a dialog box that requires additional information before a command can be completed. The following list summarizes these symbols and their meanings:

✓	Designates an item that is currently selected or an attribute that applies to everything that is currently selected.
—	Designates an attribute that applies only to some things that are currently selected.
●	Designates a document that has unsaved changes; some applications use it instead of ✓ to designate an attribute that applies to everything that is currently selected.
◆	Designates, in some applications, a window minimized in the Dock; designates, in the Classic environment's application menu, an application that requires your attention.
▶	Designates a menu item with a submenu.

Other symbols are used to specify keyboard shortcuts for menu items. Pressing a specified combination of keys has the same effect as choosing the menu item. For example, pressing ⌘+X is equivalent to choosing the Cut command from the Edit menu. The following symbols represent keys:

⌘	Command key
⇧	Shift key
⌥	Option key
⌃	Control key
⌫	Delete key

When you use a keyboard shortcut for a command in a particular menu, the title of the menu may flash briefly to indicate that the command has been issued. Learning these keyboard shortcuts is a useful method for improving your control over the OS (and impressing your co-workers).

Recognizing the Desktop

The beautiful expanse of space that appears behind the menu bar and Dock is called the *desktop*. Initially, the only items on the desktop are your installed hard drives and any inserted disks, but other icons may appear. For example, an icon appears on your desktop for each file server, if any, to which your computer is connected. All of these different icons normally appear on the desktop, but you can hide them by changing settings in Finder Preferences.

In actuality, the desktop is a folder, stored in your home folder (described later in this chapter). The contents of the Desktop folder are always displayed on-screen, so users always have a location to store and retrieve items quickly. Mac OS X keeps your desktop's contents and appearance separate from users who log in with other user account names. Each user account has its own Desktop folder.

NOTE Although the icons of hard drives, CDs, and other disk volumes may appear on the desktop, your Desktop folder does not contain these items. The icons of disk volumes appear on the desktop simply because the Finder displays them there (together with other items actually stored in your Desktop folder). This can be confusing, because it goes against the understanding of folders *containing* the items they display, but it is the only exception to this rule.

Customizing the desktop

The desktop, as you know, is the large expanse of color that comprises the background of your Mac OS environment. By default, this area has a stunning image of space (see Figure 2.7) ostensibly to lead you into the future of the Mac operating system. You may want to change the color to black, red, or your favorite color, or you may want to place a picture of your children or your favorite celebrity as a desktop picture. To make this change, you must delve into the Desktop & Screen Saver System Preference.

FIGURE 2.7

OS X's new desktop picture, Aurora, is a knockout!

Setting the desktop background

You can cover the desktop with a solid color or a picture by choosing an image file as follows:

1. **Click the System Preferences icon in the Dock (or select Apple ⇨ System Preferences).** The System Preferences window appears, showing buttons for different types of settings.

2. **In System Preferences, click the Desktop & Screen Saver button or choose View ⇨ Desktop & Screen Saver.** The System Preferences window changes to show one of the two panes in this preference panel. The settings for changing the desktop background are of course under the Desktop pane. Click the Desktop button if it isn't already selected (top left) to reveal the Desktop pane. Divided into two distinct frames, the left side contains a list of options, and the right side is populated dynamically according to which list item you select on the left. The Desktop pane is shown in Figure 2.8.

FIGURE 2.8

Mac OS 10.5 debuts a number of new desktop images.

3. **Select either a picture or a solid color for your background.**

4. **Close the window with the red Close button to complete setting the preference.** Alternately, you can select System Preferences ⇨ Quit System Preferences.

When choosing a background, you have a number of preinstalled options available. You can set your background as a solid color or as one of many stunning pictures or patterns.

- To choose a color, click the Solid Colors list item and then choose one of the preselected colors available in the right-hand window pane.
- To choose a picture, click any of the following list items:

  - **Apple Images:** This is a collection of swirled patterns. Typically these are attractive patterns, usually comprised of a single color. Click any pattern in the right-hand frame to set it as the desktop.

  - **Nature:** This is a standardized preselected list of nature-themed pictures. New images include Aurora, Earth, Earth Horizon, Golden Palace, Rock Garden, Rocks, Zebra, and Zen Garden. Click any picture in the right frame to set it as the desktop.

  - **Plants:** A collection of images of flowers and other vegetation. Grass Blades and Roses are new to this collection.

  - **Black and White:** A collection of black-and-white landscape images. The Sea Mist Blue and Wave images are nice additions.

  - **Abstract:** This is another collection of swirled patterns. These are typically much more colorful, with two, three, or more colors per pattern. Click any picture in the right frame to set it as the desktop.

  - **Solid Colors:** A collection of solid color backgrounds. Click any picture in the right frame to set it as the desktop.

  - **Pictures Folder:** If your Pictures folder (located in your Home folder) contains any images, they appear in the right-hand pane. Click any picture displayed in the right frame to set it as the desktop.

  - **iPhoto Albums:** Linked to your iPhoto library, set your personal photos as your desktop picture. Choose from Photos (all of the photos in your library), the Last 12 Months, the Last Import, and Flagged. Click any option and the results appear in the right frame, allowing you to set a picture as the desktop theme.

Saving the Screen

Originally designed as a method of preserving displays from damage, screen savers are now as much a form of entertainment as they are a hardware-protection measure. Early cathode ray tube (CRT) displays were victimized by an unfortunate condition known as phosphor burn-in. *Phosphor burn-in* occurs when a display shows the same image for too long. After a few days of displaying the same static image, the display is permanently scarred with a shadow of the image. That said, fundamental changes wrought in CRT display technology in the mid 1990s reduced the risk of phosphor burn-in to practically nil. Phosphor burn-in is also no longer a concern for CRT owners simply because lower prices and more demanding users result in the replacement of displays much more often. These factors combined to practically eliminate the need for screen savers. A new factor has arisen though. Many users are migrating to liquid crystal displays (LCD), which are again susceptible to a form of image burn-in. Screen savers are again a useful piece of software. In general though, the best protection for your screen and your electric bill is to have your monitor

completely switch off after a period of inactivity. This option is found in the Energy Saver preference pane. (For more on the Energy Saver preference pane, see Chapter 17.)

To use a screen saver, or to change the settings of the currently selected screen saver, follow these
steps:

1. **Click the System Preferences icon in the Dock (or choose Apple ➪ System
    Preferences).** The System Preferences window appears, showing buttons for many differ-
    ent settings. (Most are covered in Chapter 17.)

2. **In System Preferences, click the Desktop & Screen Saver button or choose View ➪
    Desktop & Screen Saver.** The System Preferences window changes to show one of the
    two available panes in this preference panel. Screen saver controls are of course under the
    Screen Saver pane. Click the Screen Saver button (top right) to reveal the Screen Saver
    pane. Much like the Desktop pane, the Screen Saver pane is divided into two distinct
    panels. The left side has a list of available screen savers; the right side shows a preview
    display of the screen saver in action.

3. **Choose the screen saver desired from the left panel.**

4. **Close the Desktop & Screen Saver preference pane with the Close button, or quit
    system preferences via the Application menu to enable the screen saver.**

The Screen Saver pane in System Preferences is shown in Figure 2.9. The standard preinstalled
screen savers are divided into two groups, Apple and Pictures. The Apple group includes the
following:

-   **Arabesque:** This screen saver displays colorful dots that radiate in lines and random
    alignments. After the light display is over, the dots seemingly explode into clouds of
    evolving color. The clouds then condense and become focused colorful dots again,
    forming an endless pattern of light and color.

-   **Computer Name:** This screen saver is a simple display of a platinum-looking Apple logo
    with an overlay of your computer's name on a black background. The logo and name fade
    and reappear, each centered at different points on-screen. Your computer's name is set
    during the installation process.

-   **Flurry:** Although Flurry may or may not be the most popular, it is definitely the most
    hypnotic! Flurry is perhaps best described as a single point of light erupting and spewing
    forth colorful streams of light while moving around the screen. *(You will buy Apple
    computers . . . you will buy Apple computers . . .)*

-   **iTunes Artwork:** Some MP3 files have embedded album or artist artwork. This screen
    saver cycles through that artwork in a slide show.

-   **RSS Visualizer:** Your computer can pull down headline news and topics, and display the
    headlines in columns of text that fly by. This screen saver also offers an interactive oppor-
    tunity to "read more" by pressing a key.

-   **Shell:** This screen saver is a lovely display of floating streams of color that form different
    shapes. This screen saver is similar to the iTunes visualizer.

- **Spectrum:** Various colors cycle through the spectrum. (It's like the end of the movie *2001: A Space Odyssey*, although it makes more sense.)

- **Word of the Day:** This screen saver is a simple display of a word and its definition. A new word appears approximately every three minutes. The screen saver also offers an interactive opportunity to "learn more" about the word shown by pressing the D key.

The Pictures group includes the following:

- **.Mac and RSS:** This screen saver allows you to access and display images from your .Mac account, as well as any public images from your friends' or family's .Mac accounts. It also displays any RSS feeds you subscribe to with your .Mac account. If no .Mac account is available, the slide show displays various Apple marketing images.

- **Abstract:** This is a collection of colorful patterns and swirls, cross-fading and panning across the screen. This is the first of the Ken Burns-style slide show screen savers. (Ken Burns directed a series of famous documentaries and is very creative in the use of still images that pan, fade, and zoom throughout.)

- **Beach:** This is another of the slide show-style screen savers. Rather than abstract images of color swirls, Beach is comprised of photos of various beach locations. Consider it inspiration for your next vacation.

- **Cosmos:** Like the Beach screen saver, but probably designed by a *Star Trek* fan, Cosmos is comprised of various deep space photos.

- **Forest:** Another of the slide show-style screen savers, Forest is a collection of images of various wilderness locations. (Queue your favorite Enya tracks while it plays.)

- **Nature Patterns:** This is another slide show of a collection of zoomed-in and almost microscopic images of nature, like the patterns of a snowflake. Mac OS 10.5 brings a number of new, stunning images to this collection.

- **Paper Shadow:** A collection of images of paper, forming delicate curves and shadows, like an origami party gone wild.

- **Pictures Folder:** Any images stored in your Pictures folder (located in your Home folder) become the slides in this screen saver slide show as they pan, zoom, cross-fade, and randomize. (Moving items to and from folders is discussed in detail in Chapter 5.)

- **Choose Folder:** Just as with the Choose Folder option for the Desktop Picture, by selecting this option, a dialog box opens. Choose a folder containing images you want to have as a screen saver. Click Open when you find the folder, and the dialog box closes. The screen saver displays images from the selected folder.

- **Photos:** A tie-in to iPhoto, this screen saver option uses your entire iPhoto library as the slides in the screen saver.

- **Last 12 Months:** This option displays images that have been imported only in the last 12 months as the available elements of the slide show.

- **Last Import:** This option uses images only from your last iPhoto import as the available elements of the slide show.

- **Flagged:** This option displays only the pictures that have been flagged in iPhoto.

FIGURE 2.9

Screen savers engage after a set period of inactivity, replacing your screen's displayed items by showing photos, cycling interesting patterns, or changing colors.

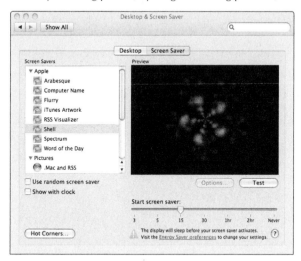

Optimizing screen saver settings

In addition to selecting a screen saver, there are a few settings available to optimize each screen saver's functionality.

- **Test:** Click the Test button under the preview area of the screen saver pane to preview your screen saver in full-screen mode. Move the mouse or click any key to return to the preference pane.

- **Start Screen Saver:** This slider, located at the bottom of the Desktop & Screen Saver window, allows you to set the screen saver's activation time. The activation time is how long the computer will sit idle before engaging the screen saver. The slider ranges from two minutes to two hours, with Never at the far right. Setting activation to Never prevents any screen saver from engaging automatically.

- **Random:** If you click the Use random screen saver check box in the lower-left area of the pane, Mac OS X chooses a random screen saver to activate.

- **Clock:** Ever wish that the time appeared while the screen saver was activated? Apple has added this capability to their screen savers. Selecting this check box displays a digital clock while your screen saver is engaged. What's especially cool is that when the screen saver is first activated, the clock counts down the seconds until the screen is locked (assuming this setting has also been turned on).

- **Hot Corners:** When clicking this push button in the lower left corner, a dialog box appears. In the dialog box, four pop-up menus in the corners surround a small window displaying a thumbnail image of the desktop. Clicking any of these menus reveals options that engage when a user moves the mouse to that corner of the screen. The options include Activate Screen Saver, Disable Screen Saver, and any of the three modes of Exposé. You can assign each corner one of these commands. Moving the pointer to the specified corner initiates that action. Activate Screen Saver immediately engages the screen saver. Disable Screen Saver prevents the screen saver from engaging at the specified activation time. The Exposé features are covered in the "Exposing Exposé" section later in this chapter. Figure 2.10 shows the Hot Corners dialog box, as well as one of the pop-up menu's options.

FIGURE 2.10

The Hot Corners dialog box not only enables you to activate screen savers, but also allows you to set Exposé options.

Setting screen saver options

Each screen saver may have a series of options available to modify its performance. When you select a screen saver on the left side of the Desktop & Screen Saver dialog box, click the Options button that sits underneath the preview. If the Options button is dimmed out, there are no available options. (For example, the Computer Name screen saver has no available options.)

Making its first appearance in Mac OS 10.5, the Display Style setting puts a new spin on the display of your Picture screen saver images. You can choose from the following styles:

- **Standard:** Presents images in the standard display. In this very simple display, images take up the entire screen.

- **Photo Prints:** This setting presents each image as a printed photo being dropped onto a surface. Options for this style include viewing images in Classic mode, with a thin white border, or Annotated, with a Polaroid-like border. If you select the Annotated layout, you can also choose to show the image name and the date, as depicted in Figure 2.11.

- **Mosaic Tile:** By far the most artistic of the new display style options, this setting works with your iPhoto library to generate a mosaic of every screen saver picture. It begins by displaying a screen saver image and then pulling outward slowly to reveal a custom mosaic created using your photos.

FIGURE 2.11

The Photo Print style is a cool, new way to display screen saver images.

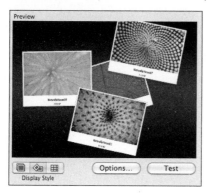

Flurry's options include the following:

- **Color:** This pull-down menu contains many options. There are six colors to choose from (each of which roots the Flurry's eruptions in a particular color space); there are four cycle speeds (each sets the Flurry's eruptions to cycle through all colors at varying speeds); and finally, there are three brightness levels to choose from (each keeps the Flurry and its eruptions rooted at a particular degree of brightness). These options are mutually exclusive. The Flurry is set by default to Cycle and an average brightness setting, and to cycle through all colors.

- **Streams:** A slider ranging from Few to Many, Streams sets how many eruptions of color come from the Flurry. By default, this is set in the middle.

- **Thickness:** A slider ranging from Thin to Thick, Thickness sets the width of the emerging streams of color. By default, this is set in the middle.

- **Speed:** Another slider, ranging from Slow to Fast, Speed sets the pace at which the Flurry itself moves about the screen. By default, this is set in the middle.

iTunes Artwork options include the following:

- **Rows:** Using the slider, select how many rows of artwork you want to appear. You can choose as little as two or as many as eight rows.

- **Delay:** A slider ranging from 0 to 5 controls how many seconds elapse between each image.

RSS Visualizer options include the following:

- **Select an RSS feed or enter one below:** Choose from the Apple-provided RSS feed, or supply your own. To change the feed, enter the URL of the feed you want to subscribe to in the Feed URL field.

- **Article Display Duration:** A slider ranging from 0 to 11 controls how many seconds elapse between each article.

Word of the Day includes the following option:

- **Dictionary to Use:** Choose from Apple's dictionary, or the New Oxford American Dictionary.

All of the slide show-style screen savers have the same options set, with check boxes to engage/disengage each option. The options include the following:

- **Present slides in random order:** This option randomly presents the images from the available slides. In the case of large image collections, this option helps to alleviate boredom. (After all, screen savers are supposed to be fun!)

- **Cross-Fade between slides:** This option enables the selected slides to cross-fade from one to the next; as one image fades away, another fades in.

- **Zoom Back and Forth:** This option causes the screen saver to zoom in and out on images, as well as to pan left and right.

- **Crop to Fit on Screen:** This option ensures that your images appear full screen, as opposed to appearing too small or radically oversized.

- **Keep Slides Centered:** This option modifies the Zoom Back and Forth option, so the slides zoom in and out only, and no longer move left to right. Having Zoom Back and Forth and Centered Onscreen unchecked disables all zooming and panning, and results in a more static (boring) screen saver.

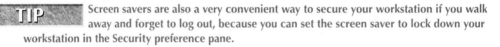 Screen savers are also a very convenient way to secure your workstation if you walk away and forget to log out, because you can set the screen saver to lock down your workstation in the Security preference pane.

Peeking into Windows

A window is literally a portal that displays content for your perusal. There are many different kinds of windows. Each serves a particular function; each offers options for control and interaction. Some windows show the contents of disks and folders. Some windows show the text of a written document or the content of a photograph. Certain windows alert you to conditions requiring your attention. Other windows even offer interaction with tools that are used to modify the contents of other windows (whew!). Most windows are rectangular and malleable. You can reshape them to maximize your screen real estate. This section describes how different types of Mac OS windows look and operate.

Recognizing different window types

There are several types of Mac OS X windows, and each is designed to display a specific kind of information. Some windows display the files and other items stored on disks. Other window types display the actual contents of files, which may be text, pictures, movies, or other kinds of information. Figure 2.12 shows examples of the different types of Aqua windows. The different types of windows are as follows:

- **Windows:** Windows show any nonstandard data, ranging from a document written in Microsoft Word, to a QuickTime movie or a video game (even when a game is running "full screen," it is still technically a window). Another type of window is the Finder window, which shows the content of folders and disks. These windows are generated by the Finder, which is covered in further detail later in this chapter.

- **Dialog boxes:** These are windows that display options that require an action before you can continue.

- **Sheets:** Sheets are dialog boxes that apply to, and are attached to, another window. A sheet ensures you won't lose track of which window the dialog box applies to.

- **Palettes:** Also called panels or utility windows, palettes contain controls or tools, or display auxiliary information for the application that you're currently using.

FIGURE 2.12

The Mac OS X Aqua environment has several different types of windows: a document (a), a dialog box (b), a sheet (c), and a palette (d).

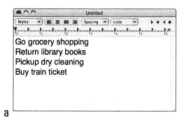

a

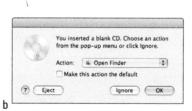

b

Window controls

As mentioned earlier in this chapter, windows are portals that display important data. They are made up of numerous control surfaces and other objects, including buttons and more. There are many different types of windows in Mac OS X, as discussed later in this chapter, but there are a slew of common control surfaces and buttons available within most windows. Of course, you won't find all types of window controls on every kind of window. For example, document windows have all or most of the available controls, whereas dialog boxes generally have fewer window controls available, and alerts have fewer still. Figure 2.13 shows a standard document window with the most commonly found items indicated.

- **Title bar:** The title bar is usually the home of the stoplight cluster of close (red), minimize (yellow), and expand (green) on the left side, as well as the location of the name of the active window (the title). The title indicates which document is currently being shown (or which folder is being shown in the case of a Finder window, which is discussed later in this chapter). Click and drag the title bar to move the window. Double-clicking the title bar minimizes the window into the Dock just as the Minimize button does.

- **Close:** The Close button is the uppermost and leftmost item in every window. Typically a round red button found at the top left of a window, when you position the pointer near the Close button, an X appears in its center. This button closes the window to which it is attached. In some applications, notably the Finder, press the Option key and click this button to close all of the application's windows. Please note that unlike Microsoft Windows, this will *not* usually quit the active application, but simply closes the displayed window. Quitting applications is covered in Chapter 5.

- **Minimize:** The Minimize button is usually a round yellow button, found to the right of the Close button, that displays a minus sign (–) when you position the pointer near it. Clicking this button minimizes the attached window, sucking it down into the Dock, for easy retrieval later. Be warned: Minimizing too many windows results in a cluttered Dock!

- **Zoom:** The Zoom button is typically a round green button, found to the right of the Minimize button, that displays a plus sign (+) when you position the mouse pointer near it. Its function is first to make a window as large as is required to display all items within, or to make that window as large as possible, without stretching off-screen if too many items are present to be displayed at once. A zoomed window may leave a margin at the bottom or sides of the screen for the Dock. After the first zoom-button click, this button then reduces the window to its original size. If a window cannot be resized, its zoom button is dim, and a plus sign does not appear in its center.

- **Scroller:** The scroller is both an indicator as well as a control item. The scroller indicates a given window's current focused position of the displayed folder contents with both its size as well as its position in the scroll bar. For example, if the scroller is at the top of the scroll bar and is taking up about one third of the bar, the window is displaying one third of the total folder's viewable material, and is showing the top third portion. Click and drag the scroller to move quickly to a desired position within a displayed folder. A scroller can appear on the right of a folder or window as well as at the bottom. This is the fastest way to shift your window's list of displayed items. Like scroll arrows, the scroller is not available if all of a folder's contents are displayed by the current window's size.

- **Scroll Bar:** The scroll bar serves as a container for the scroller. The scroll track can be clicked to refocus the window one full window display area at a time. For example, if the scroller is half the size of the scroll bar and at the top of the scroll bar, a single click in the scroll bar moves the window's focus to the bottom half. This method is useful to quickly scan a folder's contents.

- **Scroll arrow:** The scroll arrows shift a window's focus in the arrow's indicated direction slightly with each mouse click. Clicking and holding on a scroll arrow shifts the window's focus both smoothly and more quickly. These buttons are useful when trying to slowly scan through a large grouping of items.

- **Resize control:** The bottom right corner of a window is typically the control for resizing the window. This is usually indicated with a slightly rougher texture or three lines in the corner that would suggest grabbing it. Click and drag the resize corner to adjust the size of the window.

FIGURE 2.13

Windows are made up of numerous controls and objects. Learning what they all do is crucial to an efficient computing experience. The items highlighted are common to many windows.

Buttons and other controls

Window controls, as covered in the previous section, afford you the means for controlling the window itself. However, many of the windows encountered day to day contain a wide variety of controls that you also operate by clicking or dragging with the mouse. These other controls perform various functions, hopefully clearly labeled by the software designers! Examples of these other controls include push buttons, check boxes, radio buttons, sliders, little arrows for increasing or decreasing numeric values, disclosure triangles, scrolling lists, and tabs.

Using push buttons

A *push button* causes an action to take place when clicked. A label on the button indicates the action that the button performs. The label may be text or graphic. Push buttons with text labels are generally rectangular with rounded ends. Buttons with graphic labels may be any shape. An example of push buttons is illustrated in Figure 2.14.

Using standard OK and Cancel buttons

Many dialog boxes and alert windows have buttons labeled OK and Cancel. Clicking OK accepts all the settings and entries in the dialog box (or the conditions stated by the alert). Clicking Cancel rejects any changes you may have made in the dialog box and restores all settings and entries to their state before the dialog box appeared, or cancels an action. A shortcut for clicking the Cancel button is pressing the Escape key (the Escape key is labeled esc) or pressing the ⌘ and period (.) keys in combination.

Using radio buttons

Radio buttons are one way to select a single setting from a group. They're called radio buttons because they work like the station presets on a car radio. Just as you can select only one radio station at a time, you can select only one radio button from a group. To select a radio button, click it. The selected radio button is darker than its unselected neighbors. Radio buttons are shown in Figure 2.15.

FIGURE 2.14

Click a push button in an Aqua window to cause an action to take place.

FIGURE 2.15

Click a radio button in an Aqua window to select one setting from a group.

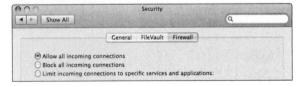

Using check boxes

A *check box* is another way to select a setting from a group or turn a setting on or off. When a setting is on (or selected), a check mark appears in the check box. When a setting is off (or deselected), the check box is empty. When a setting is partly on and partly off because it indicates the state of more than one thing, such as the format of a range of text, a dash appears in the check box. Unlike radio buttons, check boxes are not mutually exclusive. You can turn on check boxes in any combination. That being said, some applications may use check symbols in their radio button fields, allowing only one check to be seen at a time, just to confuse us all. Be careful. Clicking a check box reverses its state. Figure 2.16 shows check boxes.

Using sliders

A *slider* consists of a track that displays a range of values or magnitudes and the slider itself, also known as the *thumb,* which indicates the current setting. You can change the setting by dragging the slider. An Aqua slider is a dark color (initially blue, but you can change colors as described later in this chapter). Sliders are shown in Figure 2.17.

FIGURE 2.16

Click check boxes in Aqua windows to turn individual settings on and off.

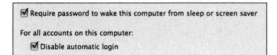

FIGURE 2.17

Drag a slider in an Aqua window to change a setting across a range of values.

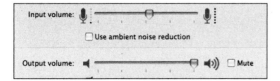

Using little arrows

Little arrows that point in opposite directions let you raise or lower a value incrementally. Clicking an arrow changes the value one increment at a time. Pressing an arrow continuously changes the value until it reaches the end of its range.

Using disclosure triangles

A *disclosure triangle* controls how much detail you see in a window. When the window is displaying minimal detail, clicking a disclosure triangle reveals additional detail and may automatically enlarge the window to accommodate it. Clicking the same triangle again hides detail and may automatically shrink the window to fit. Figure 2.18 shows an example of disclosure triangles.

43

FIGURE 2.18

Click a disclosure triangle to adjust the amount of detail shown.

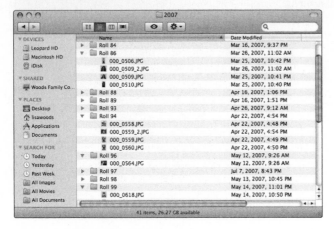

Using scrolling lists

A *scrolling list* displays a list of values in a box with an adjacent scroll bar. If there are more values than can be displayed at once, the scroll bar becomes active and you can use it to see other values in the list. Clicking a listed item selects it. You may be able to select multiple items by pressing Shift or ⌘ while clicking. See Figure 2.19.

FIGURE 2.19

Scroll a list to see an item you want and then click to select it (Shift+click or ⌘+click to select multiple items) in an Aqua window.

Using tabs

Tabs in Mac OS windows perform the same function as tabs on dividers used in card files or ring binders. They divide the contents of a window into discrete pages or sections, with each tab presenting one section of window content. Apple calls each tabbed section a *pane*. You can see only one pane at a time, and users switch to a different pane by clicking the appropriate tab. Figure 2.20 provides two examples of tabs.

FIGURE 2.20

Tabs come in many shapes and sizes.

Working with Windows

Having described windows in detail, it's important to remember that there are many additional types of windows in Mac OS X, but they all adhere to standards of command and have many of the same control surfaces. In this section, you learn how to create and control windows. You work mostly with Finder windows because they tend to have the most tools for control.

New window, please

As noted earlier in this chapter, to open an item in a new window (like a folder or document), simply double-click the item. Alternately, you can single-click to select a folder or disk and then press ⌘+O or choose Open from the File menu (or use any of the other options presented). To open a new Finder window that displays your Home folder, click on the desktop and press ⌘+N.

Active and inactive windows

When more than one standard window is open, only one window is considered active, meaning that you can interact with all the items in it, and control the surfaces it is comprised of. You may be able to interact with some window controls and other items in inactive windows (for example, you can close inactive windows by clicking their respective Close buttons), but you can't interact with everything in inactive windows.

Recognizing the active window

You can recognize the active window because it is in front of all inactive windows. Therefore, the active window overlaps all other windows except palettes belonging to the same application as the active window. (Palettes float in a layer above the active window.) In addition, the active window is conspicuous because all of its controls are full color and available for use, whereas the controls of inactive windows appear grayed out as shown in Figure 2.21.

FIGURE 2.21

The active window is in front of inactive windows, and controls and items in the inactive window appear grayed out.

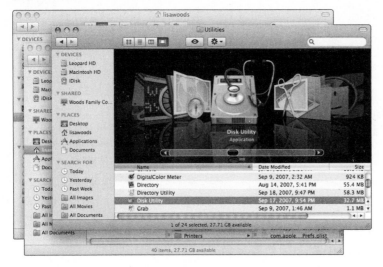

Making another window active

You can make any window the active window by clicking any visible part of it, with the exception of the close or minimize buttons. Making a window active brings it to the forefront; if the new active window belongs to an application with palettes, they also come to the front. To make all the windows of a Mac OS X application come forward together, click the application's icon in the Dock.

NOTE   If an alert or a dialog box other than a sheet appears, you may need to dismiss it (by clicking its OK button or Cancel button) before you can make another window active in the same application program.

Interacting with inactive windows

If you want to interact with something in an inactive window, you can always click the window to make it active and then click again to interact with the object of your desire in the window. In some cases, you don't have to click twice to interact with items in an inactive window. For example, you can operate the Close, Minimize, and Zoom buttons in most inactive Aqua windows, and they perform their standard functions, closing, minimizing, or in the case of Zoom, changing the window's size. In addition, some applications bring a window to the front when you click the window's Zoom button. The Finder does not behave this way; a Finder window that's in the background stays in the background when you click the window's Zoom button, but the window resizes. If you think about what the Close and Minimize buttons do, you can see why clicking one of these in an inactive window does not bring the window to the front. The ability to interact directly with an item in an inactive window is called click-through.

Some items in inactive Aqua windows respond when you interact with them, and other items in the same windows don't respond. A responsive window control in an inactive Aqua window becomes more pronounced when the mouse pointer passes over it. A responsive item labeled with text or a symbol (such as an arrow) is supposed to have a dark label to indicate that it is enabled. An unresponsive item is supposed to have a dim label to indicate that it is disabled. However, Mac OS X applications don't follow these rules uniformly. You have to learn by trial and error which items are responsive in inactive windows.

Using the Window menu

When you have multiple Finder windows displayed and want to use one in particular, figuring out which of them is the one you want can often be difficult. In Mac OS X, the Finder exhibits a Window menu that lists all the open Finder windows by name; active windows are indicated with a check to the right of the item's title. You can quickly bring a particular Finder window to the front by choosing it from the Window menu. Figure 2.22 shows an example of the Finder's Window menu. You can also flip through the windows by using the ⌘+~ (tilde) shortcut.

In Mac OS X, Finder windows can become intermingled with windows belonging to other applications. Clicking a window belonging to a particular Mac OS X application brings just that one window to the front. If you click Finder windows alternately with windows belonging to other Mac OS X applications, the windows end up stacked in the order you clicked them regardless of the application, as shown in Figure 2.23.

FIGURE 2.22

Bring a Finder window to the front by choosing it from the Window menu.

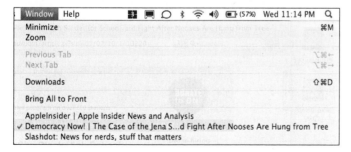

FIGURE 2.23

Finder windows can become intermingled with windows belonging to other Mac OS X applications.

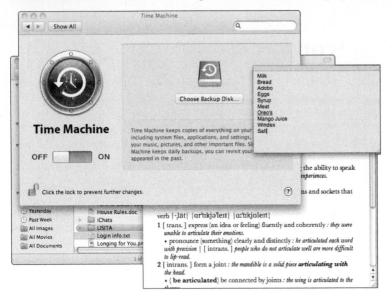

Bringing just the clicked window forward is a consistent and flexible behavior, but there are times when you may want to bring all of a particular application's windows forward. This is the *raison d'être* of the Bring All to Front command in the Window menu. Choosing Window ⇨ Bring All to Front moves all the Finder windows in front of all other applications' windows, while retaining their own front-to-back ordering. Choosing Window ⇨ Bring All to Front does not bring any minimized windows to the front; they remain in the Dock. Let us hope that developers of other Mac OS X applications follow the Finder's lead, and build this function into all applications. Many already have it, but some don't. Heck, some applications don't even have a Window menu yet!

Window Tricks

You can move and minimize most inactive windows without bringing them to the front. The following window tricks work even on windows that don't have visible controls:

- To move an inactive window, press ⌘ while dragging the window's title bar or frame.
- To minimize, close, or zoom all windows that belong to the same application as the active window, press ⌘+Option while clicking the active window's Minimize, Close, or Zoom button. In some cases, you get the same effect on inactive windows by pressing Option+⌘ while clicking the appropriate button.

> **TIP** You can also bring all the Finder's windows to the front by clicking the Finder's icon in the Dock. To bring all Finder windows to the front while hiding all other windows, ⌘+Option+click the Finder's icon in the Dock.

Worshipping Icons

Now that menus and windows have been discussed, there's one key piece of the puzzle left. Icons! Icons are small pictures that represent many objects in the Mac OS. You work with the objects by manipulating their respective icons. For example, you work with the applications, documents, folders, and disks in your computer by manipulating icons on the computer screen. This section explains how to identify the different types of icons by their appearance, and most important, how to use icons.

The icons in Mac OS 10.5 have a very different look from the icons in previous Mac OS versions. Figure 2.24 illustrates the new Finder icons. They are typically larger and much more photorealistic. Unlike the fixed-size icons in previous Mac OS versions, you can size Mac OS X icons up to 128 x 128 pixels. In some contexts, you decide how large you want Mac OS X to display icons. In other contexts, Mac OS X scales icons to fit the available space.

An icon's basic appearance often gives you some idea of what kind of item it represents. You can usually identify icons for applications, documents, and folders by common characteristics of each type.

FIGURE 2.24

In Mac OS 10.5, the folder icons look decidedly different.

Identifying application icons

Application icons come in two basic varieties:

■ **Mac OS X applications:** Icons of Mac OS X applications have several distinctive characteristics. An application icon depicts the kind of information it creates or views, such as pictures, notes, or a particular type of document. Application icons usually include a tool that suggests the type of task the application helps you perform, such as a stamp for e-mails or a musical note for music.

■ **Mac OS X utilities:** The icon of a utility application communicates the auxiliary function it performs. An icon showing a doctor's stethoscope over a hard drive suggests a utility that checks the vital signs of a hard drive, and in fact is the icon for Apple's Disk Utility. Figure 2.25 provides examples of Mac OS X utility icons.

FIGURE 2.25

Like application icons, utility icons generally advertise their function.

AirPort Utility

Directory

Migration Assistant

Identifying document icons

In Mac OS 10.5 document icons look like a sheet of paper with a preview of the data (text, image, movie, and so on), a dog-eared corner, and the file extension (of the application that created it) in the bottom half of the icon. Document files can contain text, pictures, sounds, and other kinds of data stored on your computer.

Identifying folder icons

Icons that look like manila folders represent the folders in which programs, documents, and other items are organized on your disks. A folder with a special purpose may incorporate an image that indicates the particular kind of items the folder contains.

Identifying volume icons

Volume icons are pretty easy to spot; they usually look like the type of volume they are. For example, hard drives look like real hard drives, and CD-ROMs look like actual CDs. Network drives may be depicted with a distinctive starscape sphere, or may appear as hard drives with wires emerging from the bottom, symbolizing the network connection to the drive. See Figure 2.26.

FIGURE 2.26

Volume icons represent the type of volume mounted.

Identifying alias icons

Aliases are shortcuts to a document, folder, or application. These original items often reside deep inside a hard drive, or even on a server drive. By using aliases, users can navigate to desired locations quickly, with less clicking (aliases are discussed in forthcoming sections of this chapter). The alias icon is typically a copy of the original item's icon, with a small black arrow in the lower left corner, indicating the icon "points" to an original item.

Identifying restricted folders

Some folders on your computer or on servers you connect to are restricted to particular users. This is particularly true of items within other users' home folders (covered later in this chapter). You cannot access and edit another user's folders or their contents when logged in with your account. You can spot restricted folders easily because they are marked with the "do not enter" symbol, a red circle with a white dash. Figure 2.27 shows an inactive user's home folder and all of its restricted folders.

FIGURE 2.27

These restricted folders are inaccessible to the current user. This is a view of another user's home folder. Notice that the Public and Sites folders are not restricted.

Interacting with icons

Whether you are viewing your windows in list view, column view, or icon view, the items you interact with day to day are icons. All icons respond universally to a few standard interactive techniques. This section explores some of them, preparing you for a more in-depth look at your environment in the following chapters. Opening applications and creating/editing documents is covered in Chapter 5.

Selecting icons

Everyone who uses a Mac quickly learns to select an icon by simply clicking it with the mouse, but even some seasoned veterans don't know that you can select icons individually by typing instead of clicking. In addition, you can select more than one icon at a time using various techniques.

When you select an icon, the Mac OS highlights it by creating a border around it and by highlighting the item's name. Figure 2.28 shows an example of an icon that is highlighted and one that isn't.

FIGURE 2.28

Mac OS X highlights the selected icon by surrounding it with a more distinct shadow and highlighting the title.

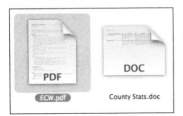

Selecting multiple icons by clicking

Ordinarily, clicking an icon selects it (highlights it) and deselects the icon that was previously selected. After selecting the first icon, you can select a group of icons in the same window by pressing and holding the ⌘ key while clicking each icon in turn. At any time, you can deselect a selected icon by pressing and holding the ⌘ key and clicking it again.

Selecting multiple items in a column view

In a window where icons appear in a list or column, you can select a whole range of icons with two clicks. First, you click one icon to select it, and then you press and hold the Shift key while clicking another icon to select it and all the icons between the first icon and the one you just selected. You can also select individual items by pressing and holding the ⌘ key while clicking an icon. In a column view, when multiple items are selected, preview data in the rightmost column is not shown, nor do selected folders expand in the next column.

Selecting from multiple folders in a list view

In a list view, ⌘+clicking affords you an additional technique for selecting. After expanding several folders in a list view, you can simultaneously select items in any of the expanded folders. To select an additional item, press ⌘ while clicking it. If you want to select consecutive items, Shift+click the first and last item. If you need to deselect a few items, ⌘+click each item. Figure 2.29 shows a list view with items selected from two folders.

Selected items remain selected if you expand or close other folders in the same window. Note that any selected items in a folder you collapse are no longer selected.

FIGURE 2.29

In a list view, you can select items from multiple folders.

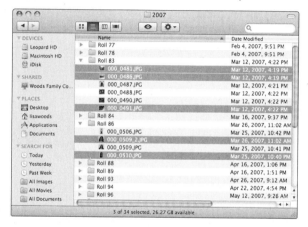

Selecting multiple icons by dragging

In addition to selecting multiple icons by clicking with the ⌘ or Shift keys, you can select adjacent icons by dragging the mouse pointer across them. As you drag, the Mac OS displays a shaded rectangle, called a selection rectangle, and every icon it touches or encloses is selected. Icons are highlighted one by one as you drag over them, not en masse after you stop dragging. All icons must be in a single window.

You can combine dragging with the use of the ⌘ key. Pressing ⌘ while dragging a selection rectangle across unselected icons adds the enclosed icons to the current selection. Conversely, pressing ⌘ while dragging a selection rectangle across selected icons deselects the enclosed group without deselecting other icons (if any).

Selecting by typing

When you know the name of an icon that you want to select but aren't sure where it is in a window, you can quickly select it by typing. Typing may be faster than clicking if the icon you want to select requires lots of scrolling to bring it into view.

To select an icon in the active window simply type the first part of its name. You need to type only enough of the name to identify the icon you want uniquely. In a window in which every icon has a completely different name, for example, you need to type only the first letter of a name to select an icon. By contrast, in a folder where every item name begins with New, you have to type those three letters plus enough additional letters to single out the icon you want. This typing must be done reasonably quickly, because any lengthy delays result in the computer assuming you are searching for a new file. This may frustrate slower typists. Also, pressing one of the arrow keys selects the icon nearest the one currently selected in the arrow's direction. In a window where icons do not appear in a list, pressing Tab selects the next icon alphabetically and Shift+Tab selects the previous icon alphabetically. Table 2.1 summarizes keyboard selection techniques.

TABLE 2.1

Selecting Icons by Typing

To Select This	Do This
An icon	Type the icon's partial or full name
Next icon up or down	Press Up (↑) or Down Arrow (↓)
Next icon left or right*	Press Left (←) or Right Arrow (→)
Next icon alphabetically*	Press Tab
Previous icon alphabetically*	Press Shift+Tab

*Applies only to a window where icons are not displayed in a list.

Contextual Menus

By simply Control+clicking an item, the contextual menu is revealed. Each item's contextual menu is different, depending on the item's type (thus the name, *contextual*). Folders, documents, aliases, disks, and applications all get their own set of options. All the commands made available in a contextual menu are available elsewhere, via the File menu, the Apple menu, or some other way, but the contextual menu is a convenient and quick way to apply commonly used commands to an item. Opening the contextual menu for the desktop and selecting Change Desktop Background opens the Desktop & Screen saver preference pane, which enables you to change the desktop background. The contextual menu for a standard document has an Open With option. This expands via a submenu to show compatible applications. It's a convenient way to open a document with a different application; it is especially fast when using a two-button mouse. We refer to contextual menus often, and strongly recommend purchasing a two-button mouse and using the right-button. The two-button method is much easier and faster than the Control+click method.

Moving icons

After selecting a few items, you may want to move them around. To move files from folder to folder, simply select the files, and then drag any of the items to the new desired location. You can drag an item by its icon or its name. In a list view, you can also drag an item by any text on the same line as the item's icon, such as its modification date or kind. The new location for your item can be the desktop, an open Finder window, or a closed folder. When you position the item you are moving over a folder icon, the Finder highlights the destination icon by making it darker. When you drag an item over a Finder window, the Finder highlights the window by drawing a heavy border inside the window frame. The highlight visually confirms your target.

When you release the mouse button, the item is moved from its original location to the newly selected one. There is one exception: If you are attempting to move a file to a different volume, the mouse pointer changes from a black arrow to a plus sign within a green dot. This symbol signifies that you are not moving the file to the new location, but rather making a copy of the file in the new location. The original item remains unaffected. You can force the file to *move* by holding down the ⌘ key while dragging the file to the volume.

Replacing items

If you move an item into a folder that contains another item of the same name, you are confronted with an alert, asking if you want to replace the file at the destination. (If you copy a group of items and more than one of them has the same name as items at the destination, you are alerted one by one for each of the duplicates.) Clicking Replace erases the items noted in the alert window from the destination folder and replaces them with the moved items. Clicking Stop cancels the operation, while clicking Don't Replace stops the file in question from being moved. You may also have the option to apply the action to all of the items you are moving, by selecting the Apply to All check box as seen in Figure 2.30.

FIGURE 2.30

You get this message when attempting to move an item to a folder where a file with that name already exists.

Spring loaded folders

To move an item from one folder to another, you do not need to have both folders open in separate windows simultaneously. You can deposit an item directly on top of another folder. This places the item within the folder. If you want to delve deeper, use Apple's extra-nifty Spring Loaded Folders

Making Corrections with Undo

If you move a file to an incorrect location, assign the wrong file name, or incorrectly label a file with a color, pressing ⌘+Z (or selecting Undo from the Edit menu) undoes the erroneous move/name/color. The function undoes only the last action performed, and the Undo operation does *not* undo an item replacement or deletion. It simply restores items to their original location or name or color, but replaced or deleted items are gone for good! Of course, it's still a powerful tool to use. In fact, after using the Finder's Undo feature a few times, we all wish the other aspects of our lives had an "undo."

feature. Drag an item over a folder to highlight it and hold it there. After a brief delay, the folder blinks twice as if double-clicked and opens to display its contents. A new window opens if there wasn't a window opened already. You can then place the item within the folder that has been sprung, or repeat the process until you reach the folder you were seeking. If you open the wrong folder with this method, either move the item out of the window (which closes the window), or move the item over a location in the sidebar to navigate there. For example, if you delve too deeply into your Documents folder, go back to the root level of the folder by dragging over its icon in the sidebar. After the brief Spring Loaded Folder delay, your window now displays the Documents folder, and you can reattempt the moving process. After you release the item into its new location, the item is placed there. It is worth noting that if the window was created by the Spring Loaded Folders feature, releasing the item places it in its new location and also closes the window.

This technique works for disks as well; dragging an item directly on top of a disk opens a new Finder window displaying the contents of the root level of the selected drive. Pressing the space bar while dragging an item on top of a folder or disk will open it into a Finder window. The length of delay time before springing is set in the Finder Preferences window, which is covered in later sections of this chapter.

Replicating your files

There will be times when you may need to replicate a file, either to make changes to one while preserving the original version, or to copy the file from one disk to another. The commands Copy or Duplicate are typically used, and are interchangeable in this context for all intents and purposes. In either case, there are a few simple techniques available.

Duplicating an item

To generate an identical copy of a selected item in the same location as the original, use the Duplicate command. To perform a duplicate operation, single-click an item and select Duplicate from the File menu. If the item chosen is a folder, the duplicate contains duplicates of everything stored in the original folder. The newly created item is placed in the same folder as the original, but with the word *copy* tagged onto the end of its name. This phrase is added to the end to help distinguish between the original and the copy, and because two files with the same name cannot exist simultaneously in the same folder. Additional copies of the same item also have a serial number added after the word *copy*. If the name does have a file extension, the word *copy* and the serial number appear before the extension. For example, the first duplicate of a folder named Untitled Folder is Untitled Folder copy, but the first duplicate of a file named Readme.txt is Readme copy.txt, and the second duplicate of the file is Readme copy 2.txt. The keyboard shortcut for Duplicate is ⌘+D. You can also duplicate a file with the contextual menu, selecting the Duplicate option when Control+clicking an item.

Copying an item

The main difference between Duplicate and Copy is that Duplicate creates the new item in the same location as the original and tinkers with the new item's name, whereas Copy does not. A copy can create items in the same folder, forcing the name change, but it can also create files in new locations, with no need to change the name, due to the alternative location (that is, no name conflict).

To copy a file, select the item and then choose Copy from the Edit menu (or contextual menu). Then, navigate to the new desired location and make it active. Select Paste from the Edit menu to initiate the copy. This method works best with a two-button mouse, because all copies can be done with one hand.

Another method is to press and hold the Option key and then drag the file. The pointer switches from its normal status as an arrow to a plus symbol in a green dot. This signifies that you are about to copy the file to the selected location, rather than just move it there.

The Finder always copies an item when you drag it to a folder that's on another disk. Again, the Finder displays a green plus sign on the pointer when you position an item over a folder of a different disk.

Replacing an item

As with moving files, when you copy an item to a folder that already contains an item by the same name, an alert asks whether you want to replace the item at the destination. If you copy a group of items and more than one of them has the same name as items at the destination, you are alerted one by one for each of the duplicates. Clicking Replace erases the items in the destination folder and replaces them with the new copies. Clicking Stop halts the copy operation.

Renaming files

After an item is selected, you can rename the item to better reflect your needs. For example, you may need to reflect changes in the document by tacking on *revised* to the name, or you may just want to rename an item to reflect its creator or content: "Letter from Chantel" or "Zanetta's Birthday Invite." Some items can be renamed with impunity, and other items are best left unmodified. Documents can be renamed with total freedom. However, applications and system files should not be renamed. Disks can be renamed with freedom, although the new name may goof up some external things, like aliases and path shortcuts. (Aliases are covered in detail later in this chapter; network paths are covered in Chapter 11.)

Creating an Archive

Archive creation is a standard feature in Leopard. This was once handled by third-party software, but Mac OS has built in this functionality. What is archiving? *Archiving* compiles and compresses any number of files selected into a single, smaller, more protected file. Select any folder, disk, item (or group of items), and select Create Archive of <*filename*> from the File menu (or from the contextual menu). When using the archive command, a progress bar briefly appears as the system is creating the archive. Archiving is often necessary to e-mail files to friends because e-mail really kicks your files around in transit (much like the post office does with your mail), and often corrupts them. This is especially true when trying to e-mail more than one item at a time. By compressing the files into a single archive, you protect them from harm as they zoom around the Internet. This archiving is also a form of lossless compression. *Lossless compression* makes a file smaller without actually reducing any of the quality (when the file is decompressed it goes back to its original size). Compression is obviously useful if you want to preserve space on your disk, or if you just want to make a particular cluster of files into a single, easily manageable item. After the archive is created, you can un-archive the files by simply double-clicking the archived file. The archive is opened and the files are safely extracted by any of a number of available tools. After extraction, the archive remains in its original form, still full of your files.

To rename a folder, file, or other item, you must explicitly select its name. After you have performed the selection correctly, the item's name is highlighted with a lighter shade of the selection color (remember, when items are selected, the icon is highlighted, and the name is surrounded by a color). The lighter shade highlighting the name indicates that the entire text is selected and ready for replacement. There are a few different methods to achieve this, depending on the way your items appear. In any view mode select the item, and then press Return or Enter. You can also select the item using any method you choose, then *wait* a couple of seconds and click the selected item's name (the text of the name, rather than the icon). If you issue the second click too quickly, the computer thinks you are double-clicking and opens the document instead of selecting the name for editing. In either case, after a brief delay, the name is selected for your editing pleasure. From the Get Info window, you can change the name in the Name and Extension panes.

When the name is first selected, the file name is highlighted. With the file name selected this way, you replace it completely by typing a new name. If you want to change only part of the name, you can select that part and replace or delete it. You can also place an insertion point and type additional text.

To replace or delete part of an item name, do the following:

1. **Select the name for editing.** Use any of the methods described above.
2. **Position the pointer where you want to begin selecting the name.** When the pointer is over the selected text, it should be shaped like the letter *I*.

3. **Press and hold the mouse button and drag the pointer to select part of the name.** As you drag, the text is selected.

    To select one particular word in a name, you can double-click the word instead of dragging across it.

4. **Release the mouse button to stop selecting.**

5. **Type a replacement for the selected part of the name or press Delete to remove the selected text.**

6. **Press Return to end your editing.** Alternatively, you can click outside the name that you're editing.

To insert text in an item name, follow these steps:

1. **Select the name for editing.** Use any of the prescribed methods.

2. **Position the pointer where you want to make an insertion.** When the pointer is over the selected text, it should be shaped like the letter *I*.

3. **Click to place an insertion point.** A thin flashing line (known as the *cursor*) marks the position of the insertion point.

4. **Type your additional text.**

5. **Press Return to end your editing.** Alternatively, you can click outside the name that you're editing.

When the desired name is entered, press Return or Enter to complete the renaming. If you decide you don't want to rename the item, but have already accidentally erased the original name, don't panic! Press the Escape key before pressing return and the original name will be restored. If you have already pressed Return and applied the name, all is still not lost. Use the Finder's Undo feature to restore the name. To use Undo, press ⌘+Z. (The Undo feature is covered in greater detail later in this chapter.)

Naming with Cut, Copy, and Paste

While editing a name, instead of typing the name from scratch, you can use the Cut, Copy, and Paste commands in the Edit menu. To copy all or part of an icon name, select the part that you want to copy and choose Copy from the Edit menu. The Copy command places the selected text on the Clipboard, which is an internal holding area. Then you can paste what you copied by selecting all or part of another icon's name and choosing Paste from the Edit menu. At this point, you can make changes to the name that you pasted. Whatever text you copied remains on the Clipboard until you use the Copy command again or the Cut command. The Cut command works just like the Copy command, but Cut also removes the initially selected text while placing it on the Clipboard. Cut, Copy, and Paste operations are covered in greater detail in Chapter 5.

NOTE Some item names cannot be selected for editing. You can't rename such an item because it is locked or you don't have Write privileges for the item. You may be able to unlock the item, but you probably can't give yourself Write privileges. Locking and unlocking is discussed later in this chapter.

Some notes on naming

Mac OS X is very forgiving with regards to naming rules. With support for 255-character-long names and all the funky symbols you can imagine, names in the Mac OS X world are limited only by your imagination. That said, Windows machines are not so forgiving. Therefore, if you ever intend to share your documents, you should obey naming convention rules.

- Avoid special characters, such as the infinity symbol (∞), the bullet symbol (•), or the euro symbol (€) in the file name because the Windows OS may not render these characters correctly. Because of having incorrectly represented characters in a name, the files may be unreadable to others.

- Names cannot include colons because the Mac OS uses colons internally to specify the *path* through your folder structure to a file. A pathname consists of a disk name, a succession of folder names, and a file name, with a colon separating each name. For example, the pathname `Macintosh HD:Applications:Spaces` specifies the location of the Spaces application on a startup disk named Macintosh HD. Putting a colon in a file name would interfere with the computer's scheme for specifying paths, so the Finder won't let you do it.

- Although the Finder won't let you use colons in a file name, it *does* let you use slashes. It is strongly advised that you *never* use slash characters (/ or \) in your file names. Windows machines read these characters as indicating the path on their disks (just like Macs use colons), and the computer will look for folders that do not exist, resulting in a completely inaccessible document (unless your friend is smart enough to figure out how to rename the files).

- A few things that *are* okay: All alphabetic letters (capital or not, for example A–Z, a–z), Hindu-Arabic numbers (0–9), the symbols in the number row (`~!@#$%^&*()=+), blank spaces, hyphens (-), and underscores (_) are universally acceptable, as are commas (,).

Get Info

Mac OS X keeps a great deal of detailed information about your files, folders, and disks beyond what's available in regular Finder windows. A time may come when you want to see or change some of this information. Hidden in the Info window (also known as the Get Info pane, or just Get Info) is the area that displays the additional critical information and enables some interesting changes to be performed on most selected items. To bring this powerful window to light, select an item and select Show Info from the File menu, or press ⌘+I. The Get Info window opens, complete with basic information and bearing multiple disclosure triangles hiding various information and control repositories.

Spotlight Comments

This field can be populated with any information you want. The expectation is that any data in this field will improve the effectiveness of Spotlight searches. Spotlight is covered in more detail in Chapter 3. This field can be helpful when managing a large host of files with similar names, because users can enter information here to help distinguish files. Also, information can be entered in the Spotlight Comments field for the benefit of others that may be using the files.

Selecting Text with the Keyboard

With an icon name selected for editing, you can also move the insertion point or change the selection by using the arrow keys.

↑	Moves the insertion point to the beginning of the name
↓	Moves the insertion point to the end of the name
→	Moves the insertion point to the right
←	Moves the insertion point to the left
Option+→	Moves the insertion point word-by-word to the right.
Option+←	Moves the insertion point word-by-word to the left.
Shift+→	Selects more (or less) of the name to the right
Shift+←	Selects more (or less) of the name to the left

Whether Shift+→ and Shift+← selects more or less depends on the direction that you dragged when you initially selected part of the name.

General

General is the main area of the Get Info window. The item's kind, size, location, creation date, modification date, and label all appear in this area. Depending on the item's type, additional or alternate information will appear. For example, if the selected item is a disk, information on the Format method applied to the disk is shown, and the size information is replaced and supplemented with total capacity, available space remaining on the disk, and the amount of space currently in use. The Get Info window for documents also gives users the option to set the file as a Stationary Pad or Lock the file for protection (discussed in detail later), and the Get Info window for volumes enables you to set the volume as a Shared Folder.

Stationery Pad

Many items have the Stationery Pad check box. Checking this box turns the item into a template. More on stationery pads and templates can be found in Chapter 5.

Locked

Like the Stationery Pad check box, many items have the locked check box. Checking this box locks the item and prevents it from being deleted or modified. Locked files are discussed in greater detail later in this chapter.

More Info

The More Info area is populated with more specific and often technical information about a particular file. For example, in the case of a Portable Network Graphics file, the More Info section provides the dimensions of the image, the color space, profile name, alpha channel, and the date it was last opened.

Name & Extension

The name of the selected item is shown in the Name & Extension section. Clicking in the box containing the item's name enables you to edit the name of the item. It is worth noting that the name of the item is shown with its extension here. The file name extension is a three- or four-letter code that delineates the document's type. Changing this extension is not recommended, because it has the potential to confuse the Finder's ability to choose the appropriate application to open the document with. See "Some notes on naming" earlier in this chapter regarding some general tips on naming files.

Open With

Each document has a parent application (that is, the application that by default attempts to open it). In this area, that default application can be changed. For example, Portable Document Format (PDF) files can be opened by Apple's built-in Preview application or by Adobe's Acrobat application. Choose which application you want to open the document with by default by using the convenient pop-up menu. You can choose to have the selected file or all related files opened by the newly selected parent application by clicking the Change All button. Beware: This action cannot be undone.

Preview

If the item is a graphic file, this area displays a preview of the image. If the file is a movie file, the preview displays a miniature version of the movie, complete with controls to play it. Some items cannot be previewed in this area, either because the preview engine cannot render them or because there is nothing to preview. Items that cannot be previewed include, but are not limited to, certain text documents, folders, and disks. In this case, the Preview field will just display a full-size rendering of the item's icon.

I'm sorry Dave, I'm afraid I can't do that . . .

Mac OS X doesn't permit you to move, rename, or copy everything, and it won't let you put stuff anywhere you want. For example, you can't move or copy your items into another user's home folder. Conversely, you can't move or rename items that belong to other users, although you may be able to copy other users' items into your folders.

The Finder won't let you move an item from its current location or rename it unless you have Write privileges for the item. If you try to move an item for which you don't have Write privileges but do have Read privileges, the Finder makes a copy of the item instead. If you don't have Write or Read privileges for an item, the Finder doesn't let you move, rename, or copy the item.

Regardless of your Write privileges for an item that you want to move or copy, you must also have Write privileges for the destination folder. If you try to move or copy an item to a folder for which you don't have Write privileges, the Finder displays an alert, saying the destination folder cannot be modified.

Sharing & Permissions

Sharing of a file and the permissions associated with the file are complex and potentially confusing. The basic concept is as follows: The creator of a file is the default owner of that file. The owner can choose to share the file with whomever he pleases. Permissions are the rules that owners apply to their files, enabling other people to work with them. The permissions can be very specific, allowing visitors only to read files, and not to edit or delete them. The permissions can be cut and dried as well, allowing total control or complete lock-out.

Locking or unlocking an item

You can use the Info window to lock files individually so that they can't be changed. After locking a file, you can open the file and copy it, but you can't make any changes to its name or contents. Additionally, the Finder does not allow you to move locked files into the Trash. The padlock in the lower left-hand corner of the file's icon indicates if a file is locked. Follow these steps to lock a file:

1. **Select the file that you want to lock.** Choose Get Info from the File menu.
2. **Select the Locked option in the Info window.** The Locked option appears under the General section of the Info window. You can't change an item's Locked option if you are not the item's owner.

Finding Out About the Finder

Ask most Mac users which application they use most often, and you will receive answers like Adobe Photoshop or Microsoft Word or Safari. These answers are all incorrect. What's the correct answer? The Finder! The Finder is the most accessed application in the Mac OS because it is at the heart of your environmental experience. Unlike the majority of other applications, you don't have to do anything to make it start running. The Finder starts running automatically when you log in and keeps running until you log out. Represented by a blue smiling computer face, the Finder's icon is always listed first in the Dock. The Finder is responsible for generating the desktop, maintaining its own windows, and controlling the interaction between files, their host applications, and the hard drive. Of course, this makes the Finder not only the most commonly used, but also the most important and potentially most fragile application. The old Macintosh OS 9 Finder was less of an application, and more of a system function. Any attempts to recover from a Finder problem would typically be met with a user shouting at the screen and/or punching the keyboard as the last few hours of work disappeared in a reboot. The Mac OS X Finder operates much like other applications; able to recover from errors — even able to be relaunch when needed — on the fly, without forcing a reboot or damaging a user's work in other applications

Finder-specific menus

Earlier this chapter discussed the menu bar in general. Most applications make their own additions to the menu bar, or they may eliminate some menu items, or remove the menu bar altogether! And, yes, even the Finder, the core system application, has its own unique menus that are added to the menu bar.

Finder menu

The application menu is the first menu after the Apple menu, and it's named for the active application. Thus, while in the Finder, the menu is named Finder. As with all application menus, this menu is populated with commands that pertain to that specific application. Selecting the About Finder option opens a window containing copyright information on the Finder as well as stating which version of the Finder you are using. (Apple releases updates all the time, which you can keep up with via the Software Update preference pane as covered in Chapter 1.) Other menu options in the Finder menu include the command to Secure Empty Trash, and the Services drop-down menu that contains various additional features and commands. The Services menu and its various elements are covered in Chapter 9.

Go menu

The Go menu is one of two Finder-specific menus available in the menu bar. The Go menu is designed to offer the user a few convenient shortcuts to commonly used locations or items. By selecting these items, a new Finder window opens, displaying the selected location. See the Go menu in Figure 2.31.

Choose Computer, Home, Desktop, iDisk, or Applications from the Go menu to display the contents of the corresponding folder in the front Finder window. (If no Finder window is currently open, a new Finder window appears.) Each Go menu item has handy keyboard shortcuts. Computer is ⌘+Shift+C, Home is ⌘+Shift+H, iDisk is ⌘+Shift+I, and Applications is ⌘+Shift+A.

FIGURE 2.31
_____

The Go menu contains shortcuts to numerous commonly used locations.

Recent Folders

The Recent Folders submenu of the Go menu lists the last 10 folders you displayed in the Finder. This submenu is similar in concept to the Recent Items menu in the Apple menu, which lists applications and documents that you have recently used. Like the Apple ➪ Recent Items submenu, the Go ➪ Recent Folders submenu has a menu choice for clearing the current list of recent folders.

Go To Folder

If you know the exact name and path to the folder you want (and you type well), choose Go ⇨ Go To Folder (or press the keyboard shortcut ⌘+Shift+G). The Finder displays a dialog box in which you type the path and name of the folder you want. This is far from the traditional Macintosh graphical interface, but it is one near and dear to the hearts of folks accustomed to Unix and MS-DOS environments.

A complete path to a folder begins with a slash character (/) and is followed by the names of every folder from the outermost folder to the folder that you want to open, with an additional slash between folder names. For example, /Applications/Utilities is the path to the Utilities folder within the Applications folder.

If you don't start the pathname with a /, the Finder looks for a relative path, one that starts in the current folder. For example, if the Applications folder is open in the front Finder window, you can open the Utilities folder by typing **Utilities** in the Go To Folder dialog box.

TIP Unix pathname shortcuts all work in the Go To Folder dialog box. For example, if you're in a folder on another volume and want to be in the Sites folder of your home folder, just press ⌘+Shift+G to display the Go To Folder dialog box and type ~/Sites to be transported. Similarly, to get to the Public folder of another user with the short name eabrahams, you would type ~eabrahams/Public. Confused? See Chapter 23 for more on Unix.

Back

If you want the front Finder window to go back to the folder or disk that it last displayed, choose Go ⇨ Back (or press ⌘+[). You can continue going back by choosing Go ⇨ Back again. When the front Finder window can't go back any more because it is displaying the first folder or disk that it ever showed, the Back item is disabled (dim) in the Go menu. The Back item in the Go menu is equivalent to the Back button in the Finder window toolbar.

Connect To Server

The Go menu's final choice provides access to file servers, either on your own network or on the Internet. Choosing Go ⇨ Connect To Server (or pressing ⌘+K) displays a dialog box in which you specify the server that you want to connect to. This dialog box provides a pop-up menu of recent servers, in addition to a browser area in which you find available servers on your local network.

View menu

The View menu contains commands that change the style and method of items presented via the Finder. In addition to switching between view modes (covered later in this chapter), the View menu enables users to edit some specific view details for each view mode. The commands apply to Finder windows and the desktop, and typically affect only the foremost window (or the desktop if no windows are selected or open). Figure 2.32 shows the View menu.

FIGURE 2.32

The View menu includes options to adjust the appearance of items in a Finder window or on the desktop.

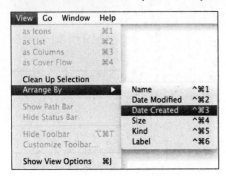

The View menu contains the following commands:

- **as Icons:** This switches the current Finder window to the IIcon view mode. You can change this setting by clicking the icon button at the top of the Finder window. The keyboard shortcut to perform this command is ⌘+1. This command is available only if a Finder window is open and active.

- **as List:** This switches the current Finder window to the List view mode. The keyboard shortcut to perform this command is ⌘+2. This command is available only if a Finder window is open and active.

- **as Columns:** This switches the current Finder window to the Column view mode. The keyboard shortcut to perform this command is ⌘+3. This command is available only if a Finder window is open and active.

- **as Cover Flow:** This switches the current Finder window to the Cover Flow view mode. Adopted from iTunes, this view is new to the Finder. The keyboard shortcut to perform this command is ⌘+4. This command is available only if a Finder window is open and active. This view is discussed in greater detail in the "Working in Cover Flow view" section.

- **Clean Up:** This command is available with icon views only. Clean Up neatens up the current window's contents by aligning the items on a grid.

- **Arrange:** This command is available with icon views only. Arrange reorganizes a window's contents both to a grid and to a specified factor. You specify the sorting factor via the submenu: The options are by Name, Date Modified, Date Created, Size, Kind, and Label.

- **Hide Toolbar:** This command does more than just turn off the toolbar in the active Finder window. In fact, hiding the Toolbar results in a very different-looking and much leaner Finder window. If the toolbar is already hidden, the menu option reads Show

Toolbar, and selecting it returns the toolbar to view. The keyboard shortcut for this command is ⌘+Option+T. This command is available only if a Finder window is open and active.

- **Customize Toolbar:** This command opens a dialog box that enables users to customize the toolbar according to their needs. This command is available only if a Finder window is open and active.

- **Hide Status Bar:** This command is available only for Finder windows that are in the simpler Hide Toolbar view. This command turns off the status bar in the active Finder window. If the status bar is already hidden, the menu option reads Show Status Bar, and selecting it returns the status bar to view.

- **Show View Options:** This menu command opens a dialog box where the current view mode can be edited and adjusted.

Finder windows

Typically, you navigate your computer's myriad of files and folders via Finder windows. Finder windows graphically represent the contents of particular folders or disks, and can present this information in many ways, each with its own characteristics and advantages. A standard Finder window is a good place to review many of the most common objects.

Mac OS X gives you a few ways to create new Finder windows:

- Choose File ➪ New Finder Window.
- Click any folder or disk icon and choose Open from the Finder menu.
- Click the Finder icon in the Dock. If there are open Finder windows, this brings the windows to the front, with the exception of minimized Finder windows.
- If the Finder is the active application, press ⌘+N. (Identifying active applications is discussed later in this chapter.)
- Double-click any folder or disk icon visible on the desktop.
- Double-click any folder or disk icon in another Finder window with the toolbar hidden.
- Press ⌘ while opening (double-clicking) a folder or disk that appears in a Finder window with the toolbar visible.

In this new Finder window, you are confronted with a number of interesting controls and surfaces. Some are large and obvious, such as the sidebar, the toolbar (both discussed later in this chapter), and a few icons in the main window pane (either the elements of your home folder or the root level of your hard disk). Figure 2.33 displays an annotated diagram of a basic Finder window.

NOTE *Root level* is geek-talk for the bottommost layer. Think of root level as the roots of a tree, with all of your files as leaves sprouting out from various branches (the folders) that pop out along the way up the trunk (the disk/volume).

FIGURE 2.33

Finder windows are the primary tools used to view available files within folders or disks. These are some items unique to Finder windows.

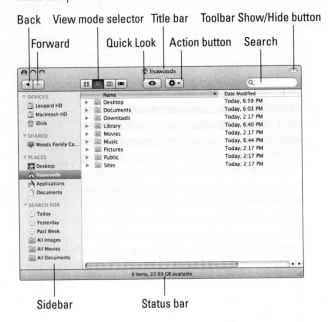

Sidebar   Status bar

Finder windows are composed of the standard window controls described earlier in this chapter, in addition to a number of unique additional tools to modify the window's appearance and behavior.

■ **Sidebar:** The sidebar is the area on the left side of a Finder window that contains short-cuts to commonly needed destinations within a user's system. The sidebar can be edited to suit your needs. Editing the sidebar is discussed later in this chapter. To use a sidebar item, simply click its icon. The current window displays the sidebar item's contents. For example, if you are currently reviewing your home folder in a Finder window, and then click the Macintosh HD icon in the sidebar, the contents of the root level of the hard disk appear in the main window, rather than the home folder. Pressing and holding ⌘ when clicking a sidebar item opens a completely new Finder window in front of the original window. The new window displays the selected item's contents. Holding down Option while clicking an item closes the original window and opens a new one displaying the selected item. The sidebar in Mac OS 10.5 has notably changed. Shortcuts are now organized into the following categories:

■ **Devices:** Lists hard disks, iDisks, CDs, and so on.

■ **Shared:** Computers on the same local area network are listed here. Not only can you share your screen or control the other computer (administrator privileges are required), but you can do so without the use of Apple Remote Desktop or any third-party applications. To share your screen, simply click the icon of the computer that appears below the Shared Computers heading in the Finder sidebar and click Share Screen. You will be prompted for an administrator password. After authenticating, the computer screen appears in a new window. See Figure 2.34. To end the session, simply close the window.

FIGURE 2.34

Using the Share Screen feature, you can check in on your child's computing activity from another room.

- **Places:** Organizes the popular destinations on your hard disk, like your Desktop, Home folder, Application folder, and Documents folder.

- **Search For:** Sorts the data that you have created, opened, or modified into three categories: Today, Yesterday, or Last Week. If on the other hand you want to sort the data by type, you can choose to see all of the Images, Movies, or Documents stored on your hard disk.

- **Toolbar:** The toolbar is located just below the title bar, and contains very useful tools to perform commonly used functions with a single click, rather than through complex commands. It functions as an adjunct to the menu bar. A new addition to the toolbar is Quick Look and the Cover Flow icon. Quick Look is a great way to peek into documents, and the Cover Flow view is a dramatic way to peruse your files and folders in the Finder. It may not be the view you choose on a daily basis, but it's an awesome way to browse through your images. The toolbar can be edited to suit your needs or style. Changing the toolbar to suit your needs is discussed later in this chapter.

- **Toolbar Hide/Show button:** Another element of the title bar in all Finder windows, the toolbar Hide/Show control is a pill-shaped button. It is located in the top right portion of the title bar. Click this button to hide the toolbar and most of the Finder-specific elements of the window. The result of turning off the toolbar is to produce a radically different-looking Finder window, with no toolbar, no sidebar, and no metallic border. The look is very minimal, which will probably make the clean-freaks or OS 9 addicts out there happy. If this reduced window mode is already in effect, click this button to show the toolbar.

- **Action button:** The Action button looks like a gear with a downward facing black triangle next to it. The Action button performs functions nearly identical to a contextual menu. By clicking the Action button, a list of commands is presented based on the type of item or window selected.

- **Quick Look button:** This new addition to the Toolbar looks eerily like an eye. Quick Look offers a full size preview of files. There are three ways to access this feature: via the Quick Look button in the toolbar, via the contextual menu, or by simply selecting an item and pressing the Spacebar (this is my favorite way); press the space bar again and the preview is closed. You have the option to view the items in full screen, or you can flip through documents that contain more than one page. Chapter 5 digs deeper into Quick Look.

- **Back:** A standard button in the toolbar, the Back button returns the Finder window to the previous folder that was opened or viewing mode that was selected.

- **Forward:** Also a standard button in the toolbar, the Forward button moves forward into a selected folder or undoes a click of the Back button.

- **View mode selectors:** The view mode selectors are four buttons to the right of the Forward and Back buttons. These buttons allow easy switching between the four Finder window view modes: Icon, List, Column, and Cover Flow views. Each mode is illustrated by a distinct icon; the Icon view selector looks like four icons arranged in a square, the List view selector resembles a list of information, the Column view selector looks like three columns, and the Cover Flow icon is a box with three vertical lines on the left and right side. Click any of these buttons to switch the current Finder window to the desired mode of view. These view modes are discussed in detail later in this chapter.

- **Search field:** It's all too easy to lose track of files or folders within the maze of your computer's directory. This tool makes finding the lost files easy. Located at the top right of every Finder window, the Search field performs a dynamic file search. Start by clicking the magnifying glass symbol next to the empty text field and select where you want to begin searching. Say for example that you are looking for an e-mail from an old friend; type the name of the sender or the subject of the message (if you can recall it). The current window depopulates and begins displaying all files and folders that contain the letters typed. This search field works dynamically, so each letter typed refines the displayed content. When you can see the file you are seeking, simply stop typing and double-click the file to open it, or open the file using any of the other methods covered in Chapter 5.

- **File Path:** The File Path displays the location of the currently selected file and appears at the bottom of the Finder window, when in the Search For mode or when searching for a file. Double-clicking a folder in the File Path field opens a new Finder window. Meanwhile, double-clicking any document in File Path opens the document.

- **Status bar:** The status bar appears at the bottom of every Finder window. However, the status bar does not appear when the Toolbar is suppressed. The status bar presents information concerning the window's contents. The status bar also displays the amount of unused storage space on the disk or other volume that contains the folder whose contents appear in the window. Also, if you do not have write privileges for a folder, disk, or other item whose contents appear in the window, a small icon that looks like a crossed-out pencil appears near the left end of the status bar. Privileges are covered in Chapter 12.

Finder window views

Each Finder window can be viewed in one of four view modes, each with its own advantages and disadvantages. These choices are Icon, List, Column, and Cover Flow views. If you think you've seen Cover Flow before, you're right. Cover Flow was first introduced in iTunes as a nifty way to view your music and album artwork simultaneously. This view mode is especially useful when browsing through images. Which mode or modes you use is completely up to your tastes or circumstances.

Choosing a view

Every view has its purpose. You can choose your view format for the active Finder window in one of two ways:

- **Choose a view style from the Finder's View menu.** Select one of the four choices: as Icons, as List, as Columns, or as Cover Flow.

- **Click the appropriate part of the View Mode Selector button in the window's toolbar.** Click the appropriate button to view as Icons, as a List, as Columns, or as Cover Flow.

Working in an icon view

The icon view is the original Finder view, dating back to the very first Macs shipped in 1984. In Mac OS 10.5, the icon view has been updated to provide more information. The icons of Text Edit, Preview, iPhoto, Portable Network Graphics, and Microsoft Office application files now give you a preview of the data contained in the file. Before Leopard, this functionality was limited for the most part to applications like Photoshop. In addition to displaying the icon view with a custom icon that gives you a preview of the file's contents, picture documents advertise the size of the image directly beneath the file name. You select an icon by clicking it, typing the first part of its name, or pressing the arrow keys. You can select multiple icons by clicking and dragging your pointer across them or by ⌘+clicking or Shift+clicking each icon in turn. The biggest advantage of the icon view is the ability to preview a document before opening it.

Cleaning up

If the icons in an icon view are in disarray, you can have the Finder align them in neat rows and columns. You clean up the active window by choosing View ⇨ Clean Up. You can clean up individual icons by pressing and holding the ⌘ key while dragging them individually or in groups.

Arrange by Name

You can also have the Finder alphabetize the icons and align them in rows and columns. Do this by choosing View ⇨ Arrange by Name. The Finder can also keep the icons in a window arranged for you. Configuring automatic icon arrangement in the Finder's View Options window is covered later in this chapter.

Working in a list view

List views pack a lot of information in a window. Although items appear in a list format, columns enable you to sort the information by the file name, date modified, size, and kind. You can use the columns to help sort and organize the items. You can sort the list by any of the column headings at the top of the view. Folder contents appear in an indented outline format. Apple has streamlined the list view by shading alternate rows, thereby making it easier to follow the facts of the file across columns from Name to Kind. The main advantages of the list view are the ability to select multiple items from different folders, the variety of navigation tools available, and the ability to sort lists by more than just name.

Changing the sort order

When you initially view a window as a list, the items are arranged alphabetically by name. A quick glance at the column headings tells you the sorting order. The highlighted column heading indicates that the items are being sorted by that column. In a Finder window, you can change the sorting order by clicking one of the column headings near the top of the window. For example, to list the items in the order in which they were last modified, click the Date Modified heading. Click the heading again to toggle between ascending and descending order. An arrowhead at the right end of the heading indicates the sort direction.

Rearranging and resizing columns

The columns of a list view are adjustable in a Finder window. This is helpful if an item's name is too long to be displayed in the current layout, as indicated by the name truncated by an ellipsis (...).

To change the size of a column, follow these steps:

1. **Position the mouse pointer to the right edge of a column heading.** (The pointer is in the right place for resizing a column when the pointer transforms into a vertical line with left- and right-pointing arrows coming out of it).

2. **Click and hold the mouse button.**

3. **Drag left or right.**

> **TIP** You don't have to widen a column in a list view just to read one long name. You can display the entire name in a help tag by positioning the pointer over the name and waiting a few seconds. If you can't wait, point at the name and press Option to see the help tag immediately.

You can also change the order in which columns appear. Simply click and drag the column heading to the left or right. As you drag, the pointer transforms to a hand and you see a pale image of the column you are moving. Unfortunately, Apple doesn't allow you to move the Name column. However, you can achieve the same end by moving other columns in front (to the left) of the Name column.

Navigating a list view with disclosure triangles

When reviewing a folder's contents in List view, you don't have to open disks or folders in new windows to navigate deeper into your folder structure. A list view allows you to expand the folders via a method similar to an indented outline. Instead of opening a folder or disk in a new window, you can see the contents of a disk or folder by clicking the disclosure triangle to the left of its icon.

Disclosure triangles appear next to folder names if the folder contains additional items, and they tell you whether the folders are expanded or collapsed. If a triangle points to the right, the folder next to it is collapsed, and you cannot see its contents. If the triangle points down, the folder is expanded, and below the folder name you can see a list of the items in the folder. The Finder displays list views in an indented outline format. The levels of indentation in the outline show how folders are nested. The indented outline provides a graphical representation of a folder's organization. You can look through and reorganize several folders all in one window. Figure 2.35 shows an example of a list view with both expanded and collapsed folders.

To expand a folder, click the triangle to the left of the folder's icon. When you expand a folder, the Finder remembers whether folders nested within it were previously expanded or collapsed and restores each to its former state.

To collapse a folder, click the down-pointing triangle to the left of the folder's icon. The triangle returns to the right-pointing orientation, and the contents can no longer be seen.

FIGURE 2.35

A list view with expanded and collapsed folders

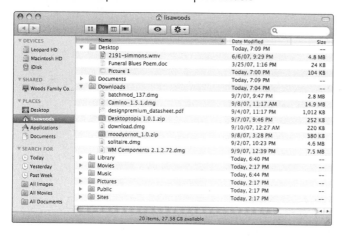

To expand a folder and the first level of all subfolders within it, press Option while clicking the disclosure triangle. Repeating this action collapses the folder and the first level of subfolders.

Working in a column view

This column view derives its layout from the NeXT browser view, and it first appeared on the Mac in the shareware utility, Greg's Browser, back in 1989. Understanding the column view and becoming comfortable with its use is relatively important because you see column views in the dialog boxes for opening and saving documents within applications (as explained in Chapter 5). The main advantages of the column view are the ease of reviewing the path to a particular item and the wealth of information displayed when previewing items. The disadvantage is the lack of the sorting options present in this view.

A column view shows a folder and its contents in the same window through the use of limitless replicating columns. When you select a folder in a column view, that folder's contents appear in the next column to the right. The deeper you explore, the more columns become available. When you select an alias of a folder, Mac OS X resolves the alias and the Finder displays the original folder's contents in the next column to the right. When you select a file, some basic information about the item, as well as its icon or a preview of its contents, appears in the next column to the right (see Figure 2.36). Whether you see a file's icon or a preview of its contents depends on the type of file. For an application, you always see an icon and some facts about the application including the name; kind; size; date the application was created (or installed), modified, or last opened; and the version of the application you are running. For some types of documents that contain text or graphics, you see a preview. When previewing a graphic in column view, all of the file information mentioned above appears, but the version is replaced with the graphic's dimensions.

FIGURE 2.36

When viewing an image in column view, a preview of the image, as well as the file name, kind, size, date it was created, modification date, the last time the file was opened, and the file's dimensions appear.

A column view differs markedly from an icon view or a list view in how much of the folder structure you can see. Where an icon view shows only one folder and a list view shows one folder plus the folders it contains, every column view can show any part of the folder structure on any disk that's available on your computer. By scrolling a column view to the left, you can traverse the folder hierarchy to the Computer level. By scrolling to the right, you can traverse the folder hierarchy in the other direction until you reach the currently selected folder or file.

Unlike list or icon views, you have no control over the sorting order in a column view. Items in each column are always listed alphabetically. (Actually, the order of items is based on the character-set ordering established for your system and language.)

Resizing columns

Column width is adjustable in a column view. You can adjust the widths of all columns uniformly or the width of a single column as follows:

- To resize one column, drag the handle at the bottom of the column divider.

- To resize *all* columns at once uniformly, press and hold Option while dragging the handle at the bottom of any column divider to the right or left.

Previewing files in a column view

One of the column view's nicest features is that, when you select certain types of document files, you see a preview of that document's contents in the rightmost column. Previews appear for several types of documents, including plain text, PDF, sound, movie, and graphics files. For a document with multiple pages, the preview shows the first page. The preview for a sound or movie appears with a small QuickTime controller, which enables you to play a song or watch a preview of a movie. QuickTime is discussed in Chapters 6 and 7.

NOTE Back in the day, preparing the preview for a long PDF document or even a very large plain text document could take a long time and cause the Mac to be unresponsive. However, with Quick Look you can preview an entire PDF or text file regardless of length.

Pathfinding alternative

As noted, a column view gives you a quick look at the path through the folder structure from the Computer level to the item or items displayed in the rightmost column. However, you don't have to be in a column view to obtain this path information. At the top of any Finder window, the title bar tells you the name of the folder you are in. When you press the ⌘ key and click the name of the folder, a menu pops up, showing the hierarchy of folders traversed to get back to the Computer level. The current folder is at the top of the pop-up menu, and the Computer level is at the bottom, as shown in Figure 2.37.

FIGURE 2.37

See the path through your folder structure by ⌘+clicking the title bar of a Finder window.

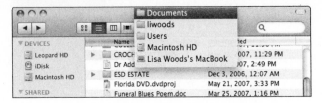

Working in Cover Flow view

Taken straight out of the pages of iTunes, Cover Flow is the newest addition to the Finder views. By far the prettiest view, the Cover Flow view is a combination of the Icon and the List view. Split horizontally, the upper half presents icons of the items in a runway-like display, and the bottom half displays the items in a list (see Figure 2.38). As a result, you can modify the sorting order of items just as you would in List view. Navigating through items in the Cover Flow view is simple: Use the scroll bar directly beneath the icons to flip through files or press the up and down arrows in the list. Double-click a folder to reveal its contents. Not only do you get a preview of the file, you can also click through multipage documents as if you were turning pages in a book, or play a QuickTime movie.

FIGURE 2.38

The Cover Flow view displays your images and documents in stunning array.

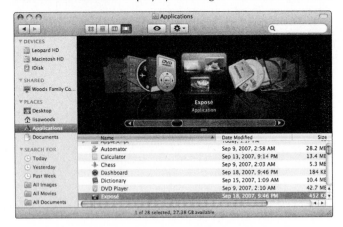

Setting Finder Preferences

The Finder has a number of preference settings that affect the appearance of icons on the desktop, the behavior of Finder windows, label colors, emptying the Trash, showing extensions on the names of files, and more. You change these preference settings by choosing Finder ➪ Preferences.

The Finder Preferences window appears. There are four available subpanes to the Finder Preferences window. Each is shown in Figure 2.39.

FIGURE 2.39

The Finder's preference settings affect desktop icons, Finder windows, the Trash, and file extensions. Note the expanded sidebar preferences.

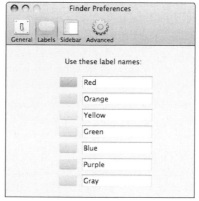

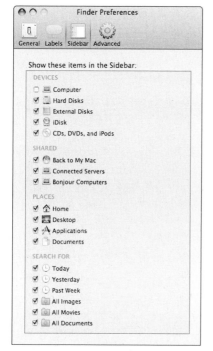

Finder Preferences offers the following options:

- **Show these items on the Desktop:** Select the types of items that you want the Finder to display on your desktop. These items are shown together with any additional items located in the Desktop folder of your Home folder. All items appear at the Computer level of your workspace regardless of the settings here.

- **New Finder windows open:** Select what folder you want to appear when you create a new Finder window. The default, and recommended, option is your Home folder. Other options include the Documents folder, Macintosh HD (root level of the disk), iDisk (if available), the Computer level of your folder structure, or Other. Selecting Other opens a dialog box, where you can select the desired folder and click Open. The Home folder is recommended because this is the main repository for all of your personal data, including documents, music, pictures, and more.

- **Always open folders in a new window:** Select this option to reverse the Mac OS X Finder's practice of navigating within a single window. This makes the Mac OS X Finder spawn windows in the same way as the old Mac OS 9 Finder.

- **Open new windows in column view:** Select this option, and the Finder opens all new windows in column view. Of course, once the window is opened, you can switch to any desired view mode through the methods covered earlier in this chapter.

- **Spring-loaded folders and windows:** If you drag an icon over a closed folder, the folder automatically opens after a brief delay. This delayed opening is called *spring-loading*. This slider sets the time delay between when you drag an icon over a folder and when that folder springs open. As the note below the slider points out, if you want a folder to open immediately, drag the icon over the folder, and then press the Spacebar on the keyboard.

- **Labels:** Each individual file or folder in Mac OS X can have a colored label applied to it, affording users another way of visually sorting through their files. In the second subpane of the Finder Preferences window, the labels can be named to more accurately reflect their purpose. By default, the names are simply the name of the color.

- **Sidebar:** This subpane of the Finder preference pane displays the list of standard items shown in the sidebar. Deselecting items here removes them from the sidebar.

- **Show all file extensions:** Select this option if you want to see the three or four character name extensions (suffixes) for all files that have them. Displaying the file extension gives you a clue as to what *type* of file you may have been given.

- **Show warning before emptying the Trash:** Deselect this option if you want the Finder to empty the Trash without first prompting you to confirm the action. If this option is off, the Finder also deletes locked items from the Trash without any warning. It is recommended to leave this option selected, to prevent accidental erasure of files.

- **Empty Trash securely:** Select this option if you want to securely empty your Trash each time you select Empty Trash.

Modifying Finder windows

So far this chapter has discussed how to view a Finder window as icons, a list, columns, or cover flow; how to clean up an icon view and change the sorting of a list view; and how to show and hide the toolbar at the top of any Finder window (which results in a rather different look!). These are only some of the ways you can customize Finder windows. Other methods for tuning Finder windows include suppressing the sidebar and customizing the toolbar. These methods are covered in this section.

Customizing the toolbar

The default toolbar consists of a number of buttons — Back, Forward, View Mode Selectors, Quick Look, and Action — and the Search field. Apple enables you to remove any of these buttons, add others, and arrange them any way you want. You can also set the toolbar to display the buttons as named icons, icons without names, or names alone. To make these changes, with any Finder window active, choose View ⇨ Customize Toolbar. The active Finder window changes to display the Customize Toolbar dialog box shown in Figure 2.40.

FIGURE 2.40

Add, remove, and rearrange buttons in a Finder window's toolbar by using the Customize Toolbar dialog box.

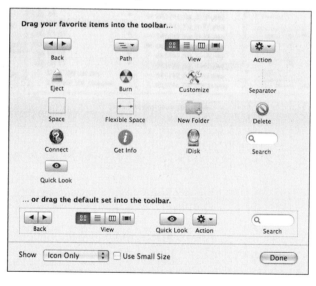

With the Customize Toolbar dialog box open, change the toolbar by doing the following:

■ **Add buttons:** Drag any of the optional buttons to the toolbar from the main part of the dialog box. You don't have to add buttons only to the right end of the toolbar. If you drag a button between two buttons in the toolbar, they move apart to make room for the button you're dragging. If the toolbar is full of buttons and you drag another button to the toolbar, buttons that don't fit on the toolbar appear in a pop-up menu. To see this menu, click the arrow that appears at the right end of the toolbar. Click the Done button to complete your toolbar customization.

- **Remove buttons:** Drag buttons away from the toolbar.

- **Rearrange buttons:** Drag buttons to different places on the toolbar.

- **Revert to default buttons:** If you've customized the toolbar and want to get back to the default set of buttons, drag the boxed default set from the lower part of the dialog box to the toolbar to replace whatever is currently there.

- **Show:** Show items as icons with names, icons only, or names only by choosing from the Show pop-up menu at the bottom of the dialog box. Figure 2.41 gives examples of each toolbar mode. The Use Small Size check box makes the toolbar icons smaller, conserving space.

FIGURE 2.41

A Finder window's toolbar displaying just icons (top), both icons and text (middle), and only text (bottom).

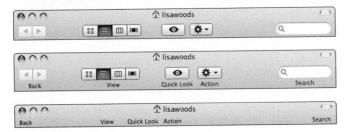

NOTE   Add icons as buttons — even without the Customize Toolbar dialog box open! Just drag folders, files, or disks from anywhere on your computer to the toolbar while pressing and holding the ⌘ key, and the items become buttons there. For example, if you create a folder for a particular project within your Documents folder, drag its icon to the toolbar to make it accessible with a single click. To remove items, use the Customize Toolbar dialog box; however, the easiest way to remove items is to press and hold ⌘ and drag the item out of the toolbar. The item disappears in a puff of smoke.

TIP   Clicking a folder button in the toolbar opens the folder in the same window. If you ⌘+click a folder button in the toolbar, the folder opens in a new Finder window.

Additional toolbar buttons

As shown in Figure 2.40, there are numerous controls available for the toolbar. Each has its use:

- **Path:** The Path tool when clicked displays a pop-up menu showing the file hierarchy path to the current folder. Selecting any of the folders in the path opens that folder within the active window. This can also be performed by ⌘+clicking the title bar.

- **Eject:** This tool ejects any selected disks or disconnects server volumes. The contextual menu for each disk or volume offers the same option.

- **Burn:** If your computer is equipped with a CD or DVD burner, this tool opens the Burn disk dialog box.

- **Customize:** This tool when clicked opens the Customize Toolbar window.

- **Separator:** The Separator is a simply vertical line that serves as a visual dividing line between items.

- **Flexible Space:** This item is simply a blank space, approximately the same width as other tools. The Flexible Space item fills all space available in the toolbar. Placing a flexible space between items pushes items on both sides to the far left and far right sides.

- **New Folder:** Clicking this tool creates a new folder in the active window. This action can also be performed by pressing Shift+⌘+N.

- **Delete:** This tool moves selected items to the Trash.

- **Connect:** Clicking this tool opens the Connect To Server dialog box. This dialog box can also be opened via the Go menu, or by pressing ⌘+K. (The Connect To Server dialog box is discussed in Chapter 12.)

- **Get Info:** This tool opens the Get Info window for any selected item. This window can also be opened by pressing ⌘+I.

- **iDisk:** Click this tool to open your iDisk (a feature of Apple's .Mac service, covered in Chapter 14).

- **Search:** Adds a search field (linked to Spotlight) to the toolbar.

- **Quick Look:** One of the many new features in Mac OS 10.5, Quick Look gives you a preview of a file without launching its supporting application.

Setting View Options

The Finder in Mac OS X provides still more ways to tweak the basic icon and list views. This section discusses the adjustments you can make to icon and list views in the View Options window, which you display for an active window by choosing View ⇨ Show View Options. The options in this window are different for Icon, List, Column, and Cover Flow view, as shown in Figure 2.42.

The View Options window displays the settings of the folder, disk, or other item whose name appears in the title bar of the active Finder window. If you make another Finder window active (bring it to the front), the View Options window changes to show settings for the item named in this Finder window's title. Therefore, you can see the View Options settings only for one folder at a time.

The View Options settings don't actually apply to the active Finder window. The View Options settings actually apply to the folder, disk, or other item *appearing* in the active Finder window. The settings for the folder shown in a Finder window remain applied even when you close the window. If you open the same folder in another Finder window later, the Finder uses that folder's previously established View Options settings. (You can alter this behavior by changing an option in Finder Preferences, as described later in this chapter.) If a background Finder window is showing the contents of the same folder as the active Finder window, both windows have the same title, and changes you make to the View Options settings affect both windows.

FIGURE 2.42

The View Options windows for Icon, List, Column, and Cover Flow views respectively.

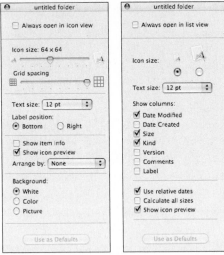

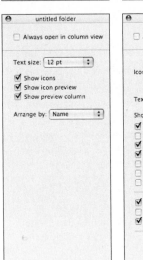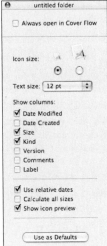

Setting Icon view options

In a Finder window set to icon view, you can set the icon size, grid spacing, text size, label position, show item info, show icon preview, arrange by, and background color or picture.

Changing the icon size in an icon view

To change the icon size in an icon view, use the Icon Size slider in the View Options window. If you set the slider for the smallest size, the icon's name appears next to the icon rather than below it. The icons of most Mac OS X applications and their documents are designed to look great at any size.

Grid spacing

Adjust the space *between* icons using the Grid spacing slider. This is a great tool for making the most of your desktop space.

Setting text size

An item's name appears in 12-point text by default. The Text Size pull-down menu offers other options ranging from 10 point to 16 point.

Label position

The name of an item appears beneath its icon by default. These radio buttons maintain this setting or force the text to be placed to the right at all times.

Item Info, Icon Preview, Arrange By

These three options alter the behavior of the items much as their names imply. The Item Info check box displays important information about many items, such as the number of items in a folder or a disk's size and available space remaining. Not all items display any additional information. Icon preview forces the operating system to generate an icon-sized preview of graphic image files. This is helpful, because many graphic files don't have a preview generated, especially items downloaded from the Web. Finally, the Arrange by setting in the View Options window determines if and how the Finder automatically aligns icons in an icon view. Using the Arrange by pop-up menu, select one of the following seven options: Snap to Grid, Name, Date modified, Date created, Size, Kind, and Label. The Finder then aligns icons on the invisible grid and places them in order according to the chosen factor. This option is an effective tool for keeping icons neatly organized.

Changing the background in icon view

In addition to specifying icon size and arrangement, you can specify the background for a folder displayed in an icon view. Here are your options:

- **White:** The standard white appears in the background behind your icons.
- **Color:** This option makes the background a solid color, which you can specify by following these steps:
    1. **After selecting the Color setting, click the small swatch of the currently selected color that appears in the View Options window.** This action displays the standard Mac OS X Color Picker window, discussed later in this chapter.
    2. **Pick the background color you want.** Depending on the type of Color Picker you selected, you pick a color for your background.
    3. **Click OK.**

- **Picture:** This option makes the background a picture, as seen in Figure 2.43. To set an image as the background, follow these steps:

  1. **After selecting the Picture setting, click the Select button that appears in the View Options window.**

  2. **In the resulting dialog box, select a graphics file that contains an appropriate picture and click Select.** This dialog box is a standard Open dialog box, which is covered in more detail in Chapter 5.

FIGURE 2.43

The background of icon view windows can be a color or a picture.

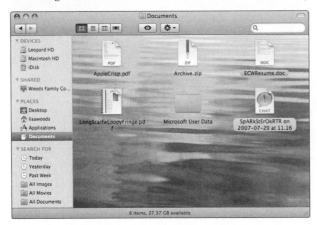

Setting List view options

For a list view, you can set the icon and text size (with the radio buttons and pull-down menu, respectively) and select which of seven optional columns you want shown. By selecting just the columns you need to see in a window, you can see most or all columns without scrolling the window. Of course, you can make more columns fit in a window by widening the window or reducing column widths, as described earlier in this chapter.

While in the list view the Name column cannot be removed; therefore, it is not listed below. The columns that you can show or hide are the following:

- Date Modified (selected by default)
- Date Created
- Size (selected by default)
- Kind (selected by default)
- Version

- Comments
- Label

Another option for list views determines whether the Finder displays relative dates (yesterday, today, tomorrow) rather than the actual month, day, and year. For dates other than yesterday, today, and tomorrow, the Finder uses the date and time formats that are set in the International pane of System Preferences (as described in Chapter 17). The column's width determines whether the Finder uses the long date format or short date format from System Preferences. For example, a standard-width column that shows Tue, Jan 2, 2001 12:00 PM would show 1/2/01 12:00 PM in a narrower column or Tuesday, January 2, 2001 12:00 PM in a wider column.

You can also set an option to have the Finder calculate folder sizes and display them in a list view. Folder size calculation takes place in the background, while you're doing other things. This is a helpful way to monitor your folder sizes, but the information is not only slow to appear; having this option checked can cause your computer to slow down when displaying a list containing many folders, because it has to calculate this information for all folders shown.

Finally, you can choose to have the Finder display an icon preview while in List view. This setting is most useful when the icon size is set to large.

Setting Column view options

Column view has five options: Set text size, Show icons, Show icon preview, Show preview column, and Arrange by. Set text size changes the size of text names. If Show icon is deselected, the Column view simply shows the text names of items, with no icons. Show icon preview displays a miniature image of the item's icon. The Show preview column check box enables the preview column to display the item preview when a single item is selected.

Setting Cover Flow view options

New to the Finder, the cover flow view options are nearly identical to the List view setting because part of the Cover Flow view includes a List view. The first two options listed are Icon Size and Text Size. Next, you are presented with the same optional columns you want shown as with the List view: Date Modified (selected by default), Date Created, Size (selected by default), Kind (selected by default), Version, Comments, and Label. Just as these options are available in the List view, you can choose to use relative dates, calculate all sizes, and show icon preview.

Using Custom Icons

If you don't want all of your folder icons to look the same, or if you don't like the default icons provided by applications for either the application itself or the documents they create, you can (on a file-by-file basis) attach custom icons of your choosing to those files through the Get Info window.

Attaching a custom icon

To attach a custom icon, follow these steps:

1. **Copy an image that you want to use as an icon.** You can do this by opening an image file and choosing Edit ➪ Copy (or pressing ⌘+C). This command puts a copy of the picture on the Clipboard, which is a temporary system storage area. It is recommended you try to copy a square image that is as close as possible to 128 x 128 pixels. If the image is larger, the Finder scales it down; if it is too small, the icon will appear jagged or fuzzy if it is displayed at a size larger than its native size.

2. **In the Finder, make sure that the Info window is showing (⌘+I) and select the file or folder whose icon you want to replace.** The selected item's information and icon appear in the General section of the Info window.

3. **In the General section of the Info window, click the displayed icon to select it.** When the icon is selected, a border appears around it. You can't select the icon if the item is locked or you don't have write privileges for the item.

4. **Choose Edit ➪ Paste (⌘+V).** The Finder pastes the image from the Clipboard into the item's icon, as shown in Figure 2.44.

FIGURE 2.44

At left, a plain folder; to spruce it up a bit, copy an icon and then paste it as a custom icon in the Info window (results at right).

Removing a custom icon

You can remove a custom icon as follows:

1. **Select the file or folder whose custom icon you want to remove.** The selected item's icon appears in the corner of the Info window.

2. **In the General section of the Info window, click the icon to select it.** You can't select the icon if the item is locked or you don't have write privileges for the item.

3. **Press Delete.** The custom icon disappears and the standard icon for the selected file or folder returns.

Working with Labels

Labels are used to color-code various items on a user's hard drive. Items have no label applied by default. To apply a label, single-click an item to select it, then open the File menu and select the desired label color from the list at the bottom of the menu. To be more individually tailored, labels can be renamed according to priority, or named for particular clients. This is done in the Finder preference pane, as described earlier in this chapter. Applying the priority- or client-named label to a file marks it visually for quick recognition.

In icon view, a colored border surrounds a labeled item's name. The items almost look as if they are selected (because selecting an item also surrounds the name with a color). The key difference to note is that selected items' actual *icons* are also highlighted with a gray box. When selecting an item that is labeled, the label color still remains as a slight border around the selection color.

In list view, a labeled item's entire line is surrounded with the colored border. Turn on the label column in the List View Options to enable sorting by label color (as described earlier in this chapter). Figure 2.45 shows the list view with label colors applied to different items.

FIGURE 2.45

Labels are especially noticeable in list view.

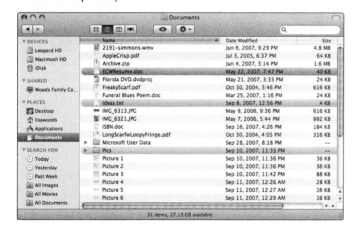

Setting Appearance Preferences

Now that you've set your Finder Preferences, it's time to add some color to your computing experience. In addition to setting the colors or pictures that appear on your desktop, you can also set the color scheme and some of the standard control features the OS uses. The Appearance preference pane controls many of these general appearance elements. To open the Appearance preference pane, click the System Preferences icon in the Dock (or choose Apple ➪ System Preferences), and then select the Appearance preference pane. Alternatively, you can choose View ➪ Appearance. Figure 2.46 shows the Appearance preference pane, and the options are listed as follows:

- **Appearance:** This option contains a pull-down menu with two possible selections: Graphite and Blue. The default setting is Blue. Switching to Graphite changes the color of certain system control elements; the Scroller, highlighted push buttons, and the Close/Minimize/Expand buttons become a graphite gray color.

- **Highlight Color:** This option consists of a pull-down menu with eight color choices and an intriguing item named Other. The color you select from this list becomes the color used to highlight selected text. You can choose any of these Highlight Color options to change your highlight color from blue (the default) to any of the eight preselected colors. Selecting Other opens the Color Picker. The Color Picker is discussed in further detail in the next section.

- **Place scroll arrows:** The two options available are Together (default) or At top and bottom. The scroll arrows that appear in all windows when needed are placed according to this setting. When set to At top and bottom, the up arrow appears at the top of the scroll bar, the down arrow at the bottom, the left arrow on the left side, and the right arrow on the right side. The default keeps the up and down buttons together at the bottom and the left/right buttons on the right side.

- **Click in the scroll bar to:** The two available options are Jump to the next page (default) or Scroll to here. The default is the preferred mode because it is consistent and predictable. Clicking in the scroll bar shifts the window one page or screen of data at a time. The alternative method, Scroll to here, causes the window to jump to the position you clicked instead of one page at a time.

- **Use smooth scrolling:** This option is only perceivable when scrolling page by page. When smooth scrolling is selected, you will see the data scroll up or down quickly. If smooth scrolling is deselected, the data is repositioned as you scroll, so that all you see is the next page.

- **Minimize when double-clicking a window title bar:** Rather than forcing you to click the minimize button, this option allows (as the title suggests) you to double-click the title bar to minimize.

- **Number of Recent Items:** Recently used applications, documents, and servers appear in the Apple menu in a pull-out menu. Increasing or decreasing the numbers here lengthens or shortens the lists. The default is 10 results for each item.

- **Font smoothing style:** OS X smoothes out on-screen fonts (called *anti-aliasing*) to improve their appearance. The styles available here tailor the degree of smoothing. The default is Standard — best for CRT because most users still use CRT displays. The other options are Light, Strong, and Medium — best for LCD displays. If you have an LCD, select Medium. Selecting any of these options results in very subtle changes that you may not notice.

- **Turn off text smoothing for font sizes:** Because font smoothing can result in smaller type being very difficult to read (the fonts get too gooey-looking, and letters blend together or get blurry), this option enables you to deactivate the anti-aliasing of fonts at a certain threshold and below.

FIGURE 2.46

The Appearance preference pane is the location of many options to adjust the general look and feel of the Mac OS X environment.

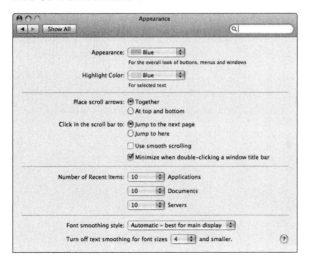

Using the Color Picker

The Color Picker is a tool designed to afford users the option of choosing any color under the sun. In the Appearance pane, it is used to pick a custom highlight color. The Color Picker comes up in other areas of the Finder, with the same controls, applying the custom color to other items. In the Color Picker, five subpanes are available, each with its own method of choosing colors. Common elements include a magnifying glass that when clicked enables users to choose a color from any visible area on-screen; the white box next to the magnifying glass fills with the chosen color. Close the Color Picker to choose the color in the box. Figure 2.47 shows each of the five subpanes.

- **Color picker subpane 1 — color wheel:** Click any area of the color wheel to choose that color. The slider to the right adjusts the overall brightness of the color wheel.

- **Color picker subpane 2 — slider-based color selector:** The pull-down menu offers different types of sliders, from CMYK to RGB to HSB. The different sliders are useful if you have to reproduce a specific color by its numeric value rather than find it by eye.

- **Color picker subpane 3 — list-based color selector:** The standard Apple list has 11 colors. Other lists are available, and custom lists can be created. The search field can be used to find a color by name.

- **Color picker subpane 4 — picture-based color selector:** This is by default populated with the Spectrum image, and contains a wide range of colors. The pull-down menu at the bottom has a New from file and Copy option, enabling you to open an image in that window, and then select the desired color from the image.

- **Color picker subpane 5 — crayons!** This pane has a collection of crayons available. Pick your favorite crayon color.

FIGURE 2.47

The Color Picker is the primary tool Apple provides to enable users to choose colors using a number of different methods.

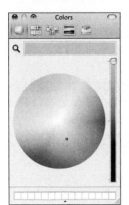

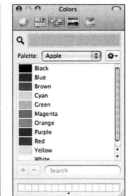

Working with Folders

So far this chapter has discussed some generic, universal commands to interact with icons and windows, including resizing, renaming, getting info, and selecting. Working with folders is slightly different.

Creating folders

Folders are very small files that create branches on the data storage tree within a volume. Put simply, folders partition files into smaller clusters of information that you organize yourself. Apple provides you with a host of useful folders within the user's home folder, but you will certainly need to create more finely tuned subdivisions. To create new folders, the Finder must be the active application. Simply click New Folder in the File menu, or press ⌘+Shift+N. This creates a new folder named Untitled Folder in the currently active window. If no window is active, the folder is created on the desktop. When the new folder is created, its name is automatically selected and ready for editing. Type a desired name, and press Enter or Return or click the mouse somewhere else on the screen. At this point, the folder is ready for action and itching to receive any and all files you throw at it. There is no limit to how much data a given folder can hold, although it makes sense to organize your data in a way that makes finding files easy. There is certainly no need to create a folder for every individual item, but it makes sense to create new folders for documents of particular types or files containing data on similar topics. Some applications have the capability to create new folders, particularly during the Save process.

Opening folders and disks

One way to navigate the folder structure of your disks is by opening disks and folders. You can open any disk or folder that you can see in a Finder window or on the desktop (with the exception of restricted folders and disks). When you open a disk or a folder, you see its contents in a Finder window. If these contents include folders, you can open one of them to see its contents in a Finder window. By opening folders within folders, you make your way through the folder structure. If you open the right sequence of folders, eventually you open the folder that contains the document or application that you're looking for.

To open a disk or folder that you have located in a Finder window or on the desktop, you can use any of these methods:

- Double-click the icon or the name of the item.
- Select the item using any of the methods previously described, and then choose File ➪ Open.
- Select the item using any of the methods previously described, and then press ⌘+O.
- Select the item using any of the methods previously described, and then press ⌘+↓.
- Control+click the item's icon to display its contextual menu, and then choose Open from the contextual menu.

Places You Cannot Create New Folders

You cannot create a new folder inside some folders because you do not have write privileges for all folders. For example, you cannot create a new folder in the System folder, the Users folder, or another user's home folder. These folders are off-limits to protect their contents. Privileges are discussed in more detail in Chapter 18. If you do not have write privileges for the folder that appears in the active Finder window, the New Folder command is disabled (dim) in the File menu and is not included at all in the window's contextual menu. The easiest way to keep an eye on your write privileges is to have the Finder window status bar showing (choose View ➪ Show Status Bar). If you see an icon that looks like a pencil with a line through it at the bottom left end of the Finder window, you don't have write privileges for the folder shown in the window.

These methods for opening items work in any Finder window viewed as icons, lists, or cover flow. The methods also work for opening items on the desktop. This method does not work when viewing items as a column because the folders are automatically opened in the next column as you select them.

NOTE   In a list view of Mac OS X 10.1.1 and earlier, you must first click an item to select it before you can display its contextual menu by Control+clicking the item. Of course, we recommend Apple's Leopard (Mac OS 10.5) for many reasons, this being one of them.

When you open a folder shown in an already open window, its contents appear in the same Finder window. Folders open in new Finder windows if the window's toolbar is suppressed. You can change this behavior by pressing the ⌘ key while opening a folder. For example, if you ⌘+double-click a folder in a Finder window whose toolbar is showing, the folder's contents appear in a new Finder window. You can also change a Finder preference setting to make the Finder normally display a new window when you open a folder; setting Finder preferences was discussed earlier in this chapter.

Opening the alias of a folder or disk has exactly the same effect as opening the folder or disk that the alias represents. If you open an alias of a folder or disk, Mac OS X resolves the alias and the Finder displays the contents of the original folder or disk.

Folder actions

In the previous OS version (10.4, aka Tiger), Apple added quite a few new tools to make your computing more efficient. A collection of AppleScripts, known as folder actions, was added, so that your folders can perform actions for you — making your day-to-day work easier. Folder actions are actually AppleScripts that run when the folder is accessed in some fashion. Some folder actions perform operations on documents that are dropped within them. Some folder actions simply edit the way a folder behaves, by closing all folders within or displaying more or less information; basically folder actions do whatever the chosen AppleScript demands.

Enabling folder actions

To enable folder actions, open the contextual menu on any folder or disk, and select Enable Folder Actions from the list. Selecting this option makes the Folder Action system active, enabling you to attach and remove actions to particular folders or volumes. After you select it, this menu option becomes Disable Folder Actions, which when selected, turns off all folder actions system-wide.

Attaching an action

Apple provides a collection of scripts that perform various functions. To attach an action to a folder, do the following:

1. **Open the contextual menu and select More/Configure folder actions.**

2. **In the Folder Actions Setup, click the plus (+) sign.**

3. **A sheet appears that looks similar to a Finder window.** Navigate to `Applications/AppleScript/Example Scripts`. You can choose from Folder Action Scripts or Folder Actions; although they have different names, the scripts contained within these folders are identical.

4. **Select the action you want to apply to the folder, and click Attach.**

This closes the dialog box and makes the selected folder action active on the folder. The folder action is now ready for use.

Using actions

The standard method to use a folder action is simply to drag an item (or items) onto the icon of the folder. This activates the folder action script, and performs the programmed action on the items selected. These scripts also create two subfolders within their parent folder: one called Original Images and another called <type> Images (<type> represents the format the image is converted into). Once an action is performed, the script then places the original unedited item into the Original Images folder, and creates the converted file in the <type> Images folder. This is a vastly easier way to save a large cluster of files in an alternate format.

Folder actions are of course not limited to simply reformatting images and don't always require that items be dropped in to activate. You can create your own folder actions that perform other operations, like e-mailing dropped-in files to certain people, renaming files according to a certain standard, or automatically uploading the files to a server and then securely deleting them from your computer. You are limited only by your imagination, your knowledge, and the capabilities of AppleScript. To learn how to use AppleScript, see Chapter 22.

Configuring actions

To add, remove, temporarily deactivate, or edit folder actions all in one convenient window, use the Configure Actions command. Select Configure Actions from the contextual menu of any folder or disk. The Folder Actions Setup application opens, as shown in Figure 2.48.

FIGURE 2.48

Configure Actions is a convenient way to turn off actions without removing them from folders; it's also a helpful tool to see how many actions are currently in place.

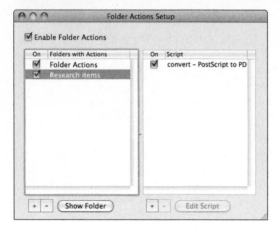

After applying a number of folder actions, it is possible to lose track of which actions have been applied where. The Folder Actions Setup application also is helpful in this eventuality. The list on the left side displays all folders that have folder actions applied. Selecting any folder on the left side populates the right side of the window with a list of the actions applied to that folder. Each item has a check box next to it. Uncheck any folder to temporarily deactivate all applied actions for that folder. Uncheck individual actions from the right side of the window if you want to temporarily deactivate only some of the actions applied to a folder.

At the top of the Folder Actions Setup window is a check box labeled Enable Actions. Unchecking this box deactivates all folder actions. (You can get this result more easily by simply selecting Disable Actions from the contextual menu from any folder or disk.)

At the bottom of the left side (the folder side) of the Folder Actions Setup application are a plus (+), a minus (-), and a Show Folder button. Click the plus sign to select a new folder to which you want to attach actions. This action generates a dialog box from which you select a new folder you want to attach folder actions to. Navigate through your drive hierarchy in this dialog box, select the folder you want, and click Open.

The newly selected folder appears in the left side of the main window. Select any item in the left side of the window, and both the minus sign (-) and the Show Folder button becomes active. To remove all folder actions on a folder, click the minus sign. An alert opens after clicking the button, confirming your intention to remove all folder actions. To see a folder that has actions applied to it, click the Show Folder button and a new Finder window opens, displaying content of the selected folder's parent (that is, the folder that the selected item lives inside of).

At the bottom of the right side (the action side) of the Folder Actions Setup window are plus (+), minus (-), and Edit Script buttons. These items are active only when an item is selected on the left side (because the right side will not be populated with any actions to edit without first choosing a folder). To add an action to a folder, click the plus sign. A dialog box appears containing the list of valid folder actions. Select the desired action and click Attach. This dialog box is shown in Figure 2.49.

To remove an action from a folder, select the action and then click the minus sign. A dialog box appears, confirming your intention to remove the selected script.

To edit a folder action, select the action and then click the Edit Script button. The ScriptEditor application opens, allowing you to tinker with or simply review the content of the action.

FIGURE 2.49

To add actions to a folder, select one from this dialog box.

Removing actions

You don't need to go to Folder Actions Setup to remove an action from a folder. To do this more quickly, use your contextual menus. From the contextual menu of a folder with folder actions attached, choose Remove Action to reveal a pull-out menu. The pull-out menu is populated with all actions attached to this folder; selecting any of them removes that action from the folder.

Editing actions

You can also edit the actions applied to a folder via your contextual menus. From the contextual menu of an item with folder actions applied, select Edit Action to reveal the pull-out menu that contains the list of attached scripts. Select the script you want to edit, and the ScriptEditor application opens, with your script ready for edit or review.

Working with Disks and Other Volumes

A volume is a fixed amount of storage. Typically, volumes exist on disks, but they can also exist on tapes or USB (Universal Serial Bus) flash drives. A volume is a location in which data can be stored. The terms *disk* and *volume* are often used interchangeably, but volumes are areas within a disk, and there can be more than one volume per disk. For our purposes in this book, though, the terms can be transposed with some freedom.

Looking at drives, partitions, and volumes

When you select a computer under the list of devices in the sidebar, the window reveals all the volumes currently available on your computer. The simplest example of a volume is a disk, such as your internal hard drive, a CD-ROM, or an external hard drive. However, as mentioned, a disk can be partitioned so that it contains two or more volumes. A partitioned disk is like a duplex or apartment building; one building holds two or more separate residences, and one disk can have two or more independent volumes. If you want to partition your hard drive into multiple volumes, you must use the Disk Utility application as described in Chapter 6.

A mounted disk image is also a volume. A disk image is actually a file that when opened creates a virtual disk available to your system. The content stored on these virtual disks is typically application installers or upgrades. Many software developers distribute software updates in a disk image file. You are able to make your own disk image files using the Disk Utility application.

File server drives and iDisks are also volumes; Chapters 12 and 14, respectively, explain how to access these volumes.

Mac OS X represents each type of volume with a distinctive icon. For example, hard drives and partitions have an icon that looks like an internal hard drive, and network drives look like something from a science fiction movie, to represent the ethereal and high-tech network connection between the server and your machine.

You decide whether volume icons show on your desktop. This is set in Finder Preferences (covered earlier in this chapter). All disks are set to appear on your desktop by default.

Ejecting disks

Server volumes, external hard drives, disk images, CD-ROMs, USB flash drives, and venerable floppy disks have one very important thing in common: They are all removable. Remove disk icons by unmounting (also known as ejecting) the disk. Although ejecting really applies only to removable disks, such as Zip disks or CDs, the same term is used throughout the Mac OS for consistency. It is generally recommended to eject disks such as USB flash drives, external hard drives, and server volumes before removing or disconnecting the drives. Eject a volume by using any of the following methods:

- **Drag the disks to the Trash (the last item in the Dock).** The Trash icon becomes an Eject symbol when dragging a disk, to reassure users that you are not "trashing" a disk, just removing it.

- **Control+click the volume's icon, either in the Computer window or on the desktop, and choose Eject from the contextual menu.**

- **Select the volume's icon and choose File ➪ Eject <name>.** (<name> is the name of the disk selected.) The keyboard equivalent for this command is ⌘+E.

- **Click the Eject symbol that appears in the sidebar next to the desired disk.**

- **For optical drives only: Press the Eject key on your keyboard.** (If your keyboard doesn't have an eject key, the F12 key works.) If your Mac has two optical drives, you can eject the secondary drive by pressing Option+eject. This method works only with your computer's optical drive (meaning your DVD, SuperDrive, combo drive, CD-RW, and so on.)

If the volume isn't in use ("in use" refers to the volume containing open files), the Finder removes it from the desktop and the Computer window. Because the System volume (the one containing the active copy of Mac OS X) is in use, you cannot eject it.

Removable disks, such as Zips and CDs, are remounted by inserting them back in their drives. Disk images are remounted by double-clicking the images and allowing the Disk Utility application to mount them. Hard drives and partitions can be remounted by logging out and logging back in to Mac OS X or by using the Disk Utility application.

Erasing volumes

Sometimes, particularly with removable volumes like external hard drives, USB flash drives, or Zip disks, you may want to return a disk to its original condition, before it contained any data. This process is called initializing or erasing a disk. You accomplish this with the Disk Utility application.

Burning discs

Most modern computers have the capability to write data to optical media. This is most commonly known as burning a disc (spelled d-i-s-c when referring to optical media, and d-i-s-k when referring to hard drives, network drives, or other removable media types). Burnable optical media includes CD-R, CD-RW, DVD-R, DVD-+R, DVD-RAM, and DVD-RW. The mad scientists at Apple realized that as more people gained access to this technology, it would be nice if it was easy to use! To this end, Mac OS X supports the ultra-easy and intuitive Finder-based burning, called Burn folders.

Using a Burn folder

Burn folders are a convenient way to burn a disc. It's a process that simply involves creating a Burn folder, organizing its content, and clicking a button. Another great benefit of a Burn folder is that the files that you choose to burn to disc remain organized as you set them, and when the original files change, the Burn folder updates its content. This is a fantastic way to back up a particular set of frequently updated important documents.

To use a Burn folder, select New Burn Folder from the Finder's File menu. The new Burn folder is created in the foremost active window, or on the Desktop if no window is active. The name of the folder is Burn Folder by default, and will be the name of the CD unless you personalize the name, to prevent confusion in the future. We suggest naming this folder something that suggests the type of information that is being burned to the disc (for example, "Photos to print"). Once named, drag any desired items onto the Burn folder. Aliases of those items are automatically placed within (read more about aliases later in this chapter). Feel free to open the Burn folder and reorganize it by dragging items around within as needed. When you are satisfied with the content of the folder, click the Burn button in the top right corner of the window. Your computer then requests a blank piece of media, and specifies the amount of room required. After inserting the blank disc and confirming your intention to complete the burn, the computer burns the disc. See Figure 2.50. Note the Burn button within the window.

FIGURE 2.50

Burn folders make burning CDs and DVDs very fast and easy.

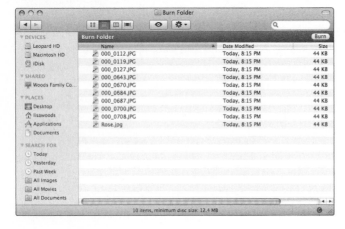

Using the Finder Burn

An alternative to Burn folders is to perform a Finder Burn. To get this process started, simply insert one piece of blank optical media of your choice. (Make sure the media is compatible with your drive. Check the documentation that came with your system and/or Apple System Profiler.) After inserting the disc, an alert appears, as shown in Figure 2.51.

The alert window gives you choices about how to use the disc. Select your desired application to prepare the disc (in the case of a Finder burn, predictably select the first option: Open Finder). You'll notice the Make this action the default check box. If you first check this box, your computer always performs this action when you insert a blank disc. It's not advisable to check this box, simply because you may want to prepare discs differently at some point. If you accidentally set the wrong default action, or want to edit the settings, open the CDs & DVDs preference pane and choose the appropriate actions from the pull-down menus. The preference pane is shown in Figure 2.52.

FIGURE 2.51

This alert appears when a blank or burnable disc is inserted.

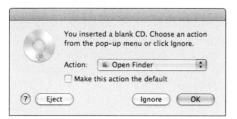

FIGURE 2.52

The CDs & DVDs preference pane gives you control of the Finder's behavior when discs are inserted. The window contains controls for blank media as well as formatted media.

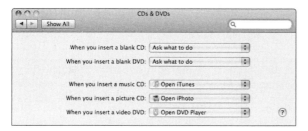

Selecting Open Finder tells the Finder to take responsibility for making your new disc. The Finder first creates an icon of a Burn folder on your desktop labeled Untitled CD, Drag any items that you want to burn onto the disc, double-click the virtual disc to reveal its contents, and then organize the files as you like. When you are satisfied with the setup of the disc, choose Burn from the upper right corner Finder menu (or from the File menu, or from the contextual menu for the disc itself), or drag the folder onto the Trash. You'll notice that the Trash icon, which would normally become the Eject symbol when removing a disc, becomes a type of fallout shelter/nuclear waste warning symbol, which is Apple's clever Burn icon.

Regardless of how you initiate the burn, the result is an alert window, requesting confirmation of your intent to burn the disc. A Burn Speed pull-down menu is also present in the burn confirmation dialog box. Though the default speed is Maximum, you can choose a slower speed (8x) from the pull-down menu. This slower speed option is useful if your media is of lesser quality or if your drive is misbehaving. There is also an option to save this disc's setup as a Burn folder for future burning. Simply check the box, and specify a location for the Burn folder.

After clicking Burn from the confirmation dialog box, the burn process begins. A progress bar appears, displaying information on what's happening behind the scenes: The Finder prepares the data, initiates the writing process, and then verifies the condition of the newly created CD.

At nearly any time during the process, you can click the Stop button in the progress meter. This usually results in a partially burned disc, which is useless. Your computer can't deal with a disc that's only half done.

The aforementioned process is used to create data discs. If you want to create a music CD, the process is different. You would select iTunes from the initial disc-preparation window's pop-up menu. Similarly, select iMovie or iDVD to create a movie disc or DVD, or select iPhoto to create a disc full of images. After selecting the appropriate application for your project, the chosen application launches and initiates its own burn controls and dialog boxes.

Discovering Your Inner Hard Drive

Now that you are aware of the basic elements of your environment, it's time to become familiar with the most important area of your computer: the hard drive. All of the data stored on your computer, from the letters you write to the digital photos you take to the actual operating system itself, are all sorted and organized on various disks. Most of the data is on your hard drive; some may be stored on external hard drives or removable CD-ROMs; and some may be stored on your digital camera or on other types of media.

On your desktop you will see a disk icon for Macintosh HD in the top right corner. That drive is the main system drive, and contains the operating system, your applications, and your user account information. All of this information is sorted in various subfolders. Figure 2.53 shows the contents of a standard Macintosh OS X hard drive:

- **Applications:** As its name implies, this folder contains applications. Applications are the tools that you use to review, create, or edit documents.

- **System:** This folder contains the actual files that comprise the heart of Mac OS X. Many of the pieces that make your computer work are stored here. Although users can explore this folder, it is not easily editable. Users cannot erase, edit, or add files within the System folder. Essentially, you can see behind the wizard's curtain, but you cannot interrupt him while he's working.

- **Library:** The Library folder contains system-wide settings files, as well as some additional files that help the computer operate. All of the settings saved in this Library folder apply to all users. For example, any fonts that are installed within this Library folder are available for all users to access. Mac OS X actually has at least three Library folders. Each performs a similar function, but at a different level of *priority*.

- **Users:** Within this folder are a number of subfolders, one for each user of the computer. Each of these folders is the central storage area for users. These subfolders comprise a user's home folder, or simply *home*. Because this folder is of great importance, it is covered in more detail in the following section.

FIGURE 2.53

The first level of a standard Mac OS X hard drive, known as the root level, contains various subfolders that perform very important functions.

Living at Home

Because Mac OS X is a truly multiuser operating system, each user is given a protected space. The operating system itself also needs a place to store settings, preferences, and other information for each user. This area is appropriately named *home*. Each user has a home of his or her own, represented by a folder in the Users folder. Each user's home folder is named for the user, and each is protected from the prying eyes and pointer of the other users on the system. When you create or save documents, the documents are stored within the home folder of the user that created the file. When you make changes to your environment, or adjust settings influencing the behavior of your computer, the operating system stores the settings in your home as well. An icon that appropriately looks like a house represents the currently logged-in user's home. The inactive users' homes are simply folders. Each user's home contains subfolders that are designed to help keep information sorted according to its purpose. Table 2.2 covers these subfolders.

NOTE Only the currently logged-in user can access his or her home folder. This security measure is designed to keep users' documents and settings private. That said, there is a built-in method to share information with the other users on your system. However, this method of sharing is a one-way street. You can *give* files to other users, and they can *give* files to you, but you cannot *take* files from each other. To learn more about sharing files between local users, see Chapter 12.

TABLE 2.2

Home Folder Contents

Name	Contents
Desktop	Contains all items on display on the desktop, with the exception of disks.
Documents	A catch-all folder where a user's miscellaneous documents are stored by default.
Downloads	New to the home folder, this folder consolidates all of the files that are downloaded from the Internet.
Library	Contains application preferences and other system elements unique to the user account. The settings in this Library folder are *not* system-wide. They apply only to this user.
Movies	The default save location for Apple's iMovie application, and a convenient place to store any other movie files.
Music	The default location for the iTunes music library, and a convenient place to store any other music files.
Pictures	The default location for the iPhoto picture library, and a convenient place to store any other image files.
Public	This is where users place items that are meant to be shared across the network or between user accounts. (Sharing files between users is covered in Chapter 12.)
Sites	The default location for Web sites that a user may want to save and a convenient location to place created Web pages.

Working with Aliases

An alias is a shortcut that points to another item. The alias looks and functions much like the original item, but it can be placed wherever you like, and the original can stay put in its original place. An important visual cue to help differentiate between the alias and the original is a small black arrow in the lower left corner of all aliases. (The arrow signifies that the item points to the original.) Methods of creating and modifying aliases are covered later in this chapter.

To use an alias, simply double-click it. The Finder opens the original item. Alternately, if you drag an item to an alias, the Finder resolves the alias (that is, figures out where the original item is located), and then takes the appropriate action. The resulting action is just as if you dragged an item directly to the alias's original item. For example, dragging an item to an alias of a folder puts the dragged item into the original folder, or if you drag a document to an alias for an application, the application attempts to open the document. Dragging an alias to a folder moves just the alias.

Using aliases

As described earlier in this chapter, aliases are shortcut files that when opened point to and open another file. In some ways, aliases act just like the files or folders they represent. In other ways, aliases may act like the independent files they actually are. Accordingly, you use many of the same techniques when working with aliases that you do when working with files and folders, although some differences do exist. This section covers many techniques for working with aliases.

Making an alias

You can make an alias for files, folders, or disks. You can make more than one alias for the same original item and put each alias in a different location.

Making an alias is a simple procedure. Do one of the following:

- **Select an item and then choose File ⇨ Make Alias or press ⌘+L.** This creates the alias in the same folder as the original item.

- **Control+click an item to open its contextual menu and choose Make Alias.** This creates the alias in the same folder as the original item.

- **Press ⌘+Option while dragging an item to the place where you want an alias of it.** You can start pressing ⌘+Option at any time while dragging, but you must hold down the keys while you release the mouse button to make an alias. While you press ⌘+Option, the pointer changes and acquires a small right-pointing arrow in addition to its normal large left-pointing arrow. This method allows you to simultaneously create an alias and place it in the desired location, saving you the step of moving the alias required by the previous two methods.

An alias has the same icon as the original item, except that the icon has a small curved arrow superimposed to indicate it is an alias. The alias also inherits the name of the original item. If the alias is created in the same folder as the original, the Finder appends the word *alias* to the alias name. The Finder also adds a number to the name as needed (to prevent a new alias from having the same name as another alias in the same folder). The word *alias* is not added when you make an alias by Option+⌘+dragging the original item to another folder. Figure 2.54 illustrates the subtle differences between an alias and an original.

 The small icons in Finder window title bars can also be used to make aliases. Just press ⌘+Option while dragging the small icon to make an alias of the original folder.

FIGURE 2.54

An item's alias (right) is primarily differentiated from the original (left) by the small arrow in the corner (always present) rather than by the word *alias,* which can be removed.

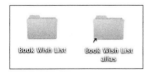

Renaming an alias

Immediately after you create an alias, its name is selected for editing. You can change the name by typing a replacement or by using the other name-editing techniques described earlier in this chapter. For example, you may want to remove the word *alias* from an alias name so the alias has the same name as its original item. An alias can have exactly the same name as its original item as long as they are in different folders. If an alias is in the same folder as its original item, move the alias somewhere else before you try to make the alias's name the same as the original item's name. Of course, an alias and its original can be in the same folder if their names are very similar but not identical.

Dragging items to an alias

Aliases function like their original item when items are dragged to them. For example, if you drag an item to an alias of a folder, Mac OS X resolves the alias and the Finder puts the dragged item into the original folder. Dragging a document to an alias of an application causes the original application to attempt to open the document. Note that dragging an *alias* to a folder or application just moves the alias or causes the application to attempt to interact with the alias.

Moving, copying, and deleting an alias

After you make an alias, you can manipulate it as you would any other item. You can move it, copy it, and delete it.

- If you move an alias to a different folder, its original item is not affected. Only the alias is moved, and the alias still knows where to find its original item.
- If you make copies of an alias, all the copies of the alias refer to the same original item.
- If you delete an alias, its original item is not deleted.

Finding an original item

You can find an alias's original item by choosing File ➪ Show Original (⌘+R). The Show Original command displays a Finder window that contains the original item, scrolls the original item into view, and selects it. Alternately, Control+clicking an alias (opening its contextual menu) also offers an option to Show Original.

Fixing broken aliases

If you try to show an alias's original item but the original item has been deleted or moved to a disk that has been ejected or removed, the Finder tells you that the original item can't be found. Figure 2.55 shows the alert that you see in the Finder if Mac OS X can't resolve an alias.

NOTE   You may not get the alert shown in Figure 2.55 if you try to use a broken alias in an application other than the Finder. In certain Mac OS X applications, the alert you see simply states the item could not be opened.

FIGURE 2.55

The Finder displays an alert when it can't find an alias's original item.

The Finder's alert has an OK button, a Delete Alias button, and a Fix Alias button. Clicking OK cancels the attempt to use the alias for now. Clicking Delete Alias moves the alias to the Trash. Clicking Fix Alias displays a Fix Alias dialog box in which you can choose a new original for the alias. This dialog box is an Open dialog box. In this dialog box, select a file or folder to be the new original item and click Choose. (Of course, you can select the old original item to be the new original item, if you know where it is.)

Selecting a new original for an alias

Instead of throwing away an obsolete or broken alias and making a new one, you can recycle the old alias by assigning it a new original item. Frankly, creating a new alias and discarding an old one is easier than assigning the old one a new original item, and recycling old aliases certainly has no positive environmental impact. Nevertheless, you may have an alias on which you have lavished great attention (having applied a fancy custom icon, elaborate comments, or a clever name) and repurposing such a work of art may be easier than recreating it. Perhaps you have an alias on your Desktop folder that refers to a project folder buried inside your Documents folder, and you want to keep using the same alias when you move on to a new project folder. It is also possible that when fixing a broken alias you selected the wrong original item, and rather than recreate the alias, you can just select a different item. Whatever your reason for taking advantage of the power that the Info window grants you to redirect an alias, here is the procedure for doing the deed:

1. **Select the alias to which you want to assign a new original item.**

2. **Open the Get Info window.** A Select New Original button appears in the General section of the Info window. This button is disabled if the alias is locked or you don't have write privileges for the alias.

3. **Click the Select New Original button.** The Fix Alias dialog box appears. This dialog box is like the column view of a Finder window.

4. **In the Fix Alias dialog box, select a file or folder to be the new original item and click Choose.**

Taking Out the Trash

At the opposite end of the Dock from the Finder icon, you see an icon resembling a wire-mesh wastepaper basket. This is the Trash, the receptacle into which you place items you want to be rid of.

Deleting files and folders is a two-step process. First, you need to move them to the Trash and then — just like at home — you need to empty the Trash. Before emptying the Trash, you can still change your mind and open the Trash to remove items from it. Unlike your trash at home, users are responsible for their own trash; you cannot see the contents of their trash, nor can they see the contents of yours.

Moving items to the Trash

Move one or more items to the Trash by using any of the following methods:

- Drag the items to the Trash icon in the Dock.
- Select the items and choose Finder ➪ Move to Trash.
- Select the items and press ⌘+Delete (which is the keyboard shortcut for choosing Finder ➪ Move to Trash).
- Control+click an item, or select several items and Control+click one of them, and then choose Move To Trash from the contextual menu that appears.

After moving an item to the Trash, the Trash icon changes from an empty wire mesh basket to a basket full of crumpled-up papers. The documents are not deleted yet, though. They are merely in your trash pail. To actually delete them, much like your kitchen trash can, you have to take out the trash. In the Finder menu, choose Empty Trash, or press ⌘+Shift+Delete. After the action is confirmed in a dialog box, a swish sound occurs and your files are deleted. Do not get in the habit of storing items in the Trash. Not only does the Trash file get bloated storing all the unwanted garbage, but it's also very easy to accidentally empty the Trash when trying to send an item to the Trash (especially with the keyboard shortcut; it's only a Shift key's difference). If you intend to trash something, do so. If you think you want to trash something, but aren't sure yet, store the files somewhere else.

Viewing and removing Trash contents

You can see the contents of the Trash by clicking the Trash icon in the Dock. The Trash contents appear in a Finder window. You can remove items from the Trash by dragging them out of this Finder window and placing them in another folder or on the desktop. (Remember, the items you put on the Mac OS X desktop are actually located in the Desktop folder of your home folder.)

Emptying the Trash

You can use one of the following methods to empty the Trash:

- Choose Finder ➪ Empty Trash.
- Press ⌘+Shift+Delete.
- Control+click the Trash icon (or click it and hold) and select Empty Trash from the pop-up Dock menu.

In the first two methods, the Finder displays a warning, asking if you really want to permanently delete the items that are in the Trash. If you use the pop-up Dock menu, the Trash is emptied without warning.

> **NOTE** If you put a file in the Trash by accident, you can remove it from the Trash by using the Finder undo feature — pressing ⌘+Z. This works only if putting the item in the Trash was the last thing you did (because the undo only undoes your last action) and, most importantly, if you *haven't emptied the Trash yet.* The emphasis is there for a reason! Emptying the Trash normally means "bye-bye files." To recover files that have been erased accidentally or prematurely (or to rescue files from disks that are damaged) you must call in a team of professionals. Check out `www.DriveSavers.com` and `www.OnTrack.com` if you need help recovering files. Get your checkbook ready, because file recovery prices range from $100 to $3,000, depending on disk size, disk condition, and how quickly you need the files back. To avoid this unfortunate situation, back up your work often, as discussed in Chapters 14 and 21.

Secure Empty Trash

If you are selling your computer, or have very sensitive information on your computer, simply emptying the Trash is not an effective way to remove the data. As noted above, it is indeed possible to get your work back! This may be a bad thing if you really want the files gone. To this end, Apple has added the Secure Empty Trash option, which truly purges the files that you are currently trashing from your computer by overwriting them with meaningless junk data. This is significant because what actually happens when a file is simply trashed is that the computer erases its record of where the file was. Because the computer no longer recognizes that there is a file there, it writes over the (still intact) file eventually as you create more work. The problem is, this may take a while, or never occur at all. A good technician (or evil hacker) may be able to restore trashed files with third-party software. By first erasing the file record, and then overwriting the file's location with meaningless data, Mac OS X makes it much more difficult if not impossible to recover the work. To use this erasure method, simply select Secure Empty Trash from the Finder menu or contextual menu. Figure 2.56 shows the alert that appears when selecting the Secure Empty Trash option.

FIGURE 2.56

Secure Empty Trash is a better way to ensure that your unwanted data is erased permanently, because a determined person can often very easily undo the normal Empty Trash command.

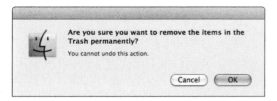

Are you sure you want to remove the items in the Trash permanently?

You cannot undo this action.

Cancel   OK

Looking At the Dock

The Dock, arguably the single most useful and unique feature of Mac OS X, gives users fast access to frequently used items within their environment. The Dock contains shortcuts to your favorite applications and documents, and shows active applications and minimized windows. You can easily edit the Dock to more accurately represent your needs. The new Dock is shown in Figure 2.57.

FIGURE 2.57

With an enhanced 3-D look and groovy glowing-orb indicators, the redesigned Dock rocks a futuristic look.

The Dock contains an initial set of icons, which you can rearrange or remove to suit your needs. The initial set of Dock icons includes the following:

- **Finder:** An application for managing the files and folders stored on your computer, always at the left end of the Dock.
- **Dashboard:** The master control application for widgets, which are covered later in this chapter.
- **Mail:** An application for sending and receiving e-mail.
- **Safari:** Apple's own Internet browser.
- **iChat:** An instant messaging (IM) client.
- **Address Book:** A contact list for people, business, and so on, integrated with Apple's Mail application and the rest of Mac OS.
- **iCal:** A scheduling application.
- **Preview:** An application for viewing graphic and PDF files.
- **iTunes:** An application for playing, organizing, and importing digital music from CDs, MP3 files, and Internet radio.
- **Spaces:** Facilitates the organization of applications and windows into various groups.
- **Time Machine:** An application that restores files or enables you to look into the history of a particular directory.
- **System Preferences:** An application for customizing Mac OS X on your computer.
- **Documents:** A shortcut to the Documents folder.
- **Downloads:** A folder designated to store items downloaded from the Internet.
- **Trash:** A container for discarding files and folders that you no longer need.

Icons are temporarily added to the Dock automatically as you use your computer. When you open an application, its icon bounces up and down in the Dock and remains there while the application is open. An open application's icon has a small white oval with a blue outline (giving you the impression of a glowing orb) underneath it to represent that the application is open. When you minimize an Aqua window, it shrinks to the size of an icon and appears in the Dock. A window shrinks to the Dock with a wavering visual effect that Apple likens to a genie going into a bottle, or the application can shrink in a linear scale progression.

Appreciating Dock niceties

The Dock is divided into two sections, separated by a broken vertical line (it resembles the lane separators on pavement) known as the Dock divider. The items to the left of the line are applications.

The right section contains the Trash along with all other item types, such as minimized windows, files, and folders. As you open new applications, they appear in the Dock to the left of the vertical line. New documents and windows minimized in the Dock appear to the right of the Dock divider.

The icons of items in the Dock sometimes provide feedback. For example, an application that requires attention can bounce up and down, as if it was excitedly raising its hand in class. Another example: The Mail icon indicates the number of new messages waiting for you, and the iCal icon displays the current date.

Identifying Dock icons

When you position the mouse pointer over a Dock icon, the icon's name appears above it. Clicking a Dock icon opens the item. When you click a minimized window in the Dock, the window emerges and becomes full-sized again.

Customizing the Dock

By default, the Dock is located at the bottom of your screen and is quite large. In addition to the ability to change its location and size, the Dock has a few additional tricks up its sleeve accessible via the Dock preference pane. Many of the Dock's settings can also be changed using the Dock's very own contextual menu. The different ways to initiate all of the commands is discussed under each heading. That said, to gain access to all of the Dock's available options in one place, open the Dock preference pane. Choose Apple ➪ Dock ➪ Dock Preferences (or Apple ➪ System Preferences ➪ Dock). The Dock's contextual menu is shown in Figure 2.58.

FIGURE 2.58

Change Dock size, magnification, hiding, position, and visual effect in with the Dock's contextual menu.

Resizing the Dock

The Dock resizes automatically as items are added or removed from it, but you can also manually resize the Dock (and the icons in it) yourself. To do this, move the Dock size slider from Small to Large and release at the desired size. Alternately, position the mouse pointer over the vertical line that separates application icons from folder and document icons. When the pointer changes to look like a two-headed arrow, drag down to make the Dock smaller or up to make the Dock larger.

Setting the Dock position and hiding

The Dock can be at the bottom of the screen or at either side. The bottom of the screen is longer than the sides and has room for more Dock icons. That said, the Dock will get in your way more often while stationed at the bottom of the screen than when located on a side. At the bottom of the screen, the Dock interferes with making windows the full height of the screen, which minimizes vertical scrolling. This has become obvious as more and more users migrate to widescreen-style displays. The increased room left to right translates to less room from top to bottom, and the Dock takes up a healthy portion of the bottom space!

The Dock, when permanently displayed, is least obtrusive on the right side of the screen because most applications display windows aligned with the left side of the screen. To reposition the Dock on the left or right side of the screen, select the appropriate radio button in the Dock preference pane. As an alternative method to reposition the Dock, press and hold the Control key, click the vertical separator in the Dock, and then click to check the desired location from the Dock position onscreen pull-out menu.

Regardless of the Dock position, to conserve space, the most desirable option is to have the Dock stay out of your way altogether. This is accomplished by having it hide until you move the pointer to one of the edges of the screen. In the Dock preference pane, select the Automatically hide and show the Dock option. (You can also Control+click the vertical line that separates application icons from folder and document icons, and select Turn Hiding On.) This option causes the Dock to retreat beyond the edge of the screen. When your mouse is moved to the area where the Dock should normally be, the Dock emerges from hiding, ready for use. This is the best way to get the most out of your available screen real estate.

Setting Dock magnification

When you resize the Dock to make the icons very small, it can become difficult to distinguish between the various items. As a solution to this, the Dock can magnify icons as the pointer approaches so they are easier to recognize. To enable this feature, click the Magnification check box. The Magnification slider will no longer be dimmed out. This slider adjusts the amount of magnification that occurs when your pointer rolls over a particular item in the Dock. Alternatively, you can Control+click the Dock's separator line to display its contextual menu and choose Turn Magnification On. When magnification is turned on, the menu command changes to Turn Magnification Off. Figure 2.59 shows the results of magnification activated and set to the middle rate.

FIGURE 2.59

With magnification turned on, iTunes, Spaces, and Time Machine dominate the Dock.

Choosing a visual effect

When you minimize a window, the Dock usually shows a visual effect that resembles a genie being sucked into a bottle. The genie-in-a-bottle visual effect that occurs when you minimize a window is impressive, but after a while, you may get tired of it and wish the window would just minimize more quickly. For this purpose, Apple has made the Scale Effect. It's simpler and faster than the Genie Effect (in which the window gradually gets smaller as it minimizes). You can set the visual effect by choosing Scale Effect in the Minimize using pull-down menu in the Dock preference pane, or you can Control+click the separator line in the Dock and then choose Scale Effect in the pop-up menu.

Adding items to the Dock

Add any item to the Dock by simply dragging it into the Dock. This creates a Dock-based alias of the item. Note that there is neither a small arrow in the lower left nor the word *alias* in its name to signify its alias status; but because the actual item remains in its original location, and this Dock item merely points to it, the icon in the Dock is a kind of alias. Applications must be placed to the left of the Dock divider; documents, folders, and disks must be placed on the right side of the divider. Placing an application's icon in the Dock gives you one-click access to the application regardless of what application is currently active. When you place a document or folder icon in the Dock, it is quickly available with a couple of clicks.

Unlike other folders in the Dock, the Downloads folder does not require files to be added to it manually. Items that you download from the Internet are automatically saved to this folder. For people that want an uncluttered, pristine desktop, this folder is heaven sent. It also serves as a centralized location for all of your downloads, making the days that you spent squinting at your screen, searching your desktop for the PDF you just downloaded, a thing of the past. What can be better?

Removing Dock icons

Removing an item from the Dock is also extremely simple. Drag the icon out of the Dock, let go, and it disappears in a puff of smoke. You can't remove the Finder or the Trash from the Dock.

Moving icons in the Dock

You can rearrange icons in the Dock by dragging them to different positions. As you drag an icon across the Dock, the other icons move apart to make room for the icon you're dragging. You can place the icon you're dragging in any space that opens up by releasing the mouse button.

Using Dock folder navigation

The real convenience and power of the Dock is recognized when you place a folder or disk icon in the Dock. In Mac OS 10.5, folders placed in the Dock behave slightly different than in previous versions of the OS X. In Tiger, clicking a docked folder would open it in a new Finder window, giving you access to your files. In Leopard, Apple has added a step to this process: When clicking a folder in the Dock such as the Documents or Downloads folder, you are presented with a pop-up menu that displays the contents of that folder (see Figure 2.60). Clicking a file in the pop-up menu opens the item, and clicking a folder opens a new Finder window revealing its contents. To put it succinctly, the pop-out menu gives you a preview of the folder contents without cluttering your desktop with another Finder window.

FIGURE 2.60

Clicking the Documents folder in the Dock presents you with a pop-up menu that gives you access to its contents.

Like the Dock, you can change the behavior of the pop-up menu for a particular folder via its contextual menu. To open the contextual menu, simply control+click the item in question. You are presented with the following options:

- **Sort by:** Sort the contents of the folder by Name, Date Added, Date Modified, Date Created, or Kind.

- **View As:** This setting determines how the pop-out menu appears. There are two options: Grid or Fan. The Fan setting is the more visually pleasing of the two. Items are opened in a stacking column illustrated in Figure 2.61. The Grid setting is more functional. The items open into a square that displays iconic representations of each item stored in the folder.

- **Remove from Dock:** Selecting this option removes the folder from the Dock. However, it does not delete the folder or its contents; the original item remains untouched.

- **Show in Finder:** Displays folder contents in the Finder.

- **Open "Folder Name":** Opens the selected folder in a new Finder window.

FIGURE 2.61

The Fan effect displays folder contents beautifully.

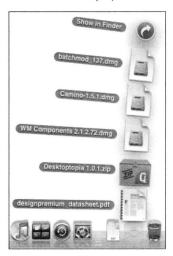

The folder icons in the Dock are dynamic. When the folders are empty, a standard icon appears. As you work and store files in these folders, their icons take on the appearance of the topmost file in the folder. This added functionality continues to make the Dock a great way to gain access to your files quickly.

Applications in the Dock

In addition to the application shortcuts that are already in the Dock, every open application adds its own icon to the Dock temporarily. When these applications quit, the icon fades, shrinking the Dock back to its original state. All open applications are identifiable by a small white orb, with a blue border that appears to be glowing below the application's icon in the Dock. When you click and hold (or Control+click) the icon of an open application in the Dock, a pop-up menu appears, giving you application-specific choices. For example, the Finder's pop-up Dock menu presents a list of available windows, and you can choose one to bring it to the front. Other applications list different commands and items in their pop-up Dock menus. Figure 2.62 shows an example of the iTunes pop-up Dock menu, displaying options to Quit, Hide (which banishes all open windows off screen, to help free up screen space), Show in Finder (which opens a new Finder window displaying the item in its location on the disk), and all the open windows that can be brought to the front by selecting them from the pop-up menu. If the application is not permanently added to the Dock, another option appears: Keep in Dock. Selecting this option is another convenient way to add an application to the Dock.

FIGURE 2.62

The pop-up Dock menu of an open application may include items specific to the application.

Minimizing windows in the Dock

When you minimize a window by clicking its Minimize button or pressing ⌘+M on the keyboard, the Genie or Scale Effect occurs, leaving you a miniature version of the window in the Dock (to the right of the Dock separator). Whatever was displayed in the window also appears, but reduced in size, in the minimized window. Furthermore, the window belongs to an application that is still running, and the application may continue updating the minimized window in the Dock. For example, Apple loves to demonstrate this capability by playing miniature QuickTime movies in the Dock. Click a minimized window icon in the Dock to restore the window to full size and its original position. If you quit the application that has a file minimized in the Dock, you are either presented with the option to save the file or the application quits (if the file has already been saved).

Exposing Exposé

For many of us, Exposé was one of the best new features to OS X. Exposé, a window control system, enables you to arrange open windows on your desktop in an impressive array. Now that you know how to create Finder windows and open documents, your screen has the potential to become a cluttered mess. Using the Window menu you can manage some of the clutter, or you can minimize the items into the Dock with the Minimize button, but that's all too slow! Exposé dissolves the clutter when you press one of three buttons. Please note that part of the beauty of this product is the animated nature of the action. To see it in action is much more impressive than these screenshots can convey!

The three modes of Exposé can be activated with the F9, F10, and F11 keys. Through the Exposé & Dashboard preference pane, you can activate any of the modes by moving your pointer to a particular corner of the screen (this is called using a *hot corner*). You can also activate Exposé with a multibutton mouse (all of Apple's desktops now ship with multibutton mice). With a multibutton mouse, you can map desired Exposé modes to particular mouse buttons, radically improving speed. Figure 2.63 shows the Exposé control panel.

FIGURE 2.63

The Exposé preference pane offers options to change the keys, hot corners, or mouse buttons assigned to activate each of Exposé's modes.

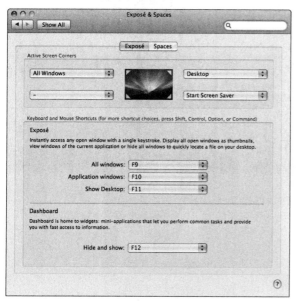

The Exposé preference pane allows you to change the keys that activate the three different modes. The keyboard area has a pull-down menu available for each mode of Exposé. Each pull-down menu is populated with a list of keys that can activate Exposé. When accessing the pull-down menu, the Shift, Option, Control, and ⌘ keys all modify the list. Pressing and holding any of those keys while selecting the items in the list results in that combination activating Exposé. For example, pressing and holding Option and selecting F10 activates the Exposé mode only when pressing Option and

F10 together. Each hot corner's menu offers each of the three Exposé modes. They engage when the pointer is moved to that corner.

NOTE   Each hot corner's pull-down menu in the Exposé preference pane also has two screen saver commands available, because the other function of hot corners can be to activate or disable screen savers. After all, a hot corner can do only one thing at a time.

Show all windows

When there are two or more applications and multiple documents open, the screen gets cluttered very quickly. Exposé's first command is the All Windows command. Click the F9 key and all the open windows shrink and rearrange themselves across the screen (accompanied by an impressive animation) so all windows are visible at once. Positioning your mouse pointer over any of the reduced windows highlights the window and reveals the application's name. (Documents and Web pages reveal their name rather than the application.) Clicking any of these reduced windows brings that window to the foreground. If you don't want to change your active window, clicking F9 again returns all windows to full size and restores the previous active window to the foreground. Figure 2.64 shows the results of Exposé's All Windows command.

FIGURE 2.64

Pick a window, any window!

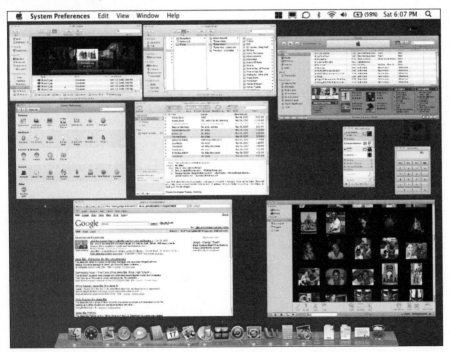

Show active application's windows

Many applications support multiple windows. Web browsers, for example, often have multiple Web pages open at once. Consider when a user who reviews a rare car part for his or her car (a 2001 Mustang Bullitt, let's say) on eBay, checks a local mechanic's Web page to determine the street value of the part, and compares that price to a Mustang-enthusiast organization's notes on their Web page. It would be easy to get lost switching between just those three windows, much less any other applications that may be open. Exposé's first command works, but when a user just wants to find a window within the current active application, the Application Windows command is the solution. With a press of F10, all of the active application's windows (in the above example, Web pages) shrink and align themselves (while dimming all other application windows). Positioning the mouse pointer over a window shows the Web page's name, making it easy to pick the desired window. Clicking that window restores all windows to normal size and makes the clicked window active in the foreground. Pressing F10 again restores all application windows to their previous position, restoring the previous active window to the foreground.

Show desktop

Even with ten windows open, there may be a need to open more documents. Getting to your desktop or opening your hard drive to open a particular document or folder can be troublesome with so many windows already open. Exposé's third command, the Desktop command, makes it easy. Press F11 and all open windows retreat to beyond the edges of the screen, showing only the bottom edge of the windows, and thus revealing the desktop. Disks and folders can be opened and searched for the desired document, all without restoring the clutter. After a document or application is opened, the windows return to their original position, with your newly opened item as the active window. Alternatively, clicking the visible edges of the retracted applications (or pressing F11 again) restores them to their original positions.

Using Dashboard

Dashboard first burst on the scene in OS 10.4. Dashboard is actually a host to a whole suite of mini-applications called widgets, which provide a nearly limitless feature set to users. Apple has developed many of these widgets, and third-party developers create many more. In OS 10.5, Dashboard is part of Leopard's application suite.

Activating Dashboard

On your keyboard, press F12 to activate Dashboard. The screen darkens, and the active widgets sweep in, ready for use. Alternately, click the Dashboard icon in the Dock. Unlike other applications, Dashboard does not take over the menu bar and as such, does not have traditionally accessible preferences and controls. Figure 2.65 shows Dashboard in the foreground, with some active widgets.

FIGURE 2.65

A view of Dashboard in action

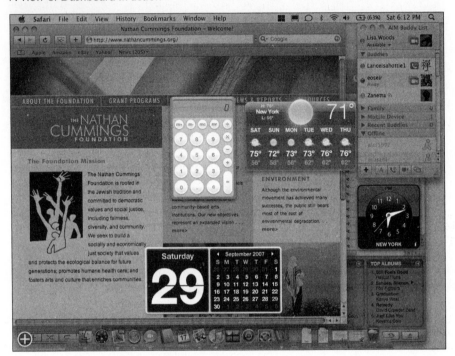

Available widgets

The following list outlines the widgets included in Dashboard:

- **Address Book:** This widget ties nicely into Apple's built-in Address Book application. It is a great way to look up the particulars of one of your contact's address card information, including phone number, e-mail address, AIM handle, address, and image.

- **Business:** Searches for business listings by ZIP code.

- **Calculator:** Unlike the scientific-style calculator in the Application folder, the widget calculator is a smaller, simpler version.

- **Dictionary:** Instead of going to the trouble of visiting www.dictionary.com, now you can use a widget to find the spelling, definition, and pronunciation of challenging words. This widget contains a Thesaurus as well.

- **Google:** This widget is a shortcut to the Google Search page. Enter your search criteria in the search field and press enter or return; a new Web page opens displaying your search results.

- **Flight Tracker:** This widget is a great tool to track an airline flight's status. Enter the airline, source city, and destination city, and then click Find Flights. The list of possible flights and status is presented.

- **iCal:** This widget is a mini-app of iCal. It presents the current date on the left and the current month on the right.

- **iTunes:** This widget offers basic control of iTunes, including Pause, Rewind, Forward, Volume control, and Playlist selection. iTunes is automatically launched when a song or playlist is played.

- **Movies:** This widget is driven by Fandango, the nation's largest online movie ticketing service. A list of current movies and the theaters in your area in which they are playing appears.

- **People:** A shortcut to the white pages, this widget makes it possible for you to search for people by first name, last name, or city, state, and ZIP.

- **Ski Resort:** This widget provides information on ski resorts including resort temperature, new snowfall, and open trails.

- **Stickies:** This widget simply adds a sticky note to the Dashboard display. This is designed to be a convenient place to jot down quick notes or reminders.

- **Stocks:** This widget is a stock tracker. Enter stock symbols and choose your favorite index, and this widget keeps you up to date on your portfolio's status.

- **Tile Game:** This widget is a simple game wherein an image is divided into 15 tiles on a 16-tile grid, and then shuffled. Unscramble the image to win.

- **Translation:** Use this widget to help translate into another language. Choose source and destination language and enter text, and receive instant translation. "Where is the bathroom?" becomes "¿Dondé está el baño?" in a flash.

- **Unit Converter:** Choose the item to be converted from a range including units of time, distance, area, volume, power, pressure, temperature, and more. After entering your source data, this widget converts the numbers to the chosen format.

- **Weather:** Choose your location by ZIP code or city/state, and your five-day weather forecast is always a click away.

- **Web Clip:** New in Mac OS 10.5, Web Clip allows you to create your very own widgets from Web pages. Apple makes it very simple, even going so far as to add a shortcut for creating Web clips into Safari's browser windows.

- **World Clock:** After choosing continent and city, this widget provides an attractive analog clock. You may add multiple clocks, with each clock tuned into different cities.

Activating more widgets

When Dashboard is first launched, the widgets that are active may not satisfy your needs. Adding more widgets is quick and easy. While active, Dashboard presents a plus-symbol icon in the lower left corner. Click this icon to review all available widgets installed on your system. Click a widget to launch it.

To close unwanted widgets, open the list of available widgets; the currently active widgets each display a large X icon in their upper left corner. Also, while the list of available widgets is open, click the Manage widgets button directly above the widget icon. Clicking this button launches a widget window enabling you to activate and deactivate widgets. If you want to add to your widget empire, click the More Widgets button and you're taken to Apple's Dashboard Widgets Web page where you can keep your widget collection fresh. Figure 2.66 shows Apple's Dashboard Widgets page.

FIGURE 2.66

Apple's widget page is everything widget. Check out the Top Widgets list.

Modifying widgets

Each widget has options available, but none is available via the menu. Simply position your mouse pointer over the widget you want to modify, and a small italicized i appears in the lower-right corner of the widget. Clicking this i displays the options for the widget in question. Once the options are set, click Done in the options screen.

Spaces

A new feature in Mac OS 10.5, Spaces enables you to organize your desktop clutter by organizing windows and applications into groups. Spaces segregates your application windows into groups that can be accessed with a click of your mouse. When a space is activated, the windows that belong to that space are brought to the forefront of the screen, and items that do not belong to that space are moved off the screen completely. You can choose to have one application or many applications in one space. Working concurrently with Exposé, Spaces takes desktop clutter removal to a new level. First, Spaces reduces the amount of windows on your screen. Next, Exposé kicks in and sorts the windows in that particular Space. It all adds up to a well-organized, clutter-free space.

Everything in its Space

Spaces is the key to a clutter-free desktop. To activate Spaces, click the Spaces icon in the Dock and click the Set Up Spaces button; the Exposé & Spaces preference pane opens. Select the Enable Spaces check box. When first launched, you are provided with two Spaces. To add applications to a Space, click the plus (+) sign and select items from the Applications folder. The application you choose is automatically added to the last Space that was selected. To change the assigned Space, click the application row under the Space column; your new Space selection will be highlighted (see Figure 2.67). In time, you may find that you need more space or have too much. You can choose to add or remove columns or rows. Simply click the plus (+) or minus (-) sign next to the respective row or column.

FIGURE 2.67

Setting a space is easy.

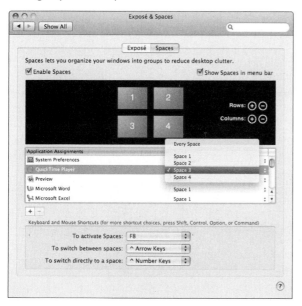

Jumping from Space to Space

After setting your Spaces straight, you'll need to get accustomed to working in them. Each Space operates independently of the other. As you launch applications, open files, and browse the Internet, each Space does its part. Use any of the following methods to switch between each Space:

- Select an item from the Dock.
- Select an item from the Recent Items menu.
- ⌘+Tab to select an application.

- Open an application or file from the Finder.

- Press and hold Control while clicking a direction arrow. If you are in Space 1 and want to go to Space 2, you would click Control+Right Arrow to be taken to Space 2 with all of the fanfare described below.

Any of these actions takes you from one space to the next. Suppose that you have set Space 1 to handle your Preview documents and Space 3 to manage your e-mail. While working in Mail, you receive a PDF attachment in an e-mail. When you open the attachment, OS X takes you from Space 3 over to the Preview application in Space 1. As you are leaving Space 3, an image flashes on the screen, displaying the number of spaces you've set up and highlighting as well as pointing to the space you are headed to. In quick succession, the screen shoves one space out of the way to make room for another.

If you aren't sure what Space your open files are in, press F8 and all of your Spaces align across your screen, displaying the open files and applications. Figure 2.68 illustrates Spaces in action. Another way to keep abreast of your position in Spaces is to select the Show Spaces in menu bar check box. This places a tiny iconic representation of Spaces in the menu bar complete with the Space number you are currently working in.

FIGURE 2.68

Hitting F8 displays all of your Spaces at once. The space in the upper-left-hand corner also shows that Exposé is active.

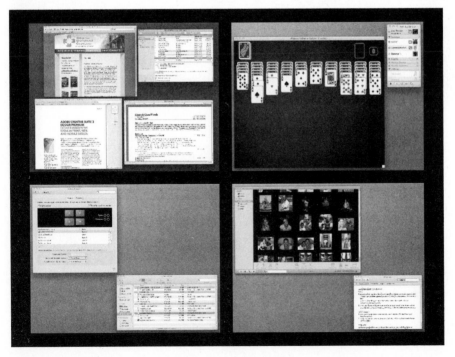

Sleeping, Shutting Down, Restarting, or Logging Out

When you want to conclude a session with your computer, you need to do one of the following:

- Put the computer to sleep to save energy.

- Log out so other people won't have access to your data. They can log in and use the computer with their own account (assuming the computer is configured for multiple users).

- Restart the computer to complete the installation of some updates or new applications or to allow the computer to run its self-tests on startup.

- Shut down the computer to save energy, ensure greater safety in case of power failure, and prolong the lifespan of components.

CAUTION If you shut down your Mac improperly, for example by disconnecting the power, you risk damaging your files. Such damage may be minor and not readily apparent, but an accumulation of minor damage may lead to mysterious, serious problems later. You can find some maintenance procedures in Chapter 21.

Making the computer sleep (and wake up)

If you're not going to use your computer for a while, you can save energy and reduce wear and tear on the computer by making it sleep. When you're ready to use your computer again, you can wake it quickly. Waking from sleep is much faster than starting up.

Going to sleep

To make your computer sleep, do one of the following:

- If you have a MacBook, MacBook Pro, PowerBook, or iBook, close the lid.

- Choose Sleep from the Apple menu.

- If your keyboard has a Power key, press it briefly and then press the S key or click the Sleep button in the resulting dialog box.

- If your keyboard has an Eject key, you can sleep by pressing the Option+⌘+Eject combination.

- If your keyboard has an Eject key, press Control while pressing the Eject key, and then press the S key or click the Sleep button in the resulting dialog box.

- If you have an Apple Cinema display or Apple Studio LCD display, press its power button.

- Configure your computer to sleep automatically after a period of inactivity by using the Energy Saver pane of System Preferences.

To Shut Down or Not to Shut Down

You do not need to regularly shut down a Mac OS X-based computer because its Unix foundation operates much more cleanly than Mac OS 9 and earlier. What does this mean? In the old days of Mac OS 9, the computer's performance would degrade over time, requiring regular restarts just to shake out the cobwebs. OS X is so clean that these digital cobwebs never get a chance to form. However, some useful maintenance operations may not happen according to schedule if you only have your computer sleep every night, as explained in Chapter 21. Most technicians recommend shutting down your computer instead of putting it to sleep. As noted earlier, during startup, your computer performs a basic self-test, where it verifies that all hardware is functioning normally. The computer's self-test functions are very useful indicators of upcoming problems, and the tests are run during startup. Another factor in the recommendation is the possibility of local power problems. The computer is much safer being shut down normally rather than having the power fail while you're away from the machine for the weekend. This is also not to mention the electric bill! You wouldn't leave the television on when you go out, would you?

Waking up

To make your computer wake up from sleep, do one of the following:

- If you have a MacBook, MacBook Pro, PowerBook, or iBook, open its lid. (This action doesn't wake all PowerBook models.)

- Press any key on the keyboard (we suggest using the Shift key because it doesn't actually type anything by itself, which would prevent you from putting a lot of gobbledygook type in a document by accident while your computer is waking up).

- Click the mouse.

Logging out of Mac OS X

You can log out of Mac OS X so that someone else can log in, or just to protect your data's security. To log out, choose Log Out from the Apple menu. A dialog box appears in which you must confirm or cancel your intention to log out.

If you click Log Out in the dialog box, Mac OS X instructs all open applications to quit. If any open application has a document with unsaved changes, the affected application asks whether you want to save the changes before quitting. After all applications have quit, the login window appears.

In this case, the login window appears after you log out even if your computer is configured to log in automatically.

TIP   You can configure your computer so that the Restart and Shut Down buttons don't work in the login window. This makes it more difficult, although not impossible, for someone to restart the computer with a CD, which may allow them to access your Mac OS X files. Chapter 14 discusses how to disable these buttons.

Restarting the computer

You need to restart your computer far less often with Mac OS X because it doesn't crash as often as earlier Mac OS versions. Nevertheless, you may need to restart your computer after installing new software or to get the computer to recognize a newly connected device.

Use any of the following methods to restart your computer:

- If your keyboard has a Power key, press it; then press the R key or click the Restart button in the dialog box that appears.

- If your keyboard has an Eject key, press Control while pressing Eject and then press the R key or click the Restart button in the dialog box that appears.

- Log out and then click the Restart button in the login window.

- Choose Restart from the Apple menu.

With any of these methods, Mac OS X tells all open applications to quit. As with logging out, any open applications that have a document with unsaved changes ask whether you want to save the changes before quitting. After all applications have quit, the computer shuts down and then automatically starts up as described at the beginning of this chapter.

Shutting down the computer

Although you can leave the computer running indefinitely and simply set it to sleep when no one is using it, you can also shut it down. Shutting down saves more energy than sleeping.

You can use any of these methods to shut down:

- If your keyboard has a Power key, press it and then press the Enter key or click the Shut Down button in the dialog box that appears.

- If your keyboard has an Eject key, press Control while pressing Eject, and then press the Enter key or click the Shut Down button in the dialog box that appears.

- Log out and click the Shut Down button in the login window.

- Choose Shut Down from the Apple menu.

When you shut down your computer, Mac OS X tells all open applications to quit. If an open application has a document with unsaved changes, it asks whether you want to save the changes before quitting. After all applications have quit, the computer shuts off.

NOTE In the event of a hard system crash, you may need to power your computer down manually, as opposed to using these safer methods of restarting, logging out, or shutting down. When a hard crash occurs, push and hold the power button on your computer for five seconds. This shuts down your computer, but it does so without saving any open documents and may result in damage to the system.

Summary

This chapter covered a lot of ground! It presented you with an introduction to the GUI, its key elements, and the Finder, your main tool to access the data stored on your machine. You learned how to interact with the windows and folders that display the applications and documents (represented by icons) within your Mac. You learned how to work with volumes, ejecting and even burning new ones! It introduced Spaces, Apple's new desktop organization tool that works in conjunction with Exposé to help you manage desktop clutter. This chapter also covered how to modify the behavior and appearance of Finder windows, icons, Exposé, Spaces, the desktop screen savers, and the Dock to better suit your needs. Additionally, you learned how to work with labels and aliases. The next chapter builds upon this knowledge and discusses working with documents and applications in greater detail.

Chapter 3

Searching with Spotlight

M ac OS X includes a powerful tool to help you search through the information on your Mac: Spotlight technology. Spotlight is a revolutionary new technology that helps you find files and folders quickly and accurately, using a variety of methods and criteria.

Searching with Spotlight can be extremely simple or very sophisticated. For example, Spotlight can simply search for a file by its name, or it can search for combinations of other attributes, such as the file's size, creator, modification date, or label color. Better still, Spotlight can search for dozens of even more specific and complex characteristics, such as for text that is embedded in a PDF or Word document, or the exposure settings for a picture imported from your digital camera. In Leopard, you can even use Boolean logic or enter a specific date range.

What Spotlight Can Do for You

No matter how carefully you organize your folders and disks, the time will inevitably arrive when you cannot locate an application, file, or folder without the frustrating task of having to shuffle through hundreds of them to find the one you need. It might also come to pass that your search criteria isn't something you can invoke simply by manually picking through your files in the Finder. What happens if you want to search through thousands of Word documents for a specific quote or phrase, find an application instantaneously, or search your music library for folk songs recorded only in 1966? Wouldn't it be nice to be able to search for all of the pictures that your Pop has e-mailed you in the past year? Spotlight makes these kinds of searches effortless, from the simplest by-name-only search to sophisticated queries involving many different kinds of attributes.

Spotlight can find anything on your Mac for you almost instantly. Spotlight can search through your e-mail, your calendars, your contacts — even through movie, image, and music files — and display them in easily understandable categories that make sorting and picking through your results a simple task. Spotlight can be very intuitive. If you're not sure when certain documents were created, you can take advantage of Mac OS X's use of relative dating and search for items created "today" or "last month." Because of the advanced technologies that Spotlight employs, it tends to be almost surprisingly (and pleasantly) fast and accurate, reaching far into the depths of your file system.

Behind the Scenes with Spotlight

To search for a file under a computer operating system's file system, there exists a search "engine" that is able to reference and point to certain pieces of data regarding the files. In Mac OS X Leopard (10.5), the search engine technology employed is called Spotlight. The pieces of information that Spotlight searches for are called *metadata*.

Metadata

Metadata is literally "data about data." Files contain data. An image file contains the data that makes up its picture. Text documents contain the data that make up their text. Distinct from their typical main body of data, files also contain metadata. From the perspective of your Mac's file system, metadata is part of a file but is separate from the data stored there. This metadata is said to be associated with the file that it is part of, and contains small strings of information that reference the file's data, as well as referencing attributes of the file itself.

Although you might not realize it, you are already very familiar with some different examples of metadata. A file's name is the simplest example of a bit of metadata. Although it might not be a part of the text of your actual Word document, it would be pretty hard to know whether or not you were viewing the correct file in the Finder if you couldn't reference it by name. The size of a file is another essential tidbit of information for an operating system to be aware of (how else would it know where the file began and ended within the file system?) and is also part of a file's metadata; again, data that is not part of the file's data itself, but data that is nonetheless part of the file. In fact, if you do a "Get Info" on a file you can see a whole bunch of information that is stored in a file's metadata right there in the Info window. One metadata option exclusive to Mac OS X is the Spotlight Comments field, to which you can add specific data for Spotlight to search through on a customized per-file basis. Take a look at Figure 3.1.

Information such as the file's creation date, modification date, label color, and location are all great examples of a file's metadata. These examples are said to be external to the file; they are easily viewed and have been visible to users of the Mac OS for many years. In previous examples of the Mac OS (before 10.4), when the Find command was initiated, it was these attributes that were searched through. The search engine was written to take advantage of these bits of data and would search each file individually for the desired results.

FIGURE 3.1

Many attributes that you can view in a Get Info window are observable examples of metadata.

More interesting, however, is the metadata that is stored inside of the files and that is not so easily visible to the file system. Many files contain a fantastic amount of metadata, just waiting to be accessed. Images taken with a digital camera, for example, can embed the make and model of the camera that was used, the exposure time, and whether or not a flash was used in the metadata of each file. When iTunes encodes an AAC file, information such as the song name, year, and genre are encoded in the metadata as well. When your buddy sends you a document over iChat, that document gets its metadata encoded with your buddy's screen name. Because the usual nature of metadata is that it's stored within individual files, searching through an entire file system, comprised of hundreds of thousands of files (such as under Mac OS X), for large numbers of complex information pieces is a slow process.

The Spotlight Store

Spotlight takes this concept of searching metadata and, well, steals the show with it, so to speak. Instead of having to search through the metadata of every individual file on your Mac, Spotlight takes all of this information and keeps it in a single database, called the *Spotlight Store*. Every single time a file is created, copied, moved, saved, or deleted, Spotlight works on-the-fly, in the background, with no tangible performance lags, to keep the Spotlight Store updated with the latest information regarding your files. The metadata portion of the Spotlight Store is called the Meta-data Store.

The Spotlight Store also serves another very important purpose: It keeps an index of the contents of your files. This means that, if you have a text document, Spotlight saves the actual text of the document into the Spotlight Store. This portion of the Spotlight Store is called the Content Index. Just like the Meta-data Store, the Content Index is updated any time a document is created, copied, moved, saved, or deleted. Once a file's contents are in the Content Index, terms appearing within the file can be searched for just as easily as the file's name or creation date. Unlike the past indexing

The Great Metadata Controversy

Interestingly, the integration (or lack thereof) of metadata into Mac OS X has been the source of a long-standing debate among those involved and committed individuals in the Mac OS X community. Way back in the era of Mac OS X 10.0 (circa 2001), Apple introduced what proved to be a controversial change in the way Mac files were "typed" by the Mac OS. Under Mac OS 9, this was handled in the metadata; the application that created a file (and thus the application that opens it) was stored in the file itself, in the "data about data." In Mac OS X, files still had the creator type stored in metadata, but Apple specifically requested that developers write that their applications *also* specify a file extension at the end of the file name (such as motorcycle.jpg), the objective being increased compatibility with other computing platforms. File extensions! What is this, Windows? Apple's new naming convention divided the Mac community; users began lobbying for their causes. On one hand were the users who were all for metadata and against the decidedly backwards usage of file extensions, which were deemed archaic, Windows-like, and forced users to give up their previous full control over naming their files. Thus, the Mac OS X Metadata Proposal was created, voicing fears that Apple was regressing from the metadata model and rallying for its future, while simultaneously requesting that users be re-granted full control over file names and not be forced to use the .txt type of model. On the other hand were those that felt that Apple was doing the right thing by using file extensions, and seemingly moving away from the metadata model, and a Mac OS X *Anti*-Metadata counter petition was released.

Well, with Spotlight in mind, it's clear that Apple chose to go the metadata route, alleviating any fears carried by the pro-metadata community. Apple still mandates that files contain extensions embedded within the file name; however, there is currently a preference in the Finder to show or hide said extensions. Those who are against Apple's metadata typically are against it for misguided fears of compatibility issues, falling prey to the common misconception that metadata and resource forks are the same thing, which they are not. (See the previous Tip for more information regarding resource forks.)

systems of the Mac, which were often slow and would require manual updating, Spotlight handles content indexing automatically and virtually instantaneously.

NOTE Be aware that Spotlight maintains one database (the Spotlight Store) per file system. This means that in the case of removable storage — say, a portable FireWire drive — its relevant Spotlight information is stored on the drive itself, and thus is not tied to a specific Mac or Mac OS X installation. Spotlight data relevant to a given set of files always stays with the files. This data becomes even more crucial when dealing with networked volumes, covered a bit later in this chapter.

TIP A common misconception is that metadata and resource forks are the same thing. This is most definitely not the case. Resource forks exist as actual portions of a file or application, and metadata is data *about* a file (but still part of the file). Classic Mac files have two portions: a data fork for storing coded information regarding the file or program, and the resource fork for storing information (resources) like graphics and sounds. It is likely that confusion has arisen from the tendency for Mac resource forks to get "stripped" off of files when transmitted through non-Mac file systems, such as over the Internet, which would cause the files to lose metadata-like information. To confuse matters further, older Mac files could indeed store the metadata within the resource forks. Although Mac OS X fully supports resource forks, going forward Apple has moved towards a single-fork model for files, and "bundles" or "packages" for applications that store their resources inside of a hidden folder. This model prevents metadata from parting with files, no matter what file systems are traversed.

Supported file types

Spotlight supports the following file types (the list is continually growing) as of the printing of this book:

- Plain text
- RTF
- PDF
- Mail
- Address Book contacts
- Microsoft Office Word documents
- Microsoft Office Excel spreadsheets
- Keynote presentations
- Photoshop images
- Applications
- Folders/directories
- Video and audio files:
  - MP3
  - AAC
  - MOV

- Images:
  - JPEG
  - GIF
  - TIFF
  - PNG
  - EXIF

The fact that these files are "supported" means that Mac OS X 10.5 already possesses the underpinnings and capabilities to seamlessly read the metadata and the contents of these files and write them to the Spotlight Store so that they can be retrieved via a Spotlight search.

This doesn't mean that "unsupported" file types are left out in the cold. Apple has made Spotlight technology extensible, meaning that for developers, the technology is open for them to incorporate within their own non-Apple applications and consequently to extend the metadata schema to include files in formats other than the ones listed in this section. Apple accomplishes this by making readily available all of the programming tools and information one would need to easily integrate this technology into new and already existing applications.

Using Spotlight

Now that you've seen how Spotlight functions, you're ready to put it to good use, namely, learning how to search. Searching is initiated by specifying the attributes of a file that you want to look for. In its most basic form, a search can be for a single word. If you have a document that you know the name but not the location of, you can search for it by typing its file name into Spotlight. More sophisticatedly, a search can be run by specifying very specific parameters, such as searching only for files within a specific folder or including only results that fall above or below a specific file size. A Spotlight search can be run in two main ways:

- From the menu bar
- Within a Finder window

Running Spotlight from the menu bar is the easiest and most convenient way to start a search; it's also the more basic method, but don't hold that against it. Running a Spotlight search from a Finder window isn't always as convenient, but it's more advanced than the menu bar searches in that it lets you set specific parameters and gives you greater control over your results. There's even a Spotlight System Preferences pane which gives you full control over the categories and locations which are searched. Read ahead to discover how to use Spotlight to search your drive in more ways than you ever thought possible.

The magnifying glass in the menu bar

Take a look in the upper right-hand corner of your menu bar. Mac OS X 10.4 introduced a brand new menu bar icon, and Leopard has refined it, as shown in Figure 3.2.

The Spotlight search icon, lying dormant in the menu bar

Clicking the magnifying glass icon in the menu bar drops down the Spotlight search field. It is here where you can type the terms that you want to search your file system for. Figure 3.3 displays how the Spotlight field looks after the magnifying glass is clicked.

Type your search criteria here.

Very simply, typing your desired search criteria is all you need to do to invoke a Spotlight search. Once you see your desired result, click it once to select it from the list and launch or open the item. Even when using the most modest of Mac hardware, you will see the results of your search start to spill into a list below the search field almost instantaneously. This expedience is the result of the fact that instead of searching your entire computer, Spotlight is searching through its own lean central databases. As the search is executed, the spinning gear appears on the right side of the search field, indicating that a search is in progress. To the left of the search text that you have entered, a ghosted X icon appears, which when clicked allows you to clear the search field. Figure 3.4 displays a Spotlight search for the term *motorcycle*.

Before going any further, it's important to keep in mind the underlying concepts of how Spotlight pinpoints its search results. Take a look at the list displayed in Figure 3.4. Some of those files seem very out of place as the result of a query for the term *motorcycle*. How did all of that stuff make it in there? The results that are displayed are due to Spotlight's uncanny ability to delve deeply within the file system and search for information (metadata) associated with the files that is not readily visible during your normal Mac usage. Whenever you invoke a Spotlight search, there are effectively three different data stores accessed to provide your results:

- **The Meta-data Store:** This is the central database that holds all of the metadata for every file on the machine, such as the composer of a song or the color space of an image.

- **The Content Index:** This is the central database that holds all of the content information for indexable files on the machine. The Content Index and the Meta-data Store are part of the Spotlight Store database, which updates its information automatically, every time changes are made to files, with no user intervention.

- **The File System:** Files that don't yet support metadata or content indexing are still searched for in the old style of searching, by searching through the file system itself and not the new Spotlight Store.

FIGURE 3.4

Perform a search by simply starting to type. Notice the variety of search results and the way Spotlight organizes them.

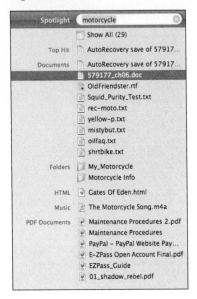

Keeping those search methods in mind, it becomes easy to imagine how some of those seemingly incongruous results showed up in our motorcycle search. The contents of those text documents could likely contain the word *motorcycle* in them (content), and there could be music files with embedded album information that contains the word *motorcycle* (metadata). Or, at a basic level, the document could have the word *motorcycle* in its name as displayed in the Finder. One of the documents displayed in the list is titled 041749 ch03.doc. That's right — it's the very chapter of this book that is being typed at this very moment. Microsoft Word, during its periodic auto-saves, has saved this file to the hard drive, and thus caused the content of this document (which as of a few minutes ago, includes the word *motorcycle*) to be written, in the background, to Mac OS X's Content Index, which, when queried for the term *motorcycle* as displayed in Figure 3.4, now returns this document as a result.

Working with your Spotlight results

Taking a look at the search results in Figure 3.4 reveals that Spotlight displays your results by kind (that is, it organizes the list into groupings of files of the same categories). In the motorcycle search list, you can see files organized in groups of Documents (text documents), Folders (Finder folders), Music (MP3 and AAC files), HTML (Web-formatted documents), and PDFs. Other file categories include Applications, Movies, Presentations, Images, AppleScripts, and even System Preference files.

The Top Hit

The Top Hit category always appears at the head of the file list. There is always a single item in this section, which is determined to be a top hit for you by using factors such as relevance to the search term that you provided, how frequently the file is used, and how often the search for your specific terms leads you to choose that file from a Spotlight search.

Spotlighting applications

When Spotlight was first introduced, it became clear that often the fastest way to find and launch an application that is not in the Dock is to do a Spotlight menu bar search. Executing a search eliminates the need to navigate through the Finder hierarchy and into the Applications folder. And because Spotlight is so fast, the application that is being searched for often comes up before you're done typing its name. In Leopard, Spotlight has been further refined to take advantage of this fact, and special prominence is now given to application files that match search results. If a query for an application yields accurate results, the application file becomes the top hit, and is preselected in the results list. Moving the mouse or the arrow keys to select the application is no longer necessary; you can just press Return after performing the search and the application launches. In Figure 3.5, a search for the Disk Utility application has been performed. You can see that it has been selected as the Top Hit, and is also highlighted, awaiting the press of the Return key to launch.

FIGURE 3.5

Spotlight makes launching applications nearly effortless.

Show All

Besides the Top Hit, there is one other option that always appears at the top of the list under a menu bar-induced Spotlight search, called Show All. When Spotlight completes a search, it is quite possible that it has found more items than can be displayed from under the menu bar, and that you want to see all of them. Or, you might want some more control over the way your search results appear. Clicking Show All closes the submenu bar list and opens a modified Finder window to display your results in their entirety. You can see the Show All option in Figure 3.6, and the Spotlight Finder window in Figure 3.7.

FIGURE 3.6

If your results list is too long to be displayed in the menu bar drop-down list, click Show All to see it all.

FIGURE 3.7

Clicking the Show All option gives you this larger, full-featured window for browsing the results of your Spotlight Search.

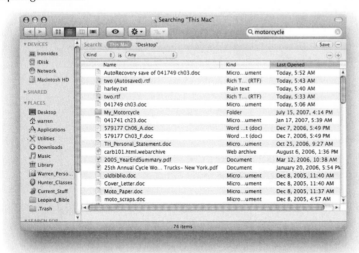

Working with basic search results

The Spotlight window displayed in Figure 3.7 is geared toward the quick and flexible browsing and organization of your search results so that you can find what you want and move on with your life. Nestled in the toolbar of the Spotlight window is the Spotlight search field (which you can use to start a new search or to modify your current one), along with a number at the bottom of the window specifying the total number of search results. Notice that the list defaults to sorting itself in order of when the files were last opened, with the most recently opened files at the head of the list. Next to each item in the list is the date and time of the file's most recent opening, which can be useful for weeding out older documents when looking for recently changed ones. You can click the Name and Kind list headings to sort the list of results alphabetically or by file kind, respectively. Clicking a heading a second time reverses the order of the list. If the Name heading is clicked once, for example, the list becomes alphabetized, starting from Apple and working down towards Zebra. If the Name heading is clicked a second time, the list becomes reversed, with Zebra on top and Apple at the bottom. The same model holds true for the date last opened and for grouping by Kind. In Figure 3.8, you can see a list of search results grouped by Kind.

These groups are provided to give you even more flexibility over viewing the way that your search results appear. By simply clicking the different options provided, you can dramatically change the look of your results. For example, by forcing the list to be grouped by Kind, you can immediately eliminate whole chunks of files that don't match the type you are looking for.

FIGURE 3.8

Clicking the Kind heading groups together files of a particular type, such as Word documents.

If the results list is monstrously huge, Mac OS X shows only a limited number of results at one time; otherwise, you might be stuck navigating a list comprised of tens of thousands of items, a daunting task. Instead, Apple caps the list after 4,000 items. If you scroll to the bottom of your results, you will find a More option, shown in Figure 3.9, which allows you to keep adding more files to the results list, should the need arise.

FIGURE 3.9

Click the More option at the bottom of the list to display the full cache of results. The bottom of the window changes to reflect the added results.

Organizing your search results

You can work with the files in the Spotlight window the same way you would treat them if they were being viewed directly from the Finder. Files in the list can be drag-and-dropped over aliases or applications in the Dock, double-clicked to launch, or dragged between folders and windows to move them around. You can even choose to show the path bar from the Finder's View menu to always see the full pathway to the files that you are looking at.

You can also use the View menu (or the toolbar shortcuts) to change the way your search results appear. The results are in the List view by default, but you may want to use the Icon view to display a small number of search results for a better visual appearance. The Cover Flow view can be especially useful if you are picking through a bunch of files like pictures and PDFs. Using Cover Flow enables you to shuffle through your files one by one and glimpse a preview as each file passes by. Cover Flow, and changing the look and feel of your Finder windows in general, is covered in the preceding chapter.

Take a peek with Quick Look

Instead of running a Get Info command, or even opening your files to see more of their attributes, you can use the Quick Look feature. On folders and generic files (see Figure 3.10) a Quick Look gives you basic information such as file size and date modified, which are external forms of metadata that were discussed earlier in the chapter. But using Quick Look on files like text documents, PDFs, images, music files, and movies, and Mac OS X gives you a preview of the file right in the Finder, without having to open a separate application, as seen in Figure 3.11. (Some of this data, such as an AAC file's album art cover, or a text document's content, actually becomes internal metadata). Using Quick Look can be a faster and easier way to preview and organize your Spotlight search results by letting you have access to files' content straight from the Finder.

FIGURE 3.10

Performing a Quick Look displays basic information for this folder.

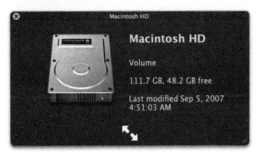

FIGURE 3.11

On files like text documents and images, a Quick Look grants you access to their contents right from the Finder.

Performing more complex searches

Besides accessing Spotlight from the menu bar icon (the magnifying glass), you can also perform Spotlight searches straight from your Finder windows just by typing your search terms into the search field that sits right in the toolbar of every Finder window. (More accurately, the search bar is there by default. If you don't see the search bar, choose Customize Toolbar from the View menu to put it back up there.) You can make a new Finder window to open the search field (⌘+N) or run a Find (⌘+F) like back in the old days.

Running Spotlight searches through Finder windows can be more convenient than running searches from the menu bar. While the Spotlight searches run from the menu bar are a kind of quick and dirty way of scanning your whole file corpus for a single word or phrase, Spotlighting from Finder windows performs searches that are more relative to the folders that you are viewing, instead of defaulting to searching everywhere all at once. Searching through a Finder window's toolbar gives you more flexible control over which locations on your system will be searched and gives you quick access for customizing searches. Provided with more options than the menu bar searches give you, your custom searches might take a bit longer to set up, but worry not — in Leopard, you can save them for later.

The location bar

When you initiate a search through a Finder window, the list of results begins to instantaneously appear directly within the window that you are looking at. One of the most apparent differences between this method and the Spotlight menu bar/window method is the presence of a bar that sits directly under the toolbar. We'll call this the location bar. The location bar is quite interesting, because its options change depending on where you had navigated to just prior to invoking a search. Take a look at Figure 3.12 to see the location bar.

FIGURE 3.12

The location bar's location options change depending on where you are in the Finder.

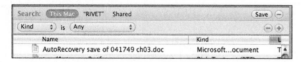

Different options in the location bar will be present depending on where you have navigated to and what your configuration is like. On basic systems, you will see two options next to the word Search: one for This Mac, which searches your entire computer, and one that reflects the current folder you are in. Clicking these buttons restricts your searches to just those locations. If you have external volumes mounted, these show up in the location bar, as do any mounted network volumes in the form of a "Shared" location.

- If your current Finder window is set to your Music folder, and you start typing a search in the toolbar, the location bar will have your Music folder listed as an option.

- If you don't have any Finder windows open, and create a new one, and then start typing a search in the toolbar, the location bar will have whatever folder is set as your default for new windows as an option. (You can change the default new window folder in the Finder Preferences.)

- If you use the Find command (⌘+F or File ➪ Find from the Finder) the location bar reflects the window you have just been in. If you didn't have any windows open, the default folder for new windows appears.

Also present in the location bar is a Save button and a plus sign. Those will be discussed soon.

Customized searches

Running a customized search really puts you in control of your Spotlight searches. Instead of using only strings of words, you can specify other attributes to search for. Go to the Finder and press ⌘+F to begin a new search. Do you see the little plus sign, next to the Save button, in the location bar? That button is the gateway to customized searching.

Click the plus button to begin adding parameters to your searches. Each time you click the plus button, another line drops down with another set of options to search by. The attributes readily available for adding to your search parameters can be viewed in Figure 3.13 and are explained as follows:

- **What:** Use the check box to tell Spotlight to search only for the file name attribute, as opposed to the file's content or creation date. You can use the second check box to tell Spotlight to search through Mac OS X's operating system underpinnings as well, which are by default left out of regular searches.

- **Kind:** You can search for a specific type of document, such as an image or a music file.

- **Last opened date:** With this option you can specify a search regarding when a file was last opened.

- **Last modified date:** This option searches files for the last time they were modified, by date, such as the last time you edited a Word document.

- **Created:** This option searches for creation dates of files.

- **Name:** This is a basic file name search.

- **Contents:** This option searches for file content, such as the text contained in a PDF or Word document.

FIGURE 3.13

The more easily accessible options for running custom searches

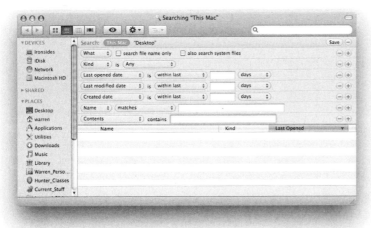

Using these search factors means that you don't even have to use a string of text to find your files anymore. You could, for example, run a search for files opened today, above 100K in size, and modified within the last month. No text typing required!

Metadata on the rise

Earlier this chapter touched upon two different kinds of metadata. One type, discussed in the last section, is considered to be external, that is, it's easily viewable by the user of the computer, and by its operating system. If you were to do a Get Info in the Finder, you could easily view the basic parameters of a file, such as the file kind, size, name, or creation date.

More elusive is the metadata that isn't so easily viewable to us humans and in many cases even to the graphical interface of the computers that we use. Look at Figure 3.14. When choosing parameters in Finder window searches, there's a tremendously important option sitting modestly at the bottom of the list, namely, the Other option. It is within this Other option that much of Spotlight's behind-the-scenes power lies. Choosing it opens a list (part of which appears in Figure 3.15) of literally *dozens* of options that you can add to your searches. It's also a great list to browse to come up with terms to search by when performing a plain-Jane text query — this is a list of *all* of the metadata options that Spotlight can search for.

FIGURE 3.14

Let the Other option be your metadata gateway.

FIGURE 3.15

This is just a taste of some of the advanced metadata options that you can search for using Spotlight.

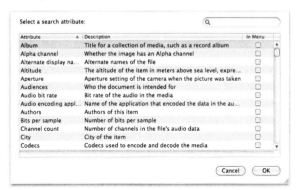

This multitude of options really deserves to be at least skimmed, so as to familiarize yourself with the types of searches that you can make. There are too many to even list here, but the scenarios that you can orchestrate blow other search technologies clear out of the, er, Spotlight. With Spotlight, a digital photographer with tens of thousands of photographs, for example, can create searches for such detailed information as the camera model, focal length, f-stop, exposure time, flash usage, camera mode, color space, and even if red-eye reduction was on or off.

Checking the Add to Favorites box as shown in Figure 3.15 places the selected search parameter in the more easily accessible menu items that appear above the Other option.

Boolean Spotlight searching

In Spotlight, Boolean searches allow yet additional flexibility for term searching. Boolean logic is an algebraic system for organizing sets of data, first synthesized by a man named George Bool in the 1800s. Since that time Boolean logic has been heavily employed in mathematics and in computer science. All of the circuits in your Mac use some form of Boolean logic to complete their function. Almost every line of code in any software program you use is based on the principles of Boolean logic. Boolean logic sets use things called operators to organize the aforementioned sets of data. The most common Boolean operators, and the ones Spotlight can employ, are as follows:

- **AND:** Normally, when a Spotlight search is invoked, although this is not typed in, the search by default is using the "AND" operator. A search for "honda motorcycle" displays results for all files only with both the word honda AND the word motorcycle. In an AND search, both conditions must be met in order to yield a true statement. This is an example of Boolean logic at its most basic. Look at Figure 3.16 to see a Boolean AND search in action.

FIGURE 3.16

Normally, Spotlight uses the AND Boolean logic operator to search for all terms in a query.

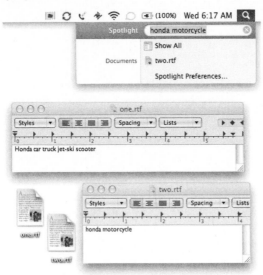

- **OR:** However, what if you don't want to be so specific, and you want to find files with *either* the term honda *or* the term motorcycle in them? Prior to Leopard, you would have to run two separate searches, one for motorcycle, one for honda, and compare the two. In Leopard, you can use the Boolean operator OR, and perform a search for honda OR motorcycle. This search yields results with files that have only the word *honda* in them, OR files that have only the word *motorcycle* in them. With an OR search, only one of the conditions needs to be met to yield a true statement. Take a look at Figure 3.17 to see an OR statement at work.

- **NOT:** What if you now want to be even more specific? Say that you want to search for documents with both the terms *honda* and *motorcycle* in them, but only files that do *not* have the term *sportbike* in them. In order to accomplish this search, you can use the NOT operator and specify a search for honda AND motorcycle NOT sportbike. This search finds all files with both the terms *honda* AND *motorcycle*, but only files that do NOT have the word *sportbike* in them. Note that in the preceding search, the AND term is actually redundant because all Spotlight searches default to using the AND operator. See Figure 3.18 to see how a NOT search can look.

FIGURE 3.17

Using the OR operator yields results that have any one of the terms in your query.

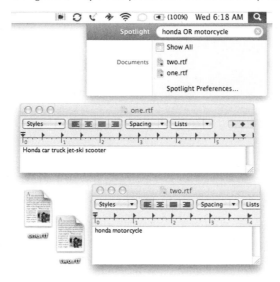

FIGURE 3.18

Using the NOT operator finds only files without the term that you single out for exclusion.

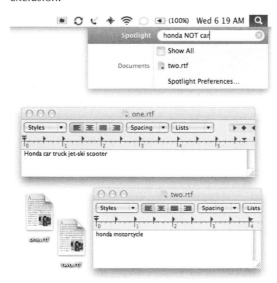

TIP Computer scientists and mathematicians use shorthand notation for Boolean logic, such as the ampersand (&) for an AND operator, the vertical bars (| |) for the OR operator, and the exclamation mark (!) for NOT operators. In the previous version of Mac OS X, some of this shorthand was active, yet undocumented. As of this writing, Leopard does not support such shorthand notation. You can, however, use the minus sign (-sportbike, for example) to indicate a NOT search.

Spotlighting shortcuts

Besides Boolean logic, Mac OS X affords you other advanced methods for finding your files. You can search for exact phrases by placing your search terms inside quotation marks, such as searching for the phrase "O the bleeding drops of red" to find your copy of Uncle Walt's famous poem.

You can also use Spotlight to search for files that have been modified before or after a specific date by using greater than (>) and less than (<) symbols. For example, performing a file search for "motorcycle >5/2/07" limits the results of the search to files modified after May 2, 2007. Using a less than symbol in the search ("motorcycle <5/2/07") limits search results to files modified before May 2, 2007.

You can use Spotlight as a shortcut for oft-repeated tasks or as a way to save you a few clicks before repeatedly opening the same applications. In Mac OS X 10.5, instead of first opening the dictionary application and then typing your word, you can type the word right in the Spotlight field. Take a look at Figure 3.19 to see Spotlight's defining action.

Spotlight can also provide simple calculations, eliminating the need to launch the calculator every time you need to do some basic math. Just about any feature found in the Calculator's basic mode you can utilize from the Spotlight field. See Figure 3.20 to see Spotlight performing some arithmetic.

FIGURE 3.19

Enter a word into the Spotlight field, and Mac OS X hands you its definition using the built-in dictionary.

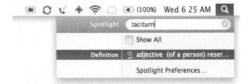

FIGURE 3.20

Type basic arithmetic equations and Spotlight solves them for you, sans calculator.

Smart folders (saved searches)

Now, after making all of these detailed, complicated Spotlights, wouldn't it be nice if you could save your searches for future usage? Of course it would, and Apple has devised a new type of folder just to handle the job. These folders, called smart folders, can be created in one of two ways:

- Choose New Smart Folder from the Finder's File menu (⌘+Option+N). This opens essentially a new Find file window, which then lets you:

- Save your searches in the Finder windows by clicking the Save button that you've seen in the location bar, under the toolbar, on the right side of the window. This opens a sheet that asks you for a location to save the folder and grants you the option of adding the smart folder to the sidebar automatically.

You can always tell a smart folder by its custom icon, as highlighted in Figure 3.21. Once you've created a smart folder, you can open it to view its contents. When viewing the contents of a smart folder, it's important to realize that the items that you see are not actually moved there; they are still maintained in their original locations. Smart folders can really change the way you organize your files by no longer forcing the file system to display a single file in one and only one location. Interestingly, depending on your specified parameters, the contents of smart folders can easily change from one moment to the next. As files' data change and time goes by, different files, at different times, will meet a constant set of search criteria specified in a smart folder.

FIGURE 3.21

Smart folders are purple and have the distinctive gear icon.

A Spotlight in your sidebar

Speaking of smart folders, there are some that already exist within the Mac OS! Before creating some smart folders of your own, take a look in the sidebar. Under the sections called Devices, Shared, and Places, is a section called Search For. In the Search For section, you can see a bunch of Apple's premade searches, which are really just prebuilt smart folders. In Figure 3.22 you can see the bunch of searches sitting in the sidebar. There are two types of prebuilt searches:

- **Chronological:** The searches that have a clock-face icon are chronological searches, that is, they specify a specific relative date range. Use these searches to look for files and folders that have been created or modified on the current day, the previous day, or within the past week.

- **Kind:** Use the folders with the standard smart folder appearance to search for all instances of specific types of files. You can see prebuilt searches for Images, Movies, and Documents in the sidebar.

FIGURE 3.22

Use Mac OS X's prebuilt sidebar searches to search your system for files of a certain kind or that were created within a specific time frame.

The Spotlight contextual menu

Remember the extensible nature of Spotlight mentioned before? Because Spotlight is a service that is supported on a system-wide level, other applications that have Spotlight support built-in can also invoke a Spotlight search that opens a window like the one shown earlier in Figure 3.7. In an open document in TextEdit, for example, you can Control+click (or right-click, for you two-button mousers) a word or selected portion of text, and choose the Search In Spotlight option that appears in the resulting contextual menu. Doing this opens a new Spotlight window with the selected text as a search field. Figure 3.23 displays the Spotlight option as it appears in a TextEdit contextual menu. Notice the Google search option that appears in the menu as well, which enables you to initiate an Internet search straight from the application you're in.

FIGURE 3.23

Control+clicking a bit of text in a Spotlight-supported application is a shortcut for initiating a Spotlight search.

You can also Control+click (or right-click, for two-button mousers again) directly within a Spotlight results window to access a few shortcuts. Depending on your results, you can choose to reveal the document in the Finder, e-mail it to somebody, or start an Automator workflow without having to manually open the application first, and find the files second.

Spotlight volume indexing

If you install Leopard over a pre-existing Mac OS X installation, you might notice the Spotlight menu bar icon (the magnifying glass) pulsating for a period of time. Mac OS X is letting you know that Spotlight is creating and updating its databases for the first time. You can also click the Spotlight icon to display the search bar, underneath which you'll see a progress bar (see Figure 3.24) for the volume indexing. Because you are essentially bombarding a brand-new Leopard installation with hundreds of thousands of files, this might take a little while. Position the cursor over the magnifying glass for a few seconds to display the percentage of your file system that Spotlight has slogged through and updated.

FIGURE 3.24

Spotlight is indexing the system named "Ironsides," which has just had its Spotlight store rebuilt and is therefore creating a fresh index.

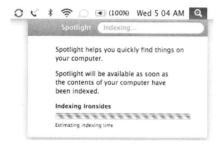

The magnifying glass icon also pulsates whenever an external volume, such as a FireWire or USB hard drive, is connected for the first time to a Mac running Leopard. This indicates that the drive is being indexed for the first time. When a drive is "indexed," all of its files are analyzed and the metadata information is copied to the Spotlight store. It is important to understand that the Spotlight store always stays with the files that it carries information about. If an external hard drive is plugged into your Mac, and then indexed, it does not need to be re-indexed when it is connected to a different Mac. Instead, other Macs can utilize the index that was created by the first Mac.

Spotlight indexing and searching on network volumes, however, is a bit trickier. When many users have access to a shared volume, they often have different sets of permissions, meaning essentially that they all don't have access to the same data set, even through they are all using the same volume. This makes it hard to create a .Spotlight database that everyone has access to. It also presents the technological challenge of creating a metadata store that everyone has access to when the need to search for files arises, but at the same time extending the same permissions that the users have to access their files into the metadata store as well. Otherwise, users will end up with search results listing files that they do not have access to.

In the previous release of Mac OS X, this problem was solved in a less than elegant manner. Instead of having a single Spotlight store local to the volume, as FireWire and USB drives do, network users created their own index of the mounted network volume and then saved it to their own file systems. Not tragic, unless it comes to pass that multiple users access the same volume simultaneously and initiate a Spotlight search. Then you have many users attempting to simultaneously create a full index of the network volume. As you might imagine, this unfortunate chain of events can bring even the most robust server to its knees. Thankfully, in Mac OS X 10.5, the problem has been solved, and Apple's servers are now smart enough to save a single Spotlight index on each network volume. Leopard also writes the file's permissions in as part of the metadata store, so that when searches are initiated across the network, users see only results lists of files they have access to.

Spotlight System Preferences

These in-depth, frighteningly quick and comprehensive searches are all well and good, but let's be honest: They can be a little *too* good. There might come a time that you don't want Spotlight to search certain categories for you. What if you want to search only for music, or only for documents? Or maybe you never want to see the names of folders in your searches ever again; after all, you know what folders you have, right? (Sure you do.) And that list that Spotlight makes from the menu bar — it might be useful to reorder that a bit as well. And come to think of it, you've got all of your e-mail backed up in a folder somewhere, but you don't need Spotlight to search though it, because it's really a duplicate folder.

Enter the Spotlight System Preferences. In Leopard, Apple provides a set of preferences to help you customize your Spotlight searches. The preferences are personal, meaning that they are configured on a per-user basis. Click the Spotlight icon after you launch the System Preferences application to access the features displayed in Figure 3.25. There are two panels in the Spotlight Preferences: one called Search Results and the other called Privacy.

Search Results

In the Search Results area is a list of categories that Spotlight divides your files into when it searches your system. Using the check boxes next to each item, you can choose whether or not Spotlight includes the specific category in its searches. All of the categories are active by default. You can also reorder the categories by selecting them and dragging them up or down in the list. When Spotlight displays its search results, it organizes them by category to reflect the order that they appear in this list.

Privacy

In the Privacy pane, you can prevent Spotlight from searching specific locations. Use the plus and minus (add and remove) buttons to add and remove your private locations to and from the list. You can also drag and drop locations directly from the Finder, or use the Delete key to remove a location. Note that you can add only folders or volumes, not individual files, into the Privacy window. Figure 3.26 shows a user who has decided not to let Spotlight search through his logged iChats folder nor through his Mail folder.

FIGURE 3.25

Customize Spotlight's overall behavior in the Mac OS X System Preferences.

FIGURE 3.26

Prevent Spotlight from searching specific locations by adding them to your Privacy list.

Using the first of the two check boxes on the bottom of the window, you can choose whether or not to enable a shortcut key for bringing down the Spotlight menu, and choose what the shortcut key should be. (The default is F8.) The second check box enables or disables a keyboard shortcut for the Spotlight window, the default of which is ⌘+Option+spacebar.

System-wide integration

So far this chapter has talked about Spotlight and its ability to search through your Mac OS X files using the menu bar icon as well as directly through the Finder. In OS X Leopard, Apple has built the Spotlight search technology into other applications as well. You can be sure that as time moves on, both Apple and third-party Mac software developers will continue to integrate Spotlight into their applications. As a start, every Mac OS X application has Spotlight built into the Open and Save dialog boxes, to make your navigation even easier.

Mail

Whenever you run a search or create a Smart Mailbox in Apple's Mail application, you are harnessing Spotlight technology. Spotlight searches quite quickly even through the body of the messages themselves for your search criteria. Just as you make smart folders in the Finder to save frequent searches that adhere to dynamically changing criteria, you can make Smart Mailboxes for searching through your e-mail.

Address Book

In the Mac OS X Address Book you can create special groups called Smart Groups. A Smart Group contains search criteria that cause the results to change dynamically. A great example is to make a Smart Group with the search criteria for upcoming birthdays in a particular time frame. As time advances, contacts with upcoming birthdays are added to the group and contacts with birthdays already passed are removed automatically.

iCal

iCal doesn't have the smart searching that its fellow applications share, but it does use Spotlight search technology to help you track down your calendar items. In iCal's upper right-hand corner is a search field that you can use to find different events and locations. If you pull down the menu from the magnifying glass, iCal lets you narrow your search criteria by the type of data you are looking for, even if it is for the attendees of an event, or just for a To Do item.

System Preferences

Instead of the icon bar, the System Preferences contains a Spotlight search field. As you type your search criteria, the System Preferences highlights (Spotlights!) the preference panes that match your search. System Preferences even helps Windows converts by matching common Windows terminology with Mac terminology. For example, if you performed a search for "wallpaper," System Preferences would know that you are looking for the Desktop and Screen Saver preferences.

Automator

Using Automator to simulate a workflow involves piecing together different actions. Weeding through the huge number of provided actions and finding the ones you need can be a difficult process. Spotlight searching is built into Automator, helping you quickly find exactly what you are looking for.

Spotlighting from the Command Line

If you'd like to delve deeper into Spotlight and get in under the hood, Apple has made it possible to do so. Besides the lovely and more commonly utilized graphical methods for accessing Spotlight, Apple has added command-line tools for power users to take advantage of. Because the core of Spotlight technology lives deep down in the roots of the operating system, Apple felt that command-line access was a natural step for rounding out Spotlight's functionality (and geek factor!).

Use the `mdls` command to view the metadata attributes of a file. Just as the standard `ls` command gives you a listing of files in a given directory, the `mdls` command displays the list of metadata attributes stored within a given file. For example, type **$ mdls warri.jpg** to display the attributes for the file `warri.jpg`.

Use the `mdfind` command to run a Spotlight search directly from the command line. For example, type **$ mdfind CB750** to search your files for any occurrences of CB750.

As previously stated, each file system has its own Spotlight Store database, meaning that there's usually a separate database per volume, so that the database stays with the files it is referencing. The database is stored as a hidden folder, called `.Spotlight-V100`, on the root level of the drive (/.Spotlight-V100). You'll need to use the sudo command (or authenticate as root) to view the contents of the folder. (See more on sudo-ing in the chapter on Unix, Chapter 23.)

If this database becomes corrupt or for whatever reason ceases to function properly, Spotlight searching will begin to flounder. New files will no longer update their changes to the database, changed content will not be reflected when searched for, and existing files may be ignored completely. If this unfortunate set of circumstances becomes your reality, fear not. Spotlight's database can be fully eradicated and then rebuilt all with a simple command. Just type **sudo mdutil –E /** into the Terminal and press Return, entering your password when prompted. (The "/" character indicates that you are erasing the Spotlight store on your boot volume.) If you've done it correctly, the Terminal should prompt you that your Spotlight database has been erased, and that a new one is being created in its stead. In a few seconds, the Spotlight menu bar icon will update to reflect that your index is rebuilt and display a progress report. In a few minutes (or more, depending on how much data is on your drive) your data will be back in the Spotlight.

Third-party utilities

In certain situations, Spotlight is known not to behave so nicely. Sometimes on older machines with frequently changing files, Spotlight can cause hang-ups. Digital video editors and photographers know all too well the consequences that continually modifying and saving multi-gigabyte-sized files can have on their systems. On older (pre-10.5, Leopard) Mac OS X servers, clients that connect and simultaneously re-index mounted volumes can even cause Mac OS X servers to crash. These incidences are very rare. Spotlight behaves wonderfully on the vast majority of systems. However, if you are having issues, or would simply like to tinker around, there are a number of third-party utilities that can make your Spotlight experience more enjoyable.

Spotless

Spotless is a simple utility that gives you greater control over the manner in which Spotlight creates and updates its indexes. In cases where you want to disable Spotlight indexing completely, you can add those volumes to the Spotless list. Although you can do this through Mac OS X's System Preferences, doing so disables all searching whatsoever, and Spotless retains its file name searching capabilities. If the Spotlight store — the .Spotlight-V100 hidden folder that was mentioned earlier — becomes corrupt, you can also use Spotless to delete the index, which can be easier than the aforementioned command-line method. Spotless also lets you see the exact size of your .Spotlight-V100 folders; if they are size-wise bloating out of control, that might be an alert that the index is having problems. Spotless can also be turned off and on at will. Spotless costs $12.95 for a single license and can be downloaded from Fixamac Software's Web site (`www.fixamac.net/software/spot/index.php`).

EasyFind and FileSpot

EasyFind is billed as either an alternative or supplement to Leopard's Spotlight. It provides you with what some users feel is a simpler interface for finding your files, and displays your results in a Finder-like window. You can launch and move your files around just as though you were in a real Finder window. You can choose what to search for, that is, only file names, only content, or only the names of folders. You can also use EasyFind to include invisible items in your searches, and even to be case sensitive (or insensitive). Best of all, EasyFind is free, and can be downloaded from Devon Technologies' Web site (`www.devon-technologies.com/download/index.html`). Give it a try — if you are frustrated with Spotlight's interface and level of control, EasyFind might make your searches easier.

FileSpot is the continuation of the older program MoRU, which was also a Spotlight enhancement utility. Like EasyFind, it is built on top of Spotlight, and is to be used either as an augmentation or replacement for the built-in Spotlight interface. FileSpot, like EasyFind, provides you with an alternate and arguably more flexible interface for finding files. FileSpot also lets you perform actions that Spotlight does not, such as tagging your files by adding metadata in the course of your search, and filtering a list of search results for further refinement. You can download FileSpot from Synthesis Studios' Web site (`http://mac.synthesisstudios.com/mac/filespot/about`).

Summary

Here's what you should know after reading this chapter:

- Use Spotlight to search for files and folders on volumes and disks attached to your computer.

- Spotlight bases its searches on the metadata and content of your files.

- Spotlight searches are extremely fast because instead of searching through the entire file system, Spotlight searches through its own databases.

- Spotlight updates its databases automatically. You don't have to do anything to keep the information current; OS X does it for you all in the background.

- By leveraging the power of metadata, Spotlight can perform searches with an accuracy and complexity never seen before in a consumer operating system.

Chapter 4

Transitioning to Intel Architecture and Universal/Binary Apps

In the simplest terms, a computer is built around several important devices. We're all fairly familiar with the basics, but to recap (again, on a very general, basic level), we've got the CPU, the hard drive, RAM, and some various busses. This chapter concentrates on the CPU, including what some of the recent changes in Apple's lineup mean to the end user.

When we talk about processor architecture, we're basically referring to the design of the chip and how it relates to the way it processes information. There are two main strategies that chip designers take: CISC and RISC. CISC stands for Complex Instruction Set Computers, and RISC stands for Reduced Instruction Set Computers. In a sense, these methodologies aren't much more than design philosophies, and in some sense were coined retroactively after the early chip design schemes had started to play out. Most early chips were CISC, when storage was at a premium. CISC chips are generally characterized by a greater number of operations built into the chip explicitly. On the other hand, RISC chips have comparatively few instructions, or operations, implemented. Generally RISC chips can perform individual instructions more quickly because they are simple and limited in scope, while CISC chips take longer to perform an individual instruction because they're more complex and take longer to call the instruction.

An example of this would be that a RISC chip generally has instructions that can be completed in a single clock cycle, while a CISC chip performs an instruction which can span more than one clock cycle. In order to get the RISC chip to multiply, you would first call an instruction to load the first number, another instruction to load the second number, one to find the "product" of the two numbers, and then you'd store the result in a register. In a CISC chip, you'd probably just call a function called MULT, which would do all of these things and return the result. This can mean that CISC chips are easier to program for because you don't have to write the code for a divide function.

It's important to note that most programmers will be writing code in one of the higher level languages (such as C+) and will not have to deal with the nuances of this; the compiler will take care of the details. However, the programmer who is creating an OS or preparing a compiler for a new chipset has to take these details into account, though there are times when a programmer must take certain low-level architecture details into account even when writing code on a high level. Certain operations won't just recompile for another chip without modification to the code and some understanding of what's going on "down there."

In reality, many of today's chips are not quite CISC and not quite RISC. They are a blend of both, trying to ply the advantages of both to create the best possible chip architecture for the task at hand.

PowerPC versus Intel

The first Macintosh computers were built around the Motorola 680x0 chip. This was a pretty fast (for the time) CISC-based chipset. For a while this was working out well for Apple, but at a certain point, Motorola had gotten about all the performance they could get out of it. RISC was becoming a hot concept, and Apple got together with IBM and Motorola to jump on the bandwagon and create the PowerPC architecture. PowerPC was a RISC chip that was very fast, and in 1994 Apple began using PowerPC chips (starting with the 601). By 2003 Apple had incorporated the G3 (for third-generation PPC), the G4, and just began releasing Macs based on the G5, a 64-bit multiprocessor-capable chipset. In order to ease the transition from the 680x0 chipset to the PPC chipset, Apple implemented a 680x0-to-PPC emulator which enabled the newer PPC-based machines to run code that hadn't been recompiled for the PPC. While not a speed demon initially, it allowed virtually all older programs to function fairly flawlessly on the new systems. Windows, on the other hand, initially started out on the Intel x86 platform, which (at least in the beginning) was also very CISC based. The two chipsets were incompatible, and programs and operating systems which were designed for one could not run on the other.

After Apple's switch to PPC, the Mac's processor was considerably faster on a megahertz basis than Intel-compatible Windows-based machines. A 400 MHz PPC machine was at least as fast, if not faster at some things, as an 800 MHz Intel-based machine. RISC was fast enough that some emulators for the Intel architecture were released that allowed you to run Windows on a Mac, albeit at a considerable speed loss. For a while though, Apple was able to keep up, at least performance-wise, with the Windows/Intel side of the world. But at a certain point, Apple began having problems getting Motorola, and then IBM, to keep the PPC architecture up to snuff speed-wise when stacked up against the Intel architecture. In 2005 Apple announced that they would be moving to an Intel-based chipset across the entire lineup.

How do you know if you've got a Mac with a PPC or an Intel chip? With the advent of the new processor scheme, Apple changed the names of their pro workstations to Mac Pro from "PowerMac G5" (or 4, or 3), and their laptops to MacBook and MacBook Pro from iBook and PowerBook. So if you've got a Mac Pro, MacBook, or MacBook Pro, then you've got an Intel Processor. If you've got an iMac or a Mac Mini, it can be difficult to tell from the outside whether you're PPC or Intel. No matter what machine you've got, you can find out fairly easily; go to the Apple menu and select

About This Mac. You'll see a whole bunch of information, but if you look at the Processor section, it will say "Intel" or "PowerPC," as shown in Figure 4.1.

You can find out what kind of machine you've got by choosing About This Mac from the Apple menu on any Mac running OS X.

Migration Considerations

All of the previous talk about CPU architecture is interesting, but few of us are programmers. So let's take a look at what Apple's switch to Intel means to the average user. The quick and somewhat incomplete answer is that it will impact the average user very little. The rest of this chapter looks at some of the things you should know about migrating and how you can best optimize your system and programs for the best user experience.

Rosetta

Rosetta is what Apple has dubbed the compatibility layer that allows you to run PPC-coded applications on your shiny new Intel-based Macintosh. Unlike the Classic application environment, it is completely transparent to the user. Rosetta also differs from the Classic application environment in that it's not an *emulation* environment, but rather a dynamic recompiling of the code so that it runs natively. While generally faster than emulation, this dynamic recompiling does take time, and applications running under Rosetta definitely suffer from some performance issues. None of Apple's "pro" applications will run in Rosetta, but all have been updated to be natively compatible with Intel-based machines. Check Apple's Web site to find out if your specific application qualifies for a free update or if a low-cost update is available. Most third-party applications have been updated as well; check with the software company to see what's required of you for an upgrade.

Universal applications

Most applications that have been written recently can be fairly easily compiled to work natively on Intel-based systems. Many developers were able to check the box in Apple's development environment Xcode that said "Make Universal," and, *voilà*, the application compiles as a *Universal Binary* — Apple's terminology for an application that has code for both PPC and Intel that can run natively on both systems.

Is my application running in Rosetta or is it native?

You can force a Universal application to open in Rosetta (though we have no idea why you'd want to do that) by clicking Get Info on an application in the Finder, and then checking the Open using Rosetta option near the bottom of the General section (see Figure 4.2).

FIGURE 4.2

Click Get Info on a Universal application and you can force it to open in Rosetta. But why?

In order to get a snapshot of your system and see what's running natively and what's not, the easiest way is to simply open Activity Monitor. Mouse to the View menu and ensure that Kind is selected. You'll now be able to see at a glance what apps and processes are running as Intel or PPC (see Figure 4.3).

FIGURE 4.3

Using the Activity Monitor to see your PPC processes

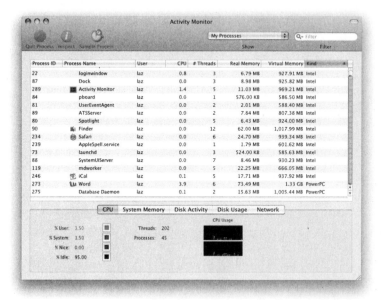

Classic caveat

The Classic application environment was Apple's way to ensure that OS X was backward-compatible with earlier applications. With the Intel change, Classic applications would have to run in the Emulation environment in Rosetta. Apple decided that there was just too much of a performance hit, and that compatibility issues would be too great to support, so Apple has dropped Classic support from the Mac OS X starting with Leopard. This is true across the board for both PPC-and Intel-based systems. There are a few different ways to get around this, if you really need to.

Drive formatting issues

In addition to a whole new processor architecture, the new Intel machines also have a completely new firmware system as well as a new boot partition scheme. The PowerPC machines used a boot partition called APM (Apple Partition Manager), and the Intel machines use a scheme called GUID. The decision to use GUID came out of the decision to use Intel's next-generation firmware scheme EFI. Older machines will not be able to boot from GUID-partitioned drives, but they should be able to mount them as long as you've formatted the partition as a HFS+ drive and are running 10.4 and above.

NOTE Macs have always been able to boot from external FireWire drives, but with the new EFI/Intel architecture, you can boot from USB as well.

What doesn't work in Rosetta?

Rosetta does not support the following (may be a bit technical):

- The Classic Application Environment and any applications built for any version of the Mac OS earlier than Mac OS X, that is, those that require the Classic environment.

- Screen savers (non-universal screen savers won't run; universal screen savers should be running outside of Rosetta)

- System Preferences, or code that inserts itself into the prefpanes

- Applications that require certain aspects of the architecture of a G5 processor, such as Virtual PC

- Applications that depend on PowerPC-only kernel extensions, or kernel extensions themselves

- Java applications that require JNI libraries

- Java applets run in the Java applet environment natively, thus applications that are running in the Rosetta environment cannot actively translate Java routines. Therefore applets will not work. For example, a browser running under Rosetta will not be able to execute Java applets.

Summary

In this chapter, you learned about the Intel and PowerPC architectures. You should now understand the difference between a PPC application and a Universal Binary. Classic support has been sidelined for a while, and with Leopard, Classic is finally gone. You should now have some understanding of the new drive formatting scheme that Apple has introduced with the Intel architecture.

Chapter 5

Working with Applications and Documents

Chapter 2 explained just how useful the Finder is, but you can spend only so much time tinkering with the look and feel of your Mac, browsing your drive, and organizing files and folders. Pretty soon, it's time to get some real work done. When that time comes, you need to open some applications and work with some documents. Applications are the tools. Documents are the tangible results of doing the work.

In this chapter, we look at the different types of applications you can use in Mac OS X and explore how you open applications to start using them. We also talk about opening documents with the Finder and with other applications. We discuss how to manage having several applications open at the same time. Then we delve into some basic methods of editing documents — copy-and-paste, drag-and-drop. We cover the ways you can create new documents and save the documents you've created or changed. Finally, we describe how to quit applications when you're finished.

This chapter covers general techniques that apply to almost all applications and documents. Other chapters get specific about particular applications that are included with Mac OS X. You can find out where we cover each application by scanning the table of contents or checking out the index.

Working with Mac OS X Applications

As discussed in Chapter 1, Mac OS X has five application environments — Cocoa, Carbon, Java, BSD, and Classic — and you use applications built on any of these different frameworks. The diversity of these frameworks reflects the parentage of Mac OS X: the traditional Mac OS wedded with NeXT's Unix genealogy. The different frameworks exist because each enables an important type of application to work with Mac OS X.

This state of bliss did not always exist. Initially, Apple wanted to move to a completely new style of Mac OS but couldn't. Apple couldn't just orphan the applications upon which Mac users had come to rely. Additionally, Apple could not get enough application developers to agree to completely rewrite all their software for a new Mac OS, which required the use of new development tools and programming languages.

To address these concerns, Apple provided developers choices for building their applications Mac OS X compatible. They can update their existing applications to benefit from the new Mac OS X features. They can develop innovative applications by using the new development tools.

The contents of this chapter primarily refer to the following application environments:

- **Cocoa applications:** These are programs written from the ground up by using the new development tools provided by Mac OS X; these Cocoa applications require Mac OS X to run. No one really expects to make Windows versions of Cocoa applications.

- **Carbon applications:** Typically, these programs run on PowerPC processors that have been around for a while. Most likely originally developed for Mac OS 9 or earlier, Carbon applications can still run in Mac OS X (with the addition of the CarbonLib system extension).

Apple's recent shift from PowerPC to Intel processors has created a sub-category of applications that can be classified as either Universal Binary or Rosetta. Universal Binary applications have been coded to run equally well on both PowerPC and Intel processors. Applications that have not been optimized as Universal Binary require Rosetta emulation, which in essence emulates PPC processor dependencies on an Intel Mac workstation, thereby allowing most PowerPC-based applications to work in an acceptable manner.

NOTE When OS X was first introduced, Classic was a godsend. It meant that programs that were not yet OS X compatible could remain in use without incurring additional cost to the user. Not only does Apple no longer ship its OS with Classic, it isn't supported. If you have any legacy applications that require Classic, your choices are as follows: Set up an older Mac with a PowerPC processor and run OS 9, or set up a PowerPC running OS X, with Classic installed. Our advice? Use Cocoa, Carbon, and whenever possible, Universal Binary applications.

Preinstalled applications

Apple preinstalls various useful applications with Mac OS X. Some of these applications are in the Applications folder or the Utilities folder, which resides on the hard drive. Table 5.1 lists the applications provided with Mac OS X 10.5 and identifies the applications that are normally located in an interior folder of the Applications folder. The contents of your Applications folder may vary because Apple adds and subtracts from the bundled software as time passes, and someone else who uses your computer may install additional applications.

Understanding Packages

Although all Mac OS X applications appear in the Finder as a single icon, many of them actually consist of a collection of folders and files. These compound applications are variously known as *packages, bundles,* or *application wrappers.* The terms are synonymous. Examples of such applications are as close as your Applications folder. Almost every application included with Mac OS X in the Applications folder is one of these application packages. Put simply, a *package* is a structured collection of files and folders that appears like a single file to users.

In Mac OS X, application packages have the filename extension .app. You don't ordinarily see this filename extension because Mac OS X hides it (unless you select the Show all file extensions option in the Finder Preferences window, as discussed in Chapter 2). You can also see the name extension in the Finder's Info window. (Choose View ➪ Show Info and then choose Name & Extension from the Info window's pop-up menu.)

Packages can be stored on volumes that have the Unix File System (UFS) format as well as on volumes that have the Mac OS Extended format (also known as HFS Plus). Thus, they're considerably more flexible than traditional Mac applications, which aren't packages. An application that isn't a package generally has a two-part file and extensive Finder information, with the part known as the *resource fork* being equivalent to an application package's Resources folder. The problem with two-fork files with extensive Finder information is that they must be stored on volumes that have the Mac OS Extended format. The traditional two-forked applications can't be stored on volumes that use the UFS format. Because of this, Apple hopes to wean application developers away from the use of resource forks, and packages are the means to do so.

When you double-click an application package, say, Preview, it opens and runs; however, Preview is not a single file. You can see what we mean if you Control+click the Preview icon in the Finder and choose Show Package Contents from the contextual menu. Doing this presents a Finder window with a folder icon named Contents. Opening the Contents folder, you see that it contains a Resources folder, and opening the Resources folder reveals the various files and folders containing the resources used by Preview, as shown in the following figure.

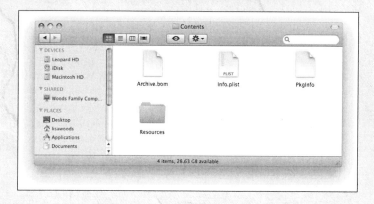

TABLE 5.1

Included Applications

Name	Folder	Brief Description — See Chapter 6 for detailed information
AppleScript	AppleScript	Create entire applications.
Script Editor	AppleScript	Create scripts of simple, repetitious tasks.
Address Book	Applications	Manage an address (postal and e-mail) and phone book. Integrated with Lightweight Directory Access Protocol (LDAP) directory searches and is linked to Mail and iChat.
Automator	Applications	An application used to create automated actions to help maximize workflow efficiency.
Calculator	Applications	A calculator, controlled from the keypad or with a mouse.
Chess	Applications	A graphical front end for GNU Chess; a pretty decent chess program with multiple difficulty settings and both 2-D and 3-D views.
Dashboard	Applications	The application responsible for generating and controlling "widgets," a class of mini-applications.
Dictionary	Applications	As the name suggests, a dictionary application.
DVD Player	Applications	The default application for playing DVDs. Will not work if your computer doesn't have a DVD drive.
Expose	Applications	Momentarily arrange windows on your computer to help you quickly get to open applications or documents, Dashboard, and your desktop. You can also use Expose to start or disable your screensaver.
Font Book	Applications	A font-management program. Use it to preview, activate, and deactivate fonts.
Front Row	Applications	Access all of your digital media in one convenient location.
iCal	Applications	A calendar-management app; basically, a digital appointment book.
iChat	Applications	Instant messaging (IM) client.
Image Capture	Applications	Download photos from compatible (USB) digital cameras and capture images from scanners connected to your Mac. Comes with a series of AppleScripts to automatically reformat and arrange pictures.
iTunes	Applications	Play songs from audio CDs, digital audio files, and Internet radio stations. Burn recordable CDs on Macs equipped with CD-RW drives; ties into iTunes Music Store, Apple's full featured music sales service.
Mail	Applications	Flexible e-mail application. Supports multiple accounts; links to Address Book.
Photo Booth	Applications	Take pictures with your Mac's iSight camera. You can add visual effects such as sepia, stretch, glow, and many more.

Name	Folder	Brief Description — See Chapter 6 for detailed information
Preview	Applications	View graphic and PDF files. Also used to access print preview from applications.
QuickTime Player	Applications	Apple's application to play and export multimedia files.
Safari	Applications	Apple's Web browser.
Spaces	Applications	Organize open applications and windows into groups that represent multiple, virtual desktops.
Stickies	Applications	Creates and manages notes windows.
System Preferences	Applications	Control Panel application for your System Preferences settings.
TextEdit	Applications	Styled-text editor (a word processor).
Time Machine	Applications	Backup utility that backs up your digital photos, music, documents, movies, and much more to an external drive.
Activity Monitor	Utilities	Shows processor, memory, network usage, and currently running processors. Allows for termination of processes to help with troubleshooting and repair.
AirPort Utility	Utilities	Changes individual settings of an AirPort base station device, including settings that aren't changed by the AirPort Setup Assistant application.
Audio MIDI Setup	Utilities	Central control for routing audio and MIDI.
Bluetooth File Exchange	Utilities	Use to create serial connections between various devices; often used to access modems in palmtop computers or cell phones.
Boot Camp Assistant	Utilities	Facilitates the installation and setup of the Windows environment in Boot Camp.
ColorSync Utility	Utilities	Verifies and repairs ColorSync International Color Consortium (ICC) profiles. These profiles are used to synchronize color input and output between various device types (monitors, scanners, printers, and the like).
Console	Utilities	Presents a window to the Unix console log for your session, letting you see messages from Mac OS X and applications. This tool is primarily useful to programmers and system administrators. Remember that underlying everything you do in Mac OS X, you're really running a Unix system.
Digital Color Meter	Utilities	Presents the RGB (or other) color information for the pixels under the pointer.
Directory	Utilities	Manages access to directory services.
Directory Utility	Utilities	Sets up the LDAP services and authentication protocols used by Directory Services and Mac OS X.

continued

TABLE 15.2   *(continued)*

Name	Folder	Brief Description — See Chapter 6 for detailed information
Disk Utility	Utilities	The Swiss Army knife of disk-control applications. Used to burn discs, verify, repair, and format disk volumes, and create disk images.
Grab	Utilities	Used to take screen pictures, either of the entire screen or a selection.
Grapher		Used to graph curves, surfaces, and inequalities.
Java	Utilities	Enables users to switch from the default version of Java to the previous version for Java-dependent applications and Web sites that do not behave as expected.
Keychain Access	Utilities	Used to store and retrieve your user IDs and passwords for files, remote sites, servers, and so on.
Migration Assistant	Utilities	Transfer files, applications, and important settings from an older Mac to a new Mac.
Network Utility	Utilities	A collection of network and Internet utility programs.
ODBC Administrator	Utilities	Open Database Connectivity (ODBC) configuration.
Podcast Capture	Utilities	Create audio or video Podcasts and distribute them using Leopard Server's Podcast Producer.
RAID Utility	Utilities	Allows you to configure internal disk arrays for Apple's RAID card.
System Profiler	Utilities	Utility to report how your hardware is configured and what software you have installed. This is a handy diagnostic tool when tracking down hardware and software problems.
Terminal	Utilities	This is your window into the Unix command-line environment. See Chapters 6, 23, and 24 for further information.
VoiceOver Utility	Utilities	A text-to-speech application. Allows the Mac to speak GUI elements, especially helpful for visually impaired users.

Installing applications

In addition to these preinstalled applications, there will come a time to add new tools to this digital toolbox. Installing additional applications is a great way to expand your options. There are a few different methods of application installations, although most are very self-explanatory. Typically, a set of paper instructions or a digital text file accompanies the application. The text file usually has a name like Read Me or Installation Instructions. Read these instructions carefully because there may be exceptions to the rules we present here.

The easiest method of installation is the *drag-install*. This method is commonly used when installing an application from removable media (CD-ROM, DVD, and so on) and from downloaded disk images. If a drag installation is called for, it will be indicated in the instructions or via a visible note within the disk that says "drag this folder to your hard drive to install." Simply drag the specified folder to your Applications folder to copy the required data there. You can choose to place the application in a folder other than Applications, although that location makes the most sense. Regardless of the location to which you copied the files, after the copy is complete, launch the newly copied application. If the application has to perform any additional setup functions, it should do so at this time. These installations do not typically require a restart. The application will copy files to various locations within your system and then proceed to ask for a serial number if needed, in addition to bugging you with the ubiquitous registration page. (We hate those things, too.) Figure 5.1 shows the Microsoft Office install disk's contents. It's pretty obvious what to do from the window's instructions.

FIGURE 5.1

The drag-install is the easiest install method available. Simply drag the folder to the desired location, and go to work!

The traditional method of installation is the installation program. Normally titled something like Install or Setup, installation programs go through the install process, querying for various bits of input from the user as they do. The most common installation programs on the Mac are InstallerVISE and Apple's installer, and typically require users to agree to a legal copyright agreement, insert serial numbers, and then select the destination drive to complete the process. Figure 5.2 shows the Adobe Photoshop installation screen in action.

FIGURE 5.2

The installation program method is a commonly used technique for adding programs.

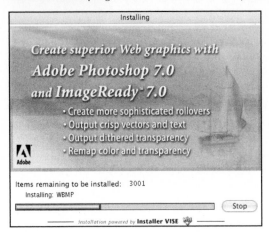

Removing applications

In the event that you no longer want an application stored on your hard drive, simply drag the application item out of the Applications folder, and deposit it into the Trash icon in the Dock. After emptying the Trash (choose Apple menu ⇨ Empty Trash), the application in question is gone. Just as with trashing a document you no longer want, be *sure* that you really want to remove it. The item won't come back from the digital graveyard very easily. Many applications spread various bits of themselves around in other folders in the system. You usually don't have to worry about them, but you may want to fully eradicate an application. The best place to look is in the Application Support folder. This folder is the standard dumping ground for extra files generated by an application. You'll find Application Support just inside the main Library folder (Hard Drive/Library/Application Support). Inside Application Support, you may find some items related to the deleted application. You can trash these files, but, again, be careful because you may be deleting files that are affiliated with the wrong application.

Opening Applications and Documents

You open an application when you want to work with it. This action is also called *launching* an application. You open a document when you want to view or edit its contents. For example, you can open TextEdit when you want to view, edit, or create a text document. (You can also work with text documents by opening a variety of other applications.) Numerous ways to open applications, documents, and other types of files and folders are available. This section discusses a variety of ways to open applications and documents.

Opening items from the Finder

The methods presented in Chapter 2 for opening folders in the Finder can also be used for opening an application or document with the Finder:

- Double-click the program or document icon that you want to open.

- Select the application or document that you want to open and then choose File ⇨ Open (⌘+O).

- Control+click the item that you want to open and choose Open from the contextual menu that appears.

- Navigate to the file location and double-click the item's icon.

Opening a document by using any of these methods automatically opens an application to handle the document. The Finder determines which application handles the document, opens that application, and then tells that application to open the document.

Suppose that you want to open multiple documents. No problem! Just select them all and then double-click one of them or use the Open command. If the documents are handled by different applications, the Finder opens each application and tells it which documents to open.

Opening documents with an application

As you work on your Mac, you may find it necessary to view or edit documents. How a file is opened greatly depends on how you work. The methods for opening documents are the following:

- Double-click the icon of a document and Finder automatically launches the application.

- Drag a document directly onto the icon of a compatible application, and the application's icon will highlight; releasing the item results in the document opening within the selected application.

- You can also open documents from within an application by choosing Open from that application's File menu. Choosing File ⇨ Open displays an Open dialog box. This dialog box enables you to move through your folders and select a file you want to open.

Mac OS X Open dialog box

When you choose File ⇨ Open in a Mac OS X application, you see an Open dialog box containing a pane reminiscent of the Finder's List or Column view, as shown in Figure 5.3. The view can be switched between Icon, List, or Column view with the familiar buttons in the top-left of the window.

FIGURE 5.3

In Mac OS X applications, the Open dialog box appears like the List or Column view in the Finder.

You can use the file browser to navigate through your folders to find the item you want to open, just as you do in the Finder. In Column view, each column shows the contents of a folder, and clicking a folder causes its contents to appear in the next column to the right. You can scroll left to see folders closer to the Computer level or scroll right to see the currently selected folder. In List view, double-clicking folders takes you deeper within the hierarchy. The pull-down menu available at the top of the window populates with the file hierarchy in addition to a few standard items. As you go deeper, the pull-down extends to offer you a way up to higher levels.

You can quickly go to a file or a folder in an Open dialog box's file browser if you can see the file or folder outside the dialog box on the desktop or in a Finder window. All you do is drag the file or folder to the dialog box.

Initially, the Open dialog box shows two columns, but you can widen the dialog box to see more columns. Drag the resize control at the lower right corner to make the dialog box larger or smaller.

You can move the Open dialog box to see items under it. Move the dialog box by dragging its title bar.

Two buttons appear at the bottom of the Open dialog box:

- **Cancel:** Dismisses the dialog box without opening anything.
- **Open:** Tells the application to open the selected file. This is the default button, so pressing Return is the equivalent of clicking Open.

Some applications have customized the Open dialog box by placing their own controls near the bottom of the dialog box. As the example in Figure 5.4 shows, TextEdit adds a pop-up menu for choosing a text encoding method, and a check box for ignoring rich text formatting when it opens the document you select.

FIGURE 5.4
_____

While opening a file, the Open dialog box may offer numerous options.

You'll notice that some documents presented in the list may be dimmed out. This is because the application is not compatible with the dimmed-out files and will not be able to open them.

To open a document, you select it in the list and click Open. Alternatively, you can double-click the document in the list, or select it and press Return or Enter.

Opening a document with another compatible application

Instead of opening a document with the application that usually handles it, you can also open it with another compatible application. For example, the TextEdit application can open documents that are usually handled by Microsoft Office.

To do this, open the desired application, and select Open from that application's File menu. Select the document from the dialog box that appears. The dialog box shows only documents that the application can open. Other documents are automatically made invisible in the dialog box.

Another method to accomplish this is to drag the document's icon onto the icon of the application you want to use (or onto an alias of the application). For example, if you have a Web page you saved from Firefox that you want to edit in TextEdit, drag the document icon onto the TextEdit icon (or onto an alias to TextEdit). In most cases, if the application is compatible with the document, the application's icon becomes highlighted. Release the mouse button while the application icon is highlighted, and the application opens the document. If the application is not already open, the Finder opens it automatically. If an application can't open a document you drag to it, nothing happens — no highlighting, no opening. If you're sure that the application should be able to open the document, hold the ⌘ and Option keys while dragging to force the action. Figure 5.5 shows how an application icon looks if it can open a document that you drag to it.

FIGURE 5.5

When you drag a document to a compatible application, the application's icon becomes highlighted.

Setting a new default application

Documents are set to open with a default application, depending on their type. For example, movie files most likely will open with QuickTime Player, pictures will open with Preview, and text files will open with TextEdit. (Or they'll open with a real word processor like Microsoft Word or AppleWorks, if installed.) The Mac OS allows you to change the default application for one document or even to have alternate applications open all files of a particular type. Select an item that you want to open with a new default application and open the Get Info window (⌘+I). The Open With area is collapsed with a disclosure triangle. Figure 5.6 shows the Open With area.

The Open With area contains a pull-down menu and a Change All button. The pull-down menu is populated with compatible applications and an Other option. Selecting one of the applications listed changes the current file's parent application to the new selection. Selecting Other opens a dialog box in which you can select a new parent application from applications not listed in the Open With pull-down menu. This dialog box is helpful if the Mac OS doesn't recognize an application as compatible, which would preclude it from being in the pull-down list, or if you want to experiment with what happens when you open an audio file with a text editor. (Lots and lots of gibberish appear within a text document.) Figure 5.7 shows the dialog box.

FIGURE 5.6

The Info window contains the means to switch a document's parent application.

FIGURE 5.7

The Choose Other Application dialog box is helpful when the Mac OS doesn't recognize your desired parent application as being compatible with a particular document.

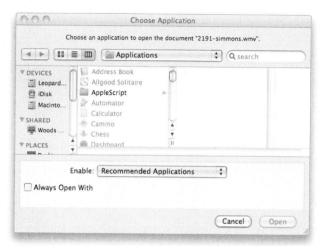

After selecting a new application, you can make this application the default for all files of this type by clicking the Change All button. Switching parent applications also changes document icons to reflect the icon of the new parent application. If you accidentally set the wrong application, undoing your mistake is easy enough. Just reverse the procedure by selecting the original parent or your desired application and clicking Change All.

Opening items in the Dock

As discussed in Chapter 2, you can place icons of frequently used documents and applications in the Dock and then open them simply by clicking the icon in the Dock. You can also place a folder in the Dock; you can click and hold on the icon in the Dock to produce a menu of files and folders you can traverse to find the item you want to open. (Dock navigation is covered in Chapter 2.)

You can also open a document by dragging it to the icon of a compatible application that is already in the Dock. When the application's Dock icon becomes highlighted, release the item. If the application is running, it opens the document. If the application is not open, the Finder launches the application and then opens the document. As with opening documents via drag-and-drop in the Finder, the application icon in the Dock may not highlight, in which case, the selected application cannot open the selected item.

Opening items with the Apple menu

Choosing Apple ➪ Recent Items displays a submenu with sections labeled Applications, Documents, and Servers. The Recent Items submenu enables you to quickly reopen an application or document that you used recently or reconnect to a server that you accessed recently. Suppose, for example, that you recently quit Microsoft Word. Rather than navigating to the Applications folder, then the Microsoft Office folder, and finally launching Word again, you can merely choose Apple ➪ Recent Items ➪ Microsoft Word, and the application reopens. Figure 5.8 shows the Recent Items submenu.

Although useful for applications, choosing Apple ➪ Recent Items is even more desirable for reopening documents because you're far more likely to have your documents distributed throughout a hierarchy of folders. (Users typically just add their favorite applications to the Dock, eliminating the need to access them in Recent Items.) Obviously, navigating your folder structure to reopen a document that you recently used takes much longer than choosing the document from the Recent Items submenu.

The Recent Items submenu in Mac OS X keeps track of 5 to 50 recent applications, documents, and servers. You can change the numbers of items tracked in the Appearance preference pane, as described in Chapter 2.

FIGURE 5.8

The Recent Items submenu is a helpful shortcut to find recently opened documents, applications, and servers.

In the Mac OS X Apple menu, the Recent Items submenu has an additional very handy menu choice: Clear Menu. This choice empties out the Recent Items submenu (but doesn't affect the actual items that were listed).

Viewing items with the Finder

Leopard's version of Finder enables you to view items *without* opening the supporting application. To use Quick Look to view items with the Finder, Control+click the item and select Quick Look from the menu. A window appears showing you the item. If you want to take a peek at a different item, simply click the item and Quick Look updates the view.

Although Quick Look doesn't launch the supporting application to view the item, you need to have the application installed on your computer. If the supporting application isn't installed on your Mac, Quick Look will not be able to give you a quick look. Quick Look works with documents, photos, Web pages, music, and movies.

Quick Look handles files in the same way their applications do. Quick Look renders saved Web pages the same way a browser does — animation and all. When taking a peek at a song, Quick Look displays the song's artwork and gives you the option of actually playing the selected song! Pictures that have some of Apple's neat effects added (personally, I can't get enough of the edge blur effect) appear in their modified form. Figure 5.9 illustrates what a photo looks like when viewed via Quick Look.

FIGURE 5.9

Use Quick Look to browse through images without launching Preview or iPhoto.

Managing Multiple Open Applications

The ability to have multiple applications open simultaneously is called *multitasking*. In Mac OS 9 and earlier, this multitasking is *cooperative,* meaning that the various open applications have to take turns using the computer's processor, memory, and other hardware. Mac OS X has *preemptive* multitasking, which means that Mac OS X dynamically parcels out chunks of time to the various open applications.

Multitasking is convenient but can be disorienting. For example, a stray mouse click may make another open program active, bringing its windows to the front and covering the windows of the program you were using. If this happens unexpectedly, you may think that the program you're using has crashed when it's actually still open and running, albeit in the background. You have to get used to having multiple layers of open programs like piles of paper on a desk. Fortunately, you instantly sort through and organize your open applications with Exposé or Spaces (as covered in Chapter 2), plus you can hide open applications on your Mac (unlike the many layers of paper on your desk) as discussed later in this section.

As mentioned in Chapter 2, only one application has control of the menu bar, no matter how many applications you have open. The application currently in control is called the *active application.*

Switching programs

When you have more than one application open, you can switch to another application by simply clicking its icon in the Dock. You can also use Exposé to show all the application windows with F9 or a specific mouse movement, and then select the desired application. You can also switch to another application by clicking any of its visible windows (or a window minimized in the Dock). Another method is to use the application switch command. Figure 5.10 shows this function in action. Here's how to do it:

1. **Press and hold ⌘, then press Tab.** Striking this keyboard combination displays a list of open applications across the screen.

2. **Continue holding ⌘, and with each additional press of Tab, a highlight window migrates to the different open applications.**

3. **Release ⌘ when the desired application is highlighted.** This application becomes the active application.

FIGURE 5.10

The application switch command in action

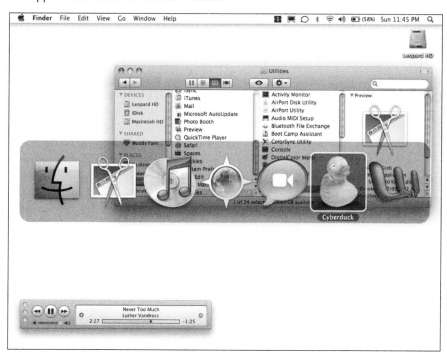

> **TIP**   When you switch to another application, its menus take over the menu bar. Its name appears as the title of the application menu, which is next to the Apple menu.

If you switch applications by clicking an application icon in the Dock, all the application's open windows come forward as a group. (Windows that are minimized in the Dock remain there.)

If you switch to a Mac OS X application by clicking one of its windows, *only that window comes forward*. Other windows belonging to the same application remain where they are in the layered hierarchy. You can bring them all to the front by clicking the application's icon in the Dock or by choosing Window ⇨ Bring All to Front. (Some applications don't have this menu command.)

Where'd it go?

With many applications open, trying to find what you are looking for is like looking for a needle in a haystack. You can reduce the clutter by using the Hide feature. Using Hide is different from clicking the Minimize button (which you'll recall places a tiny version of the window in the Dock). When you hide an application, the application and all its open windows disappear! This reduces clutter on-screen and in the Dock. To activate Hide, choose Hide Others from the application menu. This command hides the windows of all applications except the currently active one. Alternatively, you can hide only the currently active application's windows and simultaneously switch to the most recently active application by choosing Hide *Application* (where *Application* is the name of the active application) from the application menu. Additionally, you can Option+click anywhere on the desktop to hide the currently active application. Additionally, you can press ⌘+H to hide the currently active application. To restore any applications from Hide, click their icons in the Dock. (*Remember:* An open application has a small black triangle under its icon.) To make the windows of all applications visible with one click, choose Show All from the application menu.

> **TIP**   A quick way to hide all background applications is to ⌘+Option+click the active application's icon in the Dock. If you ⌘+Option+click another application's icon in the Dock, it becomes active and all other applications' windows are hidden. To hide the active application while switching to another application, Option+click the other application's icon in the Dock or Option+click a window belonging to the other application.

Attending to background applications

If a Mac OS X application that's open in the background needs your attention, its icon starts jumping up and down in the Dock (like a little kid in class waving his hand excitedly for attention). The icon jumps far enough that you can see it even if the Dock is hidden. To find out what has made the application so excited, click its icon in the Dock. When the application's windows come forward, look for an alert, sheet, or dialog box that you need to attend to. Figure 5.11 shows an example of an application jumping for attention.

FIGURE 5.11

When an application's icon jumps out of the Dock, the application needs your attention.

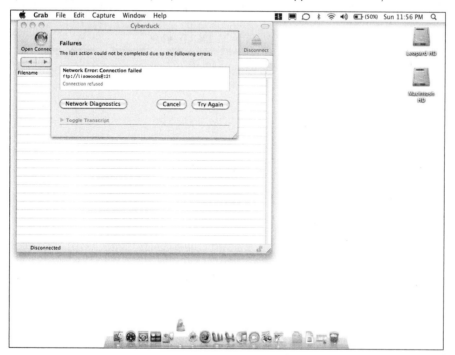

Pimping Your Document's Contents

While a document is open, you can generally tinker with its contents. Create new content, move existing content around to a different place within the same document, or even move content to other documents. Each application has its own content type — Microsoft Word works with text, Adobe Photoshop with pictures, iMovie with video, for examples — and each has its own methods of content creation and editing. For details on this, consult some of the other excellent Wiley Publishing titles available for your application of choice. This section covers the established standard techniques that many applications use, regardless of data type. For example, the traditional method to shuffle a document's content is via the Edit menu's Copy, Cut, and Paste commands. Additionally, most programs also let you drag content from one place to another or, by holding down the Option key while dragging, copy the content from one spot to another.

Copy, Cut, and Paste

One of the first things a Mac user learns is to use the Cut, Copy, and Paste commands in an application's Edit menu to transfer data from one place to another within a document or between documents.

The first thing you do is select the data you want to move. Next, you choose what to do with that data. Choose Edit ⇨ Cut (if you want to *move* the original data) or Edit ⇨ Copy (if you want to place a copy of the data in another location). Either of these actions places the data on the *Clipboard,* a temporary virtual storage area for data being moved or copied. After deciding your method of gathering the data, select where the data is to be placed. Finally, choose Edit ⇨ Paste to put it there.

Pasting does not remove the data from the Clipboard. The data remains there until you use Cut or Copy again to place new content on the Clipboard or you log out. This also means you only get one contiguous Cut or Copy at a time. If you select and Copy some data, and then Copy something else, the original Copy is gone. The two Copy contents are not stored in the Clipboard; instead, the original is overwritten with the new Copy.

You can Cut, Copy, and Paste within a single document, between multiple documents of a given application, or between the documents of different applications. This technique rapidly becomes second nature, especially after you start using keyboard shortcuts for the actions: ⌘+X for Cut, ⌘+C for Copy, and ⌘+V for Paste (and ⌘+A to select all the data in a document).

Drag-and-drop

The Mac OS provides a quick and easy way to copy text, graphics, and other material. This capability, called *drag-and-drop editing,* works only with programs that are designed to take advantage of it. Fortunately for you, this includes most Mac OS X applications that open documents.

To move material within a document, open the document and select the text, graphic, or other data you want to move. Then, position the mouse pointer over the selected material, press and hold the mouse button, and drag the selected material to its new location. As you drag, a lightened, ghostlike version of the selected material follows the cursor and, typically, an insertion point shows where the material appears after you stop dragging. If you want to copy rather than move the material, press and hold Option before releasing the mouse button. Figure 5.12 shows some text being moved within a TextEdit document.

 If you have trouble dragging selected material, try holding down the mouse button a moment longer before you start to drag.

To drag-copy material between documents, first open both documents and position them so that you can see the source material and the place where you want to drop a copy of it. Select the text, graphic, or other source material and then drag the selected material to the place in the second document where you want the copy. As you drag, an outline of the selected material follows the cursor. When the cursor enters the destination window, a border appears around the content area of the window; and if you're dragging text, an insertion point shows where the copy appears when you stop dragging. Note that you don't have to press Option to make a copy when dragging between documents. You can use the same method to copy between two documents in the same application or between documents or windows in different applications. The only requirement is that the destination window be capable of handling the type of material you're dragging. Figure 5.13 shows some text being copied from a TextEdit window into a Stickies note.

FIGURE 5.12

With drag-and-drop editing, you can move data within a document.

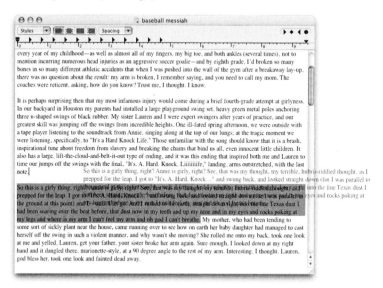

FIGURE 5.13

With drag-and-drop editing, you can also move text, images, and other data between windows and even other applications.

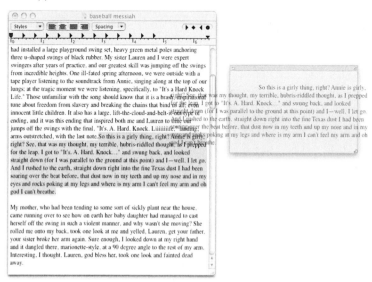

Some people prefer drag-and-drop to cut-and-paste editing because they find it easier to use. Drag-and-drop editing has one clear advantage: It doesn't use or wipe out the contents of the Clipboard, so it's a good method to use when the Clipboard contains important material that you're not ready to replace. Knowing how to use both methods in tandem is best — each has its benefits, and knowing more techniques is the key to being a better computer user.

Clipping files

You can also drag selected material from a document to the desktop or to a folder, where the Finder creates a clipping file that contains a copy of the dragged material. Clipping files can contain text, pictures, QuickTime movies, or sound, but a single clipping file can contain only one type of data. You can open a clipping file to see it in the Finder, but you can't select anything in a clipping file. To copy the contents of a clipping file to a document, drag the clipping-file icon to an open document's window. The contents will be inserted when you release the mouse button.

You can use a clipping file over and over. For example, you can keep clippings that contain your letterhead, the company logo, your signature, a list of e-mail addresses, or any other data that you use frequently.

Creating Documents

You won't always be opening documents that already exist. Sometimes you need to create new ones. Many application programs automatically create a brand-new, untitled document when you launch the application. In addition, most applications let you create a new document any time you want one by choosing File ⇨ New.

Creating copies of documents

You can also create a document by making a copy of an existing document. This method is especially useful if the existing document contains something you want to include in a new document, such as a letterhead or some boilerplate text. To make a copy of a document, use the Finder's Duplicate command or one of the other methods described in Chapter 2.

Creating documents with stationery pads

Instead of duplicating a document each time you want a copy of it, you can make a frequently used document into a *stationery pad.* (Most software developers call these items *templates,* but Apple calls them stationery pads.) When you open a stationery pad, you get a new document with a preset format and contents. It's like tearing a sheet off an endless pad of preprinted stationery (hence, the name). Some stationery pads have a distinctive icon that looks like a stack of documents and indicates which application opens the stationery pad. Other stationery pads have blank document icons or icons indistinguishable from those of standard documents.

Some applications allow you to save an ordinary document as a stationery pad or template; the next section explains how. You can also convert any document into a stationery pad in the Finder's Info window, as shown in Figure 5.14, by following these steps:

1. **In the Finder, select the document you want to make into a stationery pad.**

2. **Choose File ⇨ Get Info (⌘+I).** This command opens the Info window.

3. **Select the Stationery Pad check box.**

FIGURE 5.14

Set a document as a stationery pad in the Finder's Info window.

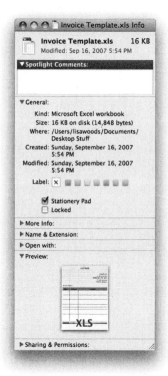

What happens when you open a stationery pad depends on whether the application that opens it knows the difference between stationery pads and regular documents. If the application is programmed to work with stationery pads, it creates a new untitled document with the identical format and content of the stationery pad. If the application is not compatible with stationery pads, the Finder should create a new document by making a copy from the stationery pad and having the application open the copy.

In the event that you need to make changes to a stationery pad, you must go back to the file's Get Info window and uncheck the stationery pad check box — this returns the document to a standard document and enables you to save changes to the stationery pad. When you've completed making your changes, follow the steps outlined earlier to set the document *back* to a stationery pad.

Saving Documents

After creating a new document or making changes to a document you opened, you need to save the document on disk for the changes to persist. Make sure that the document's window is active (in front of other document windows) and choose File ➪ Save or File ➪ Save As. For a new document, either of these commands displays a dialog box in which you name the document and select the folder where you want it saved. For a previously saved document, the Save command does not open a dialog box; the application automatically saves the changed document in place of the previously saved document (replacing the original with this modified version). The Save As command always opens the dialog box so that you can rename and/or relocate the edited version, enabling you to preserve the original and the modified file.

TIP   While you're entering a name for the document to save in a Save dialog box, the Cut, Copy, and Paste commands are available from the Edit menu. This means that you can copy a name for a document from within the document before choosing the Save command, and then you can paste the copied name into the dialog box. Instead of using the Edit menu, you can also use the keyboard equivalents: ⌘+X for Cut, ⌘+C for Copy, and ⌘+V for Paste.

The Save dialog box has a simple form and an expanded form. You can switch between the compact form and the expanded form by clicking the disclosure triangle, which is next to the Where pop-up menu. Figure 5.15 shows an example of the compact Save dialog box and an expanded Save dialog box.

A Save dialog box has a pop-up menu that allows you to choose between the current folder, the desktop, your home folder, and a hierarchical menu to your iDisk. This pop-up menu also lists recently used folders. In addition, the Save dialog box has a text field where you specify the name for the document. The Save dialog box may have an option for hiding the name extension, and the other controls for setting document format options.

The location browser visible in the expanded Save dialog box works just like the browser in the Open dialog box. The option exists to navigate in List view or Column view. In Column view, each column shows the contents of a folder, and clicking a folder causes its contents to appear in the next column to the right. You can scroll left to see folders closer to the Computer level or scroll right to see the currently selected folder. In List view, double-clicking folders takes you deeper within the hierarchy. The pull-down menu available at the top of the window populates with the file hierarchy in addition to a few standard items. As you go deeper, the pull-down extends to offer you a way up to higher levels.

FIGURE 5.15

Click the disclosure button to switch between the compact Save dialog box (first image) and the expanded Save dialog box (second image).

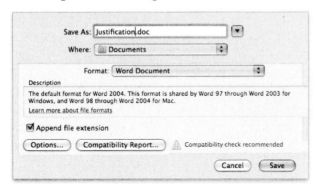

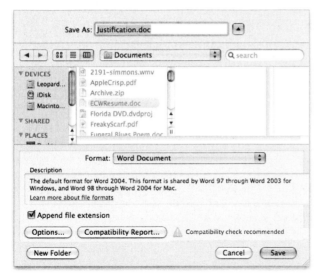

You can quickly go to a file or a folder in a Save dialog box's file browser if you can see the file or folder outside the dialog box on the desktop or in a Finder window. All you need to do is drag the file or folder to the dialog box.

The Save dialog box is also resizable. Drag the resize control at the lower right corner to make the dialog box larger or smaller.

In some applications, the Save dialog box is a sheet that's attached to the window of the document being saved. In other applications, the Save dialog box is independent, and you can move it by dragging its title bar.

Some applications give you the option of saving the file in a different application format. For example, you can save a Text Edit document as a Microsoft Word document. If you want to change the document format to a compatible application other than the one it was created or modified in, click the Format drop-down box and select the file format that you want to save the document as.

Saving a Stationery Pad

In many applications, you can designate in the Save dialog box whether to save a document as a stationery pad (template) or as a regular document. Some applications offer this choice with two radio buttons — one labeled with a regular document icon, and the other labeled with a stationery pad icon. Other applications offer many document format options, including stationery or template, in a pop-up menu in the dialog box.

Moving Documents

After creating and then saving a document, you may want to move that item to a different location within your disk or to a removable disk or server volume. The Mac OS makes this very easy. Simply drag the item from its original location to a new one. You can drag the item to an item in the Sidebar, to a folder represented in the Dock, to any area of your desktop, to the root level of your hard drive, or to any area of your user folder. This drag-and-drop method of moving should be very familiar to you by now. A new feature of Mac OS X is Cut and Paste moves. After selecting an item, select Copy from the Edit menu (or from the contextual menu of a particular item), and then, with the desired new location active, select Paste from the Edit menu and the item moves to the new location. This technique will be very familiar to former Windows users.

A Word on Home

Your Home folder has a collection of various useful subfolders for convenient organization of your data. It contains a Pictures folder for your images, a Movies folder for movies, and so on. It's recommended by Apple and by most technicians that you use these folders as much as possible and store as much of your data as possible within your Home folder. *Remember:* Items on your desktop are already within your Home because the desktop is actually a folder stored within your Home. You can create as many folders as you want within your Home, although placing created subfolders within the Documents folder is wise, to avoid cluttering up your Home folder's root level. Storing your work within your Home makes it very easy to protect your data, because you only need to create a backup of one folder to protect your most important information. Applications can be reinstalled — even the OS can be reinstalled — but your documents are much more difficult to re-create.

Playing Well with Others

Because Mac OS X is a secure multiuser environment, the elements of each user account are available only to that user account. When logged in as Tristan, you can get at Tristan's files, but you cannot get access to Vivianne's files. To get at Vivianne's files, you'd need to prove to the Mac that you are Vivianne by logging out of Tristan's account and then entering Vivianne's password at the login screen. However, as Tristan, you can give files to Vivianne, and she can give files to you. You can't *take* files from each other, but you can *give* them to each other. To share work with other users on your computer, you need to use the predetermined Drop Boxes. Within each user's Home is a Public folder. This folder is, as the name implies, a public area that is accessible by other accounts. Within the Public folder is a folder called Drop Box. This folder allows users to place files for sharing. Place a file for Vivianne into her drop box, and Vivianne can get at the file the next time she logs in. Placing files into Drop Boxes is a blind event, though. The Mac OS warns you that you cannot see the results of placing the file. It's similar to dropping mail into one of those big blue mailboxes on the sidewalk — you have to trust that the mail carrier will pick up and deliver the letter. Note that dropping a file into a drop box does not move the file but rather *copies* it there. Your original file remains in its original location.

Quitting Applications

When you're done working with an application for a while, you can issue a Quit command, to terminate the application. Mac OS X provides a number of ways to quit from a running program. Some are for normal situations; others are for use when a program stops responding.

Using an application's Quit command

Nearly every application menu has a Quit command at the bottom of the Application menu, with a standard keyboard equivalent of ⌘+Q. Using the Quit command is the preferred method for quitting from an application. When you choose this command, the application asks whether to save each unsaved document, as shown in Figure 5.16, before closing that document's window. This is the same dialog box that you see if you click the Close button of an unsaved document's window. In this dialog box, the Save and Don't Save buttons are self-explanatory. The Cancel button tells the application that you've changed your mind about quitting. If you click Cancel, the application *doesn't* quit and the document it was asking you about saving remains in the forefront.

FIGURE 5.16

You're asked to save any open and edited documents when you quit an application.

Quitting with a pop-up Dock menu

You can also quit an application by Control+clicking (or right-clicking, or clicking and holding) its icon in the Dock. When the pop-up Dock menu appears, choose Quit from it. This method is handy for quitting an application that's open in the background because you can quit the background application without making it active.

If you quit an application in this manner, the application's icon may start bouncing in the Dock. This behavior indicates that the application needs your attention. It probably wants to ask you what to do about documents with unsaved changes. Address the application's warnings as appropriate.

Quitting by logging out, shutting down, or restarting

Another way to quit all open applications is by choosing Apple ⇨ Log Out (⌘+Shift+Q) or Apple ⇨ Shut Down or Apple ⇨ Restart. After choosing any of these commands, you're asked whether you really want to quit from all open applications. If you answer affirmatively, each application quits in turn, asking what to do about unsaved changes, as shown in Figure 5.17. Canceling the Save dialog box in any document's Close dialog box cancels the Quit command in addition to the logout, restart, or shutdown.

Forcing an application to quit

Inevitably, occasions arise when an application stops, stalls, or fails to respond to input, preventing you from doing anything meaningful with the application, including quitting. Mac OS X gives you a number of ways to force the offending application to quit. Choosing Apple ⇨ Force Quit or pressing ⌘+Option+Esc presents the window shown in Figure 5.17. Select the unresponsive application in the Force Quit Applications window, and click the Force Quit button.

FIGURE 5.17

Select an unresponsive application you want to have quit.

Alternatively, you could launch the Activity Monitor utility, which is located in the Utilities folder of the Applications folder (path/Applications/Utilities). Activity Monitor presents a list of all active processes, as shown in Figure 5.18. Select the process you want to terminate and choose Processes ➪ Quit Process.

CAUTION Selecting this method bypasses any Save dialog boxes, and unsaved changes are lost. (If you frequently experience stalled application issues, turn to Chapter 21 for help on maintaining Mac OS X.)

FIGURE 5.18

The process listing in the Activity Monitor enables you to view allocation of system resources and to quit stalled processes and applications.

Summary

In this chapter, you learned how to open applications with the Finder, Dock, and Apple menu. We went through a complete list of the included applications and utilities that ship with the Mac OS and how to install and remove applications. We covered opening documents using the Open dialog box in applications, the Finder, and Recent Items menu, switching between several open applications, and attending to open windows. We introduced Leopard's nifty new Quick Look feature and went over editing documents with the copy-and-paste and drag-and-drop functions. We discussed the creation of new documents, copies of documents, and stationery pads; how to save documents with the Save dialog box; moving files around on your drive; and sharing files with other local users. Finally, we discussed how to quit applications and force unresponsive applications to quit.

Chapter 6

Working with Included Applications

With each release of OS X, Apple has included many impressive applications, each time improving functionality and raising the fun factor. Apple's latest iteration of OS X, called Leopard, is no exception.

Apple has placed all included applications in the Applications folder. There are many *classes* of applications; some applications, like Photo Booth, provide instant gratification; others, like Mail, enable you to get work done. In addition to useful applications, Apple has included various utilities — located in /Applications/Utilities — to manage and troubleshoot the technical aspects of your Macintosh. This chapter discusses the programs and system utilities included in OS X Leopard.

IN THIS CHAPTER

The Application folder

A tour of the Mac OS X Utilities folder

The Applications Folder

Let's take a closer look at the software in the Application folder. See Figure 6.1. You may find it convenient to change from Icon view to List view in the Finder. As you work with these Applications, you may find it useful to place some of your favorite and most-used apps in the Dock for quick access. The last item listed in the Applications folder is the Utilities folder; its contents are discussed later in this chapter.

FIGURE 6.1

Exposé has been upgraded to an independent application and as such is now included in the Applications folder.

Address Book

With Address Book, Apple has provided you with a personal content management system. Address Book is ideal for storing addresses, phone numbers, e-mail addresses, work contacts, and other information that allows you to keep track of friends and family. It provides all the necessary functionality to store, sort, search, and categorize that information for you. The Address Book's usefulness extends beyond the application because it is fully integrated into Mail, iCal (Apple's calendar program), iSync, synchronizes with your Yahoo! address book, and can even map directions to addresses using Google Maps.

Contact information is stored in cards. Each contact has a card with standard fields, including name, photo, address, home and work phone numbers, e-mail address, and so on. If you'd like to modify the card template, you can add and remove fields according to your needs; you can also choose to customize Address cards for individual contacts. It is easy to assign categories and define data relative to each contact. In addition, the Address Book allows for the creation of Groups and Smart Groups, which in turn allows for smart selection criteria. Leopard's version of Address Book enables you to apply video effects (choose from 18 amusing effects) to a contact's photo. See Figure 6.2.

If you need to share contacts with others or need to create a contact list, you can import information in commonly used personal information manager (PIM) formats such as vCards (essentially an electronic business card), LDIF (LDAP Data Interchange Format), tab-delimited, and CSV (comma-separated values) files. vCards are arguably the simplest way to import contacts. They carry standard contact information as well as photographs and company logos. LDIF is an interesting feature because OS X Leopard fully supports the LDAP (Lightweight Directory Access Protocol). When importing contacts from a text file, the file has to comply with the comma-separated values (CSV) standard, a common data format for the exchange of information between unrelated systems. Address Book can export information only in the vCard format.

FIGURE 6.2

Spice up your Address Book photos by adding a video effect.

Lightweight Directory Access Protocol (LDAP) provides access to user and group directory information. Not only does Address Book enable you to access shared address books via .Mac, but you can also access LDAP directories. Servers configured in Address Book also appear in Mail; this integration makes performing lookups and sending e-mails seamless. When configuring LDAP servers, set your Address Book's preferences to automatically update LDAP cards, and you'll always have the most current information available. This is especially useful when sending e-mail because you can have Mail automatically complete addresses. .Mac users can choose to share their address book with other .Mac users or subscribe to another user's address book — you will need user credentials to access the information. Chapters 10 and 14 also cover the Address Book. For more information on .Mac services, see Chapters 2 and 10.

AppleScript folder

Inside the AppleScript folder you will find the AppleScript Utility, Example Scripts, Folder Actions Setup, and Script Editor, basically everything you need to create scripts. AppleScript is a powerful language designed to create automatic operations on your Mac. It has a long history of automation and is useful to manage repetitive operations inside applications such as QuarkXPress and Adobe Photoshop. Leopard brings a number of new features to AppleScript including full Unicode support, read/write property lists, more descriptive error messages, and updated folder action support, to name a few. For more information on AppleScript, see Chapter 22.

Automator

For many of us, our jobs include repetitive tasks that we would be happy to delegate or skip all together. Wouldn't it be great if you could have your computer perform the task for you? Enter Automator. OS X Leopard brings a new, improved interface, Watch Me Do, to users; Automator enables you to record every click of your mouse and create a script that you can use again and again. It's that simple. Starting Points allow you to create workflows more easily and quickly; choose from Custom workflow, Files and Folders, Music and Audio, Photos and Images, and Text. Starting Points is shown in Figure 6.3. Automator fans will be happy to heart that Apple has included all new actions including PDF management and RSS feeds. For more information on Automator, see Chapter 22.

FIGURE 6.3

Starting Points are a great addition to Automator.

Calculator

Calculator performs standard mathematical calculations as well as a number of advanced operations. You can change the view from Basic, Scientific, and Programmer modes, according to your needs. It can also display a *paper tape* to keep track of your entries.

Among the many useful features in Calculator is the Convert menu item. To convert a figure, punch in the value you want to convert and select the conversion operation you want to perform. The list of conversion options includes Area, Currency, Energy or Work, Temperature, Length, Weights and Mass, Speed, Pressure, Power, and Volume. Calculator automatically updates the current currency exchanges.

It's easy to confuse the Calculator Application with the Calculator widget; however, the widget calculator is limited to the basic calculator.

Chess

As in many previous versions of the OS, Apple has included Chess. In this version, the game is better, faster, and more cunning than ever. Add the awesome power of the new Intel processors and you have a serious challenge. Change your chessboard style or your chess pieces; choices include Wood, Metal, Grass, Marble, and Fur.

Dashboard

Since its introduction in OS X Tiger, Dashboard has grown in popularity and usefulness. Dashboard is a collection of small applications called *widgets*. Each widget is a limited mini-application that displays important information, or provides an impressive means of distraction (Sudoku is my favorite). There's a widget for everyone, from the Google widget to the ESPN widget. Apple has included 21 widgets with OS X Leopard; some are mini-apps of the applications shipped with the operating system, and others are stand-alone applications. Many widgets require Internet access to display information. Table 6.1 lists all of the included widgets and provides a brief explanation of their function.

TABLE 6.1

Widgets Included in Dashboard

Widget	Function	Related Application	Is it Configurable?
Address Book	Accesses your address book	Address Book	Yes
Calculator	Simple calculator	None	No
Dictionary	Complete English dictionary	Dictionary	No
ESPN	Displays Sports news and scores for sports	None	Yes
Flight Tracker	Tracks airline flight status	None	Yes
Google	Searches Google from Dashboard	None	No
iCal	Displays current date and preview of the current month	iCal	No
iTunes	Plays music	iTunes	Yes
Movies	View trailers and movies playing in your area	None	Yes
People	Searches for contact information	None	Yes
Ski Resort	Displays ski resort information	None	Yes
Stickies	Displays stickies	Stickies	Yes
Stocks	Displays current stock quotes	None	Yes
Tile Game	Traditional tile game	None	No
Translation	Translates languages	None	Yes

continued

TABLE 6.1	(continued)		
Widget	**Function**	**Related Application**	**Is it Configurable?**
Unit Converter	Converts units and currency	Calculator	No
Weather	Displays weather	None	Yes
Web Clip	Creates a widget from any Web page	None	Yes
World Clock	Displays the time	None	Yes

When Dashboard is active, all open applications continue working, but they move to the background; the widgets are brought to the forefront of your screen and highlighted. If you click your mouse on the background, the widgets immediately disappear and your applications return to the front. If you would like your widgets to operate as traditional applications, Amnesty's Widget Browser is just the utility you're looking for. Widget Browser enables you to run widgets right on your desktop.

Some widgets are incredibly cool; for example, the Web clip widget uses Safari to create a widget from any Web page. To view a list of your available widgets, double-click the Dashboard icon in the Applications folder and click the plus sign in the lower left corner of the screen. If you would like to add a widget from the list to your Dashboard, simply drag and drop the desired widget onto the screen. To change a widget's configuration, click the i button, usually located in the lower right corner of the widget pane. The widget flips and presents its configuration settings. If you want to add to your widget collection, visit Apple's Web site or search the Web for OS X-supported widgets. When you are done playing in the widget world, you can return to your desktop or applications by clicking behind a widget or over the Dashboard icon in the Dock (this works only if your Dock is not set up to hide).

New to Dashboard in OS X Leopard is Dashboard sync and Dashcode. With Dashboard sync, use your .Mac account to synchronize widget preferences on every Mac you use. Dashcode gives you the power to create your very own widgets. You can choose from Apple-made templates, or build your own widget from scratch. After creating your widget, submit it to Apple's Web site so that others can enjoy your creation.

Dictionary

The Dictionary application debuted in OS X Tiger. It is comprised of four dictionary databases: the New Oxford American Dictionary, the Oxford American Writers Thesaurus, Apple Dictionary, and Wikipedia. The New Oxford American Dictionary operates like other online dictionaries in that it provides definitions for words that are queried. The Oxford American Writers Thesaurus supplies the synonym for the requested word and even includes an example of antonyms. The Apple dictionary defines common Apple terms and provides descriptions of Apple software. The Wikipedia dictionary is the coolest; you can search Wikipedia's complete online database. Look up everything from Apple Computer Inc. to the movie Se7en, without ever leaving the Dictionary application.

The VoiceOver utility does not operate inside the dictionary.

In Leopard, the Dictionary is integrated into Spotlight; when performing a search in Spotlight, the definition of the word is provided as well. See Figure 6.4. Japanese language support has been built in; the Dictionary contains over 200,00 words, while the Thesaurus includes 25,000 words.

FIGURE 6.4

Perform a Wikipedia search directly in the Dictionary application.

DVD Player

DVD Player is an instant-gratification application. Following the Apple tradition of video excellence, the DVD Player provides you with great entertainment. If your Mac has a DVD drive—all new Macs do—just insert your favorite DVD (*Shaun of the Dead* is mine) and click play. With the right equipment, you can connect your portable Mac to a TV to boost your movie-watching experience. If your Mac supports the new Apple Remote—it comes with all new iMacs, MacBooks and MacBook Pros—you can use the remote to control DVDs from across the room.

TIP
Try connecting your Mac to an HDTV monitor or HDTV with computer input capability for incredible results. Some plasma and LCD systems can display up to 1024 x 768 or even 1280 x 1024 dpi. At those resolutions, DVD playback gets an incredible quality boost from the video processing capabilities of your Mac.

The DVD player in Leopard has been updated to give you more control of your movies, create bookmarks of your favorite moments, create video clips, and limit the movies your children can see on your Mac via parental controls. A control bar has been added to the bottom of the screen. It not only has the standard DVD controls like pause, fast forward, and rewind; it also has a Time Slider that allows you to slide forward or backward to any part of the movie. You can adjust player settings for example, changing the width and height of the movie (great for viewing wide screen movies as full screen), and set streaming or the closed captioning option. The Image Bar, located at the top of the screen, allows you to view movie chapters, add bookmarks and create video clips.

For serious movie fans, now you can watch DVDs while writing e-mails, surfing the web, or doing mindless tasks — the DVD player floats above all other windows. Old DVDs that may have a few scratches can return to the play list; Leopard identifies and skips the damaged part of the disk to allow for smooth playback. Parents of young children will appreciate the new parental controls built into the DVD player. After you enable Parental Controls in DVD Player, all DVDs that are inserted into your Mac's CD/DVD drive require an administrator password to play. Talk about total control!

Exposé

Introduced in OS X Panther, Exposé provides easy access to hidden application windows. Exposé gives you the ability to temporarily arrange open windows to help you find things; it's great if you work with many different applications and multiple windows, but prefer not to minimize or hide windows. In OS X Leopard, Exposé has graduated to a full-fledged application; therefore, you can access it from System Preferences or the Applications Folder. Exposé is covered in further detail in Chapter 2.

Font Book

Apple introduced the Font Book application in OS X Panther. It is a powerful font management system that enables you to manage, install, remove, and preview fonts. Leopard updates to the Font Book include new fonts including Tahoma, Papyrus, and Wingdings, Braille support, auto-activation and a printable font book (great for previewing fonts). Font Book is discussed in further detail in Chapter 15.

Front Row

Front Row brings your digital music, movies and pictures together in a beautiful presentation. Using Front Row, you can watch DVDs, listen to music stored in your iTunes application, watch TV shows, or watch iPhoto slideshows on your Mac or a television that your Mac is connected to. If your Mac is connected to the Internet, you can view trailers from Apple's Web site, browse iTunes for music, movies, Podcasts, or TV shows. Impress friends and family as you launch your daughter's dance competition video from across the couch with your Apple Remote. Figure 6.5 shows Front Row's main menu.

FIGURE 6.5

When you launch Front Row, you are presented with a list of digital media sources.

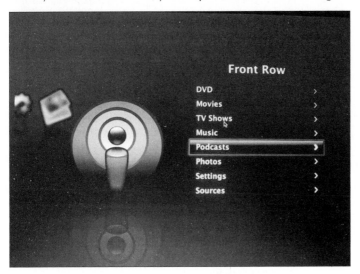

iCal

Apple's calendaring program, iCal, is a great application for keeping your time organized and planning ahead. See Figure 6.6. iCal has full Address Book, Mail and — new to OS X Leopard — iSync integration. The addition of iSync integration allows you to view and modify calendars stored on a Web server while offline; when you reconnect to the Internet, iSync synchronizes your Calendars. You can create multiple calendars, publish calendars on the Web, invite attendees, and set repetitive events with alarm notifications. With CalDAV (Cal Distributed Authoring and Versioning) and iCal Server, iCal for OS X Leopard introduces new functionality, making it a great choice for office environments.

Along with a new interface, iCal has a number of useful features making their debut in Leopard including Event Dropbox, Auto Pick, and Delegation. When scheduling meetings, utilize the new Event Dropbox to share documents, videos, spreadsheets, and so on with invitees. Further simplifying meeting scheduling, iCal automatically picks the date and time when everyone is available. Delegation, another long-awaited feature, is now built into iCal, enabling you to place someone else in charge of your calendar when you are not in the office.

CalDAV, built on WebDAV technology or the ability to edit and manage files on remote Web servers, makes iCal a true collaborative calendaring program that enables users to access your calendar and edit Calendar entries. This collaborative calendaring allows you to see another user's availability, send meeting invitations to groups, and reserve meeting rooms and equipment. At times, you will be required to collaborate with Entourage users; no need to worry — Mail can handle event invitations and adds the event to your iCal calendar.

FIGURE 6.6

iCal's interface has slimmed down; the Info window no longer appears as a side bar, but is now a pop-up box.

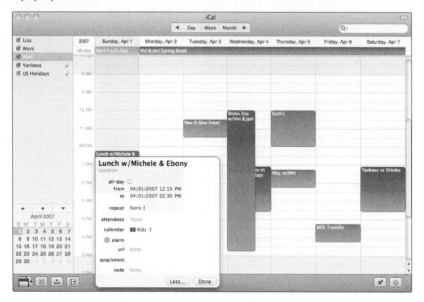

iCal Server, the first calendar server for OS X Server, enables users to share calendars, check invitee availability, schedule meetings, and organize events among workgroups. Because iCal Server is built using open calendaring protocols, it seamlessly integrates with the industry's leading calendaring software such as Mozilla's SunBird and Microsoft Outlook. iCal is discussed in further detail in Chapter 14.

iChat

iChat (formerly iChat AV) is Apple's Instant Messaging software. It's easy to configure and great for chatting with buddies over the Web or having an audio or video conference. If you plan on chatting with friends over the Web, you will need a .Mac or an AIM account. You can also chat with people on your local area network via Bonjour or the Jabber Open Source protocol, which is similar to other IM services such as AIM, ICQ, MSN, and Yahoo!. Files can be transferred via iChat using the AIM protocol. Both protocols can be enabled the first time you launch iChat.

For those of you who like to see the people you are chatting with (I'm with you), you can turn your Mac into a videoconference center by plugging a camera into your Mac (Apple's iMac and MacBook lines come with a built-in camera) and *voilà!* Magically, you're having a videoconference with your sister Margaret who lives in Virginia! When video chatting, keep in mind that due to the limitations of dial-up connections, you can have video chats only if you have a broadband connection. iChat is aware of the capabilities of your Internet connection, and provides the best possible experience depending on your bandwidth; broadband generally gives you a full video and audio session, and a standard dial-up line works fine with text or audio sessions.

OS X Leopard brings new, impressive features to iChat, including screen sharing, backdrop effects, recording, Photo Booth effects, tabbed chats, multiple logins, animated buddy icons, and an updated buddy list. Screen Sharing enables you and a buddy to share either of your screens; show a buddy your new iMovie, train a colleague on a new program, or work with your partner on your Keynote presentation. With Screen Sharing, remotely control a buddy's screen — or simultaneously control the screen — which is especially useful when working on a project. See Figure 6.7. iChat Theatre allows you to share content *without* sharing your screen with buddies. If you'd like to jazz up your video sessions, you can change your background by simply dragging and dropping any image onto your video window. Apple has even added recording capability to video chats. Record and save your audio or video chats for memory's sake or blackmailing purposes. Add Video effects from 24 different Photo Booth effects like Fisheye, Comic Book, X-Ray, or Dent. For mega-chatters, organize your chats into one tabbed window for chatting with multiple people. Chat with AIM, Jabber and Gmail buddies simultaneously. To the left of the tabbed window, iChat lists the buddies you are currently chatting with; when a buddy types a new message, a text bubble — showing the first few words of the message — appears under his or her screen name.

FIGURE 6.7

Share your computer screen with a buddy.

Apple has changed the look of the Buddy List; buddies are sorted into five categories: Buddies, Family, Mobile Device, Recent Buddies, and Offline. The Buddies category lists all of your available buddies. The Family category lists buddies that have been tagged as family members. The Mobile Device category lists available buddies that are connected to Instant Messenger via a cell phone, laptop, and other wireless device. The Recent Buddies category lists the people that you have recently chatted with. There's an Offline category that lists your buddies that are not currently online. See Figure 6.8. For those of you that want to be logged into Instant Messenger, but remain hidden from your buddies, Apple has added an Invisible status *a la* stealth mode. A word of caution:Ttext and files sent via iChat are not encrypted; third-party peepers can view them.

FIGURE 6.8

iChat indicates the type of chatting supported on your buddy's computer next to his or her buddy icon.

Image Capture

If you want to connect a scanner or a digital camera to your Mac and manage that device to copy or transfer images, Image Capture is the application for you. In OS X Leopard, Image Capture (and its integration with the core OS) works as a hub for all imaging devices connected to your Mac. Depending on the camera you have, you may even be able to take pictures and import them, all while connected to your Mac. Even more impressive, you can import images wirelessly from 802.11-enabled digital cameras and Bluetooth devices. Once opened, Image Capture looks for all imaging devices connected to your Mac. You can then start importing images into your machine from your digital camera or scanner. See Figure 6.9.

Image Capture also work with Kodak Picture CDs and other image sources. Scanners and other imaging devices are accessed as TWAIN devices. (For more information about TWAIN, see the related sidebar.)

TWAIN

Technology Without An Interesting Name, or TWAIN, was developed by a consortium of companies interested in making their devices able to operate inside important applications such as Adobe Photoshop, Microsoft PowerPoint, and others. In general, a TWAIN device provides a driver or interface that can be used by any program that has a TWAIN interface implemented. That means you can activate the device from inside an application and use the device's software to control and operate it. Once you have performed your scanning or capture operation, the resulting image is placed inside your application. So far, TWAIN has been a successful endeavor that is currently being implemented by new technologies built directly into the operating systems.

FIGURE 6.9

When importing pictures from your digital camera, you have the option to delete the files after importing or keep them.

iSync

iSync, as its name suggests, synchronizes information from your Mac with different devices including cellular phones, personal digital assistants (PDAs), and iPods. iSync makes synching quick and easy. Its interface is simple and straightforward, as shown in Figure 6.10. iSync's functionality is extendable through various third-party plug-ins that enable the synchronization of devices that Apple does not natively support. PocketMac for BlackBerry enables Macintosh users to synchronize Address Book, iCal, Entourage, Now Up-to-Date, Now Contact, and Stickies with a Blackberry.

PocketMac for BlackBerry supports 12 different BlackBerry devices, including the BlackBerry 8700c/r and the BlackBerry 8100 Pearl. The Missing Sync's Sync Together software facilitates Mac-to-Mac synchronization of Address Book contacts, Safari bookmarks, iCal calendars and tasks, and Bonjour local networks for up to three users. Users can even select the information that they'd like to keep private.

FIGURE 6.10

iSync tells you if a device you are trying to add is not supported.

The list of supported devices grows steadily, and chances are that third-party application developers will have support for your device, or it may be that your data resides in other applications. For example, PocketMac for BlackBerry is a third-party plug-in that enables iSync to synchronize information between your BlackBerry and Microsoft Entourage. Apple also provides a list of supported devices on its Web site. See Chapter 14 for more information on iSync.

iTunes

Like the iPod, iTunes is a masterpiece of design. It has been so successful that it is considered an integral part of Apple's Music Store and operating system. iTunes has made a substantial impact on the music industry. Like other success stories, there have been numerous attempts to dethrone iTunes; to date, they have all been unsuccessful. Its sleek and smooth interface is simple and intuitive — a hallmark of Apple's creativity and design. iTunes has been designed to provide music entertainment at all levels. From subscribing to podcasts, to purchasing TV shows and movies, to burning your own music CDs, iTunes provides a vast array of entertainment and capabilities. See Figure 6.11.

It is difficult to imagine a better management tool for your media. It's easy to organize music files in libraries or playlists; you can even add ratings and lyrics. You can view album art and have your screen perform visual effects tuned to the music beat.

FIGURE 6.11

The Get Info window of individual tracks allows you to view a summary of the song, change the play options, add lyrics, and add/modify album artwork.

Mail

Apple's Mail has seen many enhancements over the years. OS X Leopard is no exception. Additions to Mail include Email Stationary, RSS feeds, Notes, and To-Do's. Mail's interface has changed a bit, adding a new Mail Activity indicator at the bottom left of the Mail pane; it shows the progress as mail messages are received and sent. Under the standard Inbox, Drafts, and Sent icons are a few new ones: Notes, To Do, and RSS Feeds. Mail is a full-featured application completely integrated with Address Book and iChat. E-mail interchange choices are comprised of .Mac, POP (Post Office Protocol), IMAP (Internet Message Access Protocol), and Microsoft Exchange mail services. Mail includes standard features such as Junk Mail, LDAP support, Rules, and Signatures.

For many, e-mail is just text on a page. With Mail for OS X Leopard, you can enliven e-mail with Stationary. See Figure 6.12. Choose from more than 35 Apple-designed templates, add your own pictures from your iPhoto library, and customize the text to include fun fonts and colors. Stationary is great for any occasion, including party invitations, business meetings, birth announcements, and holiday greetings. Stationary messages are formatted in standard HTML, enabling Macs and PCs alike to read your e-mail.

FIGURE 6.12

Stationary lets you send striking e-mails that can be viewed on a Mac or PC.

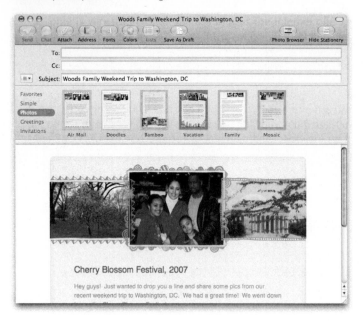

In today's busy world, going onto the Net and visiting various sites to get up to speed on news and articles can be time consuming. RSS, or Really Simple Syndication, has been a godsend for many people. Not only does Apple's Safari have RSS built directly into it, OS X Leopard has taken the convenience of RSS to a new level, by integrating it into Mail. Now you can catch up on all the news simply by clicking the RSS icon in Mail and browsing through the feeds. Choose to have the feeds updated every 30 minutes, every hour, or every day. RSS is also covered in Chapters 2 and 10.

 **TIP**   When transferring data from one computer to another or to backup your messages, utilize Mail's Archive mailbox feature to simplify the process.

Mail also doubles as a To-Do and Reminder application. We've all sent ourselves e-mails reminding us to make a call, pick up dry cleaning, research an issue, or complete a task. Now, you can jot down meeting agenda ideas, create a list of people that you need to e-mail, or add a To-Do item directly in Mail using the new Notes and To-Do features. Notes look like ruled, legal sheets and can include bulleted items, formatted text, and attached documents or photos. See Figure 6.13. Notes can be saved in Mail, printed, or e-mailed. To-Do items created in Mail are automatically added to iCal. Add a due date and completion date, prioritize, choose the calendar you'd like the task to appear on, and add an alarm and notes. A simple click can create a To-Do item from any e-mail message. You can even include To-Do items in Notes!

When performing searches in OS X Leopard, Mail items including messages, RSS feeds, Notes, and To-Do items are included in the results. Mail is also covered in Chapters 9 and 10.

FIGURE 6.13

Notes are great for integrating To-Do's and keeping track of things. When typing text, press the Esc key to automatically complete words.

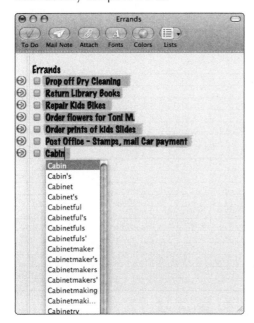

Photo Booth

When Apple upgraded its processors to Intel, they added a sweet new application called Photo Booth to its suite of applications. Photo Booth, aptly named after photo booths found at carnivals, fairs, and malls, enables you to take pictures of yourself using your Mac's built-in camera or connected iSight. You can apply various effects to your pictures including Sepia, Black and White, X-Ray, Mirror, and Stretch and Squeeze; pick from eight backgrounds; or add your own backdrop. There are three picture choices: Still, Photo Booth Burst (four quick snapshots), or a Movie Clip. When taking photos, Photo Booth counts down giving you three seconds to pose. The still photo takes one snapshot. As its name states, the four quick pictures takes just that: four photos in quick succession. Photo Booth counts down to the first snapshot, but each successive shot is taken immediately after the other. Movie Clip doesn't take a picture, but records a video snapshot.

Still photos are saved as JPEG (Joint Photographic Experts Group), Photo Booth Burst snapshots are saved as four JPEGs, while Movie Clips are saved as .mov files (QuickTime movies). See Figure 6.14. Use your Photo Booth picture as your Account picture or Address Book card photo. You can also import your favorite photos into your iPhoto Library or email them to friends and family. Use your Movie Clip or Photo Booth Burst photos as your animated buddy icon by exporting it as an animated GIF.

FIGURE 6.14

Backdrops are an awesome addition to Photo Booth.

Preview

Preview is one of the most useful applications integrated into OS X Leopard. Not only does Preview take full advantage of the awesome graphic capabilities of the Quartz core service in OS X, it can handle several file formats and is able to perform conversions among them. One of the most notable features of Preview is its ability to handle portable document format (PDF) files. PDF is widely regarded as the universal file format for sharing and transferring files. PDFs can be created from any application via the Print dialog box; the PDF files can then be opened on any computer platform.

In Mac OS X Leopard, you can rearrange the pages in your PDF document by dragging and dropping them in their new locations. Suppose you have two separate documents that you would like to combine as one PDF file: first save each file as a PDF, then open one and drop the other file(s) into the open PDF. Rearrange as desired. Perfect your PDFs with built-in image manipulation; you can crop images, rotate, resize and save images in many different formats. Speed up the process by applying these changes to a batch of photos. Preview will automatically adjust the white and black levels to reveal the best image.

Other enhancements include improved annotations, more image printing options and GPS Metadata support. Annotations are a very useful tool when numerous people are working on the same file. Leopard's Preview allows users to add Stickies-style notes to PDFs and draw attention to important areas with rectangles and highlighted text. Printing options have been expanded to allow users to print different images within a PDF or multiple copies of an individual image. Perhaps the niftiest addition to Preview is GPS Metadata support. Images that have embedded GPS Metadata (data about data) will tell you where the photo was taken; using the image inspector, you can pin-point the exact location that the image was taken.

In addition to opening PDF documents with lightning speed, Preview also supports the file formats discussed in the following sections.

BMP

BMP (short for bitmap) is a resolution-dependant Microsoft Windows image file format. It is not widely supported outside the Windows environment and not commonly used on the Internet. However, this format has been around for quite some time, and because of the sheer number of Windows-based machines, it is common to find images stored in it. Its color depth can range from 1 to 24 bits or 16.7 million colors. Sometimes it is compressed using the run-length encoding (RLE) algorithm.

JPEG and JPEG-2000

A popular image compression and presentation format, JPEG (which stands for Joint Photographic Experts Group) was first introduced in the late 1980s and is now the most widely used format for image presentation on the Internet. It is considered a *lossy compression method*, which means that when an image is created, some of the original image file's information is discarded. The discarded information is not noticeable to the human eye. Nonetheless, it can achieve very high levels of data reduction; it is common to find 10:1 compression ratios. To accomplish this, the image is first converted to a color space where the luminance and color channels are managed separately (usually LAB color space). Next, an algorithm performs a comprehensive *down sampling* of the information contained in the chrominance channels, resulting in up to 50 percent data reduction. The process does not end there. The image is then divided into portions of 8 x 8 pixels and put through another algorithm that generally performs a *discrete cosine transformation,* which results in a mathematical expression that represents the color and brightness values for each 8-x-8-pixel tile. This final step permits the selective removal of repetitive information.

The final step in this process involves discarding even more information based on the quality level selected. When using JPEG file compression, each time the image is modified and saved, information is discarded, resulting in an image that may differ greatly from the original. Therefore, it is only recommended for use with image samples and images that will be presented on the Web. JPEG is attractive due to its ability to compress image files while retaining visual quality at a particular resolution without noticeable data loss by the viewer.

There are several implementations of the JPEG compression standard. Some include multiple versions of the same image reduced to different resolutions, and others use different mathematical transformations (other than discrete cosine transformation) to remove *lossless* information from the original image. One implementation is the progressive version, which stores an image at different quality levels. When displayed, the lowest-quality image is presented first, the next lowest is presented second, and so on until the highest one is superimposed.

> JPEG images are not recommended for print production because many artifacts may appear when the images are printed on a high-quality printer.

JPEG-2000 is the natural evolution of the current JPEG standard. Many new features were included in the JPEG-2000 format that retain more of the information stored in the original image and implement metadata (data about data) inside the file format. There are many different kinds of JPEG-2000 formats, but the most common include layered files, incremental resolution, motion, multiple format (for text and images), and many other formats that will be supported in future implementations of Web browsers and other image-intensive interactive software. You can visit www.jpeg.org for more information on this important standard. Figure 6.15 illustrates the ease with which Preview can convert image formats.

FIGURE 6.15

Preview allows you to convert image formats with ease.

PDF

PDF, short for Portable Document Format, is one of the most common document storage standards in use today. Simply put, a PDF file is a visual representation of a document or its printed equivalent. PDF files keep the best possible resemblance to the original document, regardless of the program or operating system on which it was created.

Introduced by Adobe in 1993, PDF has become one of the great file format standards of our time. Although other operating systems require Adobe Acrobat Reader to view or print PDF documents, with Preview, that capability is built into OS X. Nevertheless, Adobe continues to produce an Acrobat Reader version for OS X that provides the same functionality as Preview. The importance of the PDF format has increased enormously with the widespread use of the Internet. In fact, the paperless office example presented by Adobe in 1993 is becoming a reality as new features and capabilities are built into the format.

The format preservation of extremely complex documents, image-quality parameters, and font embedding technologies present in the PDF standard now permit the creation of full PDF work-flow environments for the advertisement industry, meeting the highest pre-press requirements and enabling printers to tweak special parameters such as trapping and color spaces. PDF also supports embedded video and audio as well as presentation capabilities; annotation and collaboration environments; and forms, legal signatures, and a ton of other useful features. Investing in PDF capabilities in the corporate environment is always a win-win choice.

PICT

PICT is an Apple image file format introduced in 1984 that can be viewed in Preview and QuickTime. It is composed of bitmap images, outline objects, and QuickDraw commands. PICT files support 32-bit color depths and have many interesting uses. For example, you can save an Adobe Photoshop file in PICT format in order to use the file in a video editing or animation program. PICT files reproduce well at standard laser printer or inkjet printer resolutions and should not be used in high-quality print operations. Because PICT files contain QuickDraw commands, they are good for rendering line art objects in conjunction with bitmap images such as grayscale and even RGB. With the release of OS X Jaguar, Apple replaced the PICT format with PDF; however, PICTs are still supported in OS X Leopard. PICT files can be compressed using the RLE algorithm. PICT files can also contain JPEG-compressed images.

PNG

PNG (Portable Network Graphics) is a widely used format for storing graphics information. Its compression process is very sophisticated, and, unlike JPEG, there is no data loss when storing those files. Currently, up to 48- and 64-bit depth is supported for TrueColor images and 16-bit depth for grayscale. The PNG format was originally designed to replace GIF (Graphics Interchange Format) files; however, it does not support the multiple image mechanism that can be stored in the GIF format; the PNG format was intended for one image only. The PNG format appeared in 1995; however, its history can be traced to 1977. It has many advantages over other formats and has been gaining ground, particularly in the free software movement. Unlike TIFF, the PNG implementation is specific, and once a file is stored as PNG, all applications that support the standard can open and manipulate the image.

TIFF

Developed by Aldus (which merged with Adobe) and Microsoft, TIFF (Tagged Image File Format) is widely used in print production. Like the PNG format, all of the image information is preserved when the file is saved as a TIFF. Various compression algorithms are used to save space when storing TIFF files; however, the requirement is that all of the information must be kept intact when compressing. There is a theoretical 4GB limit for TIFF file sizes; this limit can be bypassed using compression methods.

QuickTime Player

A true technological breakthrough when introduced by Apple, the QuickTime Player has become one of the most reliable standards for multimedia distribution. A multimedia framework, QuickTime consists of: the QuickTime application, the QuickTime framework, and the QuickTime Movie. Its ability to handle nearly any media, including video, text, audio, images, and different languages; the ability to take advantage of the networking technology for video streaming over the Internet; and High Definition support and its cross-platform appeal make QuickTime an easy sell for your media needs. 3-D spaces can be defined and viewed using a special virtual reality version of the QuickTime Player, and QuickTime Broadcaster allows users to air live media.

QuickTime's popularity has made numerous plug-ins available, like Flip4Mac and Divx. Flip4Mac distributes products that enable users to export and import media into various formats. For example, Flip4Mac WMV allows QuickTime users to play, import, export, and convert Windows Media Video files. QuickTime is also covered in Chapter 7.

Safari

Since its introduction in January 2003, Safari has evolved to become a full-featured browser, able to present to you the Web in a fast, simple, and powerful way. Its interface is intuitive and supports common browser features such as page tabs and bookmarks, and its integration with the core features of OS X Leopard makes it a great choice for Web browsing. Tabbed browsing has been improved in Safari, in order for you to quickly reorder open tabs by simply clicking and dragging them to their new location. If you have many Web pages open and would prefer to have them consolidated into one tabbed window, simply select "Merge All Windows" from the Window menu on the top toolbar. If, in fact, you want the opposite effect, that is to pull a tab *out* of a window, all you have to do is select the desired tab and pull it out of the window. It will then be a stand-alone Web page. If you accidentally close a window, Safari "remembers" the sites you've visited as well as indexes the text in those sites.

TIP   Say "so long" to the three-step process of identifying an image online, saving it to your pictures folder, and setting it as your desktop picture. Safari makes this simple by enabling you to set any image as your desktop picture by Control+clicking the image and choosing Use Image as Desktop Picture. By default, the image is set to fill the screen.

If you stumble upon a new site that you would like to add to your Bookmarks toolbar, just drag and drop it onto the toolbar. Position your mouse over the tabs, and a miniature representation of the page drops down.

Tying into Apple's new Webclip widget, an icon has been placed on the Safari toolbar that enables you to create a Webclip page in Dashboard, directly from Safari. Open the Web page you'd like to create the widget from, and click the Webclip icon; a bar appears below the search bar and Safari suggests a section to serve as your clip. If you'd like to select another section, simply click the area and hit Add. See Figure 6.16. When searching for text within a Web page, Safari highlights each occurrence of the word for your review.

FIGURE 6.16

Create a Webclip widget directly from Safari.

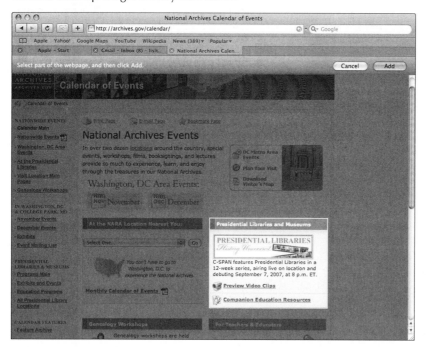

The intimate integration of Safari into the Mac OS enables it to maximize the execution of Java applets. The incorporation of RSS allows you to access hundreds of news sources simultaneously. An extension of the RDF language and an XML application, RSS is a multipurpose, extensible metadata format for news syndication and other content. RSS-aware applications such as Safari are called *news aggregators*. See Chapter 10 for detailed information on Safari.

Spaces

Like Exposé, Spaces helps users locate open windows and reduce Desktop clutter. Simply, Spaces allows you to create multiple *virtual* desktops and organize your applications into their own individual space. See Figure 6.17. Chapter 2 discuss Spaces in further detail.

FIGURE 6.17

Organize your applications into different Spaces.

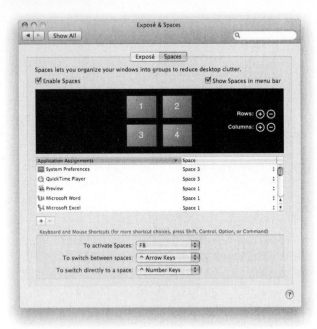

Stickies

Stickies is a useful application that has been carried over through many Mac OS versions. In general, the Stickies application works exactly as Post-it brand notes by 3M — you attach them to your desktop and their information is available whenever you activate the application. If you want to save a Stickie, you can export it as a plain text, RTF (Rich Text Format), or RTFD (Rich Text Format Directory) file. You can also print Stickies; when printing Stickies, you can choose to print the active note, or print all notes. OS X Tiger added Stickies to Dashboard.

 **NOTE** Stickies created in Dashboard are not viewable on the Desktop.

System Preferences

The control center for many of OS X Leopard core functions is the System Preferences application. See Figure 6.18. You can access System Preferences via the Apple menu at the top left corner of the screen (or from the Applications folder). In OS X Leopard, the Exposé and Spaces system preference panes also appear in the applications folder; however, they are not applications, but another method to access the preference. New preference panes include Spaces (part of the Expose & Spaces pane), Parental Controls, and Time Machine.

The Network Preferences pane has been streamlined to provide more information and granular control of network connections. The simplified interface combines network locations in a column to the left and location configurations to the right. Advanced options are available for all network locations including preferred AirPort networks and 802.1X settings. The network preference pane is shown in figure 6.18.

Many parents, like myself, will be impressed by the improvements to Parental Controls. No longer buried in the Accounts preference pane, Parental Controls is all grown up. Parents can control whether their children can change passwords, modify the dock, administer printers, choose what Applications can be used, restrict Web site access, determine who they can receive email from and what buddies they can chat with, limit the amount of time they can spend on the computer (broken up into Weekdays, Weekends, and Bedtime), and generate logs of their child's computer activity (this one is my favorite). Leopard sets itself apart as an Operating System that empowers parents.

Another new feature includes .Mac sync of System Preferences on each Mac you use, and improved Expose and Dashboard control with your mouse. System Preferences are discussed at length in Chapter 17.

FIGURE 6.18

The Network Preference pane has been completely redesigned.

TextEdit

Often mistaken to be a simple word processor, TextEdit is a powerful, full-featured application capable of handling most text-related operations and working with many file formats. TextEdit is the default text editor in Mac OS X. Whether receiving attachments via e-mail or creating a new document, TextEdit can handle all text files (with the .txt extension), RTF (Rich Text Files), OpenDocument file formats, as well as Microsoft Word documents. With new autosave abilities, new header and footer support, smart quotes, and enhanced OpenDocument and Word 2007 format support, Text Edit makes an impressive turn with Mac OS 10.5 Leopard.

Time Machine

Leopard introduces a new concept to old-school Mac users: built-in backup. For years, Mac users have dragged and dropped their files to the relative safety of external hard drives or burned their way to data protection. Not only is this process time consuming, it isn't reliable; suppose you forget to include that Excel spreadsheet you were working on until 1 a.m. or lose the backup CD. With Time Machine you don't need to worry; simply set the backup schedule and let it be. You need only be sure that your drive is connected.

You will need either an external hard drive or a partitioned hard disk (Time Machine does not support optical media). If you have an external hard drive, the first time you connect it to your Mac, Time Machine prompts you to back up your data to the connected hard drive. If you say yes, Time Machine backs up everything on your machine including documents, movies, pictures, applications, system files, and accounts—make sure you allocate a generous amount of time for this—and it backs up your machine according to the default schedule. If you would like to modify Time Machine's settings you can access the application in the Applications folder or under its Systems Preference pane. See Figure 6.19. You can change the backup disk, select what data you *don't* want backed up, and turn Time Machine on or off. There's no need to worry about the security of your documents, either. Time Machine preserves your file's access privileges as it backs up your data.

After performing the initial backup, Time Machine backs up only what changes on your system, thereby maximizing the space on your drive while preserving a complete blueprint of your system. Time Machine backs up your data every hour of every day and keeps hourly backups for 24 hours, daily backups for a month, and weekly backups until your backup drive is full. When you need to restore a file, application, or contact, simply launch Time Machine and click the arrows on the lower right-hand corner to scroll to the backup date that your data was stored on; when you've located the missing data, click Restore and Time Machine restores the data to its original location, or returns your system to its previous state. See Figure 6.20. You can even search for your data— Spotlight is built into Time Machine. A piece of advice: Your backup is only as good your backup plan. For sensitive data it's best to have multiple backups and to store that content off-site.

FIGURE 6.19

The Time Machine application has a simple, very user-friendly interface.

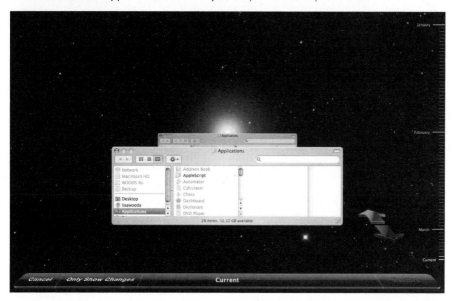

FIGURE 6.20

In Time Machine's preference pane, set your backup drive, how long your backups will be retained, and what time your system will back up each night.

A Tour of Mac OS X Utilities

Mac OS X Leopard comes with a treasure chest of utility applications that empower you to access and control intimate aspects of the operation of your Mac. A brief description of each utility is discussed in the following section, with some emphasis being placed on particularly useful ones.

Activity Monitor

Have you ever wondered if your Mac is just hung-up or if it is working on some demanding task after your last click? The Activity Monitor, shown in Figure 6.21, presents a visual depiction of the current activity load in your CPU. It also lets you stop processes being executed in your machine.

NOTE You should take extreme caution when stopping executing processes if you are not familiar with their purpose or dependencies. If you must stop and quit applications, we recommend using the Force Quit command; in that way you make sure OS X Leopard takes care of quitting all of the processes related to an application.

FIGURE 6.21

The Activity Monitor shows you what is going on in your Mac.

If you suspect that your computer is "hung up" on a process, the Activity Monitor is the first place to start investigating. If you want to monitor your CPU usage, launch Activity Monitor (in /Applications/Utilities) and select Window ⇨ CPU Usage for a small window with a vertical gauge, or Window ⇨ Show Floating CPU Window on the menu bar. Both are useful for keeping tabs on how hard your CPU is working.

 When you quit Activity Monitor, the CPU Usage window closes.

AirPort Utility

Apple offers two wireless networking devices: the AirPort Extreme Base Station and the AirPort Express Base Station. The latter operates under the 802.11b (11 Mbps) and 802.11g (54 Mbps) wireless standards, and the former utilizes the new 802.11n wireless technology. All new Macs are capable of using the 802.11n standard, but older Macs need a hand to get it going. Intel Core 2 Duo processors — with the exception of 17-inch, 1.83 GHz iMacs — MacBooks, and Mac Pros need Apple's AirPort Extreme 802.11n Enabler in order to take advantage of this new technology. OS X Leopard includes the AirPort Extreme 802.11n Enabler software free, as part of the AirPort Utility application. See Figure 6.22.

FIGURE 6.22

The new AirPort Utility not only premieres new features, but also sports a new interface.

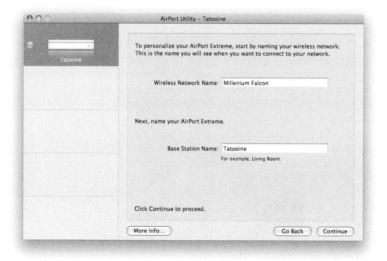

The AirPort Utility allows you to do the following:

- Assign a name and password to the AirPort in order to identify and secure it. The first thing you should do when installing your AirPort is assign a password. Next, you need to assign a name to the AirPort network, select a wireless channel, and select what kind of wireless security you will utilize. Keep in mind that wireless networks without security are public networks — anyone can access them. Maximize your network's security by selecting to create a closed network. By entering the exact name of your network in addition to your password for protocol encryption, you ensure that your network is invulnerable to snooping and other intrusions.

- Select what type of network configuration you will be using to connect to the Internet, including managing connectivity using a DSL line (PPPoE protocol). Notice that you can choose to configure your network parameters manually instead of using the Dynamic Host Configuration Protocol (DHCP); this enables you to assign a fixed IP address to your station. You can also set your AirPort to work as a repeater or relay for another AirPort.

- Configure the network settings such as IP addresses and other network settings that will be distributed to the computers that will connect to your AirPort.

- Manage port mappings for Web, FTP, or other server services on your network, or remap protocol settings according to your needs.

- Designate computers that are allowed to communicate with the AirPort using their MAC Address, which is a unique hardware ID used to verify that only the designated devices are able to talk to the AirPort. You can also utilize a RADIUS server to authenticate the devices.

The new AirPort Extreme Base Station can support up to 50 users and boasts up to five times the speed and two times the range of older AirPorts. If your home network is like mine, and you have multiple Macs using one printer, simply plug your printer into the USB port on the back of your AirPort Extreme Base Station and the printer is instantly available to everyone on your network. The same concept applies to sharing an external hard drive: connect the hard drive to the USB port of your Base Station and all users on your network can save documents or back up files to the drive using Time Machine.

For many of us, the security of wireless networks is a major concern. The upgraded AirPort Extreme includes a built-in firewall and incorporates industry-standard encryption technologies including WPA/WPA2 and 128-bit WEP, making it difficult for unauthorized users to access your network, while authorized users can connect to your AirPort seamlessly. Finally, you can use your AirPort Extreme Base Station to transfer music, videos, and movies from iTunes to Apple TV. For more information on AirPort, see Chapter 11.

Audio MIDI Setup

The Musical Instrument Digital Interface (MIDI) is designed to connect digital audio equipment (keyboards, drums, and so on) to a Mac. Because Apple has always been on the leading edge of audio technology, MIDI-interface support is fully implemented into OS X Leopard via the Audio MIDI Setup utility, which facilitates the addition of devices or linking them across a network in a snap.

Collaboration between systems is also supported, enabling the user to get input from different computers, even from remote locations. Taking full advantage of the many features offered by the Audio MIDI Setup enables you to create professional-grade musical mixes as well as other sound-related operations.

Bluetooth file exchange

Mac OS X Leopard fully supports the Bluetooth Personal Area Network (PAN) standard, intended for simple information interchange on a peer-to-peer basis. To use Bluetooth technology, your Mac must have the necessary hardware built into it. If your Mac does not have the necessary hardware, you can purchase a Bluetooth link device that fits neatly into one of your available USB ports.

After a Bluetooth pair has been created, and the devices support the requested operation, data interchange may start. See Figure 6.23. Although many devices support the Bluetooth standard, many have poor implementations that cause communications and pairing problems.

FIGURE 6.23

Once paired, the device services are accessible. Notice that some devices do not fully support synching operations.

Once your devices are paired, you can initiate file exchanges. Browsing and file transfer operations are available from the Bluetooth menu. File transfers happen fast after the communication channel is established. OS X Tiger saw the integration of many options for Bluetooth in the Bluetooth Preferences pane. You can control the Bluetooth Serial utility from System Preferences, and all of the necessary options to configure ports using the Bluetooth protocol are accessible there. There are different options available with each paired device. Bluetooth is discussed in greater detail in Chapter 11.

Boot Camp Assistant

OS X Leopard is the first Apple operating system that provides a means to install the Windows operating system on your Macintosh. Boot Camp Assistant facilitates the installation of Microsoft Windows on your Mac, enabling you to run Mac or Windows. If you decide to delete Windows, Apple has made this process very simple; delete Windows and restore the disk space to OS X. Working with Window files has been improved, enabling you to copy, paste and delete files between both operating systems. Boot Camp is discussed in further detail in Chapter 19.

ColorSync Utility

In 1993, Apple Computer Inc. led an initiative to formalize a device-independent color management system called ColorSync. Apple's intention was to enable its devices to match the color displayed in monitors, from input sources such as color scanners and other imaging technologies, as well as enable the publishing industry to accurately reproduce color from the (then emerging) desktop publishing phenomenon. The term WYSIWIG (What You See Is What You Get) was coined at that time. When Adobe embraced the initiative and included the then-new International Color Consortium (ICC) profiles to work with Adobe Photoshop, the ColorSync technology became an industry standard. See Figure 6.24.

FIGURE 6.24

The ColorSync utility enables you to repair and check ICC profiles installed in your system. It also enables you to select profiles that match a color space, select a profile for a particular device, and apply useful filters such as PDF/X. It even includes a special calculator for profile conversion and color matching.

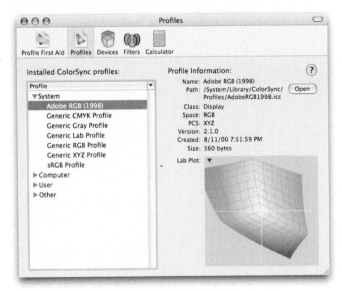

ColorSync is a technology that keeps Apple at the forefront of desktop publishing technology, allowing for device calibration and profile sharing with remote printers. The ColorSync implementation in OS X Leopard is part of the Quartz core services, making it part of every color-related operation performed by your Mac. After a profile is selected it is applied to your system monitor, printer, scanner, and so on.

Console

Used primarily by support technicians, Console is a useful troubleshooting tool. Console stores the messages your software sends detailing the activities between various parts of your system and sorts them into *logs*. These logs can be of great use when trying to understand an error message or why an application has crashed; you can even send a copy of your log to technical support personnel for further diagnosis.

DigitalColor Meter

For immediate information about a color displayed on-screen, the DigitalColor Meter utility illustrates the color information in RGB percentages, decimal (actual value), hexadecimal, CIE 1931, CIE 1976, CIE L*a*b, or tristimulus formats. Not all devices provide color translation tables for CIE or tristimulus. The DigitalColor Meter can also be used to copy the color of an image or pixel on your screen into HTML or graphics documents.

 CIE is short for *Commission Internationale de l'Eclairage*, which is the French title of the international commission on light. Tristimulus is a 3-D color space in X, Y, and Z coordinates.

Directory

New to the Utility folder, Directory is a consolidated list of all directory services including People, Groups, Locations, Resources, Maps, and Shared Contacts available to users. The Directory is a Lightweight Directory Access Protocol (LDAP) utility that duplicates some of the functionality and information stored in the Address Book. Directory is also discussed in Chapter 19.

Directory Utility

As you move through the world with your Mac, you may need to connect to different network environments. Simply stated, a Directory is a centralized database that can contain a list of computers, groups, and users, and is categorized into organizational units. Directory systems come in two different varieties: static and dynamic. The Directory Utility application is where you configure your computer to access the directory system. It doesn't provide services; it facilitates permissions to access those services such as SMB, AFP, Email, and so on. You will have little use for the Directory Access Utility if you use your Mac in a stand-alone environment. However, if you need to bind your Mac to a directory system, you need to use the Directory Utility. OS X Leopard includes the Directory Utility to assist you with these connections.

When you launch Directory Utility, you are presented with an empty window stating that no Directory Services have been configured. If you would like to add a Directory Server, you will first need to authenticate. When adding Directory Servers, you can choose from two types, Open and Active, and enter an IP Address. Click Show Advanced Settings to mount servers, add services, or search for a policy. See Figure 6.25.

FIGURE 6.25

The Advanced Settings pane gives users access to additional configuration options.

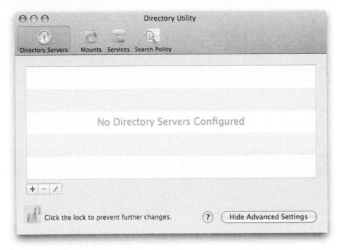

Active Directory

Found mainly in Microsoft Windows network environments, Active Directory provides security and information about available services. In reality, it is Microsoft's implementation of the LDAP standard. Many Macintosh systems find themselves connected to servers and printers that operate under the Windows environments and have been updated from NT domain-based security to Active Directory. It is recommended that you ask your network administrator to manipulate the Active Directory parameters, which are specific to each network infrastructure. The Active Directory utility supports the following connections:

- **BSD Flat File and NIS:** A native UNIX authentication methodology, the Network Information Service (NIS) is used to enable access to Network File System (NFS) resources. Developed by Sun Microsystems, NIS is a distributed security system widely used in Unix-based network services.

- **LDAPv3:** Short for Lightweight Directory Access Protocol version 3, LDAPv3 is a security and network directory services standard developed as a simplified version of the X.500 Worldwide Directory Service, therefore the *lightweight* prefix. In essence, LDAP utilizes distributed relational databases to store and access user, system, and service information across a network and match it against a list of users and their access privileges. Unlike X.500, LDAP can operate over TCP/IP.

■ **Local:** The directory system formerly known as NetInfo is, in essence, a database that contains information about each user defined on a Mac running OS X. In Mac OS X servers, NetInfo is used to access network resources, as well as user information such as names, positions, phone numbers, and so on. Use caution when modifying the information stored in the NetInfo database, because losing or changing that information can cause serious problems on your Mac.

In versions prior to OS X Leopard, the NetInfo application was used to enable, disable, and configure the Root account; the Directory Utility now handles these functions. The Directory Utility is also discussed in Chapter 19.

Disk Utility

As you work on your Mac, the need may arise to burn a disk, check the health of your hard disk, repair permissions, or create a secure image of a selection of files. At first sight, Disk Utility displays all volumes. See Figure 6.26. Once all physical volumes are identified, you can perform the functions outlined below.

FIGURE 6.26

Disk Utility presents all identified physical volumes on the left side of the window. Note the progress bar, at the bottom, when repairing permissions.

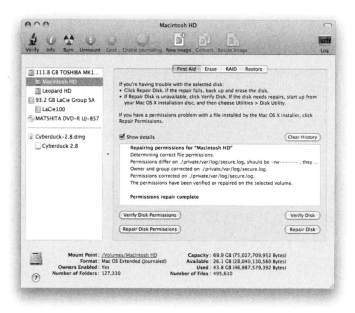

First Aid

First Aid is your main line of defense for disk failure. You are allowed to repair permissions and fix simple disk problems. It is a good idea to repair disk permissions after all software upgrades or installations. It is recommended that you perform regular verifications of your hard disks to maintain an optimal performance.

Erase

Erase is a useful function that should be undertaken carefully. You can erase your hard disk and CDRW disks. If your Mac starts misbehaving constantly and repairing your disk seems to have no effect, it is probably a good idea to erase and reinstall Mac OS X and its applications. Given that performing an Erase destroys all of data on your hard drive, we strongly suggest backing up all of your applications and documents before reinstalling your system — just make sure to place the data (or image) on a drive other than the one you intend to erase.

> **NOTE** When Erasing a drive as preparation for imaging, choose your Journaling settings wisely. Mac OS Extended (Journaled) may not be the best idea for systems that are dependant on disk performance as journaling can put quite a load on Input/Output performance.

Partition

When a disk is partitioned, it is divided into more than one logical entity. If you want to have two different versions of Mac OS X (see Figure 6.27), or you want to have your disk separated into more than one storage space on the same physical disk, partitioning is the way to do it. However, partitioning should be performed at installation time. Generally, you boot your Mac from an installation DVD or CD and then use the Disk Utility to perform a partition operation. OS 10.5 Leopard enables you to resize partitions without wiping your entire machine and rebuilding it. Instead, erase the unwanted partition using Disk Utility and reallocate the space to another partition.

RAID

RAID is a technology used to protect information from hard disk failures by combining the storage capacity of several devices into a unified storage entity. Disk Utility supports a number of RAID formats, including Mirrored, Striped, and Concatenated. The Mirrored RAID set takes two identical disks and unifies them as one entity. This ensures that if one fails or is lost, the other contains an identical copy of the information. If you need to extend the storage capacity of your drive, the Striped RAID set can be used. Striped RAID uses at least two hard disks of the same capacity and pairs them to form a logical entity whose storage capacity is the sum of all disks. When information is written to a striped disk, chunks of data are sequentially sent to each disk, thus improving performance and distributing the information across all units. The major drawback to this configuration is that if one unit is lost, all information is lost. Concatenated RAID sets create a storage unit that combines the available capacity of several disks, in which more than one disk, physical or logical, are combined to create a logical storage entity. Like the Striped RAID set, if any member of the Concatenated Disk array is lost, all data is lost. Generally, software-based RAID systems are not recommended because they lower overall performance and are subject to software glitches; if an array becomes corrupted, all data can be lost. It is important to note that Disk Utility only supports software-based RAID configuration.

FIGURE 6.27

When partitioning a disk, you choose a different system format, different disk sizes, and other options.

Restore

One of the nice features of the Disk Utility is its ability to create images of disk volumes, effectively creating a backup of the *imaged* disk. These images can be stored in any of the available volumes in the system, including network-based resources. When created, images can be compressed to minimize space and you can choose to erase the destination location as the image is written. This technique is commonly used to install new systems based on a master image, which is generally stored on a network server, facilitating the simultaneous configuration of multiple systems. Disk images are true backups of entire volumes. These images can be saved on any available device (local or network) with enough storage space to retain the image.

TIP   For diagnostic purposes, Disk Utility can access S.M.A.R.T. (Self-Monitoring Analysis and Reporting Technology) information from SATA or ATA drives installed in your machine. S.M.A.R.T. was developed to predict disk failures and diagnose the media and mechanics of a hard disk. Disk Utility displays the S.M.A.R.T. information on the selected disk (if supported) and indicates the current status of the drive. If the words "About to Fail" appear in red text, it is recommended that you immediately make a backup of your disk (using disk image, for example) and replace the defective disk.

Grab

The Grab utility enables you to takes snapshots of windows, areas, or your entire screens. Four options are available:

- **Selection Grab (⌘+↑+A):** Captures an area you define in the screen. Use your cursor to drag a rectangle around the area that you want to capture.
- **Window Grab (⌘+↑+W):** Allows you to capture a window displayed on the screen. A dialog box will appear prompting you to select the window you want to capture.
- **Screen Grab (⌘+Z):** Captures the entire screen. A dialog box will appear; you can capture the screen by clicking outside of the dialog box.
- **Timed Screen (⌘+↑+Z):** Executes a full screen capture 10 seconds after you start the clock in a dialog window. It is a useful tool for capturing ongoing actions, or menu selections that otherwise will not be included when taking a snapshot of a portion of the screen or a window.

What's the difference between the Grab utility and the keyboard shortcuts that have the same capability? Grab generates TIFF files and you can assign a file name and choose a location to save them. The keyboard shortcuts, on the other hand, produce PNG images, save them on your desktop, and assign them the file name Picture#.png.

Grapher

The Grapher application is a computerized version of a graphing calculator; it is a powerful tool designed to present mathematical equations as graphs. The original Graphing Calculator was included with the first PowerPC Macs and System 7, during the transition from the Motorola 68000–based Macs to the then-new PowerPC systems. It was the first program that was developed to take advantage of the full capabilities of the PowerPC processor. At that time, it showcased the great power of the PowerPC CPU and opened the door for many scientific applications to take advantage of its RISC design.

The Grapher is an impressive tool that can represent expressions in two and three dimensions, as shown in Figure 6.28. It can be used as a teaching tool in schools and can export graphics in several formats. When the 3-D mode is enabled you can see the graphic representation of an expression rotate on the screen.

Expressions can be defined and represented in 2-D or 3-D views. Intersecting lines show solution points for equation systems. With OS X Leopard, Apple has continued its tradition, showing again that scientific applications will achieve excellent performance on a Mac. However, its power goes beyond the simple representation of mathematical equations. You can evaluate, differentiate, integrate, and time-step functions and other mathematical definitions.

FIGURE 6.28

The Grapher utility can graphically represent, evaluate, integrate, differentiate, and even time-step mathematical expressions.

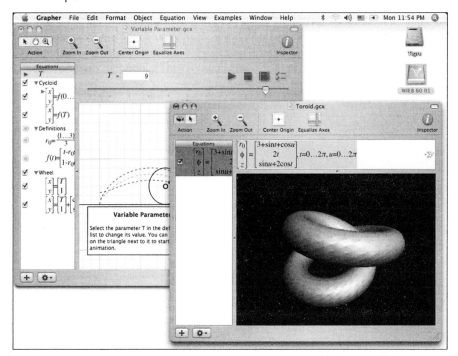

The Java folder

Mac OS X Leopard is the only mass-marketed OS that includes a full Java operating and development environment. The Java Run-Time Environment (JRE) and the Just In Time Compiler (JIT) are integrated with OS X Leopard. For developers, the Java Development Kit (JDK) is included, as well as the J2SE 1.4.X execution environment and the HotSpot Virtual Machine. Some of the components of the Java-language support on OS X Leopard are installed in the `Applications/Utilities/Java` folder.

The Java language was developed by Sun Microsystems, Inc. and was formally announced at the SunWorld conference in 1995. It has been implied that Java was the natural evolution of a sophisticated language called Smalltalk, widely used in Sun workstations. Sun's concept of a universal and standard environment that was platform-independent, Web-enabled, and efficient, was a powerful message. Many companies joined the Java bandwagon, including IBM, Netscape, and Microsoft. At that time, there was a big battle between many software giants, competing for the fastest, most reliable and easiest way to use software development environments. However, Java's JIT (Just In Time) compiler technology paired with the JVM (Java Virtual Machine) presented an interesting alternative to programmers and software development companies. The birth of the Internet and its exponential growth created an opening for a standard environment capable of extending the functionality of Web browsers; Java was just the platform.

Today, Java is widely used. Java programs, called applets, are used in Web browsers and other Internet-enabled systems. Market forces and competition led to divergence between Java implementations from Sun and Microsoft, which engaged in a bitter battle over the Java language and other related technologies. Those divergences have created a confusing arena, which stands in direct opposition to the original, platform-independent environment conceived by Sun, and is the cause of many headaches and Internet browser problems. Java is a powerful, well-designed language; its components enable programmers to create highly sophisticated applications and systems. Many large corporations have big investments in custom applications developed in Java. As with any other major language, Java is evolving and adapting its power to the current technological requirements of our times.

Keychain Access

Keychain Access manages a repository of username/password combinations, authentication certificates, security keys, and secured notes. It is especially useful when accessing secure sites over the Internet or authenticating into secured networks in the workplace. However, Keychain Access is not just a password-management system. It is also a complete Security Certificate Management System. When online, certificates provide a safe way to authenticate systems across networks, protecting your identity and ensuring you are connected to the right system.

With Internet theft a 30-billion-dollar-a-year criminal industry, it is important to protect your private information. It can be dangerous to keep all of your security information stored in one place. If you forgot your access information, it may become a serious problem to gain access to important services such as online banking and credit card sites. Keychain Access is not infallible; there can be problems with accessing keychains — especially when changing your login password. When issues arise, you can use Keychain First Aid to repair most problems. Keychain First Aid can be accessed under Keychain Access on the top menu bar. As a safety measure, it is wise to back up your keychain file regularly on a USB Key or CD and store it in a safe place. The keychain file is usually located in the ~/Library/Keychains folder.

Keychain Access makes accessing corporate network environments an easy task, because it presents the right credentials to the network every time accessing a protected resource is requested (such as accessing MS Exchange servers or MS Windows shares). Another great feature is Secure Notes, which are protected text annotations that may be useful to keep private information about financial records or very personal information in your system.

Migration Assistant

After breaking out that beautiful new Mac, the Migration Assistant will probably be your next step. Apple has provided a simple way to move your information from machine to machine. See Figure 6.29.

FIGURE 6.29

Migration Assistant transfers information from another Mac or partitioned volumes when you connect them with a FireWire cable.

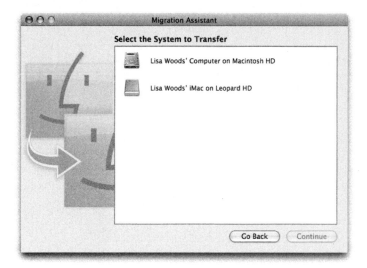

Before beginning, make sure that your older Mac has a FireWire port; once you have the two systems connected, you will be instructed to restart the old Mac and press T while it comes back online. The Migration Assistant transfers your system configuration, applications, and data. Mac OS X Leopard then makes sure that all files related to an application are copied and placed in their proper locations on your new computer. If your files have related settings, those too will be copied and configured. Your network and user settings will be moved as well, carrying with them all security-related settings. However, it is recommended that you migrate only your data and reinstall the applications on your new system.

Network Utility

A powerful collection of diagnostic tools, the Network Utility enables you to check the operation of network resources and how your Mac is using those resources. Mac OS X Leopard includes those tools to help network administrators pinpoint networking problems and diagnose network services. A brief explanation of each tool follows.

Info

Info provides general IP information on each network port installed in your Mac. The information includes the Hardware Address (also known as MAC address), the IP address of the port, the link speed, the status, the manufacturer, and the model. You can also see statistical information for that particular port. FireWire ports are also included.

Netstat

A powerful network analysis tool, Netstat presents network routing information, protocol statistics, multicast protocol information, and all of the socket connections active on your machine. Looking over the reports displayed will help you understand how your Mac is talking to devices and accessing the Internet.

AppleTalk

This utility is very useful when trying to diagnose sporadic connectivity errors or if you experience disappearing network resources while using AppleTalk.

Ping

A command of the IP/ICMP protocol, Ping is used to discover if your Mac can reach a network device by providing its IP address or its Universal Resource Locator (URL). If you are not able to open your default page when calling up Safari, you can test if the site is up by "pinging" it. However, because there are some Internet network attacks based on this command, many networks do not reply to the ping request. Ping is able to measure the distance to the target host timed in milliseconds.

Lookup

To investigate a domain or if an IP address is related to a domain, Lookup finds the information you need. Just type the IP address or the URL of the site you want and a report on the address or URL will appear. This utility is useful in local network environments.

Traceroute

Using the same principles behind Ping, Traceroute maps a list of hops or transitions from network to network as packets (network traffic) that are routed until they reach the destination address. Traceroute is helpful if you need to know where your network traffic is going before reaching its destination. Sometimes it is used to pinpoint faulty routers that lead to delays.

Whois

The Whois utility identifies who owns a particular domain, where the domain is registered, and other information, such as Domain Name Server (DNS) configuration and so on.

Finger

If you want to know information about a user, Finger is your utility. Finger gives you important information about a user in your system or network. Additional information can be added from the directory, including the user's name, address, or phone number.

Port Scan

Port Scan presents a wealth of information about how a network device responds to service requests. If you understand the way networks and protocols work, you may find those reports useful. If your Mac cannot see a service, printer, or device in your network, you can use Port Scan to check if the service (port number) is open and responding to requests. Network Administrators use

Port Scan to test their firewalls and servers for security vulnerabilities. Hackers also use Port Scan to identify network vulnerabilities.

ODBC Administrator

Relational database systems have become increasingly popular and are used by companies to organize information in a comprehensive and consistent way. SQL (Structured Query Language) servers allow applications to perform lookup operations called *queries* and make the resulting information available to the requesting application. SQL systems and other databases (mostly hierarchical systems such as 4D) are hosted in powerful computers that are able to sift through great amounts of data in a very short time. ODBC, short for Open Database Connectivity, is a standard developed by Microsoft, to access any data from any application regardless of the database management system handling the data.

Any application that needs to connect to a SQL server (such as MySQL) can use an ODBC, which is made using DSN (Data Source Name) definitions. See Figure 6.30. Those definitions are address locations such as Volumes and Folders where information resides. Application developers visit the ODBC Administrator often, using Tracing to track errors, and then Connection Pooling to improve performance.

FIGURE 6.30

The ODBC Administrator allows you to set DSN (user and system) connectors, install ODBC drivers for specific platforms, and enable tracing operations to debug applications and faulty connectors.

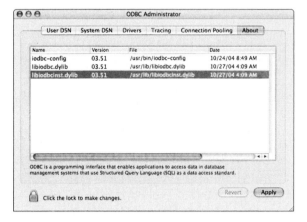

Podcast Capture

A digital media file (or a series of such files), a *podcast* is shared over the Internet using syndication feeds for playback on portable media players such as iPods and computers. Podcasting began spreading like wildfire in late 2004; there is a podcast out there for everyone, history buffs, hip hop fans, techies, and even public broadcasts. For people who are looking to get into podcasting, Podcast Capture is the client to Mac OS X Leopard's server application Podcast Producer. For the slowpokes that haven't joined the podcast bandwagon, Podcast Capture may be just what you've been waiting for. Podcast Capture enables users to create podcasts. Capture audio or video using your Mac's built-in iSight camera, digital video records connected via Firewire, or microphones connected via USB, and upload it to Podcast Producer for encoding and distribution. Podcast Producer is part of OS 10.5 Server.

RAID Utility

New in Mac OS X 10.5 is the RAID Utility. The purpose of the RAID Utility is to configure internal disk arrays via Apple's hardware RAID card. As previously mentioned, Disk Utility is the application one would use to configure software based RAIDs. Xserve RAIDS are configured via their dedicated management software called RAID Admin. RAID Utility will not open unless your Mac has an Apple RAID card installed. Intel-powered Xserves and Mac Pros are the only shipping Macs that have the Apple RAID card as an installable option. The amount of physical drives installed will dictate what RAID configurations can be made, which are RAID 0, 1, and 5. The RAID Utility is seen in figure 6.31.

FIGURE 6.31

The RAID Utility can also be used to migrate data from an existing JBOD volume to a RAID volume.

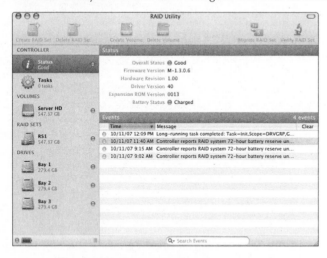

System Profiler

The System Profiler keeps a database of details for each important component in your Mac, divided in three main components: Hardware, Network, and Software. See Figure 6.32.

FIGURE 6.32

The System Profiler can present a complete list of all programs installed on your computer.

Having access to the information related to each component of your machine is useful when troubleshooting sporadic problems and software issues. An experienced technician will check for file versions and drivers installed using the System Profiler. When experiencing problems and requesting assistance from Apple, you can send your system profile via e-mail to help Apple's technicians diagnose the problems on your Mac. The quantity of detail, presented by the System Profiler, can be controlled by selecting View from the System Profiler menu bar. Experiment with the three different views presented. You can also access the System Profiler by clicking the Apple menu (top left corner) and select About This Mac, then clicking the More Info button at the bottom of the pane.

Terminal

For Unix users, the Terminal is a godsend. Many Unix systems are managed by text instructions called commands, an unheard-of operation for Mac users accustomed to the graphical interface. That may have been true for System 9, where the only textual commands were given to troubleshoot hardware problems when a crash occurred, and were the realm of the most dedicated technicians. OS X Leopard introduces tabbed Terminal windows that can be moved around easily by dragging and dropping. A tab can become its own window by pulling the Tab outside of the Terminal window. Similarly, a bunch of individual windows can become one, tabbed window by merging all windows into a single, tabbed window. Users who prefer the Terminal application to the GUI will be happy to hear that the Terminal now allows users to save workspaces. Save window and shell settings as a profile that can be used over and over again. See Figure 6.33.

System and Network Administrators have found that the Terminal is a great tool for completing many tasks. In fact, there are commands that can be performed in Terminal that do not have GUI (Graphical User Interface) equivalents. Another useful feature of the Terminal utility is the execution of shell scripts. Shell scripts are sequences of Unix instructions, contained in a text file that executes one after another. Examples of shell scripts include clearing your cache files, removing suspect system preferences, or performing Internet file clean-up operations. The Terminal is also discussed in Chapter 24.

FIGURE 6.33

The Terminal in tabs.

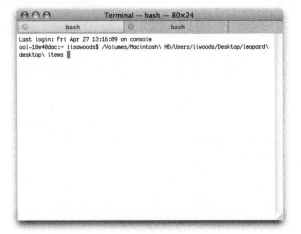

VoiceOver Utility

The VoiceOver Utility, shown in Figure 6.34, could be considered an extension of the Universal Access pane in the System Preferences. This utility literally reads what is on the screen, under the mouse pointer. Apple has always been noted for its devotion to facilitate the usage of their systems to all people with disabilities. The VoiceOver Utility is a worthy addition to this effort. Included in OS X Tiger for the first time, the utility has many options that can be configured to provide the most understandable voice reading what is on-screen.

As with many innovations, it is still somewhat primitive, but the idea behind it is very compelling. One of the nicest features is the ability to add chat text combinations, such as a smiling face (:-) or ;-) or lol, and so on) and have them substituted with sound. This is accomplished by typing the character combination and assigning a substitution string, which is read by the utility and the application on which it is used.

FIGURE 6.34

You can access the VoiceOver Utility from the System Preferences Universal Access pane or from the Utilities folder.

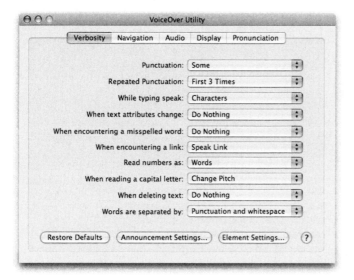

X11

OS X is built on UNIX and, as a result, supports various UNIX tools and environments. Mac users who want to run X Window System applications can use X11 for Mac OS X. Apple supplies a complete X Window System including standard X11 display server software, developer toolkits, client libraries, and utilities. X11 is installed as part of a standard installation of OS X and is an essential tool for programmers that wish to develop X Window applications for OS X. X11 is also discussed in Chapter 23.

Summary

In this chapter, the highlights and benefits of each included application and utility in OS X Leopard were presented. Some users will touch nearly every application and utility in Leopard, while other users will only browse the Web and send and receive e-mail. We've gone over it all. We reviewed the cool new video effects in Address Book; discussed new additions to the Applications folder like Front Row and Time Machine; perused the Stationary templates added to Mail; and examined items in the Utility folder like the new AirPort Disk Utility, the updated AirPort Utility, and Network Utility. Apple has provided an impressive suite of applications with Leopard, continuing its reputation for excellence.

Chapter 7

Working with QuickTime and Included Media Applications

The beginnings of QuickTime were understandably humble, with the first version focusing mainly on providing the ability to watch small, jumpy videos in a "player" window on your Mac.

Sixteen years later QuickTime is now the foundation of the amazing multi-media capabilities of Mac OS X and a widely used cross-platform Internet file format standard. Thanks to QuickTime, you can use your Mac as an audio jukebox with the iTunes application, buy music online with the iTunes Music Store, and take it with you in your iPod. You can store and work with the images from your digital camera with iPhoto. You can take raw digital videos from your camcorder and convert them into edited, polished home movies with iMovie. And you can take photos from iPhoto and movies from iMovie and save them on an impressive, slick-looking DVD, with the iDVD application (and an Apple SuperDrive). Using GarageBand you can record your own music using a line-level input or compose your own songs with the included audio loops. QuickTime is at the center of GarageBand's ability to use MIDI instruments and to record and play back sound.

These five applications — iTunes, iPhoto, iMovie, iDVD, and GarageBand — are part of what Apple markets as the iLife Suite. They are at the center of the digital hub, Steve Jobs' concept of the Macintosh, facilitating work with handheld digital devices; and QuickTime is its core.

QuickTime also makes it possible to watch video DVDs on your Macintosh, play video files over the Internet (even on a Windows PC), or view video streamed from a QuickTime Streaming Server. You can even view or create virtual reality files with QuickTime VR.

In this chapter, you find out about QuickTime technology and how it works in Leopard. We also give you a concise overview of the five iLife applications.

IN THIS CHAPTER

Playing QuickTime movies

Configuring and updating QuickTime

Watching streaming QuickTime media

Making a QuickTime slideshow

Understanding basic QuickTime movie editing

Finding out what's in the iTunes Music Store

Using iTunes

Playing with Front Row

About QuickTime

QuickTime is not only a core technology of Leopard; it is also a file format that is a pervasive Internet standard. QuickTime files, usually called QuickTime movies, can combine sound and video in a single file, or hold only sound or only video. QuickTime files can have file name extensions of .qt, .mov, or .moov, with .mov being the most common.

QuickTime files can include the following content, technologies, and capabilities:

- **Motion pictures:** What you watch on TV or at the movies.
- **Digitized sound recordings:** Music and other sounds that play in CD-quality sound (44.1 kHz, 17-bit stereo).
- **Synthesized music:** Based on the MIDI (Musical Instrument Digital Interface) standard that takes far less disk space to store than digitized sound, yet sounds realistic and plays in CD quality.
- **Surround Sound:** QuickTime 7 includes extensive support for surround sound, so you can get the ultimate in DVD movie experience.
- **Text:** For closed-caption viewing, karaoke singalongs, or text-based searches of movie content.
- **Sprites:** Graphic objects that move independently, like actors moving on a stage with a motion-picture backdrop.
- **MPEG:** Movies that use the common MPEG-1 and new MPEG-4 and H.264 video and audio standards; MPEG-2 playback is an additional component available for a small fee.
- **AVI:** Movies common on Windows; the file type actually covers a broad range of movie codecs (although not all varieties of AVI are currently supported by QuickTime — for example, Intel has not ported the Indeo 2.63 codec to the Mac).
- **Graphics:** QuickTime 7 includes support for Macromedia Flash 5 and JPEG 2000.
- **Panoramas and objects:** Permits viewing objects in 360 degrees using QuickTime VR methods.
- **Timecode information:** Displays elapsed hours, minutes, seconds, and frames at the bottom of a playing movie.
- **Functional information:** Tells QuickTime how other tracks interact.

QuickTime is built into Mac OS X as one of its five graphics and media technologies (the other four being CoreImage, CoreAudio, CoreVideo and OpenGL). QuickTime makes multimedia ubiquitous in Mac OS X. The Finder lets you view QuickTime files as thumbnails without even opening an application. You don't need a special application to watch QuickTime movies. Many applications (such as the Microsoft Office applications) let you copy and paste movies into documents as easily as you copy and paste graphics, and you can play a QuickTime movie wherever you encounter one in a document.

What's in QuickTime Pro?

What do you get when you purchase an upgrade from the basic edition of QuickTime to QuickTime Pro? The upgrade similarly enables the QuickTime plug-in for Web browsers to save movies from the Web, as well as offering the ability to capture movies from an attached video camera with one- click ease.

Moreover, the upgrade brings many improvements to the QuickTime Player application. You can see what functionality is enabled by the upgrade by examining the menus in the QuickTime Player — features that are not available in the standard player are grayed out and have a PRO icon next to their name. Here's some of what QuickTime Player Pro can do that the basic QuickTime Player cannot:

- Create new movies
- Open a sequence of still images as a movie (a slide show)
- Import and export to and from a large number of additional video formats
- Export sound tracks to several additional sound formats
- Apply video and audio compression
- Edit movies by drag-and-drop editing and with Cut, Copy, and Paste commands
- Extract individual tracks from a movie
- Show and set the movie poster frame
- Present a movie centered on a black screen
- Play a movie at full-screen size on a second display while working on a different display (requires dual display setup)
- Play a movie in a back-and-forth loop
- Play only the selected part of a movie
- Adjust the size and orientation of each video track in the movie frame
- Show and set the following additional movie, video track, and sound track information
- Capture video using an attached camera

For more information on the differences between QuickTime 7 and QuickTime Pro, visit Apple's QuickTime Pro Web site at www.apple.com/quicktime/upgrade.

What's in a movie

The motion pictures, sound, and other types of time-based data in a QuickTime movie file exist in separate tracks. A simple movie may consist of one video track and one sound track. A more complex movie may have several video tracks, several audio tracks, and closed-caption text tracks for text subtitles. Each video track can be designed for playback with a specified number of available colors (for example, 256 colors, thousands of colors, or millions of colors), each audio track can provide dialog in a different language (English, Spanish, Japanese, and so on), and each closed-caption text track can provide subtitles in a different language.

243

If a QuickTime movie contains MIDI-synthesized music, sprites, or a QuickTime VR scene or object, each item is in a separate track. QuickTime takes care of synchronizing all tracks so that they play at the proper time.

Getting QuickTime software

You get the basic QuickTime software as a part of the standard installation of Mac OS X. You can upgrade to QuickTime Pro, unleashing many additional editing features, for $29.95 by phone (1-888-295-0648) or from Apple's QuickTime site on the Web (www.apple.com/quicktime/). In some cases, you can get a free upgrade to QuickTime Pro when you purchase a retail version of the Mac OS or various software packages, such as Final Cut Pro.

 You can enter your QuickTime Pro registration information in the Registration sheet by choosing the QuickTime System Preferences and clicking the Registration button.

Playing QuickTime Movies

QuickTime makes it possible to play movies in all kinds of applications, and it establishes standard methods for controlling playback in all applications. You can use a standard QuickTime movie controller and other standard methods for controlling playback when the controller is absent. The QuickTime Player application included with QuickTime has additional features used to play movies. If you play movies that contain MIDI-synthesized music, you may be able to affect how they sound by setting some options in the QuickTime System preference pane.

Using the QuickTime movie controller

You usually control playback of a QuickTime movie in an application other than QuickTime Player with a standard collection of buttons and sliders along the bottom edge of the movie. With this controller, you can play, stop, browse, or step through the movie. If the movie has a soundtrack, you can use the controller to adjust the sound level. The controller also gauges where the current scene is in relation to the beginning and end of the movie. By pressing certain keys while operating the controller, you can turn the sound on and off, copy and paste parts of the movie, play in reverse, change the playback rate, and more. Figure 7.1 illustrates the functions of a standard QuickTime movie controller for a music file. (Some applications have variants of the standard controller and may put the controller in a palette that floats above the document window.)

Playing and pausing

To start a movie playing, click the Play button. This button has a right-pointing triangle like the play button on a tape recorder or VCR. While a movie is playing, this button becomes a pause button (with two vertical lines on it); press it a second time to pause.

FIGURE 7.1

Use controls below a movie file to play, pause, browse, or step through it and adjust its sound volume.

Duration: 01'38
Dimensions: 320 x 135

Stepping forward and backward

The two arrow buttons to the right of the play bar step backward and forward at the rate of one frame per click. The step buttons have different effects on movies that don't have frames. For example, in a movie that has only sound or music tracks, each click of a step button skips ahead or back a quarter of a second.

Going to another part of the movie

The gray play bar in the middle of the movie controller shows the position of the currently playing frame relative to the beginning and end of the movie. To go to a different place in the movie, you can drag the playhead in the play bar or simply click the play bar (at or near the location of the movie segment that you want to see).

You can also go immediately to the beginning or end of the movie. Option+click the backward-step button to go to the beginning of a movie. Option+click the forward-step button to go to the end of a movie.

Adjusting the sound

To adjust the sound level, use the button labeled with the speaker. Click and hold down this button to pop up a slider (shown in Figure 7.1) that you can use to raise or lower the sound level. You can turn the sound off and on by Option+clicking the speaker button. You can set the sound level to up to three times louder than its normal maximum by holding down the Shift key while adjusting the level with the slider. If the speaker button is absent, the movie has no sound.

QuickTime Controller Shortcuts

The QuickTime movie controller responds to all kinds of keyboard shortcuts. Pressing Return or the Spacebar alternately starts and pauses play forward. You can press ⌘+→ (right arrow) to play forward and ⌘+← (left arrow) to play backward. Press → to step forward and ← to step backward. To raise or lower the sound level, press ↑ (up arrow) or ↓ (down arrow). Shift+↑ raises the sound level beyond its normal maximum.

Changing playback direction and speed

To play the movie backward, ⌘+click the backward-step button. In some applications, you can Control+click either step button to reveal a jog shuttle that controls the direction and playback rate. Dragging the jog shuttle to the right gradually increases the forward playback rate from below normal to twice normal speed. Dragging the jog shuttle to the left has the same effect on playback speed, but makes the movie play backward.

Choosing a chapter

A text area appears to the left of the step buttons in the movie controller for some movies. This chapter list button lets you go to predetermined points in the movie, in the same way that index tabs let you turn to sections of a binder. Pressing the chapter list button pops up a menu of chapter titles, and choosing a chapter title takes you quickly to the corresponding part of the movie. If the chapter list button is absent, either the movie window is too small to show the chapter list or the movie has no defined chapters.

Playing movies without controllers

Applications may display movies without controllers. In this case, a badge in the lower left corner of the movie distinguishes it from a still graphic. To play a movie that has a badge and no controller, double-click the movie. If you press Shift while double-clicking the movie, it plays backward. Clicking a playing movie stops it. You can also display a standard movie controller by clicking the badge. Figure 7.2 shows a QuickTime movie with a badge.

FIGURE 7.2

A badge identifies a movie without a controller, here seen in a Microsoft Word document.

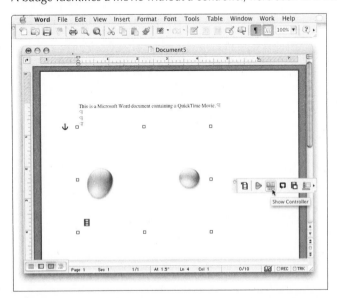

 Badge is a term for a distinguishing mark superimposed on an icon or image to indicate that it isn't a standard icon or image — such as the little arrow to indicate an alias icon.

Viewing with QuickTime Player

Although you don't need a special application to view QuickTime movies, QuickTime includes one called QuickTime Player. With the QuickTime Player menu commands, you have more control over playing a movie than in some other applications. In some cases, however, you have less control over a movie. That's because the QuickTime Player application sports a sleek interface that has traded some features to look more like a consumer device. Some of the controls are more like those found on a VCR.

The controls of QuickTime Player are enhanced when you upgrade to QuickTime Pro. The following descriptions of QuickTime Player commands indicate the QuickTime Player versions in which the described command is available.

Using QuickTime Player controls

When you open a movie in the QuickTime Player application, you find a number of slight differences from the QuickTime controls found in other applications, as shown in Figure 7.3.

FIGURE 7.3

QuickTime Player has controls for movie playback seen on most DVD players.

Most of the differences in QuickTime Player controls are cosmetic. The play bar and playhead are located above the play/pause and step controls, which are larger in QuickTime Player than in the QuickTime controller of other applications. QuickTime Player has separate controls for going to the start or end of the movie, which are discussed later in this chapter. QuickTime Player also displays some extra information, including the elapsed time display to the left of the play bar and the audio equalizer display to the left of the play bar. A few features are missing. For example, you can't ⌘+click the step buttons to open a shuttle jog control.

In addition to the clearly visible volume control, QuickTime Player has some additional audio controls that don't appear in the main player window. To see the advanced audio video controls — Balance, Bass, Treble, Jog Shuttle, and Playback Speed — choose Window ⇨ Show A/V Controls or press ⌘+K. See Figure 7.4. The new feature, Jog Shuttle, acts like a jog dial on a professional video editing deck. You can "scrub" through the video by sliding the slider left and right. The farther you move the slider to the right or left, the faster the video plays, allowing you to quickly close in on the exact second of the clip you want.

 You can change the slider settings quickly by clicking in the slider track instead of dragging the slider. For example, to set full volume, click at the right end of the slider track. To raise the sound level beyond its normal maximum, press Shift+↑.

FIGURE 7.4

QuickTime Player has hidden audio controls.

Using QuickTime Player Favorites

QuickTime Player can keep track of your favorite movies to make playing them more convenient. You designate which movies are your Favorites, and then you can play one by choosing it from a menu or clicking an item in a list window.

To see a list of your favorite movies in a window choose Window ⇨ Favorites ⇨ Show Favorites. The Favorites window is empty until you add movies as Favorites. To make a movie a Favorite, drag its movie file from the Finder to the Favorites window. You can drag several movie files at the same time to make Favorites of them all. You can make a Favorite of a movie that's open in QuickTime Player by bringing the movie to the front and choosing Window ⇨ Favorites ⇨ Add Movie As Favorite or by pressing ⌘+D.

To play a favorite movie, double-click it in the Favorites window or choose it from the Favorites submenu.

You can rearrange the Favorites window by dragging icons to different positions in the window. You can remove a Favorite by selecting an item and then pressing the delete key; you'll be prompted for confirmation before the favorite is actually deleted.

Using controls within movies

For the most part, you'll probably confine your mouse clicks to the QuickTime Player controls. Occasionally, you may find it useful to actually click inside the movie window. For example, QuickTime can display Macromedia Flash documents, which may include buttons and links that can be clicked in the movie window. If you're viewing an image, especially one that's available via a streaming QuickTime connection over the Internet, you may be able to click a button or link in the QuickTime Player movie window.

Changing the QuickTime Player window size

Unlike many other applications that can show QuickTime movies, the QuickTime Player application displays QuickTime movies in windows with resize controls. If you resize a movie window, QuickTime resizes the movie to fill the window. QuickTime normally forces movie windows to maintain their original proportions to ensure optimal viewing. To resize without this constraint, press Shift while dragging the resize control.

A movie looks best at an even multiple of its original size, such as half size or double size. QuickTime Player constrains a movie to an optimal multiple of its original size if you press Option while dragging the movie window's resize control. To quickly change a window to the nearest even multiple of its original size, Option+click its resize control.

In addition to dragging a movie window's size box, you can use QuickTime Player menu commands to resize it. The basic edition of QuickTime Player has Half Size, Double Size, and Normal Size commands.

Presenting a movie

Instead of displaying a movie in a window, you can present it centered on a completely black screen. In QuickTime Player Pro, choose View ➪ Present Movie (⌘+Shift+F). (The Present Movie command is not available in the basic edition of QuickTime Player, though you can use Full Screen Mode without Pro in version 7.2.)

The Present Movie command displays a dialog box in which you can set the movie size and specify whether you want to play the movie normally or in slide show fashion (one frame at a time, for example). If your computer has more than one display, this dialog box lets you select the display on which you want the movie presented. Setting a movie's presentation size in this dialog box to Double or Full Screen usually produces better results than resizing the movie manually before presenting it.

To stop a movie presentation, click the mouse button. With a slide show presentation, clicking the mouse button advances to the next movie frame; double-clicking goes back one frame. Pressing Esc or ⌘+. (period) stops a slide show presentation.

Searching for a text track

While viewing a movie that contains a text track, you can search for specific text in the movie. In QuickTime Player Pro, choose Edit ➪ Find (⌘+F). If there are no text tracks, Find is disabled (grayed-out). (Text searching is not available in the basic edition of QuickTime Player.)

The Find command displays a dialog box in which you search forward or backward to find text. If QuickTime Player finds the text you're looking for, it immediately shows the corresponding part of the movie and highlights the found text. You can search for another occurrence of the same text by choosing Find Again from the Edit menu.

Choosing a language

QuickTime movies can have sound tracks in several languages. To select the language you want to hear, choose View ⇨ Choose Language. QuickTime Player displays a dialog box that lists the available languages. If the Choose Language command is disabled (grayed out), the movie doesn't have sound tracks in multiple languages.

Playing continuously (looping)

You can set QuickTime Player Pro to play a QuickTime movie in a continuous loop, either always playing forward or playing alternately forward and backward. Choose Loop or Loop Back and Forth from the Movie menu. (These commands are available in the basic edition of QuickTime Player.)

Selecting part of a movie and playing it

In QuickTime Player Pro, you can select part of a movie and then play only the selected part. (You can't select part of a movie in the basic edition of QuickTime Player.)

To select part of a movie while playing that part, follow these steps:

1. **Drag both of the selection triangles to the far-left edge of the play bar.**
2. **Move the playhead to the place in the movie where you want to begin selecting.**
3. **Shift+click the Play button to start the movie and begin selecting the movie segment.**
4. **Release the Shift key to end the selection and stop playing.** The selected part of the movie appears gray in the play bar.

To select part of a movie without playing it, follow these steps:

1. **Drag the left selection triangle to the first frame you want to select.**
2. **Drag the right selection triangle to the last frame you want to select.**
3. **Adjust the selection by doing either of the following:**

   - Drag a selection triangle.
   - Click a selection triangle; then use the left (←) and right (→) arrow keys to adjust the selection frame by frame.

To play the selected part of a movie, follow these steps:

1. **Choose View ⇨ Play Selection Only (⌘+T).**
2. **Click the Play button.** When a check mark is next to Play Selection Only in the Movie menu, all the movie controls and QuickTime Player commands apply only to the selected part. For example, the Loop command causes only the selected part to play continuously, and the first-frame and last-frame buttons go to the beginning and end of the selection.

To cancel a selection, drag both selection arrows to the far left side of the play bar.

Playing every frame

In QuickTime Player Pro, you can prevent QuickTime from dropping any video frames to keep the video and audio tracks synchronized. If you want to see every frame, even if it means playing the movie more slowly and without sound, choose View ➪ Play All Frames. (The Play All Frames command is not available in the basic edition of QuickTime Player and is disabled if there is no video track.)

Playing all movies

You can have QuickTime Player Pro play all movies that are currently open by choosing View ➪ Play All Movies. (This command is not available in the basic edition of QuickTime Player.)

Saving QuickTime Movies from a Web Browser

When you view a QuickTime movie in a Web browser window, the movie is downloaded from the Internet but is not saved permanently on your hard drive. You may be able to save the movie from the Web browser as a movie file on your hard drive so that you can watch the movie again in QuickTime Player without downloading it again. You can save a QuickTime movie from a Web browser only if you have QuickTime Pro and only if the author of the movie allows saving the movie.

To save a QuickTime movie that's displayed in a Web browser, Control+click the movie and choose Save As QuickTime Movie from the contextual menu that appears. You can also make the contextual menu appear by clicking a movie in the browser window and holding the mouse button down for a few seconds. (The Save As QuickTime Movie choice does not appear in the contextual menu if you do not have QuickTime Pro or if the author of the movie does not allow saving the movie.)

Configuring and Updating QuickTime

QuickTime is highly configurable to suit your situation and use. This section covers some of the settings you can adjust in QuickTime.

QuickTime System Preferences

The Registration panel is the first panel in the QuickTime System Preferences, which is shown selected in Figure 7.5. Use this panel to enter your registration code to upgrade to the QuickTime Pro feature set.

FIGURE 7.5

The QuickTime pane showing the registration tab

In the Browser panel, the settings allow you to set the way QuickTime functions with your Web browser. You can use the check boxes to choose whether or not to play a movie automatically, save a movie in the Web browser's disk cache, change the size of the disk cache, and empty the disk cache.

Click the Update panel to view the information shown in Figure 7.6.

FIGURE 7.6

Use the Update panel to find and install new QuickTime components and applications.

If you click the Update Now button on the Update panel, QuickTime checks for new codecs and other QuickTime software. This QuickTime update feature is separate from the Software Update in System Preferences for OS X.

The Streaming panel lets you set your system's connection speed with the pop-up menu so that QuickTime knows how fast to request data and at what rate to display the audio or video so as to avoid creating gaps while you wait for the next part of the data to download. For most people the Automatic setting is just fine, as is shown in Figure 7.7. If you have a fast connection, you may want to click the Instant-On check box to shorten the wait at the beginning. Drag the slider below the Instant-On check box to change the delay before QuickTime begins playback.

FIGURE 7.7

Use the Streaming panel to change the streaming speed and enable instant-on playback.

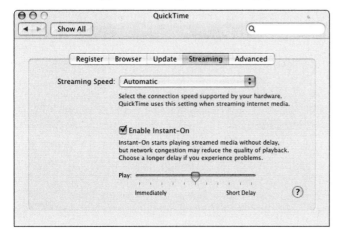

The Advanced panel allows you to set the default synthesizer if you have any alternates installed. You can also change the transport settings, but most applications require the automatic setting. Enabling Kiosk mode sets QuickTime into a more limited mode, which is useful when setting up a public computer.

If you click the MIME Settings button you see the MIME sheet shown in Figure 7.8. Here you can decide what media types the QuickTime browser plug-in will handle. Most people will want to stick with the default selections, which you can return to by clicking the Use Defaults button.

The Media Keys button allows you to add and configure any media keys to enable the playback of encrypted content that you have purchased.

FIGURE 7.8

Clicking the MIME Settings button displays a sheet that allows you to customize your MIME settings and change which types of media the QuickTime software will play back.

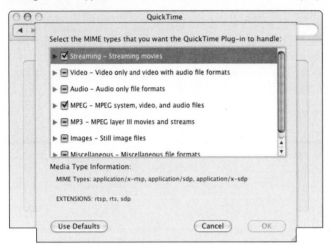

QuickTime Player Preferences

With QuickTime open, choose QuickTime Player ⇨ Preferences. Here you can alter the settings pertaining to the QuickTime Player for movies, sound, showing Apple's Hot Picks movie, and for pausing a movie when logged out in Fast User Switching. Again, the default settings will be best for most people. If you have a broadband connection, you may want to check the Use high quality video setting when available check box. In addition, you can configure the number of displayed recent items at the bottom of the dialog box.

Using the Full Screen Preferences (new to QuickTime 7.2), you can choose how you want the movies to play when in full-screen mode. In addition, you can choose the background color, and whether to show the full-screen controls or have a floating controller box. Figure 7.9 shows General Preferences, while Figure 7.10 shows the new Full Screen Preferences.

FIGURE 7.9

Set the behavior of the QuickTime Player application in Player Preferences.

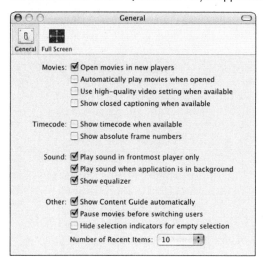

FIGURE 7.10

Additional options are available in Full Screen Preferences.

Watching Streaming QuickTime Media

QuickTime 4.0 introduced a new technology to the world of QuickTime — *streaming media*. QuickTime 7, the version included with Mac OS X 10.4 and above, has significantly improved the performance of streaming media. With streaming media, QuickTime movie files (whether they contain video, audio, text, or other elements) are sent over the Internet a piece at a time. Those pieces are reassembled in QuickTime Player and played back almost as quickly as the data arrives over the Internet. In this way, movies can be viewed (or listened to) more quickly over the Internet. Likewise, live events can be displayed in real time over the Web.

> **TIP** For optimum streaming, QuickTime Player consults the settings on the Streaming tab in your QuickTime System Preferences. If you are having any trouble viewing movies on the Web, you may want to change the default Automatic settings to match the speed of your connection so that you get better playback from streaming movies.

With some streaming media movies, you can pause, play, and move back and forth within the movie file by using the play bar or the forward and reverse controls. In others, especially live events, you won't have as much control — pausing and playing again takes you to the current moment in the live event instead of picking up where you left off.

QuickTime streaming media uses an Internet protocol known as RTP (real-time transport protocol). RTP is similar to the familiar HTTP protocol used for Web pages, but RTP is designed specifically for the special requirements of streaming media. With RTP, movies are not downloaded to your computer. Instead, a continuous data stream is sent to your computer, and QuickTime plays it immediately.

QuickTime movies can also be sent to your computer via the HTTP or FTP protocols. With HTTP or FTP, the entire movie is downloaded to your computer. (If you don't have QuickTime Pro, the movie may be downloaded to a temporary file that is deleted automatically.) You don't necessarily have to wait for the entire movie to finish downloading before it begins playing. Many QuickTime movies use a technology called *fast start* or *progressive download*. In practice, fast-start movies may seem like streaming video as the header information is compressed in order to ensure a near-instant start. In fact, QuickTime begins playing the first part of the movie while it continues to download the remainder.

Interacting with QuickTime VR Images

You can do more with QuickTime than play linear movies. Apple's QuickTime VR software lets you explore places as if you were really there and interact with objects in the scene. When you view a QuickTime VR panorama of a place, you can look up, look down, turn around, zoom in to see detail, and zoom out for a broader view. When you view a QuickTime VR object, you can manipulate it to see a different view of it. As you explore a panorama, you can move from it into a neighboring panorama or to an object in it. For example, you could move from one room to another room and then examine an object there.

You can interact with a QuickTime VR panorama or object from any application in which you can view a linear QuickTime movie. You can use QuickTime Player, a Web browser, TextEdit, AppleWorks, or any other application that can play QuickTime movies.

When you view a QuickTime VR panorama or object, a QuickTime VR controller sometimes appears at the bottom of the window. It's in the same place as the controller for a regular QuickTime movie (especially those viewed with the conventional controller in applications like AppleWorks). As with regular QuickTime movies, the QuickTime VR controller in QuickTime Player looks different than the VR controller in other applications. The cosmetic differences don't affect the functions of the controller buttons.

Actually, you don't use the QuickTime VR controller as the primary means of interacting with a QuickTime VR image. You simply drag the mouse pointer to explore a QuickTime VR panorama or investigate a QuickTime VR object. The remainder of this section describes how to use the mouse pointer and the VR controller to interact with a QuickTime VR image.

Exploring VR panoramas

To look around a QuickTime VR panorama, you click the picture and drag left, right, up, or down. The picture moves in the direction that you drag, and the pointer changes shape to indicate the direction of movement. Figure 7.11 shows a QuickTime VR panorama being moved to the left.

FIGURE 7.11

When you pan a QuickTime VR panorama, the pointer indicates the direction of movement.

Investigating VR objects

To manipulate a QuickTime VR object, you drag it left, right, up, or down. As you drag, the object, or some part of it, moves. For example, it may turn around so that you can see all sides of it, or it may open and close. The author of the VR picture determines the effect.

When viewing a QuickTime VR object, you can also place the pointer near an inside edge of the VR window and press the mouse button to move the object continuously. Figure 7.12 shows two views of a QuickTime VR object.

FIGURE 7.12

Drag a QuickTime VR object in any direction to see another view of the object.

Images courtesy of John Greenleigh/Flipside Studios.

Revealing the VR controller

When you view a QuickTime VR image in a Web browser window, the VR controller may not appear at the bottom of the image. If you have QuickTime Pro, you can view the VR image with a VR controller by saving the VR image as a QuickTime movie file on your hard drive and opening the movie file in QuickTime Player. The method for saving a VR image is the same as the method described earlier for saving a regular QuickTime movie. To recap: Control+click the movie or click the movie and hold the mouse button until the contextual menu appears, and choose Save As QuickTime Movie from the contextual menu. (The Save As QuickTime Movie choice does not appear in the contextual menu if you do not have QuickTime Pro, or the author of the VR image does not allow saving it.)

Zooming in and out

While viewing a QuickTime VR panorama or object, you can zoom in or out:

- **To zoom in:** Click the VR controller button that looks like a plus sign or press the Control key.

- **To zoom out:** Click the button that looks like a minus sign or press the Shift key.

As you zoom in on a VR object, it eventually becomes too large to see all at once in the QuickTime VR window. You may be able to view another part of a zoomed-in VR object by clicking the controller button labeled with a four-way arrow and then dragging the object or by pressing Option while dragging. Either way, the object holds its pose as it moves around in the window. To resume normal operation, click the button again or release the Option key. (You don't need to use the four-way drag button or the Option key with a VR panorama, which you can pan just by dragging across it.)

Interacting with hot spots

A QuickTime VR panorama or object can contain hot spots. You click these areas of the picture to cause some action to occur. Typically, the action involves going to another panorama or object. A hot spot can trigger another kind of action, such as displaying text in the empty area of the VR controller or taking you to a Web page.

Hot spots are normally unmarked. One way to find them is to move the pointer around the panorama or object. When the pointer is over a hot spot, the pointer's shape changes. A variety of different pointer shapes may indicate a hot spot. One common shape is a large white arrow pointing up.

You can also have QuickTime VR show the hot spots in the picture. To highlight the hot spots with shaded rectangles, click the VR controller button labeled with an up arrow and question mark. If you double-click this button, it stays down and you can see all hot spots as you drag the pointer to move the picture. Figure 7.13 is an example of an outlined hot spot in a QuickTime VR panorama.

FIGURE 7.13

Hot spots are revealed in a QuickTime VR panorama (the highlighted area).

If clicking a hot spot takes you to another panorama or object, you can go back to your previous location by clicking the back button, which is labeled with a left arrow in the VR controller. If you've progressed through several hot spots, you can retrace your steps by clicking the back button repeatedly.

Making a QuickTime Slide Show

Telling a story or delivering a message through a sequence of pictures—as they say, a picture is worth a thousand words—is a very common use of computers. Major applications, such as Apple's Keynote or Microsoft's PowerPoint, are devoted to this task. Presenting slide shows from images on your disks is also a major feature of such applications as GraphicConverter and iView Multimedia.

QuickTime allows you to create slide shows from images on your disk, as well. However, QuickTime combines them into a platform-independent file that you can view on any computer with QuickTime support.

Of course, going to the effort of importing multiple image files, placing and orienting them just so, and then saving the result as a QuickTime file in PowerPoint seems like an awful lot of effort. QuickTime Pro makes the task a whole lot easier, as follows:

1. **Collect the image files you want in your slide show in a single folder.**

2. **Give them a common name followed by a sequential number.**

3. **In QuickTime Player, choose File ⇨ Open Image Sequence and select the first file in your sequence of pictures.**

4. **Choose a Frame rate in the Image Sequence Settings dialog box that appears.** The default of 15 frames per second is useful for animations, but you will probably want something a bit slower for a slide show.

QuickTime Player Pro then creates a movie, showing each picture in sequence. If you want to save this QuickTime movie, choose File ⇨ Save As and then name the movie in the Save dialog box that appears. The default radio button selection, Save normally (allowing dependencies), requires you to transport the folder of images along with the QuickTime movie. To add audio to your slideshow, choose Show Movie Properties from the Window menu and select the audio track you'd like. To add the extracted track to your movie, return to your slideshow and select it (or the portion of it you want your pasted media to fit into) and choose Edit ⇨ Add to Movie.

> **TIP** If the audio sequence is longer than your slide show, its play is sped up to fit the length of your show; conversely, if it is shorter than your slide show, the clip is slowed down to fit the slide show's length. You should choose a clip as close in length to that of your slide show as possible. You can find the length required by choosing View ⇨ Get Movie Properties (⌘+J) and choosing Time from the right-hand pop-up menu.

Basic QuickTime Movie Editing

As is usually the case if you want to use QuickTime for much more than a viewer, editing your QuickTime movies and tracks requires an update to QuickTime Pro. One of the first changes you may notice if you've upgraded to QuickTime Pro is that the play bar has two markers at the bottom. You use these to mark the beginning and end of a selection. Another change is that the Edit menu has added a slew of extra options, including the ability to Delete Tracks, Extract Tracks, and more. The Movie menu has added a Present Movie option so that you can have your QuickTime movie take over the whole screen.

The selection markers and additional Edit menu options give you the tools to do a significant amount of editing—either to create a new movie or to modify an existing movie. With these options you can add, eliminate, and rearrange scenes and then save the movie under the same or a new name.

Fine-tuning a selection

Of course, you can drag the selection triangles to the point where you want them. However, this sort of gross movement tends to make positioning on a particular frame of your movie somewhat difficult. Use the drag technique to get the triangle into the general vicinity of the frame; then click a selection triangle and press the left or right arrow keys to move the selection triangle one frame in that direction, or hold down the appropriate arrow key to move the selection triangle in that direction in slow motion.

Working with selections

After you've made your selection, you can play just the selection by choosing View ⇨ Play Selection Only (⌘+T). You can even drag the picture from the movie screen to the Desktop or a Finder window to create a movie clipping—just double-click it to view the clip.

You can cut, copy, or clear the contents of a selection using the corresponding Edit menu commands, or trim everything but the selection from the movie by choosing Edit ⇨ Trim.

To paste a cut or copied selection in another location within your movie (or even in a different movie), position the playhead where you want the insertion to occur and choose Edit ⇨ Paste (⌘+V). The pasted information appears, and the selection markers show you where it begins and ends.

TIP A quick way to add a title or silent-movie-style text block is to paste text in at the current frame. This inserts a two-second block of white text against a black background— QuickTime makes use of any font and style information that was with the text on the Clipboard. This also works to insert still pictures. You can even drag text files directly to the QuickTime Player screen to get the two-second inserts.

These editing techniques work with all editable QuickTime movies—even sound files such as AIFF. AIFF is the standard file format for CD audio and is short for Audio Interchange File Format. It is an uncompressed format, which means that AIFF files are generally much larger than other formats such as MP3, AAC, or Apple Lossless.

NOTE Some media types, such as MPEG-1 files, which are playable in QuickTime Player, are not editable with these tools. If the movie is in one of these noneditable formats, all the Edit menu choices are disabled.

Adding a Sound Track to Your Movie

By using QuickTime Player Pro's editing capabilities, you can add an audio (sound) track to your movie before saving it. Import the audio file to a new movie and copy the desired portion (or all of it) to the Clipboard. Now, select the slide show movie and choose Edit ⇨ Add Scaled.

Adding QuickTime Text Tracks

QuickTime lets you include multiple tracks in a single movie. One of these track types is the *text track*. Text can be used for credits, subtitles, title screens, or teleprompter text.

You can create text tracks very easily in any word-processor or editor that allows you to save as plain text (sometimes called *ASCII* text). If you use TextEdit, be sure to choose Format ⇨ Make Plain Text (⌘+Shift+T). To create a text track, follow these steps:

1. **Create and save your plain text file.**

2. **Copy the text to the Clipboard.**

3. **In QuickTime Player Pro, position the playhead where you want the track to begin.**

4. **Choose Edit ⇨ Add (⌘+Option+V) to position the text file at that point, overlaying the image.** The default duration for a text track inserted in this manner is two seconds. If you want a different duration, make a selection covering the duration and choose Edit ⇨ Add to selection and Scale (⌘+Option+Shift+V). The text track is added with each paragraph of your text file covering its own sequence of frames.

Applying QuickTime Effects

Concealed in the Export dialog box (File ⇨ Export, or ⌘+E), QuickTime Pro includes a number of *filters* (special effects) that you can apply to your movie. You find these filters by first setting the Export dialog box's Export pop-up menu to Movie to QuickTime Movie, next clicking the Options button in the Export dialog box, and then clicking the Filter button in the Movie Settings dialog box that appears.

QuickTime Pro even enables you to save filter settings for later use via the Save and Load buttons in the Choose Video Filter dialog box. Unfortunately, you can apply only one filter to a movie on export. Therefore, if you want to accumulate effects, you need to export with one effect, load that movie, apply another effect when exporting it, and so on — cumbersome, but possible.

The available filters (14 of them) let you adjust brightness, color, and contrast, apply blurs or sharpen, and add film noise (simulating scratches and dust) or a lens flare (similar to what happens when you have the sun in front of the lens).

Using iTunes

The free iTunes application enables you to burn CDs, which makes purchasing third-party software tools less necessary if all you want to burn are audio CDs. In addition to *ripping* (recording audio CDs and encoding them in AAC, Apple Lossless, MP3, AIFF, or WAV format) audio from CDs, iTunes also writes audio CDs from music collections called *playlists,* by using a compatible CD-RW drive. In addition, you can download music files to a variety of music players, such as the Rio or iPod, and play streaming audio from a huge assortment of Internet radio stations. One of the best legal ways to obtain music is to purchase songs in AAC (advanced audio coding) format online from the iTunes Music Store.

Playing MP3 and CD audio with iTunes

The iTunes window, as shown in Figure 7.14, is divided into panes. The tall, slender pane on the left of the window is the *Source* pane. In the Source pane, you determine from where you select your audio. You can make audio selections from your iTunes Library, Internet radio, a mounted audio CD, a connected MP3 player, or a playlist.

Playing songs

To play songs, you can do the following:

- Double-click the song.
- Select the song and press Return or Enter.
- Select the song and click the Play button.

You can also move between adjacent songs by using one of the following methods:

- Press ⌘+← (previous song) and ⌘+→ (next song).
- Choose Controls ➪ Previous Song or Controls ➪ Next Song.

When a song is playing, iTunes displays your choice of a timeline or equalizer. The timeline with playhead is shown in Figure 7.15. You can position or reposition playing to any point in a song by dragging the playhead (the diamond) to the desired location in the timeline. To view the equalizer display in this area, all you need to do is click the little arrowhead to which the arrow pointer is pointing in the figure.

In Figure 7.15, you see the song title shown at the top of the progress area. Click this line of text to switch between song title, artist, and album name. Over time, this information automatically cycles among the three possibilities.

NOTE   iTunes takes title, artist, and album information from what are called ID3 tags — textual information stored within an MP3 file. A number of other fields are also described by ID3 tags, which are discussed later in this chapter.

FIGURE 7.14

The basic iTunes interface

Library   Volume control   Search field

Play controls   Information pane   View control

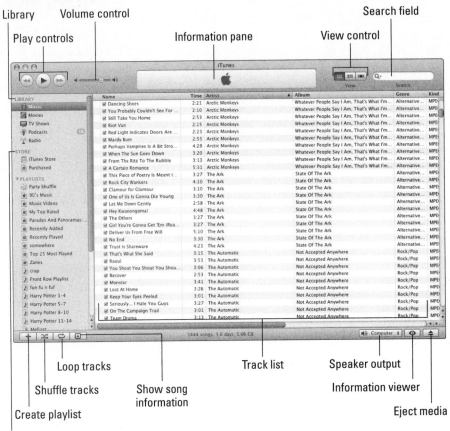

Loop tracks   Track list   Speaker output

Shuffle tracks   Information viewer

Create playlist   Show song   Eject media
                   information

iTunes store
and purchased
music list

FIGURE 7.15

The iTunes progress bar lets you position the playhead anywhere within a song if you only want to listen to a part of the tune, or if you want to replay a passage.

Below the title-artist-album line is the timeline. To the left of the timeline you'll see the elapsed time, and on the right you can click on the time display to switch the display between Total Time and Remaining Time.

The equalizer display gives you a "light show" depicting what is happening on the two output channels (left and right speakers). If you hear an imbalance in the sound, you can utilize it to see if your problem is the result of one of your speakers or if the recording is unbalanced. You can adjust the equalization with the Equalizer window. Clicking the Equalizer button shows the Equalizer window shown in Figure 7.16. Clicking the pop-up menu shows a wide range of preset equalization options.

FIGURE 7.16

The iTunes Equalizer window adjusts balance of audio ranges.

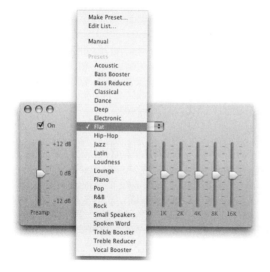

TIP Clicking the iTunes window zoom button (+) reduces the window to just the controls at the top left and the progress area. Further, the buttons are now positioned vertically at the left edge of the window with close (X) on top, minimize to Dock (–) in the middle, and zoom (+) on the bottom. Clicking zoom again pops you back to the original size, which is an easy way to keep the window around in an unobtrusive manner.

Managing your iTunes Library

The iTunes Library is the collection of all the songs you've played in iTunes (less those you've deleted from the iTunes Library), plus all those you've added using File ⇨ Add to iTunes Library or by using the Import button when a CD is selected. The iTunes feature adds the song to your iTunes Library whether you've double-clicked an MP3 file on your Desktop or in a Finder window or imported it from an audio CD. If you look in your home folder's Documents folder, you see an iTunes folder. This folder contains a database file, which keeps information on the 32,000 songs that iTunes can handle. This iTunes folder also contains an iTunes Music folder, and inside it are more folders that contain the songs in your iTunes Library. The folders inside the iTunes Music folder are named for performers, and each performer's folder contains folders with the names of album titles.

If you download MP3 files from the Internet, you can add them to your iTunes Library by performing the following steps:

1. **Choose File ➪ Add to Library.**
2. **Locate the item (folder or file) you want to add.**
3. **Click Choose.**

> **NOTE**   You can change the format iTunes uses to encode your music in the iTunes ➪ Preferences menu in the Importing pane. As mentioned previously, you can choose from several formats including AAC, MP3, AIFF, and Apple Lossless.

Listening to Internet radio

iTunes supports an ever-changing and growing list of Internet radio stations, divided into categories. Just click the disclosure triangle next to the genre of interest and then select the radio station of interest. You need to have an active Internet connection first because iTunes doesn't initiate one for you. Of course, if you have an always-on broadband connection, such as a T1, DSL, or cable modem connection, remembering to make sure you have an Internet connection isn't a problem. (Chapter 10 explains how to connect to the Internet.)

> **TIP**   Select stations where the bit rate field is lower than your connection speed. For example, if your modem cannot actually get a 56K connection, you should avoid 56 Kbps streams. If you have a decent broadband connection (cable or DSL) you should be fine with most stations, however. Who doesn't have a broadband connection these days though?

Downloading to digital MP3 players

Digital MP3 players are well supported by iTunes. As long as your MP3 player is on the list of supported devices (see Apple's iTunes Web page because this list changes), you can hook it up by using the supplied USB cable and have it show up in your source list. Select your MP3 player in the source list and see its contents, from which you can delete or add items. Adding items to your MP3 player is very simple: Just select the songs you want to add from the iTunes Library or a playlist and then drag the songs to the MP3 player in the source list. You cannot play items on the MP3 player in iTunes or move items from the MP3 player to iTunes, nor will your player (unless it's an iPod) play music from the iTunes store.

Using Apple's iPod MP3 player

The iPod MP3 player is tightly integrated with iTunes. If an iPod is connected to a Macintosh and the iPod is selected in the Source list of iTunes, an iPod window appears and the Eject button becomes an Eject iPod button. Clicking the iPod button displays the iPod Preferences window.

> **TIP**   If you connect your iPod to multiple computers, you will most likely want to set your iPod to be manually managed. This way you can take parts of each library, instead of only the entire library of one.

Making use of playlists

The playlist is a powerful and useful feature in iTunes. A *playlist* is like a folder containing aliases to your audio songs. You can create a playlist by clicking the Create a playlist button and then naming it in the source list. Playlists let you group songs that you like to hear together and put them in the order you want to hear them. Just select them from the iTunes Library and drag them to the playlist group in the source list.

NOTE An alternate and often easier method of creating a playlist involves selecting the songs in the iTunes Library list and choosing File ➪ New Playlist from Selection (⌘+Shift+N). iTunes creates a new playlist entry with the name selected for your editing pleasure. When you then select the playlist, the selected songs are shown in the song list window. Doing this is a great way to create a playlist containing songs by a particular artist.

Clicking the Shuffle button, the Playlist button with the crossed arrows, you can randomize the order of items in a playlist. Clicking it again reverts you to the original order. You can also click the Repeat button to *loop* a playlist.

You can also work with subsets of a playlist without creating a new playlist just by deselecting the boxes next to the names of the songs you don't want played.

If you want your playlist to open in its own window, just double-click the playlist's icon. To delete a playlist, for example after burning your own CD of it (see the next topic), just click the playlist's icon to select it and press Delete or choose Edit ➪ Clear.

Smart Playlists are a new feature of iTunes in version 3 and up. With Smart Playlists, you can have iTunes automatically create and update playlists as you add and remove music from your iTunes Library. Go to File ➪ Create Smart Playlist and choose the selectors of files you'd like iTunes to create a playlist for.

Smart Playlists allow you to automate the creation of playlists using search-like criteria. Smart Playlists automatically update as you add music to your library that fits the criteria. To create a Smart Playlist, chose File ➪ New Smart Playlist. See Figure 7.17 for an example of the creation of a Smart Playlist.

Recording your own audio CDs

Possibly the most useful feature of a playlist is that, when combined with a compatible CD-RW drive, it lets you write audio CDs suitable for use in most standard CD players. Just create your playlist by dragging the songs into the order you want them to appear, checking the time at the bottom of the window to make sure that your material fits on a CD (usually either 74 minutes or 80 minutes), and clicking the Burn CD aperture in the lower right corner of the window. iTunes asks you to insert a recordable CD into your CD burner and then to click the Burn CD button. At that point, just sit back and relax while iTunes creates your CD. You can listen to music while iTunes burns the CD.

NOTE You can set iTunes to automatically start whenever a blank CD or DVD is inserted into the drive with the CDs and DVDs pane of System Preferences, covered in Chapter 17.

FIGURE 7.17

To create auto-updating Smart Playlists, choose from the criteria in the Smart Playlist dialog box and make sure "Live Updating" is checked.

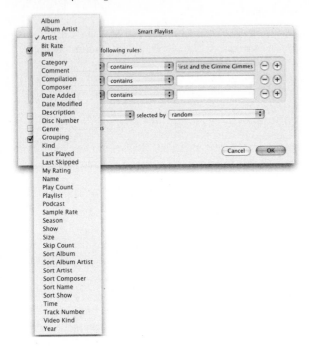

Although you can record to a CD-R or a CD-RW and have no difficulties reading the disc on your computer, your experiences using such discs in commercial audio CD players can vary widely. Many standard CD players, especially those made more than three or four years ago, have problems reading CD-R media. Even more have difficulty with CD-RW media. The reasons for these difficulties are rooted in the methods used to record the data on the different media. Standard CDs have physical pits in an aluminum (or other metallic) surface, below the transparent layer encasing the metallic disc. A player's laser detects those deviations in the surface to read the stored data. A CD-R emulates this pitting with charged layers of a photosensitive dye. A CD-RW emulates this pitting with a chemical compound, which crystallizes when heated to the correct temperature, but returns to its liquid state when heated even more and then allowed to cool. In any event, the lasers in many older CD players do not operate at a wavelength that allows them to read CD-R or CD-RW media. Before purchasing a CD player, check to see whether its specifications are compatible with CD-R media.

Blank CD-R media typically has two sizes listed — one in minutes and one in megabytes. The two most common sizes are 74 min/640MB and 80 min/700MB. When you're recording audio to a CD, only look at the time figure. The megabytes figure refers to data CDs.

Another type of CD player can play both audio CDs and what are called MP3 CDs. These MP3 CDs are actually data discs, which are written in a format known as ISO 9660 and can contain literally hundreds of MP3 files. iTunes can create these CDs, but not all CD players will play them. You can play them on your Macintosh computer. You may also archive music to DVDs with iTunes if you have a DVD burner such as Apple's SuperDrive.

Working with iTunes song and album information

The iTunes window (refer to Figure 7.16) has a large pane dedicated to displaying information about the songs in the currently selected source — playlist, audio CD, MP3 player, or iTunes Library. By choosing View ➪ View Options, you can control which of the tag fields defined in the ID3 standard (and some that are not) are displayed.

With the exception of the song field, which iTunes keeps on the left, you can rearrange the order of the other columns by dragging a column header over another column header. The column with the dark header is the column by which the display is sorted. The small arrow at the right of the selected column header indicates whether it is an ascending (A–Z) or descending (Z–A) sort, and you can reverse the order by clicking the header.

iTunes can also display album cover artwork. Choose View ➪ Show Artwork (⌘+G), and a panel appears under the Source section of the iTunes interface. If there is already artwork associated with a particular song, it will appear there while the track is playing. Music purchased from the iTunes Store automatically has album artwork associated with it. To add your own album art, you just select the songs you want to update and then drag a picture into the Now Playing pane of the iTunes interface. To remove artwork, select a song and choose File ➪ Get Info (⌘+I). Select the artwork you don't want, and press Delete.

Looking up album information

Not only can iTunes stream radio from the Internet, it can make use of the CDDB (Compact Disc Data Base) at www.gracenote.com to look up information about your CDs, retrieve song names, album title, artist information, and other pertinent information.

If you select the Automatically retrieve CD tracks names from internet box in your iTunes Preferences (on the Importing tab of the Advanced pane), iTunes automatically connects to the Internet when you insert an audio CD. If you want iTunes to check manually, choose Advanced ➪ Get CD Track Names.

The information in the CDDB has been submitted by various people and sometimes more than one person submits album information for a CD, resulting in slightly different entries (spelling differences and the like) for the same CD. CDs are recognized by the number of songs and the respective lengths of those songs. Thus, if two different CDs have the same number of songs and each corresponding song is the same length, you may have to choose the appropriate entry. The CDDB is a useful tool, but it isn't infallible.

Special iTunes Symbols

iTunes employs some graphic symbols for specific purposes. The following are the ones you're most likely to encounter:

Moving waveform: Indicates the song is currently being imported

Circled exclamation point: Indicates the song can't be located

Speaker: Indicates the song being played

Entering song information manually

You can enter or edit song information manually by using in-place editing or a dialog box for songs that are on your hard disk. You can even edit song information for songs on CD-ROMs and other locked sources. iTunes holds the information you enter in its database, overriding any information previously obtained from the Internet. Naturally, iTunes can't change the song information on the CD-ROM or other locked source itself. You may have some songs stored in locations that prevent you from editing their information. Songs on noneditable media, such as CD-ROMs, are not editable in this way because iTunes cannot write the information back to the read-only media. For example, you can't edit the information of songs that are located in a folder to which you have read-only access, such as the Public folder of someone else's home folder.

In-place editing is a straightforward Macintosh editing operation. Just click to select the record, and then click the text field to select it and start typing. To avoid the typing hassle, you can select a song and choose File ➪ Get Info (⌘+I) to display the Song Information panel, as shown in Figure 7.18. You can navigate to adjacent songs by using the Previous Song and Next Song buttons.

Watching iTunes visual effects

If you find the iTunes song lists boring while you're listening to your favorite tunes or a book on disk, you can replace the window's contents with iTunes Visual Effects.

You start and stop the show by clicking the Visuals On/Off button, which is located in the lower right corner of the iTunes window (review Figure 7.16). Alternatively, you can choose Visuals ➪ Turn Visual On or Visuals ➪ Turn Visual Off (⌘+T). You can also use the Visuals menu to set the size of the visual effects show. Three sizes are available for show within the iTunes window (Small, Medium, and Large) as well as a Full Screen (⌘+F) mode.

Pressing the I key while the effects are on displays information about the song, which gradually fades out. Pressing the question mark key presents a list of some of the key options. This list is not comprehensive — maybe that's why it's called *Basic* Visualizer Help. Some other keys that affect the Visualizer are Q, W, A, S, Z, and X, all of which switch among the effects being used. The first two cycle forward and backward through the lists of first effects, the next two through the list of secondary effects, and the last two through the list of tertiary effects.

FIGURE 7.18

Use the iTunes Get Info window's Info panel to enter information about a song.

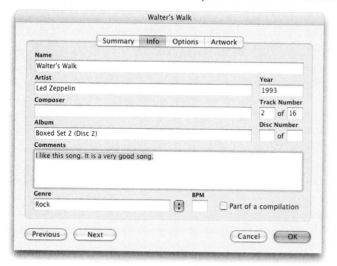

Searching your iTunes Library

As described earlier in this chapter, you have control over which columns appear and how the song list is sorted. The Search area at the top of the window acts as a filter. Any text you enter there limits the songs presented in the song list area to those that contain the text in one of the displayed columns.

When the iTunes Library is selected in the Source pane, a Browse button appears in the upper right corner of the iTunes window (where the Burn button is for a playlist). Clicking the Browse button reveals extra filtering control lists.

 For the Genre column to appear, you must select the Show Genre When Browsing check box on the iTunes Preferences General tab.

Making a choice in one list restricts the choices to only those for the given selection in lists to the right. For example, selecting Comedy under Genre narrows the choices in Artist to only those artists who have songs with Comedy in the Genre tag field. If you select an artist, only the albums for that artist are listed in the Albums column. For this reason, filling in the ID3 Tags is very important if you want to browse your iTunes Library effectively. Only the genres, artists, and albums you have in your iTunes database appear in the various lists. ID3 tags are discussed in more detail shortly.

Removing songs from your iTunes Library

Removing a song from your iTunes Library is simplicity itself. All you need to do is select the song in the Library's song list and press the Delete or Clear key. Doing so does not remove the song from your disk, though.

If you want to remove the song from both the disk and the Library, the easiest method is to perform the following:

1. **Select the song in the Library's song list.**

2. **Control+click it and choose Show Song File from the contextual menu to display the file in a Finder window.**

3. **Drag the file into the Trash (⌘+Delete).**

4. **Return to iTunes and press the Delete key with the song highlighted.**

Managing ID3 tags

Songs you download from the Internet may appear in iTunes with incorrect or unreadable titles and other information. This can be due to the file having been created with a program that stores song information differently than iTunes. Song information is stored in MP3 files in what is called ID3 tags, and you may be able to convert them into a version iTunes can use.

If no tag data exists, as is all too often the case with music obtained over the Internet, iTunes displays the file name in place of the title information, and the other fields are blank. Enter the song information manually, as described earlier in this chapter.

The ID3 Tag format has gone through a number of versions, and each is slightly different from its predecessors. iTunes can convert the data format between the different versions of ID3 when you select songs and choose Advanced ⇨ Convert ID3 Tags. If you're going to exchange MP3 files with Windows users, you should be aware that many Windows users are using MP3 player software that does not handle ID3 Version 2 tags well, and you may want to convert to an appropriate Version 1 variant.

If you have a group of songs that have the same information, such as a whole album that wasn't in the CDDB, you can select multiple files at the same time, choose Get Info, and edit common information all at once.

Using Shared Music Libraries

Under the iTunes preferences (iTunes ⇨ Preferences), you'll see the Sharing panel. Use this to enable shared music Libraries, which allows iTunes users on a network to see each other's music and play the music on their own computers. The computer that has the music file in its library streams the file to the person's computer who wants to listen to it. No files are transferred between iTunes Libraries, but people can share their taste in music temporarily. Click the Look for Shared Libraries check box to see other user's shared music on your local network. You can also configure your own iTunes Library to be shared, either wholly, or as specific playlists. If you are concerned about other people on your network using your computer to listen to music without your authorization, you can password-protect the stream.

The iTunes Store

Once upon a time, you had to buy music on the media it was encoded on: player piano rolls, then phonograph records, then tapes, then compact discs. And then along came MP3 and a little outfit called Napster. There was an instant explosion of trading of MP3s via the Internet, which made the record companies very, very angry. But no one seemed to know what to do. Except Apple.

And so it came to pass that in April, 2003, Apple introduced the iTunes Music Store and sold over one million songs in the first week — and that was only to Mac users, for no others could access the iTunes Music Store. Suddenly, it was easy, legal, and affordable to download and use digital music files. There was a revolution in the way people thought about music distribution — again. Soon there were several sites selling music on the Internet in emulation of the iTunes Music Store, but none of them were as successful. Still, said the critics, Mac users are just three percent of computer users — small potatoes.

Then in October, 2003, Apple announced that Windows users could now access the iTunes Music store via iTunes 4.1 and QuickTime 6.4 for Windows. Soon the 25 million members of America Online would gain access to the iTunes Music Store, and so it seemed that the iTunes Music Store was poised to conquer the online music-selling business. A real fairy tale!

If you have iTunes and an Internet connection, and you are not one of those people who doesn't like music, you would be doing yourself a grave disservice to not visit the iTunes Music Store and at least browse around.

To visit the Music Store in iTunes, simply click Music Store in the Source list. There you will find hundreds of thousands of songs from virtually every category of music, from the five major U.S. labels and over 200 independent labels.

The music is encoded in a format called AAC (for advanced audio coding). The AAC format is part of the MPEG-4 specification, and it features more efficient compression and better quality than MP3 format. In fact, the quality of AAC encoding rivals that of uncompressed CD audio. The iTunes Music Store currently requires iTunes 4.7 and at least QuickTime 6.2 (version 7 ships with Leopard).

If you are sick of most of the popular offerings of the large labels, you are not alone. The iTunes Music Store offers music from independent labels that is not available elsewhere online, and is virtually impossible to find anywhere offline. You will also find exclusive tracks from major artists that are available only through the Music Store.

You can spend endless hours browsing to your heart's content, or zero in quickly if you know what you want. There are simple search and Power Search options. Editorial write-ups, reviews, and lists of recommendations can guide you, as well as playlists picked by celebrities, and all from the comfort of your own home, or wherever you have a computer connected to the Internet.

And there is not just music. A large library of audiobooks — more than 5,000 titles — is available. There are also episodes of a variety of interesting radio shows.

At the Music Store, you can preview for free whatever you are interested in; then you can buy a song or an album with a single click. Songs cost 99 cents each. You can listen to your purchase as soon as it downloads—instant gratification. After you buy the audio, you own it; no monthly fees or tricky rules to follow. You can burn songs onto an unlimited number of CDs. You can use your audio on up to three different computers at once. You can also use iTunes to share music with Macs and PCs on a local area network. Allowance accounts can be set up for children, and gift certificates are available.

Album Covers and iTunes Views

New to iTunes is the ability to associate album covers with music in addition to ID3 tags. Apple has added album covers to make the iTunes library seem more like browsing a library of physical CDs, in an attempt to make purchasing online music more attractive to music collectors. You can manually add album artwork (or any graphic, for that matter) to your music by selecting it and choosing APPLE-I on your keyboard. Drag a picture to the empty square next to the song's (or collection of song's) title. See Figure 7.19 for an example.

Alternatively, you can choose Advanced ⇨ Get Album Artwork, and if you have an iTunes Store account, iTunes goes through Apple's online store and attempts to match up artwork with the music you have in your library. It's important to note that this involves iTunes sending information to Apple, in order to evaluate what music you have in your library. The iTunes Store stores cover artwork only for songs that are sold through it, though you don't have to have purchased the music from Apple in order to download covers. In addition, iTunes can only download music that it successfully matches up (by comparing ID3 tags), so it might not be able to determine a match even if the artwork exists in the iTunes Store if the tags don't compare correctly. There are several applications that can assist in finding alternative sources of cover artwork, and help you make the association if you are unsuccessful in obtaining all of the artwork for your music from the iTunes store.

iTunes Views

There are three views of your library that iTunes provides to help you quickly find the music you are looking for. The first is a mere List view, which can be seen in Figure 7.14. It is a basic list of the music contained in your library or a playlist. The second is called Cover view, and the third is Cover Flow view.

You can switch between views in two different ways: View ⇨ List View, View ⇨ Album View, and View ⇨ Cover Flow View, if you like menus, or by clicking the view buttons in the main iTunes window (Figure 7.20). Album view displays a list of your songs, grouped by album, with the cover artwork displayed (if available) to the left of the list of songs. Cover Flow is an innovative view of your music that displays your music grouped by album much like Cover view. Unlike Album view, however, Cover Flow is a 3-D representation of your albums, much like a flip book, allowing you to "flip" through your albums by using the slider control underneath the view of album covers.

FIGURE 7.19

Manually adding album artwork to your songs

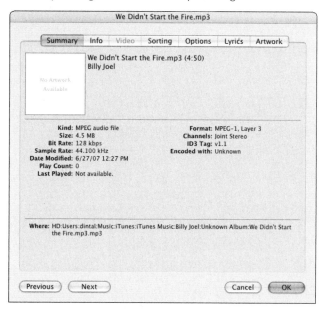

FIGURE 7.20

The view buttons in the main iTunes window, allowing you to switch between the three views

Front Row

Front Row is Apple's attempt at making OS X even more media-centric than it has ever been. If you have a machine that supports it (Intel-based laptops, Minis, and iMacs, though there were a few PPC iMacs and Minis that support Front Row), Front Row can be a fun and useful way to display your pictures, play your music, watch videos, and play DVDs.

The most common means of entering the Front Row application is through the remote control that was included with your computer. Push the small Menu button that is the bottommost button on the remote, and Front Row should pop up (Figure 7.21). The screen goes black and you see four giant icons appear in a circular arrangement, one for each of the types of media you can control: music, photos, movies, and DVDs. Use the forward and back keys to switch between applications, and the center "play" button to make your selections. You will need to have a music library in iTunes, and photos in iPhoto to be able to access their functions. The Videos category allows you to view your iMovies, should you have any, theatrical trailers from Apple's Web site, or purchased TV shows and movies from the iTunes store.

If you don't have your remote with you, you can enter Front Row using Apple+Escape on your keyboard and navigate using the arrow keys. To quickly quit Front Row, press Apple+Option+Escape (force quit) on your keyboard.

FIGURE 7.21

The main Front Row window

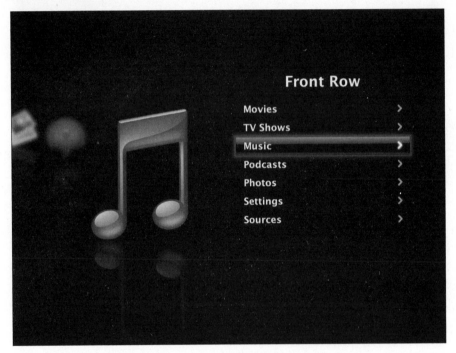

Summary

This chapter covered QuickTime, Apple's multimedia technology, and some of Apple's applications that rely on it, known as the iLife Suite.

■ QuickTime is a powerful technology that brings time-based media to the Macintosh. It is built into Mac OS X, so that you can view QuickTime movies without an application.

■ iTunes is a digital jukebox, and enables you to rip and burn CDs, listen to music on your computer, and access your iPod and the iTunes Music Store.

■ Front Row is a fun way to display your pictures and control your movies, music, and DVDs.

Part II

At Work with Mac OS X

Chapter 8

Getting Help

I n this chapter, you find out how to take advantage of Mac OS X's built-in help systems. Anyone who has ever used a computer at one time or another needs help. When the need arises, Mac OS X provides several types of built-in assistance. The principal help system is integrated into the OS, and the contents are displayed through a browser-like application, aptly named the Help Viewer. The Help Viewer application provides explanations for most basic tasks. Another type of assistance within Mac OS X is help tags. When provided, help tags are labels that appear when the mouse is positioned over various GUI elements. Typically, these GUI elements are unlabeled buttons, such as the ones found in AppleWorks or Microsoft Office's toolbars. Another form of built-in assistance is the man pages. Man pages provide help with the command-line tasks and are accessed through the Terminal application. In addition to the built-in help systems of Mac OS, many applications also provide their own built-in help. If all else fails, you can always break out the manuals or visit a products support site, if one is provided. Let's take a closer look at the various Mac OS X help systems.

IN THIS CHAPTER

Using the Help Viewer application

Displaying help tags

Getting command-line help

Exploring other avenues for help

Using the Help Viewer Application

The Help Viewer is the main source of general how-to help for Mac OS X. It also provides separate sections of specialized help on Apple technologies, such as AppleScript and QuickTime. In addition, some applications add their own sections of specialized help to the Help Viewer. In the Help Viewer, help is available by browsing a table of contents or by searching for words that describe the help you need. Some of the articles include links that you click to see related material as well as shortcuts to System Preference panes or OS X—included applications related to the assistance being sought. All the available help sections are listed in a table of contents in the Help Viewer, as explained in the following paragraphs.

To display on-screen help in the Help Viewer application, select Help from the menu bar or click the Help button. The application you're using determines what you see in the Help Viewer. You may see a list of all available help contents, a list of help article titles, or a single help article related to the product in which help is being sought.

As a convenience, some windows include a Help button that you can click to get help for that window. The Help button is the round button with a question mark on it. Clicking a Mac OS X Help button opens the Help Viewer application and displays a Spotlight-like search bar, relevant help article, or a list of relevant articles. For example, while using the Print dialog box in a Mac OS X application, click the Help button to display the article about setting printing preferences.

Getting help within Mac OS X

While you're using the Finder, the Help Viewer lets you browse a list of common Mac help topics. It also lets you see what's new to Leopard (Mac OS 10.5), provides help with top customer issues, and offers a starting point of assistance for those who are new to Mac OS. To use the Help Viewer, follow these steps:

1. **If you're not currently using the Finder, switch to it.** For example, click any Finder window or click the Finder icon at the beginning of the Dock.

2. **Choose Help ⇨ Mac OS Help to display a list of Mac help topics in the Help Viewer, as shown in Figure 8.1.**

FIGURE 8.1

You can also open the Help Viewer application within the Finder by pressing ⌘+?.

Browsing Mac OS Help

The Help Viewer application contents are based on subject matter that Apple has determined are the most commonly queried Mac OS X help issues. To view the list of central topics of help, select a topic under the Top Customer Issues on the right side of the Help Viewer window. For more topics click the Look up topics easily link. A list of help topics sorted alphabetically appears; to get more information on a particular issue, click the first letter of the item you need assistance with and select it from the list. Figure 8.2 shows the contents of Index.

FIGURE 8.2

What's New in Leopard displays a consolidated list of Leopard's new features.

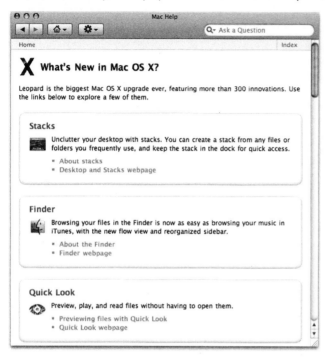

Getting help for the active application

If the application you're using provides on-screen help via the Help Viewer, you can generally display this help by choosing a command from the Help menu. For example, while using Mail, choose Help ➪ Mail Help to display a list of Mail-related topics in the Help Viewer, as shown in Figure 8.3.

FIGURE 8.3

Opening the Help Viewer from Mail shows Mail-specific help. As with the Finder, you can also open the Help Viewer application within Mail by pressing ⌘+?.

Browsing Help Viewer links

The Help Viewer works in a similar way to that of a Web browser. The blue text in the Help Viewer represents links that you can click to see related material. For example, if you click one of the subjects listed below Top Customer Issues in the Help Viewer, while in the Finder, a list of relevant articles appears. Articles themselves may also contain links to view related material as well as shortcuts to System Preference panes or OS X 10.5-included applications related to the assistance being sought. Figure 8.4 shows an example of searching for the words *keychain* and *password* with the second link selected, and Figure 8.5 shows that help article.

FIGURE 8.4

Perform a search in the Help Viewer by placing keywords in the search field.

FIGURE 8.5

Depending upon the Help article, it may contain shortcuts to Utilities or OS X 10.5-included applications related to the assistance being sought.

Retrieving Help from the Internet

At times, the Help Viewer must retrieve help articles from the Internet. For example, an application may initially have only its most popular help articles installed on your computer and keep less commonly read articles on the Internet. If you click a link to an article that's on the Internet, the Help Viewer automatically caches it on your computer. If you later want to read an article that the Help Viewer has already retrieved from the Internet, the Help Viewer displays the cached article on your computer. If there is an updated version of the article, the Help Viewer checks the Internet and retrieves the newer version. The Help Viewer also adds additional articles as they become available. Of course, the Help Viewer can retrieve articles from the Internet only if your computer has an Internet connection. If your computer has a dial-up connection to the Internet or you must go through an authentication procedure to make an Internet connection, the Help Viewer displays a dialog box asking whether you want to make the connection.

If your computer isn't connected to the Internet, and the Help Viewer needs to retrieve an article, you must approve the connection.

Using Help Viewer Quick Clicks

Quick Clicks are links in articles that take you to many places inside and outside the Help Viewer. If the author of the help article writes clearly, you should have a good idea about where the link takes you. The possibilities include the following:

■ A link may show you another article in the Help Viewer window.

■ An Open link probably opens the application that the article describes.

■ A More link at the bottom of a list of article titles takes you to a continuation of the list.

- A Supported Articles link takes you to Apple Service and Support pages.

- A Go to the Website link shows you a related Web site in your Web browser. Other links may also go to Web sites, which is especially likely if the link includes an Internet address or is near an Internet address in the help article. However, clicking an Internet address that is not underlined in a help article does nothing. Text that isn't underlined is not a link in the Help Viewer.

Navigating using the Help Viewer buttons

Besides clicking links, you can go places in the Help Viewer by clicking buttons.

- Click the Back button (left arrow) to go back to the previous page in the Help Viewer.

- After going back, click the Forward button (right arrow) to go forward in your help Viewer History.

- Click the Home button to return to the opening screen of the topic being viewed within the Help Viewer application and see its list of available help selections.

- Click the drop-down arrow to the right of the Home button to see a list of common help topics.

Searching within the Help Viewer

If you're looking for help on a specific subject and don't want to browse through links until you find it, use the search function to query for the help you need. The Help Viewer uses Spotlight search technology; to do a query, you type some words that are associated with a subject you need help with in the Ask a Question search field at the top of the Help Viewer window, and then press the Return key on your keyboard. When typing words to search for, you can include special characters to describe the help you need more precisely. Table 8.1 describes these special characters.

TABLE 8.1

Special Characters for Help Viewer Searching

Character	Meaning	Search Example	Search Results
+	and	desktop + Finder	This example finds articles that include both "desktop" and "Finder."
|	or	desktop | Finder	This example finds articles that include either "desktop" or "Finder."
!	not	desktop ! Finder	This example finds articles that include "desktop" but exclude "Finder."
( )	grouping	picture + (Finder | desktop)	This example finds articles that include "picture" and either "Finder" or "desktop."

Displaying Help Tags

Help tags are another form of help. Some applications allow you to get immediate information about GUI elements on the screen by displaying their help tags. If an object has a help tag, it automatically appears when you position the mouse pointer over the object and wait a couple seconds. You can recognize a help tag by its distinctive small yellow box, which contains a very short description of the object under the pointer. If no such box appears when you hover the pointer over an object on-screen, the object has no help tag. You don't have to click anything or press any keys to make a help tag appear. Figure 8.6 shows an example help tag.

FIGURE 8.6

A help tag describes the object under the pointer in a Mac OS X application.

Mac OS X provides help tag capability, but not all objects have help tags. Commonplace objects, such as window controls and scroll bars, usually do not have help tags. Menus and menu items never have help tags. Buttons and other objects have help tags only if the application that they are part of provides descriptions to be displayed inside the help tags. Classic applications can't provide help tags at all, and many Mac OS X applications don't provide any help tags.

If you've used Balloon Help in Mac OS 9 or earlier, you probably realize that the help tags are the Mac OS X equivalent of Balloon Help. On the downside, help tags provide much less detailed information than Balloon Help. On the upside, help tags are less intrusive and don't need to be turned on and off.

Getting Command-Line Help

In addition to the various GUI-based help systems, Mac OS X's command line has an integrated help system referred to as the *man pages*. The man pages are accessed with the man command, which is short for *manual*. The man pages provide an online manual that contains information on just about every command available when using the command line. (The man command and its uses are reviewed in more detail in Chapter 23.)

Exploring Other Avenues of Help

Many applications add how-to help, on-screen reference material, or other items to the Help menu. For example, many applications published by Adobe, FileMaker, and Microsoft list on-screen help commands in the Help menu. The help may appear in the Help Viewer or in your Web browser. Some applications use other help systems to display their on-screen help. For instructions on an application's own help system, check the documentation that came with the application.

On the Web, you can find additional help for your Macintosh computer, Mac OS X, popular applications, and add-on hardware. Check the following sites:

- **AppleCare Service and Support:** `www.apple.com/support`
- **AppleCare Knowledge Base:** `http://kbase.info.apple.com`
- **Apple Manuals:** `http://www.apple.com/support/manuals/`
- **Apple Mac OS X Support:** `http://www.apple.com/macosx/leopard/`
- **MacFixIt:** `www.macfixit.com`
- **The Web site of the company that makes the software or hardware for which you need help**

Summary

Here's what you should know after reading this chapter:

- Mac OS X displays on-screen help in the form of help tags and Help Viewer articles.
- The Help Viewer application displays short how-to articles, and you can display them by choosing items from the Help menu or by clicking a Help button in a window that has one. The kind of help that you get varies from application to application.
- Some Help Viewer articles include links that you click to see related articles, open related applications, or connect to an Internet site.
- You can search all Help Viewer articles for words you specify, optionally using the special characters +, |, !, and ( ) to pinpoint what you want to find.
- If an object has a help tag, you view it by positioning the mouse pointer on the object and waiting a few seconds. A help tag appears in a small yellow box and succinctly describes the object under the pointer.
- Some applications use help systems not provided by Mac OS X.
- As a last resort, you can always turn to the manual or to the product's Web site for help.

Chapter 9

Utilizing Services

I n Mac OS X, certain applications are able to share useful functions with other applications. Apple refers to these functions as *services* (yes, with a small s), and they can save you time and effort. However, using them can seem a little tricky because the way services are set up is somewhat counter-intuitive until you know what you're doing. Here our objective is to provide you with all the information you need to make use of services.

This chapter takes a look at the services available in Leopard and shows you how to work with them. We spotlight the services provided by the Finder, Grab, Mail, Stickies, Speech, Summarize, and TextEdit. The other services available in Mac OS X are described at the end of this chapter.

About Services

Services appear as an item in the Application menu of every Mac OS X-com-patible application. (The Application menu is the one that appears when you click the application's name in the menu bar. But you knew that.)

Choosing Services in Leopard opens a submenu containing 12 items, none of which seems to work! But looks can be deceiving. Yes, at first glance, some of these items appear grayed-out, most of their commands are inaccessible, and their functions are not immediately apparent. How very mysterious! No wonder many people move on and don't give the Services item a second thought.

The idea of services is to allow the applications and functions listed in the Services submenu to share their capabilities with other, compatible applications.

Here's how it works: First, you select some data in an application, such as the string of text, "We're coming to visit on Sunday." Then you choose a command from the Services submenu, such as the Mail application's Mail Text command. The command is executed on the selection, invoking Mail to create a new mail message with "We're coming to visit on Sunday" already placed in the message body. Very convenient!

For another example, in TextEdit you could invoke the Grab service's Selection command to allow you to select a part of the screen to be inserted as an image in your TextEdit document.

Using services often seems as though Mac OS X invisibly copies your selected data from one application and pastes it into another; the latter application modifies the data and most often copies the result back into the original application before you know it.

The content you can use with services may include text, graphics, pictures, or movies.

There's just one catch. It is important to note that services mainly work with applications and utilities written to run in Mac OS X's Cocoa environment, such as Safari, Mail, TextEdit, and many of the other programs included with Mac OS X. There are also hundreds of third-party Cocoa applications and utilities.

Carbon applications cannot take advantage of services, except in the rare event they're written to support services. Most commercial Carbon apps such as the Microsoft Office applications, Adobe Photoshop and Illustrator, and QuarkXPress, do not currently support services. This may have something to do with the fact that it is reportedly quite difficult for developers to adapt a Carbon application to use services. Perhaps they'll eventually get around to it — or perhaps not.

Now you can guess why the Services submenu items often have their commands dimmed; if you're looking at them from a typical Carbon application, none of them will work. But they also appear unavailable from inside a Cocoa application; that is, unless you first highlight the content you want the service to work on. This is a critical point — the not-quite-so-intuitive "secret" trick to taking advantage of services. Only Grab's service commands will be typically available before you select anything because the entire screen is available to choose from. Also, a service appears dimmed in the submenu if you've selected a type of content that the service doesn't work with.

You may find that, after taking all this into account, the services command you want to use is still dimmed! The explanation: Some applications may not support every service. The application's developer decides which services will be supported.

Here's another critical point to keep in mind: Services can't create documents. They can only work with a document that is open in a services-compatible application. For example, the Grab *utility* can create documents, but the Grab *service* can only work with an open document in a Cocoa or services-compatible application. That's why the Grab service commands remain dimmed if you access them from the Finder; the Finder cannot create a document for the service to place results in.

Mac OS X services will (hopefully? should? with any luck?) become increasingly useful as more and more Cocoa applications are developed that can use them, and as Apple and third parties develop more programs that make services available.

Services are really the current continuation of Apple's longtime dream of fostering communication and data exchange between individual applications. Some old-timers may still have enough functioning memory on their personal motherboards to recall the ancient notions called Publish and Subscribe. Another example would be Apple Events, still used in Mac OS X by those who make AppleScripts. Services are but a modest echo of such ambitious schemes; then again, services are more accessible and helpful.

The Finder

The Finder application provides three services to other applications — Open, Reveal, and Show Info, as shown in Figure 9.1.

FIGURE 9.1

After content is selected (here, the name of a file highlighted in TextEdit), use the Finder's services to Open, Reveal, and Show Info.

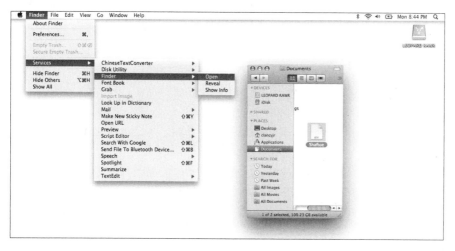

■ **Open:** Opens the file with its default application, opens a selected folder or volume and displays the contents in a Finder window, or launches an application. Essentially, the Open command in a menu acts the same way as a double-click on the item's icon. If you type the path to a folder in a text file, highlight the pathname, and choose Services ➪ File ➪ Open, the folder opens in a new Finder window.

- **Reveal:** Reveals the item in the Finder by opening a Finder window and selecting the item.
- **Show Info:** Displays the Info window for the selected item.

Grab

Apple has long made it easy to "take snapshots" of your Mac screen and parts thereof. Mac OS X provides this capability via the Grab utility.

Grab lends its services to other applications, allowing you to take a snapshot of the entire screen, a selection, or a timed screenshot.

For example, while working in TextEdit, you can choose TextEdit ➪ Services ➪ Grab ➪ Screen and a full-screen picture will be inserted in your TextEdit document at the current insertion point. Figure 9.2 shows a partial screen capture inserted into a TextEdit document.

FIGURE 9.2

The Grab service has captured part of the screen and inserted it into a TextEdit document.

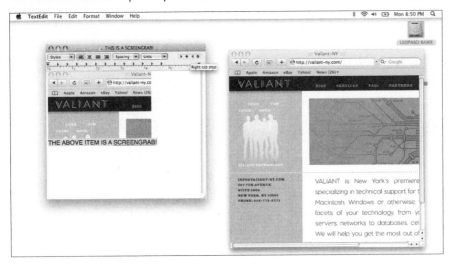

Screen Capture without Grab

Incidentally, you can capture the full screen or a selected area without using the Grab utility. This has nothing to do with services, but it's such a helpful thing to know that it is included here for your convenience. The following keystrokes do the trick:

- ⌘+Shift+3 captures the full screen.
- ⌘+Shift+4 provides a cross-hairs pointer to select the area you want captured. Drag the pointer diagonally to define the selection rectangle.

With either keystroke, the screenshot is saved as a PNG file on the desktop.

As mentioned previously, the Grab service's commands appear dimmed when you try to access them from the Finder. Many users have found this a tad confusing. But the Finder cannot produce a document for the Grab service to place its results in; it only produces Finder windows. Instead, use the Grab utility with the Finder, or use Mac OS X's screen capture commands, described in the sidebar "Screen Capture without Grab."

Mail

The Mail application supplied by Mac OS X provides two services to other applications, Send Selection and Send To:

- **Send Selection:** Your selection will appear in the body of a new e-mail message.
- **Send To:** Your selection will appear in the address of a new e-mail message.

A typical use of the Mail service is as follows:

1. **Select a name or e-mail address in the body of your TextEdit document (or other word processor — it has to support services).**
2. **Choose Services ➪ Mail ➪ Send To from the Application menu.** The Mac OS X Mail application opens with a new e-mail message addressed as you specified, as shown in Figure 9.3.

FIGURE 9.3

Use Mail's Send To service to create a mail message addressed to the selected name.

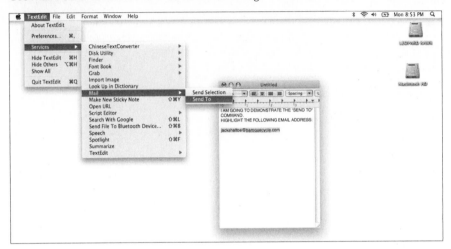

Be aware that the Mail ⇨ Send To service does not check for a valid e-mail address or name. It merely takes the text you provide and places that text into the To field of a new mail message.

Similarly, select a block of text, an image, or other material and choose Services ⇨ Mail ⇨ Send Selection from the application menu to create a new e-mail message in Mail with the selected text or image in the body of the e-mail message.

In addition to the Send Selection and Send To commands available to all compatible applications, Mail also provides a Send File service to mail an entire file from the Finder. To use this service, select a file or an entire folder in the Finder and then choose Finder ⇨ Services ⇨ Mail ⇨ Send File, as shown in Figure 9.4. This command will not be visible in the Finder unless a file is selected.

FIGURE 9.4

From the Finder, select a file and choose the Mail service's Send File command (top), and a new message will open with the file included as an attachment (bottom).

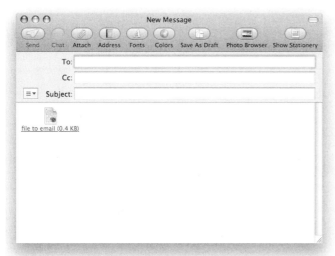

Using Stickies

For those fans of Post-it notes and their digital counterpart, Mac OS X Stickies offers a service. Any selected text in an application that supports services can be made into a Sticky note by choosing Services ➪ Make New Sticky Note (⌘+Shift+Y) from the application menu. Stickies is launched, if it isn't already, and a new Sticky note containing your selected text (up to the maximum size of a Sticky note) appears.

 Although Stickies can contain graphics in Mac OS X, the service ignores any graphics within the selection when it creates the Sticky note.

You can also access any of the supported services from within the Stickies application.

Speech

In a Cocoa or services-compatible application, any selected text can be sent to the Speech service to be read aloud, by selecting the text and choosing Services ⇨ Start Speaking Text, as shown in Figure 9.5. To stop, choose Services ⇨ Stop Speaking. To change the settings for Speech, use the Speech pane in System Preferences. (System Preferences are covered in more detail in Chapter 17.) This service is helpful for comparing long numbers or exact wording (listen to one as you look at the other).

FIGURE 9.5

Use Speech's Start Speaking Text command to hear the text, notes, or e-mail read aloud.

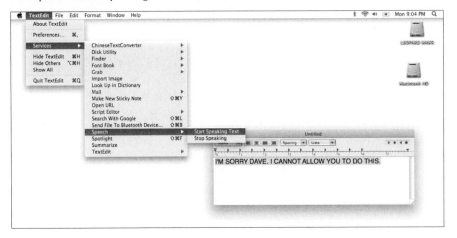

If you select an icon in the Finder and choose the Start Speaking Text command, Speech will speak the item's path! For example, if you select the application that makes this possible, `System/Library/Services/SpeechService.service`, and invoke Start Speaking Text, you'll hear "System, Library, Services, SpeechService.services." This is mostly just a nifty trick, because you could more easily hold down the ⌘ key and click the title of the Finder window to see the path. If you have to type the path, hearing it as you do so would perhaps be helpful.

Summarize

An interesting service takes selected text and quickly summarizes it by extracting key sentences or paragraphs. This service is unusual because it's provided by an application that you don't use otherwise. The service is called Summarize, and it's provided by the Summary Service application, which you won't find in the `Applications` folder — rather, it is located in the `System/Library/Services` folder.

To use this service, you select some text in a document and choose Services ➪ Summarize from the application menu. The Summary Service application opens, prepares a summary of the selected text, and displays the summary in a window. Figure 9.6 shows an example of the Summarize service.

TIP　If you select some text but the Summarize choice is disabled (dim) in the Services submenu, the Summarize service is not available in the application you're using. You can summarize the selected text by copying it to a document in the TextEdit application. Then select the text in the TextEdit document and choose TextEdit ➪ Services ➪ Summarize. You can use this same basic concept to use the other services, too.

When the Summary window appears, you can control the degree to which the text is summarized by sliding the Summary Size pointer; dragging it to the left causes the results to become shorter and less detailed. Slide the pointer and you'll see the text dynamically respond, growing or shrinking as you do so. This way you can easily pick the perfect length for your summary.

The two radio buttons, Sentences and Paragraphs, control the style of summary produced. When Sentences is selected, Summarize extracts key sentences from within paragraphs in your selected text. When Paragraphs is selected, Summarize extracts the key paragraphs from the text, keeping them intact in the result. You can switch back and forth to see which style suits your needs.

Click the Clear All button to clear the contents of the Summary window and begin a new summary.

You can save the summary as a text document by choosing File ➪ Save As. In addition, you can edit the summary by using the Edit menu and other regular text editing methods. You can even check the spelling in the summary by choosing Edit ➪ Spelling or Edit ➪ Check Spelling.

Does the Summarize service use some new advance in artificial intelligence to do what heretofore one required a human to do? Disappointingly, no. A statistical analysis is performed on keyword frequency, parts of speech usage, sentence structure, and the like. Rules are applied, the high-tech voodoo occurs, and the results spit out — all apparently within the realm of what current computer technology can do. No wonder the results can sometimes be of somewhat less quality than a human editor could achieve; but then again, *that takes work. . . .*

FIGURE 9.6

Use the Summarize service (top) to prepare a summary of selected text (bottom).

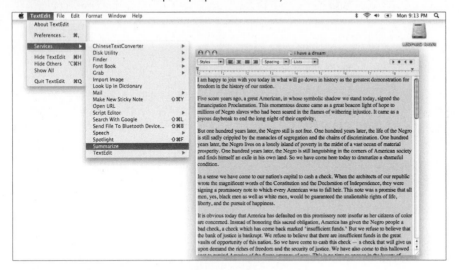

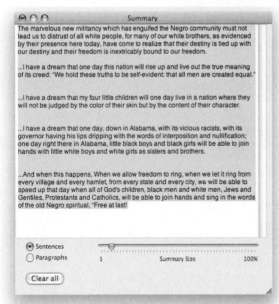

TextEdit

The TextEdit application, the versatile text editor and word processor included with Mac OS X, provides two services:

- Open a file by name.
- Create a new file containing selected content.

To open a file by name, as shown in Figure 9.7, you select text that specifies a full path to the file and then choose Services ➪ TextEdit ➪ Open Selected File from the application menu. If the file cannot be found, an error message appears stating that the file could not be opened; however, the error message doesn't tell you why the attempt failed. Note that the selection must be a file that TextEdit can open.

FIGURE 9.7

Select a full path and choose the Open Selected File command.

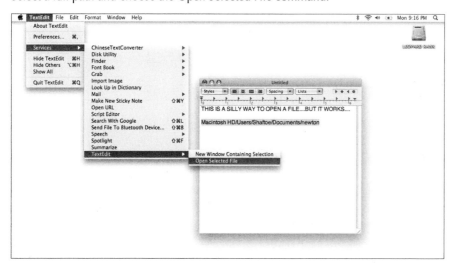

You can also select a block of text and other media, and then choose Services ➪ TextEdit ➪ New Window Containing Selection from the application menu to create a new TextEdit document using the selected media. Because both text and other media are combined, you can edit the result. This service is a useful adjunct to clipping files.

Other Services

These services also appear in the Leopard Services submenu:

- **Import Image:** Works only when you have a device connected to the computer that can be accessed through the Image Capture application. This device is typically a digital camera or a scanner. Select the image you want to import via the Image Capture interface, and it will be imported into your document. This service is helpful for quickly e-mailing a few photos you just took without importing all the photos in the camera.

- **Open URL:** Highlight a URL in your document, and select this command to open your default Cocoa Web browser (usually Safari) to show the Web page in a new window.

- **Script Editor:** Uses services provided by the Script Editor application for working with AppleScripts. These commands are meant for AppleScript developers (which could, and perhaps should, be you — see Chapter 22 for more on AppleScript). Three commands are available:

  - The **Get Result of AppleScript** command can be invoked by pressing ⌘+Shift+*. This command replaces the selected text, which must be an executable AppleScript, with the result of the executed script. For example, type **123/45 * pi** into a TextEdit document, select it, and run this command. The text is replaced with the *result* of the AppleScript calculation (in this case, 8.587019919812). Throw those calculators away!

  - The **Make New AppleScript** command transfers the selected text, which should be part or all of an AppleScript, to a new script window in the Script Editor application.

  - The **Run As AppleScript** command executes the selected text, which must be an executable AppleScript.

- **Search with Google:** Highlight any text, select this command, and your default Cocoa Web browser (usually Safari) opens to display the results of a Google search using your text.

- **Send File to Bluetooth Device:** This service is provided by the Bluetooth File Exchange utility and is enabled only when you have a Bluetooth transmitter/receiver, either inside your Mac or connected to a USB port. Selecting this command opens the Bluetooth File Exchange utility to the Select File to Send window for you to navigate to the desired file. Clicking Send opens the Select Bluetooth Device window for you to pick the device to send to. Click Send to transmit the file to the device.

Other Cocoa applications that you install may provide additional services. Services provided by a newly installed application may not become available until the next time you log in.

You can also obtain third-party services to install on your Mac OS X machine; many of them are freeware. Perhaps the best way to browse for them is to visit `VersionTracker.com`, click the Mac OS X tab, and enter **services** in the search field.

A good example of a third-party service is AtYourService, which allows you to add a selection of items to your Services menu. This shareware can look up selected text at `Dictionary.com`, `AcronymFinder.com`, VersionTracker, Yahoo! Stocks, and the Internet Movie Database (IMDb).

The six services installed with Mac OS X 10.5 live in /System/Library/Services. They are AppleSpell.service, ChineseTextConverterService, ImageCaptureService, SpeechService.service, Spotlight.service, and SummaryService. Third-party services install to either the `Library/Services` or a user's ~Library/Services folder

Summary

In this chapter, you learned that services allow the applications and functions listed in the Services submenu of the application menu to share certain helpful capabilities with other applications. Usually, only Cocoa applications can utilize these services. To enable the services commands in the menu, you must first select content in an open document. The services perform varied actions on this selected content, which were described in detail for most services available by default in Leopard. You can also install third-party services.

Chapter 10

Getting on the Internet

If your Macintosh is running OS X, and especially if you have made the effort to read this book (whether you're browsing in the computer section of a Barnes and Noble or perusing the pages in the comfort of your living room), there is no doubt about it: your computer needs an Internet connection. Having access to the World Wide Web is an essential component of the OS X experience, not only for information and communication, but also for downloading Apple's frequently provided and often massively sized software updates. Most software today can be purchased online and downloaded immediately.

This chapter discusses the very basics of getting your Mac onto the Internet, and how to use the Internet after you are successfully connected to it. This chapter walks you through the Network Setup Assistant as the means to configure your Mac for Internet connectivity. (For advanced configuration and setup, see Chapter 11.) The Internet Connect application is described here, as well as Mac OS X's menu bar icons that are related to connecting you to the Internet. This chapter also provides a detailed overview of Apple's Safari Web browser and Mail application for surfing the Web and sending and receiving e-mail, and a brief description of newsgroups and news readers.

Why You Need the Internet

Using the Internet used to be less than enjoyable. Access was slow, clumsy, and expensive. Information was erratic, unreliable, and difficult to find. Although certain difficulties still exist, lately the Net is a pleasure to use.

Apple and the Internet

Apple is very aware of all the advantages the Internet offers, and has been gradually and more intensely centering the Mac user experience around the Internet. In the summer of 1998, Apple released the original iMac, which at the time was a revolutionarily designed, low-cost, and peppy machine. The first in a long-standing and still-existing tradition of their consumer product monikers, the *i* in iMac, iBook, iTunes, and so on, stands (or at least, used to stand) for Internet — a reminder of our interconnected world and how our digital devices are an integral part of it. Since that time, which spans the introduction and release of OS X, Apple has been making it easy for OS X users to get on the Internet, including step-by-step software setup assistants, bundling a full suite of applications such as Mail and Safari, and keeping their hardware up to date with the latest connectivity options. With additional Apple applications such as iPhoto and iTunes, Mac users are able to purchase prints of digital photography, and purchase and download music and movies straight from their Macs, using the Internet.

Information is readily available. Access is cheaper and faster than it has ever been. Often, it is faster and easier to find things on the Web than by using more traditional methods, and often the case turns out to be that certain information is available by Web only.

Nowadays, it's almost unheard of that any company or business (or for that matter, anyone or anything that wants attention) does not have a Web site. Companies have spent immense amounts of time and money on informative and well-designed sites that provide support and details. The Web makes information and communication almost instantaneous. Newspapers and magazines publish articles and stories and place them online, immediately viewable to millions of readers. People who can't place the face of that one character in a lazy Sunday afternoon movie can find out who it is in seconds by searching the Internet Movie Database (`www.imdb.com`). When the Gap doesn't have the correct size in their stores, you can get clothing shipped to your house, ordered off of the Web.

E-mail has evolved into an extremely popular method of communication, thanks largely to its speed and worldwide span. It is common for people to spend several hours a day on the Web, for both business and pleasure. Online banking has changed the way people pay their bills and manage their money. With just a few clicks, the credit cards and the electric company get paid! These are just some of the reasons why you need Internet access.

Connecting to the Internet

Getting on the Internet can be a relatively simple process, and after initial setup, no configuration from that point forward is usually needed. Still, understanding the concepts and some basic behind-the-scenes action makes using and troubleshooting your Mac and the Internet a much more positive experience.

The first thing you need to access the Internet is an agreement with an Internet service provider, or ISP. Much like the way your phone company provides the services necessary to make telephone calls, an ISP provides the services necessary to access the Internet from your computer. The Internet is essentially a huge, worldwide network of people's computers, with many different types of services available. The World Wide Web (WWW) stems from this worldwide network concept, and refers to the Internet service that you are likely most familiar with: reading Web pages.

Whenever a Web browser is launched, or an e-mail message sent, your ISP is responsible for your computer's ability to communicate with this world of computers. EarthLink (`www.earthlink.net`) and AT&T (`www.att.net`) are examples of ISPs. Usually an ISP charges a monthly flat rate for their services and provides unlimited usage. You can find ISP services advertised on television and in local newspapers. Changing your ISP for better and/or less expensive service can be a healthy move, but keep in mind that an ISP switch usually means that your e-mail address changes as well. For this reason, it can be advantageous to have an e-mail address that is ISP independent, such as Apple's .Mac services, which is covered in Chapter 14. In the past, services were usually billed on a per-minute basis, which quickly got expensive, and discouraged frequent partaking. There are still some pay-as-you-go plans for travelers on laptops using services throughout the country or worldwide, and for people who use the Net infrequently. America Online (AOL) is another example of an ISP, although their focus has shifted towards their application services recently. AOL is a special case because it does more than just provide an Internet connection service, as is described later in this chapter.

Types of Internet Connections

Presently, there are two main categories of Internet connection types, especially for the consideration of the home user: broadband and dial-up. Dial-up has been around in its current form for many years. A dial-up connection is initiated by an analog modem (MOdulator/DEModulator), which actually dials a telephone number in order to contact the ISP. Modem signals travel over regular telephone lines, the same ones that voice conversations go over, and at the same frequencies that voice services use. The function of the modem (there will be one on either end of the connection) is to translate the digital information coming from the computer, send it over the analog phone lines, and retranslate the signals back to digital. Every time a dial-up connection is made, there is a waiting period while the connection is initiated and authenticated. When you initiate a disconnect, there is a wait lag as well. Dial-up is slow, and because the signals are often traveling over antique telephone lines, often unreliable. Because dial-up monopolizes the phone line it is using, most frequenters of dial-up connections obtain a dedicated phone line. In many locations, especially ones away from larger urban areas, dial-up is all that is available. Dial-up is also suited for the traveler and portable owner — anywhere there is a phone line, an Internet connection can be initiated. As of today though, many hotels offer their guests (for a fee, usually) broadband connections straight from your hotel room. Because a dial-up connection is not always on, there are security advantages as well, because your computer is not connected to the Internet full time.

continued

continued

Broadband is so named because of its speed, which can be hundreds of times faster than a dial-up connection. This means that a 3MB music file that would take 20 minutes to download over an analog modem would take just seconds to transfer using a broadband connection. If broadband is available to you, get it. Mac OS X thrives with it; it's the way the Internet was meant to be experienced. Web pages load instantaneously, movie previews come up in seconds, and there is very little waiting or frustration overall. Gone are the days of reading a magazine and waiting for a Web page to load. Consumer-level broadband typically comes in two flavors: cable or DSL. Some ISPs have recently introduced an even faster kind of broadband based on fiber-optic connections. Verizon's service, called FiOS, can be faster than a regular broadband connection to the same degree that a regular broadband connection is faster than dialup. This screamingly fast connection is becoming more widespread and is often cheaper than a cable or DSL connection. If fiber is available to you, it's an absolute must.

Cable services are usually provided by the same company that provides your cable television, and the Internet signals typically arrive over the same lines that the television signals are sent over. When cable Internet is installed, a splitter is used to divide the incoming cable TV wire into two separate leads. One goes to the television, as before, and the other goes to a cable modem. The cable modem is then connected to the computer. Although a modem is used, there is no phone number to dial and no lag time in initiating a connection. Cable's inherent advantages are its "instant on" connection (no waiting to dial-up), its ease of setup, and its speed. Disadvantages are that it's usually more expensive than dial-up, it's not as widely available, and that because it's a shared connection (with other subscribers in your neighborhood) its speeds can decrease under heavy usage. To find out if cable service is available in your area, contact your cable television provider.

Broadband also comes in the form of the digital subscriber line, or DSL. Like dial-up, DSL uses the same phone lines that voice travels over, but uses different protocols and frequencies than voice data to substantiate a much faster connection. Like cable, DSL is fast connection. DSL can be used at the same time the telephone is used, so a separate phone line is not needed. A telephone cable is run from a wall jack to the DSL modem, and then the modem is connected to the computer. DSL's advantages are that its minimum speed is guaranteed (unlike cable, which can slow down under heavy neighborhood usage) and that it's fast. Its disadvantages are that its setup is marginally more difficult (on the computer-configuring side) and that, because its lines are the old telephone copper in the streets, you are often left at the mercy of the phone company — which may or may not be the ISP — for repairs and maintenance. On a consumer level, DSL is comparable to cable in the services that are provided, so we do not recommend one over the other. On a professional or enthusiast level, DSL can offer more options and more flexibility than cable, which we discuss further in Chapter 11.

Two other connection types worth mentioning are ISDN (Integrated Services Digital Network) and satellite. ISDN is technically a dial-up connection and is configured in the same manner. Years ago, it was a faster and much more expensive alternative to dial-up, but today it is rarely seen or available. Satellite is a form of broadband and an alternative to cable or DSL, especially if neither is available in your area. Satellite can be provided by companies that also provide satellite television, or by independent providers. Satellite's advantage is that it is often available in more remote areas.

However, it is often slower than its other broadband counterparts and can be adversely affected by the weather.

It is important to make a distinction between general network connectivity and true Internet connection types. Connecting to a local network in an office or in a school's computer lab might provide you with an Internet access, but the network itself is not the Internet connection type. The network is being provided with an Internet signal by a connection that is distributed among all the machines (usually a high-end DSL). The same goes for connecting to an AirPort wireless network; this is not your connection type to the Internet, it's a bridge that's connecting you to the network, which in turn is being provided with an Internet connection shared among its devices.

Making the connection

After you have secured the capability for Internet access, the next step is to configure your Mac. To help you get your computer on the Internet, Mac OS X includes a Setup Assistant to walk you through the configuration process. The Setup Assistant appears in two forms: it initially runs automatically after a fresh installation of Mac OS X (as long as network settings from a previous installation have not been preserved) and is more readily available through the Network preferences pane, under the System Preferences application. This chapter focuses on the latter version and uses its various configuration options to familiarize you with your Mac's network capabilities. For more information on networking, look at Chapter 11, Setting Up a Local Network.

If you are not sure if your Mac has a Net connection, the easiest way to figure that out is to launch a Web browser. Click the Safari icon in the Dock. If the home page loads, you are all connected and your computer does not need to be configured. You can also try manually typing in a Web site address and pressing Return. If nothing loads, read onwards!

To launch the Network Setup Assistant:

■ The best way to launch the assistant is through the System Preferences application. Go to the Apple Menu, click System Preferences, and click Network. Clicking the Assist me button shown in Figure 10.1 opens the dialog box also shown in Figure 10.1, which asks if you need assistance setting up a new network connection, or help solving a problem with an existing connection. Click the Assistant button.

■ You can also launch the Network Setup Assistant by navigating to it through the Finder. Although the Network Setup Assistant is just another application, it is buried within the confines of the System folder. The System folder contains a Library folder, which in turn contains a CoreServices folder. You can find the Network Setup Assistant inside of this CoreServices folder. See Figure 10.2 for the full pathway.

FIGURE 10.1

Use the Network preferences to access the Network Setup Assistant.

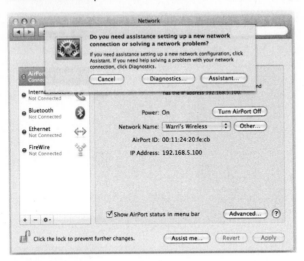

FIGURE 10.2

You can also launch the Network Setup Assistant by navigating to it through the Finder.

Internet configuration via the Network Setup Assistant

The following section walks you through using the Network Setup Assistant. If you are unfamiliar with configuring your Mac for network and Internet access, the Setup Assistant is a great way to both walk you through configuring your Mac and to familiarize yourself with the connection options that Mac OS X provides. If you want to configure your network settings manually, you can just use the Network preferences as shown in Chapter 11.

Introduction

Figure 10.3 shows the introductory screen of the Setup Assistant. The assistant asks you to provide a name for the network "location" that you are creating. Your Mac defaults to naming the location with the date and time you are configuring it, and that is fine for now. You can also change the name to reflect your current location, such as "work" or "home." This terminology is used because later on, you will have the ability to create different sets of network configurations depending on the physical location of your Mac — handy if you have a MacBook and are connecting frequently from a few different places. You can read more about network locations in Chapter 11.

FIGURE 10.3

Give a name reflecting your physical location.

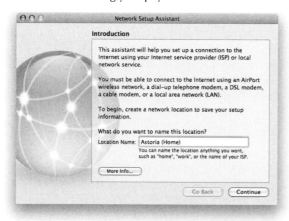

How *do* you connect?

You can connect using the five following options (see Figure 10.4):

- I use AirPort to connect to the Internet wirelessly.
- I use a telephone modem to dial my ISP.

- I use a DSL modem to connect to the Internet.
- I use a cable modem to connect to the Internet.
- I connect to my local area network (LAN).

FIGURE 10.4

Tell the Setup Assistant how your computer is connected to the Internet in the "How Do You Connect" section.

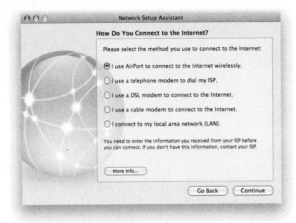

Each of these should hopefully sound familiar because they were discussed in the beginning of the chapter. Each of the possibilities is discussed in the following sections. You can also click the More Info button for a neat graphic and concise descriptions of the five types of connections, as shown in Figure 10.5. Keep in mind that most of these configurations require some information relating to your ISP.

TIP   Each of these connections, except for the AirPort, is a physical connection to the Internet. A wire needs to be plugged into your computer on one end, and the Internet connection device on the other. Just keep the make-sure-it's-plugged-in concept in mind when your computer refuses to connect for you; it's a great first troubleshooting step.

FIGURE 10.5

Clicking More Info gives you a neat description of the different types of Internet connections.

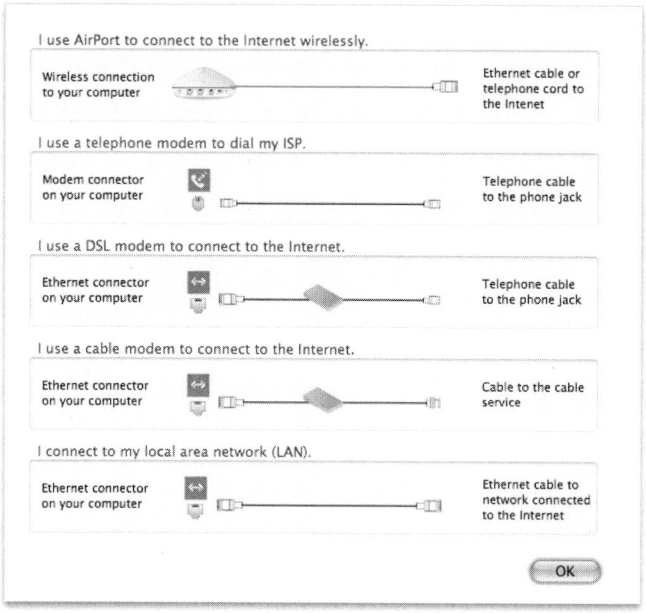

If you have an AirPort wireless network connection

Lucky you, no cables to plug in! Choosing the AirPort option at the How Do You Connect screen and clicking Continue presents you with the AirPort wireless connection screen (shown in Figure 10.6), which lets you choose the wireless network you want to join. Networks that are within your signal range should show up in the list. When you see the one you want, select it by clicking it once. If the network requires a password, a password field is provided for you to type it in. For security purposes, some networks are not readily visible, and only the privileged that know their names can have access. If that is the case, you'll need to select Other Network and type the invisible network's name and password. Clicking Continue brings you to the Ready To Connect? screen. It is most common for AirPort connections to automatically provide your computer with the information it needs to connect. If your Mac detects that is indeed the case, clicking Continue brings you to a Congratulations screen, informing you that your computer has been successfully configured. If your network does not provide your Mac with its required connection information, the next screen gives you the opportunity to enter information manually. Use the TCP/IP Connection Type pull-down menu to select the Manually option, and track down the network administrator (or a computer-savvy friend or co-worker) to find out what numbers to type in. After that's set, click Continue to bring you to the final screen. Click Done and you're home free.

FIGURE 10.6

Choose your wireless network from the list, or specify an invisible one by name.

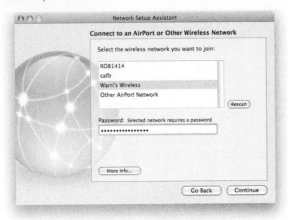

The modems, they are a disappearin'

Just a few short years ago, all new Macs shipped with a built-in modem, unless you specifically elected not to have one included. Today, no new Mac even has the capability of being configured with a built-in modem; if you want one they are external devices available for $49 extra. This modem marginalization is a testament to the increasing availability of broadband Internet and Apple's encouragement of its customers to move towards faster connections. If you have a new Mac and have purchased an external modem, you need to connect it using the USB port. If you have an older Mac that supports Leopard, it may have a built-in modem. Whether external or internal, the modem port has a picture of a telephone handset with some diagonal dots. Think of it as a phone jack; it accepts a regular phone cable, and its official name is RJ-11.

If you use a telephone modem to dial up your ISP

Welcome aboard! Plug in that phone cable and follow along. The first screen, shown in Figure 10.7, asks for your account name, password, ISP phone number, and if you need to dial a number for an outside line (necessary in some offices and schools). If you have call waiting, you can select the Yes box, and the following screen gives you the option to turn off call waiting by typing a code (*70) while you are on the Internet. This is useful if the phone line you are using is not a dedicated Internet line, and you do not want a telephone call to interrupt your Internet session. The next screen asks you what kind of modem you have, which should default to either the external or internal Apple Internal 56K Modem (V.92). Choosing to ignore the dial tone is useful if you are using an infrared or Bluetooth modem (see Chapter 11) or if you have a phone service with an inconsistent dial tone, such as a phone system that changes dial tone to alert you of a new voice-mail message. Clicking Continue takes you to the Ready To Connect? screen, which asks you to make sure that your information is correct, and then tests the connection for you. The Congratulations screen is the last to appear; click the Done button. Setup Assistant transposes your information into the Mac OS for you, and you are ready to go!

> **CAUTION** Modems are analog. Many telephone systems are digital. Although there is no physical difference in the jacks, plugging your computer into a digital telephone jack is a surefire way of ruining your modem. Hotels sometimes have dedicated analog lines for modems to circumvent this. Many business buildings are all digital, and where there are digital lines, there are often dedicated network (Ethernet) jacks. If you're not sure, don't risk it, and use a digital line tester, available from resellers like CDW (www.cdw.com).

FIGURE 10.7

Set your Mac to dial-up by typing in your name, password, and telephone information.

If you have a DSL modem connection

Click that Ethernet cable into your Mac and hold on. Back at the How Do You Connect? screen, click the DSL modem option, and click Continue. With a DSL modem, you'll typically connect in one of two ways. If your DSL modem connects automatically, or your computer is going through a switch or a router before getting to the DSL modem (more on switches, routers, and automatic connections in Chapter 11) your Mac can figure this out automatically and set up your connection for you. If your Mac can connect automatically, you're taken through to the Congratulations screen and you don't have to do anything else.

Most DSL modems connect using the Point-to-Point Protocol over Ethernet, or PPPoE. If you are connected straight to the modem, you must configure your Mac to use said PPPoE connection. No problem — when your Mac can't connect automatically, the Network Assistant shows you the screen shown in Figure 10.8. Here you can type your name and password information, and optionally, the name of your ISP in the PPPoE Service Name box, which can make finding your account settings later a bit easier. If you do not know this information, you can call your ISP and obtain it. If you do not connect via PPPoE, you have to select the More choices option and click Continue, where you are given the option to type a static address, a number assigned by your ISP that should be provided to you. You can see how this configuration looks in Figure 10.9. When your DSL configuration is complete, click Done.

FIGURE 10.8

Type your DSL account information to configure the commonly used Point-to-Point Protocol over Ethernet (PPPoE).

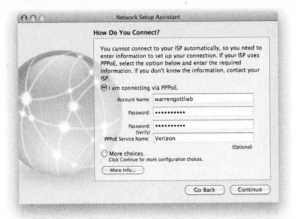

FIGURE 10.9

Use the More choices option for static IP address settings.

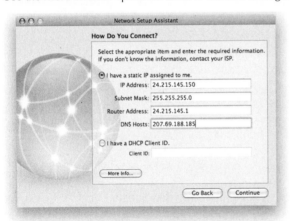

If you use a cable modem to connect to the Internet

What a fast connection you have! String that Ethernet cord from the cable modem to your Mac and you're almost there. Clicking the Continue button takes you to the screen shown in Figure 10.10, the Ready To Connect? screen. The most commonly used connection method for cable modem is via the Dynamic Host Configuration Protocol, or DHCP. Because DHCP is an automatic connection, this usually means that you don't have to enter any other information, and that clicking Continue completes your setup. In rare cases, your cable modem will connect using a Point-to-Point Protocol over Ethernet (PPPoE), or require you to type something called a DHCP client ID. If your Mac is not connecting automatically, you will be prompted to enter this information, which you must obtain from your ISP.

FIGURE 10.10

Because DHCP is the most common method for connecting with a cable modem, your Mac can usually connect you automatically.

If you connect to a local area network connection (over Ethernet)

Plug that Ethernet cable into your machine and get started by selecting the local area network option in the Setup Assistant. If you've already got a network set up (again, see Chapter 11 for more on networks), whether it is in your home, office, or elsewhere, chances are that your Mac can simply plug in and use an automatically obtained configuration, which the Setup Assistant tests for you. If an automatic connection cannot be obtained, the Setup Assistant asks you to enter the information manually, as shown in Figure 10.11. At this point, you need to enter a whole bunch of numbers that specify your network settings. Unless you've set up the local network yourself, these numbers must be provided to you by your network administrator, or at least someone who may know them, like the guy in the cubicle next to yours. (Make sure not to type in the exact same numbers though — your Mac must have a unique number in the IP Address field.) Click Continue when you have finished entering the numbers, and if your Mac can use them to make a successful connection, you are brought to the Congratulations screen and are finished.

FIGURE 10.11

Setting up your local Ethernet connection manually involves typing a lot of numbers (more on these numbers in Chapter 11) and looks something like this.

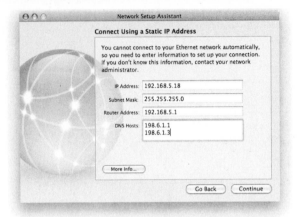

Making and breaking the connection

Ahead we discuss the making and breaking of your Internet connection using Leopard's menu bar icons. These menu bar icons are effective only if you have already configured your Mac for Internet access — they are just pointers that affect your underlying settings. It should be noted that cable and local Ethernet connections are handled automatically by the Mac OS. These are considered to be *instant-on* connections and do not require user intervention to connect; you are permanently online. Dial-up, AirPort, and DSL connections do (or can) involve some user intervention, and therefore they are covered in the following sections. For future reference, it should also be noted that defaults for dial-up and DSL are such that you must manually make the connection, but it is a common choice to automate this by configuring it in the Network preferences pane, covered in Chapter 11. You can also choose to have the session disconnect automatically or manually. Disconnecting from your Internet service when you are done is a good idea if you pay for service based on your time spent online or if you are paying phone-number charges to connect.

Going through the numbers with dial-up

You hear a brief dial tone, and then some screeching noises. What you are hearing is digital data, modulated to analog signal, being transmitted over phone lines. It might sound terrible, but it's perfectly normal, and it's a great cue as to what your Mac is doing. (In fact, if you're in the computer support field and you're troubleshooting a modem connection, that screeching noise becomes your *Rocky* theme song, which you can even dance to, if no one is looking.) If you select the option to "Show modem status in menu bar" from the Network System Preferences, (see Chapter 11) a modem pull-down menu, with an icon just like the modem icon on the back of your computer (if it has an internal modem), appears in the menu bar. Pulling down the menu displays some important options — you can choose between configurations, and choose whether or not to show the time that you are connected for, and the status of your connection when it is being made and unmade. Most importantly, the menu displays the Connect option, which is shown in Figure 10.12. Choosing Connect causes your modem to start dialing your ISP and attempts to make a connection. If you have checked the show time and/or show status options , you will see that information appear in the menu bar along with the modem icon. When you are connected, the Connect command changes to a Disconnect command, and you can choose that command to end your session.

FIGURE 10.12

Click the telephone icon in the menu bar to display modem connection commands and options without opening a separate application.

Zoom through the phone lines with DSL

A DSL connection can be initiated from the menu bar as well. In the Network preferences, a Show PPPoE status in menu bar option appears in the form of a check box. Selecting this option puts an Ethernet port icon in the menu bar, which can be used to initiate a PPPoE connection (see Figure 10.13). Pull down the menu and select Connect, and within a few seconds, you should be wired to go. A successful connection displays a Disconnect option in the pull-down menu; select this to terminate the session. Connectivity can be verified by the PPPoE icon's darker, filled in color, and launching Safari to see if a Web page loads.

FIGURE 10.13

Click the little picture of the Ethernet symbol in the menu bar to initiate a PPPoE connection.

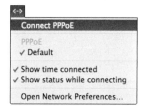

Ditch your cables and head for the AirPort

If your Mac has AirPort wireless capability, there will be an AirPort menu bar icon, the different states of which can be seen in Figures 10.14–10.16. If you do not see this icon, you can choose to enable the AirPort menu using the Network System Preferences. The first option in the pull-down list is the most basic: powering AirPort off or on, which disables or enables your computer's wireless capability. Connecting via AirPort requires that this capability be turned on. Powering AirPort off is useful on portable machines, to save battery power at the expense of an Internet connection. Click the Turn AirPort On button, if it's powered off. The next portion of this list displays the names of the wireless networks that your Mac is in range of. Select the wireless network to which you want to connect; because wireless networking is a standard, it means that your AirPort-equipped Mac should be able to connect to any wireless network that it sees..An AirPort Base Station is but one way to make a wireless network, and there are many other companies besides Apple whose products produce a wireless network signal that the Mac can access.

Often, in both residential and commercial buildings, or if you're lucky enough to be outside in a city park, multiple networks will be in range, and you'll need to choose one. If the network is password protected there will be a lock icon next to the network name, and, you'll need to type in the valid password when prompted. An error message stating "There was an error connecting to the AirPort Network" can mean an incorrect password was typed, but often signifies that you're too far out of range to sustain a connection. Solid black curved lines indicate signal strength; a muted gray display of lines indicates little or no signal. If AirPort is powered off the icon appears as an outline. The AirPort signals are shown in Figures 10.14, 10.15, and 10.16.

FIGURE 10.14

Full AirPort signal appears as thick black lines.

FIGURE 10.15

No AirPort signal is shown with gray lines in place of black ones.

FIGURE 10.16

AirPort powered off appears as an outline of the signal strength indicator.

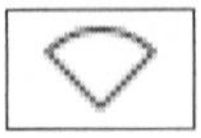

Browsing the World Wide Web

Of course, the whole point of learning and configuring your Internet access is to gain access to the wealth of information and communication available on the Internet.

One service available through this giant, globe-spanning Internet is known as the World Wide Web. Emerging gradually and booming within the mid-nineties, this technology brought the Internet to public prominence and made terms such as "surfin' the Web," or "browsin' the Net" household phrases of the previously nongeeky. Using the World Wide Web implies somehow experiencing and perusing this myriad of information, whether it is a newspaper article or a movie preview.

Safari in the Web jungle

You can access the Web with a program called a *Web browser*. In 2003, Apple released its own Web browser, called Safari, which is now part of the Mac OS. Since its release, Safari has soared in popularity; it's fast and lean, and has a fantastic interface. Safari is discussed in more detail later in the "Taking a Safari Through the Wild Web" section. Until Safari's takeover, Microsoft's Internet Explorer was the reigning browser king in OS X. Soon after Safari's release, Microsoft canceled development of IE for the Mac, stating that their Apple-oriented customers were better served by using Safari, and that they lack the access to Apple's OS that they need to compete on that level. (Funny how the plethora of other third-party browser developers haven't mentioned that issue.) A key truth that will make your Web life much better is this: always have more than one browser handy. A secondary browser is an essential tool. Not all Web sites are created equal (nor are the browsers), and what looks fine in one browser may look terrible, or not work at all, in another.

> **NOTE** Different browsers use different rendering engines to decode and display Web pages, which is why certain pages look different in different browsers. Safari and OmniWeb use Apple's WebCore library, based on the open source KHTML engine. Netscape, the Mozilla family, and the new AOL browser are based on the Netscape Gecko engine. Internet Explorer used its own proprietary Microsoft engine, which, of course, was still different from the Windows version.

Other browsers for your toolkit

A great advantage of the OS X platform is that many different browsers are available. You don't need all of them, but they're all worth a look. Each can be downloaded by using Safari.

- **Firefox:** Firefox is the premier browser offered by the Mozilla organization, available at www.firefox.com. It should be your primary alternative. Firefox is available on many operating systems; this cross-platform nature means that many Web site developers will make sure to test their pages using Firefox, even if they ignore more proprietary browsers like Safari. Other Mozilla browsers such as Camino can be downloaded from www.mozilla.org.

Understanding Web Terminology

To use the Web, it helps to know a bit of its terminology. Web browser programs display information in *Web pages,* which can contain text, pictures, and animation as well as audio and video clips. The machines that store all this information and that serve it to you on request are called *Web servers.* On a Web page, the underlined text usually indicates one or more *links,* which are also known as *hyperlinks.* Pictures can also be links. A link can be discovered by positioning the mouse pointer over it; if it's a link, the arrow changes into a pointing hand. Clicking a link takes you to another Web page. The intriguing thing about a link is that it can take you to a page on the same Web server or a page on any other Web server on the planet. So, it's possible to click your way around the world and not even know it!

- **OmniWeb:** OmniWeb is just one of many useful programs made by the Omni group. With a beautiful interface and some unique features, it's another excellent alternative. Get it at www.omnigroup.com.

- **Opera:** The Opera browser is optimized for Leopard and can be downloaded from www.opera.com.

- **Netscape:** The Netscape browser is alive and well (if not a little bloated) and downloadable at www.netscape.net.

Taking a Safari Through the Wild Web

Open Safari by clicking its icon in the Dock. When Safari opens, it displays a browser window and goes to a Web page that has been previously designated as the home page. With Mac OS X, the home page is initially set to an Apple start page, with tips, news, and other Apple-related links. Try going to Apple's main Web site by typing **www.apple.com** and pressing Return. Besides being a Web site that every Mac-head should know and love, it is a great example page for our demonstration. You can even go as far as to set this to your home page by going under the Safari menu and choosing the Preferences option. Where it says Home Page, type **www.apple.com**. If Safari is displaying the Apple Web site already (because you've typed its name into the address field), you can click the Set to Current Page button, which changes the homepage to whatever the browser is displaying. Click OK to save the change.

Navigation basics

All the buttons and fields you see in front of you in the Safari Web browser are tools designed to help you navigate the Web. You can type the names of the Web sites that you want to visit, do searches, travel to your previously saved bookmarks, and shuffle backward and forward to places you have recently been. Notice that the toolbars in Finder windows have a similar look to them. Apple has actually taken the Web-browsing concept and applied its logical simplicity to browsing the files in Mac OS X as well. A walk-through of Safari's toolbar and basic features follows.

Backward and Forward buttons

Say that you're at Apple's Web site, and Wow! You've simply got to read more about that iPhone that was just released. So you click on the iPhone header, which is a link that takes you to Apple's iPhone page, where you can read more about said iPhone. The overview, however, just isn't enough, so you click the Tech Specs section to see exactly how small it is. When you're done with that, how can you get back to Apple's main page? Clicking the Back button (the one with the left-pointing arrowhead on it) once takes you one page back, from the tech specs back to the overview. Clicking Back again takes you from the overview page back to Apple's main page. Want to go back to the overview? Click the Forward button (with the right-pointing arrowhead) to take you forward to the page you just came back from. If you are buried many pages deep in a Web browsing session, you can click and hold on either the Back or the Forward button, and a list of pages that you have been to appears. Scroll down the list and click the page that you want to visit.

Stop and Reload buttons

Perhaps you are browsing the homepage of the *New York Times*. You've read a bunch of articles and clicked your way back to the main page, but it's an hour later, and you've got a hunch that a new tidbit of information might have been posted to the site. Clicking the Reload button (the one with the curved arrow) reloads the Web site from the *New York Times'* server, and if anything new has posted, your display will reflect that. Some Web pages, however, automatically refresh themselves, sometimes eliminating the need for manually initiating a reload. Pressing Shift while clicking the Reload button fully reloads the page from the server, which can be more effective than a regular reload, which only appends new content.

As often happens while browsing the Web, you clicked a link, and man, that page is taking forever to load. You've gotten through a full e-mail to your boss with the top ten reasons why you should be able to work from home, and that page still isn't quite halfway done. You can see bits and pieces of text and graphics, but nothing useful, and you can just feel it. That page just isn't coming along. Look at the toolbar. Instead of a circle-arrow indicating a reload, the button has changed to display an X. In fact, any time a page is loading, even if it's not stuck, an X appears instead of a reload symbol. The X is the Stop button. Clicking it ceases the download of whatever page load you were attempting. After the page has stopped, you can attempt to do a reload, or just move on with your life.

Bookmark button

It's happened. You've found the definitive Web home of Arlo Guthrie, and you need to save that page for future reference. Click the Add Bookmarks bar (shown in Figure 10.17), and Safari not only saves it for you, but first asks where you want to save it and what name to give it. You can choose to save it in the bookmarks bar (which places it on the toolbar next to the currently displaying Amazon and eBay ones), the Bookmarks menu (you can get to it by going to the Bookmarks menu), or any number of folders that exist within Safari's unique bookmark management system. This system is covered a bit later in the chapter. For now, you can save it to the toolbar or in the menu.

FIGURE 10.17

FIGURE 10.17

Clicking the Add Bookmark button presents you with the option to name your bookmark and save it to the location of your choice.

Address field

As often happens, you need to go to a Web site, it's not bookmarked, but you know its address. Typing its full name (such as www.apple.com) and pressing Return gets you there. A Web address is officially called a URL, or Uniform Resource Locator. (For more in-depth information, see the sidebar "Understanding URLs" later in this chapter.) Many times, you do not need to type the full name of the site; for example, just typing in the word **maclife** should take you to *MacLife* magazine's Web site (www.maclife.com). If you have been there before, and if it's bookmarked and you don't know it, Safari might try to fill in the name for you. This can be helpful at times, but irritating when you don't want Safari to think for you.

The address field serves another purpose, a visual one, in Safari. As a Web page is loading, the background of the address turns into a page-load status bar; as the page loads further, the blue background gradually makes it all the way across the field. When a page has finished loading, the background turns back to white, as shown in Figure 10.18.

FIGURE 10.18

A page in the process of loading displays a progress bar in the address field.

Just Google it

For a noun to make its way into verb status (at least in common language) is an esteemed achievement. Google is the very popular and very effective Web search engine (www.google.com) that now has become an action verb as well. If you ever hear someone tell you to just Google something, they're asking you to go to Google's Web page, type the term, and hit Return. It's so popular and effective, in fact, that Apple has built this capability directly into the Safari toolbar. Typing something into the Google field and hitting Return is identical to first going to the actual Web site

Understanding URLs

The technical name for a Web address is a *URL,* which stands for Uniform Resource Locator. An example of a URL is http://www.macworld.com. A URL begins with a code that specifies a kind of Internet protocol. The http stands for HyperText Transfer Protocol, which is the protocol for viewing Web pages. Often a Web URL is shown without the http:// portion, and beginning with www. This is because most browsers are smart enough to assume that anything beginning with a www is specifying the http protocol, and the browser inserts that automatically.

Another protocol is the File Transfer Protocol, which is signified by ftp, and is used for transferring files over the Internet. Protocols also exist for local networking; for example, afp signifies Apple Filing Protocol, used by many Mac OS file servers. The remainder of the URL specifies the domain name, (macworld.com) and the specific server to access (www). Internet addresses are all based on numbers. The names you type exist because they are easier to remember than the numbers. The catch is that the name has to resolve, or be properly tied into, the proper number, in order for the Web site to be located. This kind of information is stored on *DNS,* or Domain Name Service, servers.

and searching from there. Safari's field even stores recently searched-for items, accessible by clicking the magnifying glass inside of the field. If something is typed into the field and you want to remove it, click the *x* that appears in the right-hand side.

Bookmarks bar

Below the toolbar with the previously mentioned features lies the bookmarks bar. When you save a page by clicking the Add button, Safari gives you the option of saving the location in this easily accessible place. After it's in the bookmarks bar, its name — that is, the name that you have specified (shorter names are ideal for the bookmarks bar) — becomes a button that you can click to open the Web site. Folders of bookmarks can be displayed in the toolbar as well and are evident by the presence of a disclosure triangle next to the folder's name. Clicking the name displays a list of items residing in the folder.

More features, and customization

Now that you know the basics of Web navigation and of Safari's visible features, it's time to hike around to where Safari really shines: all of its special features and customization. Apple has included many slick features to make your Web browsing experience quick and enjoyable.

Preferences

A great way to get to know a program is to go poking around in its Preferences window. Safari's are located under the Safari menu.

General

The first option is the General preferences, shown in Figure 10.19. Here, you can change your Mac's default Web browser to something other than Safari using the pull-down menu. If you hate that your home page opens every time you make a new window, you can set Safari to do something else, like open nothing. The next item is a pop-up menu that lets you change the amount of time Safari saves your browsing history. You can specify as long as one year, as short as one day, or use the manually setting to never erase the locations of your previously visited pages. You can also change which folder to save your downloaded files to, and whether to automatically remove items from the download list. In previous versions of Mac OS X, the default downloads folder was your Desktop folder. In Leopard, Apple has created a new folder inside of your Home, designated for the task, called Downloads. A check box lets you decide whether to let Safari automatically launch certain files after you download them, which is easier than double-clicking every file you save from the Web. Sometimes other applications link to Safari, such as an e-mail program; the last option lets you choose to have Web sites from linked applications open in a new window or in the current window. (Having links load in the current window runs the risk of taking you off of the page you were just reading; therefore many people like to have links open in a new one.)

FIGURE 10.19

Change the default Web browser or maybe your home page in Safari's General preferences.

Appearance

The Appearance section lets you choose the fonts in which to view the World Wide Web. When pages don't specify in their formatting what font to use, Safari uses the ones that you can specify here. The standard font is what you see the most; the fixed width is used less often. If you have a really slow connection, or just hate pictures, you can choose not to have Safari load any graphics (meaning you'll just see text and colors).

Bookmarks

This section lets you choose what bookmark features show up where. In the bookmarks bar, you can choose to display a link that will access the bookmarks found in the Address Book (see Chapter 6) or from Bonjour, Apple's zero-configuration networking technology (see Chapter 11). You also have similar options for the Bookmarks menu (with the added option to display the book-marks also appearing in the bar) and in the bookmark collection, which is discussed later.

Tabs

Tabs are very useful, and are described later in this chapter. Briefly, tabbed browsing lets you view multiple Web pages within the same window, instead of having 20 or so open Web pages cluttering your screen at once. Choose New Tab from the file menu (⌘+T) to watch them in action. In the Tabs preferences, you can choose to allow ⌘+clicking links to open new tabs, whether or not to bring newly created tabs to the foreground, and whether Safari should warn you when you are closing a window with multiple open tabs.

RSS

RSS stands for "Really Simple Syndication" and exists as a different kind of Internet protocol used primarily for viewing information that is subject to frequent change, such as news headlines or weblogs. RSS readers have existed for quite some time, but now this capability has been built into Safari, negating the need for a separate application. Apple's Mail application, which is covered later in this chapter, has also gained the ability to read RSS feeds. Under the RSS preferences, you can choose your default RSS reader (if you don't want to use Safari) and how frequently Safari automat-ically updates articles. You can even set a custom color for new news and set how long Safari keeps older articles present. RSS is discussed in more detail later in this chapter.

AutoFill

Instead of typing your name and address every single time you buy something, Safari can do it for you if the AutoFill options are checked. Choose the names and passwords box to have all of your names and passwords saved; they will show up automatically every time you visit the site. This can be a great time saver, but it's potentially hazardous if many people have access to your machine — they'll be able to get into anything you'd normally have to use a password for, such as your Web-based e-mail or your online banking. When you enter a password for the first time, or change an existing one, Safari asks if you want to save passwords for that particular site. You can select Never for this Web site, Not Now (meaning that you can decide to choose later on), or Yes, as shown in Figure 10.20.

FIGURE 10.20

When you tell Safari to save names and passwords in the AutoFill preferences, it lets you choose how to handle individual pages when you enter or change a password.

Would you like to save this password?

To review passwords you have saved and remove them, open the AutoFill pane of Safari preferences.

(Never for this Website)   (Not Now)   (Yes)

Protect Yourself

The fewer things you load onto your Mac from the Web, the less risk to your Mac. In general, you should feel free to leave all the Java options enabled; they affect your ability to view certain Java-programmed Web sites. If you customize only one thing about Safari (and we *do* tell you this more than once) make sure it's the Block Pop-up windows option. If this is checked (it can also be enabled from the File menu) you'll almost never again see another of those maddening, frustrating, and annoying pop-up advertisements that assault your screen. Unfortunately, some pop-up windows are especially nefarious and actually load as multimedia overlays within the same page you are trying to view. Others are more like pop-behinds because they appear behind the window and are usually discovered when the windows in the foreground are closed. Safari can't block these trickier types of advertisements.

Cookies are pieces of information that are stored on your computer after you visit certain Web sites. `Amazon.com` knows you've been there before (and might greet you by name) because the first time you visited and signed into your account, `Amazon.com` uploaded a piece of information to your computer that is now read from you every time you access that particular Web site; so, ostensibly, they know it is you. Selecting the option to accept cookies from only the sites that you navigate to prevents cookies from advertisements and sites that you have not elected to visit from installing themselves on your computer. If you choose the option to "ask before sending a non-secure form to a secure Web site," you will be alerted every time this happens, as can occur when you switch, for example, from a secure online banking site to a Macintosh news site.

Advanced

For the visually impaired, the Advanced section gives the opportunity to never let Safari use fonts below a certain size. For those who have difficulties maneuvering computer mice, you can check the next box to enable the Tab key to highlight each item on the Web page, which enables you to select links with the Return key. Selecting a custom style sheet overrides the look and feel of the sites that you go to. If you know HTML (Hypertext Markup Language), the language that Web pages are written in, you can code your own. Clicking the button to change proxy settings sends you to the Network preferences pane.

Apple Cares!

Apple Cares about how Safari is doing, plowing along through all those Web pages. Under the Safari menu, there's a Report Bugs to Apple command. Choosing this opens a screen that inputs the name of the active Web page, a field for your comments, and a Submit button. Click More options for greater specificity. If something doesn't work right, or a Web page that you go to doesn't load properly, tell Apple! They'll usually fix it.

Security

Most Web surfers are lax about security. Internet security, as it relates to you, is the idea that other Web users do or do not have access to information that you don't want them to see. This includes any information that you transmit, from your birth date, to your e-mail password, to your credit card numbers. In general, when typing sensitive information into a Web page (like when you are buying something), make sure of two things in Safari: one is that the URL begins with https:// instead of just http://. The *s* means "secure." Also, in the upper right corner of Safari's window, you see a little icon of a locked padlock. If these two indicators are present, consider the site safe. See Figure 10.21.

FIGURE 10.21

You know you're in a secure site by the presence of the lock icon in the upper right-hand corner, and by the https:// instead of just http:// in the address field.

Other ways to customize Safari

Safari's customization can go even further than we have discussed. By using Safari's menus, you can do things like change the items you see in the toolbar, see pages you have previously visited, and manage your bookmarks.

View menu

Use the View menu to customize Safari's general look and feel. Here you can add or remove portions of the main window such the Bookmark bar or the Tab bar. You can also use the Customize Toolbar option to add or remove buttons like the Forward, Back, or Homepage button. Choosing to show the status bar is a recommendation; doing so places a thin bar at the bottom of every window. When you mouse over a link, the full URL appears in the status bar. When a page is loading the status bar keeps you apprised of the page's progress. You can also use the View menu to stop loading or to reload the page, and to make the text larger or smaller. If you want to go behind the scenes, the View menu also incorporates a View Source option; choosing this lets you see the source code (HTML) of the active Web page. If you've got no programming experience, it'll look like gobbledygook, but it's a good window into what makes up a Web page, whether written out by hand or laid out in an application such as Adobe's Dreamweaver or Apple's own iWeb application.

History menu

This menu's main function is to provide an interface for your browsing history. Safari keeps track of all the sites you have visited for a specified period of time, which you can set in the General preferences. Its true usefulness is appreciated only through experience. When you forget that great site that you were just at the other day, you can scroll through the pages that show up in the history and find it. Clearing the history deletes all the locations that Safari has saved, useful if you don't want another person poking around where you've been. The History menu also lets you mark a page for snapback. Snapback is discussed a little later.

Bookmarks menu

This menu grants you access to your saved bookmarks. Bookmarks are created by saving the locations of previously visited Web sites. This is the most convenient spot to access bookmarks that you have saved to the menu. Select a location on this menu and Safari takes you there.

Window menu

This menu is used for navigating through Safari's various windows, which appear in a list towards the bottom of the menu. Here, you can select to view the Activity window, which shows you detailed information regarding the Web sites that you are loading and their various components, such as images or movies. The Downloads window keeps track of all of your downloads and pops up whenever a file is downloaded. You can also view any open windows by selecting them from the list, and select tabs and move tabs between different windows.

Advanced navigation

Some of the following features are unique to Safari, and others can be found in other browsers, but as usual, the interface wizards at Apple just know how to do it better. Read on to learn time-saving and easier ways to browse.

Avoiding the Back button

Web browsing can be a bit stressful. There's so much information, so many links, and the lurking fear of something getting lost in the searching! Using the Back button is a tried and true hallmark of Web navigation, but there are better and more organized ways.

SnapBack

You've Googled something (through Safari's toolbar, of course), say, an ex-boy- or girlfriend's name. Convince yourself that you're not a stalker. You've found some great sites and lots of useless information. In fact, you want to keep reading from the list that Google gave you, but you're currently eight clicks deep into a fascinating read on how llamas make great pets.

Instead of clicking the Back button a whole bunch of times, you might have noticed the little orange arrow that appeared in the Google search field. Clicking the arrow takes you back to the original list of search results that Google returned, without backtracking for a few dozen hits to the Back button. Safari accomplishes this by marking the first page you visit on a site. And, if you visit a page that you know you will be returning to, you can manually mark the page for snapback, by choosing to do so under the History menu.

Tabs

You're reading the *New York Times* site. There are tons of great articles. You can either open each one in a new window, which gets cluttered and unorganized pretty rapidly, or make generous use of the Back button and have only one article loading at a time, or, you can use Safari's tabs feature. Using tabs gives you the ability to open multiple Web pages in a single browser window, separated by little tabs that protrude down from the toolbar, as shown in Figure 10.22.

Tabs are enabled in the Tabs section of the Safari preferences. You can create a new tab by selecting that option from the File menu, or pressing ⌘+T. Notice that the tab displays a progress wheel to show that a page is loading. Holding down the ⌘ key while clicking a link opens the link as a new tab, as opposed to in the same window, replacing what you were just viewing. If you've chosen to select new tabs as they are created (in preferences), the tab opens in the foreground. If you have not, it opens in the background without taking the current page off the screen. You can also right-click (or Control+click) a link to display a contextual menu, which, among other options, gives you an opportunity for opening it in a new tab. If the status bar is being displayed, mousing over the link while the Control or Option keys are held down reveals what will happen when the mouse button is clicked. Opening tabs in the background is a great strategy for managing links that you have come across while still browsing. Instead of interrupting your reading, you can open as many links as you want as tabs in the background and read them all as you choose.

After all your tabs are open, you can click among them with reckless abandon. Cycle through them by holding down ⌘+Shift and either of the bracket keys (located to the right of the P key on any Apple keyboard). If there are too many tabs to view on-screen at once, Safari displays a double arrow in the toolbar to indicate more tabs to the right. Tabs can be closed by clicking the little *x* that appears on each tab, or by typing ⌘+W. If no tabs are open, ⌘+W closes the whole window. In addition, Control+clicking a tab opens a contextual menu with the option to close all tabs, or even reload them.

FIGURE 10.22

Tabbed windows look like this.

Open Web pages in the Dashboard

DashClip is a Safari feature that simply allows you to turn any portion of a Web page into a Dashboard widget, which updates itself the same way the Web page would. You can activate DashClip by clicking its icon in Safari's toolbar, or by selecting Open in Dashboard from the File menu. Once DashClip is activated, as shown in Figure 10.23, you can use the selection box to select any portion of the Web page you want to turn into a Dashboard widget. When you are satisfied with your selection, you can click the Add button, and your Mac automatically activates Dashboard and displays your newly created widget, as seen in Figure 10.24. You can also click the widget information icon and choose a customized border for your newly gestated widget, also visible in Figure 10.24.

FIGURE 10.23

Use the selection box to choose your desired widget area, and click the Add button to place your widget into the Dashboard.

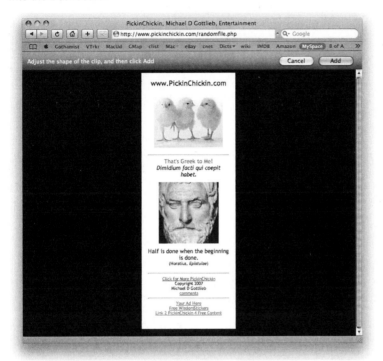

Safari RSS: it's really simple (syndication)

In Leopard, Safari has the ability to view RSS feeds right in your browser window. RSS stands for really simple syndication, and exists as a different kind of protocol that many news and weblog sites use to publish new information. Using Safari's RSS feature, it's possible to view all of your news and information headlines in a single browser window, instead of having to visit each site individually. When a site broadcasts information using RSS, it is called a *feed*. Safari saves you from visiting the sites individually by viewing feeds from all different sites on the same page. You can tell when Safari is viewing RSS feeds by looking in the address bar. Instead of the usual http:// prefix, the Web site begins with feed://.

FIGURE 10.24

Behold, your newly created widget added to the Dashboard, complete with customizable borders.

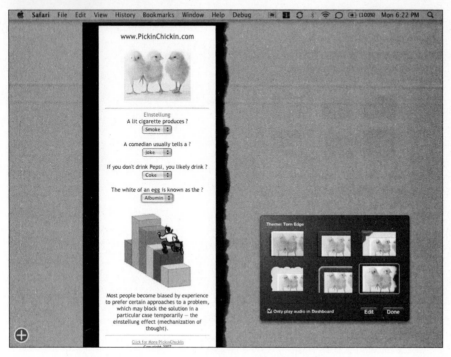

Safari displays articles from RSS feeds in a list of headlines with brief article summaries, as shown in Figure 10.25. Clicking the headline or the article summary takes you directly to the regular Web site content. On the right-hand side of the feed page is a grouping of controls for further control and customization of your feeds. You can use the Search Articles field to search your RSS feeds for specific content. If you bookmark the results, Safari can dynamically update for new content as it becomes available. (Bookmarking is discussed a bit later in this chapter.) There is also slider control for dynamically changing the length of the summaries as they appear in the Web page and sorting controls that let you view by date, title, and source.

FIGURE 10.25

RSS feeds can make it easier to stay updated with the latest news.

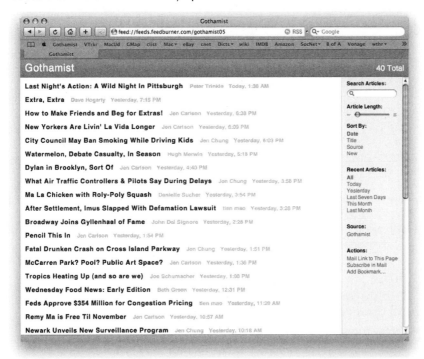

Safari tells you immediately if a Web site has an RSS feed coming from it. Once you've navigated to a Web site that has a feed, Safari displays a blue and white RSS icon in the Web address field, visually alerting you to the feed's presence. To view the RSS feed, simply click the RSS icon and Safari loads the RSS feed instead of the standard page. You can see the RRS icon in Figure 10.26.

FIGURE 10.26

The presence of the RSS icon in the Web address field is indicative of an RSS feed available for viewing with Safari.

NOTE   Although there are different RSS standards that are currently in use on the Internet, Safari is compatible with all of them. The current RSS standard is RSS 2.0. Older RSS standards include RSS 1.0 and 0.90, with RSS standing for RDF (Resource Description Framework) Site Summary, and RSS 0.91, with RSS standing for Rich Site Summary. RSS formats are created using XML.

Protect yourself, private!

It's easy to be hesitant when it comes to accessing your personal information on Macs open to the general public, or even a machine that might belong to a friend or family member. It is well known that Web browsers can save information about you, such as the sites you've visited (under Safari's History menu, for example) or even your login and password information if you inadvertently or absentmindedly choose to save them from force of habit of being on your personal machine. Who wants to worry about leaving a trail of sensitive information (such as your e-mail or online banking password) behind?

Worry no more. Under the Safari menu, you can choose to "Start Private Browsing." Once Private Browsing has been enabled, Safari ceases to store *any* information regarding your Web browsing. Nothing is cached, no passwords are saved, and nothing is added to the history. To any other user, it would appear as though you were never there at all.

Keeping organized

A great strength of Safari is its capability to keep your Web browsing organized. By blocking your pop-up windows, managing your bookmarks, and keeping your downloads managed, Safari can reduce your Web clutter.

Block those pop-ups

Pop-ups are windows that jump to the front of the screen when you are browsing the Web. You haven't asked to see these windows. They just appear. They are advertisements. They slow down your Web browser and your Mac. With Safari, you can banish annoying pop-ups forever by choosing to do so under the Safari menu. That's it. Select that option and Safari blocks them all automatically, simply by refusing to display information from a site that you have not chosen to visit. You can also choose to enable this feature in the Security preferences; in this case, Safari warns you that some Web sites might use pop-ups for legitimate reasons, and those will be disabled as well. This is true, but very rare, and a small price to pay for blocking all the illegitimate ones.

Bookmark management

Safari has a concept of bookmarking that goes way beyond the ordinary. *Bookmarking* refers to saving a current page location for future visitation. Safari gives you two immediately visible places to put them — in the Bookmarks Bar (for pages you access very frequently), or the Bookmarks menu, for pages visited every so often. But when you choose to save a bookmark, you are greeted with another option in the form of a bunch of listed folders. Saving a bookmark in one of these folders obviously saves it there, but to retrieve it?

Choose Show All Bookmarks from the Bookmarks menu, or click the little book icon in the Bookmarks Bar. What appears is Safari's Bookmark Manager (shown in Figure 10.27) — an iTunes-like interface for complete control and organization of your bookmarks — because, let's face it, they're hard to organize. You tend to accumulate lots of them and don't even want them all in that menu all the time. You can even initiate a Spotlight search through your multitude of bookmarks by using the search field at the top of the Bookmark Manager's window (which is visible in Figure 10.27).

FIGURE 10.27

Keep your bookmarks out of the menu and the toolbar with Safari's Bookmark Manager.

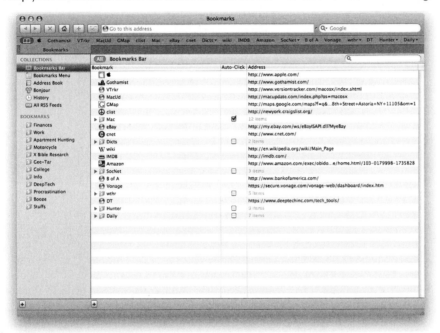

You'll notice that the sidebar is divided into two areas, called Collections and Bookmarks. In the Collections area reside specific categories of bookmarks, such as the list of bookmarks stored in the Bookmarks Bar and in the Bookmarks menu. You'll also see an entry called Address Book in the list, which creates a dynamic list of the URLs that you have entered for your Apple Address Book contacts. Under Address Book is Bonjour, which uses Apple's zero-configuration networking to automatically populate itself with Bonjour-enabled network locations. Although some Web sites make themselves evident under the Bonjour collection, the neat thing about using Bonjour is that you can access network devices like printers and webcams. Instead of manually typing the devices' addresses, they appear automatically, if they are Bonjour compatible. Under Bonjour you will find your browsing History, in which you can remove individual URLs manually. Finally you find the

RSS collection, which provides an interface for all of the RSS feeds that you have subscribed to using Safari. The Bookmarks area, below the Collections, provides you with an area for storing your personal bookmarks in custom-made folders.

What's great about the Bookmarks area is that it's a way to save tons of bookmarks without having your Bookmarks menu scroll down and off of your screen for five solid minutes. Bookmarks stored in the folders of the Bookmarks section get themselves out of the usual bookmark menu but still remain easily accessible. Clicking the plus sign at the bottom left of the manager window creates a new folder, which you can rename and drag any of your existing bookmarks into. Apple has pre-created a bunch of folders — you can choose to keep them or get rid of them by clicking them and pressing Delete. If you select a number of bookmarks in the right-hand pane and Option+click the plus sign in the right-hand window to make a new folder, Safari makes a new folder and moves the selected bookmarks into it. From now on, when creating a bookmark, you can choose to file it in a categorized folder, as opposed to slapping it onto the end of a menu.

URLs (whether in the address bar, or in the form of a bookmark) in Safari are draggable. You can drag an address by its icon, either into a folder when it's being viewed in the Bookmark Manager, or into the Bookmarks Bar directly from the address field. Shift+clicking the Add Bookmark button (the plus sign) is a shortcut for adding a bookmark directly to the Bookmarks Bar. To make use of your bookmarks, go to the Bookmark Manager and double-click a bookmark. You can also ⌘+click to open them in tabs.

Storing folders in the Bookmarks Bar is a great way to have easy access to a bunch of sites at a time. A great customization to this feature is called Auto-Tab, which, instead of displaying a list of the bookmarks in the folder when you click on the folder's name in the Bookmarks Bar, opens every bookmark inside of there as a separate tab (shown in Figures 10.28 and 10.29). The Auto-Tab option is available only when viewing the Bookmarks Bar collection within the Bookmark Manager. Check the box in the Auto-Tab column to activate. Beware, because clicking an auto-tabbed folder overrides any tabs currently being viewed in that window.

FIGURE 10.28

Clicking an Auto-Tab folder in the Bookmarks Bar (notice that there are no tabs open) takes you from this...

FIGURE 10.29

...to this! (Notice all of the tabs now present.)

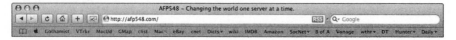

Safari, along with the aid of your .Mac account, gives you the ability to sync your bookmarks between your different Macs, as well as access them from any Web browser, eliminating the frustration of managing and remembering different sets of saved locations between different computers, and keeping a single set constant among all of your machines. You can choose to enable this preference under the Bookmarks section of the Safari preferences.

Downloads window

Downloading a file is a common practice, whether it is an instruction manual for your new outdoor grill, a new piece of software, or a movie preview. To *download* is to save a file to your computer. In most cases, clicking the download link opens Safari's Download window, which is a list of items that have been recently downloaded, as well as items that are in the process of being downloaded. As an item is being downloaded, there will be two icons opposite from the item's name, on the right side of the list. The rightmost icon is a magnifying glass. Clicking the magnifying glass switches you to the Finder and highlights the currently downloading file, effectively alleviating the where-did-that-file-go problem. You can always see what the default file download location is by going to Safari's General preferences, from the Safari menu. The other icon that appears when a file is in mid-download sits just to the left of the magnifying glass, taking the form of an X. Clicking the X stops the download. Once the download has been halted, the X icon turns into an orange arrow (which looks very similar to the SnapBack icon). Clicking this arrow restarts a paused download.

After a file is downloaded successfully, its name remains in the list. The Cancel/Resume button disappears, but the magnifying glass remains, which when clicked continues to show the file's location in the Finder, as long as it has not been removed from its original location. You can set Safari's default download location in the Safari preferences; Apple's default is the Desktop folder, which makes retrieving downloaded files pretty painless. At the bottom of the Downloads window is the Clear button, which removes all of the items that currently appear in the list.

> **TIP** Sometimes, instead of downloading the file as you had intended, Safari actually opens the file in a browser window. Pictures, sounds, and movies generally open all right (even if that is not what you intended to happen), but some files (and these are often compressed files of one kind or another, such as files ending with .zip, .bin, .hqx, and .dmg) might display as a Web page full of gobbledygook text. Although Safari is usually smart enough not to fall prey to this, when this occurs, it's usually because the Web server that is hosting the files that you requested isn't encoding them in a way that lets Safari (or any Web browser, for that matter) know how to handle the data. If this happens, click the Back button in your browser, and instead of just clicking the file's link to download it, try Option+clicking the link instead. This forces your browser to download the file directly to your Downloads folder, instead of opening it in a browser window.

Further Safari enhancements

When Apple's built-in features just aren't enough to suit your tastes, you can look towards more advanced or to third-party enhancers to customize Safari even further. Here, we discuss a hack that enables the hidden debug menu, two useful third-party utilities, and a great reference Web site.

Caching Out

Safari stores the pages you visit in a cache (pronounced "cash," not "caché"), which is a store of information located on your hard drive. Instead of reloading the page fully from the server each time, a revisit to the page usually causes Safari to access this cache, which is faster than downloading the page again because accessing your local hard drive is faster than accessing the Net (although with today's superfast connections this discrepancy is becoming less and less apparent). Information that changes frequently might be hindered by this cache, and necessitate a manual reload of a page by clicking the Reload button. In some cases, pressing and holding the Shift key and then clicking the Reload button is necessary; it forces the browser to take a brand new copy of the page and not just poll the server for changed information. In rarer cases, a page becomes stuck in the cache and not even a reload loads the page's contents from the Internet properly. If this is the case, it is necessary to empty the cache, which deletes all locally saved Web pages from your computer's hard drive. Go to the Safari menu and choose to empty the cache. You'll be given a warning, but click Empty anyway. Resume browsing with a clear cache.

Using the Debug menu

Safari has a hidden feature called the Debug menu. It's got a lot of information for troubleshooting things like JavaScript exceptions and World Leaks — not especially useful for your everyday user. There are, however, a few useful things that accessing the Debug menu can grant you. The Safari Enhancer utility discussed in the next section can enable the Debug menu, as can the Cocktail utility mentioned in Chapter 20, but it's more satisfying to enable it using the Unix command line interface. To do so, try the following:

1. **Open the Terminal from the Utilities folder.**

2. **Type the following after the prompt:**

    ```
    defaults write com.apple.Safari IncludeDebugMenu 1
    ```

3. **Press return.** To hide the Debug menu, you can use the same command, but substitute a zero for the one. It's binary — one is true, or on, and zero is false, or off. The command that you type is simply writing a change to the Safari preferences file that you can't make using the graphical interface. For more on the Unix command line, see Chapter 24.

That should be it! The next time you open Safari you should see a Debug menu to the right of the Help menu, as displayed in Figure 10.30. One important thing that you can do with this is to fool a Web site into thinking that you are a non-Safari user, even a PC user. Why would you want to do this? Some Web sites consciously block access to certain platforms and browsers, whether out of spite or incompatibility worries. Under the Debug menu, choose the User Agent option and tell the Internet what browser you want to masquerade as. Sometimes choosing Internet Explorer for Windows (Windows MSIE 6.0) can grant you access that Safari was previously barred from. Two other useful options are the ability to display a window with all of Safari's keyboard and mouse shortcuts and the ability to disable and enable RSS support.

FIGURE 10.30

Safari's Debug menu provides a myriad of options.

SafarIcon

The appropriately named SafarIcon provides you with a way to add additional, custom icons sets and graphics to enhance Safari's look to suit your taste. SafarIcon automatically installs these so-called "themes" which you can preview and choose to use. SafarIcon also grants you control over the look and feel of the Safari window, whether you would like the Tiger-style brushed Metal, non-metal Aqua, or Leopard Unified appearance themes. SafarIcon also gives you a graphical interface that grants you control over options that Apple does not normally let you tinker with. It is downloadable from `http://web.mac.com/reinholdpenner/Software/SafarIcon.html` and runs as a stand-alone application. It accomplishes its trickery by editing OS X preference files options that you normally would not be able to change. SafarIcon lets you do things like enable the Debug menu without typing anything into the Terminal, remove underlines from hyperlinks, and disable all of Safari's caching ability. Look at Figure 10.31 to see SafarIcon in action.

FIGURE 10.31

Edit hidden options with SafarIcon.

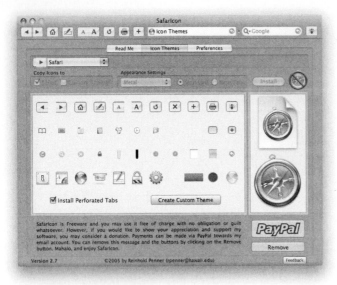

Sogudi

Sogudi is a Safari augmentation that achieves a high level of Safari integration. When installed, Sogudi is available directly from the Safari menu any time Safari is running. Why is it called Sogudi? According to its developer (and we quote): "So far-ee, so good-ee . . ." Safari, Sogudi . . . so good, indeed—Sogudi gives you the ability to create shortcuts instead of typing lengthy URLs. Even better, after typing your custom shortcut into the address bar, you can type a term to search for and Sogudi queries the Web site that corresponds to your shortcut for your specified search term. If you spend a lot of time using Safari, Sogudi can save you a lot of time and retyping of information. See Sogudi in Figure 10.32. You can download it from `www.kitzkikz.com/Sogudi`.

Pimp My Safari

The Safari browser, despite having no official extension architecture, has a plethora of add-ons created by Mac OS X developers. The Pimp My Safari Web site (`http://pimpmysafari.com/`) is an excellent centralized resource for such Safari enhancements. The site's proprietors hand-pick the best Safari software and post regular updates of the software and of Safari-related topics. Head on over to see the bevy of enhancements that are available, and learn what, according to Pimp My Safari, the three Safari essentials are.

FIGURE 10.32

Sogudi lets you type shortcuts and searches directly into the address bar.

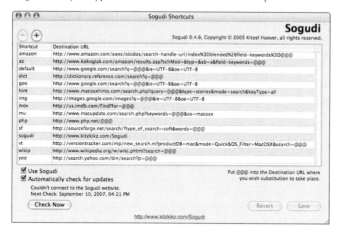

Searching the Internet

Google, though the popular favorite, is not the only search engine in town. Here are a few more, along with their URLs, to get the searches going:

- **Clusty** at `clusty.com`
- **WiseNut** at `www.wisenut.com`
- **Yahoo!** at `www.yahoo.com`
- **Excite** at `www.excite.com`
- **AltaVista** at `www.altavista.com`
- **Ask** at `www.ask.com`
- **Metacrawler** at `www.metacrawler.com`

Internet search engines use a variety of methodologies for searching, so performing the same search with different engines will likely yield different results. Google's accuracy is derived from its underpinnings; it displays results based on a Web site's frequency of access and number of sites that link to it.

Apple's Dashboard feature provides a unique method of accessing the Internet: by gathering information without having to actually launch a Web browser and view a Web page, effectively providing a GUI (graphical user interface) for the Internet. Every time you check a flight or update the weather widget, Web queries are being performed behind the scenes. (More on Dashboard in Chapter 2.)

AOL Is Not the Internet

America Online deserves special mention here. It's an interesting concept and unique in its existence. Instead of separating your Web browser, your e-mail, your text chatting, and your content into separate entities, AOL is all of these things combined. Using a standard Internet connection, you might browse the Web with Safari. You check your e-mail with Entourage. You chat with iChat, and you search with Google. AOL, however, is your Web browser, your e-mail, *and* your chat application. Although this might sound well organized, the downside stems from the fact that AOL *also* provides you with their own content. This content is *not* the World Wide Web. It's stuff that AOL generates; and because they get paid to place said content, they try to keep you in their world as much as possible, and it's not the same thing as being truly on the Web.

It's easy to feel trapped by AOL, especially if you've been with it for a while. It's your e-mail address, your screen name, and it's a pain to give that up. The good news is that AOL in its older age has become much more flexible. Historically, it was nearly impossible not to be trapped by AOL because in addition to providing your Web browsing and correspondence, they also dialed you up to the Internet, making them your ISP as well. These days you can retain your AOL contact information and browse their content for free, provided that you have an Internet connection of your own. Although with the proliferation of free email, (such as Yahoo! and Google mail) and excellent dedicated Web browsers, (like Safari and Firefox) using AOL truly begs the question, why?

AOL *does* have some plusses. As a longtime provider of dial-up Internet access, they still have local dial-up access numbers in some of the remotest areas on the globe (Siberia!), and in not-so-remote areas that haven't been reached by broadband yet. If you travel a lot, an AOL account can be very handy. AOL also provides a level of content filtering, for blocking offensive material, although this too is built into most major operating systems, Mac OS X being no exception. The point is that AOL is okay to use, just don't be fooled: AOL is not the Internet.

The explosion in the number and popularity of Web pages has spawned a corresponding increase in the number of search sites. These sites use different methods for collecting and displaying pages. Sites such as Yahoo! are primarily directories; Yahoo! lists Web sites, organized hierarchically by category, that have been submitted by Web site developers and manually reviewed by the Yahoo! staff. Other popular search sites, such as Google and AltaVista, use *robots* or *spiders* to automatically crawl through the Web and gather information, which is collected in a database and made available for searching via keywords or phrases. Many robot-driven sites also feature part of their database of Web sites in directory-style lists of links, for those users who prefer browsing rather than searching with keywords. The directory-style sites take advantage of the automated sites' technology as well. As of this writing, if a search turns up nothing in the Yahoo! categories, Yahoo! automatically forwards the search to Google.

All Web sites need to pay their bills, and search sites are no exception. In addition to the usual banner advertisements, many search sites are becoming *portals*, which provide not only search functionality but also links to online shopping, weather, news, and just about any other kind of information they think you might need. The search sites partner with other providers, such as online bookstores. You can continue your search for information or products at that provider's site.

Don't be too disappointed if a new site of yours doesn't show instantaneously in searches. It takes a while for automated robots to crawl through the billions of pages on the Web, and some directory sites make editorial decisions about which sites to include. The bots that Google uses, for example, recognize only the text contained within Web pages; if all of the writing on a Web page is embedded in pictures and graphics, the bots won't recognize the information the Web site contains.

Sending and Receiving E-mail

Electronic mail, or e-mail, lets you communicate with people all over the world. Unlike regular mail, your correspondents can be reading your messages within seconds after you send them, no matter whether the recipients are across the street or halfway around the world.

Mac OS X includes an e-mail application simply named Mail (also called Mail.app, pronounced "mail-dot-app" to distinguish its application status), and it has an icon in the Dock for easy one-click access. With Mail you can check mail from multiple Internet e-mail accounts, send and receive messages formatted with styled text and embedded pictures, view RSS feeds, manage your To Do items, and set up rules to automatically filter your mail based on content. Mail even has Safari's KHTML rendering engine built right in, which displays HTML-formatted e-mail messages easily.

Setting up e-mail information and preferences

Before Mail can send and receive e-mail for you, it must know your e-mail address, password, and other information. If you've preconfigured a .Mac account in the .Mac System Preferences, Mail should open and begin to check your account. If not, the first time you open Mail, it displays a dialog prompting you to add a new account, as shown in Figure 10.33.

Selecting an E-mail Application

Although Mac OS X includes the Mail application, you don't have to use it. You may prefer to stick with another e-mail application that you're already using, or your company may require that you use a particular application. E-mail applications have their respective strength and weaknesses. Mail has an excellent junk-mail filtering capability. Microsoft's Entourage is great all-around, but isn't free. Other e-mail apps include Eudora, Mulberry, Netscape, SeaMonkey, and Thunderbird. If you access an exchange server, you'll need that capability built in — both Entourage and Mail.app include this feature-set.

FIGURE 10.33

The first time you launch Mail, you are asked to create a new account.

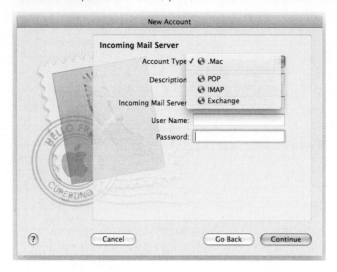

Mail supports four different types of accounts:

- **Mac accounts:** Apple's e-mail service; .Mac addresses end with @mac.com
- **POP accounts:** Post Office Protocol, which is used by ISPs such as EarthLink
- **IMAP accounts:** Internet Mail Access Protocol, which is used in many schools and businesses
- **Exchange accounts:** Microsoft's big corporate kahuna of e-mail service

Each of these types of accounts needs to be configured so that Mail can access your e-mail for you by connecting to your e-mail server(s), and so that the e-mail you send to other people is clearly recognized as being from you. Mail supports multiple accounts. If you want, you can have e-mail from a few different accounts coming in. Following is a list of the different pieces of information that Mail asks you for when you begin to configure your account settings.

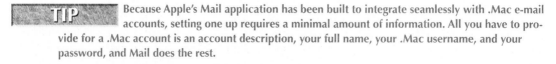

TIP   Because Apple's Mail application has been built to integrate seamlessly with .Mac e-mail accounts, setting one up requires a minimal amount of information. All you have to provide for a .Mac account is an account description, your full name, your .Mac username, and your password, and Mail does the rest.

- **Account Type:** The first thing you need to do is specify which type of account you'll be configuring.

- **Account Description:** Give your account a title. This title is used by the Mail application to tell you which account you are using, which is especially helpful if you have more than once account configured.

- **Full Name:** This is the name you want people to see in their inbox when you send them an e-mail.

- **E-mail Address:** This is the address where people send you e-mail, for example: `warren@notmyrealemailaddress.com`.

- **Incoming Mail Server:** This is the Internet name for the server from which Mail receives your e-mail, for example: `mail.mac.com`.

- **User Name:** This item is usually the first part of your e-mail address (the part before the @ symbol). In some cases, it might be different, so check if you are unsure.

- **Password:** This item is optional here. If you omit the password here, you must enter it every time you open Mail; but you are less likely to forget it if you need to check your mail from another computer, and no one else will be able to get your e-mail if you let them use your Mac OS X account.

- **Outgoing Mail Server (SMTP):** This is the Internet name for the computer through which Mail sends your e-mail, for example: `smtp.mac.com`. Some SMTP servers require authentication. For example, if you will be sending e-mail through an EarthLink account and your computer will not be accessing the Internet using EarthLink's services, you need to specify a different SMTP server (for example, `smtpauth.earthlink.net`) as well as your e-mail username and password.

After the previous information is entered, at each stage in the setup process, Mail verifies the information by trying to contact your e-mail servers. If this fails, you are given a warning asking you to double-check your information. If it still won't go through properly, Mail lets you continue anyway, but warns you that you won't be able to send or receive mail. If you don't know the information that Mail needs, check with your Internet service provider or other organization that provides your e-mail service, such as Apple for a .Mac account, or EarthLink if you've got an EarthLink address. Don't forget to make sure that your Mac has a valid Internet connection while setting up Mail.

After you've configured your account for the first time, Mail asks you if you want to import any e-mail from a previous e-mail application. If you choose yes, you will be walked through this process, which involves telling Mail what your old e-mail application was, and finding its relevant information. Entourage, Eudora, and Netscape are all importable to Mail. Don't sweat it if you've skipped or want to skip this step: you can choose to import old e-mail at any time by choosing to Import Mailboxes from under the File menu.

After Mail is open, you can always add additional e-mail accounts; having more than one is common for lots of people nowadays. Choose Preferences from under the Mail menu, and click the Accounts section. Click the plus sign button on the bottom of the window to add another account. To update or add information to an existing account, highlight its name in the column to access the account's options, as shown in Figure 10.34.

FIGURE 10.34

Customize your existing account(s) and add additional ones in Mail's account preferences window.

The preferences window includes many other settings. Under the General section is where you tell OS X what its default e-mail application is; so even if you don't use Mail, you'll still need to configure this here. Use the Junk Mail area to customize how Mail deals with junk mail, or spam. It can be turned off or tweaked to more advanced levels. Mail's fonts and colors can be played with here, as well as settings concerning Mail's column views, what happens when you compose an e-mail, and configuring a signature and rules for messages.

Using Mail's viewer window

After your e-mail information is set up, Mail opens to its main viewer window. It has a toolbar at the top, a list of messages below, and a message preview area at the bottom. A panel on the left side of the window lists your mailboxes, which contain your e-mail messages (shown in Figure 10.35).

POP versus IMAP E-mail

The provider of your e-mail account may let you set it up as a POP account or an IMAP account. With a POP account (Post Office Protocol), you transfer (download) your incoming messages from the POP server on the provider's computer to the Mail application's database on your computer's hard drive. Normally, your messages are deleted from the server after they have been transferred to your computer. Call your computer "Mac A." This means that if you then check your e-mail from a second computer (call it "Mac B"), the new messages that just showed up on the original computer (Mac A) will not show up on the second (Mac B), because they have been removed from the provider's computer and are now only on Mac A. To help alleviate this disappearing e-mail problem, now that many people check their e-mail from more than one machine, most e-mail programs let you choose to leave your POP messages on the server. Because the messages are still on the server, after they are checked, Mac A and Mac B will both get the messages. Doing this can, however, be quite hazardous to your e-mail health, manifested by messages never, ever being deleted from the server, not for years and years. It's often not obvious, but deleting a message from your inbox often does not actually delete it from the server, and messages that might not appear in any of your inboxes will sit on the server anyway. Guarding against this requires maintenance: The best thing you can do is have your e-mail program automatically delete messages from the server after a certain period of time.

Does all that sound like pain in the rear? Enter IMAP, the Internet Message Access Protocol. With an IMAP account, all the mail is stored on the server, all the time. Mail is also stored on your computer, all the time; in fact, so that your computer and the IMAP server stay synchronized, they mirror each other. If you delete a message from your computer, it's deleted from the server as well. This means that you can configure any number of computers to read your IMAP mail, and your inbox looks the same each time. Messages that have been replied to or forwarded are tagged to reflect their respective statuses, even on machines that you didn't actually send the message from. Furthermore, you can also store other folders on the server, so that items like drafts or sent messages are always present no matter which machine or Web browser you access your account from. IMAP is sometimes defaulted to downloading only the e-mail headers (subject lines) until you specify to read an entire message. Although it makes for a fast inbox download, you can get stuck if you're offline and haven't fully downloaded a message that you need to read. And of course, if you accidentally delete your entire inbox, it will be deleted from the server too, as well as from any of your other computers when they connect. As you might imagine, IMAP e-mail is much more complicated and expensive than POP e-mail for hosting companies to maintain. That is why almost all free e-mail services (Yahoo!, Gmail, Hotmail) only let you access their servers using the POP protocol from within a Mail type application, and higher-end (and paid-for) e-mail like .Mac or University e-mail can be accessed using IMAP.

FIGURE 10.35

Mail's main window. Notice the toolbar, the Mailboxes sidebar, and the one unread message.

To see a list of messages in any mailbox, select the mailbox by clicking its name in the mailbox pane. If you see only the message "No mailbox is selected" in the title bar of the Mail window, it means that nothing is selected. If you have more than one account set up, you'll see a disclosure triangle next to the inbox, and in some cases the other folders. Instead of lumping all of your messages from multiple accounts into one inbox, Mail gives you the option to view them each separately, by selecting each of the individual mini-inboxes independently. If you want to see everything at once, do click the main Inbox icon.

Use the plus button in the lower left-hand corner to add a folder to the list. If you've got an IMAP account, you have the option of storing the folder on the server, or on your Mac, as shown in Figure 10.36. Use folders for organization and for storage. Click the action button for easy access to general functionality, like emptying the Deleted Items folder or taking an account on- or offline manually.

If you have an IMAP account, Mail gives you the option to save a folder on the server, or locally on your Mac, as shown here.

You can easily tell if your account is online (connected to your e-mail server) or offline (not connected) just by looking at your mailboxes. Online accounts appear as shown in Figure 10.35. Offline accounts have grey lightning bolts next to the mailboxes.

You can work with the messages listed in a viewer window as follows:

- **Preview a listed message:** Clicking a message in the list displays its contents in the preview pane. Doing this causes an IMAP or POP message to be downloaded, and the message changes in status to "read" if the message was new.

- **Select messages in the list:** Click any information listed for a message. ⌘+click additional messages to select them also, or Shift+click to select a range of messages. After messages are selected, they can be dragged into different folders.

- **Search the messages:** Type in the toolbar's Search box and use the adjacent pop-up menu to specify which part of each message to search. If Mail finds messages that meet your search criteria, it lists only those messages. Searching is covered more in detail later in this chapter.

- **Resize the list and preview areas:** Drag the divider bar at the bottom of the list up or down.

- **Hide or show the message preview area:** Double-click the divider bar at the bottom of the list.

- **Sort the list by a column:** Click a column heading. The heading becomes highlighted to indicate that it is the sort key. Click the highlighted column heading to switch between forward and reverse sort order. Alternatively, you can choose a sort column and direction from the Sort submenu of the View menu.

- **Rearrange columns:** Drag a column heading left or right to move the column.

- **Resize columns:** Drag a column heading's right borderline left or right to make the column narrower or wider.

- **Show or hide columns:** In the View menu, choose the appropriate command to show or hide the Number, Flags, Contents, or Message Sizes columns. The Read Status, From, and Date & Time columns always appear. The Buddy Availability column bullets messages whose sender is signed into iChat, if they are in your address book.

- **See more or fewer columns at once.** Click the window's Zoom button or resize the window.

Receiving e-mail

To get your e-mail, click the Get Mail button at the top of the viewer window in the toolbar (or choose Get New Mail from the Mailbox menu). If you want to monitor the progress, choose Window ➪ Activity Viewer. You can also have Mail check for new mail automatically by setting how often you want this to happen in the Accounts section of Mail's preferences dialog box.

The number of unread messages appears as a subtle, encircled numeral next to the mailbox name in the mailbox sidebar. Unread messages are marked with a blue bullet in the list of messages below the buttons in a viewer window. The number of unread messages also appears superimposed, in red, on the Mail icon in the Dock.

You can read a message in the preview area at the bottom of a viewer window, but you won't have to scroll as much if you open the message in its own window. To read a message in its own window, double-click it in the list of messages.

Composing messages

Of course, receiving messages is only half the fun. Mail gives you several options for your e-mail correspondence. You can reply to messages you receive, forward them to other people, or compose new messages.

Replying to messages

To reply to a message you are reading, click the Reply button or the Reply All button at the top of the window. Reply and Reply All both create a new message. Reply addresses the new message only to the sender, and Reply All addresses the new message to the sender and everyone else who received the original message. Instead of clicking these buttons, you can choose equivalent commands from the Message menu.

The new message appears in a separate window. It has the same subject as the original message, except that Re: is prefixed to the reply subject. The body of the reply includes the text of the original message.

Type your reply message above the original message, and click the Send button (or choose Message ➪ Send Message) to send your message flying to its destination. If you've got the sound on, there's a satisfying rocket-swoosh that accompanies a sent message.

When replying to a message, especially a long one, it's generally considered good *neti-quette* (etiquette on the Internet) to trim the text of the original message down to the essentials. You can adjust how the text from the original message appears in the Fonts & Colors section of Mail's preferences dialog box.

Forwarding messages

Forwarding a message sends a message that you have received to somebody else. If you've got to share a message with someone, click the Forward button at the top of the window (or choose Message ⇨ Forward Message). The original message appears in a new window, with Fwd: prefixed to the subject. You need to supply the e-mail address of the person to whom you are forwarding the message. You may want to add some introductory text above the forwarded message. Click the Send button (or choose Message ⇨ Send Message) to send the message on its way.

Composing new messages

To compose a new message, as shown in Figure 10.37, click the New button at the top of a viewer window or choose File ⇨ New Compose Window. Type each recipient's e-mail address separated by commas on the To line. On the Cc (carbon copy) line, add any additional recipients who should receive a copy of the message (but aren't necessarily expected to reply). Type a subject on the Subject line and type the message in the bottom pane. If you want to get fancy, you can select different text styles, colors, and fonts from the Format menu. When you're done, click Send.

FIGURE 10.37

A new message (click the New button) may look like this.

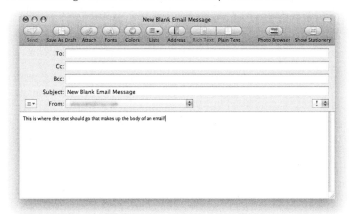

Mail remembers the addresses of people to whom you have recently sent e-mail. When you start to type an address on the To line, Mail autocompletes the address for you or provides a drop-down list if more than one address matches what you're typing. If you don't want to use Mail's suggested address, just type over it. Mail also makes addresses draggable items — you can drag addresses, even from the body of an e-mail text, into any of the sending fields that you want.

NOTE By default, Mail uses rich text format (RTF) to compose messages so that you can send messages with styled text and inset pictures. Not all e-mail programs can read this format, however. To change the format of an individual message, choose Make Plain Text from the Format menu when you are composing the message. If you know most of the people you send e-mail to use e-mail programs that don't support formatted messages, you may want to change your preferred message format to plain text. Choose Mail ⇨ Preferences, click Composing, and choose Plain Text from the Default message format pop-up menu.

Using Stationary

If you *really* want to make your e-mails fancy, Mail includes a plethora of stationery templates that allow you to send professionally designed e-mails with a few clicks — text and image placeholders are employed to make using the templates a foolproof exercise. The stationery is sent to your recipients in standard HTML format, so almost anyone with an e-mail account can read them. To access the stationery, all you need to do is click the Show Stationery button, and as shown in Figure 10.38, a new section drops down revealing the different types of stationery. The different options are sorted by the type of message you will be sending, such as a birthday invitation or a photo announcement.

FIGURE 10.38

A new message (click the New button) may look like this.

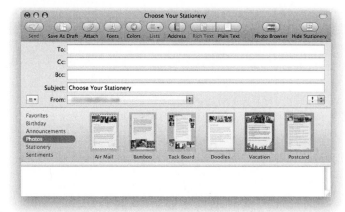

Reminders

If you have looked in the sidebar, you may have noticed a "Reminders" heading sitting under your mailboxes. The Reminders section contains two different items that are new to the Mail application in Leopard: Notes, and To Dos.

Notes

If you have an IMAP account such as Apple's .Mac e-mail, Mail's notes can be extremely handy. Instead of sending yourself oodles of reminder e-mails and having them clog up your inbox, Mail now has a dedicated note-taking feature that, with the power of IMAP e-mail, can be accessed from anywhere. You can make new notes by clicking the Note icon in the toolbar or by choosing New Note from the File menu. You can see a note being created in Figure 10.39.

FIGURE 10.39

Apple has taken the notepad concept quite literally with the new notes feature in Mail.

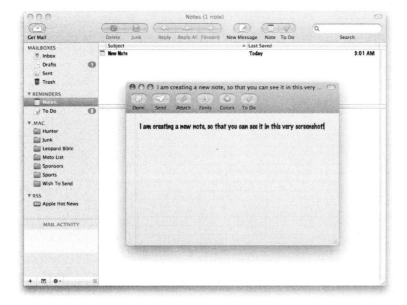

To Dos

In Leopard, Apple has turned To Do items into a central database that is accessible system-wide, and Mail is no exception. Also under the "Reminders" designation is a sort of To Do inbox, which, if you have an IMAP account such as .Mac, you can access from anywhere that you can read your e-mail. You can create To Do items by simply highlighting any text that falls within an e-mail, and choosing the To Do item from the toolbar button or through the File menu command. Doing so creates a new To Do item that can link back to the e-mail from which you created it. Even better, when you open iCal, the To Do items that you created in Mail also appear in your calendar application. Take a look at Figure 10.40 to see some To Do items in action.

FIGURE 10.40

Use existing e-mail text to create new To Do items within the Mail application.

RSS

Another item new to Leopard's Mail application is RSS feeds. That's right — just as you can sub-scribe to and view the automatically updating news feeds in Safari (see more about RSS earlier in this chapter), you can also view them in Mail. You can even use Mail's preferences to set Mail and not Safari as the default RSS reader. Instead of bunching them all on a single Web page like Safari does, Mail treats each RSS item like an individual e-mail. These e-mail items can be moved around and deleted just like you can do with real e-mail. Look at Figure 10.41 to see the way RSS feeds were meant to be read!

Using the Address Book

The Mail application is linked to the Address Book application, which you can use to store fre-quently used e-mail addresses and related contact information (such as phone numbers and birth-days). You can access the Address Book data by choosing Address Panel from the Window menu or by clicking the Address button in a message composition window. The Address Book can contain individual contacts, also known as *virtual address cards* (V-cards), and groups of contacts. Mail, along with applications such as iChat and iCal, directly interfaces with the Address Book without actually launching the application; it instead accesses its database and reads the information. You can either choose the person's name or group contact from the Address Panel, as shown in Figure 10.42, or just start typing the name into the address field in your e-mail, and the person pops up.

FIGURE 10.41

Use Mail.app to view RSS feeds and read internet articles as though they were e-mails.

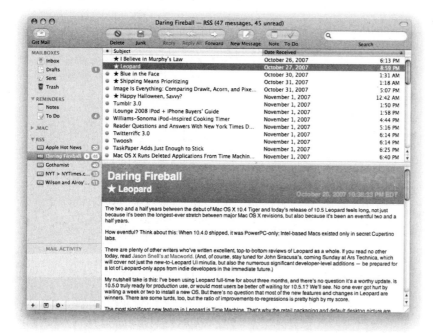

FIGURE 10.42

Choose an address from your Address Book by clicking the Address button in the message's toolbar.

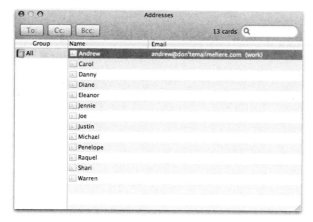

Modifying Toolbars in Mail

Many windows in the Mail application have toolbars, and these toolbars normally have buttons and other items displayed as icons with names. You can hide a toolbar or modify it in other ways by using the toolbar's contextual menu or a toolbar item's contextual menu. (You can display the toolbar's contextual menu by Control+clicking the toolbar, and you can display a toolbar item's contextual menu by Control+clicking the item.) You can modify the toolbars in Mail as follows:

- **Hide the toolbar, or show it if it is hidden.** Click the lozenge-shaped toolbar button in the upper right corner of the window.

- **Show items as icons with names, icons only, or names only.** Choose the style you want from the toolbar's contextual menu, or ⌘+click the lozenge-shaped toolbar button in succession to view all the different options.

- **Add items.** Choose Customize Toolbar from the toolbar's contextual menu or from the View menu, or ⌘+Option+click the lozenge-shaped toolbar button. Either action displays a dialog box that contains items you can drag into the toolbar.

- **Remove items.** Choose Remove Item from the button's contextual menu. Alternatively, ⌘+drag an item away from the toolbar to see it vanish in a puff of smoke. If the Customize Toolbar dialog box is displayed (as described in "Add items" in this list), you don't have to press ⌘ to drag an item away from the toolbar.

- **Move items.** ⌘+drag an item right or left to a different place on the toolbar. If the Customize Toolbar dialog box is displayed (as described in "Add items" in this list), you don't have to press ⌘ to drag an item to another place on the toolbar.

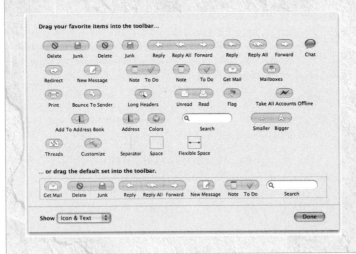

Sending e-mail attachments

In addition to text messages, you can send files with your e-mail messages. Documents, archives of multiple files (which you can create in the Finder by using the Archive command), and other programs and files can be sent as attachments to an e-mail message by using special protocols. Sending files as attachments can be useful if you'd like to send, for example, a Microsoft Word document or a picture to somebody.

Adding an attachment in Mail is simple; just look for the paper clip. With new e-mail (or reply e-mail) open in its window, click the Attach button in the toolbar. In the dialog box that appears, select the file you want to attach, and click Open. To attach multiple files, press and hold Shift while selecting each one before clicking Open. You can attach additional files by clicking the Attach button again. Alternatively, you can just drag any file from the Finder into an open composition window, and Mail attaches the file.

Your attachment is represented in your message by an icon, as shown in Figure 10.43. If you select a picture to attach, that picture may be embedded in the body of your message. When you send the e-mail message, attachments and embedded pictures go with it.

NOTE It's generally considered good netiquette to send an attachment only to recipients who expect it or would want it. Large files can cause trouble when sent through e-mail, whether it be the time it takes to download over a slow connection, or the size limit restrictions imposed by someone's e-mail service provider.

Receiving attachments

When you receive a message containing an attachment, you see the icon of the attachment in the body of the message. If the attachment is a multimedia file (picture, sound, or video clip), you may see it embedded in the body of the message, depending on the format of the attached file. Double-click the icon or single-click the name to open the attachment. Control+clicking opens a menu with the option to save the attachment to your hard drive, as opposed to just opening it. You can also drag an attachment icon or embedded picture from the body of the e-mail message to the Desktop or a Finder window to save the file.

NOTE In the Windows world, opening e-mail messages and their attachments is a risky business; it's the most common way for a virus to be transmitted to a computer. Companies invest millions in e-mail and virus protection. The top-selling software for Windows machines are virus protection utilities. Because most viruses are actually mini-Windows applications, on a Mac, they can't harm your computer. Viruses that Macs catch are called Word macro viruses and come in the form of infected Microsoft Word documents. If you transfer a lot of these files with Windows users, some virus protection software like Symantec's Norton AntiVirus or Intego's VirusBarrier is a good idea.

FIGURE 10.43

Mail displays attachments that you are sending inline with the text of the e-mail.

Junk mail

Junk mail in the form of e-mail, or spam, (to put it bluntly) just plain stinks. It clogs up your inbox. It forces you to see offensive material. Worst of all, when your e-mail application beeps to inform you of your new message, it's a false alarm, just an advertisement for augmenting . . . something. Spammers can retrieve your e-mail address from many places: Anywhere you've posted it on the Web is searchable, and they'll find it. Anything you've subscribed to or signed up for has probably sold a list with your name on it to spammers. The only way to completely rid yourself of spam is to get a new e-mail address, but this isn't an option, or is just too inconvenient, for most. Because of the back-door techniques spammers use, there's no real way of stopping them — yet. Even so, most e-mail providers, even free ones like Yahoo! mail (`http://mail.yahoo.com`), have some protection. But it's often not enough, and the junk still makes it to the inbox in droves.

Mail provides protection at the inbox level, that is, it employs a filter that identifies messages as junk before they make it there. Mail's junk mail filter starts off in *training mode*. Under training mode, a message that Mail thinks is junk appears in brown in your inbox, and has a header displayed with the message telling you that it has been identified as junk (shown in Figure 10.44). If Mail is correct, you can go ahead and delete the message. If Mail is not correct (a situation called a *false positive)* you can click the button for Not Junk, and Mail categorizes it as a regular e-mail. Mail employs something called a *Bayesian* filter, and the great thing about the filter is that it learns. After a while, its accuracy should be excellent, meaning no false positives and few false negatives. When this is the case, you can switch from training mode to automatic mode (under the preferences) by telling Mail to put all its junk mail in a special junk mail folder, after which you shouldn't see too much junk mail in your inbox. For advanced customization, click the Advanced button in the Junk Mail preferences to manually edit the junk rules, as shown in Figure 10.45.

FIGURE 10.44

Mail thinks this is a junk mail message.

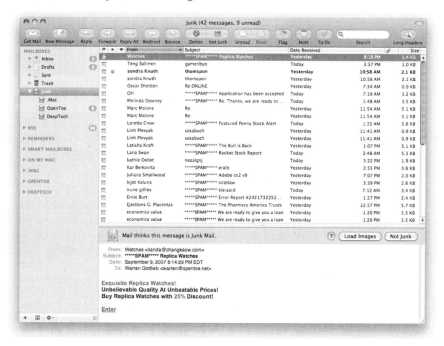

If you've been clicking all those "take-me-off-your-list-and-you'll-never-get-spam-again" links at the bottom of your junk mails, congratulations—you've just informed the spammer that there is a warm body at the end of your e-mail address and have inadvertently subscribed to even more junk mail. In most cases, spam comes from a fake address, meaning you can't reply to it. If the address is legitimate, Mail provides a way of *bouncing* the message back to the sender; on the spammer side it appears that your e-mail address is not a valid one, and you might get taken off of the list. To enable easy bouncing, customize the toolbar to show the Bounce button. To bounce a message to the sender, click the Bounce button while the offending message is selected, heed the warning Mail gives you, and off it goes. If you get a message saying that you got a returned mail, the bounce didn't work.

FIGURE 10.45

Change the junk mail filter from training mode to automatic by choosing the option in the junk-mail preferences.

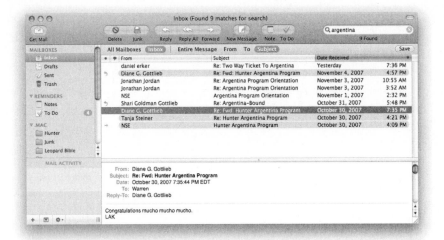

Threading

One of the more frustrating organizational issues is to easily locate all the messages from a single e-mail conversation. Mail incorporates a feature called *threading*: When any message in a conversation is selected, all the others are highlighted as well! You can turn this feature on or off in the View section of Mail's preferences as well as change the highlight color, as shown in Figure 10.46.

Smart Mailboxes

When iTunes 4 came out, Apple introduced a revolutionary feature with it called Smart Playlists. As opposed to manually categorizing your songs by dragging them into static playlists, a smart playlist can be configured with a custom rule set, which dynamically accommodates changing data. As data changes for a song file (the play count, for example) to match a specific rule set (the number 100, for example), that song is added to the smart playlist when it matches that criteria.

Apple has now created the same idea for their Mail application; instead of organizing music, however, you're organizing e-mail, notes, and to-do items. For example, there are two pre-created smart folders for you. One is called Today and the other is called Last 7 Days. Clicking the Today folder displays for you all of the e-mail messages, notes, and to-dos that you have received or created on whatever day that today happens to be. (See Figure 10.47 to see a smart folder in action.) It's important to note that Mail is not moving your e-mail around. It is simply displaying a list of your messages that are adhering to a specific set of rules that you have created.

FIGURE 10.46

Selecting one message subtly highlights other messages from the same e-mail conversation.

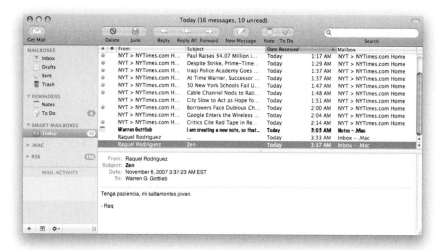

FIGURE 10.47

The Today smart folder views only the messages received today.

Click the Last 7 Days folder and use the Action menu to edit the smart mailbox. A rule set specifying that the date received is in the last seven days should be clearly visible (see Figure 10.48).

You can easily customize the rules for Smart Mailboxes.

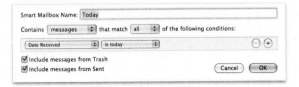

You can create your own smart folders for viewing messages in a way that you specify by clicking the action button and choosing to create a New Smart Mailbox.

Summary

Mac OS X makes it easy to harness the incredible power of the Internet:

- Getting on the Internet with Mac OS X is simple. All it takes is a quick walk through the initial Mac OS X Setup Assistant.
- If you skip the Internet setup steps in the Setup Assistant, you can run it manually through the Network preferences pane.
- After you've set up an Internet connection via cable modem, DSL, local network, or AirPort wireless, you're ready to browse the Web, get your e-mail, and use other Internet services.
- Mac OS X provides easy means of making a Net connection, either through the Internet Connect application or the menu bar icons.
- Mac OS X includes Safari for browsing the Web, although other browsers are available.
- Mac OS X also includes an e-mail application named Mail, which you can use to send, receive, and organize your e-mail messages. Mail coordinates with the included Address Book application, which stores e-mail addresses and other contact information.

Chapter 11

Setting Up a Local Network

I f you have more than one computer in your office or home, you can benefit by connecting them in a network. The idea may seem intimidating, but a simple network is easy to set up and doesn't cost much. Here are some things that you can do with a simple network:

- Share one Internet connection among several computers
- Share printers
- Share files from other computers as if they were on your computer
- Allow other computers to access the files on your computer
- Play games designed for multiple players
- Access a central database while other computers do likewise
- Maintain a group schedule or calendar
- Back up hard disks of all networked computers to a central location (tape, hard drive, offsite, and so on)
- Chat with others on your network or on the Internet
- Share your iPhoto library
- Share your iTunes library

This chapter focuses on setting up a network so that you can use some of these services. We start by discussing the fundamental concepts of a network and how to use these concepts to connect your computer to an Ethernet or AirPort (wireless) network. You also find out how to configure your network connections in the Network pane of System Preferences and how to easily switch from one configuration to another by using network locations. Additionally, we show you how to set up an AirPort Base Station and how to share files and connect computers using Bluetooth.

The Networking Concept

Mac OS X is built around the idea of networking. To fully utilize the power of Mac OS X, you must have a solid understanding of networks and how they work.

Understanding a computer network

The smallest possible network consists of two devices connected directly to each other. No Internet is required. If you have broadband Internet access at home, such as DSL or a cable modem, you are connected to someone else's network (the Internet connection) (see Figure 11.1).

A network's real strength is in its numbers. A network could allow you to share your broadband Internet connection between several computers. This same network could allow you to share a networkable printer. You could use iChat to notify someone down the hall that he or she has a call on line 4. You can use iTunes to listen to your roommate's music collection, share your own, or watch videos on your TV sent from your computer. All sorts of things become possible when you connect your computer to a network. What happens, though, when you want to connect more than just your computer and your cable modem? How do you connect several devices, not just two?

With two devices, it was simple: Connect them to each other. With several devices, however, you're going to need something else: a central networking device, such as a hub, switch, AirPort Base Station, or a standard router. The network hub or switch connects every device to every other device. This includes printers, computers, scanners, and so on. A router splits an Internet connection to allow multiple computers to share it. Most modern routers contain a switch or hub that allows for easier multi-computer connections.

The basic principles of networking are actually fairly simple. However, to build your own network, you need a little more background on how a network actually works. Although the basic concept of plugging devices into a hub is very simple, a familiarity with the inner workings of a network as well as basic networking terminology can help you to tailor a network just for you. If your network ever has any trouble, this working knowledge can help you to troubleshoot those problems. At the very least, having a basic understanding of the vocabulary of networking allows you to communicate with technical support when they ask you network-related questions.

Understanding layered networks

In computer networking theory, seven layers define networks (defined by the OSI model). Layers stack on top of one another to work together seamlessly, one on top of the other, to get your information where it needs to be.

For the sake of simplicity, we will focus these seven layers into three groups: the physical, communications, and applications layers. The physical layer contains two separate layers: the physical layer and the data-link layer. The communications layer can be broken down into three or even four separate layers. Although this refinement is important for an advanced understanding of networking, it's beyond the scope of this book.

FIGURE 11.1

A simple network without Internet and a simple network with Internet

**Simple network
without the Internet**

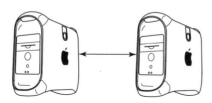

**Simple network
with the Internet**

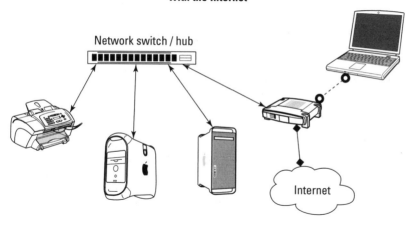

> **TIP**   To learn more about the OSI model, refer to `http://en.wikipedia.org/wiki/OSI_model`.

The Physical Layer

The first and most obvious aspect of any network is the physical components and how they interact. This is called the *physical layer*. The physical layer is the hardware. It's the wires and all the devices that they connect. Parts of this layer include the network ports on your computer or printer, the network cables, network hubs or switches, AirPort Base Stations, an AirPort Card installed in a computer, and much more. Together they make up the physical connection between every device.

These components of the physical layer require a lot of configuration. How fast does your network port send information to the network switch? Which cable leads from the network switch to the printer? What happens when your network card has to send and receive at exactly the same time? Will this cable modem work with my cable company? These are incredibly daunting tasks! Fortunately, these components can actually configure themselves. They do this by talking to each other using a common language, or *protocol*. There are several different hardware protocols. However, the Ethernet protocol is the only one that you're likely to see.

Ethernet protocol

For most people, the term *Ethernet* is synonymous with *network,* and they aren't far off. Ethernet is by far the most common wired and wireless network in use in homes and offices. An Ethernet network can include computers using Mac OS X, earlier Mac OS versions, Windows, Unix, and many other operating systems as well as appliances such as digital video recorders and others. If it can be networked and you've heard of it, you can bet it uses Ethernet.

Token ring networks are another type of networking. Like Ethernet, the components of a token ring network speak to each other. But instead of using the Ethernet protocol, the components use the token ring protocol. This makes Ethernet components and token ring components incompatible. As such, you are very unlikely to see a token ring network.

Every Ethernet port — whether it is on a computer, printer, cable modem, or any other device — has a unique address called an Ethernet address, or MAC address. (MAC is an acronym for Media Access Control, by the way, not an abbreviation for Macintosh.) This address is a long series of hexadecimal digits, twelve numbers (0–9) and letters (A–F) in the form 00:30:65:00:C2:4B. This Ethernet address is how network devices identify each other; it is a unique identifier for a physical piece of hardware. Table 11.1 shows OS X 10.5–compatible Macintoshes and their built-in Ethernet capabilities.

TABLE 11.1

Macs with Built-in Ethernet Capabilities

Mac Model	Gigabit	100Base-T	10Base-T
iMac G4 — all models		✓	✓
iMac G5 — first model		✓	✓
iMac G5 (ALS) and iSight	✓	✓	✓
iMac Intel — all models	✓	✓	✓
eMac — all models		✓	✓
iBook G4 — all models		✓	✓
MacBook — all models	✓	✓	✓
PowerBook G4 Titanium (400 and 500 MHz)		✓	✓

Mac Model	Gigabit	100Base-T	10Base-T
PowerBook G4 Titanium (550 MHz and 1 GHz)	✓	✓	✓
PowerBook G4 15 (Aluminum, 1.0 and 1.5 GHz)	✓	✓	✓
PowerBook G4 17 (1.25GHhz and1.5 GHz)	✓	✓	✓
PowerBook G4 12 (Aluminum, 867 MHz and1.33 GHz)		✓	✓
MacBook Pro — all models	✓	✓	✓
Power Mac G4 — PCI Graphics		✓	✓
Power Mac G4 — AGP Graphics		✓	✓
Power Mac G4 — Gigabit Ethernet	✓	✓	✓
Power Mac G4 — Digital Audio	✓	✓	✓
PowerMac G4 — Quicksilver	✓	✓	✓
PowerMac G4 — Mirrored Drive Doors	✓	✓	✓
PowerMac G5 — all models	✓	✓	✓
Mac Pro — all models	✓	✓	✓
Power Mac G4 Cube		✓	✓
Mac Mini G4 — all models		✓	✓
Mac Mini Intel — all models	✓	✓	✓
Xserve — All models	✓	✓	✓

Ethernet devices communicate with each other using very small bundles of data called *frames*. Ethernet frames are the post office envelopes of your network. Each frame has the sender's address, the destination's address, and a piece of your data. Data sent over the network is broken up into pieces that can fit into a frame. Those frames, then, are delivered to the destination. Finally, the destination's network port reassembles these pieces back into the original message.

Making the Ethernet connection

All Macs that are qualified for Mac OS X are ready to be connected to an Ethernet network. Older Macs commonly used another type of wiring called LocalTalk, but this type of network can't be used with Mac OS X. A LocalTalk-to-Ethernet adapter can enable these older Macs for use on an Ethernet network.

Ethernet cabling

When you think of an Ethernet network, you probably think of wires. But technically, AirPort wireless networks also use the Ethernet protocol as their physical-layer language. AirPort networks are actually wireless Ethernet networks. However, they're rarely, if ever, called that. The common practice is to refer to wired networks as Ethernet networks and to wireless networks as AirPort networks or wireless networks.

Looking at Ethernet cables

Ethernet networks may be wired with several types of cable, the most popular being unshielded twisted-pair (UTP). This type of cable looks like telephone cable and uses RJ-45 connectors that look like modular phone connectors, only a little larger. Other kinds of cable include Thinnet, thick coax, and fiber-optic Ethernet cables.

Twisted-pair cable is used in three different capacity networks: 10baseT, 100baseT (also called Fast Ethernet), and 1000baseT (also called Gigabit). All twisted-pair cable is graded according to how well it protects against electrical interference. Category 3 (Cat 3) cable is adequate for 10baseT networks, which have a maximum data-transfer rate of 10 Mbps (megabits per second). Although adequate for many small networks, this type of network is considered slow by today's standards.

100baseT networks require at least Category 5 (Cat 5) cable, properly installed. These networks have a maximum data-transfer rate of 100 Mbps. The rules for installing cable on a 100baseT network, however, are more stringent than for 10baseT. For example, sharp bends in the cable aren't allowed.

Gigabit networking requires at least Category 5e (Cat 5e) cable and can sometimes require Category 6 (Cat 6) cable. Gigabit networks have a maximum data-transfer rate of 1000 Mbps, or 1 gigabit per second (Gbps). The rules for installing cable on a Gigabit network are stringent as well.

Some have successfully used Cat 5 cable to run a Gigabit network. Although this may work for them, don't count on it. The costs of any cable are insignificant when compared to the costs of reinstallation of the correct cable if it doesn't work. If you're going to the trouble of installing the cabling, don't waste your time and money on the hope that Cat 5 will suffice. Get the right stuff: Cat 5e or Cat 6. Always prepare for the future. If you don't need it now, you may need it later.

Using crossover cables

Twisted-pair cables contain eight separate wires, twisted into four pairs (hence the name). 10baseT and 100baseT networks use only two of the four pairs, and the other two pairs are unused. Gigabit uses all four pairs. In each case, however, half of the wires in use are for inbound traffic, and the other half are for outbound traffic. Your computer sends data on the outbound wires only and it receives data on the inbound wires only.

Connecting two computers using a standard Ethernet cable doesn't usually work. All the *outbound* connectors on one computer end up going right into the *outbound* connectors on the other. This won't work! You need some way to cross over the wire somewhere along the line so that outbound goes into inbound and vice versa.

Hubs, switches, and sometimes devices such as broadband modems and routers do crossing over for you inside the port. To reflect this fact, for example, the ports on a 100baseT switch are designated 100baseTX—the X indicates that the port performs this crossover. Sometimes using a hub or switch between two computers isn't an option, though. For example, what if your friend brought her laptop over and wanted to connect it to your computer for a while? In that case, you would need a special cable called a *crossover cable*. Crossover cables are specially made cables that cross over on one end, turning outbound wires into inbound wires.

Most devices designed to plug into your computer do so by using a standard Ethernet cable. Put more technically, connecting a 100baseT network port to a 100baseTX network port requires a standard Ethernet cable. The same is true for both 10baseT and Gigabit. Connecting a computer (100baseT) to a cable modem or a network hub (100baseTX) is a good example of this very common kind of configuration.

But when you want to connect two similar devices, such as two computers or two hubs, you need a crossover cable. Put more technically, connecting two 100baseT devices to each other or two 100baseTX devices to each other requires a crossover cable. Connecting a computer (100baseT) to a computer (100baseT) or a hub (100baseTX) to a hub (100baseTX) are good examples of this kind of configuration.

 If you try to connect a computer to a hub or switch using a crossover cable, you've just double-crossed yourself! Keep crossover cables clearly labeled so that you don't make this mistake.

Smart network ports

Wouldn't it be nice if each network port could just switch automatically? Then every cable could be a standard cable. Well, someone figured it out. Some devices now have network ports that automatically change from 10baseT to 10baseTX, or 100baseT to 100baseTX, or 1000baseT to 1000baseTX whenever they need to. They also ignore the type of cable plugged in, which automatically crosses or uncrosses as needed to make the proper connection. Any Macintosh model with built-in 1000baseT (Gigabit) Ethernet has this feature, as do certain versions of Apple's AirPort Base Station. Some of the more expensive network switches also do this. This feature typically requires at least a standard, four-pair Category 5 cable. For more information please visit http://docs.info.apple.com/article.html?artnum=42717.

Hubs and switches

At the center of a network is the hub or switch. Both devices serve the same purpose: to connect the various devices on your network at a central point. For many purposes, the subtle differences between a hub and a switch are not important. You could take a hub or a switch and plug in a few computers, a printer or two, a router, and a broadband connection without needing to know the difference between the two devices. The subtle differences, however, quickly become important — even critical — as the demand on your network grows. The wrong device in an otherwise fast network can bring your network to its knees in short order.

Remember that when you send information on an Ethernet network, it's broken down into frames for the journey. Each frame has both the sender's address and the destination's address. So, when your computer sends your document to the printer, that information is broken down into frames and sent down your Ethernet cable to the hub or switch. The hub or switch then magically sends your frames down the correct cable to the printer. The difference between hubs and switches lies in how they get the right information down the right cable to the right place.

When a hub needs to get the right frame down the right cable, it takes a very simple, brute-force approach: Just send that frame down *every* cable. When you send an Ethernet frame through a hub to your printer, the hub duplicates that frame and sends it to every single device on the network. Only the destination device, however, recognizes the destination address of the frame and lets it in. Everything else on your network just ignores it.

Imagine trying to drive to work and there were no stop signs, stoplights, traffic cops, and traffic signs. It wouldn't be so bad if you were the only car on the road. However, what if there were a lot of cars on the road? It would take a long time to get there. You might even run the risk of a collision or a traffic jam. This is exactly what happens when you use a hub.

The more computers and devices on the network, the greater the volume of network traffic; the greater the traffic, the slower the network. On networks with only a handful of computers, something as ordinary as backing up a computer over the network could cause a very large number of collisions, noticeably reducing the speed of your network. Hubs, therefore, are only appropriate on very small networks.

Switches are smart. Take your commute to work, and add stoplights, stop signs, traffic cops, and traffic signs. You would get to work much more safely intact and efficiently. Instead of broadcasting every single frame to every single device, switches send each Ethernet frame only where it needs to go, creating private paths between devices on your network. Without all those duplicate frames that a hub generates, your switch can accomplish the same task with significantly less network traffic. More importantly, however, a switch dramatically reduces the number of collisions on your network, even under heavy traffic. This makes switches far more efficient on busy networks or any medium or large network.

It also makes them more secure. If you're either astute or paranoid, you might have noticed something disconcerting about the nature of a hub: Everything you send over the network ends up going to every single device — including every single computer and printer on the network. How can you be sure they aren't reading the information that you send? In short, you can't. This type of network assumes that every other device is going to dutifully ignore your information. And they do — usually. Setting up a computer to listen to all the data it receives is possible, albeit difficult. If this computer is connected to a hub, receiving every frame on the network, the computer is able to listen to all the traffic on the network. This is called *sniffing* a network. A network switch, on the other hand, sends the information only where it needs to go. From a security standpoint, this makes listening to all the traffic on a network significantly more difficult because your computer is receiving exactly what you're being sent. But chances are, if you're using a hub, your network is very small. So, if your network uses a hub and you have a hacker on your network sniffing around, the problem is the hacker in your bedroom, and not your insecure hub.

Hubs and switches come in many different sizes, measured by the number of network ports they have. The most common sizes are 4-port, 8-port, and 16-port, although you can also find 24-port and 48-port sizes readily. Even larger configurations are available, but these tend to be expensive and very sophisticated. Prices start at about $20 for a generic 4-port 10baseT hub and rise with the number of ports. 100baseT hubs cost more than 10baseT hubs, and switches cost more than hubs. Generally, if a hub or switch supports 100baseT it also supports 10baseT. A hub or switch that supports both speeds will say that it's a dual-speed or 10/100 hub or switch. Generally, only switches support Gigabit. Switches that support Gigabit will say so. These switches may or may not support both Gigabit and the slower speeds. Some Gigabit switches offer full support for all three speeds.

This is usually indicated by the phrase "10/100/1000." Some Gigabit switches offer only one or two Gigabit-only ports while the rest offer the more standard 10/100 ports. You'll often have to look very carefully at the documentation for a switch to determine which ports support Gigabit.

Connecting hubs and switches

If you use up all the ports on one hub or switch, you can connect another hub or switch to it. You can even use hubs and switches together. Connecting hubs is called *daisy chaining*. Up to four hubs can be daisy-chained with twisted-pair cable. Switches are not subject to this restriction.

If you want to connect two hubs or switches, you can do so easily using a crossover cable between any two network ports. Most hubs and switches, however, have a specially designated port for this kind of connection called an *uplink port*.

You don't need a crossover cable if your hub or switch has an uplink port or a port that you can make into an uplink port by setting a switch. Plugging a regular cable into an uplink port has the same effect as using a crossover cable because the uplink port's wiring is reversed. On some hubs and switches, the uplink port and the port next to it cannot be used at the same time because they're actually the same port, only with two different jacks. Choose one and use it. On other hubs and switches, the uplink port has a button or switch that allows you to change the port from a regular port to an uplink port. In either case, simply use a regular cable to connect the uplink port on one hub or switch to any regular port on the other hub or switch. Note that connecting two uplink ports would require a crossover cable.

NOTE Do not under any circumstances plug a network cable from one port on your hub or switch to another, or if you have daisy chained hubs don't plug more than one wire in to "chain" them together. This will cause your hub or switch to crash.

Understanding the lights on a hub or switch

All hubs and switches have lights on them indicating all sorts of information. The most important lights on any switch or hub — aside from the power light, of course — are the *link lights*. Each port has a link light associated with it. Link lights are usually either right next to each port or listed all together on one end of the hub or switch. When two network ports on either end of a cable are connected properly, they automatically establish a *link*. When this happens, the port's link light turns on. Multiple-speed hubs and switches show you what speed a port is using. Hubs and switches also indicate traffic and collisions by using lights to indicate such occurrences. Look at the front panel of your device or check the documentation.

The Communications Layer

As strange as it may seem, your Web browser and your e-mail program on your computer don't speak Ethernet. Programs on a computer require a far more sophisticated language than Ethernet to meet their needs. Macintosh computers typically use one of two different languages, or protocols: AppleTalk and TCP/IP. These two protocols, in addition to several other less common protocols, are central to the communications layer.

In our layered approach to understanding networks, each layer uses the layer below it to achieve its goal. The communications layer, therefore, depends on the physical layer to do its work. In this case, Ethernet frames are responsible for ferrying TCP/IP and AppleTalk packets from place to place. If there is ever a breakdown in the layers, communication can't happen.

AppleTalk

AppleTalk has been used on the Macintosh for a long time. Designed in the early 1980s, AppleTalk was intended to allow small workgroups of computers to exchange files and share printers, and to allow for remote access. Often called LocalTalk, this early protocol was actually a combination of both the physical and communications layers of the network. These networks used LocalTalk cables rather than Ethernet cables to connect devices. Due to limitations built into this early version of AppleTalk, early AppleTalk networks could have no more than 254 devices on them.

In 1989, with the growing prevalence of Ethernet and token ring networks, Apple introduced AppleTalk Phase 2. This new version of AppleTalk supported more-sophisticated service discovery and a far greater address range of over 16 million possible network devices. AppleTalk is an easy-to- use network protocol in a small or medium-size Macintosh-based network because it's completely autoconfiguring.

AppleTalk is to use; however, it has its limitations. Windows-based PCs don't talk AppleTalk without additional software. In addition, some of the more sophisticated networking equipment no longer supports AppleTalk. And although AppleTalk supports up to 16 million network devices on a network, it doesn't scale well to very large networks. AppleTalk networks often run into problems far before they reach the 16-million-device barrier. Because of these limitations, Apple is phasing AppleTalk out in favor of a more modern protocol called Bonjour (discussed later in this chapter).

TCP/IP

TCP/IP is the king of network protocols. It is the most widely used network protocol today. It's the language of the Internet. Web pages, e-mail servers, FTP servers, the iTunes Music Store, instant-messenger programs, and so much more all use TCP/IP. The very name has the word *Internet* in it; IP actually stands for *Internet protocol.*

What's in a name?

TCP/IP stands for Transmission Control Protocol/Internet Protocol. If that sounds like two protocols instead of just one, you're right. Both *TCP* and *IP* are actually subprotocols of the Internet Protocol Suite. Most people, however, refer to the Internet protocols as TCP/IP. So we will, too.

TCP/IP has many strengths. It can handle incredibly large networks. (AppleTalk cannot handle the vast number of computers on the Internet.) TCP/IP was designed from the ground up to handle a virtually unlimited number of computers. This ability to handle incredibly large networks turns out to be good and makes possible TCP/IP's second strength: It's everywhere. Whether it's a Macintosh, a Linux workstation, a network printer, a Windows-based PC, or a cell phone, chances are it uses TCP/IP.

Ethernet is Multilingual

Ethernet networks support multiple protocols simultaneously. So you can print to your printer using AppleTalk while you surf the Web using TCP/IP. Modern AppleTalk and TCP/IP can coexist very peacefully. In fact, for several years now Macintosh computers have supported AFP (Apple File Protocol) over IP, which is the AppleTalk protocol for file sharing using TCP/IP instead of AppleTalk.

TCP/IP is at the heart of Mac OS X and is tightly integrated. Although AppleTalk is well supported in Mac OS X, many of the services it performs are being replaced by similar functions in TCP/IP. Given its central role in Mac OS X, the following section takes an in-depth look at TCP/IP and how it works.

TCP/IP's weakness, however, is usability. It requires configuration and lots of cooperation. Not surprisingly, however, Apple has been hard at work turning TCP/IP into as friendly a protocol as AppleTalk ever was. By working closely with the Internet Engineering Task Force (IETF) on projects such as SLP and ZeroConf, Apple is bringing easy-to-use networking to the rest of us through a new protocol called Bonjour. Apple used to call this protocol Rendezvous protocol and changed its name to Bonjour as the result of a lost copyright infringement battle. Apple has released Bonjour source code and Software Development Kits so as to enable its implementation and development under Windows, Windows CE, Linux, and VxWorks platforms. Bonjour is discussed in greater detail a bit later in this chapter.

How TCP/IP works

Every device on a TCP/IP network needs a unique IP address. The standard form for noting an IP address is in the standard *dotted decimal number* format, which looks like this:

```
192.168.216.105
```

The IP address consists of 4 octets. Each octet is separated by a period. Each IP address has two parts: a network address and a host address. Every address on a single network must have the same network address. Then each address has a unique host address. Together, these two parts make up a unique address.

But which part of this address is the network address and which is the host address? Well, that depends on the needs of your network. Because the network address and the host address both come from the same number, the longer one is, the shorter the other one is. Remember, too, that the longer a binary number is, the more possible unique numbers it can make. If your network address consists only of the first few bits, your host address is very long. In this case, you have a smaller number of possible network addresses but a huge number of possible host addresses for each one of those network addresses. This would be useful for a huge, international corporation with a gigantic network because they'll need many addresses all on one network.

For example, if you define the first octet as being the network address, the remaining three octets are used to define the host addresses for each network address. Because the first octet cannot be 0, the theoretical maximum number of network addresses is 255. For technical reasons, this number is actually much smaller — only 126. The host address, then, consists of three octets. So although the total number of possible network addresses is tiny, the possible number of host addresses for each of those network addresses is staggering: over 16 million addresses each!

On the other hand, if your network address consists of most of the first bits of the IP address, the host address is very short. In this case, you have a very large number of possible network addresses but a small number of possible host addresses for each network address. This would be perfect, for example, for an Internet service provider (ISP) with hundreds of customers, each of whom has a very small network. Each customer needs only a few host addresses for his or her small network (at home or in a small office). But the ISP needs a very large number of network addresses, one for each customer.

For example, if the network address consists of the first three octets, the remaining octet is used to define the host addresses for each network address. This means that there are millions of possible network addresses but only 254 (0 and 255 can't be used) possible host addresses for each network address.

As a result of this 126-network maximum, in 1993 the classful network was replaced with the CIDR (Classless Inter-Domain Routing) system. This incorporates a technique called VLSM (variable-length subnet masking), which breaks the barriers of fixed octet subnet masks. This allows for variable amounts of Class A, B, and C networks.

 To learn more about the CIDR system visit `http://en.wikipedia.org/wiki/Classless_Inter-Domain_Routing`.

Subnets and the subnet mask

Each device on a TCP/IP network needs a unique IP address. This address consists of two parts: the network address and the host address. If all you have is an IP address, however, there is no way to know which part is the network address and which is the host address. So you need a way of specifying which bits of the address are for what. To do this, you use a setting called the *subnet mask*. The subnet mask is a 32-bit binary number broken down into four 8-bit octets, very similar to the IP address. The subnet mask defines the network-address part of the IP address by masking it out. *Masking* is taking the binary representation of two numbers (in this case the IP address and the Subnet Mask) and performing a mathematical OR operation on the two numbers. For example, if there is a 1 in any position, the mask produces a 1. A machine with a subnet mask ending in a zero can see all of the machines in that group, without the aid of a router. A machine with a subnet mask ending in 255 would only see itself. For every bit in the IP address that is used for the network address, the subnet mask's corresponding bit is set to 1. For every bit that is used for the host address, the subnet mask's corresponding bit is set to 0.

For example, if your IP address is 192.168.216.105 and your subnet mask is 255.255.255.0, this is what they look like in their native binary:

Subnet Mask: 11111111.11111111.11111111.00000000

IP Address: 11000000.10101000.11011000.01101001

Broken into network-address and host-address components based on the subnet mask:

	Network Address	Host Address
Subnet mask:	11111111.11111111.11111111.	00000000
IP address:	11000000.10101000.11011000.	01101001
Resulting mask:	11111111.11111111.11111111.	01101001

Translated back into dotted decimal form:

	Network Address	Host Address
Subnet mask:	255.255.255.	0
IP address:	192.168.216.	105
Resulting mask	255.255.255.	105

Now you can determine the network address and host address of your own IP address. Your network address is 192.168.216 and your host address is 105. More importantly, however, you can also determine which other host addresses are on the same range of addresses as you are. A range of host addresses that all share the same network address is called a *subnet*.

For technical reasons, both first and last addresses in a range may not be usable. So the possible host addresses for your network address are from 1 to 254. Knowing the IP address and the subnet mask of your computer, you can determine which IP addresses are on your subnet and which are outside of your subnet. This determination is central to delivering information from one computer to another regardless of whether the computers are right next to each other or on different sides of the planet.

When your computer wants to send data via IP to another device, it must answer only one question: Is the destination address on the local network or not? If the destination address *is* on the local subnet, your computer delivers the information directly to that destination. If the destination address is *not* on the local network, your computer delivers the information to a special device on your network called a *router*.

Routers

Routers route network traffic. Whether you're from New York City, Los Angeles, or anywhere in between, regardless of how you otherwise pronounce the word *route,* on a network it always rhymes with the word *shout* not *boot.* (If you're from Australia, this makes it much less fun than it might otherwise be.) In a sense, routers are very uncomplicated devices. A simple router has two network ports. These ports are often called the Local Area Network (LAN) port and Wide Area Network (WAN) port. The LAN port is connected to your network and has an IP address within the range of your network's subnet. The WAN network port is connected to a second network and has an IP address within the range of that other network's subnet (generally the Internet). In the router is a table of information telling the router exactly which addresses are on which side of the router. All this router has to do is direct traffic in the appropriate direction.

When your computer determines that a destination address is not on the local subnet, it passes that data, in the form of an IP packet, to the router. Your computer knows the address of the router from the TCP/IP settings on your computer. Under Mac OS X, this setting is called the *router address*. The router then asks the same question: Is the destination address of this packet on the local subnet of this second network or not? If it is, the packet is delivered. If it isn't, the packet is forwarded to the next router. This repeats itself until the correct destination is contacted.

IP addresses

For a device to work on the Internet, it needs an IP address that has been assigned from a pool of available addresses. IP addresses are usually assigned by your ISP or your local network administrator. Whatever the case, IP addresses are not arbitrary.

Public and private

There are two classes of IP addresses: public and private. Public IP addresses are standard, fully functional addresses. If there were enough of them, there would be little need for private IP addresses. As it is, however, we're running out of public addresses. So to conserve addresses, private addresses were created.

Private IP addresses are not fully functional addresses. Without any help, in fact, a private IP address could never communicate with any device out on the Internet at all. This is because private IP addresses are not routable. In order to use a private IP address on the Internet, your router has to be configured to do so. This feature of a router to route private IP addresses is called Network Address Translation (NAT). With NAT, your router's WAN port gets one real IP address. Your network, however, gets private IP addresses. When a device on your network wants to get information from the Internet, it asks the router for help. The router pretends to be that device for a moment and makes the request for you. When the router receives a reply, it then forwards that reply back to that device on your network. From the outside world, then, the only device that ever makes a request for information is the router. For the purposes of a transaction, your private IP address is translated into a public address and then back again on the return trip. Through this method, you can have thousands or even millions of devices all accessing the Internet without using more than a single real IP address.

From the Internet's point of view, however, your network is mostly invisible. The only part of your network that anyone else can see is the WAN port of your router. This is both a blessing and a curse. The blessing is that this makes your network very difficult to hack. The curse is that some network services don't work very well with private addresses. If you had a server, for example, such as a Web server, an FTP server, or even a hosted network game such as Quake or Unreal Tournament, it would be more difficult for your computer to be seen from the Internet.

> **NOTE**   Some voice-over IP technologies such as Apple's iChat have difficulty with private IP addresses. If you have trouble connecting to such a service, check your router's configuration to make sure the correct services are allowed through.

Private IP addresses are easily identified because they fall into one of three different ranges:

> 10.0.0.0 through 10.255.255.255
>
> 172.16.0.0 through 172.31.255.255
>
> 192.168.0.0 through 192.168.255.255

There is a fourth range of addresses — 169.254.0.0 through 169.254.255.255 — that is not a public set of addresses. Although it isn't classified as a private range either, it's private in effect. This range is special and is discussed in the following section.

TCP/IP configuration

Devices can be configured to use TCP/IP in many different ways. This section covers the reasons for each method. The end of the chapter walks you through setting up the configuration method you choose.

Manual configuration

The most obvious method for configuring a device is to do it by hand. This is called *manual configuration*. In this method, you're prompted to enter all the pertinent information in appropriate places. Each device that needs to be configured in this manner needs to be done individually. In the example shown in Figure 11.2, my network administrator gave me the following network information: IP address 10.0.3.2, Subnet Mask 255.255.255.0, Router 10.0.3.1, and DNS Server 4.2.2.2

FIGURE 11.2

Network preferences pane using manual configuration

DHCP and BootP configuration

Although this would be a simple matter for a small network, for a large network you would have to visit each machine and manually set each IP address. That method is too time-consuming. Fortunately, there is a more automated way to configure a device to use TCP/IP. A device may be able to obtain its TCP/IP configuration from a special server on a network called a *DHCP server* (Figure 11.3). DHCP stands for Dynamic Host Configuration Protocol and is often used to configure the TCP/IP settings of a whole network of computers automatically. Some DHCP servers require that the client have a DHCP Client ID specified in order to obtain the configuration settings, although BootP is rarely used in today's modern networks. In this example the DHCP server gave my computer an IP address of 10.0.3.24, subnet mask of 255.255.255.0, a router address of 10.0.3.1, and DNS of 167.206.3.206, and 167.206.3.205. When a computer that is set up to receive its TCP/IP configuration from a DHCP server cannot contact that server, it configures itself by choosing a random IP address from the range 169.254.0.0 through 169.254.255.255.

 In previous versions of MacOS X, the DNS settings were not visible in the network system preference pane. In Leopard, they are displayed in light gray text.

FIGURE 11.3

Network preferences pane using DHCP configuration

In theory, an entire network of computers set to use DHCP to configure themselves would work together perfectly in the absence of a DHCP server. However, because each computer chooses its address randomly, if it can't contact a DHCP server, it would be impossible to intelligently provide different network services for your network needs, such as Internet access and file servers, due to the high probability of duplication.

PPP, PPPoE, and AOL configurations

Dial-up modem communications are also able to automatically configure the connecting device with the appropriate TCP/IP settings. Standard modem connections to the Internet use a protocol called Point-to-Point Protocol (PPP) to establish the connection. The PPP connection is responsible for configuring the TCP/IP settings of your computer in this case.

Many DSL providers use a protocol called PPPoE for connecting you to the Internet. PPPoE stands for PPP over Ethernet. In this case, your DSL connection creates an Ethernet network over the telephone line all the way to your ISP. PPPoE is a version of PPP for Ethernet networks. Just as with a dial-up modem connection, PPPoE is responsible for configuring the TCP/IP settings of your computer.

Finally, AOL modem connections have their own proprietary method for configuring TCP/IP. You can connect to AOL using a telephone line as well as an already established Internet connection.

Static versus dynamic IP addresses

If your computer is configured to obtain its TCP/IP configuration from a DHCP server, it does so automatically whenever you need to connect to the Internet. When it contacts the DHCP server, it asks for a lease on an IP address. If the DHCP server grants the lease, that lease is good for a certain predefined time. At the end of that time, your computer will have to get a new lease. This happens automatically whenever it needs to happen. There is no guarantee, however, that you'll always get the same address each time your computer asks for an address. This is called a dynamic IP address because it can change.

Not all DHCP servers give out dynamic IP addresses, although it is very common. A DHCP server can be set up so that it always gives the same address to the same device. In this case, the DHCP server would be giving out static IP addresses, even though it would be doing so automatically whenever they were needed. From the perspective of the workstation it is receiving a dynamic address. BootP and PPP servers can be configured the same way as well. The only kind of TCP/IP configuration that is always static is a manually assigned IP address.

Domain name service servers

Every device on the Internet is identified by a unique IP address. But when you open your Web browser and go to a Web site, you don't type in the IP address of the Web site you want to go to. Who could remember all those numbers? To make it easier to get around, the Internet has a naming scheme to help. Now instead of having to remember that Apple's Web site is at the IP address 17.112.152.32, all you have to remember is www.apple.com.

But how does your browser (or your e-mail software or your FTP client) know that www.apple.com equals 17.112.152.32? The answer is that your computer asks a Domain Name Service (DNS) server. DNS servers are responsible for keeping a comprehensive list of which names go with which addresses. To function properly then, every computer must know the address of at least one DNS server. If your computer cannot contact a DNS server to resolve a name into an address, you won't be able to contact the destination. To prevent this kind of problem, most computers hold a list of several DNS servers if you want them to. If the first DNS server in the list doesn't respond, the computer automatically asks the next server in the list.

It is impossible for a DNS server to contain all name to IP address cross-references. Just as an IP packet gets transferred from router to router until it reaches its destination, the DNS lookup does the same thing. If the first DNS server can't find the name and IP address you are looking for, that DNS server queries other DNS servers until it finds the answer. Then it sends the information back to your computer. At this point your computer contacts the correct IP address based on your request.

Bonjour

Bonjour is a collection of technologies that work together to provide automatic network configuration and service discovery. (Bonjour was called "Rendezvous" prior to the release of Tiger.) The technical name for this project is Zeroconf. In particular, Bonjour uses three core technologies: link-local addressing, Multicast DNS, and DNS service discovery. All these technologies are open projects of the Internet Engineering Task Force. Apple's code for Bonjour is open source.

Bonjour can automatically configure a device to use TCP/IP (for local use) *without* a DHCP or BootP server. When a device is added to a network without any means of automatic configuration, such as a DHCP or BootP server, Bonjour automatically configures the device using *link-local addressing*. In link-local addressing, the device randomly chooses an address from a range of addresses set aside by the Internet Assigned Numbers Authority (IANA) for link-local addressing and assigns that address to itself. It then broadcasts a message over the network to determine if that address is in use. If it is in use, it randomly chooses another address and tries again until it finds an address that is not in use. After the device has assigned itself an unused address, it's ready to send and receive IP traffic.

Bonjour can also automatically and dynamically discover new services on a network, such as printers and servers. To do this, Bonjour uses a combination of Multicast DNS and DNS service discovery to advertise servers on a network and then to find those services when needed.

The two functions of Bonjour — automatic network configuration and service discovery — may sound familiar. This isn't the first time we Macintosh folk have been able to just turn on a computer, plug it into a network, and find all the servers on a network without having to configure anything. That's because AppleTalk can already do these things. But AppleTalk didn't do it as well as Bonjour does.

First, Bonjour is far more efficient. Whether it's AppleTalk or Bonjour doing the work, all this automatic configuration and service discovery generates network traffic. Bonjour is much more intelligent, however. Bonjour is also very extensible. AppleTalk really worked only for finding printers and file servers. Adding completely different kinds of services would have been daunting. Bonjour supports just about any service you can imagine. But most importantly, Bonjour manages to do what AppleTalk did using TCP/IP (an industry standard) instead.

IPv6

The IP address range that we've discussed so far is called IPv4. IP addresses in this range are 32-bit addresses. There are approximately 4.2 billion possible addresses in this range, although many of those addresses are not useable. Although this may sound nearly infinite, it's barely enough. Some estimates suggest that we're using about 65 percent of the usable addresses already. Consider how quickly the remaining 35 percent will go when every cell phone, every TV, every refrigerator, and every air conditioner also has its own IP address. Or, more important, imagine what will happen when all of China goes online in the next decade. Suddenly 4.2 billion doesn't sound so big anymore.

To alleviate this problem, the people who brought you IPv4 have been hard at work designing an upgrade. This upgrade is called IPv6. Among the many benefits incorporated into IPv6, the most obvious is the size of the new IP addresses. Instead of using 32-bit addresses, each address is now 128-bits long. A 128-bit-long binary number has a lot of possible combinations: 2^{128} possible combinations, to be exact. This works out to be 340,282,366,920,938,463,463,374,607,431,768,211,456.

Understanding the size of that number really isn't possible by just looking at that string of digits. So consider this: According to the United States Census Bureau, the population of this planet as of mid-year 2003 is approximately 6,302,486,693. If we were to divide up the IPv6 addresses, giving each person on the face of the Earth an equal number of addresses, each person would get 53,991,762,854,316,031,771,016,167,424! Each of us could have his own IPv4 Internet to himself without having to share a single IP address with anybody else on the planet. Even then, each of us would still have more than 12 million billion entire Internets he wouldn't be using!

For years now, manufacturers of network devices such as routers have been working to add support for IPv6 into their products. Apple added support for IPv6 into Mac OS X quite some time ago. But Mac OS X 10.5 adds an easy-to-use graphical user interface for configuring those settings. Currently, most networks do not use IPv6. Getting an IPv6 network to work with the rest of the Internet requires some configuration on the network level. If your network uses IPv6, your network administrator will be able to tell you what settings to make on your computer. But whenever the rest of the world decides to move to IPv6, Mac OS X will be ready.

The Application Layer

The final layer of a network is the application layer. When a Web browser receives a requested Web site and displays it for you, when your e-mail program checks for new e-mail messages, or when you print, your computer uses the communications layer to get the information to and from the destination. The application layer is responsible for coordinating communications.

A computer can be a Web server and an e-mail server at the same time using the same IP address. But how does your browser know to download a Web page, and your e-mail program know to download your new e-mail? It turns out that each IP address is broken down into *ports*. These ports are numbered 1 through 65,535. Only one service can use a port at a time. For example, Web servers use port 80, which is the http protocol, by default. Technically, when you type in the address for Apple's Web site `www.apple.com/`, you should have to specify not only the IP address but the port as well. So, Apple's Web server is at `172.112.152.32` port 80. The shorthand for specifying the full IP address would be `172.112.152.32:80`. Web browsers, however, know that most Web sites are on port 80. This is identified by the `http://` in front of the Web site's address. So, unless you specify otherwise, they'll assume you mean port 80.

Using Firewall Protection

A firewall is a protective gateway for network traffic, preventing and allowing traffic based on a set of rules. Firewalls are typically in one of two places: They're either installed on your computer as software to protect your computer, or they're hardware devices on your network that protect your whole network from outside attacks.

In this sense, a NAT-enabled router is a kind of firewall by default: It allows only certain packets back through to the inside. But NAT-enabled devices are not very good firewalls. A good firewall analyzes each packet as it comes or goes and either accepts or rejects it based on a set of rules that are defined.

For example, if you had a Web server on your network and a firewall protecting your network, you would want to set up a rule that would allow any traffic going to your Web server on port 80 to pass through, while traffic to any other address and any other port would be denied. Managing a firewall can be tricky, however. Depending on the services you need to use, you may find that a firewall prevents certain services from working through it. When in doubt, check the documentation for the service in question. If you're trying to use Timbuktu through a firewall for example, check the Timbuktu Web site for help on configuring a firewall for use with Timbuktu. You can usually get detailed instructions about which ports the service uses. Another good reference is the Internet Assigned Numbers Authority (IANA), which keeps a list of well-known ports for reference at `http://www.iana.org/assignments/port-numbers`.

Every service you use on a network has at least one port associated with it. The reason for ports is because one machine that has one unique IP address may be running multiple applications. It may be an FTP, Web, e-mail, SSH server. The http (Web) protocol uses port 80. When your e-mail software checks for e-mail, it checks a POP e-mail server using port 110. Sending e-mail is usually done using an SMTP server on port 25. When you log onto an FTP server and browse the contents, your FTP software connects to the server using port 21. Downloading files from an FTP server is usually done using port 20. For a full list of common Internet ports used with certain services, visit `www.iana.org/assignments/port-numbers`.

The Network Preference Pane

Although, at first, using tools like the Internet Connect application and the Setup Assistant is easiest, as your OS X and networking prowess increase, you'll want to begin poking around in the Network pane of System Preferences. Doing so provides you with more-advanced troubleshooting and more-accurate information than the simpler methods, and gives you full manual customization and control over your Mac's network-related behavior. After setting up or connecting to your network, you may want to change or add some settings here. Because Mac OS X does a phenomenal job of automatically handling and sensing network connections, you may not need to make any changes at all. Access the Network preference pane by opening the System Preferences and clicking the Network icon.

Understanding ports and locations

Max OS X handles your network connections through a kind of hierarchy. The first stage is your computer's location. Setting up a location implies that you'll really be connecting from different physical locations, but it can be simply creating a specific preference set for a specific connection type that you have. You don't have to have a portable machine to set up locations. For example, say your cable connection also gives you a free dial-up connection. You can set up a separate dial-up location for use if your cable service is ever out.

The next stage is the network ports. Under each location, you can configure multiple ports for connections. A port is a way you connect to a network, like your Ethernet port, or your AirPort Card. The default is to have different ports active on a single location, thereby allowing you to connect in multiple ways per location.

The final stage we'll call *priority*. Within an individual location, OS X lets you specify the priority in which ports are used. For example, you can have your modem, your AirPort, and your Ethernet port all configured for one location. But, if you have a good AirPort signal, you wouldn't want your Mac to start dialing up! To avoid this, OS X lets you choose which port to use first. If you have Ethernet set for first priority, after the Mac senses a good Ethernet signal, it will still take IP addresses from, say, an AirPort connection, but it won't connect to the Internet with that IP unless the top-priority one, the Ethernet, drops off. Then OS X will fall over to the other connection, more than likely without you even noticing. Because your Mac can actually have multiple IP addresses at the same time (from different ports), it may seem difficult to determine how, indeed, you're actually connected. A bit later, we discuss the first thing that you see when you open the Network Preference pane: the Network Status screen, which helps you determine just how you're connected. You can also change locations from this initial screen, by selecting different ones from the Location menu. You can edit and create new ones from this menu as well. Notice that the default location of a new Mac is always the Automatic setting, a preconfigured hierarchy of ports to make automatic sensing of a connection as effective as possible. Port order/hierarchy and locations are discussed later in this chapter.

TIP   **You can have OS X assist you in configuring network settings. Clicking the Assist Me button opens a specialized version of the Mac OS Setup Assistant for aiding in the setup and basic troubleshooting of a network.**

Network status display

Open the System Preferences application by choosing it in the Apple menu. The System Preferences application is located in the `Applications` folder. It's also in the Dock, if you haven't dragged it out of there. After System Preferences is open, choose the Network pane by clicking its icon. The first thing you see is called the Network Status area (see Figure 11.4). This is an overview of what's going on, network-connection-wise, in your Mac's world. You'll notice two different pull-down menus. One is for choosing your location (we get to that later) and the other is entitled Show. What's being shown on the Network Status screen is a list of all your active network ports and their status as related to Internet connectivity.

FIGURE 11.4

The Network System Preference pane provides a quick display of your network connectivity.

When looking at the Network System Prefernce pane, you see a column on the left side with very important information. There are iChat-style colored status-indicator dots, the name of the network port, and a brief summary of how the port is connected. A green dot means that the port is active (that is, you have an IP address and you're connected to a network), an orange dot means you are connected without an IP Address, and a red dot means you are not connected. As you click on each port, the details of your connection are revealed on the right side of the dialog box.

In Figure 11.4, the Mac in question tells you that it's connected through a base station called Almond MandMs, and that it's getting a DHCP address from it (10.0.3.26). The Ethernet port indicates that the cable is physically plugged in but has been given no IP address. In Figure 11.4, the Ethernet DHCP port has an orange dot, and OS X tells you exactly why this is so: The Ethernet cable is plugged in, but the Mac doesn't have an IP address. Further troubleshooting reveals that the TCP/IP settings were incorrectly set for a manual address.

The order in which the ports appear in the list is important because it designates in which order your Mac prefers a connection. As long as the connections are active and functional, the topmost connection receives the highest priority. If the port has a red light it moves to the bottom of the list regardless of the priority you have given it. In Figure 11.4, Ethernet is first in the list and, thus, the Mac connects over the Ethernet cable. If it is unable to communicate for whatever reason, the Mac defaults to the next available usable connection, and so on down the list. In this way, you can have many different IP addresses at the same time. You could be connected to an AirPort Base Station and have a valid IP address from it, an Ethernet cable plugged in, a valid IP from that network *and* be dialed up with your internal modem, and have an IP address from that connection as well. Each port would show up in the Network Status as having a valid IP address and, thus, display a green light in the left column. Although you can have multiple IPs, you can only be connected with one at a time, and again, the Network Status will tell you which port you're actually connected to the Internet with, even though there are multiple ports with IP addresses. In Figure 11.5, both Ethernet and AirPort have valid IP addresses, but because the Ethernet connection is first in the list, your Mac tells you that it's actually connected to the Internet with the Ethernet port. If the Ethernet connection fails, the AirPort connection takes over.

FIGURE 11.5

Let the colored dots be your guide. The Network Status display shown here indicates how you're connected; in this case, both AirPort and Ethernet are being given IP addresses, and Ethernet takes priority because it's first in the list.

Configuring the port settings

Now that you're aware of your network status, you can configure your ports and your connection methods. After viewing the Network Status, you may determine that your Mac is set up and accessing the Internet with reckless abandon. For AirPort and Ethernet, the default connection type is DHCP. Therefore, all you should have to do is plug in the cable or select the AirPort network, and if your network is set up to do so, your Mac will automatically take an address, plug and play, no configuration necessary. Whether or not this is the case, you should become familiar with all the wonderful things that Network preferences has to offer. The following section covers configuring AirPort, Ethernet, modem, Bluetooth, and infrared ports.

Unlocking Network preferences settings

Before you can change any settings, you may need to unlock the Network preference pane. If you aren't an administrator of the machine, you'll need to get an admin name and password before you can make changes.

After changing network settings, click the Apply button at the bottom of Network preferences to retain them. If you forget to click Apply, Mac OS X asks whether you want to save your changes as needed.

Common settings panes

It's important to recognize that certain settings are available from more than one port. For example, AppleTalk settings are available under both the Ethernet and AirPort settings. Proxies and TCP/IP are also available under multiple ports, and moreover, can be configured individually per port. This multiple availability is due to the fact that different connection methods still call upon some similar configurations. Because of this arrangement, we first look at the non-port-specific panel settings, and then move on to configuring the individual port settings. You can access the network port settings by selecting the port you would like to modify on the left column and then clicking the Advanced button on the bottom right of the pane. This brings up the configuration pane for that port.

TCP/IP

The TCP/IP configuration is available under every port — AirPort, Ethernet, modem, and USB Bluetooth modem adapter — because your TCP/IP settings are the very numbers by which you're granted Internet access, no matter how you connect. Typical Ethernet TCP/IP settings are shown in Figure 11.6.

Every port has TCP/IP settings. These belong to an Ethernet port.

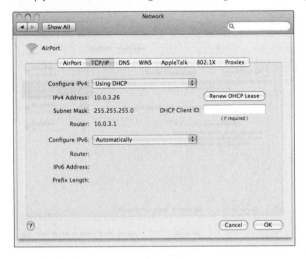

An IP address, subnet mask, router address, and DNS servers are the minimum settings you'll need to connect to the Internet. This can be set manually or automatically, depending on your network. When using Ethernet and AirPort ports, simply enter the relevant information in the appropriate fields or choose a dynamic connection method. When using a modem, PPP is the usual configure option. In the following list, you find the options that are present in the TCP/IP configuration screen:

- **Configure:** The method for obtaining some of the other TCP/IP settings for the network connection, such as Manually (see Figure 11.2), Using PPP, Using DHCP (see Figure 11.3), Using DHCP with a Fixed IP Address, or Using BOOTP.

- **IP Address:** The numerical address for the network connection. This address is a set of four numbers separated by periods, such as 17.254.0.91. This setting is provided automatically by some Configure methods.

- **Subnet Mask:** Works in tandem with the IP address.

- **Router:** The IP address of a machine that connects your local network to other networks or the Internet. This setting can be changed only when the Configure method is Manually. Leave this setting blank if your network has no router or gateway.

- **Configure IPv6:** This is the area where you configure your IPv6 settings. This is a future need, however, because most networks today are IPv4.

DNS

The DNS pane, shown in Figure 11.7, is where your Domain Name Servers are set. If your TCP/IP configuration is set to automatic, the current DNS settings are listed in gray in the left window. You can add additional DNS Servers by clicking the plus sign below the DNS Servers window. If you place your own DNS information into the pane, they take precedence over the ones designated by your DHCP server. The following options are present in the DNS configuration screen:

- **Domain Name Servers:** One or more IP addresses of computers that translate alphabetic addresses, such as www.apple.com, to IP addresses. Put each address on a separate line. This setting is provided automatically by some Configure methods. Domain Name Servers is usually abbreviated DNS.

- **Search Domains:** One or more domain names, such as nps.gov or berkeley.edu, that Mac OS X uses to resolve a partial Internet or network address. For example, if Search Domains contains apple.com, then Mac OS X resolves the partial Internet address www as www.apple.com, livepage becomes livepage.apple.com, store becomes store.apple.com, developer becomes developer.apple.com, and so forth.

AppleTalk

AppleTalk is available under the AirPort and Ethernet connection methods. If you need to use AppleTalk (you may have a network printer or a file server that requires it), you can enable it by checking its box in the AppleTalk pane, as shown in Figure 11.8.

If your computer is connected to a network divided into multiple AppleTalk zones, the AppleTalk tab of Network preferences also specifies the zone in which your computer resides. If your computer is connected to a network with only one zone, you won't have any zones from which to choose.

FIGURE 11.7

Every port has DNS settings. These belong to an Ethernet port.

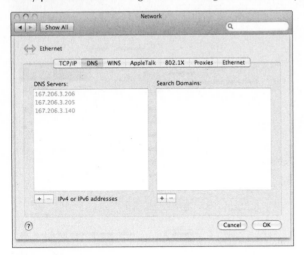

FIGURE 11.8

Activate AppleTalk with a single click.

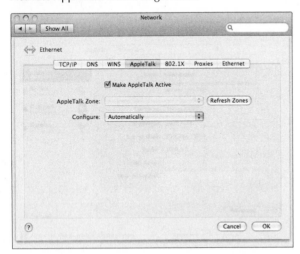

You should leave the Configure setting at Automatically unless you're an AppleTalk expert. If you are an expert, you know how to set the AppleTalk Node ID and Network ID, which are the settings that appear when you change the Configure setting to Manually.

NOTE   AppleTalk can be enabled on only one port at one time. IF you need to access two devices on separate networks using AppleTalk, they must be accessed separately.

Proxies

The Proxies pane looks the same from every port. If your computer connects to a local network that is protected from the Internet by a firewall, you may need to configure a port's proxy settings. Here, you can specify the proxy servers, which some firewalls use as buffers between a local network and the Internet for privacy, security, and speed. Figure 11.9 shows the Proxies pane.

FIGURE 11.9

Bypass proxy restrictions in the Proxies pane.

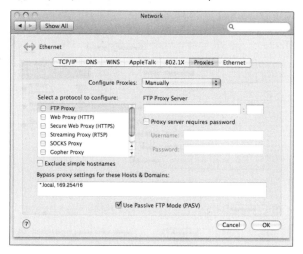

If your Internet connectivity is fine, and you can access everything you need, you don't need to worry about proxies. A network that does have proxy servers almost certainly has a network administrator who can tell you how to configure the Proxies settings. On the left side, you select the proxy server to configure. Check the box if you need to use it. On the right side is a space to type in the proxy server address; the colon separates the port number that the proxy is set for. Some proxy servers need a password, which can be set by clicking the relevant button. Toward the bottom of the pane you can type in hosts and domains whose proxy settings you want to bypass; for example, if you're on the same network that your e-mail server is on, you may not want to go through the proxy server to access your own local network.

The Proxies pane also lets you choose whether or not to use Passive FTP Mode. In active FTP mode, the server contacts two adjacent random ports within a specified range on the client side, and then the communication is facilitated between ports 20 and 21 on the server and X, and X+1 (where X is the random port) on the client side. This becomes a problem when the client has a firewall, because there are incoming FTP requests on random ports. Passive mode solves this problem somewhat by letting the client make all the port requests. If you are behind a firewall, you should turn on passive mode so the FTP traffic can peacefully pass to your computer.

802.1X

Generally there is not much security with Ethernet and AirPort communications from the network administrator's standpoint. If someone has a network port and DHCP is turned on at the server side, they can connect to the Internet or the network. 802.1X is generally used for wireless communications, but it has been added to Ethernet communications as well. Here you set the method of authentication. If the authentication fails, when prompted for a password, network communication is blocked. If your network administrator has 802.1X authentication turned on in your network, the 802.1X configuration window looks like Figure 11.10. This preference used to be in the Internet Connect program, which is now defunct.

FIGURE 11.10

802.1X configuration

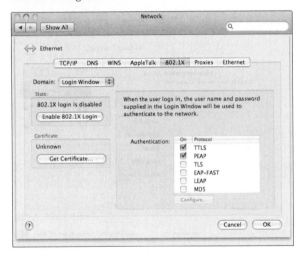

Domain

This is where the username and password is requested for 802.1X authentication. It can be requested at the Login Window, the User level, or the System level.

- **Login Window:** Takes the specific username and password used to log in to the system to ask the 802.1X server if this specific user is granted or denied access to the network.

- **System:** A designated username and password is used for the entire system. It is possible that you want to grant this particular computer access to a network, but not all users have access to the 802.1X authenticated network. Here you can designate an user account which applies to the entire system for authentication.

- **User:** Some users specifically need access and others don't. Here you can specify profiles for individuals so some people have access and others don't.

State

Here you can enable or disable 802.1X authentication.

Certificate

Some 802.1X networks have a certificate for security. If you click on Get Certificate it asks for a username and password. The computer then contacts the 802.1X authentication server for the valid certificate. If there is no certificate to be had, you can select the appropriate protocols in the box on the right side of the window.

WINS

Windows Internet Naming Service is a method of Windows computer naming. It relates the NetBIOS name of a computer to an address. Here you can set the NetBIOS Name of your computer, which workgroup your computer belongs to, and which WINS servers your computer will communicate with. These settings used to be in the Directory Access application and have been moved into the Network System Preference pane for easier access. Figure 11.11 shows the WINS preference pane. In this case the NetBIOS name of this computer is SZMBP, and the Workgroup it is connecting to is MSHOME. This setting used to be in the Directory Access program but it has been moved to the Network System Preference pane.

FIGURE 11.11

The WINS settings for the Ethernet port

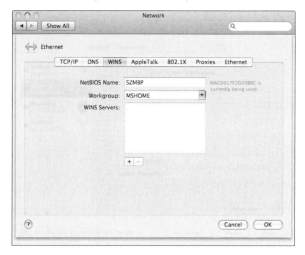

Configuring AirPort

Click the Configure button from the Network Status screen after clicking AirPort in the list, or use the Show menu to choose it. Under the AirPort section are four panels. Figure 11.12 shows the AirPort configuration screen.

AirPort

The settings on the main Airport pane are very basic, as shown in Figure 11.12, until you click the Advanced button on the bottom right of the pane. Here you have the option in the pull-down menu to connect to an AirPort network. If the network is hidden, select Join Other Network in the pull-down menu. Here you can select to ask to join new networks. When selected, this option brings up a window automatically (Figure 11.13) when you are not connected to a wireless network, to allow selection of wireless networks in range. Here you can also show the AirPort status in the menu bar, just to the left of the time and date.

FIGURE 11.12

The basic AirPort settings

FIGURE 11.13

The Automatic AirPort selection window

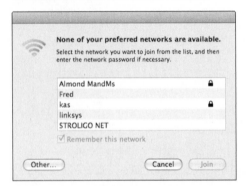

The advanced pane, Figure 11.14, allows for much more customization of your AirPort settings. This pane shows your AirPort card's hardware address, also called a MAC address, or AirPort ID. In certain situations, such as a secure wireless network that recognizes computers by their hardware address, you'll need to know how to find yours. In this pane, you can specify the behavior of your AirPort connection (that is, how your Mac joins networks). There is a list of Preferred Networks, which causes your Mac to connect to any of the wireless networks on the list. You can add the networks that you "prefer" to connect to in order of preference. Your Mac always looks for one of your Preferred Networks before searching for other available wireless connections. You can drag the names within the list to reorder them. Use the plus sign to add, and the minus sign to delete networks from the list. Click the Edit button to change the password to an encrypted network.

FIGURE 11.14

The Advanced AirPort settings pane

At the bottom of the window are three options. One is to remember any network this computer has joined. As you connect to networks, MacOS X automatically adds them to the Preferred Networks list. Second is to disconnect from a wireless network when logging out. Since each user has specific passwords for a wireless network stored in their keychain, one user may not want to allow another user access to their wireless. The last option is to require an administrator to control AirPort settings. Click Apply to save your changes.

TCP/IP

This is the place. Time to type or select your Internet configuration settings. These terms should all be familiar — they were discussed at the beginning of this chapter. Choose the appropriate information and type it all in, or make your selections for receiving a dynamic address. If you're having trouble getting an IP address automatically (via DHCP) try clicking the Renew DHCP Lease button.

This requests a new lease on the address that you have signed out or, if you have no address, a new one altogether. You also have the option to configure IPv6 (as opposed to IPv4), which is a new form of IP addressing that allows for a greater number of total addresses. As of now, it's pretty rare, and you may need a network admin to tell you how to configure it, if necessary. Click the button to turn it from automatic to manual or to turn it off.

DNS

See your current DNS and search domain settings. You can manually add DNS servers and search domains to the list.

AppleTalk

Click the AppleTalk box to make AppleTalk active. Because it seems certain that AppleTalk is slowly being phased out, you may not need to use it; in fact, it's turned off by default.

Proxies

Configure your AirPort connection to use proxy servers in the Proxies pane. Click the Apply button to save changes.

WINS

Configure your AirPort connection for a Windows-based network.

802.1X

Configure your AirPort connection for an 802.1X-authenticated network.

Configuring Ethernet settings

If you need to configure your Ethernet port, click Built-In Ethernet from the Status menu, or scroll to it in the Show menu. The Ethernet option, within the Ethernet configuration screen, appears as shown in Figure 11.15.

TCP/IP

Same deal here as with AirPort. Configure as necessary, whether it be for a manual IP address or a dynamic one. Click the appropriate button to renew your DHCP lease if you need to. If you need to use IPv6, do so.

Proxies

If you need it, you'll know it. Configure as necessary.

FIGURE 11.15

Take charge of your Ethernet-specific settings here.

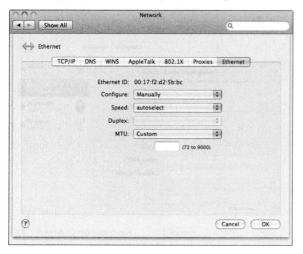

Ethernet

A special Ethernet section (within the Ethernet section) lurks. The first thing that appears is your Mac's hardware Ethernet address, or MAC address. Most commonly, Ethernet will be set to Configure: Automatically and doesn't need to be changed. If you're troubleshooting a network issue, or tinkering around, you might want to switch from automatic to manual. Doing so gives you the ability to select the speed of your Ethernet port manually (you might want to set it slower, at 10BaseT, to test stability on a problem-prone network) and to control the size of the packets that your Mac sends over the network, the MTU.

NOTE   If you are having trouble connecting to the Internet and all of your network settings are correct, you may want to change the MTU (Maximum Transmission Unit) to something smaller than 1500. Check with your ISP first. Commonly DSL connections have an MTU of 1492, smaller than the default 1500. Generally your router handles this automatically. That doesn't always happen. If your computer's MTU is larger than the IPS's, the Internet will not work as "high speed" as you anticipated.

Click Apply to save changes made to your Ethernet settings.

Configuring modem settings

Select the internal modem port to configure settings for dial-up Internet Access. Figure 11.16 shows the Modem configuration area.

FIGURE 11.16

Take charge of your internal modem settings here.

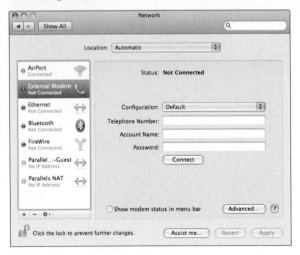

PPP (Point to Point Protocol)

PPP is how modems connect to the Internet. Here in the modem system preferences, you can add the destination phone number, account username, and password. You also can create different configurations for PPP connections. If you have an EVDO card and an external modem, you need a separate configuration for each connection type. For more advanced options, select Advanced.

- **Connect automatically when needed:** Starts a PPP session when an application, for example Mail, attempts to access the Internet.

- **Prompt every *x* minutes to maintain connection:** Causes a dialog box to appear periodically, asking if you want to stay connected, and ends the PPP session if no one responds to the dialog box.

- **Disconnect if idle for *x* minutes:** Automatically stops the PPP session if no Internet activity occurs on the PPP connection during the specified time interval.

- **Disconnect when user logs out:** Automatically stops the PPP session when you log out of Mac OS X, so the next person to log in can't inherit your PPP session.

- **Redial if busy:** Specifies how to redial the service provider's telephone number if it's busy.

- **Send PPP echo packets:** Makes Mac OS X periodically ask your Internet provider's computer to respond and ends the PPP session if your Internet provider's computer stops responding. If your Internet provider doesn't support PPP echoing, turning on this option may cause your PPP sessions to end prematurely.

- **Use TCP header compression:** Makes Mac OS X try to compress TCP header information for efficiency. Leave this option turned on because the service provider can refuse header compression without causing a problem.

■ **Connect using a terminal window (command line):** Causes a terminal window to appear while you're connecting so that you can type commands and enter requested information for your service provider.

■ **Use verbose logging:** Creates a detailed connection log for troubleshooting purposes. A detailed log uses more disk space.

Proxies

Configure as you would for either AirPort or Ethernet. Because most dial-up connections are commonly away from offices and firewalls, configuring Proxies while using a dial-up connection is rare but sometimes necessary.

Modem

Click the Modem pane to identify the type of modem you have and to set certain dialing options. Your Mac should default to the correct modem type, but you can find out just what type of modem you have by viewing the modem area of the Apple System Profiler. (Find Apple System Profiler in the Utilities folder, or by going to the Apple menu, choosing About This Mac, and clicking the More Info button.) The *V* number that comes after the modem type represents the speed and features supported by the modem. Newest modems use the V.92 protocol, which supports 56 Kbps connection speeds and can use call waiting to receive voice calls even if you're dialed up to the Internet. The V.90 script supports the 56 Kbps speeds, but not call waiting. Lower numbers are for lower speeds. If you're not sure which to use, try the higher one first and work your way down.

The first check box is for enabling error correction and compression. If you want to use speeds above 33.6 Kbps, you'll need to have this box checked. If you're having trouble maintaining a faster dial-up speed, unchecking this box can lead to more stability. The second check box tells the computer to wait for the dial tone before dialing. If your phone doesn't always give a clean dial tone (for example, if you have a voicemail system with a dial tone that changes to alert you of new messages), you'll want to uncheck this box.

If your phone is a pulse-dialing model, you'll need to select that option. Almost all phones are tone, so you should probably not select this option.

If you want the modem sound off, you can select the sound off option. Leaving the sound on is usually a good idea, as an aural indicator that your Mac is dialing up properly.

If you have call waiting, you can set your Mac to warn you when an incoming call is received when you're dialed up. You can choose to have an alert sound play and to be warned before being disconnected.

If you change countries, you should alter the modem settings to reflect your new location.

You can show or hide the Modem status icon in the menu bar by selecting or deselecting the option labeled Show Modem status in menu bar. You see the effect of changing this setting immediately. If the Modem status icon is hidden and you select this option, the Modem status icon appears to the left of other icons on the right side of the menu bar. You can use the Modem icon to connect to the Internet, disconnect from the Internet, and monitor the connection status, as described in Chapter 10.

If you have a slightly older Mac, you might have an infrared port. All the PowerBook G3s have them, as well as the earlier PowerBook G4s, and the original Bondi Blue iMac. You can use the infrared (IR) port to connect to the Internet through an IR-equipped Palm device or cell phone. Configuration is almost identical to both the regular internal modem and a Bluetooth modem (which is covered in the next section). IR is much slower and requires a direct line of sight between the devices.

Configuring the USB Bluetooth modem adapter

One of the niftier features of OS X is the ability to use a Bluetooth-enabled mobile phone to dial your Mac up to the Internet. This is especially cool (although a bit slow) if you have a PowerBook and are without the Internet, whether you're in a cab riding through Central Park or you're actually *in* Central Park. You'll need to set up your phone using the Bluetooth Setup Assistant first (covered later in this chapter). After you're dialed up through your cell phone, you can even go as far as to set your computer to share its connection over AirPort (see Chapter 12) and broadcast an Internet signal to other computers.

The Bluetooth modem is configured the same as the internal modem would be with respect to the TCP/IP, PPP, and Proxies panels. The unique panel is the Bluetooth Modem panel under Advanced. Instead of choosing a modem script to reflect your Mac's internal modem, the modem script needs to reflect your cell phone model or carrier (see Figure 11.17). If it's not present, you can go to www.apple.com/bluetooth for information and downloads. You're also given the option to show the Bluetooth status in the menu bar on the main Bluetooth pane. Otherwise, you initiate a connection just like you would a regular dial-up. You can click Dial Now right from the PPP panel, use the Internet Connect application, or use the modem menu-bar icon.

FIGURE 11.17

Choose the correct modem corresponding to your phone or cell phone carrier.

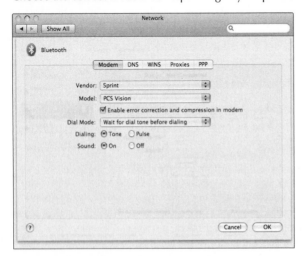

Configuring network ports

Mac OS X lets your computer have more than one network port active at the same time. Therefore, as previously stated, your computer can have concurrently active configurations of AirPort, Ethernet, and modem connections. You can even have multiple configurations of the same port, all of them operating in conjunction.

Multiple port configurations can provide overlapping services. On a PowerBook that you use in different locations, Ethernet can provide fast Internet access from the local network at your desk. AirPort can provide wireless Internet access when you're in meetings. A modem can provide Internet access when you're at home. On this PowerBook, the Ethernet, and AirPort configurations are active all the time, and Mac OS X is able to determine which configuration to use for Internet access at any given time and/or location.

Somehow, Mac OS X has to determine which of the available port configurations to use when you start to check your e-mail, browse the Web, print, or use some other network service. Mac OS X has a simple method of prioritizing port configurations. It goes down a list of available port configurations, trying each in turn, and uses the first one that works. By default, Mac OS X tries port configurations in the following order: internal modem, built-in Ethernet, and AirPort. (This port hierarchy is default for the Automatic location.) If your computer doesn't have one of these interfaces, it skips to the next one on the list.

You can change settings in Network preferences that affect which port configuration Mac OS X uses. You can do the following:

- Change the priority of port configurations
- Turn each port configuration on or off
- Create additional port configurations that use the same ports as existing configurations
- Rename port configurations
- Delete port configurations

Displaying network port configurations

When you open the Network Preference pane, the current status and configuration are displayed in the left column. Figure 11.18 shows an example of Network Port Configurations settings.

The status window includes a list of all ports, their current state, their priority, and activity. In this configuration the Ethernet port and AirPort are active and connected. The FireWire port is not connected, and Bluetooth is disabled. The Ethernet port (because it is on top) has the highest priority followed by the Airport.

Duplicating a Port Configuration

You can duplicate a port that currently exists on your Mac. If you wanted to create an additional Ethernet configuration, select the port you wish to duplicate. Click the cog at the bottom left of the window and click Duplicate Service. A dialogue box pops up, where you can edit the name of the new duplicate port.

FIGURE 11.18

Change the Network Port Configurations settings in Network preferences to affect which port configuration Mac OS X uses.

Renaming a Port

In the event you mislabeled a port or you would prefer a more descriptive name for a current port, you can rename it. First, select the port you wish to rename. Then click the cog at the bottom left of the window and select Rename Service. The same dialogue box pops up and you can rename the port.

Activating and Deactivating Services

You can turn a service on or off. For example, if you are at work and you want to turn off your wireless connection, you can turn AirPort off. First, select the port you wish to deactivate. Then click the cog at the bottom left of the pane and Make Service Inactive. If you wish to re-activate the service, follow the same steps. This time click Make Service Active.

Setting a Service Priority

By default, Mac OS X tries port configurations in the following order: internal modem, built-in Ethernet, and AirPort. If you wish to change this, click the cog at the bottom left of the pane and Select Service Order (see Figure 11.19). First you select the location you wish to have the service order apply to, and then you can drag each port up and down to change the priority. Items on top, if active, receive priority over items on the bottom.

Prioritizing network ports

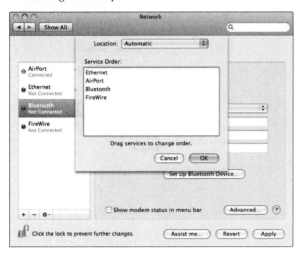

Exporting Port Configurations

If you would like to make a backup copy of your network settings for an individual port, you can do so! Select the port you want to export the settings for. Click the cog again, and select Export Configurations. Here you can export an individual user's network configuration as well as the system's network configuration. You can also include passwords for PPP sessions and other connections if you choose. Just select "Include items from the user's keychain." Select a destination for the configuration file, and click Save.

 If you include items from the keychain, the passwords are no longer secure. If you are not an administrator you can only export your users configuration.

Importing Port Configurations

If you have a backup copy of your port configurations, you can easily import them into the system. Select the port you want to import settings for, click the cog again, and select Import Configurations. Select the configuration file, then Apple, and you are done!

Managing Virtual Interfaces

You can create virtual interfaces such as VLANs and port aggregates. VLANs allow you to be more granular in the location of specific network services. Parallels in particular creates a VLAN device. Port aggregates are the reverse of duplicating a port. It takes two ports and aggregates their speed to create one really fast interface.

 VLANs are beyond the scope of this book. If you would like to learn more about VLANs, visit http://en.wikipedia.org/wiki/Virtual_LAN.

To delete a port configuration

You delete a port configuration by selecting it in the Network Port Configurations settings of Network preferences and then clicking the Delete button. An alert appears asking you to confirm that you really want to delete the port configuration.

When you create a new or duplicate port configuration, Mac OS X puts it at the bottom of the list. You can drag it higher to raise its priority as discussed previously in this chapter.

Working with network locations

You may find that you need to make regular changes to settings in Network preferences. For example, you may use your computer in locations that need to have different network settings. Every time you change locations, you have to remember what changes to make and then click and type repetitiously to make the changes. You can simplify the process of changing locations by letting Mac OS X do the repetitive part.

So far this chapter has discussed how to view the status of the entire network, then how to configure and work with individual ports. This section covers how to create locations of different groups of ports or a single port. You can create additional network locations in Network preferences to facilitate making regular changes to network settings. Each network location is simply one specific arrangement of all the various Network preferences settings. When you create a network location, you give it a name. The names of network locations appear in the Apple menu and in the Location pop-up menu at the top of Network preferences. In fact, the network locations appear in these places for all users of your computer; they're system-wide settings. (User accounts don't have private network locations.)

After you create a network location for a particular arrangement of network settings, you can quickly change to that arrangement by choosing the network location by name from the Apple menu. This method of reconfiguring the Network preferences settings is much quicker and simpler than changing all the individual settings involved in the reconfiguration.

Here are some situations in which you may want to create network locations:

- **You use the computer in more than one place,** such as at home and at work or school, with different port configurations at each place.
- **You connect to different networks from the same port,** such as a modem connection to your Internet provider and a modem connection to your network at work or school.
- **You set different port priorities** to determine which port configuration your computer uses for network services that are available on more than one network port, such as file sharing on Ethernet or AirPort.

You use the Location pop-up menu near the top of Network preferences to manage network locations. You can also use this pop-up menu to switch network locations, but the Apple menu is usually more convenient.

Creating new network locations

You can create additional network locations by making new ones or by duplicating existing ones. To make a new network location, choose Edit Locations from the location pop-up menu in the Network System Preference Pane. Click the plus sign, and enter the name in the box that appears. When done, click Done. To duplicate a network location, again choose Edit Locations, choose Edit from the Location pop-up menu, select the location that you want to duplicate, click the cog, and select Duplicate Location. The duped location now appears in the list with the suffix *Copy* and its name highlighted, ready to be changed. Change the name and click the Done button.

Switching network locations

We already revealed the easiest way to switch to another network location, which is to use the Apple menu. Specifically, you choose the network location by name from the Location submenu in the Apple menu.

You can also switch the network location by choosing the one you want from the Location pop-up menu in Network preferences, but you must click the Apply button at the bottom of Network preferences to make the switch take effect. This allows you to view your different locations without changing your current network settings at the same time.

Reconfiguring network locations

Location settings can be changed at any time by going into Network preferences and changing the port settings or the ports themselves. Network locations can also be renamed or deleted by using the Edit Locations option under the Location pop-up menu.

Getting assistance

If you're having trouble with your network settings, or just want to do some Mac OS X exploration, Apple provides a means to do so within the Network Preference pane. Toward the bottom of the main Network Preference pane window is a button called "Assist me." Clicking this button opens a window offering you the option to cancel, solve problems by checking network diagnostics, or launch the Network Setup Assistant.

Diagnostics

Clicking Assist Me and selecting Diagnostics launches the Network Diagnostics application, a feature created in Mac OS X 10.4. This utility is provided in order to aid the troubleshooting of network problems. Network Diagnostics polls all of your Mac's network ports and searches for a valid connection. If the computer's network connection seems to be functioning correctly, the Diagnostics application tells you so and asks if you still want to continue going through the Diagnostics. If your connection does indeed seem nonfunctional, Network Diagnostics asks you which port configuration you would like to use, and walks you through returning your connection(s) to a functional state. Check out Figure 11.20 to see Network Diagnostics in action.

FIGURE 11.20

Use Network Diagnostics to troubleshoot a misbehaving network connection.

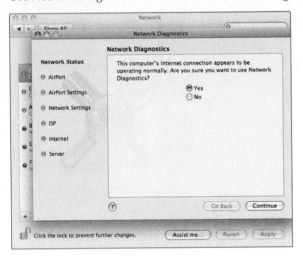

Network Setup Assistant

Clicking the Assist me button and then clicking the Assistant button launches the Network Setup Assistant. The Assistant is in place to help walk you through setting up new connections from scratch, without having to manually edit and apply settings deep within the resources of the Network Preferences, as discussed earlier in this chapter. For example, if you had previously been using a dial-up connection and have switched your service over to a broadband connection (such as cable or DSL), you could use the Network Setup Assistant to walk you through configuring your new connection type. Take a look at Figure 11.21 to see the Network Setup Assistant aiding with the configuration of a cable modem connection.

Other roads for help

Apple has also built a bit more intelligence into some of its network-savvy applications. For example, let's say that in the middle of a feverish eBay bidding war, your AirPort connection suddenly drops out, leaving your computer Internet-less. In the past, Safari might have spun its gears and timed the connection out, leaving you in wonder as to what went wrong. Under Leopard, Safari, sensing no Internet connection, will display the message shown in Figure 11.22 directly in a browser window. Not only does it tell you that you are no longer connected to the Internet, but it also gives you the option to launch the Network Diagnostics and find out exactly what has faulted.

NOTE You can also launch both the Network Diagnostics and the Network Setup Assistant manually by navigating to their location in the Finder and double-clicking them. They are both located within the CoreServices folder, inside of the System Library folder. (The pathway is /System/Library/CoreServices.)

FIGURE 11.21

Use the Network Setup Assistant to create new connections. In this example, a cable modem connection is being configured.

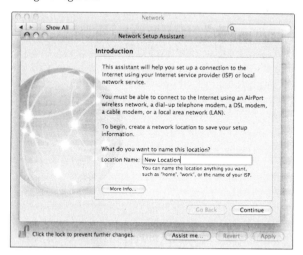

FIGURE 11.22

When Safari doesn't have a valid Internet connection, this message appears.

AirPort

The following section is a more in-depth look at AirPort networking, including installation of the card in your machine and setting up a base station. AirPort now comes in three flavors, AirPort (802.11b) and AirPort Extreme (802.11g and 802.11n). AirPort Extreme is faster and is available only on Macs manufactured after January 2003. If you would like the 802.11n capabilities, most Intel-based Macs have that card built in. An AirPort Extreme (802.11g) card is small and silvery. An original AirPort Card is white and the size of a regular PCMCIA card. Most Macs come with wireless built in, and as a result it is not user-upgradeable. When we speak of an AirPort-capable/equipped Mac, unless otherwise specified, it won't matter if it's AirPort or AirPort Extreme.

Installing AirPort cards

Macs ready for AirPort have a built-in antenna or antenna port and a special slot for Apple's AirPort Card. If your Mac doesn't have one of these cards installed, you may need to obtain a card, connect the antenna to the port on the card, and install the card in the slot. Of course, you don't need to install an AirPort Card if you order one with the computer or if someone else already installed a card.

All iBooks and all slot-loading and flat-panel iMacs that are Leopard-compatible are AirPort-compatible; the iBook G4s are AirPort Extreme-compatible. For the most part, iMacs produced after February 2003 support AirPort Extreme. All Intel-based Macs have wireless built right in. Table 11.2 shows the AirPort capabilities of all 10.5-compatible Macs.

TABLE 11.2			
AirPort Capabilities			
Macintosh Model	**AirPort Capable**	**AirPort Extreme 802.11g**	**Airport Extreme 802.11n**
PowerMac G4 Quicksilver	✓	—	—
PowerMac G4 Mirrored Drive Doors (2002)	✓	—	—
PowerMac G4 Mirrored Drive Doors (2003)	—	✓	—
PowerBook G4 Titanium (867Mhz–1 GHz)	✓	—	—
PowerBook G4 Aluminum (12", 15", 17")	—	✓	—
IBook G4	—	✓	—
iMac G4 17" 1 GHz	—	✓	—
iMac G4 (USB 2.0)	—	✓	—
iMac Intel	—	✓	—
iMac Intel Late 2006 & newer	—	—	✓ *
PowerMac G5 — all models	—	—	✓

Macintosh Model	AirPort Capable	AirPort Extreme 802.11g	Airport Extreme 802.11n
Macbook	—	✓	—
Macbook Late 2006 & newer	—	—	✓ *
Macbook Pro	—	✓	—
Macbook Pro Late 2006 & newer	—	—	✓ *
Mac-Pro	—	—	✓

 Some early model Intel Mac's require the 802.11n enabler from Apple to turn on the 802.11n capabilities.

All computers with a G4 processor are AirPort-compatible with either an AirPort 802.11b (original) card or an AirPort 802.11g (extreme) card, or it is built in. All Intel Macs except for the Mac Pro have AirPort built right in. All Intel Macs built after late 2006 have 802.11n wireless capabilities.

Not surprisingly, the procedure for installing an AirPort Card is different for each Mac model. Instructions for installing an AirPort Card in your computer are in the manual that came with it. You can also find detailed, illustrated instructions for your Mac model in Apple's Knowledge Base (www.apple.com/support).

Creating a computer-to-computer AirPort network

If you have two or more computers with AirPort Cards installed, you can create an ad hoc wireless network. Apple calls this a *computer-to-computer network*. This network connects the AirPort-equipped computers without an AirPort Base Station. One computer creates a computer-to-computer network, and other computers within about 150 feet can join it.

 Any computer with a wireless card that complies with revision b, g or n of the IEEE 802.11 standard should be able to join a computer-to-computer network created by Mac OS X. The IEEE 802.11b, g, and n standards cover ad hoc wireless networks called Independent Basic Service Set (IBSS), and the Mac OS X AirPort software complies with IBSS.

Computers connected to an ad hoc wireless network can share files and participate in multiplayer games. They can also access multiuser databases and use other software designed for multiple users.

The easiest way to create a computer-to-computer network is to choose the Create Network option under the AirPort menu bar icon. Figure 11.23 displays the result of choosing to create a computer-to-computer network.

Click the Require Password button. This gives you the ability to set a password for your network. Select the type of password using the Security pull-down menu. Setting a password for your network is a good habit to get into, for security reasons. Type the name and the password in the appropriate fields. You must retype your password in the Confirm field for verification.

FIGURE 11.23

Behold, the birth of a computer-to-computer wireless network.

You may need to change the Channel setting if other wireless networks are in the vicinity. Each wireless network listed in the Network pop-up menu should use a different channel. When two networks share the same channel, their performance decreases. Because adjacent channels actually overlap, you should leave two unused channel numbers between each used channel for best network performance. Also, because 2.4 GHz cordless telephones use the same frequency range as 802.11b, g, and n wireless Ethernet devices, they can interfere if they're on the same or an adjacent channel.

After you've created your network, users on other computers can join it. If you've set a password, they'll need to type it in. See Chapter 12 for more on sharing files.

Setting Up an AirPort Base Station

The computer-to-computer AirPort network described earlier has some limitations. For one, it doesn't inherently let you share an Internet connection. What's more, a computer-to-computer network is transitory; it ceases to exist after all computers have left it.

An AirPort Base Station has neither of these limitations. It lets all AirPort-equipped computers share an Internet connection, share files, participate in multiplayer games, and use other multiuser software. Additionally, it can bridge (combine) a wireless network and an Ethernet network. Wireless computers gain access to network services on the Ethernet network, such as network printers. Computers on the Ethernet network gain access to services on the wireless network, such as the shared Internet connection. Computers on either network can share files, participate in multiplayer games, and use other multiuser software with computers on the other network. An AirPort Base Station has all the benefits of a computer-to-computer wireless network and more.

Setting up an AirPort Base Station

An AirPort Base Station can connect to the Internet via its built-in 56 Kbps modem (on some models) or its WAN Ethernet port. The WAN Ethernet port enables the AirPort Base Station to connect via a cable modem or a DSL modem. Use the LAN port to connect to an existing local network that already has an Internet gateway or router. The AirPort Base Station shares its one Internet connection with multiple computers concurrently. The computers must have AirPort cards or other wireless equipment that is compatible with the 802.11b/g/n standard. For example, an iBook or PowerBook G4 with an AirPort card can access the Internet completely untethered. Adding an AirPort Base Station to your wireless network is the easiest and most efficient way to provide wireless Internet access, but it isn't the cheapest way.

Preparing for base station setup

When you set up an AirPort Base Station, you need to know all the details about how your base station will connect to the Internet. The details you need to know depend on how the base station connects to the Internet, as follows:

- **Base station internal modem:** You must know the name and password for your ISP account, ISP phone number, country, and dialing method (tone or pulse). You also specify whether to dial automatically as needed and how long to wait idle before disconnecting automatically. Additionally, you can enter one or more IP addresses of name servers (also known as DNS addresses) and default domain names.

- **Local network (Ethernet):** For a manual configuration, you need to know the base station's IP address and subnet mask on the local network. You also need to know the IP address of your network's Internet router or gateway. For a DHCP configuration, you need to know the DHCP client ID, if the DHCP server requires one. For either type of configuration, you can also enter one or more IP addresses of name servers (also known as DNS addresses) and default domain names.

- **Cable modem or DSL using DHCP or a static IP address:** For a manual configuration, you need to know the static IP address, subnet mask, and router IP address assigned by your ISP. For a DHCP configuration, you need to know the DHCP client ID, if your ISP requires one. For either type of configuration, you can also enter one or more IP addresses of name servers (also known as DNS addresses) and default domain names.

- **Cable modem or DSL using PPPoE:** You must know the name and password for your ISP account. You also specify whether to connect automatically as needed and how long to wait idle before disconnecting automatically. In addition, you can specify your ISP name and PPPoE service name, and you can enter one or more IP addresses of name servers (also known as DNS addresses) and default domain names.

You can learn the details of a modem, DSL, or cable modem connection from your ISP. You should know the details of a local network connection if you set up your local network. If you didn't set up your own local network, consult the person who set up or administers the network.

Using the AirPort Utility

With the details about your base station's Internet connection in hand, you're ready to configure the base station settings. You can configure an AirPort Base Station device by using the AiPport Utility program that's included with Mac OS X. The AirPort Utility can be found in the Applications/Utilities folder. Proceed as follows:

1. **Plug in the base station's power adapter.** The base station flashes its lights as it starts up, which takes about 30 seconds. The middle light glows white when it's ready. (It's okay if you plugged in the base station ahead of time.)

2. **Select the wireless in your Airport menu:** It usually reads Apple Network XXXX.

3. **Make sure that the base station's middle light is glowing white, then start the AirPort Utility program select the airport base station, and click continue.** The AirPort Setup Assistant, shown in Figure 11.24, asks you to enter the following information:

    *   **Network password:** The Setup Assistant asks for this password only if the base station has been set up previously with a network password.

    *   **Base station password:** The Setup Assistant does not ask for this password if the base station has the default password, which is *public.*

    *   **Type of network connection:** The base station can connect to the Internet via its built-in modem, DSL, cable modem, or local Ethernet network as described previously.

    *   **Internet connection details:** The details you enter depend on the type of Internet connection, as described previously.

    *   **Network name and password:** You give the base station network a name and password. The password is optional but strongly recommended.

    *   **Base station password:** The base station can use the same password as its network, or you can give it a different password. A person must know this password to change base station settings.

> **NOTE** Apple has released five versions of the AirPort base stations. The first version was graphite (gray) with three multicolored status lights. The second version is snow (white) with three white status lights. The third, the Extreme version, is white with a silver Apple. The fourth is the Express version, which is small, rectangular, and portable. The fifth version is square and half the size of a Mac Mini. Accordingly, the status is displayed in different ways on the three versions of the base stations. Apple has an article in the Knowledge Base defining the differences in AirPort Base Station light status.

FIGURE 11.24

The AirPort Setup Assistant leads you through setting up a base station device.

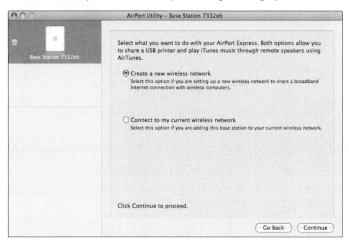

Administering an AirPort Base Station

Both the AirPort Base Station device and the AirPort Base Station software have advanced features that the AirPort Utility application wizard doesn't set up. These features include the ability to do the following:

- **Provide Internet access to computers on an Ethernet network** in addition to wireless computers.

- **Turn on a DHCP server to automatically assign private IP addresses** to computers on your AirPort network and, optionally, on an Ethernet network.

- **Change individual Internet connection settings,** such as the phone number for a modem connection.

- **Allow computers on the Internet to penetrate your local network** to access Web sites, FTP sites, and other services hosted by computers on your network.

- **Limit base station access** to computers with specific AirPort Cards so that unauthorized computers can't join the base station's wireless network.

- **Change individual base station settings** such as the network password, channel number, and encryption.

To configure the advanced features of a base station device, you use the AirPort Utility program, found in the Utilities folder. Select the base station, then click the Manual button. Figure 11.25 shows the Admin Utility and some of the settings that can be changed by using it.

FIGURE 11.25

Change many settings on an AirPort Base Station device by using the AirPort Admin Utility application.

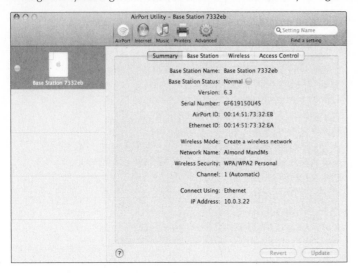

Going into full AirPort setup detail is beyond the scope of this book. Use the very capable built-in help, or go to Apple's online support area for further information.

Bluetooth Networking

Although Bluetooth is better suited for connecting peripherals, like cell phones and mice (think of it as a wireless USB), OS X does have quite a full set of features for connecting computers over the Bluetooth protocol. This is a simple way to create a computer-to-computer network. It provides a direct connection and the ability to browse the files on other machines. Bluetooth is slower than AirPort, so you'll want to use AirPort for wireless file transfers if you can. Open the Bluetooth preference pane by first opening System Preferences and clicking Bluetooth. (If you don't see a Bluetooth Preference pane, your computer is not Bluetooth-capable.)

Settings panel

The Bluetooth pane has been simplified significantly in Leopard. The main panel has plus and minus signs to add and remove Bluetooth devices. You can make your computer discoverable, as well as turn power on or off to Bluetooth. If you never use Bluetooth, you should turn it off; it will marginally increase your computer's performance. In addition, the advanced button gets you to Bluetooth settings such as power and additional serial connections.

If there are no Bluetooth devices added to your computer, the main window states in big bold letters "No Devices." Click Set Up New Device to open the Bluetooth setup assistant. If you already have a device paired with your computer, click the plus sign on the bottom left of the window.

A few options are available in the Advanced location. You can force the Bluetooth setup assistant to start when no keyboard and mouse is present. The computer can respond to Bluetooth requests by waking up from sleep(generally not a good idea, especially if someone accidentally tries to pair their device with your computer). You can force your computer to respond when Bluetooth audio devices, such as a Bluetooth headset or microphone, connect to the computer. You also can share your Internet connection with other Bluetooth devices.

Finally, you can choose to show the Bluetooth status in the menu bar. A solid black B indicates that Bluetooth is on but no devices are paired. A grayed out B indicates that Bluetooth is turned off. A B with a dashed line through it indicates that a device is paired with the Mac, and a gray B with a jagged line through it usually indicates that the external USB Bluetooth adaptor has been unplugged or, for whatever reason, is not being recognized.

FIGURE 11.26

The Bluetooth System Preference Settings panel

Sharing

You can share your files on your computer using the Bluetooth connection. If you have two Bluetooth-enabled devices such as two computers or a computer and a phone, you can share files between your computer and that device. This is covered in more depth in Chapter 12.

Setting up Bluetooth devices

If you're a Bluetooth aficionado, you'll be spending a lot of time pairing devices using the Setup Assistant. The Bluetooth Setup Assistant is accessible via the plus sign in the Bluetooth System

Preferences as well as your Applications folder on your hard drive. Whether it's another computer, a mouse, a cell phone, or a printer, you always need to *pair* the device with your Mac before you can use it. The steps to pair a device are very straightforward.

In the example shown in Figure 11.27, the computer in use has found one device: a Smartphone. Select the device you want to pair, and click Continue. It asks you to enter a passkey into the device to which you are trying to connect. If all goes well, you enter the passkey (when prompted) on your second device and click Continue on your computer. You have now successfully paired two devices via Bluetooth. After you have a successful pairing, you're given the option of adding it to or removing it from your favorites (depending on if it's already there or not), deleting the pairing, disconnecting from the device but not deleting it, or pairing a new device.

FIGURE 11.27

When you choose to pair a device, available Bluetooth devices show up in the list that appears. In this case, SZ, a mobile phone, is available.

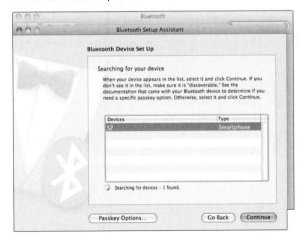

Bluetooth menu bar icon

If you've set the Bluetooth menu bar icon to be displayed, pulling it down gives you a few new options. Choosing the Send File command lets you send your files to another Bluetooth device, like another mobile phone. You can also choose to browse a device for files to take from it.

Bluetooth file exchange

Many devices support the Bluetooth Personal Area Network (PAN) standard. Mac OS X Leopard fully supports the standard intended for simple information interchange on a peer-to-peer basis.

Bluetooth

In 1994, Ericsson Mobile Communications started research on a technology that would enable wireless communications between devices at short distances. By February 1998, Nokia, IBM, Toshiba, and Intel had joined Ericsson in this endeavor and announced the Bluetooth standard in May 1998. In 1999, the Bluetooth 1.0 Specification was released to the public.

Currently the Bluetooth 2.0 standard is in use, and 3Com, Lucent Technologies, Microsoft, and Motorola have joined the original group of sponsor companies. The idea behind the research is to create what is called a *Personal Area Network*, in which devices such as mobile phones, laptop computers, PDAs, headsets, and so on, can communicate relevant information between each other at short distances, and perform a function in unison. For example, your Mac can use your Bluetooth phone to call somebody and then play the audio from the phone in your computer speakers; or your PDA automatically passes your new appointments and contacts once you are in close proximity to your machine.

The name *Bluetooth* comes from King Harald I Blåtand (literally translated to Bluetooth, meaning great dark man, from the original Danish roots), who ruled Denmark between 940 and 985 AD. During his reign, King Bluetooth united Denmark and conquered Norway. The expansion of his kingdom was continued by his son Sweyn I, who conquered England in 1013, and then his grandson Canute, who ruled over an Anglo-Scandinavian kingdom that included parts of Sweden. Because of King Bluetooth's unifying influence in Denmark and Norway, the name was chosen for a technology that will unify the operations of several handheld devices. However, King Harald I Bluetooth had no blue teeth and no PDA either.

Bluetooth is a great technology that was conceived to support the highest security standards as well as a plethora of services and operations. However, the required security is not always implemented in the devices, only communication capabilities.

There are many security risks when using Bluetooth technology. Like in the wired and wireless Internet there are hackers trying to *bluejack* your devices; there are also *bluesnarfing* and *bluebugging* techniques that work on some devices. The companies behind Bluetooth are improving security and enforcing proper implementations of their protocols to ensure data link privacy and security. The communication happens at 2.4 GHz and it has a *supposed* range of 30 feet. There is a two-way 1-megabit link for voice and a 768-kilobit link for data interchange. When using a 2.4 GHz phone or wireless access point at that frequency, you may lose connectivity or have other communication problems. The low power link used by Bluetooth will be blanked out by the transmitters in those devices.

Once a Bluetooth pair has been created, and the devices support the requested operation, data exchange may start. To discover which devices are available to you, open the Bluetooth System Preferences, and click the device in question. On the right you can see what type of Bluetooth functionality the item has. In general, File Exchange is available to all Bluetooth-enabled computers and PDAs (as long as you have checked allow Bluetooth File Exchange).

To send a file to a Bluetooth-enabled device, click the Bluetooth menu, and then send file. Choose the file you want to send. Next select the device you want to send a file to, then click Send. Depending on how you setup your other device, it will accept, deny, or ask for acceptance. If the file is accepted, the computer will progress and send the file to your device. You are now done!

NOTE   Bluetooth has many additional functions that are not covered in depth in this book.

Summary

Here's what you know about setting up networks after reading this chapter:

- Setting up a network makes it possible for your computers to share an Internet connection, share printers, share files, participate in multiplayer games, and use other multiuser software.

- Wiring an Ethernet network involves running a twisted-pair cable from each computer and other network device to a hub or switch.

- Establishing an AirPort wireless network involves installing an AirPort Card in each computer. Then you can create a computer-to-computer wireless network. An AirPort Base Station is optional but allows AirPort-equipped computers to share an Internet connection and to communicate with computers on a wired Ethernet network, if you also have one of these.

- After making a network connection — Ethernet, AirPort, or modem — you may need to configure some settings in the Network pane of System Preferences. You configure settings for each network connection separately. Each network connection has several groups of related settings, and you switch between groups by clicking tabs in Network Preferences. The tabs include AirPort, TCP/IP, AppleTalk, PPPoE, Proxies, PPP, and Modem.

- The Active Network Ports settings of Network preferences lets you change the priority of network port configurations, turn each port configuration on or off, create additional configurations that use the same ports as existing configurations, rename port configurations, and delete port configurations.

- Network locations facilitate making regular changes to network settings. Each network location is one specific arrangement of all network settings. You can switch to any network location by choosing it from the Apple menu.

- An AirPort Base Station can be a free-standing device or software running on an AirPort-equipped Mac. A base station lets all AirPort-equipped computers share an Internet connection, and it can bridge a wireless network and an Ethernet network. You set up either kind of base station with the Setup Assistant application.

- You can share files between computers using the Bluetooth protocol.

Chapter 12

Sharing Files and Network Services

Viewing Web pages over the Internet is just one type of network service that you can access with your computer. Just as the Internet is one way of obtaining information and viewing files, so is file sharing over a network and the Internet. Using different types of connection protocols and interfacing with Macintosh, Windows, and Internet servers, your Mac can connect to an abundance of devices and trade files back and forth between them all. This chapter explains how to access files from other people's machines, how to use Mac OS X's Keychains to keep track of all of your passwords for you, how to set up your own Mac for sharing files so that other users can get them from you, and how to secure yourself from intruders.

Accessing Files

The sharing part of file sharing implies a give-and-take scenario. On a network and over the Internet, you can take and use files from other people's computers, and, if you set your computer to allow it, they can do the same from you. Computers that provide files and storage space are known as *file servers*. A file server is said to be a dedicated server when it's a computer that is not used for personal work. Its primary job is to share files. A file server can also be someone's personal computer (also called a *workstation*) that, aside from being used for regular work, is set up to share its files with other network computers. For files to be moved between the machines, a specific client-server protocol must be used. These protocols are the language with which different hardware and different operating systems can speak to each other. Mac OS X supports quite a few protocols, all of which are accessible through the Finder.

Apple has had its own file sharing protocol called AFP, or Apple Filing Protocol. Macintosh file servers typically use the AFP protocol. The address of an AFP server begins with `afp://`.

Windows servers typically use the SMB (Server Message Block) or CIFS (Common Internet File System) protocols for file sharing. Your Mac can connect to these without problem. Windows file server addresses usually begin with `smb://`.

Sharing files over the Internet is often done through a protocol known as FTP, or File Transfer Protocol. An `ftp://` at the beginning of a server address designates it as an FTP server. (More about connecting to FTP servers later in this chapter.)

Other protocols supported in OS X include WebDAV and NFS. WebDAV stands for Web-based Distributed Authoring and Versioning, and is usually used in Web server applications where live changes need to be made to online material. For example, the iDisks from Apple's .Mac services are connected via WebDAV. WebDAV servers are connected to using `http://` and the server address. NFS stands for Network File System, and is the native file-sharing protocol used by Unix. An NFS share is recognized by `nfs://` at the beginning of its address.

One great thing about OS X is that Apple has made connecting to all these different kinds of servers and protocols extremely uniform. Although specific messages and dialog boxes will appear slightly differently between each protocol, the basic concepts are the same. To use any of these kinds of file servers or protocols, all you need is the Finder. With the Finder, you can connect to a file server, mount server volumes, see your access privileges on the server volumes, and copy files. You can also use the Finder to open files from a server, or you can open server files directly from within other applications. When you're finished using a server, use the Finder to disconnect from it.

> **TIP** You can also connect to AFP, FTP, and WebDAV servers by typing their addresses into the address field in Safari. When you press the Return or Enter key to connect, Mac OS X opens an authentication dialog box, just as if you connected through the Finder.

Connecting to a file server

In previous versions of Mac OS X, the only way to connect to a server was to pull down the Finder's Go menu, and choose the Connect To Server option (⌘+k). See Figure 12.1. This presented you with a dialog box in which you could either browse the network for local servers, or type an address and connect to a remote one. Puzzling to many people was that there was a "Network" (see Figure 12.2) globe visible at the Computer level of the Finder, which seemed as though it would be a convenient way to browse the local network. This was true in special circumstances only (when in the presence of a NetInfo server) and was often left unused. To enable the Network globe, in the Finder, click the Finder menu ⇨ Preferences. Click Sidebar at the top, then select the Computer icon.

Starting in Mac OS X 10.3, and continuing the trend in OS 10.4 and 10.5, Apple now separates the methods for connecting to servers. The Connect To Server dialog box still exists, but it is mainly used for specifying a known or remote server whose address you already know. Local servers are accessible through the Finder and automatically appear under the Shared list in any Finder window (see Figure 12.2). If you are in the Connect To Server dialog box, you can click the Browse button to open a new Finder window with the Network globe selected. A remote server, however, will not show up when browsing locally, and its location must be specified. Yes, it is possible to connect "remotely" to a local server by using the Connect To Server dialog box and not browsing, but for our purposes in this book, local servers will be accessed through the Finder's Network icon and remote servers will be accessed by choosing the Connect To Server command. Choosing the Connect To Server option from the Go menu opens the dialog box shown in Figure 12.1.

FIGURE 12.1

Your journey to a file server connection begins with the Connect To Server dialog box.

FIGURE 12.2

The network globe for browsing for servers

Connecting remotely

The main idea here is to type the address of a server and click the Connect button to engage. If you want to view the servers that are available locally, click the Browse button. Although there are a bunch of different servers that you can connect to, the basic way in which you do so is the same. The following list is a breakdown of the elements found within the Connect To Server dialog box:

- **Server Address:** This is the field in which you specify the location of your server. Just as you type in a URL for connecting to a Web site through Safari, you also must type in a URL to connect to a server. A Web site is specified by its `http` (hypertext transfer protocol) beginnings. When connecting to a file server, instead of specifying the hypertext transfer protocol, you need to specify a file sharing protocol, such as FTP. For example, take the server at address `192.168.1.3`. It is possible for this machine to have services active for connecting over many different protocols. The URL that you type in (for example, `ftp://192.168.1.3` for an FTP connection) is what specifies which service to connect to.

- **Add to Favorites:** The Add to Favorites button (the button with the plus sign) is used to save server addresses for future connection. Essentially, you are bookmarking the address, just as if you were bookmarking a Web site. If you are about to connect to a server and think that you may want to visit it later, click the plus sign to add it to your list of favorite servers.

> **NOTE** If your Mac has file sharing turned on, you see your Mac listed as one of the file servers on the network. If you try to connect to it, Mac OS X fails the connection.

- **Recent Servers:** Clicking the Choose a Recent Server button (the button with a clock face icon) pulls down a list and displays the servers to which you have recently connected. The Mac OS saves your recent connections so you don't have to. If you have never connected to a server before, the list will be empty.

- **Favorite Servers:** In this portion of the dialog box is a list of the servers that you saved by clicking the plus sign. Clicking an item in the list places its address into the address field. Double-clicking an item initiates a server connection.

- **Remove:** Clicking the Remove button removes a selected favorite from the favorites list.

- **Browse:** Use the Browse button if you don't know the address of the server that you want to connect to, or if you just want to view all of the servers that are available over the network. Clicking the Browse button takes you to a new Finder window within the network.

- **Connect:** Click the Connect button to initiate your connection to the server.

In all cases, if the address is valid and the server is online, after you click the Connect button, you are presented with another dialog box. This box confirms that a connection has been achieved and has fields for entering your name and password so that you can authenticate to the server. Depending on whether you are connecting to an AFP, FTP, or SMB volume, the box will look slightly different. In any case, the end goal is to access the files of these volumes from within the graphical interface of the Finder. Ahead, we look at the different possibilities.

AFP connections

After typing in the URL of the Apple File Protocol server you want to connect to and clicking the Connect button, you are presented with an untitled dialog box that prompts you to connect either as a guest (if this is enabled) or as a registered user of the server, as shown in Figure 12.3.

Connecting to AppleTalk File Servers

Although just about any connection you make to an Apple server involves a TCP/IP connection nowadays, it is possible that some servers will need to be connected to using the now-legacy standalone AppleTalk protocol. (The capability of accessing AppleTalk and/or the AFP over IP originated back in Mac OS 9.) Making these types or connections requires two things: First, AppleTalk must be enabled under the Network pane of the System Preferences dialog box; and second, you must specify the AppleTalk protocol in the Connect To Server dialog box (instead of the usual TCP/IP protocol).

The AppleTalk address of a file server differs from a TCP/IP address in that AppleTalk identifies file servers by name, and not by IP address (or by domain name, which is really just a pointer to a numbered IP address). This necessitates two important changes when typing in an AppleTalk address.

Instead of beginning the address with `afp://` and then the server name, you have to add `at` (meaning AppleTalk) between the slashes. The `at` between the slashes forces the Mac to initiate an AppleTalk connection, instead of the default, which would be an IP connection. An AppleTalk connection to a machine called "ECCSERVER" looks like this: afp://`at://ECCSERVER/`.

If a file server's AppleTalk name includes spaces or symbols, these characters have to be encoded when you type the name in the Connect To Server dialog box. For example, the AppleTalk address of a file server whose name is Mikey's PowerBook appears as `afp:/at/Mikey%27s%20PowerBook` in the Address box. The code `%27` stands for an apostrophe, and the code `%20` stands for a space. These codes are based on ASCII code of the character, expressed as a hexadecimal number (see Table 12.1).

You can also connect to an AppleTalk server using TCP/IP. Begin the address with `afp://`. You can add XYZServer.local, the server's IP address, or the server's FQDN (fully qualified domain name) such as XYZserver.XYZcompany.com.

Clearly, browsing the network for AppleTalk servers is easier — you don't have to specify the entire name and address, just select it. Depending on your network configuration, however, the full pathway might have to be specified.

FIGURE 12.3

Establish your identity as a guest or registered user of a file server in this dialog box.

TABLE 12.1

Table of Decimal/Hexadecimal/Symbols

Dec	Hex	Symbol	Dec	Hex	Symbol	Dec	Hex	Symbol	Dec	Hex	Symbol
0	0	NUL	32	20	(space)	64	40	@	96	60	`
1	1	SOH	33	21	!	65	41	A	97	61	a
2	2	STX	34	22	"	66	42	B	98	62	b
3	3	ETX	35	23	#	67	43	C	99	63	c
4	4	EOT	36	24	$	68	44	D	100	64	d
5	5	ENQ	37	25	%	69	45	E	101	65	e
6	6	ACK	38	26	&	70	46	F	102	66	f
7	7	BEL	39	27		71	47	G	103	67	g
8	8	BS	40	28	(	72	48	H	104	68	h
9	9	TAB	41	29	)	73	49	I	105	69	i
10	A	LF	42	2A	*	74	4A	J	106	6A	j
11	B	VT	43	2B	+	75	4B	K	107	6B	k
12	C	FF	44	2C	,	76	4C	L	108	6C	l
13	D	CR	45	2D	-	77	4D	M	109	6D	m
14	E	SO	46	2E	.	78	4E	N	110	6E	n
15	F	SI	47	2F	/	79	4F	O	111	6F	o
16	10	DLE	48	30	0	80	50	P	112	70	p
17	11	DC1	49	31	1	81	51	Q	113	71	q
18	12	DC2	50	32	2	82	52	R	114	72	r
19	13	DC3	51	33	3	83	53	S	115	73	s
20	14	DC4	52	34	4	84	54	T	116	74	t
21	15	NAK	53	35	5	85	55	U	117	75	u
22	16	SYN	54	36	6	86	56	V	118	76	v
23	17	ETB	55	37	7	87	57	W	119	77	w
24	18	CAN	56	38	8	88	58	X	120	78	x
25	19	EM	57	39	9	89	59	Y	121	79	y
26	1A	SUB	58	3A	:	90	5A	Z	122	7A	z
27	1B	ESC	59	3B	;	91	5B	[	123	7B	{
28	1C	FS	60	3C	<	92	5C	\	124	7C	|
29	1D	GS	61	3D	=	93	5D	]	125	7D	}
30	1E	RS	62	3E	>	94	5E	^	126	7E	~
31	1F	US	63	3F	?	95	5F	_	127	7F	DEL

To connect as a registered user, make sure the Registered User option is selected and enter your account name and password in the appropriate fields. To be a registered user means that the owner of the server has set up a user account for you with the proper access privileges, and assigned this name and password to you. If your own computer is set up as a file server (which is covered later in this chapter) and you're connecting to it from another computer, enter your own Mac OS X account name and password. When you enter your password, you must type it correctly, including uppercase and lowercase letters (it's case-sensitive). Then click Connect.

Enabling people to log in as a guest user means that anyone, including those without a user account and a password, can log into the server and access certain files. If you're not a registered user and the Guest option isn't disabled (grayed out), you can select the guest option to connect that way. However, guests usually have far fewer privileges on a file server than registered users. If the Guest option is grayed out, it means that guests are not permitted to access the file server.

Setting preferences for file server connections

While identifying yourself as a registered user or a guest, you have the opportunity to set some preferences concerning the handling of your password and your connection. In the initial dialog box, you are presented with options for handling your password and your connection type. You can choose to save the password in the Keychain (covered later this chapter) by clicking the check box under the password field.

The Cog icon in the lower left-hand corner is a pull-down menu. Clicking it displays the options that it provides to you: changing your password. This can be seen in Figure 12.3. Changing your password requires you to enter your old password once, and the new one twice, for confirmation. Clicking OK saves the new password.

Selecting network volumes

After you click the Connect button from the identification box, you see the Select a Volume dialog box. This dialog box tells you the name of the server to which you're connecting and the various volumes on that server that you can mount, as shown in Figure 12.4.

Connecting as a registered user gives you the choice of any folders or volumes to which you have access as one of the following:

■ Any folders or volumes to which the authenticated user or group the user is part of is the owner.

■ Any folders or volumes to which everybody has access

■ The Public folders of all other accounts on that Mac OS X machine

FIGURE 12.4

Select the volumes you want to mount from the file server in this dialog box.

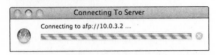

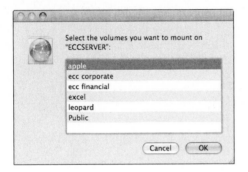

If you are connecting to your own machine, you will typically see three categories of items. First is a listing of all volumes on the computer. The second is your home folder, which you are always the owner of. The third is any folder you have specifically shared that you have access to. If the server allows Guest access and you choose to connect as a Guest, you'll see a separate volume for each user that has a public folder. You'll also see any folders or volumes specifically set up for Guest access. You can double-click the volumes you want to mount or select them (⌘+click or Shift+click for multiple items) and click OK. Mac OS X's default behavior is for the servers to show up in the sidebar of its Finder windows, as well as on the Desktop. The Finder preferences can be customized to alter these behaviors.

After the volumes are mounted, you can treat them like any other disk and begin working with files. Refer to Chapter 18 for more discussion of access privileges, which are set through the Get Info windows in the Finder (or by Unix commands in the Terminal application).

Connecting to Microsoft Windows file servers

In a world dominated by Microsoft Windows (at least on the computing front), being able to access files on a Windows file server is important. Beginning with Mac OS X Version 10.1, you can use OS X's built-in capabilities to access Microsoft Windows file servers, which include Windows NT, Windows 98, 2000, ME, XP, and 2003 machines, if the proper services are enabled. Windows servers typically use the SMB/CIFS protocol.

A Windows server address is entered in the Server Address box. The address of a Windows file server has the following form: `smb://server/share/` where *server* is the name or IP address of the file server and *share* is the name of the volume or folder that you want to connect to. For example, the address `smb://10.0.3.2/public/` connects to the public folder of the Windows file server whose IP address is 10.0.3.2. If you use a file server's name instead of its IP address, you may need to type the name in all capital letters. If you do not know the specific share, you can just type the fully qualified domain name or IP address of the server.

After entering the address of a Windows file server and clicking Connect in the Connect To Server dialog box, one of two dialog boxes appears, as shown in Figures 12.3 and 12.4. In prior versions of MacOS X the dialog boxes looked different. Because the method of connection is similar, Apple has changed the dialog boxes for an SMB and AFP connection to be the same.

TIP In the server address window you can bypass the authentication window by typing your username and password in the address window — that is, smb://username: password@10.0.3.2/public.

NOTE Mac OS X 10.1 can't connect to a Windows file server if the server name or share name includes any spaces, even if you encode them as %20, but all subsequent versions of OS X (10.2, 10.3, 10.4, 10.5) do not suffer that ailment.

Connecting to an FTP server

Files are commonly sent over the Internet using File Transfer Protocol (FTP), as discussed earlier in this chapter. A computer can make files available using this protocol by running a type of program called an *FTP server*. This term also refers to the combination of the server program and the computer that's running it. You may sometimes hear people refer to an *FTP site,* which is a collection of files on an FTP server that are available for downloading. An FTP site has the same function on the Internet as a file server on your network.

In Mac OS X, you can connect to FTP servers directly from the Finder. Interestingly, a Finder-based connection to an FTP server is a read-only connection; that is, you can copy files from the server to your Mac, but you cannot copy files from your Mac to the server. For more advanced functionality you can use a program specially made for FTP transactions, called an *FTP client.* One such application is called Transmit or Fetch (which lets you upload as well as download).

An FTP server address goes into the Server Address field of the Finder's Connect To Server dialog box, just like AFP and SMB addresses. Clicking Connect causes one of two things to happen:

- A successful connection is made, and no login or password information is requested, nor specified. If an FTP server has anonymous access enabled, users can connect without logging in individually, much like guest access on an AFP or SMB server.
- Mac OS X opens the FTP authentication screen, where you'll need to type your name and password to be granted server access. See Figure 12.5.

When you log in successfully, you'll be prompted to choose the volume you want to connect to. When the volume is selected, the Connect To Server dialog box disappears and the FTP volume is mounted in the Finder, free for your perusal.

TIP Because Mac OS X has full Unix underpinnings, you can use the command line to access FTP servers by launching the terminal and using the FTP command.

FIGURE 12.5

An FTP authentication window

Connecting locally

Local servers are servers that appear dynamically to your Mac without having to specify their location, whether by name or IP address. Local servers are advantageous because you can browse for their existence. (And browsing for local servers is accomplished directly from the Finder.) There are two ways to accomplish this. One is browsing, and the other is using the Shared shortcut:

- **Browsing for servers.** If you're already in the Connect To Server dialog box, clicking the Browse button opens a new Finder window with the Network globe pre-selected. All the servers that are locally accessible on your network show up in the Network globe window. You also can access the Network globe directly by opening a new Finder window, clicking your computer icon (in this case Expert CC MBP), and then double-clicking Network. You also can also browse for servers from the Go menu, or by pressing ⌘+Shift+K on the keyboard. Figure 12.6 shows how browsing in the Finder looks.

- **Using the Finder window.** In the left column of the Finder window is a new list called SHARED. This is the listing of all local identifiable and connected remote servers on your Mac. Just click the server.

Whichever method you use to connect, and whichever view you are in (icon, list, or column) double-clicking the server you want results in one of two things. If guest access is enabled, the guest accessible shares automatically show up. This is indicated by the text underneath the computer icon (Figure 12.6) or underneath the toolbar (Figure 12.7).

If there is no guest access, or you want to authenticate as a different user, you can click the Connect As button. After you do this, the Connect To Server authentication box opens, as shown earlier in this chapter in Figure 12.3. At this stage, the connection methods and options are the same; type your name and password and click Connect.

FIGURE 12.6

Browse for local network servers in the Network window. This network has multiple servers available, including Sharon's Room and ECCSERVER.

NOTE   If the computer you are connecting to happens to be a recognized type of computer (a Mac or Windows machine), the icon for the server changes to the appropriate type. In Figure 12.6 I am connecting to a G4 Tower and the icon has changed accordingly.

If you are browsing in list or icon view you have the same options, but the layout is a little different. See Figure 12.7.

NOTE   If the remote computer has VNC or screen sharing enabled, an additional button, Share Screen, sits alongside the Connect As button.

FIGURE 12.7

Viewing Sharon's computer in icon view. Click the Connect button from the column view to access the server.

Connecting with a favorite

When you are in the Connect To Server dialog box, or after the volume is mounted and you are in the Finder, you can create a favorite from a server location for more streamlined connections in the future. Opening a server location from a favorite skips the Connect To Server dialog box and takes you right to the identification screen. If your password is saved in the Keychain, you don't even have to type in anything. A favorite is simply a double-clickable data file that contains the network path to a specific server (not, however, the individual volume). You can make a favorite by clicking the plus sign as discussed earlier in the chapter (when you're in the Connect To Server dialog box). Favorites show up in the Finder as document files, named with either the name or the IP address of its server. These documents can be double-clicked, placed in the Dock, or even set as login items in order to connect to the servers.

Although it is possible to make aliases of server volumes (which can be more convenient because individual volumes can be referenced, as opposed to the entire server, which is the case when using favorites), making favorites is the best option under OS X. Because of the operating system's Unix underpinnings, aliases that reference files and volumes across networks are less reliable than favorites, which encode the true network pathway within the files. AFP volumes can work as an alias fairly reliably. Other connection protocols, notably SMB, deal very poorly with aliased files and volumes.

 Your favorites are located in Macintosh HD ⇨ Users ⇨ Home ⇨ Library ⇨ Favorites.

Recognizing your access privileges

Just as you can recognize your access privileges to folders on your Mac in the Finder, the same indicators are present for server volumes and the folders they contain. The symbols for each type of privilege and description of access are as follows:

- **Read-Only Access:** A small icon that looks like a pencil with a line through it appears in the status bar for a folder or volume where you can see the contents but may not change them. See Figure 12.8.

- **No Access:** A folder icon with a circled red do-not-enter sign in the lower right corner is a volume or folder that you cannot open or otherwise manipulate.

- **Write-Only Access:** A circled blue down arrow in the lower right corner marks a *drop box* folder. You can put files into a drop box, but you cannot open it.

- **Full Access:** The folder is blue with no icons associated with it.

Figure 12.8 shows examples of these folder icons and the read-only indicator in the bottom left corner of the Finder window, the pencil with the line through it. The Drop Box is write only. Desktop, Documents, Library, Movies, Music, and Pictures are No Access. Public is read only.

FIGURE 12.8

Special folder icons and an icon in the status bar indicate your access privileges. The bottom left indicates the Public folder is read only as shown by the icon with a pencil through it.

Transferring network files

When you've got a server volume mounted in the Finder, OS X treats it like any other disk; that is, you can copy files to and from it (if you have the correct access privileges), you can open files from it in Open/Save dialog boxes from any application, or you can open files directly from the server without copying them to your drive first.

Depending on your network and the types and sizes of the files that you are working on, opening and editing files directly from the server can be a great way to streamline work, or it can be an excruciatingly slow, crash-prone, data loss nightmare. In general, the faster your network is, the more reliable your connection is, and the smaller your files are, the better shape you will be in. For example, on a network of even very modest speeds, opening and saving Microsoft Word documents off of the server can be fine and purposeful, thereby eliminating the need for first copying the file to your hard drive and then copying it back when you are finished with your work.

An issue to be aware of when working on a file you have copied off the server to your desktop is versioning. It's possible for another co-worker to edit the same file without your knowledge while you have it on your workstation. You then run the risk of copying over their saved changes when you copy your edited file back. A Word document opened directly from a server by a second user will manifest as a read-only document, until the original editor closes the file. If, however, you are editing gigabyte-sized Adobe Photoshop files, working over the network would be a slow and frustrating process, and well as prone to data loss, and thus, ill advised. In more advanced setups that utilize the Directory Services of Mac OS X Server, it is possible to have your entire home folder located on the server, instead of locally on your machine. In this case, all your files are accessed from the server (even your preferences and fonts stored in your Library folder).

Opening network files

Because Mac OS X treats mounted server volumes exactly as though they are local disks, you can navigate to them in an Open dialog box, as shown in Figure 12.9, and open them. Similarly, you can save to the network server in a Save dialog box.

Open a file from a server just as though it were stored on a local disk.

Disconnecting from network volumes and servers

When you finish using a network volume, you can remove it from the Finder by using any of the following methods:

- Double-click your hard drive. On the left column where the server name is located, select the server you want to disconnect from. Click Disconnect from either underneath the computer icon (in Column view) or at the top of the finder window (in Icon, Cover Flow, or List view).

- On a non-MacOS X server, select the volume's icon and choose File ➪ Eject (*Name of Disk*) or press ⌘+E.

- Click the eject icon that is visible next to the server's icon as it appears in the sidebar within Finder windows.

Removing a network volume from the Finder is also known as *unmounting* or *disconnecting* (not dismounting) the volume.

Disconnecting from a network file server involves no more than removing all that server's volumes from the Finder. It can be common to get errors upon attempting to unmount a network volume; these errors generally say something to the effect that the volume is still in use. A volume is in use as long as any files that are stored on it are in use. These can take the form of open files or applications, or more sneakily, resources that are still in use, such as fonts or temporary files. If you can't eject, then this may be the case; quit any of your open programs and try again. If it *still* won't unmount, there might be resources in use behind the scenes. Try relaunching the Finder by using ⌘+Option+Escape (force quit) and, as a last resort, logging out and/or rebooting.

Using the Keychain

Virtually every file server to which you connect, some of the Web sites you visit, and any number of network services you invoke require you to identify yourself with a name and a password. These combinations of name and password are called *access keys,* or just *keys* for short. A computer key is analogous to a physical key that you'd use to unlock the door to your house — each key grants you access to specific resources that you need. If we have lots of different locked doors that we need to get through, we also have lots of different keys to unlock them. Instead of having individual keys strewn about, we humans usually put them on key chains, which keep them all (relatively) in the same, easily accessible place.

Having lots of different logins and passwords for all kinds of different services gets confusing, making the keys difficult to keep track of. Because of this, Apple created their Keychains as a method of storing all of your different types of keys in one secure and easily retrievable location. Essentially, the *Keychain* is a database file (`~/Library/Keychains/`) that stores your keys as individual records, which can be viewed and edited through the use of the Keychain Access application (located in the Utilities folder). When you access a service that requires a login and password (checking your e-mail, for example) your login and password that have been saved in the Keychain will automatically be provided, as long as the Keychain itself is unlocked.

Apple first introduced the concept of the Keychain with System 7 Pro's AOCE (Apple Open Collaborative Environment), also known as PowerTalk, a decade ago. Because AOCE's acceptance was less than inspiring, even the well-liked pieces, such as the Keychain, were not widely used. PowerTalk disappeared from Apple System Software releases after System 7.5.5. Apple revived the Keychain in Mac OS 9 and, because it didn't bring with it the overhead and clumsiness of AOCE, many more users started taking advantage of it. Now, with Mac OS X, the Keychain continues to be even better integrated with Mac OS and its software.

Mac OS X automatically creates a Keychain for each user at the user's initial login, in the form of a file called `login.keychain` or your OS X shortname, stored in the Keychains folder within the user's Library folder. The Keychain has a password tied to it, which is used to lock and unlock it. In most cases, the password to your Keychain is identical to your login password. Thus, as you log in to OS X at the login window, your Keychain is unlocked automatically. If your login and Keychain passwords differ, each time an application tries to access a service that calls upon the Keychain to retrieve a saved login and password, you'll be prompted to enter the Keychain password, so as to unlock it. (This can be easily solved by manually assigning your current login password to Keychain, discussed just ahead in this chapter.)

For the most part, the Keychain remains invisible, and behind the scenes to the average user, manifesting only as an occasional checkbox when we're asked to save our password so that we don't have to type it in again and again. Operating almost universally behind the scenes, most of us never have a need or a reason to delve into the Keychain file.

The Keychain Access application

Behold the Keychain Access application, which is located in the Utilities folder. See Figure 12.10. The main function of Keychain Access is the management of your keys and the maintenance of your Keychain file.

FIGURE 12.10

View all of your keys from the Keychain Access window.

Locking and unlocking your Keychain

Keychain Access' iTunes-like interface has two main areas: the sidebar, for viewing your Keychains and their different item categories, and the main window, which displays a list of your keys, as well as a summary of the selected key's attributes.

The most immediate and obvious visual cue that the Keychain Access application can give you is whether the Keychain is locked or unlocked. Most of the time, your Keychain should unlock automatically when you login, thereby eliminating the need to manually unlock it. In the upper left corner of the application window, you'll see a padlock. If the lock is in the open position, your

Keychain is unlocked. If the lock is locked, your Keychain is too, and any application requesting a stored key will prompt you to enter your Keychain password to unlock it.

Types of records

Keychain Access holds four different types of records:

- **Passwords:** Anytime a login and password of yours is saved, it shows up in Keychain Access as an individual record. Keychain Access, as shown in Figure 12.10, divides passwords up into three categories: AppleShare (for server logins), Application (for Applications with saved passwords, such as Microsoft Entourage), and Internet (for Web page logins). You might specify for a password to be saved, such as when you check the box during the server login process, or you might say yes when Safari asks you if the password should be saved for a particular Web site login.

- **Certificates:** Certificates are digital pieces of information that help to keep your identity secure when transmitting information across a network. It is possible for a certificate to be assigned to you, from a mail server, for example, or for you to create your own certificate (called a *self-assigned* certificate) or create a Certificate Authority (CA) that you can assign to other people. Certificates can be created using the Certificate Assistant found under the Keychain Access menu.

- **Keys:** In a bit of a redundancy in terminology, Keychain Access also stores records called keys. *Keys* are pieces of information used for the encoding and decoding of other information, which is usually in the form of text. A common application for using keys is the public and private key encryption scheme employed by PGP (Pretty Good Privacy) for the secure transmission of encrypted e-mail messages.

- **Secure Notes:** Keychain Access can store strings of text in items called Secure Notes. A Secure Note is encrypted and is available for viewing only if you have unlocked your Keychain.

Viewing and editing record attributes

Now that you have been introduced to the types of records that Keychain Access can hold, you can begin to examine their contents and glean the useful information that they can provide:

- **Passwords:** Double-clicking a password record opens an information window with greater detail than in the main preview pane. These windows have two sections, Attributes and Access Control. Under the Attributes pane (shown in Figure 12.11) you can view and edit the Name and Kind of password, as well as see the network location of whatever you're logging into, in the "Where" field. Checking the box next to the Show Password field displays the saved password in clear text, so that you can read exactly what it is (which is useful if you forget a saved password). The Access Control section of the information window (shown in Figure 12.12) enables you to set all or specific applications to have access to the particular record. You can use the plus and minus signs to add and remove applications from the list.

FIGURE 12.11

The Attributes pane of an AppleShare record

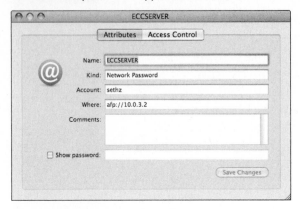

FIGURE 12.12

Control how and which applications have access to your record in the Access Control pane.

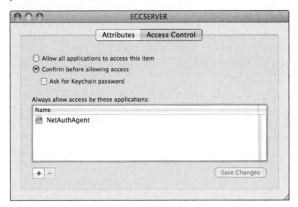

■ **Certificates:** Double-clicking a certificate opens a detailed information window regarding your certificate. Included are the name and e-mail address of the issuer, as well as the dates that the certificate is valid.

■ **Keys:** Double-click your key records to bring up a detailed information window regarding your saved key.

■ **Secure Notes:** If you want to read a secure note that you have previously saved, you'll have to double-click the record to open it. The resulting window displays the title of the note (which you can edit) along with creation and modification dates. Check the box next to "Show note" to display the text. See Figure 12.13. If you have not checked Always Allow in the password box, you are asked for a password for access.

FIGURE 12.13

The oh-so-secretive text from a secure note requires a password before it appears.

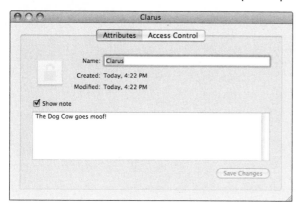

Creating and deleting records manually

Most functions of the Keychain are taken care of automatically, behind the scenes, and with little user intervention. If you need to, however, you can create and delete Keychain records manually.

You can manually add new password items by choosing New Password Item from the File menu, and entering the appropriate item name, account name, and password.

You can add secure notes by choosing File ⇨ New Secure Note Item. The resulting dialog box lets you title your note and enter the text.

You can also add additional Keychains by choosing File ⇨ New Keychain, which saves an additional Keychain file in your ~/Library/Keychains folder. The authors agree that it is best to stick with one Keychain, if only for reliability purposes (we don't really see the point of multiples). You can also copy Keychains between computers. Once the Keychain file has been placed on the destination machine, you can double-click the file right from the Finder to import the file.

Keychain first aid

The saying tends to go that an application with its own built-in first aid feature is never a good sign, and in Keychain Access, it makes us a bit wary. The reality is that because there tend to be lots of records, and some that are updated and accessed frequently, sometimes the Keychain files get corrupted. If bad things begin to happen when you try to access your Keychain (consistent crashes from other applications, records not being saved, and so on) running the Keychain First Aid feature might get you out of trouble. To do so, go to the Keychain Access menu and select Keychain First Aid. Enter your password and click Start to either verify or repair your Keychain. Keychain First Aid checks all of your records and their associations and makes sure that the proper information is carried in each record. See Figure 12.14 for a look at Keychain First Aid in action.

FIGURE 12.14

Keychain First Aid at work

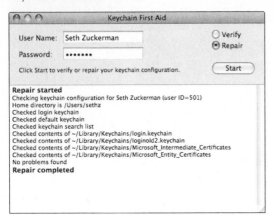

Keychain preferences

One helpful feature of the Keychain Access application is that it displays its status in the menu bar. One glance at the icon and you can quickly tell if your Keychain is locked or unlocked. See Figure 12.15. You can also choose to lock and unlock the Keychain manually from the menu bar icon, as well as launch the Keychain Access application.

 **To turn this feature on, open Keychain Access and click the Keychain menu ⇨ Preferences. Next select Show Status in Menu Bar; this turns on the Keychain Menu.**

FIGURE 12.15

Keychain Access, menu bar style

The preferences in Keychain Access also enable you to search .Mac and Directory Services for certificates, set specific logging features of the First Aid portion, and alter the security requirements for your certificates.

Sharing Your Files

The beginning of this chapter explained how to access files that other computers are sharing. This section of the chapter explains how to do the opposite: make your files available for other people to access. First, you plan for file sharing and identify your computer on the network. Next, you start the file-sharing feature in Mac OS X. Finally, you create user accounts for people you want to have more or less access to your files.

Using file sharing in a small network enables all or some of the computers on that network to function as both personal computer and file server, saving the cost and space of a dedicated machine functioning as a server.

Planning for file sharing

The personal file-sharing capabilities of Mac OS X make sharing files and folders across a network surprisingly easy but not without some cost. This section discusses the capabilities and limitations of Mac OS X file sharing to help you decide in advance whether or not it meets your needs. The alternative to personal file sharing is a dedicated, centralized file server, usually running Mac OS X Server.

Deciding between distributed or centralized file sharing

Your network can implement file sharing in a distributed or centralized fashion. With distributed file sharing, also known as *peer-to-peer file sharing*, each computer makes files, folders, and disks available to other computers on the network. While your computer shares your files with other computers, you are free to use your computer for other tasks.

The price you pay for a distributed system includes the following: Making files from your computer available does lead to a reduced performance of your computer. While you are doing your work, other computers are accessing your files. Also, this can lead to a big mess of files with no one knowing where the original might be located. There may be multiple versions of a certain file on many computers. This can be very confusing and lead to errors. In addition, Mac OS X file sharing limits the number of people that can share the same folder or disk at the same time, making file sharing unsuitable for serving files to large numbers of computers.

In contrast, a network with centralized file sharing dedicates one computer (or more) to providing file-sharing services. The file sharing occurs between the centralized computer and the client computers, not between the client computers themselves. The dedicated computer runs file server software, such as Apple's Mac OS X Server, enabling the computer to serve files to a large number of other computers. A dedicated file server must be fast and must have one or more large hard disks. Although the underpinnings are the same in both Mac OS X client and Mac OS X Server, the huge difference lies in the management tools that OS X Server provides, and thus the capabilities that it can provide for the average user. Mac OS X Server costs $499 for up to ten simultaneous users, or $999 for an unlimited number of users. If you purchase an XServe, Apple's specially designed enterprise-level rack-mountable server, OS X Server is included with the hardware purchase.

Mac OS X Server

Apple's software for centralized serving is Mac OS X Server. This server package, built on the Unix underpinnings of Mac OS X, offers Apple File Services support as well as sharing of many Ethernet-capable PostScript printers. Designed as a full-service Web, Internet, e-mail, and network server as well as an Apple File Services server, Mac OS X Server offers impressive performance and capabilities. One of those capabilities, called NetBoot, actually allows most late-model Macs to start up from the Mac OS X server machine, making it possible for a roomful of such Macs to receive their system software and applications from a centralized server. You can choose to boot from a Network volume in the Startup Disk pane of the OS X System Preferences window. Another impressive capability is OS X Server's client management, offering individualized control over the user environments of the clients that connect to it, through the use of its Open Directory databases and Directory Services.

Centralized disk storage reduces the amount of local disk storage required by each networked computer while providing a way for people who work together to share information. People can store files on the server's disks where other people can open or copy them. Many people can access the server's disks and folders simultaneously, and new files become available to everyone instantly. Unlike the file sharing provided by Mac OS X, no one uses the server's computer to do personal work because it is dedicated to providing network services. Conversely, your computer is not burdened when someone else on the network accesses one of your shared items on the server's disks.

A centralized file server is set up and maintained by a trained person called a *network administrator*. Mac OS X Server includes organizational, administrative, and security features to manage file access on the network. The network administrator does not control access to folders and files on the server's disks; that is the responsibility of each person who puts items on the disks.

The Mac OS X Server software runs on any Macintosh that came with built-in USB ports (PowerBooks and iBooks are officially unsupported, but you can swing an install if you have the laptop mounted in FireWire disk mode on a supported machine) as long as there is a minimum of 512MB RAM and 10GB free on the hard drive. These are, however, the bare minimum requirements. OS X Server is quite RAM hungry, and the more you give it, the happier it is.

Although Mac OS X client's file-sharing capabilities are designed for distributed file sharing, you can use file sharing on a dedicated computer to create a file server for a small network. Folders or entire hard disks on that file-server computer can be made available to other computers on the network as described in the remainder of this chapter. (Going forward, any mention of "Mac OS X" is referring to the client — the one that ships on your Mac — version. The server version is specifically referenced as "Mac OS X Server.")

The problem with such a file server is its performance. Mac OS X assumes someone is using the dedicated computer for more than sharing files. As a result, Mac OS reserves more than 50 percent of the dedicated computer's processing power for tasks other than file sharing and runs the file-sharing activities at a lower priority than other tasks.

Guidelines for file sharing

The following guidelines and tips for sharing folders and disks help optimize file sharing and help prevent problems:

■ **To share a write-only folder (a drop box), it must be inside another shared folder that has read permission.**

■ **The greater the number of accessed shared folders, the greater the memory and processing demands on your computer.** Too many sharing connections slow your system to a crawl.

■ **Check or review any applicable licensing agreements before sharing programs, artwork, or sounds.** Often, licensing agreements or copyright laws restrict use of such items to a single computer.

■ **Select a single computer and dedicate it to acting as a file server for the shared information.** Create a regular user account (not an administrator account) on this computer for everyone to use when connecting for file sharing. Everyone who connects for file sharing with this account's name and password has access to the contents of the account's home folder. This method is often the most efficient way to share numerous files or to share folders with several users simultaneously.

■ **Use a router rather than a hub if your network has a DSL or cable modem connection to the Internet and each network computer has a public IP address assigned by your ISP.** If you use a hub, network traffic from one machine travels to another machine on your network via your ISP. In addition to upsetting most ISPs, this can result in significant performance degradation. This situation does not occur if the computers on your network have private IP addresses and your network has an Internet connection that shares a public IP address among the network computers.

Identifying your computer

Before your Mac can share files, it requires a network identity. There are two components to a network identity:

■ **Computer Name:** You establish the computer name in the Services tab of the Sharing pane of System Preferences, as shown in Figure 12.16.

■ **Computer IP address:** The current IP address is displayed, established, and changed in the Network pane of System Preferences.

> **TIP** After you have your settings the way you want them in Sharing preferences and Network preferences, you may want to click the lock button to prevent accidental changes. You are asked for your password to unlock the settings if you want to make changes later.

FIGURE 12.16

The Sharing pane in System Preferences with Expert CC MBP as the Computer Name

Turning file sharing on and off

After you establish your computer's network identity in Sharing preferences, and Network preferences if necessary, you are ready to turn on file sharing in the same Sharing preferences window. You don't need to turn on file sharing to access files from other computers, for example, by using the Finder's Go ➪ Connect To Server command. However, you do need to turn on file sharing to allow users of other network computers to access the shared files on your computer. If some other computer users need to access your shared files via the AppleTalk protocol, you also need to turn on this protocol in Network preferences.

Unlike previous versions of Mac OS (Versions 9.2.2 and earlier), simply turning on file sharing does not significantly slow down your Mac OS X computer. You may, however notice your computer performing more slowly while other computers are opening or copying your shared files. During this activity, your attempts to open, save, or copy files as well as network activities of your own take a bit longer.

Starting and stopping file sharing

To start file sharing, simply check the File Sharing box on the left column of the Sharing System Preference pane. The right side of the preference pane will change to tell you that file sharing is starting up, and then it will change to say that it is turned on. The gray light next to the File Sharing status turns green if File Sharing is turned on. See Figure 12.17.

FIGURE 12.17

File sharing is enabled as indicated by the green light.

Changing folder and file permissions

File and Folder permissions have drastically changed in Leopard. You can add multiple folders for sharing. You also can define privileges for more than one group and user on a folder:

- **Adding additional folders to share:** In the Shared Folders window, click the plus sign. Select the folder you want to share. In this case I have added the Applications folder for sharing. See Figure 12.18.

- **Changing user and group privileges:** You can add, change, and delete individual rights to a folder that is shared. First, select the share you want to modify in the Sharing Folders box. In the right-hand window, Users, select the user or group whose privileges you want to change. Here you can change the permissions to Read & Write, Read Only, Write Only, or No Access.

- **Adding a user or group to a folder:** First, select the share you want to modify in the Sharing Folders window. Then click the plus sign at the bottom left of the Users box. Select the user or group you want to grant or deny access to the highlighted folder. The same privileges apply from changing user and group privileges. See Figure 12.19.

  Figure 12.20 shows the result of adding a My Sharing account.

FIGURE 12.18

Applications folder added to sharing

FIGURE 12.19

Adding a user or group to the selected share point

FIGURE 12.20

Added My Sharing (sharing only account) to the Applications folder

It is important to recognize that the permissions in your Sharing pane are identical to the permissions on the folder itself. The same rules apply as listed previously. If you would not apply the permissions you want to the folder or file in the Finder, don't do it here! You can seriously break many things if you change permissions incorrectly.

When file sharing is turned on, Mac OS has a neat way to indicate to the shared computer user that a particular folder is shared. When navigating your computer to that folder, a black bar at the top of the finder window shows up and states that it is a shared folder. See Figure 12.21.

Sharing with Microsoft Windows

Whatever the reasons may be, far more people use Windows PCs than all other personal computers combined. Because the Windows PC is the lowest common denominator, other operating systems need to be able to coexist — something that became much more seamless with the advent of Mac OS X. Not only can Mac OS X read and write PC-formatted disks, use Windows fonts, and share many hardware peripherals with Windows PCs, but it can share files with Windows PCs as well. You can also enable SMB/CIFS file sharing by choosing to turn on Windows File Sharing in the Services tab of the Sharing pane of System Preferences.

FIGURE 12.21

The gray bar at the top of the Applications folder indicates the folder is shared.

Enabling FTP, SMB, and AFP

Here is where you enable FTP, SMB, and AFP. In prior versions of Mac OS X, this was broken up into separate areas in Sharing. It has been simplified into one File Sharing option. To change any of these settings, click the Options button on the bottom right of the File Sharing option in the Sharing pane. A pop-up shows up with each option. See Figure 12.22. The following options are available:

- **Share files and folders using AFP:** Checking this box allows Macintosh computers to access your files. If it is turned on, the number of active users connected is listed just below this check box.

- **Share files and folders using FTP:** Checking this box allows FTP users to connect to your computer. Keep in mind this is not a secure method of sharing files.

- **Share files and folders using SMB:** Checking this box allows Windows users to connect to your machine. Each user you want to have connect using SMB must be individually enabled. When you enable an account you must enter that user's password.

Enabling multiple protocols for sharing

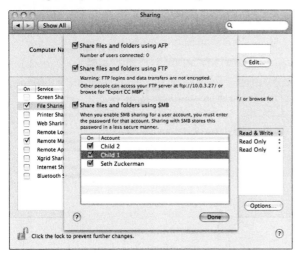

Enabling file sharing via AppleTalk

Mac OS X usually uses the TCP/IP protocol for file-sharing services, but it can also use the AppleTalk protocol simultaneously. If some other computer users need or prefer to use the AppleTalk protocol for file sharing, you can configure Mac OS X to use it. You turn on AppleTalk in the Network pane of System Preferences, which is described in Chapter 11.

Identifying who can connect for file sharing

In Mac OS X, unlike in Mac OS 9 and earlier, you do not create users, groups, and passwords specifically for file sharing. In Mac OS X, the user accounts that are created in the Accounts preference pane are identical to user accounts that are accessed when people log into your Mac for file sharing services. As soon as you turn file sharing on, any administrator-level user has access to the hard drive as a mounted volume, as well as his or her user folder. As long as file sharing is on, anyone is able to log in as a guest and have access to every user's public folder.

Designating your shared items

Inside every user account's home folder lies a Public folder. By default, the Public folder is a read-only folder for all users, that is, anyone can copy an item *from* the folder, but cannot copy anything *to* the folder. Within the Public folder, by default, is a Drop Box folder. The Drop Box folder is a write-only folder for all users. This means that users can copy information *to* the folder, but do not have access to anything inside of it, and therefore cannot take items *from* it. If you want to share items so that any user can copy them, place them in the Public folder. People who give items to you place them inside of your Drop Box folder.

CAUTION   A user gains access to your entire hard drive and other volumes by connecting for file sharing as an administrator of your computer. For obvious security reasons, be careful whom you allow to connect to your computer for file sharing as an administrator. Ensure that user accounts created on your computer solely for file sharing purposes are not administrator accounts. For each of these accounts, the option in the Accounts pane of your System Preferences that allows the account to administer Mac OS X on your computer should be turned off.

A special folder called Shared exists in the Users folder in Mac OS X. All registered users of a Mac OS X machine have only local access to this folder. If you want to make items accessible to all users of the machine, but not to guests logging in remotely for file sharing, place the items in the Shared folder that is inside of the Users folder.

Setting specific access privileges

This section explains how to use the Finder's Info window to set separate access privileges for an item's owner, group, and for everyone else.

You set access privileges for a folder or volume in its Get Info window. Select a folder or volume in the Finder and Choose File ⇨ Get Info (⌘+I) to display the Info window. (⌘+Option+I opens the inspector window that displays information for whatever is selected in the Finder.) By default, the ownership and permissions section is partially disclosed, and a summary of the privileges that you have are displayed. For anything within your Home folder, expect the permissions to be read and write. Clicking the disclosure triangle next to the word *Details* brings down the full permissions area, giving you the option to set specific privileges for owner, for group, and for others. See Figure 12.23.

As discussed in Chapter 18, each file and folder in Mac OS X can have different access privileges for three user categories: Owner, Group, and Others (everyone else). Anyone connecting to your Mac as a guest falls into the Others category. Even if a person connects with the name and password of a login account on your computer, this person falls in the Others category for every file and folder unless this person is either the owner of the file or a member of the file's group.

You can set one of four privilege levels for each user category in the access privileges pop-up menus:

- **Read & Write:** This level permits users to open and copy the file or folder. In the case of a folder, users can also see enclosed files and folders and can put items into the folder. In the case of a file, users can also make changes to the file.

- **Read only:** This level permits users to open and copy the file or folder. In the case of a folder, users can see also enclosed files and folders.

- **Write only (drop box):** This level permits users to put files and folders into the folder, but does not allow users to open the folder. (Files can't have write-only permission.)

- **None:** This level denies access to the file or folder. Users can see the item but can't open it or change it.

FIGURE 12.23

The Info window for my Documents folder. sethz (the owner) has Read & Write Access; Office People (the group) has Read only access; and Others (The Other selection) has No Access.

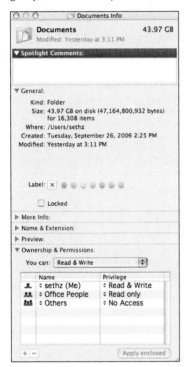

NOTE To establish write-only access to a folder, you must give the person or group read privileges or read and write privileges to the folder containing the folder. For example, your Public folder has read-only privileges for Others. Inside the read-only Public folder is a folder named Drop Box, which has write-only privileges for Others. Other users couldn't access the Drop Box folder if you put it inside another folder with write-only privileges. That would defeat the purpose.

The Owner privileges must be at least as broad as the Group privileges, and the Group privileges must be at least as broad as the Others privileges. In other words, if you give Others read and write privileges, both the Group and the Owner are automatically set to read and write.

If you want to set the same privileges for all folders enclosed within the current folder, click the Apply to enclosed items button. Remember that this is an all-or-nothing operation; once you close the info window, it cannot easily be undone.

For more information on Accounts and Privileges see Chapter 18.

Dealing with Security Risks

File sharing poses security risks. Allowing other users to connect as guests is a relatively low risk if you are careful. If your computer has multiple administrator login accounts, the risk is much greater. The risks are magnified if your computer has a public IP address and is thus directly exposed to the Internet, as opposed to being Network Address Translated and having a private IP address. (See Chapter 11 for more on Network Address Translation and the difference between public and private IP addresses.)

Assessing the risks of guest access

Mac OS X usually allows everyone on your network to access your Public folder as a guest, without supplying a name and password (if file sharing is turned on). Therefore, you should be careful what you put in your Public folder. The Public folder itself is usually read-only, and you can set restricted access privileges individually for items that you put into your Public folder. However, if everyone has write access to a folder inside your Public folder, such as to the Drop Box folder, a guest can still cause mischief by filling your disk with file after file.

Assessing the risks of administrator access

An administrator's special ability to connect to all disks and work without certain restrictions can threaten the computer's security much more than guest access does. In Mac OS X 10.1 and earlier, someone who connects to your computer for file sharing with an administrator's name and password can actually access the contents of all home folders and the main Library folder on your computer. This is more freedom than Mac OS X allows when you log in locally as an administrator. Under Mac OS X 10.2 and higher, an administrator logged in through file sharing has the same privileges and restrictions as that user would if logged into the machine locally.

Assessing the risk of your Internet connection

The security risks of file sharing are amplified by the fact that file sharing is usually available via the Internet's TCP/IP protocol. A potential hacker does not have to be physically near your Macs. The hacker could enter over an Internet connection. If your computer is connected directly to the Internet, anyone in the world who learns your computer's IP address can access your Public folder anonymously via the Internet. Someone who also knows the name and password of an administrator account on your computer has very broad access via the Internet. The Internet exposure is relatively high if your computer has a static IP address from your ISP. The Internet exposure is relatively low if your ISP assigns your computer a different IP address every time you connect, as is usually the case with a modem connection, a cable modem connection, or a PPPoE connection (the protocol with which most DSL subscribers utilize). If you share a connection via an Internet router, your computer may have a private IP address that can't be accessed from the Internet unless the router is explicitly configured to allow such access.

Improving file-sharing security

Here are some techniques you can employ to improve file-sharing security:

■ **Be very sure to turn off the administrator option on any account that does not absolutely require it.**

■ **Don't allow write permission for guests, even to Drop Box folders.** Set the Others category of every guest-accessible shared folder to read-only.

■ **Do not overvalue the security of passwords.** Someone may connect to your computer with a password and then leave his or her computer without disconnecting. A passerby can then use this computer to access all your shared files (subject to the access privileges you set). Remind people who connect to your computer for file sharing that they must put away all your shared folders (by ejecting them) when they are finished. Also, remind users to lock their Keychains or log out of their machines when they leave them unattended. If they do not, unauthorized users may be able to access shared folders using their account, even if they do not know the password.

Particularly if you have high-speed Internet access, such as cable modem or DSL, you might want to set up a firewall to protect your local network. Firewalls provide a barrier to unauthorized access from outside your local network.

> **TIP** When installing Mac OS X for the first time, create an Administrator account as well as a regular user account. Use your computer as the standard user, not Administrator. This prevents anyone installing unwanted programs onto your computer without the Administrator account password. If you share your files, it also prevents someone from erasing important programs and files on your machine if logged in remotely.

Using a personal firewall to improve security

A *firewall* is an application that runs on a computer or a piece of separate network hardware that exists to improve security by blocking access to that computer or network. Mac OS X includes a firewall application that is integrated in the Security preference pane. In previous versions of OS X it was located in the Sharing preference pane. Although this is not a replacement for a true hardware-based firewall, it can still be an effective barrier.

The Mac OS X Leopard has been changed to an application-based firewall. This has been done to ease the setup of the firewall. A port-based firewall (which is what Apple used to use) is more complicated to configure, but more customizable. An application-based firewall is much easier to set up but doesn't give as much flexibility to block specific services. To see the firewall configuration, open System Preferences, open the Security pane, and then click the Firewall panel, which is shown in Figure 12.24.

FIGURE 12.24

Use the Firewall panel of the Security pane to switch the built-in firewall on and off and to change its settings.

In this pane you have three options:

- **Block all incoming connections:** This is the most conservative mode. Mac OS X will block all connections except a limited list of services essential to the operation of your computer.

- **Allow all incoming connections:** This is the most "open" mode. Mac OS X will not block any incoming connections to your computer. This is the default mode for Leopard.

- **Set access for specific services and applications:** This mode offers you the most flexibility. You can choose whether to allow or deny incoming connections for any application on your system.

To turn on the firewall and block all traffic (including file sharing traffic), click Block all incoming connections. The firewall automatically stops all incoming network traffic for all services (except system essential ones), even if you have file sharing turned on. This is the most secure method of protecting your computer. If you plan to keep all of your files private, choose this option. However, if you plan to share files, this won't work!

To turn off the firewall, that is, without exceptions, click Allow all incoming connections. Selecting this option allows all incoming traffic to connect to your computer. Having file sharing turned on allows the connection to take place. This turns off the firewall, and is generally not a good option because it gives you no security whatsoever!

TIP To troubleshoot a connection problem, for example, file sharing, turn off your firewall and test again. Oftentimes a service is blocked by your firewall and turning it off tests to see if this is the case.

The most optimal method of using a firewall is turning it on with exceptions (set access for specific services and applications). This mode offers you the most flexibility. You can choose whether to allow or deny incoming connections for any application on your system:

- You can click the + button to add an application to this list. You can select an application and click the – button to remove it. Control+clicking the application name gives you the option to reveal the application's location in Finder.

- Once you've added an application to the list, you can choose whether to allow or deny incoming connections for that application. You can even add command line applications to this list.

- When you add an application to this list, Mac OS X digitally signs the application (if it has not been signed already). If the application is later modified, you will be prompted to allow or deny incoming network connections to it. Most applications do not modify themselves, and this is a safety feature that notifies you of the change.

- All applications not in the list that have been digitally signed by a Certificate Authority trusted by the system (for the purpose of code signing) are allowed to receive incoming connections. Every Apple application in Leopard has been signed by Apple and is allowed to receive incoming connections. If you want to deny a digitally signed application you should first add it to the list and then explicitly deny it.

  If you run an application that is unsigned and not in the Application Firewall list, you are presented with a dialog with options to Allow or Deny connections for the application. If you choose Allow, Mac OS X 10.5 signs the application and adds it to the Application Firewall list. If you choose Deny, Mac OS X 10.5 signs the application, adds it to the Application Firewall list, and denies the connection.

NOTE Some applications check their own integrity when they are run without using code signing. If the Application Firewall recognizes such an application it does not sign it, but then it continues to show the dialog every time the application is run. This may be avoided by upgrading to a version of the application that is signed by its developer.

If you want a port-based firewall, you can still use the previous firewall system ipfw. Ipfw is a port-based firewall and is still accessible via the command line in Terminal. If a port is blocked by the ipfw firewall, the new firewall does not overrule this decision.

Sharing Your Internet Connection

A nifty feature of the OS X Sharing preference pane is the ability to share an Internet connection between more than one Mac. In the Internet pane under sharing, you choose what connection of yours other Macs share *from,* and then what connections of your Mac they can connect *to.* For example, if you are using a Bluetooth cell phone to give your laptop an Internet connection, you specify that you are sharing *from* a Bluetooth modem. If you have an AirPort card, you can allow other Macs to wirelessly connect to your Mac, and therefore share your Bluetooth Internet connection among them, over a self-created AirPort network. To do this, choose to share your connection from your Bluetooth modem and check the box next to the AirPort connection that shows up in the To computers using list. This is but one of many different possibilities; you could, as a further example, share your AirPort network connection to another Mac connected to your Ethernet port, or share your dial-up modem connection to a Mac connected to yours through your AirPort connection. See Figure 12.25.

FIGURE 12.25

The AirPort Internet connection is shared with computers connected via Ethernet.

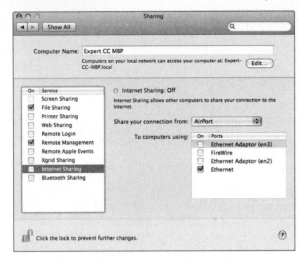

Summary

This chapter showed you how to connect to and work with files and use storage space located on file servers on your local network. The file servers can be dedicated file servers, or they can be personal computers running file sharing. We covered using the Finder to connect to AFP, SMB, and FTP servers. To determine your access privileges to a folder, you can look at the folder's icon, open it, and look for a small icon in the status bar of its window. This chapter also discussed transferring and opening files on the network. In addition, you learned how to disconnect from shared folders and disks.

You can use the Mac OS X Keychain to automatically provide your name and password when you connect to a file server, and you can streamline subsequent connections to a file server by making a favorite.

This chapter discussed the peer-to-peer (distributed) file sharing provided by Mac OS X. Peer-to-peer file sharing in Mac OS X is great for small groups, but a dedicated file server (such as AppleShare IP or Mac OS X Server) is generally better in a large environment.

You learned how to activate and deactivate file sharing, specify privileges for folders, and take basic security precautions. You also learned how to share your Internet connection between other Macs.

Chapter 13

Deploying More Network Services

You know from previous chapters that with Mac OS X you can share files and some USB printers with other computers on your local network. In this chapter, we look at the following additional services that Mac OS X can provide on your network or the Internet:

- Web sharing for hosting a Web site from your computer
- FTP access for unprotected file copying between your computer and others
- Remote login for protected file copying between your computer and others, and for control of your computer from others using encrypted Unix commands
- Remote control of your computer if you are away from the office or home

In addition to all these network services, your computer can respond to messages sent from other computers on your network. These messages, called *remote Apple events,* are sent by AppleScript programs that are running on other computers. We cover this capability along with AppleScript in Chapter 22.

Making Network Services Available

All network services described in this chapter require a local network, an Internet connection, or both. The local network can be an Ethernet network or an AirPort wireless network. If you're not sure how to set up a local network or an Internet connection, look back at Chapters 10 and 11.

When a network service is enabled on your computer, it's available as soon as your computer is powered up. While a service is available, other computers on the Internet or your local network can access it, depending on firewall rules. The service remains available until someone deliberately turns off the service or shuts down your computer. If you enable a network service while you're logged into the machine and then log out, the service remains available. Network services are even available while no one is logged in (that is, while the login window is displayed). Logging in as another user does not affect availability, because network service settings are not in any way tied to user account settings or privileges.

Shutting down or sleeping your computer ends its network services, but only temporarily. The next time the computer is started up, Mac OS X automatically turns on network services that are configured to be available.

If your computer goes into sleep mode, it's the same as shutting down the computer with regard to network services. For this reason, if you're configuring your Mac OS X computer to offer any network services, you'll want to use the Energy Saver preference pane to disable sleep functionality, or to put the display to sleep after a certain amount of time, as described in Chapter 17. If another computer is connected to your computer for Web sharing, FTP access, or remote login and your computer goes to sleep, the other computer is unable to access that service until your computer wakes from sleep. When your computer wakes up, computers with existing connections to your computer's network services may resume access.

Your computer's IP addresses

Other computers need to know your computer's network identity to access the network services that it provides. For Web sharing, FTP access, and remote login, your computer can always be identified by a numeric IP address. You can think of your computer's IP address as its telephone number.

Actually, your computer can have more than one IP address. It has different IP addresses for each network port that it's connected to. Your computer could be connected to an Internet provider via modem, an Ethernet network via its built-in Ethernet port, and an AirPort wireless network. Each connection has its own IP address.

Displaying your computer's IP address

To see the IP address of the port currently used to provide Web sharing, FTP access, and remote login, open System Preferences and then click the Network button (or choose Location ⇨ Network Preferences from the Apple menu). Click on the port you want to know the IP address of. The IP address is displayed to the right of the window. See Figure 13.1.

FIGURE 13.1

See the IP address of the Airport network in the Network pane of System Preferences.

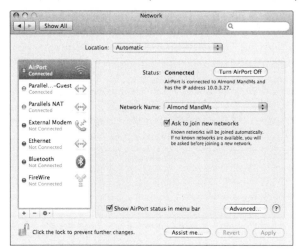

Punching holes in your firewall

If your computer is at home and is connected via broadband (DSL, cable), you likely have an Internet gateway or router that shares a single public IP address among the computers on the network using special reserved private IP addresses. If your IP address is 192.168.*x.x*, 10.*x.x.x*, 169.254.*x.x*, or 172.16.*x.x*, it is likely a private IP address. You'll have to check your gateway or router to be completely sure. Computers on the Internet see only the shared public IP address. They can't see the private IP addresses of computers on the local network. Therefore, they have no way of contacting computers on the local network for Web, FTP, or remote login services. Because the gateway keeps Internet computers out, it provides a kind of firewall for your local network. If you want to let Internet computers through your firewall, you need to punch holes in the firewall. Each type of service — Web sharing, FTP access, and remote login — needs a separate hole in the firewall.

You may be able to configure your Internet gateway so that it directs all incoming requests for a particular service, such as FTP access, from the shared public IP address to one computer's private IP address. This scheme is usually called *inbound port mapping*. This scheme is like an office with a main phone number and a receptionist who routes incoming calls to a different private extension for each department. Within the company, departments call each other by using the private extension numbers. With inbound port mapping, your local network has one public IP address and a gateway that routes incoming service requests to private IP addresses according to the type of request. Computers on your local network use your private IP address to access your computer's network services.

The details of configuring inbound port mapping are different for each gateway product. Consult your Internet gateway's manual for specific instructions.

Dynamic and static IP address

Your computer's IP address may be dynamic or static. A *dynamic IP address* may change each time you begin an Internet session or each time your computer starts up. A *static IP address* doesn't change. Your computer probably has a dynamic IP address if it connects to the Internet via modem or DSL with PPPoE. Most cable modem connections also provide a dynamic IP address. In fact, most consumer Internet connections will come with dynamic IP addresses because static addresses are usually more costly to provide.

A computer on a local network, Ethernet, or AirPort may get an IP address from a DHCP server on the local network each time the computer starts up. The IP address could be different each time, so it is a dynamic IP address. (The *D* in DHCP stands for Dynamic.) The AirPort base station includes a DHCP server, as do many Internet gateway and router products. If you are behind a router with an IP address similar to 192.168.xxx.xxx or 10.xxx.xxx.xxx you can give your internal computer a static IP address to make configuring your network services more accessible to others. This varies by router manufacturer and each one is different. Consult your router manufacturer or network administrator to determine how to configure a static address.

Having a dynamic IP address makes your computer hard for other computers to find, which means that your network services are hard to find. It's like a business whose phone number changes every day.

Getting your computer a name

Although your Mac has an IP address for the Web sharing, FTP access, and remote login services that it provides, an IP address is not as convenient as the names that people normally use to access Web sites and FTP servers on the Internet. In addition to its IP address, your computer can have a name for the services that it provides on the Internet and on your local network. The name is actually just another way of referring to your computer's IP address. When another computer tries to contact your computer by name, a name server on your local network or on the Internet looks up the name in a directory and finds your IP address. These name servers are known as *DNS servers* (Domain Name Server).

The Mac OS X client does not include an interface to the built-in DNS server, nor can Mac OS X help get a name assigned to your computer and listed with DNS servers on the Internet or your local network. How you get your computer a name address for its Web sharing, FTP access, and remote login services depends on how it connects to the Internet and whether it is on a local network. The details are beyond the scope of this book, but here are some general guidelines:

■ You need to register a domain name if you do not already have access to one. Historically, Network Solutions (www.networksolutions.com) provides this service in the United States for the major domains (.com, .net, .org, and so on); however, now many other companies provide this service. If you're looking for a domain name, you would be well served to spend some time comparison shopping, because there are many lower-cost alternatives that offer different feature packages from Web hosting to e-mail services that may appeal to you. A good place to start would be to feed the following term to your favorite search engine: *domain name registrars*.

- Most Internet service providers, such as `www.godaddy.com`, provide name-based hosting, for a fee.

- If you have a static IP address and have your own domain name, you can get free DNS service from Granite Canyon Group, LLC (`www.granitecanyon.com`).

- If you don't need your own domain name, you can get a free name like `myname.dnsalias.com` from an organization that provides dynamic DNS service, such as Dynamic DNS Network Services (`www.dyndns.org`). If you have a dynamic IP address, you also need to install software on your computer that notices each time you get a different IP address and automatically sends your new IP address to your dynamic DNS service provider. An example of this software is the free DNSUpdate, available at `www.dnsupdate.org`.

- If you want to use names instead of private IP addresses on your local network, set up a DNS server on the network. Some Internet gateway products include DNS, and DNS software is available for Mac OS 9. Your Mac OS X installation actually includes BIND, the Internet standard DNS server for Unix; however, it is not recommended to run DNS on your personal workstation. Configuring the included DNS server is out of the scope of this book, but if you are curious enter **man bind** at a shell prompt in the Terminal application. Also a trip to your favorite search engine with the query *Mac OS X bind* will provide a plethora of results.

NOTE A computer name is displayed above the IP address in the Sharing preference pane. This name is used for file sharing and other AppleTalk services, not for such TCP/IP services as Web sharing, FTP access, and remote login.

Hosting Your Own Web Site

Have you ever wanted to host your own Web site? All you need, other than a network or Internet connection, is Web server software and some Web pages. Mac OS X includes the Apache Web server, which is in use at many commercial sites hosting large, active sites. This industrial-strength Web server is easy to set up thanks to Mac OS X's Web Sharing feature. It gets your Web site on the Internet or your local network in about a minute. (No, this does not include the time it takes to actually create your Web pages!)

Although you could use Web Sharing to host a large Web site, you probably wouldn't want to. Web Sharing is best suited to hosting a personal Web site. Your Web site is as sturdy as large Web sites, thanks to the Apache server software and Mac OS X's Unix core. System resources, not reliability, are the limiting factor. Unlike administrators of large Web sites, you probably don't want to dedicate your computer to hosting a Web site. Most likely, you want to host some Web pages for others' use or convenience, or perhaps you would like to have access to some pages on your computer from any location, be it home, work, or elsewhere. However, this being your personal computer, you'll probably use other applications at the same time. If you use Web sharing to host a large, busy Web site, you'll probably find that your computer is not responsive enough when you use other applications at the same time. Web sharing is ideally suited for distributing information to co-workers on a local network or to family and friends on the Internet.

If you want to host a Web site on the Internet, your computer needs a continuous, high-capacity Internet connection. A DSL or cable modem connection should be adequate for a personal Web site. However, many DSL and cable modem connections *upload* files (send to the Internet) much slower than they *download* files (receive from the Internet). For example, your computer may download files at over 140KB per second but only be permitted to upload at less than 14KB per second. If this is the case with your connection, visitors to your Web site will receive Web pages from your computer at the slower upload rate. Nevertheless, DSL and cable modem connections are much faster than a modem connection. You don't want to frustrate your Web site visitors with spotty, slow service via a modem connection.

Starting Web sharing

You can get a Web site set up on your local network or your Internet connection in a minute or less. Simply open System Preferences and choose View ➪ Sharing (or click the Sharing button). Click the check box next to Web Sharing. Web sharing takes a few seconds to start up. Unchecking the Web Sharing box turns off Web Sharing. Figure 13.2 shows the Sharing preference pane with Web Sharing turned on.

FIGURE 13.2

Start Web sharing in the Sharing pane of System Preferences.

If the Sharing preference pane settings are locked, you must unlock them before you can start Web sharing. When the settings are locked, they're dim and the lock button at the bottom of the window looks locked. To unlock the settings, click the lock button and enter an administrator's user account name and password in the dialog box that appears.

Loading Web site files

Turning on Web sharing in the Sharing preference pane gets a Web site on the air, but it's not your Web site until you put your site's files into the right folder. In the meantime, you have an introductory site supplied with Mac OS X, as shown in Figure 13.3.

FIGURE 13.3

Visitors to your personal Web site see a provisional home page until you place your Web site's files in your home folder's Sites folder.

 127.0.0.1 is the internal loop-back test IP address. If you are not connected to a network and want to test your Web site, use this IP address.

Loading a personal Web site

You can put files for a Web site in two places. Files for a personal Web site should go in the Sites folder in your home folder (Figure 13.4) where other users of your computer can't change them. Naturally, other users of your computer can create their own personal Web sites, and you can't change them. Each user's personal Web site has a unique URL.

FIGURE 13.4

The Sites folder is highlighted in the sethz home folder.

Loading the common Web site

Files for a joint Web site that all administrators of your computer can change go in the Documents folder in the WebServer folder in the main Library folder; the path is `/Library/WebServer/Documents/`. This folder initially contains a provisional home page in several languages. Each language has a separate HTML file. These files all have names beginning with `index.html` and ending with a suffix that indicates the language. For example, `index.html.en` is the English version and `index.html.es` is the Spanish (Español) version. You can make any of these HTML files the provisional home page for your Web site by removing the language-designation suffix so that the filename is just `index.html`. (You do not need to rename the `index.html.en` file because the Mac OS X Apache Web server automatically uses it if no files are named `index.html`.) Figure 13.5 shows the joint Web site's provisional home page in English.

> **TIP**   If you have no other use for your computer's common Web site, make it an index to your computer's personal Web sites. This index can be a simple Web page containing a list of links to the sites. For example, if users sethz and Laz both have personal Web sites, the index page would have a link to `/~sethz/` and another link to `/~laz/`. Note that the personal Web sites are named for the User's short name, which is always lowercase.

FIGURE 13.5

Visitors to your computer's common Web site see another provisional Web page until someone using your computer puts Web site files in the `/Library/WebServer/Documents/` folder.

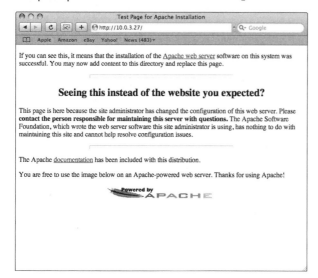

Designing and Creating a Web Site

Designing a Web site and creating all the files that go into it can be a lot of work. If your needs are simple, you may be able to produce a satisfactory Web site with a word processing application. For example, recent versions of Microsoft Word and AppleWorks can convert a word processing document to an HTML file. Word or AppleWorks word processing documents can include formatted text, tables, graphics, and links to places in the same document or to other documents. If the original word processing document includes graphics, the graphics are converted to separate image files. You must put the image files together with the HTML file in your Sites folder or the `/Library/WebServer/Documents/` folder.

Both Microsoft Word and AppleWorks convert simple documents more accurately than complex documents. You can experiment to see whether your word processing application can generate Web site files that meet your needs.

Of course, if you have experience with HTML authoring, you'll be comfortable using TextEdit to create raw HTML files, or you can use either Adobe's GoLive or Dreamweaver for a more WYSIWYG (What You See Is What You Get) approach to authoring. If you purchased the iLife suite you can use iWeb to easily publish a Web site as well.

Setting up a file listing

Instead of displaying a home page, your Web site can display a list of the files in your Sites folder or in the Documents folder of the WebServer folder (path `/Library/WebServer/Documents/`). To make this happen, simply remove the file named `index.html` or `index.html.en` from the folder. If the folder doesn't contain a file by either of these names, the Mac OS X Web server creates a Web page that is a list of the folder's contents, as shown in Figure 13.6.

FIGURE 13.6

If your Web site folder does not have a home page, visitors see a listing of the folder's contents.

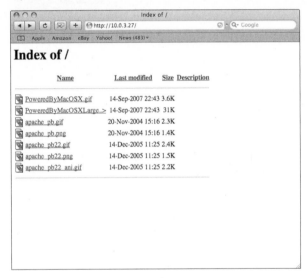

Visiting your Web site

People visit your personal Web site (the one in your Sites folder) at an Internet address (URL) like one of these:

- `http://10.0.3.27/~sethz/`

- `http://mycomputer.mydomain.com/~sethz/`

Substitute your computer's IP address or name, and substitute the short name of your user account at the end of the Internet address. Be sure to include the ending slash (/) or Apache will not know exactly which file to deliver, and an error message will appear. Notice that neither of these Internet addresses has a www prefix. Your Web site's Internet address doesn't include the www prefix unless it is part of the domain name you've obtained for your computer as described at the beginning of this chapter.

The joint Web site (the one with files in `/Library/WebServer/Documents/`) has an Internet address like one of these:

- `http://10.0.3.27`
- `http://mycomputer.mydomain.com`

Substitute your computer's IP address or name. Here again, your Web site's Internet address doesn't include the www prefix unless it is part of the name you have obtained for your computer.

> **TIP**   If your computer has only an IP address, put a note on your home page advising people who connect to it to add a bookmark for your page so that they don't have to remember and retype the IP address to visit again. If you have set up an account with DynDNS as discussed earlier, use the link to your DynDNS hostname.

Allowing FTP Access

The Mac OS X Web sharing feature is of little help when you want to share files rather than Web pages. Another feature that Mac OS X has in common with Unix is a built-in FTP Server. *FTP* (File Transfer Protocol) enables other computers on your local network or the Internet to copy files to and from your computer.

Turning FTP access on or off

The software that provides FTP service is built into Mac OS X, and you can turn it on or off quite easily. First, open System Preferences and choose View ➪ Sharing (or click the Sharing button). When the Sharing preference pane appears, check the File Sharing box. To turn the FTP service on click the Options button at the bottom right of the window. Check the Share Files and Folders Using FTP box. You can uncheck File Sharing or the Share files and Folders using FTP box to turn it off. Figure 13.7 shows FTP ready turned on in the Sharing preference pane.

Comparing FTP and Personal File Sharing

If you've never used FTP before, you may think that it sounds like Mac OS X's personal file-sharing feature, which is described in Chapter 12. Actually, FTP differs from file sharing in a couple of significant ways. For one, file sharing is mainly for Macs, but FTP works across all platforms. Computers running Windows and Unix operating systems can copy files to and from your computer using a native FTP client program.

Another key difference concerns how people use your files on other computers. With file sharing, other computer users see your shared files in Finder windows and Open dialog boxes. These computer users can open and save files directly on your computer. With FTP, other computer users see your files in FTP client applications, and these other users must copy files between your computer and theirs. They work with copies of your files on their computers.

FIGURE 13.7

Turn the built-in FTP server on or off in the Sharing pane of System Preferences.

If the Sharing preference pane settings are locked, just like Web Sharing, you must unlock them before you can turn FTP access on or off. The settings are dim when they're locked, and the lock button looks locked. To unlock the settings, click the security button and enter an administrator's user account name and password in the dialog box that appears.

Avoiding file damage

FTP was designed to transfer plain text files. Other kinds of files such as pictures, software, and formatted text files lose vital information unless first encoded as binary files before being transferred. Files that must be encoded before being sent over the Internet are known as *binary* files. Encoding Mac files also preserves information used by the Finder, such as the type of file and which application created it. Encoded files must be decoded after being received before they can be used. Read on for information regarding encoding and decoding.

Unlike other FTP software for Macs, the FTP server in Mac OS X is not able to automatically encode Mac files before sending them to another computer. Nor does the Mac OS X FTP server recognize encoded Mac files and automatically decode them when it receives them from another computer.

Because the Mac OS X FTP server doesn't handle any encoding or decoding automatically, you should encode files that you want other people to download from your computer. Conversely, if other people upload encoded files to your computer using FTP, you must decode the files before you can manipulate them. You can use the .zip Archive utility application included with Mac OS X to decode .zip files. You can encode files using the built-in Archive application or DropStuff by Allume systems (www.allume.com).

A future version of Mac OS X may include an FTP server that automatically encodes and decodes transferred files.

Considering security

Although convenient, allowing FTP access to your computer poses a security risk. Anyone who knows the name and password of a user account on your computer can connect to your computer from anywhere on your local network, and if your computer has an active Internet connection, from anywhere on the Internet.

Additionally, in FTP transfers both username and password information used to connect to your server is unencrypted. If someone is listening in to network traffic, either on your side or on the network you're connecting to, he or she can see your username and password as you connect to the server.

Additional information on SFTP, the secure FTP client distributed as part of OpenSSH and installed by default on Mac OS X computers, is provided later in this chapter. Refer to Chapter 24 for further discussion on FTP security, as well as information on configuring the SFTP server if you want to provide FTP access to your machine.

Unprotected passwords

FTP's authentication method, a user account name and password, protects your computer against casual snooping, but it is no defense at all against a skilled attacker. FTP does not encrypt the name and password before sending them across the network or the Internet. An attacker can use well-known tools and methods to capture names and passwords of everyone who connects to your computer for FTP access. Your name and password are just as vulnerable as those of other users of your computer. If you use FTP to get files from your computer while you're away from it, your name and password can be captured.

TIP   If you allow FTP access to your computer, change your password frequently and have all other users of your computer do likewise. Never use the same password for FTP that you use for anything else, such as online banking! You could also set up a separate user account specifically for FTP protecting your main account.

Unprotected file transfers

Similarly, FTP does nothing to protect files transferred to and from your computer. Sure, you can encrypt files on your computer using privacy tools such as GPG and Apple's FileVault, and encrypted files are secure from snoops if they're transferred as encrypted files. If you follow this route, remember to give the key to the people you are sharing files with, or else they will be unable to open your documents.

Protecting with privilege settings

The privilege settings for files and folders are the same for SMB and AFP access. This can be modified in the Sharing System Preferences panel. Details of how to modify permissions and access are explained in more detail in Chapter 12.

Prevent FTP Access Outside Home Folders

The FTP server normally allows remote users to go outside their home folders, but it can be configured to restrict users individually to their own home folders. This configuration requires the use of the Terminal application and an Administrator account.

First, you create a text file containing a list of user accounts that you want to restrict. You put the short name of each user account on a separate line, making sure to press Return after the last name. For example, the following list restricts users *sethz* and *ender* to their home folders when they log in for FTP access:

```
sethz
ender
```

In addition to restricting FTP access for individual users, you can restrict access for groups of users. For each group that you want to restrict, you simply add a line to the text file consisting of an "at" sign (@) followed by the group name. Because all Mac OS X user accounts belong to the staff group, a file containing the following lines (the last line being blank) restricts all users to their home directories when they log in for FTP access to your computer:

```
@staff
```

When you save the text file, name it `ftpchroot` and put it in your home folder. This file must be plain text. If you want to use the TextEdit application to create this file, you must choose Format ⇨ Make Plain Text before saving the file. After saving the file, change the filename so that it does not end with `.txt`.

After saving the file `ftpchroot` in your home folder, open the Terminal application and type the following command:

```
sudo mv ~/ftpchroot /etc/ftpchroot
```

When you're prompted in the Terminal window to enter a password, enter your own account password. Done!

Back door to network volumes

The Volumes folder (located in the root of the FTP connection) in prior versions of Mac OS X was actually an insidious security problem on a network where people use file sharing or file servers. The Volumes folder gave everyone who logs in to a computer's FTP server a back-door entrance to all network volumes mounted on the computer.

For example, suppose your computer has FTP access turned off but file sharing is turned on. Sue connects to your computer as a file-sharing guest, and your Public folder is mounted on Sue's computer. Sue has FTP access turned on. Using a third computer, Tim logs in to the FTP server on Sue's computer, goes to Sue's Volumes folder, and through it can access your Public folder. If Sue connects to your computer as a file-sharing administrator and mounts your hard drive as a network volume, Tim would have access to your entire hard drive through Sue's Volumes folder. If Sue has permission to access your files via File Sharing and has connected to your computer, anyone who logs on to Sue's computer as Sue (in any way) has access to what Sue has access to. As a result, if someone connects to Sue's computer as Sue and she is logged onto your computer, that person has permission to access your files.

 **This problem seems to have been corrected in Mac OS X Leopard.**

Allowing anonymous guest access

Considering the security problems that FTP access has, you may understandably balk at allowing guests to connect without user account names and passwords. Yet ironically, anonymous FTP access is arguably more secure than FTP access with a name and password. One reason is that anyone who connects anonymously is restricted to the contents of one folder. They can't ransack your other folders as users with passwords can. Furthermore, if everyone connects anonymously, their names and passwords aren't being sent over the network or Internet; what isn't there can't be captured. With that said, providing anonymous guest access to your machine can make your computer a very attractive target to some of the more unscrupulous users on the Internet. It is very likely that an unmonitored anonymous FTP server will be used for a purpose not intended by its owner. Although you may not think there is anything special about your home computer, its disk space and bandwidth are very attractive to file swappers and other network hoodlums.

Although it is possible to use the FTP Server provided by Apple in a default Mac OS X installation to enable and provide anonymous FTP access, we recommend replacing the Apple-provided FTP Server with one that allows greater control over access to the server, and one with much greater logging facilities.

Connecting to your FTP server

If your computer has FTP access turned on, people can use any FTP client application to connect to your computer's FTP server. They can also use a Web browser, although Web browsers have limited abilities with FTP.

Connecting with an FTP client

The FTP client needs to know the identity of the server or host, and this is just your computer's IP address or name. The client also needs to know the user's account name and password on your computer. If you have set up anonymous FTP access on your computer, the user can specify *anonymous* as the name (also called username or user ID) or leave the name blank.

There are many FTP clients available for Mac OS X. For this chapter, we use Transmit by Panic Software. Transmit is available at www.panic.com/transmit. Transmit has a very simple two-pane interface, as shown in Figure 13.8. When you open the program, the left window is labeled *your stuff*, and it shows you your home directory. You can navigate through your hard drive in this window. The right side initially is waiting for you to type in login information for a remote server. This typically is the server address, your username, and password, as described earlier. There is a space to enter the initial path, if you want to start somewhere other than your home directory. In addition, Transmit offers a choice between traditional FTP and secure FTP, which is described later in this chapter.

FIGURE 13.8

Use Transmit to log into a remote FTP server.

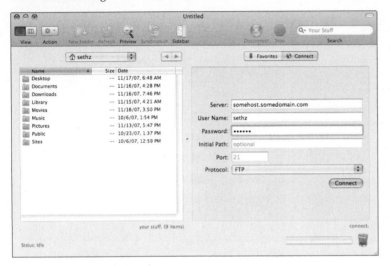

Connecting with a Web browser

Instead of connecting to your FTP server with an FTP client, people can use a Web browser, such as Safari, Internet Explorer, or Netscape Communicator. A Web browser can download files from your computer but can't upload files to it. With a Web browser, people connect to your FTP server with an Internet address (URL) like one of these:

- `ftp://username:password@/10.0.3.27`
- `ftp://mycomputer.mydomain.com`

Substitute your computer's IP address or name. As the Web browser is connecting to your computer, it displays a dialog box asking for a user account name (also called the username or user ID) and password. For FTP access to your computer from a Web browser, specify `ftp://` and your computer's IP address or name as the Internet address, and then enter a user account name and password in the resulting dialog box. Figure 13.9 shows Safari with the Internet address for an FTP server and the dialog box for entering name and password.

Using Safari for the FTP URL mounts your FTP site in the Finder. Figure 13.10 shows this. The FTP site is denoted by the IP address or name.

FIGURE 13.9

FTP File System Authentication

FIGURE 13.10

FTP 127.0.0.1 mounted on the desktop through Safari

Allowing Remote Login

Although FTP isn't secure, Mac OS X includes a different service that is. This service provides encrypted communications between your computer and others on the Internet or any network that is not secure. Other computer users can log in to your computer and copy files back and forth. These remote users of your computer can also control it with Unix commands that they type on their computers.

Mac OS X provides remote login through included OpenSSH server software. OpenSSH is a public version of SSH (secure shell), which provides secure, encrypted communications between two computers over the Internet or any network that is not secure. OpenSSH encrypts all communications and data transfer, preventing eavesdropping, hijacking of connections, and other network attacks.

OpenSSH is actually several software tools that replace several insecure Unix tools. The ssh tool provides remote login and command-line sessions, replacing login and telnet. The scp tool provides file copying, replacing rcp and some FTP functions. The sftp tool provides easier file transfer, replacing FTP.

Because OpenSSH is better for file transfer than FTP, you may wonder why more and better FTP client applications are available. The reason is simple: FTP has been around for decades and OpenSSH has been around only a few years.

Turning remote login on or off

You can turn remote login on or off easily. First, open System Preferences and then choose View ⇨ Sharing (or click the Sharing button). In the Sharing preference pane, click the check box next to Remote Login in the Service list on the left. Figure 13.11 shows remote login turned on in the Sharing preference pane.

FIGURE 13.11

Remote Login turned on with only Administrators having access

If the Sharing preference pane settings are locked, you must unlock them before you can turn remote login on or off. The settings are dim when locked, and the lock button looks locked. To unlock the settings, click the lock button and enter an administrator's user account name and password in the dialog box that appears.

NOTE The first time you turn on the Remote Login option, you may have to wait a minute or so before a check mark appears in the check box. While you're waiting for the OpenSSH service to start up, don't become impatient and click in the check box repeatedly, or you may induce the condition where remote login appears to be turned on but the OpenSSH service is not actually started. If this happens, remote login may appear to be turned on, yet no one is able to connect to your computer by using an SSH client application on another computer. In this case, you can fix the problem by restarting your computer.

In the Remote Login selection in the Sharing pane you can select which users have SSH access. Previously, remote login was on or off for everyone. By default all users have SSH access.

To start specifying which users have access to SSH, first select the Only these users radio button. Click the plus sign at the bottom and select a user you want to give access to SSH. In this case, as shown in Figure 13.11, only Administrators have access. To remove access to a particular user or group, select the user or group and click the minus sign.

Connecting for remote login

When your computer has remote login turned on, other computer users can connect to your computer using SSH client software.

Connecting with the Terminal application

Mac OS X includes an SSH client that can be used from the Terminal window. This means another Mac OS X user can log in to your computer by opening the Terminal application and typing a Unix command similar to the following:

```
ssh -lusername 10.0.3.111
```

In this command, -lusername must be replaced with the remote user's short name on your computer — for example, -lsethz. The -l stands for login; it passes that username to ssh. The -lusername part of the command can be omitted if the remote user has the same short name on your computer and on the remote computer he or she is using.

The IP address must be your computer's IP address or your computer's name, if you have obtained one for it as described at the beginning of this chapter.

The first time you connect to a computer using SSH, Terminal asks you if you want to accept the RSA key fingerprint. This has to be done only once in order to connect.

NOTE You may need to wait a moment or so after entering an **SSH** command for the remote computer to respond, depending upon the speed of the network between your computer and the remote computer.

After logging in to your computer, the remote user can type additional Unix commands in the Terminal application to control your computer. Figure 13.12 shows a Terminal session in which sethz connects remotely to the computer whose IP address is 10.0.3.111 and then uses the w command to see who is using the remote computer.

FIGURE 13.12

Use the ssh command in the Terminal window to log in remotely and control the remote computer with Unix commands.

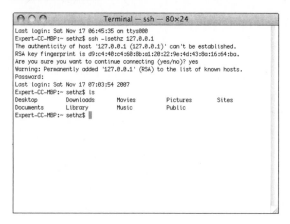

```
Last login: Sat Nov 17 06:45:35 on ttys000
Expert-CC-MBP:~ sethz$ ssh –lsethz 127.0.0.1
The authenticity of host '127.0.0.1 (127.0.0.1)' can't be established.
RSA key fingerprint is d9:c4:40:c4:60:8b:a1:20:22:9e:4d:43:8a:16:64:ba.
Are you sure you want to continue connecting (yes/no)? yes
Warning: Permanently added '127.0.0.1' (RSA) to the list of known hosts.
Password:
Last login: Sat Nov 17 07:03:54 2007
Expert-CC-MBP:~ sethz$ ls
Desktop      Downloads    Movies       Pictures     Sites
Documents    Library      Music        Public
Expert-CC-MBP:~ sethz$
```

Using Transmit for SFTP transfers

SFTP is part of the OpenSSH package. It is designed to be a replacement for a standard FTP client. SFTP uses an encrypted ssh transport to transfer files from your computer to an SFTP server. Think of SFTP as a safer alternative to FTP. Because the transport is encrypted, neither your login information nor the files you're transferring are visible to an outsider. If someone does sniff the network traffic, all he or she will see is encrypted noise rather than clear text information. SFTP is installed as /usr/bin/sftp and is available as a command-line client from the Terminal application.

If you want to use a GUI front end to SFTP, Transmit includes an SFTP mode for copying files between computers via SFTP using Transmit's familiar FTP browser interface. Simply select Secure (SFTP) from the protocol pop-up menu item in the right pane of the Transmit window, where you enter your login information. See Figure 13.13.

FIGURE 13.13

Transmit can log into another computer's SFTP server and securely copy files by using the same two-pane view as it uses for FTP.

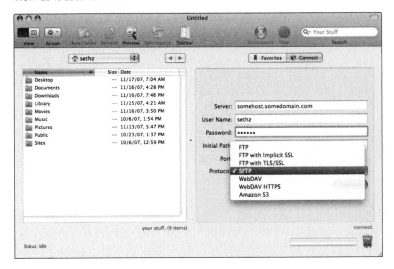

Remote Control

Mac OS X has always had remote control features built into it. In Leopard they are easier to unleash than ever before. There are two ways to initiate Remote Control: one is Screen Sharing, and the other is Apple Remote Desktop. For home users and small installations, Screen Sharing works very well. If you would like more granular control of services and deploying software, Apple Remote Desktop is the way to go.

 **Apple Remote Desktop is not built into Mac OS X. It is a separate application for purchase from Apple.**

Turning on Remote Control

All remote control options are accessible via the Sharing panel in System Preferences. There are two options: Remote Management and Screen Sharing. They perform similar functions.

Remote Management

Remote Management is a new category of feature in Mac OS X. Previously this was called Apple Remote Desktop. This feature allows two things:

- Screen sharing via the Leopard Finder
- The ability to control and manage the computer using Apple Remote Desktop

To turn this feature on, check the box to the left of Remote Management in the Sharing pane of System Preferences. As with Remote Login, you can specify who has access and who doesn't.

Computer Settings

This is where you can specify computer-wide settings and preferences. See Figure 13.14. The following options are available:

- **Show Remote Management in menu bar:** If this option is checked, a small pair of binoculars shows up at the top right of the screen. If a computer monitor surrounds the binoculars, it indicates the computer is being observed.

FIGURE 13.14

Options for Remote Management. Managers can observe but not control the screen.

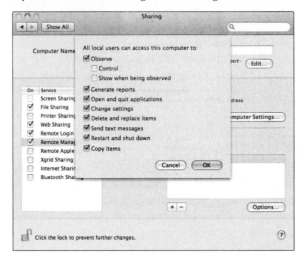

- **Anyone may request permission to control screen:** If you would like guests to request permission to control a computer (such as a presentation computer in a conference room) you can enable this feature.

- **VNC viewers may control screen with password:** VNC (Virtual Network Computing) is an open source remote control software. It is cross-platform, so if you want a Windows machine to control your Mac, enable this option.

- **Computer Information:** When using Remote Desktop you may need a better description of what computer you are controlling or reporting on. Here you can add four lines of text to make reports more descriptive.

Specifying access

You can define who has access to your computer and who doesn't. By default all users have access to remotely manage your Leopard system.

- **Specifying privileges:** Select Options at the bottom right of the window in the Remote Management portion of Sharing in the System Preference pane. Here you can allow users to observe, control, show when being observed, generate reports, open and quit applications, change settings, delete and replace items, send text messages, restart and shut down, and copy items. Each of these settings can be turned off and on.

- **Specifying users:** Select the Only these users radio button. Click the plus sign at the bottom left of the window. Then select the users you want. After you select the user, the Options pop up. Each individual user has his or her own options. You must set that for each user account.

Once the Remote Management service is turned on, the remote computer is accessible in the Apple Remote Desktop software. See Figure 13.15.

FIGURE 13.15

Sharon's Computer and Expert CC MBP have Remote Management turned on.

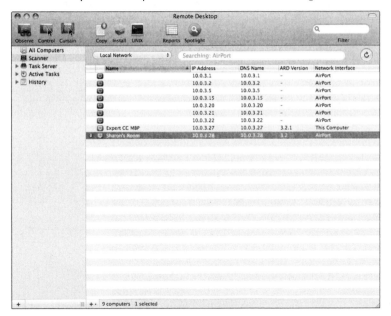

Screen Sharing

This feature is similar to the Remote Management feature. It is only the sharing of your screen. This feature removes any of the file management and reporting aspects available in Remote Management.

Just as in Remote Management, you can specify the computer settings. Here only two options remain, VNC and guest access. In addition, you can specify specific users having access. The process is the same as in Remote Management.

NOTE You cannot have Screen Sharing and Remote Management turned on at the same time. If you only want to control screens and you don't own Apple Remote Desktop, just enable Screen Sharing.

Controlling a computer

After you have turned on Screen Sharing or Remote management, you can control the remote computer. This is accessible via the Finder as well as Apple Remote Desktop.

Remote Desktop

As shown in Figure 13.15, the computers that have Remote Management turned on are listed in the main window of the Remote Desktop application.

If you select the computer you want to control and select Control at the top left of the window, you are prompted for the username and password for that machine. Once you enter it correctly, you will see that computer's screen. See Figure 13.16.

Advanced Apple Remote Desktop usage is beyond the scope of this book. To learn more, visit Apple's Web site at `http://www.apple.com/remotedesktop/`.

FIGURE 13.16

Controlling Sharon's computer using Apple Remote Desktop

476

Using the Finder

You can control any computer screen that has VNC or Remote Management enabled. Just as you can browse computers on your local network to share files, you do the same for screen sharing. Here is how:

1. Double-click your hard drive.

2. In the left column you will see your computers listed under SHARED. Select the computer you want to control.

3. In the upper right of the window, click Share Screen. See Figure 13.17.

FIGURE 13.17

The Finder window connecting to Sharon's computer

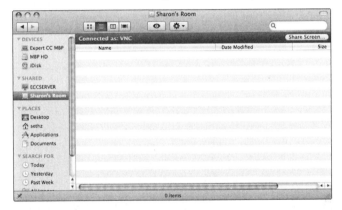

4. Another window pops up asking for a name and password,. See Figure 13.18. Enter your name and password for that machine.

FIGURE 13.18

Asking for credentials for ECC FTP SERVER

You are finished! The Sharing Screen application opens and you see the computer you want to control. See Figure 13.19.

Connecting in other ways

Sometimes the computer you want to connect to is not located locally, or it is not visible via the Finder. You can connect in several other ways.

Using the Sharing Screen application

If you can't see your computer in the Finder, or it is located across the Internet, you can use the Sharing Screen application to connect using the computer's IP Address. The Sharing Screen application is located at /Macintosh HD/System/Library/CoreServices.

You can open this application directly. When you do, it asks you for a Host address. You can enter the IP address or FQDN (Fully Qualified Domain Name), and you're asked for a username and password.

FIGURE 13.19

Controlling Sharon's G4 Tower

Using the Connect To Server option

Just as you can connect to an AFP or SMB volume remotely, you can do the same with screen sharing. In the finder click the Go ⇨ Connect to Server menu or press ⌘ + K. In the Server Address box, type **vnc://WWW.XXX.YYY.ZZZ/** where WWW.XXX.YYY.ZZZ is the server IP address. The Sharing Screen application opens automatically.

Controlling a non-Leopard Mac OS X computer

Screen Sharing uses the Apple Remote desktop service to control screens. It is a derivative of VNC. As long as you have Remote Desktop turned on in System Preferences on the non-Leopard computer, the procedure for connecting to it is similar to connecting to Leopard-based computers. Figure 13.20 shows a Tiger-based Mac being controlled remotely.

FIGURE 13.20

Controlling my Tiger-based Mac using Screen Sharing and Remote Desktop service

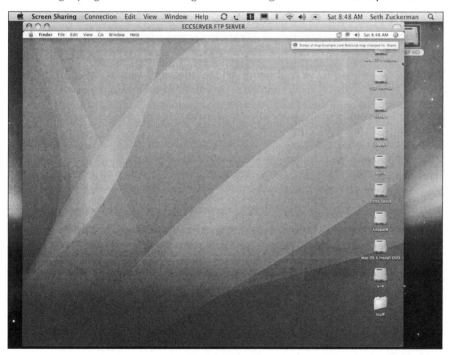

Summary

Here's what you know about Web sharing, FTP access, remote login, and remote control after reading this chapter:

- Every computer on a network or the Internet has an IP address. With Mac OS X, a computer can have a different IP address for Ethernet, modem, AirPort, and other network ports.

- If you have a public IP address, computers on the Internet can use your computer's network services. If you have a private IP address, Internet computers must go through a gateway on your network to use your computer's network services.

- A dynamic IP address may change each time you begin an Internet session or each time your computer starts up. A static IP address doesn't change.

- You can host a Web site by turning on Web sharing in the Sharing preference pane. Your Web site files go in the Sites folder inside your home folder. Files for a joint Web site shared by all users of your computer go in the Documents folder of the WebServer folder in the main Library folder (path /Library/WebServer/Documents/).

- The URL for your personal Web site has the form http://192.168.0.X/~user/ or http://mycomputer.mydomain.com/~user/. The URL for your computer's joint Web site has the form http://192.168.0.X or http://mycomputer.mydomain.com. (Substitute your computer's address or name and the short name of your user account.)

- Mac OS X does not normally allow anonymous FTP access, but you can enable it.

- SFTP is secure FTP and is superior to FTP in terms of security. If the remote host supports SFTP, you should use an SFTP client if possible.

- Turning on the Remote Login option in the Sharing preference pane enables other computer users to securely log in to your computer, copy files, and send Unix commands.

- Remote screen sharing can be enabled on any Mac OS X-equipped Mac.

- You can connect to any computer locally or remotely to control its screen for remote assistance.

Chapter 14

Harnessing .Mac

At the July 2002 MacWorld Expo in New York, Apple CEO Steve Jobs announced that the free suite of Mac-only Internet-based applications and services previously known as iTools would now be fee-based, and its name would be changed to *.Mac* (pronounced "dot Mac").

The .Mac services greatly expand on iTools, and have evolved into a remarkably powerful combination of software and services that help you easily store, share, and protect your files as well as communicate in text, voice, or video. As a result, the number of users willing to pay $99.95 for .Mac has been steadily growing.

Previous versions of Mac OS X had been designed to work with the .Mac services, and Mac OS X 10.5 continues this tradition by integrating .Mac further, now providing a separate .Mac System preference pane, as well as including with it several integrated applications that can take advantage of .Mac services.

In this chapter, you find out about the Internet services .Mac has to offer, including .Mac mail, iCards, Homepage, and the iWeb service. We discuss the applications included with Mac OS X 10.5 that interoperate with each other and with or without the .Mac service: Address Book, iCal, and iWeb. You also explore the main utilities you can download as part of your .Mac membership: Backup and Slides Publisher.

About the .Mac Service

For the .Mac membership fee, you receive the following services:

- **Mac.com e-mail:** The Mac.com e-mail service provides e-mail service from Apple's servers (up to 10GB of storage space), featuring a nifty membername@mac.com address, and Web mail access from any computer with a supported Web browser. You have the option to purchase additional storage.

- **.Mac Web mail:** The Web mail service enables you to access your Mac.com e-mail account from any Web browser.

- **.Mac Address Book:** With the Address Book you can store your contact information on the Web so you can access your e-mail addresses whenever you use .Mac Mail via the Web.

- **iDisk:** iDisk is file storage space on Apple's Internet servers, which can be used to share files with anyone you want, transfer files between computers, or back up your computer's files. The combined e-mail and iDisk initial storage space is 10GB and can be upgraded to a maximum of 30GB of space.

- **iDisk Utility:** The iDisk Utility allows .Mac users to quickly open their iDisk, view or add to their iDisk storage, assign a password and read-write access to their Public folder, or connect to the Public folder of another member's iDisk. Mac OS X 10.3, 10.4, and 10.5 users can access similar functionality through the .Mac System preferences pane. The iDisk Utility is available for Mac OS X and for Windows XP.

- **Backup:** Backup is a utility that can make manual or scheduled copies of your chosen files to your hard disk, a CD, a DVD, or your iDisk.

- **HomePage:** The HomePage service simplifies the creation of personal Web sites to publish text, photos from iPhoto, or movies.

- **iWeb:** Similar to HomePage, a Web site with multimedia content can be created. This includes blogs, RSS feeds, video, and pictures.

- **iCards:** iCards is a digital greeting card service for e-mail, with a wide range of photos or messages to choose from. Standard iCards can be sent without a .Mac membership, but create-your-own iCards, using your own images, requires .Mac membership.

- **Slides Publisher:** This service is an application that creates a slide show of photos on your iDisk that can be viewed over the Internet by anyone with Mac OS X 10.2 and above as a slide show screen saver.

- **Member Benefits:** This is a constantly changing assortment of free downloads, discounted software, and special offers.

- **iCal Publishing:** This allows users to publish their iCal calendars to their iDisk so others can view them over the Internet.

- **.Mac Sync:** This service (located in the .Mac System Preferences) allows the subscriber to synchronize various pieces of data (like contacts and calendars and Keychains) between all of his or her Mac computers by using Apple's .Mac servers as a central synchronization point.

- **Back to My Mac:** Access and control your remote Mac running Mac OS X Leopard from any other Leopard-based Mac.

Requirements to use .Mac

Apple's stated requirements to use the .Mac service are provided in the following list:

- You must be age 13 or older.

- iDisk is accessible using a Macintosh or Windows PC. A Macintosh requires Mac OS 9 or higher. A Windows PC requires Windows 98 (XP or higher). The iDisk utility requires Windows XP. Unix or Linux-based computers can access your iDisk or a Public folder using the Internet file sharing protocol WebDAV.

- Backup requires Mac OS 10.3.9 and higher.

- Back to My Mac requires 10.5 and higher

- .Mac Slides publisher requires 10.2 or higher.

- Mail requires an IMAP- or POP-compatible e-mail client.

- Mac Web browsers: Safari 1.3 or later (Safari 2.0 or later required for Web Gallery); Firefox 1.0.4 or later (Firefox 1.5 or later required for Web Gallery).

- Windows Web browsers: Safari 3 Public Beta; Firefox 1.0.4 or later (Firefox 1.5 required for Web Gallery); Microsoft Internet Explorer 6.0 or later.

NOTE A membership to .Mac costs US $99.95 for one year. If you don't live in the United States, Apple accepts payment in nine other currencies. Check the details on the .Mac "learn more" page at www.mac.com. You can try a limited version of .Mac free for 60 days.

Signing up for a .Mac account

Apple has made signing up for .Mac membership very easy; in fact, we count four different ways to join. Take your pick.

The retail box option

You can buy a .Mac account at any Apple Store or at many other Apple retailers. You get a shrink-wrapped cardboard box that contains a CD, a "Getting Started" instruction card with a .Mac activation key sticker, and two Apple logo stickers.

The CD contains the Backup and iDisk utilities, along with some more in-depth instructions. This software either comes with Mac OS X 10.5 or can be readily downloaded. To ensure that you have the most recent copies, it is best to download them.

To activate the membership, go to www.mac.com/activate, where you enter your activation key, create a new account or upgrade a trial account, and pick your member name and password. You are also asked to provide your contact information, and you have the option to renew your membership automatically by entering credit card information.

The .Mac retail package is a nice way to give a .Mac membership as a gift, but if you already use Mac OS X 10.2 or above and have Internet access, you can join .Mac immediately by signing up online without having to go to a store. (See the following section.)

The online sign-up option

To become a .Mac member by signing up online from any computer with an Internet connection, go to either www.mac.com or to Apple's home page at www.apple.com/dotmac. You will see a

Web page detailing the benefits of a .Mac membership, as shown in Figure 14.1. Here you can sign up for the free 60-day trial. To become a member, click Ready to Join?

FIGURE 14.1

The .Mac welcome Web page

Web page courtesy of Apple, Inc.

The Mac OS X installation option

Signing up for a .Mac account is possible during the initial setup process that follows installation of Mac OS X. If you already have a .Mac account at that time, the Setup Assistant program offers to configure Mac OS X to use your account. If you don't already have a .Mac account, the Setup Assistant offers to create one on the spot. You can also choose to skip either choice and not sign up.

The .Mac System Preferences option

If you are already running Mac OS X and did not create a .Mac account during installation, or if you'd like another .Mac account, you can easily create one at any time. To do this, perform the following steps:

1. **Launch the System Preferences by choosing Apple ⇨ System Preferences or by clicking the System Preferences icon in the Dock.**

2. **Click the .Mac icon or choose View ⇨ .Mac.**

3. **Click the Account panel and then click the Learn More button.** Your Web browser opens and displays the .Mac sign-up page.

Details about signing up

Whichever option you use to join .Mac, you end up at the .Mac sign-up page, shown in Figure 14.2. This page's format could change slightly, but should look very much like what you see here.

You are asked to fill in personal information and select a member name and password. Your member name is what precedes `@mac.com` in your .Mac e-mail address. For example, if you choose "phaedrus" as your member name, your e-mail address will be `phaedrus@mac.com`.

NOTE Your member name cannot be changed after your account is established; however, you can change the password you select at any time.

After you fill out and submit the form, you are informed if your account request was accepted. If you failed to provide some required information, you are asked to resubmit the form with the missing information included. Another possible reason for a rejected request is if your selected member name is already in use. If that problem arises, you are asked to try a different member name, and .Mac suggests some variations of the one you originally proposed.

Next, you are asked to pay for your membership with a credit card (unless you have already entered the activation key from the retail package). Your account automatically renews each year using your credit card information unless you deselect the Auto-Renew check box.

FIGURE 14.2

The .Mac sign-up page

Web page courtesy of Apple, Inc.

After your account exists, you're informed that a copy of your sign-up information has been sent to your new e-mail account. (See Chapter 6 for information on using Mac OS X's Mail application to access your .Mac e-mail.) Following that, you are asked whether you want to send announcement iCards (electronic greeting cards) to people informing them of your new e-mail address. Figure 14.3 shows the .Mac welcome Web page that members see after logging in.

Updating or upgrading your .Mac membership

You can update your address, billing information, or password at any time by going to www.mac.com and clicking "Account" under the .Mac tab. Here you can also upgrade your account to include additional iDisk or e-mail storage space, or additional e-mail-only accounts.

FIGURE 14.3

Apple's .Mac welcome page after logging in

Web page courtesy of Apple, Inc.

You can buy up to 30GB of combined e-mail and iDisk storage, and 10 additional e-mail accounts, whose storage cannot be increased. Recently, Apple increased the total default storage space to 10GB, likely a response to the storage increases given by *free* e-mail accounts, such as the unlimited space offered by Yahoo! and 6GB of Goggle's Gmail. Very thoughtfully, Apple lets you control the allocation of your resources, by allowing you to specify separate storage amounts for your e-mail and your iDisk. You can have as little as 15MB of storage for your e-mail and as much as 30GB of storage for your iDisk, or on the other end of the scale, have as much as 30GB reserved for e-mail and as little as 15MB for your iDisk.

The amount you pay to upgrade is proportional to how much time is left in your yearly membership; that is, the closer it is to your expiration date, the less you pay. It should be noted that holders of free accounts, achieved through certain promotions, cannot upgrade their storage or add e-mail-only accounts. When your free account's renewal period is up, you can choose to convert it into a paid account, which grants you the ability to access these options, but you'll never be able to change it back into a free account.

Configuring Mac OS X for your .Mac account using the .Mac System preference pane

When you get a new .Mac account, you can (and should) configure Mac OS X to use that particular .Mac account. Configuring Mac OS X to use a .Mac account enables you to connect easily to that account's iDisk in the Finder. Doing so also sets up the Mail application to use the account for e-mail the next time it is launched.

To configure Mac OS X for a .Mac account, follow these steps:

1. **Launch System Preferences.** Either choose Apple ➪ System Preferences or click the System Preferences icon in the Dock.

2. **Click the .Mac icon or choose View ➪ .Mac.**

3. **Click the Account pane and then enter your .Mac member name and password.** Figure 14.4 shows the .Mac pane.

FIGURE 14.4

Set up your .Mac account under the Account section of the .Mac preference pane.

If you enter your .Mac member name and password in the Setup Assistant following the installation of Mac OS X, this information is automatically entered into the .Mac System preference pane.

 **NOTE**   If you change your .Mac password (using the mac.com Web site), you must enter the new password in the .Mac System preference pane.

Using the Mac.com e-mail service

.Mac Mail is Apple's premium e-mail service. The following list provides the service's key features:

■ .Mac Mail is a Web-based e-mail account that is ISP (Internet Service Provider) independent. You can keep your Mac.com address if you change your ISP, and send and receive .Mac mail no matter which one you have.

- Your e-mail address is your .Mac member name followed by @mac.com.

- You can use any standard e-mail program to read your mail.

- You can send and receive your e-mail from any Mac or Windows machine with an Internet connection via .Mac Mail on the Web.

- You have a 15MB mailbox that is expandable up to 30GB.

- You can auto-reply to incoming e-mail, which you can set up if you will be away from your e-mail for a while.

- You can forward messages to an alternate e-mail address.

- You can add a text or photo signature to outgoing e-mail messages.

You have two choices to read your .Mac Mail messages. You can configure your e-mail program to receive .Mac Mail messages, or you can use your Web browser to access .Mac Mail on the Web, as described in the following sections.

Setting up Mac OS X Mail to receive .Mac Mail messages

Mac OS X's included Mail application must be set up to receive messages from .Mac Mail. Follow this procedure:

1. Follow the instructions provided earlier in this chapter under the heading "Configuring Mac OS X for your .Mac account using the .Mac System Preference pane."

2. Open the Mail application.

3. Choose Preferences from the Mail menu.

4. Click the Accounts icon.

5. **Click the Add Account (plus sign) button.** See Figure 14.5.

6. From the Account Type pop-up window, choose .Mac.

7. **Enter your account information into the fields.** Your e-mail address is entered automatically from the information in the .Mac System preference pane. See Figure 14.6.

8. Click Continue.

9. After the mail program verifies your account information the Account Summary window appears.

10. Click Continue.

11. You can create another account or click Done.

FIGURE 14.5

The Mail Accounts preferences pane

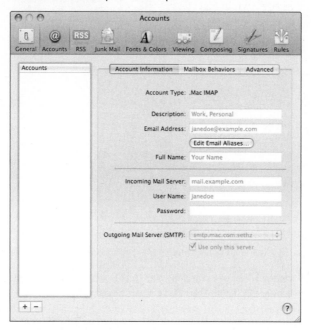

FIGURE 14.6

The Accounts information screen

.Mac Mail on the Web

You can access your .Mac mail account with any Web browser on any Internet-connected computer via its Web interface, shown in Figure 14.7.

FIGURE 14.7

Mac Mail Web interface in two-pane mode

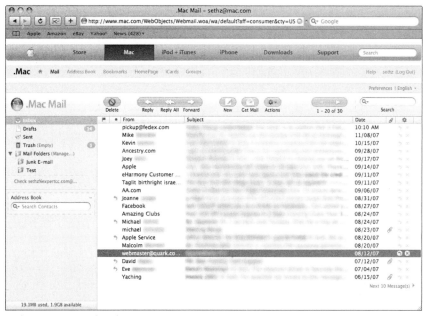

Web page courtesy of Apple, Inc.

To use Mac.com Web mail, follow these steps:

1. **Go to the .Mac Webmail page at** `http://webmail.mac.com/`

2. **Enter your member name and password.** If you have forgotten them, they were sent to you in your .Mac Mail Welcome e-mail message.

3. **The .Mac Mail Web interface opens (see Figure 14.7).**

4. **From here you can reply to current messages, and create new ones and drafts.** These icons are at the top of the screen.

 **All messages created on the Web site will mirror in your e-mail program.**

Setting .Mac Mail preferences

To set preferences for .Mac Mail, click the Preferences icon in the toolbar. Figure 14.8 shows the .Mac Mail on the Web Preferences interface.

FIGURE 14.8

The .Mac Mail on the Web Preferences page

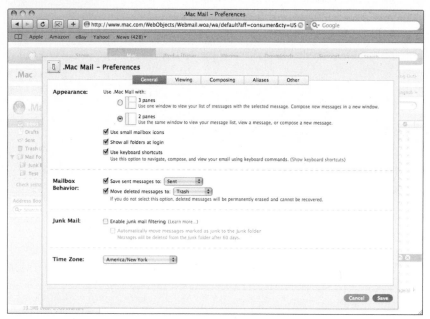

Web page courtesy of Apple, Inc.

The .Mac Web mail Preferences page has five sections: General, Viewing, Composing, Aliases, and Other.

General

In the General section, you can set up the Web mail appearance, mailbox behavior, and time zone. In the Appearance section you can choose two or three panes for viewing your e-mail. Figure 14.7 shows the two-pane view. Figure 14.9 shows the three-pane view. Also, small mailbox icons, showing folders, and keyboard shortcuts can be enabled.

- **Three-pane view:** This option is the default in .Mac Web mail. It is most similar to the Mail program. The main window views the selected message. New messages, replies, and forwards open in a new window.

- **Two-pane view:** This mode keeps all messages in the same window. This includes viewing messages, composing, replying, and forwarding. When you are viewing or editing a message, the message list is hidden with the new message.

- **Small mailbox icons:** When you select this option, small icons in the left column of the main mail page replace the large ones. This allows for more information to be listed on the Web page.

■ **Show Folders at login:** Normally only the Inbox, Drafts, Sent, and Trash folders show, and your Mail Folders that you have created, such as Junk e-mail, are collapsed as shown in Figure 14.7 ("Mail Folders"). When you select Show all folders at login, those Mail Folders will be uncollapsed.

■ **Use Keyboard Shortcuts:** This option allows you to navigate, compose, and view your e-mail using keyboard shortcuts (see Table 14.1).

■ **Save sent messages to:** Most people agree that having copies of their sent messages to reference in the future is a good thing (the author likes to use them as a confirmation that the message was actually sent), but not everyone likes to save them, and they take up room, which is a consideration if space is limited. Use the check box to turn the saving of sent messages on and off. The pull-down menu allows you to select the default sent folder, or one you created.

■ **Move deleted messages to:** Use the appropriate check box to either save a copy of your deleted items to a periodically emptied folder or have them deleted immediately. Those with itchy-deletion-click tendencies will do well to save their deleted items to a separate folder first.

■ **Enable junk mail filtering:** Here you can enable .Mac's built in junk mail filter. If you check this feature, make sure (if you are using the Mail application) you check the "store junk messages on the server" button in the Junk mail Mail preference pane.

■ **Time zone:** Here you can select your time zone so the time stamp is correct when composing messages. If you are on the East Coast, make sure you have Eastern Standard Time selected; otherwise your associates may think you get no sleep!

FIGURE 14.9

.Mac Mail in three-pane mode

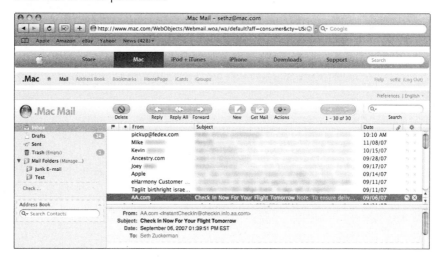

TABLE 14.1

.Mac Web Mail Keyboard Shortcuts

Action	Shortcut
View message	Enter
Compose new message	n
Send message	D
Forward message	f
Reply	r
Reply to all	R
Delete message(s)	Delete key
Next message	Down arrow key
Previous message	Up arrow key
Next batch of messages	Right arrow key
Previous batch of messages	Left arrow key
Mark message(s) as read and unread	u
Flag and unflag message(s)	l
Move message(s) to folder	m
Select all	a
Back to folder	b
Search	/
Print message	p

In the Mailbox Behavior section you can turn on and off saving sent and deleted messages to a specified folder. Depending on where you are located, you can change the time zone as well.

Viewing preferences

In the Viewing section, you can set the number of messages to appear per page, what type of message previews to view, and preferences for HTML e-mails.

- **Message previews:** These are in light gray text located next to the e-mail subject. This is shown in Figure 14.7. Long previews show up to four lines of the message subject and preview. Short previews show one line including the subject and preview.

- **Automatically load images in HTML messages:** This HTML setting is for avoidance of spam and to increase message-loading speed. If you don't enable automatic image loading, when you view an HTML message there will be a link at the top of the message to download images. They do not automatically load. Enabling this option automatically downloads the e-mail images and slows the loading of the message.

- **Enable Show long headers:** Long headers include detailed information about the message, including its return and delivery paths, the Reply-to field, its content type, the original recipient, and more.

Composing preferences

In the Composing section, you can choose an image from your hard drive to use as your photo signature, to appear on outgoing e-mail messages. The image looks best if you use iPhoto to create a 64-x-64-pixel image. You can also enter text in the Signature field to add to each message you send; many people type their name and contact information here, and sometimes a favorite quotation or saying. You can also choose these options:

- Quote original when replying is on by default. It quotes the original message in a reply to a received message. This is very helpful when the recipient may not remember the topic of the message you are replying to.

- Add a Bcc (blind carbon copy) header to every e-mail message, which you can use to add e-mail addresses that will not be visible to the rest of the recipients.

- Encoding outgoing messages in UTF-8: Mac Mail automatically encodes your outgoing messages based on the language used to compose them. Sometimes, however, recipients are still unable to properly view your messages. In this case, you may want to change your encoding preference to UTF-8. This is a universal encoding that is compatible with a wide range of e-mail clients.

- Check Spelling before you send, which brings you to an intermediary spell-check screen before your message is sent, where you can correct misspellings. You can also choose the language of the dictionary.

- Change the appearance of your "Send mail as" name. This field represents the name under which your e-mail messages appear in the inboxes of the people to whom you send your mail.

Aliases preferences

In the Aliases section, Apple has provided a unique service for .Mac subscribers. To help their users (that's us) in the never-ending war on spam, and for the preservation of some anonymity (or just to have a little fun) you can now create up to five aliases to your main .Mac e-mail address. Once you have established an alias, you can use it for things that you'd rather not use your main account for, such as online purchases and those frustrating sites that require your e-mail address for anything you access from them. If your alias becomes prone to spam, or if you're tired of it, you can turn it on and off at will or even delete it permanently!

Tips for Using .Mac Mail on the Web

The following list provides you with helpful tips on using .Mac Mail on the Web:

- A .Mac Mail message must be 20MB or smaller to be sent or received successfully, including any attachments.

- You can create new folders to organize your messages by clicking Manage next to Mail Folders in the left column. Enter the folder name in the dialog box at the bottom, and then click the New Folder button. When done, click Done on the bottom right. The folders you create appear in the left column under Mail Folders; select the folder here to view its contents.

- To move messages to a particular folder, open the message, click the cog at the top of the window, and select move. A window pops up with the list of folders, and there you can select which folder to move the message to.

- Deleted messages are moved to the Deleted Messages folder, where they are saved for 30 days before being permanently deleted. You can manually empty the folder any time you want by clicking Empty next to the trash icon on the left column.

- You can change the folder where deleted messages are saved. Click Preferences and choose a folder from the "Move Deleted Messages To" pop-up menu.

- Search for a specific message in the current folder using the Search field box at the top right of the main .Mac mail screen. You can refine the search in the results window by changing "Show results in:" from All fields to Subject, From, To, and Cc.

- To format a message so that the printed version only contains header information and body text, open the message and then click Print from the cog at the top of the message window. Otherwise, your Web browser prints the .Mac tabs and the .Mac Mail toolbar.

- To make e-mail move faster, you may want to enable the keyboard shortcut commands so you don't have to use the mouse and click to accomplish reading your messages.

- Use the .Mac junk mail filter. As .Mac gets more popular, more and more junk gets sent there. Just make sure you check the Junk folder every few days to make sure something didn't get in their by accident.

To create an alias, click the Create Alias button on the left side of the screen. This brings you to a screen where you can create an alias, which would be an e-mail address that forwards to your main account. Just as when you created your account, the alias must be unique to .Mac.

Other preferences

In this preference section, you can add an external POP account other than .Mac to retrieve your e-mail to the .Mac Web interface. Forwarding and vacation messages can also be set in this preference pane. The following options are available:

- **External Account:** Here you can add another POP account to retrieve e-mail. Simply check the box and enter your e-mail address, incoming mail server, user name for the server, and password. You can also select to leave a copy of the message on the server so you can retrieve e-mail later at home as well as where the e-mail retrieves into. By default it retrieves into the Inbox.

- **Forwarding:** Click the Email Forwarding check box to forward your mac.com e-mail to another address and then enter the destination address in the field. This affects all incoming e-mail, whether you read it using a desktop e-mail program or .Mac Mail on the Web. If you want to keep a copy of the forwarded messages, make sure you check the "Keep a copy of forwarded messages" box. This function is useful when you want have a work e-mail and you want to read your .Mac e-mail, but your office may block the `http://webmail.mac.com` Web site.

- **Automatic reply:** If you are going away and cannot check your e-mail for a while, check the Auto Reply check box and compose your outgoing message in the field below. Every message that comes to your .Mac e-mail address will receive this auto-reply. Keep in mind this does include spam messages as well.

 **AOL's e-mail program cannot be used to view .Mac Mail messages directly, but you can set your .Mac Mail account to forward e-mail to your AOL account.**

Using the .Mac Address Book

The .Mac Address Book exists on the Web for your use when addressing a message in .Mac Mail on the Web. You can add addresses manually, or better yet, have .Mac synchronize it with the Address Book application on your Macintosh.

Add addresses manually to the .Mac Address Book by using the following procedure:

1. Go to `www.mac.com`.
2. Click Address Book.
3. Click New.
4. Enter the contact information.
5. Click Save when done.

You can easily add the sender of a message to your .Mac Address Book from .Mac Mail by opening the message and clicking the sender's e-mail address or name.

To insert an address from the .Mac Address Book to a message you are composing:

1. Click the Address icon on the composing page.
2. Choose an address field from the pop-up window. Click the check mark next to To:, CC:, or Bcc: just to the right of the contact you want to use. That address will be inserted into the field you choose.
3. Click OK.

 If you have not selected Bcc in your preferences, it will not be an option in the Address window.

Using iDisk

An iDisk storage is 10GB or more of space on Apple's Internet Servers that can be mounted on your desktop just like another hard drive on your local system.

Apple calls iDisk "Your personal hard disk on the Internet." You can use iDisk to hide sensitive information you don't want others to find, because iDisk is password protected. You can use iDisk to transfer files between computers that are not otherwise connected. Your iDisk contains, for your convenience, the latest Macintosh software. Your iDisk is an integral part of other .Mac services.

iDisk is tightly integrated into Mac OS X 10.5. The functionality of iDisk Utility, which works with Mac OS X 10.1, 10.2, and 10.3, has now been integrated into the Mac OS X 10.4 and 10.5 .Mac System preference pane. Starting under 10.3 and continuing in 10.5, you can now even create a local copy of your iDisk and synchronize it with the Internet iDisk automatically. Doing this gives you access to your iDisk even without an Internet connection.

All you need to use an iDisk in Mac OS X is the Finder, which is specially designed to work with iDisks.

Connecting to iDisks with Mac OS X

After configuring Mac OS X for your .Mac account, as explained earlier in this chapter, you can connect to your iDisk through the Finder. You can connect to another iDisk if you know the name and password of the corresponding .Mac account. You can also connect to an iDisk with a Web browser.

Connecting to your iDisk with the Finder

If you have configured Mac OS X with your .Mac member name and password, you can open your iDisk with the Finder, which mounts its icon on your desktop and allows you see its contents and copy files to or from it. To open your iDisk in Mac OS X 10.5, follow these steps:

1. Click the Finder in your Dock.
2. Under the Go menu, click iDisk. The iDisk submenu appears.
3. Click My iDisk. Note that you have options to open another user's iDisk or Public folder in the submenu. See Figure 14.10.

After a short time, the iDisk icon appears in the left column of your Finder window with your member name. A window showing its contents should automatically open. You can also press ⌘+Shift+I to connect to your iDisk if you are in the Finder.

Alternatively, you can click the iDisk icon in the sidebar of any Finder window to mount your personal iDisk set in the System Preference pane.

 You must be connected to the Internet to mount an iDisk on your desktop.

FIGURE 14.10

Choose My iDisk from the Finder's Go menu to connect to your iDisk.

Connecting to another member's iDisk with the Finder

If you want to connect to the iDisk of other .Mac members, they need to provide you with their .Mac member name and password. This is a good way to allow someone you trust to transfer files to you. Follow these steps:

1. **Switch to the Finder.**
2. **Under the Go menu, click iDisk.** The iDisk submenu appears.
3. **Choose Other User's iDisk.** The Connect to iDisk dialog box opens.
4. **Enter their member name and password.**
5. **Click Connect.**

After a moment, the iDisk icon appears on the desktop. Its name is the .Mac member's name. A window showing its contents should automatically open.

Connecting to another member's Public folder with the Finder

Each iDisk contains a Public folder that can usually be easily accessed by others without entering your .Mac password. All they need to know is your .Mac member name, unless you change your Public folder's default settings in the .Mac System preference pane (which is described in the next section) to require a password.

The Public folder of your iDisk is interesting because it enables you to share files with other Internet users, whether they are using a Mac or PC. Anything you place in this folder is automatically available to users who access it. Only you can change the contents of your Public folder. Conversely, you can see and copy, but can't change, files in the Public folder of anyone else's iDisk.

Follow these steps to connect to another member's Public folder:

1. **Switch to the Finder.**
2. **From the Go menu, click iDisk.** The iDisk submenu appears.
3. **Choose Other User's Public Folder.** The Connect to iDisk Public folder dialog box opens.
4. **Enter the Member Name.**
5. **Click Connect.**

After a short delay, the Public Folder icon appears on the desktop. You see an iDisk icon suffixed with a `-public` extension after the member name. A window showing its contents should automatically open.

Connecting to an iDisk with a Web browser

Apple's recommended method of connecting to an iDisk from Mac OS X is to use the Finder, and from Windows to use the iDisk utility. If those methods do not work, it might be possible to use your Web browser. In the Web browser, go to `http://idisk.mac.com/membername`, and enter the appropriate member name and password when prompted. Clicking OK should grant you access to your iDisk in the OS X Finder or in Windows Explorer.

Viewing an iDisk

If you double-click an iDisk, it opens and you see a regular Finder window containing several folders, some of which have the same names as the standard folders of your home folder. You also see a document that you can open to read what Apple has to say about iDisks.

You may notice that items appear slowly in an iDisk window. The iDisk performance is limited by the speed of your Internet connection, as well as the speed of Apple's servers where your files are stored. However, Mac OS X improves subsequent performance of the iDisk by caching a directory of the iDisk contents. Figure 14.11 shows the folders of an iDisk.

The folders that your iDisk contains are

- **Documents:** Anything can be stored in this folder. Only you have access to items inside of it.
- **Pictures:** JPEG or GIF files copied here can be used to create custom iCards or display them on your Web pages via HomePage.
- **Movies:** QuickTime movies copied here can be displayed on your Web pages via HomePage.
- **Public:** Files copied here can be shared with others who know your .Mac member name. HomePage can create a file-sharing Web page that permits any and all Internet users to copy items from your Public folder. You can also password protect this folder and assign read-only or read-and-write access to it.

FIGURE 14.11

The folders inside an iDisk

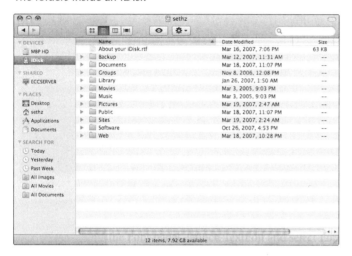

- **Sites:** HomePage stores your Web pages in this folder. You can also put Web pages you create with other applications in this folder to publish them.

- **Music:** This folder can be used to store your music files.

- **Backup:** This folder is read-only and contains files copied here by the Backup utility. Files can be copied from this folder, but can be deleted only with the Backup utility.

- **Groups:** This folder contains folders for each of the .Mac groups you belong to. Each group's folder in turn contains six subfolders — Sites, Pictures, Movies, Documents, Public, and Web — accessible to members of that group.

- **Library**: This folder contains files that support the iSync software.

- **Web**: This folder is the place where iWeb publishes its Web pages and RSS feeds.

- **Software:** This folder is read-only and contains Apple's changing selection of the latest software for downloading. Files cannot be copied to this folder, and its contents are not included in your iDisk capacity.

 Folders on your iDisk are similar to the folders in your computer's home folder except for a few additional folders.

Copying items to and from an iDisk

You can copy files and folders to and from an iDisk just as you copy files to and from any other disk. For example, you can copy an item by dragging it from one Finder window that shows your home folder to another Finder window that shows a folder on an iDisk. Be prepared for the copying of large files to take a while. Copying to or from an iDisk is akin to uploading and downloading files over the Internet, which is far slower than the speed of your computer's hard drive or optical drive.

Opening files

Instead of copying files from an iDisk and then opening the copies from your home folder, you can open files directly from an iDisk. An iDisk is just another disk, and files on it can be opened using the usual methods for opening files from your home folder. Opening a file from an iDisk takes longer than opening the same file from your hard drive because the file contents are transferred at the speed and reliability of your Internet connection. Therefore, you should avoid opening applications or large documents directly from an iDisk.

Getting software from an iDisk

One folder visible from every iDisk, the Software folder, doesn't actually take up any of the storage capacity allotted to the iDisk. The Software folder works like an alias, giving you access to a number of applications from Apple and third-party software developers, which you may find useful.

Because the contents of this folder are constantly changing, it is not possible here to enumerate the files in it. Just remember that it is a handy place to look for software — from games to productivity tools. To use an application from the Software folder, copy the application's disk image or installer file to your home folder, and then double-click the copied file to install the software.

CAUTION   Be aware that many of the applications from the Software folder are without any warranty of fitness and can even be preliminary or limited versions of commercial products. Read the accompanying documentation files before installing the application.

Using your iDisk with Mac OS 9

Mac OS 9 does not natively support WebDAV, the file connection protocol used for Apple's iDisks. WebDAV is a way of transferring files back and forth using an http connection. Apple recommends downloading the WebDAV software from www.webdav.org/goliath and installing it in order for Mac OS 9 users to access their iDisks.

Using your iDisk with Microsoft Windows

If you're not near a Mac and need a file from your iDisk, you can open your iDisk on a computer with Microsoft Windows XP, Windows ME, Windows 98, or Windows 2000.

- In Windows XP, download the iDisk utility from the .Mac downloads section of the www.mac.com Web site.

- In Windows ME or Windows 98, double-click the My Computer icon, double-click the Web Folders icon, and double-click Add Web Folder. As the location to add, enter http://idisk.Mac.com/membername where membername is your .Mac member name.

- In Windows 2000, open My Computer, choose Map Network Drive from the Tools menu, and click Web folder or FTP site. As the location to add, enter http://idisk.Mac.com/membername where membername is your .Mac member name.

Disconnecting from an iDisk

When you finish using an iDisk, you can disconnect from it by dragging its icon to the Trash. When you drag an iDisk in Mac OS X, the Trash icon changes to look like an Eject symbol (a triangle with a line below it) and its name changes to Disconnect. Disconnecting an iDisk removes it from the Finder and terminates your connection to it.

You can leave an iDisk connected as long as you like. Connection time is unlimited in Mac OS X. (In Mac OS 9, connection time is limited to one hour or 30 minutes of inactivity.)

iDisk's .Mac System preference settings

One of the areas within the .Mac System preferences pane is called iDisk. This iDisk section gives you information regarding the status of your iDisk storage space and grants you control over certain settings and functionality, as shown in Figure 14.12.

FIGURE 14.12

The .Mac System preference pane's iDisk panel with the iDisk public folder is set to Read only.

In the iDisk panel, you can:

- Check the amount of iDisk space you are using with the graphic display. (There is a graphical representation of the space currently used, and the iDisk's total capacity.)
- Purchase additional iDisk space by clicking the Upgrade Storage button.
- Start and stop iDisk syncing, which creates a local copy of your iDisk, and choose to synchronize its files either manually or automatically. (In the default setting, syncing is disabled.)

■ Configure your Public folder to allow others Read only or Read & Write access. (The default setting is Read only.) Figure 14.13 shows the icon for an iDisk Public folder.

FIGURE 14.13

The icons for a mounted iDisk Public folder and a local iDisk

■ Enabling the Sync feature, allowing multiple Macs to mirror each other, including the dock, applications, bookmarks, widgets, mail settings, and so on.
■ Back to my Mac remote control software can be enabled. This allows other Macs with Leopard installed and connected to your .Mac account to control the enabled computer.
■ Configure your Public folder to use a password you set to protect your Public folder.

Figure 14.14 shows the preference pane's Accounts section.

FIGURE 14.14

The .Mac system preference pane

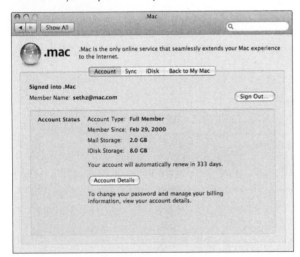

Making a local copy of your iDisk

Mac OS X 10.5 has a feature that debuted in OS X 10.3 and makes it possible to have your iDisk permanently visible and accessible on your desktop, even when you are not connected to the Internet. Mac OS X does this by creating a local copy of your iDisk on your hard drive, and automatically synchronizing it with the remote iDisk when you are connected.

To create a local copy of your iDisk, open the .Mac System preference pane to the iDisk panel and click the Start button, which turns syncing on. Then close the System Preferences window; the process of copying immediately begins. If you open a Finder window, a wheel with two arrows appears next to the iDisk icon, as shown in Figure 14.15. A progress bar appears at the bottom of the window if you select the iDisk. When the creation process is finished, you can choose to sync your iDisk manually as well as automatically.

Working with this Instant iDisk has a few key advantages. Now you can make changes to your iDisk anytime, even from a PowerBook as you travel. The changes you make happen faster because your Internet connection speed is no longer a factor. The changes can be synced with the remote iDisk whenever you next connect to the Internet.

FIGURE 14.15

The two arrows in a circle next to the iDisk icon appear as you are creating a local copy of your iDisk.

Copy in progress

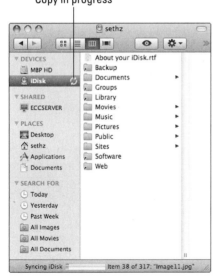

After the copying process begins, you cannot cancel it. If you have lots of files, this initial synchronization can take a very long time.

When the process of copying is complete, the wheel with two arrows next to the iDisk icon disappears. Your local copy of your iDisk is represented by your member name on the desktop, as opposed to the iDisk icon in the Finder window. They are essentially seamless. Apple wants you to consider the local and remote iDisks as a single entity, as well you should. As soon as you write data to your iDisk, it begins to copy said data back to Apple's servers. You can tell that this process is ongoing by the progress bar that appears under the iDisk window.

 This is different from the Sync portion of the preference pane. It has a similar name, but this syncs the entire iDisk. The other one syncs your settings.

After you have created a local copy of your iDisk, any changes you make to it are automatically synchronized with the remote iDisk at set intervals when you are connected to the Internet. If you log out, restart, or shut down your Mac during the syncing process, it continues after you log in again.

You can check when your iDisk was last synchronized in a Finder window. Click the iDisk icon in the sidebar and information at the bottom of the window shows the date and time of last synchronization. If your iDisk is in the process of syncing, a progress bar appears. Figure 14.15 shows the complete iDisk synchronization.

You can also manually synchronize your iDisk at any time — for example, before you log out or shut down the computer — to ensure that any changes you made were duplicated.

To manually synchronize your iDisk, choose the manual synchronization option in the iDisk panel of the .Mac System preference pane. You might want to turn off automatic synchronization if you are on a slow Internet connection, or you notice that the background synching is really slowing your system down. To force synchronization, right-click (or Control+click) your iDisk on the desktop and click Sync Now. You can also open a Finder window and click the two arrows in a circle next to the iDisk icon.

You can turn off the local/remote synchronizing all together by clicking the Stop button that now appears (in place of the Start button) in the iDisk section of the .Mac preferences. Once this button is clicked, Mac OS X changes the local copy of your iDisk into a disk image that it saves on your Desktop. The disk image will have a copy of everything that was in your local copy of your iDisk, preserving your access to files that had not been transferred (by synchronization) to the remote copy. If you now connect to the remote copy of your iDisk, the files that had been successfully transferred will still be there.

A synchronization conflict can occur when you make different changes to the same file on your iDisk from more than one computer. You are asked which version of the file you want to save. To replace the file on the remote iDisk with the version on the local iDisk of the Mac you are using, select This Computer and click Keep Selected. To keep the version on the remote iDisk, select .Mac and click Keep Selected. You can save both versions of the file to your iDisk by clicking Keep Both.

You can compare the files on the local and remote iDisks in order to decide which choice to make, by opening each version of the file. In the Finder's Go menu, choose iDisk and My iDisk in the submenu. Double-click the file to open it.

Back to My Mac

A new feature in Leopard is Back to my Mac. This allows any Leopard-equipped Mac that is attached to your .Mac account to be controlled by another Leopard-equipped Mac also tied to your .Mac account. You can enable screen and/or file sharing with this feature.

To enable this feature, follow these steps:

1. **Click the Start button in the "Back to My Mac" panel in the .Mac system preference.**
2. **Select the services you would like to enable in the Back to My Mac feature.**
3. **Turn on the appropriate service in the Sharing system preference.** You can click on the "Open Sharing Preferences" button or navigate to it using the view menu in System Preferences. How to enable these specific features is covered in more detail in Chapter 13.

Once you have enabled "Back to My Mac," you can use these features when on another Leopard-equipped Mac. If both computers are connected to the Internet and connected to your .Mac account, you are ready to go! Your shared computer(s) will show up in the Finder on the second computer in the left column under "Shared." Select the computer, and you will see the folders that are shared on that computer. You have access to them by clicking on them just like your iDisk. You also can click the "Share Screen" button to control your other Macintosh computer.

Back to my Mac requires either an AirPort base station with NAT-PMP (NAT Port Mapping Protocol) or a third-party Internet router with UPnP (Universal Plug and Play) technology. You must enable this in your router or AirPort base station to allow Back to My Mac to work. See `http://docs.info.apple.com/article.html?artnum=302510` to understand how to configure an AirPort to allow NAT-PMP.

The following AirPort products work with Back To My Mac:

- AirPort Express
- Airport Extreme Base Station (all models)

The following AirPort products do not support Back To My Mac:

- AirPort Base Station (Graphite)
- AirPort Base Station (Dual Ethernet)

For a list of third-party routers that support Back to my Mac visit `http://docs.info.apple.com/article.html?artnum=306803`.

 You will have varied success with Back to My Mac. At present it does not work consistently. In the future, Apple presumably will come out with bug fixes to address these issues.

Security concerns

Almost immediately after Leopard shipped, security users started raising concerns about Back to My Mac. It opens up remote access to machines that are otherwise protected. For the record, .Mac passwords and the .Mac authentication process have never been cracked, but phishing or a malicious Web site could fool someone into revealing their password.

iDisk Tips

The following list provides you with helpful tips on using iDisk:

- Check the amount of storage available in your iDisk on a regular basis. If you exceed your iDisk storage quota, you receive a warning message in your Mac.com e-mail account. If you do not promptly delete enough files to be within your quota, iDisk automatically deletes the excess files! You might want to buy more storage space at this point.

- You may become alarmed if you are not prompted to enter a password when opening your iDisk. Not to worry; this is actually normal. The password information is automatically pulled from the .Mac System Preference iDisk panel, and is stored in the Keychain, so you don't need to enter it. If you are concerned that others can fiddle with your iDisk while you are away from your computer, log out, or set the screen saver to activate after a specified interval of time and to prompt for a password to disable it, or upon waking from sleep.

- If you are trying to open the .Mac System preference pane to the iDisk panel, a message can appear that says "There's a problem connecting to the iDisk server at this time. Please try again later." However, your iDisk seems fine. If you get this message, check to see if the date and time settings are correct in System Preferences. These settings can change by themselves under certain circumstances, and this can interfere with the iDisk's communications with System Preferences.

- If you connect to an iDisk from a Windows or Unix computer, or from the Mac OS X Terminal application, you may see two .HSicon files on your iDisk that you do not recognize. Don't delete them! They provide the iDisk icon images for Mac OS 9 users.

- If you use multiple computers, consider turning on the Sync feature. It aids in standardizing your computers.

- If you are a mobile user and need access to a home office workstation, consider Back to My Mac. It is a great way to keep in touch with your home computer in case you leave something on your other computer and you need to access it.

.Mac Password Authentication

To use Back to My Mac, as noted earlier, you have to have an active .Mac account and enter your account name and password in the .Mac preference pane. .Mac uses a secure authentication process to validate your account information with .Mac, which, if successful, hands back a couple of certificates that are used to validate your account . These certificates can be viewed in Keychain Access. They're named starting with your .Mac account name and then "(.Mac Sharing Key)" and "(.Mac Sharing Certificate)."

Kerberos Tickets

Back to My Mac relies on a security system developed at MIT called Kerberos. Kerberos lets two parties who have previously identified themselves to each other — in this case, through .Mac digital certificates — to validate each other's identity and share information securely. The system can issue tickets, which authorize certain access for specific periods of time.

In the case of Back to My Mac, the .Mac sharing key and certificate are used to validate one Back to My Mac computer to another, after which a ticket is issued that lasts for 10 hours and allows remote control or remote file sharing. Tickets can be viewed via Keychain Access by selecting Kerberos Ticket Viewer from the Keychain Access menu.

IPsec Tunneling

The connection between two Leopard machines is established with a pair of IPSec tunnels. IPSec is a basic VPN protocol used by Apple and other VPN devices. This is discussed more in detail in Chapter 11.

Despite these strong measures, concerns still exist. One troubling basic bit of bad behavior is that the Leopard firewall doesn't prevent the use of Back to My Mac even when its most restrictive setting is applied to block all incoming connections. Blocking UDP connections to port 4500 through a third-party firewall package prevents Back to My Mac from functioning. Newly updated firewall software for Leopard can accomplish this task. DoorStop X from Open Door ($49) and Intego NetBarrier X4 ($69.95) can both block ports. I would expect this Back to My Mac flaw to be fixed or at least better explained in a Leopard security update.

More concerning is the single password. This enables such broad access to one's computer. This is despite the measures taken to secure the .Mac authentication process and Back to My Mac.

Back to My Mac is a new technology for Apple. As more issues arise, and features are added, it will change and grow. Just like most Apple technologies, they usually improve as time goes on. For more information on Back to my Mac visit `www.apple.com/dotmac/backtomymac.html`.

HomePage

HomePage is a .Mac online service that easily creates professional-looking, personalized Web sites that you can use to share photos, movies, text, or files. Anyone with a computer with an Internet connection and Web browser can access your sites, unless you choose to password-protect them. To access tools to create and edit your HomePage, follow these steps:

1. **From your Web browser, go to** `www.mac.com`.
2. **At the .Mac home page, click HomePage on the top navigation bar.**
3. **Log in using your member name and password.** The HomePage welcome page appears.

On the HomePage welcome page, note the category tabs on the left. These are the categories of Web site designs you can choose from. Each tab is connected to the large area to its right that shows thumbnails of the theme pages available in the selected category.

Creating a Web page with HomePage

If you are making a Photo Album, first drag your pictures to the Pictures folder on your iDisk. Create a folder with the group of photos you want to use. If you are making a file-sharing page, first drag the files you want to share to the Public folder on your iDisk. To create a Web page using HomePage, follow these steps:

1. From the HomePage welcome page, click the category tabs and look at the thumbnails until you find a theme design that you like. See Figure 14.16.

FIGURE 14.16

Select a theme from the category tabs.

2. **Click the desired theme thumbnail.**

3. **Select the folder that contains the photos you want on your new page.** See Figure 14.17. Clicking Choose when you are done with your selection takes you to the Edit your page theme page where your chosen images already appear.

Select the source for the homepage.

4. **Next the Edit your page window opens with the theme you have selected.** If you don't like what you see, click the Themes icon on the upper right, and you are returned to select another theme from that category. Selecting the theme brings you back to the edit page.

   You will see self-explanatory instructions and labels to help you identify various text entry fields, such as image captions and page titles. Some theme pages allow you to select from a choice of layouts. See Figure 14.18.

5. **Drag images to the correct positions.** If you are unhappy with the organization of the photos on the page, you can drag them around the page to reorganize them.

FIGURE 14.18

Customize captions and label.

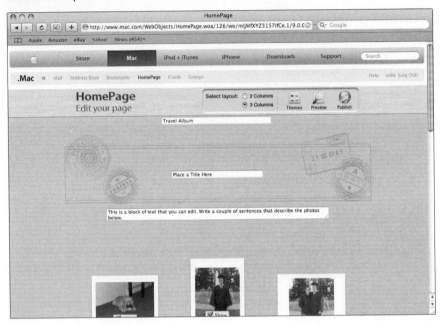

6. **Choose to display a visitor counter or a Send me a message button that enables visitors to send you an iCard with their feedback.** Click the Show check box next to these features to include them in your Web page. Some pages allow you to type in links so your visitors can view your other pages.

   If at any time you want to start over, click the word HomePage in the title bar. You will be returned to the HomePage welcome page.

7. **When the page looks the way you want, click the Publish icon at the top right.** Your page is placed on the Web.

   The Congratulations page appears. You have the option to click the link and see your page, send and iCard to tell your friends about the page, or click the Return to HomePage button to do just that.

If you click the Return to HomePage button, you notice that the HomePage welcome page now features a new area at its top that is customized for your Web site. Here you will find the new URL to reach this page (it changed when you published your first page). There is a list of pages you have published, and you can add, delete, or edit the pages using the buttons under the list. With the buttons on the right, you can announce your site, learn about new features, protect this site, or add another site.

Updating a Web page

You can make changes to any of your Web pages at any time. Follow these steps:

1. **From the HomePage welcome page, select the site that contains the page you want to change from the Site list.**

2. **Select the page you want to change from the Page list.**

3. **Click the Edit button below the lists.** The page appears in Edit mode.

4. **Make your desired changes.** Changes are performed the same way you created the HomePage.

5. **Click Publish when you are done.** The updated page will be available on the Web immediately.

To update a Photo Album page, first put the new pictures in the folder on your iDisk that contains the original pictures.

To set up or edit Web links or e-mail links (only on certain types of HomePages), in Edit mode find the link you want to edit. To set up a Web link, click the Edit Link button. The Edit your links page appears, as shown in Figure 14.19. Click the tab for what you want to do. My Pages allows you to pick another of your pages to link to; Other Pages allows you to type the URL for a page outside of your site; and Email allows you to enter an e-mail address. Click Apply when done.

FIGURE 14.19

The HomePage Edit your links page

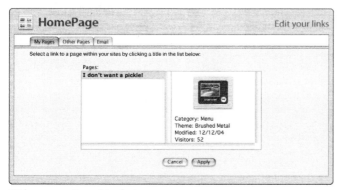

Web page courtesy of Apple, Inc.

Creating another Web site

You can create more than one Web site in HomePage. A Web site is a collection of Web pages with a designated start page (which visitors see first) and its own Web address.

1. **From the HomePage welcome page, click the Add another site button.** (The name of this button changes to Add if you already have more than one site.) The Create a site page appears, as shown in Figure 14.20.

2. **Type a name for the site.** If you want the site to have password protection, click the On check box and enter the password you want.

FIGURE 14.20

The HomePage Create a site page

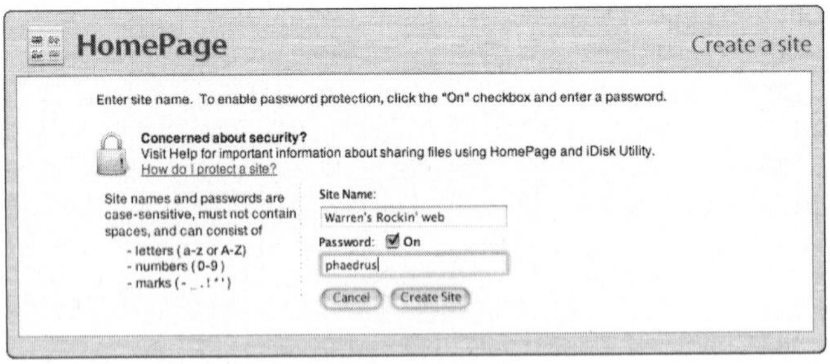

Web page courtesy of Apple, Inc.

3. **Click the Create Site button.** The site is created.

4. **You are returned to the HomePage welcome page, where you can now see the new site name in the Sites list and the new URL at the top.**

> **TIP** Creating additional Web sites creates subfolders inside your Sites folder to hold them, bearing the name of the site within. The contents of these folders may be viewed in the Finder, but any attempt to modify the folder or its contents results in an alert. If you want to store files or Web pages in your Sites folder, you can store them at the root level of the Sites folder or create new subfolders with the Finder.

Deleting a page or site

You can remove pages from your Web site or delete the entire site whenever you want. Follow this procedure:

1. **From the HomePage welcome page, select the page you want to delete in the Page list, or the site you want to delete in the Site list.**

2. **Click the Delete button below the lists.** The selected items disappear.

HomePage Tips

The following list provides you with helpful tips on using HomePage:

- If others frequently must access your iDisk's Public folder to retrieve files you have left for them, consider creating a .Mac HomePage file-sharing Web page. To do so, in the HomePage welcome page, click the File Sharing tab. If you do not password-protect the page, anyone on the Internet can see and download the files in your Public folder from this page.

- You can change the order of the links to other pages in your site that HomePage automatically puts at the top of each Web page you create. Just drag the page titles in the Pages list into the order you want. The page at the top of the list is the start page for the site, and is listed in bold type.

- Before you put files, pictures, or movies on your Web pages, you should prepare them in the following ways:

  - **Files:** Special characters in some file names may be incompatible with naming conventions on other computers accessing the files. So to be safe, alter the file names to conform to these rules. Use only uppercase letters (A–Z), lowercase letters (a–z), numbers (0–9), and the underscore (_) in your file names. Never begin a file name with a period (.), or the file will become invisible, and only use the period to separate a file name extension from the rest of the name. Include these extensions (such as Report.doc or Photo.jpg) in the file name, so all computers will know how to open them. Because some computers use short file names, use eight or fewer characters to name them — 12 if you count the three-letter extension. Don't forget to copy the files to your iDisk's Public Folder.

  - **Pictures:** Save your pictures in JPEG or GIF format, and add the extension .jpg or .gif to the end of the file name. Name the pictures files in accord with the rules listed in the previous section about file naming conventions. Don't forget to copy the pictures to your iDisk's Pictures folder.

  - **Movies:** Export your iMovie as a QuickTime file, and add .mov to the end of its file name. Don't forget to copy the movie to your iDisk's Movies folder.

- You don't have to use the HomePage service; you can use any HTML authoring tool to create your .Mac Web site pages. For example, you can use applications such as BareBones Software's BBEdit (www.barebones.com), Adobe GoLive (www.adobe.com), or Macromedia Dreamweaver (www.macromedia.com). After you prepare the Web pages, put them in the Sites folder on your iDisk, in a subfolder if there is already more than one site there.

- Looking for more functionality? Consider using iWeb; there you can add multimedia, Weblogs, and RSS feeds.

continued

continued

- You can password-protect your HomePage Web sites so that they are accessible only to people with a password you have provided. On the HomePage welcome page, if you have only one Web site, click Protect this site. If you have more than one site, select the site in the Sites list and click Edit below the list. On the Edit your site page, put a check in the password check box, type a password, and click Apply Changes. Change the password any time using the same steps. Don't forget to also password-protect your Public folder! Visitors see this page when you password-protect your HomePage Web site.

Deleting a site also deletes all that site's pages. If you have only one site, delete all the pages in the site to delete the site. Don't forget to remove pictures from the Pictures folder after you have deleted a page containing them in order to conserve space on your iDisk.

NOTE The first site you create with HomePage cannot be deleted like any of the other sites you create, because it is the "root" site. If you no longer want to use it, leave it empty, and the Start Site automatically changes to a site containing published pages.

.Mac Slides Publisher

If you are a .Mac member, .Mac Slides Publisher is an application you can use to share your digital photos as a slide show screen saver using your iDisk. Anyone using Mac OS X 10.2 or higher can view the slide show after it downloads from the Internet. When users subscribe to your slide show, they automatically receive updates to your slide show whenever you change it and publish it.

Download .Mac Slides Publisher from the .Mac Web site at www.mac.com or from your iDisk in the Software section, and run the Installer. The application is installed to the Applications folder. You may want to put an alias of it in the Dock to drag photos to it more easily.

If you attempt to launch .Mac Slides Publisher, you will see that it has no interface; it shows you a window with simplified instructions. You just drag photos to it and it does the rest.

To share your photos in a slide show, follow these steps.

1. **Make sure that all of your photos are in the JPEG file format.** It is helpful to first put the photos in a folder.

2. **Select the photos you want.** Remember that you can make a multiple selection by pressing and holding the ⌘ key as you click each photo, or by pressing and holding the Shift key and clicking the first and last photos to select them and all the photos listed in between.

3. **Drag the selected photos one at a time or all at once to the .Mac Slides Publisher icon.**

4. **Click Publish.** The photos are copied to your iDisk.

5. **When the photos are copied, click the Announce Slideshow button to tell others how to subscribe to your slide show.**

A .Mac membership is not required to subscribe to the slide shows.

To subscribe to a slide show, follow these steps:

 NOTE To subscribe to a slide show, you must be using Mac OS X 10.2 or higher.

1. **Open System Preferences.**

2. **Click Desktop & Screen Saver.**

3. **Click the Screen Saver button.**

4. **Select .Mac and RSS in the Screen Savers list.**

5. **Click the Options button.** The Subscriptions and Display Options sheet drops down, as shown in Figure 14.21.

6. **Click the plus sign to add a .Mac or RSS connection.** Choose .Mac or RSS feed.

7. **Select the slide shows you want to see, enter the .Mac member name or RSS feed in the box, and check the Display Options you want.**

8. **Click OK.** The slide show is downloaded to your computer.

After the slide show has been downloaded, it appears when the screen saver is activated. An Internet connection is no longer necessary and is used only when available to check for updates.

FIGURE 14.21

Select the slide shows you want to view in the Desktop and Screen Saver System Preference Subscriptions and Display Options sheet.

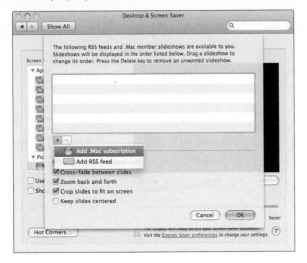

To unsubscribe from a slide show, follow these steps:

1. Open System Preferences.

2. Click Desktop & Screen Saver.

3. Click the Screen Saver button.

4. Select .Mac and RSS in the Screen Savers list.

5. **Click the Options button.** The Subscriptions and Display Options sheet drops down, as shown earlier in Figure 14.21.

6. To temporarily disable a slide show, uncheck the Selected check box to the left of the Slide Show name.

7. To remove a slide show from the list, select it and click the minus button.

iChat AV

In recent years, the use of instant messaging (IM) has rapidly increased. Millions of people enjoy its unique advantages. IM lets you type a short message and send it instantly to a recipient, who sees the message on-screen and can respond with a message of his or her own. With IM, you are having a live conversation, called a *chat*.

America Online enabled the popularity of instant messaging with its AOL Instant Messenger (AIM) system. Because of its great success, it has had many emulators, but it has endured as the most popular chat protocol by a wide margin. Apple's iChat brings instant messaging to Mac OS X and supports AIM. As of Mac OS X 10.4, Jabber, an alternative IM protocol, is also supported.

At the 2003 World Wide Developers Conference, Steve Jobs announced iChat AV, which adds live voice and video capabilities to iChat's text messaging capabilities. He also introduced the iSight video camera, the first Web camera to bear the Apple logo, which works seamlessly with iChat AV. Under Tiger, iChat can handle video and audio chats with multiple participants; up to four people in a single video chat, and up to 10 people in a single audio chat. iChat makes use of the new H.264/AVC (Advanced Video Coding) video codec, also known as MPEG-4 Part 10, for high resolution and excellent quality.

The result is that you can easily use your Mac as a telephone or video phone, and the call is free; it takes place over your broadband Internet connection. The quality of the sound and picture is impressive, and in typical Apple fashion, everything is beautifully designed and could not be easier to use. No longer do you have to manipulate the hardware and the software that was an integral part of earlier live-video-over-Internet setups.

In particular, a live video chat using iChat AV and the iSight camera is one of the more remarkable experiences you can have with your computer. These features are useful to far-away friends, grandparents and grandchildren, and travel-weary businesspeople. This author has even used iChat video chat to avoid taking the subway from Queens to Brooklyn (there's just no good way to do that).

iChat AV is included with Mac OS X 10.5, although when you look for it in the Applications folder, you find it is still just called iChat.

Setting up iChat

To use iChat with the Internet, you need to have a *screen name,* also known as an instant messaging name. If you are a .Mac member, you can use your full .Mac e-mail address as your screen name. If you have an America Online or AIM screen name, it will work with iChat, and is available for free. Although iChat under 10.5 does work with the Jabber messaging service, iChat does not work with other instant messaging systems such as MSN or Yahoo!, so you cannot use screen names from them.

You can also use iChat on a local network without needing AIM screen names, such as with a classroom, home, or small office network. In this situation, iChat automatically locates other iChat users on the network via the Bonjour protocol (which Apple used to call "Rendezvous"), and lets you chat or send files to them. The Server version of Mac OS X 10.5 has an iChat server built in, to help host your own internal network chats.

To use iChat's audio capabilities, you need a microphone connected or built into your computer. All of Apple's Leopard-compatible laptops have internal microphones built in, as well as their eMacs and iMacs. If you have a Web camera with a built-in microphone, such as iSight, iChat selects the camera microphone automatically. If not, you need to select the microphone via the iChat ⇨ Preferences ⇨ Video drop-down menu. It can be a good habit to get into to check these preferences regularly if you participate in lots of video and audio chats to make sure that everything is being recognized properly. If you really want to have a telephone-like experience with iChat, you can use the provided button to set up your Bluetooth headset, which gives you a wireless all-in-one microphone and earpiece by outputting iChat's audio to the headset speaker and taking sound input from the headset's microphone.

To use iChat's video capabilities, you need a FireWire video camera connected to your computer, and a broadband Internet connection. Almost all Intel Macs other than the Mac Mini have a camera built in as well. You can also use any Digital Video (DV) camcorder with a FireWire cable; oddly enough, you must turn the camera on for it to work — unlike the iSight camera, it does not take its power from your computer's FireWire port.

iChat guides you through its configuration process with an assistant. After the Welcome to iChat AV panel, you go to the Set up iChat Instant Messaging panel, shown in Figure 14.22.

FIGURE 14.22

Set up iChat Instant Messaging in the Set up iChat Instant Messaging panel.

The Account Type pop-up menu allows a choice between .Mac and AIM accounts.

The Get an iChat Account button opens your browser to a Web page called Try iChat, which describes the various irresistible benefits of .Mac membership and suggests you register for an iChat account. If you do so, you get a 60-day trial of .Mac services.

After you have entered your information and clicked Continue, the Assistant asks if you want to add Jabber instant messaging. See Figure 14.23.

FIGURE 14.23

Setting up a Jabber instant messaging account

When you finish the Assistant setup, iChat opens its Buddy List window, shown in Figure 14.24. When you enter someone's screen name into iChat, it appears in the Buddy List. The entries in your Buddy List are stored on the Internet, so if you log into iChat for the first time on a newly installed copy of Mac OS X, you see all of your previously entered buddy names!

In Figure 14.24, the Buddy List shows the user (this author) and a bunch of buddies who are online and their icons (which now can animate!).

FIGURE 14.24

iChat's Buddy List

Contact your friends to get their screen names. Follow these steps to add people to your Buddy List:

1. **Choose Buddies ⇨ Add A Buddy or click the plus sign button in the lower left corner of the Buddy List window.** A sheet drops down, showing the contents of your Address Book.

2. **Select someone's name and click Select Buddy.** The name is added to your Buddy List. In order for this to work, you have to have manually added a screen name in the person's address book contact.

3. **Click New Person to see another sheet asking for the Account Type and Account Name and then click Add.** You can also have the option to enter the person's first and last names and e-mail address. The information is copied to the Address Book, and the name is added to your Buddy List.

 If you want to chat with someone, but you don't want to add the person's name to your Buddy List, choose File ⇨ New Chat with Person and enter his or her screen name.

TIP You can also add a cell phone number to text message a buddy. Instead of the screen name put in +1XXXYYYZZZZ, where XXXYYYZZZZ is the phone number in question. If you have added the person's cellular phone number to your address book, you can SMS them by Control+clicking the buddy and selecting Send SMS.

Checking the status of iChat buddies

The Buddy List window shows the screen names or their Address Book names (if they are added to your Address Book) of the people you have added, with some visual indicators to let you know when they are online and if they are available for chatting. To the left of their name is the status indicator, which looks like a red, green, or yellow jewel.

The green jewel means they have set their status to Available, meaning they are online and ready to chat.

The red jewel means they have set their status to Away, meaning they are online, but don't want to chat. You can still send a message to them, but they may not answer it. "Away" users can still continue to chat even if their status is set to Away.

The yellow jewel means that a user is idle. They were available at one point and have not set an Away message, but the idle indicates that they have not physically used their computer in a while. iChat monitors mouse and keyboard movements. If it does not detect any for ten minutes, it sets your status to Idle.

The grey jewel means the user is either invisible or forwarding their messages to their cell phone. If you IM the person and the message is forwarded to their cell phone, AIM messages you back and tells you where the message is headed. You can also tell if someone is forwarding messages to their cell phone or they are invisible, when the radio signal icon (kind of like an airport signal) is just to the right of their screen name.

If their status is Offline, meaning iChat is not running, no jewel appears and their name is grayed out. You cannot send them a message.

Your name appears at the top of the Buddy List window. Under it is a pop-up menu where you can set your own status, as shown in Figure 14.25. iChat is all about customization! Choose Edit Status Menu or Custom to make up your own messages. You can display custom messages for when you're available and when you're away. You can even choose to have your current iTunes track displayed as your status message.

New to iChat 4 is setting yourself as invisible. This allows you to be online and message anyone you want. Everyone else, however, sees you as offline until you message them.

You can see status information and change your own status setting without opening iChat by using the iChat status menu item in the menu bar. The status menu is off by default; you can turn it on by choosing iChat ➪ Preferences ➪ General, and checking Show status in menu bar.

FIGURE 14.25

iChat's Buddy List shows this user pulling down the status menu to change his status.

Reviewing Buddy List features

A video camera icon next to a buddy's name means that he or she has a video camera attached, and you can have a video chat if the buddy is available. A telephone icon means the buddy is set up to have an audio chat. No icon means you can only text message the person.

IM users can choose to have a picture appear next to their names on your Buddy List. This same picture, the buddy icon, appears in the chat window next to their messages.

You can edit your own picture by clicking the picture next to your name at the top of the window and selecting Edit Picture from the pop-up menu. This opens the Buddy Picture window, where you can drag a picture, choose a picture, or take a video snapshot using your Web camera. Click Set to change your picture. You can also drag a picture directly onto your name.

TIP   For best results, use a picture for your buddy icon that is 64 x 64 pixels in size. If you drag a larger picture to the Buddy Picture window, or to your name, you can resize and crop the image to the right size.

To edit or view your buddy's information, select his or her name and then choose Buddies ⇨ Get Info.

You can sort your Buddy list by name and availability, hide names that are offline, or view by groups by choosing those options from the View menu.

At the bottom of the Buddy List window are five buttons:

- **Plus sign:** Adds a buddy to the list
- **"A" button:** Starts a text chat with the selected buddy
- **Telephone button:** Starts an audio chat with the selected buddy
- **Video camera button:** Starts a video chat with the selected buddy
- **Superimposed rectangles button:** Starts a screen sharing session with the selected buddy

The four buttons that start chats are grayed out until you first select an online buddy in the list.

TIP   To send a file, picture, or movie to a buddy, drag it to the buddy's name. You can also select his or her name, choose Buddies ⇨ Send A File, and navigate to the file you want. Only one file can be sent at a time.

Sending instant messages

To send an instant message to someone on your Buddy List, follow these steps:

1. **Double-click the buddy's name.** A chat window opens.
2. **Type a message.**
3. **Press Return to send the message.**
4. **If your buddy responds, the response appears in the chat window below your message.** Have a conversation with your buddy by sending messages and back and forth.

To send a file or picture with your message, drag it to the message entry area. Pictures will be displayed beside your text in the chat window; buddies must accept a file, which is then transferred, saved, and opened separately.

Chatting on a local network

If you want to use your Mac to chat with other Mac users on a local network, you do not need an instant messaging account or Internet access.

Chatting Tips

Chatting is fun and easy. The following list provides tips for chatting:

- You can have many chat windows open at once, instant messaging several people at the same time.

- You can choose to invite multiple people into an already-created chat session by choosing View ⇨ Show Chat Participants. To add participants, click the plus sign button and choose a person from your Buddy List, or choose Other to invite someone who is not in your Buddy List. You can also add participants by dragging them from your Buddy List.

- You can change the appearance of your text chats. This can be accomplished using the iChat ⇨ Preferences ⇨ Messages pane.

- To view a chat as plain text, choose View ⇨ Messages ⇨ Show as Text.

- To change the font or balloon color used in your messages, choose iChat ⇨ Preferences ⇨ Messages. These settings affect how your messages look on both your and your recipient's screens.

- To override other people's font and color settings, select Reformat Incoming Messages in the message preference pane.

- To set an image to show in the background, choose View ⇨ Set Chat Background and then select an image file.

- To embed a hyperlink to a Web site in your message, type a name for the link, highlight the text, and choose Edit ⇨ Add Hyperlink. The Insert Hyperlink window opens; enter the URL (you can copy it from the Web browser). Click OK and complete your message. Press Return to send the URL.

- You can send or receive files over iChat, and unlike e-mail, there is no limit to the file size. Select a recipient in your Buddy List, choose Buddies ⇨ Send a File, select the file, and click Send. Or, just drag the file to the buddy's name in the Buddy List. Only one file can be sent at a time. Large files can take a long time to transfer.

- Instead of having individual windows for each buddy chat, you can group all of your buddy messages in one window. Click iChat ⇨ Preferences ⇨ Messages ⇨ Collect chats into a single window.

- You can also have your name or screen name automatically highlighted in a chat. This can be done via the Messages preference pane and clicking Watch for my name in incoming messages.

- If you use iChat for business you can also log all your chat sessions. In the Messages preference pane, you can select Automatically save chat transcripts to: and then choose a location. The default location is in your Documents folder, in the iChats folder.

Bonjour (originally called "Rendezvous") is Apple's networking technology that is based on the Zeroconf networking standard, and it automatically recognizes other computers on the network, enabling iChat to communicate with them. Bonjour is on by default in iChat; if you want to turn it off, you can do so in the Accounts pane of iChat Preferences.

To chat on a local network, follow these steps:

1. **Choose Window ⇨ Bonjour.** In the window appear other iChat users on the same subnet (network segment) that you are on.

2. **To send an invitation to chat, double-click a person in the list.** If the person accepts your invitation to chat, by default he or she can see you type each character of the message, unlike in Internet chatting, where the entire message is sent only when you press Return. You can change this default setting, Send Text As I Type, in the Messages pane of iChat Preferences.

NOTE If you connect to the Internet with a cable modem, you may see other iChat users via Bonjour, because with cable you're technically on a shared network segment. You will not see other users if you connect to the Internet via dial-up or DSL.

TIP If firewall protection is turned on in the Security pane of System Preferences, you may be unable to chat with other Bonjour users. If you need the firewall on but would like to chat, allow activity on port 5298.

Video and audio chats

You can invite anyone in your Buddy List to a video or audio chat if a camera or telephone icon appears, respectively, next to his or her name. Figure 14.26 shows an example of iChat's video window. To start a video or audio chat, follow these steps:

1. **Click the camera or telephone icon, or select the buddy and click the camera or telephone button at the bottom of the list.**

2. **If you are already in a text chat with someone who has a camera or telephone icon next to his or her name, choose Buddies ⇨ Invite to Video Chat or Buddies ⇨ Invite to Audio Chat.** For video chats, a preview window opens momentarily, showing your video image as seen by your camera.

   If your buddy accepts the invitation, his or her image appears in the chat window, and your preview image shrinks to a corner. You can move your image to another corner by clicking where you want it to go.

   For audio chats, an audio status window with a meter that measures your sound input appears, alerting you that a connection is being attempted with your buddy. When you connect successfully, the window reflects your connection, and you can begin to speak!

3. **Resize the video chat window, if you want, by dragging the bottom right corner.** To fill the entire screen with the image, choose Video ⇨ Full Screen. Use the button with double arrows at the bottom of the video chat window to toggle between normal and full-screen modes.

FIGURE 14.26

iChat's video chat window shows a multi-way video chat in progress with two users with a camera, and one without.

You can mute the audio during an audio or video chat by choosing Audio ⇨ Mute or Video ⇨ Mute. (The Audio menu becomes a Video menu if you have a camera connected.) Or, you can click the microphone button at the bottom of either chat window. When the audio is muted in a video chat, a microphone icon with a slash appears in your preview image window, and your chat buddies won't be able to hear anything that you say. (But remember, they may still be able to read your lips!) When the audio is muted in an audio chat, your buddies can no longer hear you.

Pause a video chat by choosing Video ⇨ Pause Video. Alternatively, Option+click the microphone button in the video chat window. This button becomes highlighted during a pause, and the audio is muted. Click the microphone button to resume the chat.

Video Effects

Apple has incorporated a few neat video effects into iChat video chatting. This includes all of the features of Photo Booth into the video chat feature in iChat. You can place yourself in any background Apple has provided. You can add video effects such as fisheye or mirroring.

To preview your video effects, click the View menu ⇨ Show Video Effects. This brings up a small window that looks like the Photo Booth preview window.

Have it multi-way

The ability to not just video or audio chat with one person at a time, but to chat with multiple people at the same time started in Tiger and continues into Leopard. This had been a huge feature request from Apple's avid iChat users, and the results are quite elegant.

In order to chat with multiple people over video or audio, all you have to do is select multiple people from your Buddy List, and then click the camera or telephone icon at the bottom of your Buddy List window. Rather than inviting an individual, you're inviting a group! Alternatively, you can select your participants from your Buddy List and choose to video or audio chat from the Buddies menu.

If you're already mid-chat with someone, either audio or video, and you'd like have others join in, you can do that as well. Click the plus sign within the video or audio chat windows and you can add subsequent participants. You can have up to four video chatters and up to ten audio chatters.

> **TIP** By default, the video chat takes up as much of your Internet connection's bandwidth as possible. If you want to share your connection with others on your network, or with another application such as a Web browser, you can adjust the speed at which your video chat is transmitted. Choose iChat ⇨ Preferences, click the Video icon, and choose a speed from the Bandwidth Limit pop-up menu. The slowest setting is 100 Kbps (kilobits per second) and the fastest is 2 Mbps (megabits per second).

> **TIP** You can invite buddies who do not have cameras to a one-way video chat by choosing Buddies ⇨ Invite to One-Way Video Chat. Your buddies can see and hear you, and you can hear them if they have a built-in or attached microphone configured.

Screen Sharing

iChat version 4 has a new feature that allows you to share your screen or share the user's screen: it is an electronic white board. This feature is an extension of the iChat video feature. This feature is iChat version 4 only! It does not work even one-way with previous versions of iChat. To initiate a screen sharing, follow these steps:

1. **Select the buddy that has iChat 4 and that you want to screen-share with.**

2. **Click the Buddies menu ⇨ Share my screen or Share your buddies screen.** If you request to take control of your buddy's screen, your buddy receives a pop-up window asking for permission to give control.

   If you ask to share your screen with your buddy, the other user receives a pop-up window asking if he or she wants to accept a screen share. See Figure 14.27.

FIGURE 14.27

A screen-sharing initiation window from the controlling side

iChat Theater

iChat has become the leading instant messaging client on the Mac since its introduction. It has led the way on breakthrough features such as video and audio conferencing as well as multiway video conferencing. Its tight integration into OS X has made it extremely easy to use and, as a result, popular.

iChat in Leopard ships with an expanded Instant Messaging framework. This allows iChat to take audio, video, and photos from other supported applications and use them in an instant messaging conversation.

To share a presentation or slideshow, click the File menu and click "Share a file with iChat Theater" or "Share iPhoto with iChat Theater." You are brought to a window to select an album of your iPhoto library, a picture, video, keynote presentation, or QuickTime movie. Once you select the file you want to share, a window pops up telling you to initiate a video chat. See Figure 14.28.

FIGURE 14.28

The start of an iChat Theater session

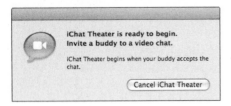

At this point you proceed with inviting people to a video chat or a multi-way video chat. Once the user(s) accept the video chat, your presentation or slideshow shows up next to your video. See Figure 14.29.

 This used to be a secret feature of iChat AV, but it became so popular Apple incorporated it into the final release of iChat.

FIGURE 14.29

An iChat Theater session in progress

The Address Book Application

Mac OS X includes the Address Book application to help you manage your contact information. Address Book is located on your hard disk, in the Applications folder. When you synchronize your contacts with your .Mac account, this is where it pulls the information from initially.

You can use iSync to synchronize your Address Book contacts with your .Mac Address Book, your handheld personal digital assistant (PDA), or your cell phone.

Mail, iCal, iChat, Safari, and Spotlight use the information from Address Book to address e-mail messages, invite contacts to chats or events, fill in online forms automatically, and customize driving instructions.

You can use Address Book to:

- Store and look up contact information
- Organize and change the formatting of contact information
- Print phone lists, mailing labels, and envelopes
- Send contact information by e-mail to an individual or group
- Automatically merge duplicate contacts
- Back up your contact information
- Use Smart Groups to dynamically manage your information
- Connect to your Bluetooth cell phone

Setting up the Address Book

The main Address Book window displays three columns. The first column shows the directories and groups defined in the Address Book. The second column shows the names in the selected group, one name per line. The third column shows the card selected in the second column.

Figure 14.30 shows the Address Book window as it appears when you first open the application.

FIGURE 14.30

The Address Book window

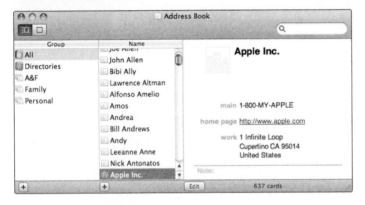

Notice that your name already appears in the Name list. If you click your name, you see your address card, which may be filled with information from the .Mac System preference pane, if you have entered it there.

TIP Even if you do not use .Mac, and even if you do not intend to manage contacts with Address Book, it's still a good idea to enter your personal information on this card, which is marked "me" in the lower left corner of your user picture. As mentioned earlier, this information is used by other applications.

To set up your contact information, follow these steps:

1. **Select your card.**

2. **Click the Edit button below the card display area.**

3. **Add your contact information to the empty fields.** Press Tab to move from field to field. You can return additional lines to the address field only by pressing Return.

4. **If one of the fields does not apply, skip it; it will not be shown on the final card.**

5. **To add more fields for additional phone numbers, click the green plus button next to the field's name.** This button appears after you have used the initial fields provided. To remove a field, click the red minus button.

6. **Unclick the Edit button to save your changes.**

Using the main Address Book window

You can work with contacts in the Address Book window as follows:

- **Select contacts in the list.** Click the name or any other information listed for a contact to select the card, ⌘+click additional contacts to select them also, or Shift+click to select a range of contacts. If you select one contact, its basic information appears in the third column of the Address Book window.

- **View the list by group.** Choose a group from the Group column.

- **Filter the list.** Type in the Search box. The Address Book looks for the search text in the information listed for each contact and hides all contacts whose listed information doesn't include the search text. In other words, the Address Book lists only address cards that have the search text in at least one column in the list.

- **Resize columns.** Drag a column heading's right borderline left or right to make the column narrower or wider.

- **Set View.** Switch between Single Contacts view or the Lists Plus Contact view by clicking the buttons in the upper right corner of the Address Book window. You can also choose View ⇨ Card Only or View ⇨ Card and Columns. When viewing a single card, advance to the next or previous card with the arrow buttons in the lower left of the window.

Setting Address Book preferences

The Address Book's Preferences window's General pane, shown in Figure 14.31, displays options for display order, sort order, address format, and font size. The check box to Notify people when my card changes is grayed out and unavailable unless a group has been created.

The Synchronize with Exchange check box enables the Configure button, leading to a sheet where you can set up Address Book to synchronize with a Microsoft Exchange mail server. In order to do this you'll need to know the URL for the Webmail server along with your Exchange user name and password. Synchronize with Yahoo has been added as well, to synchronize your contacts with Yahoo Mail. The General pane is also where you set your Address Book contacts to synchronize with .Mac; check the box to enable synchronization, and click the .Mac button to open the .Mac System Preferences, where you can customize the data that you are synchronizing. .Mac synchronization is covered a bit later in this chapter.

In the toolbar, note the icons for other preference panes. The Template pane enables you to customize the configuration of fields and labels for every new address card. The Phone pane turns on and off automatic formatting of phone numbers selected from a pop-up menu; use this to make your phone numbers conform to the standards used in a particular location.

Address Book stores its contact information in the popular vCard format. The vCard format is a common standard used in many applications and uses, from mail programs to PDAs such as Handspring Visors and Palm OS handheld devices, and many newer models of cellular phones. The vCard pane sets the version of the vCard format used, enables a private "Me" card, and enables notes from your address cards to be included in your exported vCards.

FIGURE 14.31

The Address Book's Preferences window's General pane

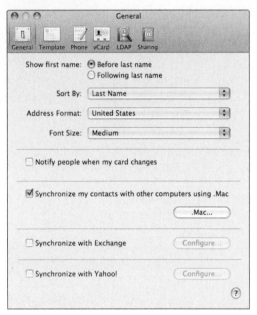

The LDAP pane is for setting up Address Book to access contact information on a server that uses the Lightweight Directory Access Protocol. LDAP is an Internet protocol used by e-mail programs to look up contact information on a network directory server. Such servers are often used by larger companies. Contact your network administrator for the information to enter here. Click the plus sign button to drop down a sheet with fields for name, server, search base, port, scope, and authentication details to be entered. Once this information is entered, click Directories in the Group column of the Address Book main window, and type in the search field to look up results from the network directory.

The Sharing pane lets you set up your Address Book contacts to be visible by other people over the Web, in accordance with your .Mac account. Click the appropriate check box to begin sharing your contacts, and use the plus and minus signs to add and remove the .Mac users with whom you want to share your information. You can click the Invite button to send an e-mail message to the people in your list, letting them know that your information has debuted!

Working with Address Book contacts

To add a contact to Address Book, follow these steps:

1. **Open Address Book.**

2. **Choose File ⇨ New Card.** A new card is created.

3. **Add the contact information to the empty fields.** Press the Tab key to move from field to field. You can add additional lines to the address field only by pressing Return.

4. **If one of the fields does not apply, skip it; it will not be shown on the final card.**

5. **To add more fields for additional phone numbers, click the green plus button next to the field's name.** This button appears after you have used the initial fields provided. To remove a field, click the red minus button.

6. **If you want to change the field labels, click the label, choose Custom from the pop-up menu, and enter the new label name.** The custom label appears on this contact only. If you want to add a label to all contacts, choose Address Book ⇨ Preferences and click Template.

7. **Add notes of any kind to the contact field at the bottom of the card.**

8. **You can add a picture by dragging a picture file to the square box at the top of the card.** You can also double-click the picture area, click Choose, and navigate to a picture file. Use the slider to enlarge and crop the picture. Click the video camera button to use a connected video camera to take a snapshot. The resulting picture is used by other applications that access Address Book information, but will never be seen by the person it represents (except for your own picture).

9. **When done, click the Edit button to see the completed card.** Click this same button to edit the card at any time, using the techniques described earlier. See Figure 14.32 for an example.

FIGURE 14.32

A new contact has just been created in Address Book.

> **TIP**   The Notes field at the bottom of each card can be set up with keywords associating that contact with a specific group. You can then use the search field to enter the keyword and quickly locate all the members of this group. For example, if you search for "enemy," all contacts with the keyword "enemy" in the Notes field would be listed.

To remove a contact from the Address Book, select the contact you want to remove and press Delete or choose Edit ⇨ Delete Person. Click Yes when asked if you are sure that you want to delete the card for "contact name." The contact is removed from the name list, and from any groups it might belong to.

Importing contacts

It is possible to import contacts from another application you may be currently using to store them only if the application supports exporting in vCard, text file, or LDIF format (LDAP Interchange Format Files). LDIF is the format an LDAP server uses to exchange information with other LDAP servers.

To import contacts into the Address Book, first check your application's documentation to see if it supports exporting addresses in vCard of LDIF formats and then follow these steps:

1. **Export your addresses from the other application as either vCards or an LDIF file.**
2. **In Address Book, choose File ⇨ Import, revealing a submenu.**
3. **Choose the format from the Import submenu.**
4. **Select the file that contains the exported addresses.**

You can view the last batch of addresses imported to Address Book by clicking Last Import in the Group column. This list is updated when you import addresses.

Creating and working with groups

After you add a few contacts to the Address Book, you can create groups to make mailing to several people at once easier. If you're synchronizing your contacts to your cell phone, you can make a Cell Phone group so you don't have to sync your entire contact list to the device. To add a new group, do one of the following:

- Click the plus sign button at the bottom of the Group column.
- Choose File ⇨ New Group.
- In the Name column, select several contacts that you want to be in the new group and then choose File ⇨ New Group From Selection.

Any of these actions displays a new Group Name in the Group column. Type the name for the new group and then press Return.

You can add contacts to a group by selecting them in the Names column and dragging the selected names to the group.

To drag a contact successfully, position the mouse pointer over the contact's icon in the Names list, press and hold the mouse button, and then drag. As you drag, a small address card icon follows the pointer, and a green plus sign icon appears, indicating that what you are dragging will be added to the destination.

You can remove a contact from a group by selecting the group, selecting the contact, and pressing Delete. You can also choose Edit ⇨ Remove From Group. A sheet drops down that asks "Are you sure you want to delete *contact name* or simply remove it from the group *Group Name*?" Click the Remove From Group button. The contact is not removed from the name list using this technique. Click the Delete button to remove the contact from all groups and lists.

Delete a group by selecting its name and pressing Delete, or by choosing Edit ⇨ Delete Group. A sheet drops down that asks "Are you sure you want to delete the selected group?" Click Yes.

You can even set up a group to contain other groups. Drag the groups you want to include to the destination group.

To see which group or groups a contact belongs to, press and hold the Option key while selecting the contact's name in the Name column. The groups the contact belongs to appear highlighted in the Group column.

If group members have multiple e-mail addresses, choose which e-mail address to use when sending mail to the group. Choose Edit ⇨ Edit Distribution List. Select the group in the left column. The e-mail address listed in bold on the right is the one which will be used when sending mail to the group. Change the e-mail address used by clicking the one you want to use; this address is now shown in bold. You can also change the phone numbers, fax numbers, or mailing addresses used when printing a distribution list by selecting a choice from the pop-up menu at the column heading of the right column. Click OK when done.

Using Spotlight technology (see Chapter 3), you can create Smart Groups, which are groups whose criteria you can set using a set of rules and parameters. As time goes by, and as your data changes, different contacts will match the criteria and thus dynamically fall in and out of your Smart Groups. For example, you can set a smart group to display the contacts whose birthdays or anniversaries are coming up in the next month. As the date changes day by day, different contacts will be dynamically added and removed from the group.

To create a new Smart Group, follow these steps:

1. **Choose File ⇨ New Smart Group.**
2. **Using the drop-down sheet, give the group a name.**

3. **Use the pull-down menus to set your group criteria.** Use the plus and minus signs to add and remove additional rules. For the upcoming birthday and anniversary example described earlier, set all conditions to meet birthdays in the next 31 days, and anniversaries in the next 31 days.

4. **Check the box if you want to highlight the group whenever it is updated.**

5. **Click OK to save your group.** You can edit the parameters of your Smart Group at any time by selecting Gear ⇨ Edit Smart Group.

Exchanging contacts

You can copy contacts as vCards to the desktop, to the body of an e-mail message as an attachment, or to a chat window to send to the person you are chatting with. Select the contacts you want to copy in the Name column and drag them to their destination.

Multiple selected contacts are copied into a single vCard, unless you press and hold Option while dragging them, resulting in separate individual vCards. You can also make your selections and choose File ⇨ Export vCard.

To keep certain information private before you send your vCard, follow these steps:

1. **Choose Address Book ⇨ Preferences.**

2. **Click vCard.**

3. **Select Enable Private Me Card.**

4. **Close the Preferences window.**

5. **Select your card in the Name column.**

6. **Click Edit.** Select only the check boxes next to the information that will be sent.

To send a group an update of the information on your vCard, choose File ⇨ Send Updates. In the Send Updates dialog box, select the group, type a subject and message, and click Send. A group e-mail message goes out via Mail containing your updated vCard. If you want this process to happen automatically whenever a change is made to your vCard, select Notify people when my card changes in the General pane of Address Book preferences.

When someone sends you a vCard, first save it to any location you choose, and then double-click it. Address Book launches if it is not already running and a sheet drops down from the Address Book window, giving you one of the following sets of choices:

■ If the contact is not a duplicate of a contact already in your Address Book, you are asked to OK or Cancel its addition.

■ If the contact is a duplicate, you have three choices. You can click OK to update the existing card with the new card, click Cancel, or click Review Duplicates to open a window showing the new card with a red Update ribbon at the top right. Compare this card to the one already in your Address Book, and click a button to Keep Old, Keep New, Keep Both, or Update the old card with the new information. If you select Update, the information to be updated is displayed in red, and newly added information is blue.

- If you are sent a vCard with multiple duplicate contacts, the Review Duplicates window shows them sequentially after clicking the Next button. You can apply your chosen action to all the contacts by clicking the Apply to All check box (see Figure 14.33).

FIGURE 14.33

A single vCard (upper left) bears the contact's name, but a vCard with multiple contacts (lower left) is called vCards. Double-clicking vCards brings down the Importing cards sheet, and clicking Review Duplicates opens the Reviewing Card window.

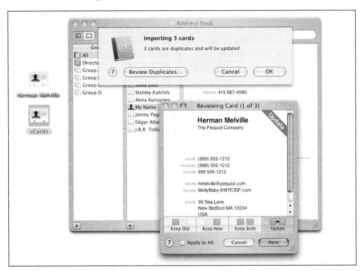

Combine duplicate contacts to retain all of their information on a single card. Use the Search field to get the duplicates to show in the Names column. Press and hold the ⌘ key as you select the contacts you want to combine, and then choose Card ➪ Merge Cards. Review the resulting card to delete any unwanted information.

Printing address lists and labels

Address Book can print address lists, mailing labels, envelopes, and even pocket address books from its contacts database. You can format them to look just right for your purposes using Address Book's sophisticated Print dialog box.

To print an address list, follow these steps:

1. **Choose File ➪ Print.** Address Book's Print dialog box opens as shown in Figure 14.34.
2. **From the Style pop-up menu, choose List.**
3. **In the Attributes box, select the fields you want to see listed.**

To print a mailing label, follow these steps:

1. Choose File ⇨ **Print.** Address Book's Print dialog box opens.

2. From the Style pop-up menu, choose **Mailing Labels.**

3. Click Layout.

4. From the Page pop-up menu, choose a type of label.

5. Choose Define Custom from the Page pop-up menu to set up how many labels to print on a page, the page margins, and the gutter space between labels.

6. From the Address pop-up menu, choose the type of address.

7. From the Sorting pop-up menu, choose Last Name or Postal Code to sort the labels based on one or the other.

8. Use the check boxes to Print Country and Except My Country, or leave them empty.

9. If you want, change the font and color, and drag any image you want to print on the label to the well.

10. As you make changes, the print preview on the left shows what the labels will look like.

11. Select the number of copies and click Print.

To print envelopes, follow these steps:

1. Choose File ⇨ **Print.** Address Book's Print dialog box opens as shown in Figure 14.34.

2. From the Style pop-up menu, choose **Envelopes.**

3. In the Attributes window, use the pop-up menus to select the type and size of your envelopes.

4. Use the additional panels to customize your labels and set the orientation of the envelopes.

5. **Choose your number of copies and click Print to begin printing.** Make sure to load your envelopes into your printer properly. You might want to send a singular test print to make sure the formatting and orientation are correct.

To print a pocket address book, follow these steps:

1. Choose File ⇨ **Print.** Address Book's Print dialog box opens as shown in Figure 14.34.

2. From the Style pop-up menu, choose **Pocket Address Book.**

3. Choose your paper size and orientation.

4. Use the Attributes window to check and uncheck the boxes to reflect the fields you want to print out.

5. Set your flip style to either Indexed or Compact, and choose your font.

6. Choose your number of copies and click Print.

FIGURE 14.34

The Address Book Print dialog box, set to the Layout panel

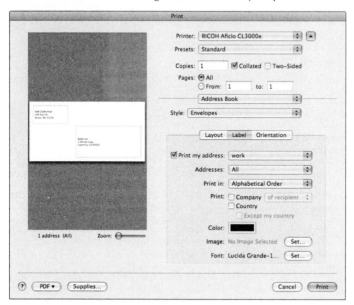

Backing up Address Book

Once you start using Address Book, the information it contains becomes valuable. It's a good idea to make frequent backups, which can be done with Address Book's Back Up Database command. It should be noted that synchronizing your contacts with .Mac is an effective way to back them up, because your information is uploaded to Apple's servers, but it's not error-proof, and it's always beneficial to keep a local backed-up copy with you at all times.

To create a backup of Address Book information, follow these steps:

1. **Choose File ➪ Export ➪ Address Book Archive.** A location selection sheet drops down.
2. **Choose a location for the backup file.**
3. **Click Save.** The backup file appears as a document icon with the Address Book icon and the acronym ABBU, for Address Book Back Up.

To restore your Address Book information from a backup file, follow these steps:

1. **Choose File ➪ Import ➪ Address Book Archive.** A navigation sheet drops down.
2. **Navigate to the desired backup file.**
3. **Click Open.** An alert appears: Reverting will cause your current database to be overwritten. Note that the operation cannot be undone.
4. **Click OK.**

Address Book Tips

Using the Address Book is an easy way to manage your contact information. The following list provides you with tips on using the Address Book feature:

■ You can tell if contacts are currently available via iChat. A circle next to the contacts' pictures indicates their status; if the circle is green, they are available. Click the circle to invite a contact to a chat.

■ If your contacts have .Mac account name e-mail addresses, there is an easy way to send them e-mail messages: Start an iChat, open your contacts' Public folders on their iDisk, visit their HomePage, or send them a vCard right from their address card. Click the field label (for example, home or work) next to the .Mac e-mail address. The resulting pop-up menu offers the following choices: Send Email, iChat, Visit HomePage, Open iDisk, or Send Update. Choose what you want to do, and the appropriate application is launched.

■ Copy an address as a mailing label to paste into another application by clicking the address field label and choosing Copy Mailing Label from the pop-up menu.

■ Get a map showing an address's location (if you are connected to the Internet) by clicking the address field label and choosing Map Of from the pop-up menu.

■ Keep track of birthdays by choosing Card ⇨ Add Field ⇨ Birthday. To track anniversaries or other important dates, choose Card ⇨ Add Field ⇨ Dates.

■ If a contact has more than one instant messaging account, you can add them all to their address card. Click the Edit button and then add the first address. Select the type of address from the pop-up menu to the right of the address. Click the green add button to add another address. Repeat until all the addresses are entered, and then click Edit to view the results; next to each address, the name of the service appears in parentheses.

NOTE   The Revert operation *can* be undone, in effect, if you first make a backup file; then you can revert to that file if you want to undo the previous revert.

TIP   If you have a .Mac account, you can use the Backup application to back up your Address Book to your iDisk. For more information, see "Using the Backup Application" later in this chapter.

Groups

.Mac has added the ability to communicate and collaborate with multiple people. This feature is called Groups. Here you can create a Web site specifically for that group, manage a group calendar, share photos, exchange messages, and share files.

Adding a group

You must add the group to your .Mac membership in order to communicate. There are a designated group owner (the person who creates the group) and members. You can define the look and feel of the group as well. To add a group, follow these steps:

1. Visit `http://www.mac.com/` and click the Groups icon at the top of the screen.

2. Log in using your .Mac member name and password.

3. You are taken to the .Mac Groups page, where you can create a new group. Click Create a new group at the top right of the window.

4. Fill out the form with your group name, desired e-mail address, description, view, time zone, and referral information.

5. Click Submit. Your group is created.

Modifying a group

To add members to a group, cancel a group, or change any of its settings, you must edit the group. Follow these steps:

1. Visit `http://www.mac.com/` and click the Groups icon at the top of the screen.

2. Log in using your .Mac member name and password.

3. You are taken to the .Mac Groups page. Look for the group you want to edit and click Edit underneath the group's name.

   Here you can add members to your group, change the description, group picture, time zone, announcements, storage, messages, layout, and referral.

   You also can subscribe to iCal published calendars. These are created in iCal and published to your .Mac Web site. Any published calendars can be chosen here.

To view a groups page, the Web site is `http://groups.mac.com/groupname`. Here you can add photos, view the group calendar, and add links and messages. It is an electronic bulletin board for all intents and purposes.

Neat group features

A few neat features are available in Mac OS X Leopard when you create a group. They make collaboration much easier.

If you create a calendar in iCal, you can publish the calendar to your .Mac account. Once it is published in the .Mac account you can subscribe the group to the calendar. Do this by logging on to your .Mac Groups page. Edit the group. Under Select Calendar, you can choose the calendar you want to subscribe to. When you edit this calendar on iCal, it updates on the group page as well.

You also can exchange files with your group. This can be done using your iDisk. As stated previously in this chapter, connect to your iDisk. Select the Groups folder and then the name of your group. Here all of the files are accessible to members through the Groups Web page.

Additional features and functionality of Groups are beyond the scope of this book. This book covers Groups to the extent they integrate with Mac OS and Leopard.

iCal

iCal is the Mac OS X calendar application (see Figure 14.35). You may assume that it is a basic application that lets you schedule appointments and events on a calendar and not much else.

iCal is simple to use, but its capabilities are quite astonishing, especially when used with the .Mac service. In fact, like the other "iApps," iCal makes a play to be the ultimate application of its kind, at the very least attempting to exceed your expectations by quite a bit.

Check out this summary of what you can do with iCal:

- Create digital calendars containing your schedule, viewed by day, week, or month, to keep track of events, appointments, meetings, deadlines, birthdays, anniversaries, reminders, and other time-related information.

- Create separate, color-coded calendars for different aspects of your life, such as work, home, school, kids, sports, and so on. The calendars can be viewed all at once or in any combination, superimposed transparently on each other.

- Invite others to events automatically by e-mail sent by Mac OS X Mail.

- Create To Do lists.

- Search for events, with the results listed so you can click an event to go directly to it.

- Set alarms to notify you of upcoming events, by sounds, on-screen messages, e-mail messages, launching applications, playing a song, or running a script.

- Share your calendar with other iCal users on the same computer, or over the Internet, using .Mac or your company's WebDAV server.

- Subscribe to the calendars of other iCal users that have been published on the Internet.

- Synchronize calendars between more than one computer using .Mac Sync.

- Synchronize calendars between your computer and your handheld devices with iSync.

Working with calendars

iCal gives you two default calendars: Home and Work. You can create other calendars for different aspects of your life or areas of interest.

FIGURE 14.35

The iCal main window

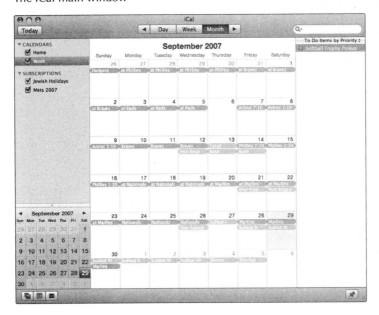

To create a new calendar, follow these steps:

1. Click the plus sign button at the bottom left of the iCal window or double-click the white area below the calendars listed in the Calendars list.

2. A new calendar appears in the Calendars list, with its name (Untitled) highlighted.

3. Type a name for the calendar.

4. Press Return.

You can rename a calendar at any time by double-clicking its name and typing a new one.

To delete a calendar, follow these steps:

1. Click the name of the calendar in the Calendars list.

2. Choose Edit ⇨ Delete.

Use a different procedure to delete a calendar that you have published over the Internet; see the instructions for this later in this section.

Working with events

Any item that appears on an iCal calendar is called an *event*. Once an event is created, its details can be set or later edited in the Info drawer that you can slide out from the right side of the iCal window or hide as necessary.

To add events to a calendar, follow these steps:

1. **In the Calendars list, click the name of the calendar you want to add an event to.**

2. **In Day or Week view, drag from the start time to the end time of the new event.** As you do so, a colored rectangle forms, with the start and end time appearing. When you release the drag, the name New Event becomes highlighted.

   In Month view, double-click the blank area of the day you want the new event to appear. The event appears as a colored bar with its name, New Event, highlighted.

3. **Type a name for the new event.**

4. **Press Return.**

To edit an event, follow these steps:

1. **Create a new event or select an existing event.**

2. **Double-click the event, and then click Edit in the pop-up that appears.** The event editor appears, listing the editable details of the event.

3. **Edit the details of the event.** You can:

   - Change or delete an event.

   - Change the time or day by dragging the event to a new position in the calendar view.

   - Change the duration, in Day or Week view, by dragging the event's top or bottom edge. (If it is an all-day event, drag its right or left side.)

   - Change the name of the event by double-clicking its name, and type a new name.

   - Delete an event by selecting it and pressing Delete.

To automatically delete events after they are due, choose iCal ⇨ Preferences. The iCal Preferences window appears, as shown in Figure 14.36. Select the Automatically delete events and To Do items check box. Enter the number of days after which the items will be deleted, click Yes in the alert box that appears, and close the Preferences window.

To create, edit, or view an event that takes place in a different time zone, follow these steps:

1. **Choose iCal ⇨ Preferences ⇨ Advanced.**

2. **Click the Turn on time zone support check box to turn on the feature.**

3. **From the time zone pop-up menu which now appears in the upper right of the iCal window, choose Other.** A world time zone map appears.

4. **Click the location the event will take place in.** A menu appears with the names of big cities in that time zone.

5. **Select a city closest to where the events take place.** Note that the exact details of time zones change in different areas. For example, some areas keep only a half-hour difference between neighboring time zones, instead of a full hour; iCal knows which ones.

6. **Click OK.** The time zone you selected appears next to the time zone label, and appears in the pop-up menu from now on.

The event appears in your calendar at the time the event takes place, adjusted for your time zone (based on your computer's settings in the Date & Time System Preference).

To view all of your iCal events adjusted for a different time zone, choose a time zone from the pop-up menu in the upper right corner of the iCal window. If the desired time zone does not appear, choose Other, and repeat Steps 4 and 6 to add a new time zone to this menu.

Events created in a particular time zone automatically shift to the correct adjusted time when you change the calendar's time zone.

iCal makes it easy to invite someone, or several people, to an event via e-mail. You might want to do this if you are planning a meeting or a party.

FIGURE 14.36

iCal's Preferences window

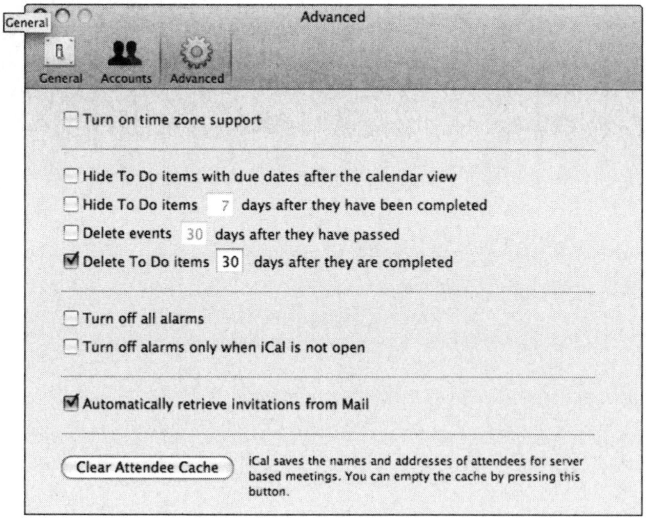

Inviting someone to an event is easy when you use iCal. To create and send an invite, follow these steps:

1. **Select the event so its information appears in the Info drawer.**

2. **Next to the label attendees, click None.** It becomes selected and you can now edit the label.

3. **Begin to type the e-mail address of the person you want to invite.** As you type the first letters, any matching names from the Address Book appear in a submenu, with any associated e-mail addresses. (If you want a new name to appear in the submenu, add it to the Address Book.)

4. **Select an e-mail address from the submenu.** The auto-completed name now appears next to the attendees label, highlighted in a colored oval.

5. **Click elsewhere to deselect the name or click the name to highlight it again.**

6. **To invite more than one person, type a comma or press the Return key after each name.**

7. **Click the triangle to the right of a highlighted name to reveal a pop-up menu with the associated e-mail addresses and the commands Edit Attendee, Remove Attendee, Open in Address Book, or Send Email.**

8. **You can also add attendees by dragging names from Address Book to an event in the iCal window.** Click the attendees label and choose Open Address Book from the pop-up menu.

9. **Drag the contacts you want to invite from Address Book to the event in the iCal calendar view.**

10. **After you have added all of the attendees, click attendees and choose Send Invitations from the pop-up menu.** E-mails are sent by Mac OS X Mail with the details of the event to the people listed.

Question mark icons now appear before each name to show the attendees have not yet confirmed. These icons change to check marks when the invitation is accepted, and X marks when declined.

iCal keeps track of the status of events — Tentative, Confirmed, or Cancelled — with status indicators that appear on the events in the Day and Week views.

You can use iCal to set up weekly meetings. Follow these steps to set up recurrent events:

1. **Select the event so its information appears in the Info drawer.**

2. **Next to the label repeat, click None.** A pop-up menu appears with the choices None, Every Day, Every Week, Every Month, Every Year, and Custom.

3. **Select the repeat interval you want to use.** If you choose Custom, a box opens to help you configure the repeat interval.

4. **From the Frequency pop-up menu, choose Daily, Weekly, Monthly, or Yearly.** The box changes to reflect each choice.

5. **Make your Custom selections and then click OK.** Your selection appears next to the repeat label. A new end label appears under the repeat label.

6. **Click the word to the right of the end label to see the choices Never, After, and On date.**

7. **Make your selection for when the repeat will end.** If you choose "on date," the date appears; click the date to edit it.

If you make any other changes to a recurring event, a dialog box opens asking if you want to change only this occurrence of the event, or all occurrences.

You can set an alarm to warn you of an impending event with an on-screen message, an e-mail message, or by opening a file of your choice. To receive an alarm before an event:

1. **Select the event so its information appears in the Info drawer.** You can set an alarm only for an event that has a due date.

2. **Next to the label alarm, click None.** A pop-up menu appears with the choices None, Message, Message with sound, Email, and Open file.

3. **Make your selection for the type of alarm you want.** Depending on your selection, other pop-up menus appear, enabling you to set the details of the alarm. Below the details you see a pop-up menu allowing you to set the alarm time before the start time of the event. You can choose to do the following:

   ▪ Select Open file to enable iCal to open an application before the event occurs. Select the application in the Navigation dialog box, and the application's name appears in a pop-up menu.

   ▪ To add another alarm, click the label alarm and choose Add Alarm from the pop-up menu, and then repeat Step 3.

   ▪ To remove an alarm, click the label alarm and choose Remove Alarm from the pop-up menu.

NOTE When the alarm goes off, you can choose to "snooze" it (temporarily silence it and remind you again later) by choosing an item from the repeat pop-up menu in the upper right corner of the iCal Alarm window.

Adding a URL to an event is a way of attaching additional information that is on the Web to an event. This feature is especially helpful for online calendars. To add an associated URL to an event follow these steps:

1. **Select the event so that its information appears in the Info drawer.**

2. **Next to the label URL, click None.** The word becomes highlighted and editable.

3. **Type a URL.** To add more than one URL, separate each with commas, or drag a URL from your Web browser's address field.

4. **Click a URL to go to the Web page in your browser.**

Creating To Do lists

In our busy modern world, it always seems that keeping track of what needs to be done is a difficult chore. iCal can help. To create a To Do list and work with To Do items, follow these steps:

1. **Click the To Do button (with the push-pin icon) in the bottom right corner of the iCal window.** The To Do list appears to the right of the calendar. To hide it, click the To Do button again.

2. **Double-click anywhere in the white area of the To Do list.** A new To Do item appears with its name selected and editable.

3. **Type your desired name for the To Do item and press Return.**

4. **If you want to assign settings to the To Do item, click the Info button at the bottom right of the iCal window.** The Info drawer slides out.

5. **When you complete the item, click the Completed check box.** The word Today appears to the right. When viewing previously completed To Do items, the date of completion appears here. You can also click the check box next to the item in the To Do list.

> **NOTE** If the item is past due, a triangle with an exclamation point shows up to the left of the event. To make this go away and make the checkbox appear, click the warning triangle.

6. **To give the To Do item a priority rating, click the increasing status bar icon to the right of the To Do.** A pop-up menu appears with the choices None, Low, Medium and High. Select the priority you want.

7. **To give the To Do item a due date, double click the To Do. A pop-up window shows up (see Figure 14.37)** Check the due date box, and select a date it is due.

8. **To receive an alarm before the due date passes, double-click the To Do and under the alarm pull-down menu, select the type of notification you would like:** None, Message, Message with Sound, Email, or Open file. If you previously had set a file to open, it appears below these choices on the menu. You can set an alarm only for items that have a due date. You can add as many alarms as you like for any To Do.

9. **After the type of alarm has been selected, select the details from the pop-up menus below your selection.** Select the amount of time before the item is due.

10. **To switch the calendar the To Do item appears on, click the name of the present calendar to the right of the calendar label.** Select from the calendars listed. The To Do item changes its color to match the calendar.

FIGURE 14.37

I must go pick up the softball trophy on 11/15/2007. Can't forget that!

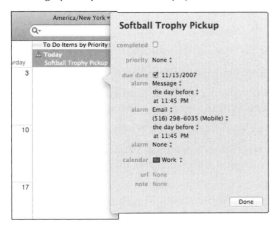

Sharing calendars

You can use iCal to share your calendars with others and to see calendars others have chosen to share. Calendars published on the Internet can be viewed by anyone with a Web browser, or viewed in iCal after they are subscribed to. You can also export your events and send them to someone else, who can import them into iCal.

Publishing a calendar puts a copy of it on a Web server to be accessed by a URL that you send to those you want to share it with. If you are a .Mac member, you can publish your calendar to your iDisk. If you have access to a private Web server that is running WebDAV, you can publish your calendar using it, to be shared with other users who have access to the server. Users viewing your published calendar cannot make changes to it; it is read-only to them.

Exporting a calendar creates a file containing your event information which can be sent to the people you want to share it with, so they can import it into iCal. Once imported, the events can be edited; the users have read/write access to them. Changes they make on the imported copy are not duplicated on your original calendar.

You can also use the exported information to back up your calendar or transfer your iCal information to another computer.

If you are a .Mac member, you can share your calendar with anyone you want via the Internet. Imagine allowing your friends, family members, and business associates to check your availability themselves instead of having them contact you.

To publish a calendar on the Internet, follow these steps:

1. **Connect to the Internet.** In the Calendars list, click the name of the calendar to be published.
2. **Choose Calendar ⇨ Publish.** A sheet drops down.
3. **In the Publish calendar as field, type the name of the calendar visitors will see.**
4. **Select the location in the Publish on menu (.Mac or Private Server).**
5. **Click the Publish changes automatically check box if you want changes you make to your calendar to be automatically copied to the published version.**
6. **Click the other check boxes to control which information is published.**
7. **From the pop-up menu, choose where you want to publish your calendar, either on .Mac or on a WebDAV server.** If you choose WebDAV the sheet lengthens, providing fields for entering the server's URL and the login name and password.
8. **Click Publish.** Figure 14.38 shows the iCal Publish sheet.
9. **Watch the Status bar to see the progress as your calendar is uploaded to the Web server.** The Calendar Published alert appears, informing you that your calendar was published successfully, and providing you with the URL for it. Click Visit Page to go to it, Send Mail to inform others and give them the URL, or click OK.

    After it is published, a broadcast icon (a dot with three short curving lines) appears next to the calendar in the Calendars list.

FIGURE 14.38

iCal's Publish sheet. I am publishing my Work calendar.

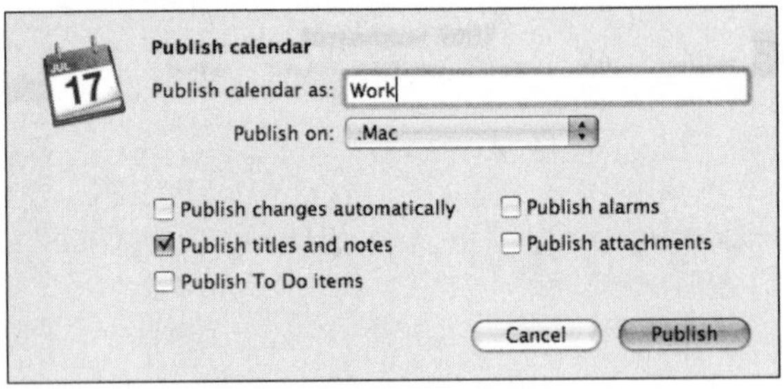

As long as Sync services are turned on in the .Mac System Preference under .Mac, the calendar will be updated automatically.

If you want to stop publication of your calendar, select the name of the calendar, choose Calendar ⇨ Unpublish, and then click Unpublish. The calendar's broadcast icon disappears. It remains available on your computer. People who subscribed to it can still see the last published copy, but no one will be able to subscribe to it.

To subscribe to and update someone else's calendar, follow these steps:

1. **Connect to the Internet.**
2. **Choose Calendar ⇨ Subscribe.** A sheet drops down.
3. **Enter the URL for the calendar you want to subscribe to.**
4. **Click Subscribe.** You'll see a progress bar apprising you of iCal's status.
5. **Choose the display name, the refresh interval, and whether or not to remove alarms and To Do items, and click OK.**

Watch the Status bar, shown in Figure 14.39, to see the progress as the calendar is downloaded from the Web server. The calendar you have subscribed to appears in the Calendars list with a curved arrow icon next to it. If you want to rename the new calendar, double-click its name. You cannot make any other changes to its events.

You can also subscribe to any of the general interest calendars available at `www.iCalShare.com`. These include holidays, professional sports team schedules, movie openings, DVD releases, rock band tour dates, TV schedules, moon phases, and Apple Store events. If you create your own general interest calendar, you can upload it to this site to share it with the world.

FIGURE 14.39

iCal's Subscribe status bar

You can export your calendar information as a file which can then be imported by any iCal user you send it to. This is another way of sharing your calendar. Figure 14.40 shows the iCal's Export command.

To export your calendar information, follow these steps:

1. **In the Calendar list, click the name of the calendar.**
2. **Choose File ⇨ Export.**
3. **Select a name for the file and a destination for it to be saved to.**
4. **Click Export.** The exported file appears as a .ics file (for iCal Standard).
5. **Send the file to the person you want to share it with, transfer it to the Mac you want to import it on, or store it in an archive folder as a backup.**

FIGURE 14.40

Using iCal's Export command produces a .ics file.

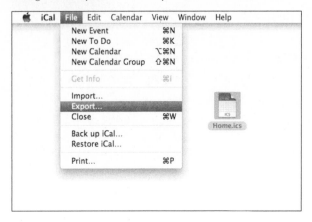

You can also import calendar information. Follow these steps:

1. **Choose File ➪ Import.** You can choose to import iCal files, vCal files, or Entourage Data.

2. **Navigate to the calendar data file you want to import.** The Add Events dialog box appears.

3. **Select the calendar you want to add the imported events to.**

4. **Click OK.**

5. **You may briefly see a progress bar as the events are imported.** The new events appear in the calendar you chose.

Printing calendars

You may find you have a need to print calendars to distribute them to others in a format that does not require a computer. You can also put them in an organizational notebook, scribble updates on them, and transfer the changes when you get back to your computer.

To print a calendar or a To Do list, follow these steps:

1. **Choose File ➪ Print.** The Print dialog box opens.

2. **Customize your print settings.** Choose your view (month, day, week, or event list) and your paper size. Choose your time duration for the print job to include, and check and uncheck the calendars you want to print or not print.

3. **Click Continue to proceed to the OS X print dialog box.** Click Preview to check what your printout will look like.

4. **Click Print.**

iCal Tips

The following list provides you with tips for using iCal:

- In iCal 1.5.1 and later, you can quickly perform the most common actions with an enhanced set of iCal-specific keyboard shortcuts. For example, you can skip to the next day, week, or month by pressing ⌘+→. Or, to duplicate a selected event, press ⌘+D. Anyone who uses iCal frequently may save quite a bit of time by using the shortcuts. You can print a comprehensive list of them from iCal Help, and post them nearby until you learn them. As Apple says on its Web site, "Efficiency is iCal's highest priority."

- To change the order of calendars in the Calendars list, drag them to where you want them.

- You can copy and paste events in the main calendar window. To select multiple events for copying, press and hold the Shift key as you make your selections. Press ⌘+C to copy, as usual. Click where you want to place the first event, and press ⌘+V to paste. The original time difference between the events is maintained.

- To see a handy shortcut menu, hold the Control key while you click an event. You can choose Cut, Copy, Paste, or Duplicate; switch the event to any calendar; or make an All Day Event, Stop Recurrence, or Email Event. Selecting this last choice opens Mail to a new message. All you need to do is supply an address, and all the recipient needs to do is click the .ics file included as an attachment to have it added to his or her calendar.

- In Month view, an ellipsis (...) at the top of the day means all the events in the day could not be shown due to size limitations. Double-click the ellipsis to see all the events in the Day view.

- Events that span several days can be created by dragging an All Day Event across the desired days.

iSync and .Mac Sync

.Mac Sync combined with iSync make up the Mac OS X synchronization software. Information is synchronized between different Mac OS X computers, Apple's .Mac servers, and also between devices such as mobile phones, Palm OS handheld devices, and iPods. Although iSync is a stand-alone application that handles synchronization between your physical devices, .Mac sync is built into the System Preferences and handles the actual data being synced. Before Mac OS X 10.5, synchronization accessed a small portion of information: your iCal calendars, Address Book contacts, and your Safari bookmarks. Instead of lending all of the functionality to the separate iSync application, under 10.4 Apple has built a full sync engine right into the operating system, enabling you to sync much more than just contacts, calendars, and bookmarks between devices. If you're using Leopard, you can really keep your Macs in sync by having the sync engine update your system settings, such as your desktop patterns, your Keychains, and your Exposé settings.

What exactly does synchronization mean? In this case, iSync and .Mac sync *compares* the information on separate computers or devices and then *changes* the information to be the same on them all. They both know to ask you how to resolve conflicting information so that nothing is lost. Anything deleted on one device is deleted on all the other devices after they are synced.

You can synchronize with or without a .Mac account. Without a .Mac account, iSync and the sync engine functions as a basic synchronization utility by keeping your changes updated and constant between your computer and your devices. With a .Mac account, however, the .Mac sync component becomes prevalent, with the incredibly powerful ability to sync data between multiple machines. .Mac Sync treats your .Mac account just like another device that is configured for synchronization; and just as iSync compares data from a phone or a Palm handheld device, .Mac Sync compares the information from your .Mac account.

For example, you could have no devices and only a .Mac account and two Macs. When you make changes on one Mac, and .Mac Sync performs a synchronization, those changes are uploaded to your .Mac account. When a synchronization is performed on the second Mac, the changes that the first Mac made are downloaded from your .Mac account and changed on that computer as well. Any changes subsequently made on the second Mac can then be synced again and thus uploaded to your .Mac account, from where your first Mac can then download those changes. Adding more computers complicates the comparisons and the work of .Mac Sync, but the principles of synchronization remain the same.

Before any syncs happen, you have to configure your Macs for sync capabilities. First, go to the .Mac System Preferences pane, click Sync, configure the information that you want to sync, and register your Mac's hardware to be recognized under your .Mac account. Once your .Mac settings are complete, you'll open iSync and add your devices that you want to synchronize (see Figure 14.41).

Setting .Mac preferences

Open the .Mac System Preferences and look at the Account panel, which was discussed earlier in this chapter. If you haven't yet, type your .Mac account name and password in the specified fields. This tells the .Mac preferences to access your information from Apple's servers.

You set up .Mac for synchronization by configuring two of the four available sections of the .Mac preferences: the Sync panel and the Advanced Panel.

Sync

Clicking the Sync area initiates a connection to the server, and you'll see a progress bar indicating that information is being transmitted. When your account is successfully verified, you are presented with a bunch of options that control how your data is synchronized. See Figure 14.41 for a look at the Sync area of the .Mac preferences.

FIGURE 14.41

The Sync portion of the .Mac preferences pane shows you what kinds of data you are syncing, along with your timed sync preferences.

In the list are the different kinds of data that you can sync between your .Mac account and your Macs. Notice that you can sync much more than just personal lifestyle information. .Mac can sync your e-mail account settings, your Keychains, and your Desktop Screensaver preferences as well. The items that appear in this list do so because of their respective settings within their own separate applications. For example, the Address Book application has a preference for choosing whether or not to sync its contacts, as does iCal for its calendars, Safari for its Bookmarks, and Mail for its e-mail accounts.

New to Leopard is the ability to sync more items than in previous versions of Mac OS X. You can sync dashboard widgets, Dock layout, Keychains, Mail rules, System Preferences (user settings), and notes. Some third-party applications also work, such as Entourage Notes and Transmit Favorites.

Click the check box to enable your .Mac synchronization, and use the pull-down menu to specify your desired sync interval. You can set your Mac to synchronize as frequently as once every hour, or leave the setting on Manual, which performs a sync only when you tell it to. If you don't have a constant Internet connection, manually syncing might be your best bet. If you run around often, it can be good for your data to be synchronized every hour.

You can also click the check box to show the status of the Leopard synchronization in the menu bar. This places the Sync icon in the menu bar, which gives you handy access for making manual syncs, or for opening the .Mac Sync Preferences to edit these very settings.

Advanced

Click the Advanced tab of the .Mac Preferences to finish getting your Mac sync-ready. You can choose to unregister any computers that appear in the list by selecting them and clicking the button that says Unregister. See Figure 14.42 for a glimpse at the Advanced settings under the .Mac pane.

FIGURE 14.42

Your registered Macs appear in the Advanced section of the .Mac System Preferences pane. Also visible is the screen for managing your sync information.

You will also notice a button labeled Manage Sync Info under the Advanced section. Click this button to open the screen shown in Figure 14.41. Syncing lots of information to lots of different places can get a bit hairy, be it a lost or corrupt device, or a poorly functioning sync process. Sometimes the easiest thing to do is to reset your synchronization from a single device. Using the Reset Sync Data button, you can choose to replace all of your data using the most current set of information, whether it is on your computer or the .Mac servers. You can even delete the contents of your .Mac account first to ensure the data from your Mac is written to a clean area. Clicking the Sync Now button erases all of your devices and replaces them with the information from the machine you are currently using.

Using the iSync application

After you've gotten the .Mac preferences worked out, the next step is to use iSync to set up your devices (other than your .Mac account) for synchronization. Figure 14.43 shows the main window of iSync.

The main iSync window before any devices have been added

iSync and Mac OS X 10.5 support the following types of devices:

- A Bluetooth-enabled mobile phone (from a Bluetooth-enabled Macintosh)
- An iSync-compatible USB mobile phone
- A Palm OS handheld device via USB or via Bluetooth (from a Bluetooth-enabled Macintosh)

iSync obviously can't synchronize system-specific settings like your desktop patterns and screen savers to your iPods and cell phones. iSync focuses on your more basic, handheld-typical information, like calendars and contacts.

In order for any device to be compatible with iSync, it has to have an iSync conduit. You can check Apple's Web site at `www.apple.com/isync/devices.html` for the most up-to-date information regarding iSync-compatible devices. Apple has been excellent regarding the rapid release of conduits for new hardware under currently supported cell phone and handheld lines.

> **TIP** You should plan on syncing a device with only a single computer. For example, if you have three computers, one at home, one at work, and a PowerBook, you cannot sync the device with all of them; you have to pick one. You can change which one later by removing the device from iSync and then adding it to iSync on another machine; see the instructions below for removing a device. Information may not sync correctly when you violate this rule.

Instructions for setting up devices may change with each new revision of iSync. For the most up-to-date information on how do set up your device, refer to the specific instructions in the "Setting up your computers and devices" section of iSync Help.

Although the details vary, in general the set-up process for phones goes like this: First, ensure connectivity between your Mac and the phone, via Bluetooth or USB. Second, open iSync, choose Devices ⇨ Add Device, and double-click the phone in the Add Device window to add it to iSync. When the phone is added, a phone icon appears on the iSync interface. You only need to add the phone once.

To set up a Palm OS device, you need to install the latest iSync Palm Conduit software on your Mac. Download this software from `www.apple.com/isync`. After the software is installed, choose the Enable Palm Syncing option from the iSync Devices menu and follow the instructions.

Enabling Palm syncing basically disables the Palm conduits that sync the Palm information to the Palm Desktop software, and instead enable the iSync conduit that allows the Palm to sync with information in Apple's iCal and Address Book.

Synchronizing your information

After you have set up all the devices you want to sync, and icons for them appear in the iSync window, you are ready to synchronize!

Even if you have the .Mac preferences set to automatically sync, it's a good idea to manually initiate your first sync to make sure everything goes as planned. To manually sync a device, follow these steps:

1. **The first time you synchronize a device, click its icon in the iSync window.** From the For first sync pop-up menu, choose Merge to combine the information from all computers and devices, or Replace to replace the information on the current computer or devices with synced information from your other computers or devices.

   If you want to choose what information will be synchronized, click a device icon in the iSync window, and make your selections. Selecting less information here speeds up the sync process.

2. **To start the sync between the computer and devices (for everything but a Palm OS device), click Sync Now in the iSync window.**

3. **To do a sync between the computer and devices, including a Palm OS device, perform a Hot Sync operation on the device.** To do this, push the Hot Sync button on the device's cradle or on the device's screen, select the Hot Sync application, and press the Hot Sync button.

   Starting the Hot Sync operation when a Palm device has been added to iSync is equivalent to pushing the Sync Now button, in that all the added devices and the computer will be synchronized. When the sync starts, the iSync window temporarily hides your settings. If more than five percent of the information on any device will be changed by the synchronization, a Safeguard window appears to inform you of how much information is going to be changed and give you an opportunity to cancel the sync process. (You can change the setting for this window in iSync Preferences.)

All registered devices are synchronized with the computer, as long as they are connected either by wire or within Bluetooth range. The first sync takes longer than subsequent syncs because all the information is being synchronized and not just the changes.

If any of the registered devices are not connected or available at the time of the sync, iSync saves the information meant for them, and updates them as soon as a connection to them becomes available.

If iSync detects that the same record has been changed on different source computers or devices and the changes are not identical, iSync asks you to resolve the conflict. In the dialog box that appears, select the source that will be used. If there is more than one conflict between sources, you will see a message to this effect. To resolve all conflicts with your selected source, click the check box next to this message. You can also click Later to resolve the conflicts at your next sync.

> **NOTE** After a sync, you may notice a new calendar in iCal called Unfiled. iSync creates an Unfiled calendar to hold date-related information from a mobile phone or Palm device that you have not specified should be added to one of your iCal calendars. You can keep the Unfiled calendar, or delete it after transferring its events to another iCal calendar.

Using the Backup Application

Backup is the .Mac service's backup application, and provides a convenient way to back up important information on your computer to your iDisk or to recordable CD or DVD discs. To use Backup, you must be a .Mac member.

Backing up

A backup is just a copy of a file or files, but the copy is made to safeguard the data. If something bad happens to the original, the backup copy should still be fine, especially if it is on a different disk.

The hard drive mechanism in your computer will fail at some point; drives are typically rated for five years of constant use but can fail *at any time*. And the magnetic medium which holds your precious data becomes demagnetized spontaneously as time progresses; at this very moment, your data is *deteriorating*!

Any time your computer crashes, data corruption may occur. Files can be unintentionally erased. A computer virus may damage your data. Your computer could be lost or stolen or simply die.

The Backup application is the very model of a modern personal backup application. It is easy to understand, easy to use, and free with your .Mac subscription.

You need to manually or automatically make back-up copies of your important files to a folder on your hard drive, an external FireWire hard disk, your iPod and iDisk, or a recordable CD or DVD.

With Backup, you can:

- Back up files in your home folder in a few clicks
- Back up your personal data such as contacts, calendars, and Safari settings
- Back up iLife data quickly
- Back up your iTunes music
- Schedule automatic backups
- Restore files from a backup

Setting up Backup

If you did not purchase the .Mac shrink-wrapped box, which contains a CD with the Backup application, you must download it from the .Mac Web site (www.mac.com) and install it on your hard disk. Put an alias of Backup in your Dock; its orange umbrella will remind you to use it often.

Using the Backup interface

When you first open Backup, you see screens similar to those shown in Figure 14.44. This is a summary of the basic items you can back up using this program. This includes your Home Folder, Personal Data & Settings, iLife applications, and iTunes library. Select the type of backup you want to execute, and the schedule shows up in the main Backup window. Each backup type, except for the Home Folder Backup, defaults to a destination of CDs or DVDs. The following backup types are available:

FIGURE 14.44

This window appears when Backup is first launched.

- **Home Folder Backup:** This selection is for an easy backup of your home folder. This includes your documents, movies, photos, music, library, and settings. If you properly store your personal data, this is a nearly complete backup of your information. By default it also selects the Backups folder as a destination, as well as CDs/DVDs.

- **Personal Data & Settings:** This selection is an easy backup for your Address Book, iCal, Keychain, Safari Settings, and Stickies.

- **iLife:** This backs up your Garageband, iDVD, iPhoto, iMovie, iTunes, and iWeb projects. Even though iTunes is not part of the iLife suite, it is placed here as the most logical place for it.

- **iTunes Library:** This backs up your iTunes library.

- **Custom:** This allows you to select which items you would like to back up or exclude from the backup. You can choose from any of the preceding options in this backup.

If you want to edit the schedule, destination, or source files, doubleclick the backup job and the job details window pops up.

Backup window

After you select the type of job you want to schedule, the computer places the job into the Backup window. Here you can see the name of the job to be executed, time of next execution, and destination of the backup job.

You can easily add another job by clicking the plus sign in the bottom left of the window. Again the quick job reference window shows up, as shown in Figure 14.45, and you can select the type of job you want to add. To modify, delete, execute now, or restore a backup, select the job you want to execute this command to. Then click the cog at the bottom left of the window and choose the action you want to perform.

FIGURE 14.45

The Job Reference window with one of each type of job

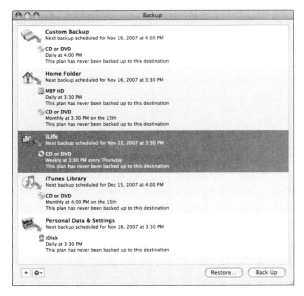

Job detail

When you double-click a job or select Edit from the cog, the job detail window pops up. See Figure 14.46. Here you can see the items being backed up, set the destinations, see history, and restore.

Job detail window with the source history and restore

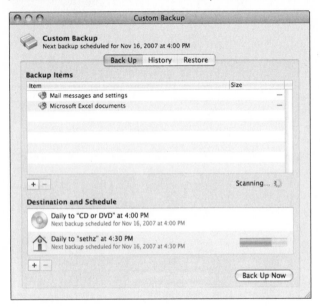

The Backup Items box is where you can add and remove the items being backed up. Click the plus sign underneath the Backup Items part of the pane. A pop-up window shows up with three tabs, as shown in Figure 14.47. Select which item you would like to add to your backup. The following tabs are available:

- **QuickPicks**: QuickPicks are groups of important related files that Apple has decided are the most helpful to back up. Take a quick look at the list and you will quickly understand the concept. The QuickPicks include files in Mac OS X that most users would not think of or know to back up.

- **Files & Folders:** Here you can specifically designate a folder to backup. For example, if you have a folder on your hard drive that everyone shares, you can designate it for backup.

- **Spotlight:** Here you can use Spotlight to search for specific files or folders you would like to back up. This is especially helpful if you don't remember where you saved an item.

The Destination and Schedule box allows you to add and remove multiple destinations. Click the plus sign below the Destination and Schedule box. Here you can select a destination, folder and a schedule:

- **Destination:** This is where you can select the drive, home folder, your iDisk, or CD.

- **Folder:** If you selected your hard drive or home folder you can choose a specific folder where your backup will go.

- **Schedule:** Here you can set the frequency (Day, Week, Month, 3 Months, 6 Months) and the time the backup executes.

For each destination you would like, click the plus sign.

FIGURE 14.47

Adding files to your backup

Choosing a destination disk

- **Back up to iDisk:** This is a good option if you are connected to the Internet, have enough space on your iDisk, and would like to have access to your backed-up files from any Internet-connected Macintosh. Remember that iDisk backups can be slow, and that you've got a limited amount of space on there, unless you opt to purchase more.

- **Back up to CD/DVD:** This is a good choice if you want to back up a lot of information. A recordable CD holds 650MB; a recordable DVD holds 4.7GB. If you have more information than will fit on a single CD or DVD disc, you can use more than one to hold your backup. Backup informs you of how many discs your backup will use. You can use a combination of CD or DVD disks, if you want. The last disk in a set is called the *master disk* because it contains the information needed to restore files Backup has split between discs.

- **Back up to a Drive:** A hard drive can hold the most data and give the fastest access of these storage options. The hard drive you use can be an internal hard drive or an external FireWire drive; this includes the iPod, which must be mounted on the desktop before it can be used. You can back up files to a folder or partition of your main hard disk, although this largely defeats the purpose of a backup and is not really recommended; but Backup will do it. You can also select a folder on a mounted network server as the destination.

TIP   As you add files, keep an eye on the storage capacity of your destination disk. The meter in the bottom right of the job reference window shows how much space is left in your iDisk if it is selected as the destination disk. Dark green means how much is already on the iDisk now, before the backup. Light green means how much space the current backup will use.

Viewing the History of a job

To view the history of a job that has executed, double-click the job in the job Reference window. Click the History tab. Here you can see the dates and times of previous executions as well as success or failure. See Figure 14.48.

FIGURE 14.48

The history of Personal Data & Settings backup

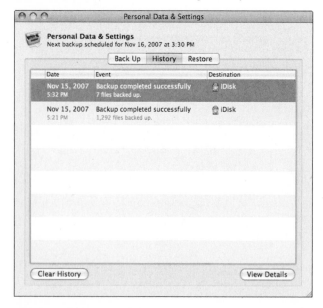

Backup Tips

Backing up is vital. Follow these tips when backing up your files:

- Do not try to use Backup to copy files from one computer to another. Apple says Backup is meant for personal backups from a single computer only. If you try to use Backup to copy files to a location (like your iDisk) that already contains files put there by Backup running from another computer, the older files will be completely erased. Use Sync instead.

- If you spot an alert icon (a triangle containing an exclamation point) next to an item in the backup list, it means that Backup can't locate the item; it may have been moved, renamed, or deleted. To back up the item, delete it from the backup list, and add it again.

- If you deleted one or several QuickPicks, and you change your mind and want them back, choose Edit ➪ Restore All QuickPicks.

- Files that you copied to a location using Backup can only be deleted using Backup! If you want to remove them to save space, choose the restore location (iDisk or Drive), select the items to be removed, and choose Edit ➪ Remove from List, or click the minus sign button in the lower left of the window. If the item is in a folder, select the folder and delete the item from the Info drawer window.

- If you want to remove all the files from the Backup folder on your iDisk, Backup must be used to clear the folder's contents. From the destination pop-up menu, choose Back up to iDisk or Restore from iDisk. Choose Edit ➪ Clear iDisk Backup Folder. Click OK.

- Backup cannot be used to back up applications.

- You must be a paid .Mac member to back up your files to a CD or DVD disk.

- You need to have at least the same amount of space free on your hard drive as the size of the recordable media you will use for your backup. For example, if you are backing up to a DVD-R disc, you would need at least 4.7GB free on you hard drive to perform the backup. Backup uses this space to temporarily assemble the backup before it copies it to the disc.

- For a restore, Backup cannot recognize files on a CD or DVD put there by another application, or dragged there manually. Backup can see files only it has backed up.

- Restores do not work to files that are write-protected. To change a file's privileges to Read & Write, select the file in the Finder, choose File ➪ Get Info, click the disclosure triangle for Ownership and permissions, and select Read and Write from the Owner and Others pop-up menu.

Here you can clear the history of a job. If you don't need it as reference, this is a great idea. You also can view the details of a job by double-clicking the execution or clicking View Details. This brings up the Console, where you can see the details of the job execution. This option is for more advanced users. See Figure 14-49.

FIGURE 14.49

The console showing the details of the Personal Data & Settings backup execution.

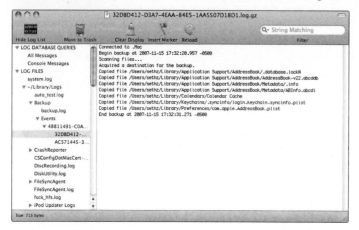

Restoring backed-up files

To restore backed-up files to your hard disk, follow these steps:

1. **From the main Job Reference window, double-click the job you want to restore.** Click the Restore button.

2. **Select the date you want to restore your files from.** Then follow the columns to the file or setting you want to restore.

3. **Click the Restore Selection button.** This restores the item. If you want to restore it to an alternate location, click the checkbox Restore to an alternate location.

To stop an install in progress, click Cancel. Only the files that were restored up to that moment will appear on your hard disk.

iCards

iCards are digital postcards that you can send via e-mail. Your recipients see the iCard appear right in the e-mail message body, and don't need to click a link to visit a Web site in order to see the card as in similar services.

iCards is the only part of the .Mac services that is completely free. You don't need to be a .Mac member to use iCards, or even a .Mac 60-day trial tire-kicker.

iCards can be sent or viewed on any Macintosh or Windows computer, via the default Web browser and standard e-mail programs.

Over 400 designed iCards are available from the iCard Web site, organized into categories such as Birthday, Love, and Holidays, to name a few. If you are a .Mac member, you can also create your own custom cards featuring digital photos or artwork from your iDisk. If you design a really beautiful iCard, you can submit it to the Member's Portfolio, and Apple will review it and consider adding it to the public selection. If you are an artist, you can offer your artwork for others to send by submitting it to the Featured Artist category.

To send an iCard, follow these steps:

1. **Visit the iCards Web site at** www.mac.com, **and in the .Mac menu bar, click iCards.** The iCards welcome page, Main Categories, appears.

2. **Choose an image category you want to explore by clicking a category image**.

3. **Choose an image from the category by clicking it.** Some categories have more than one page of images to explore, and you will see links to additional pages in the top right corner. Also notice that your path through the process is displayed at the top left; to go back, click the path you want to return to.

4. **Compose a message in the Write your message here field on the edit page, shown in Figure 14.50.** Select a font from the list on the right. When done, click Continue. On the Address Card page, you see your card at the bottom, complete with your message as it will appear to your recipients.

5. **Enter your name and e-mail address in the fields on the left, and check Send a copy to myself if you want a copy.** Check Hide Distribution List if you don't want your recipients to see your other recipients.

   To send a card to one recipient, type his or her e-mail address into the field on the top right.

   To send a card to several recipients, type the first person's e-mail address in the field, and then click Add Recipient. Repeat until the Recipient list contains all the addresses you want.

   Remove an address from the Recipient list by selecting it and clicking Remove Recipient.

6. **Click Send Your Card.** The Thank You page appears.

You can return to the Main Categories page from here by clicking the Return to Categories button, or click Send Same Card to send the same card to someone else.

FIGURE 14.50

The iCards edit card page

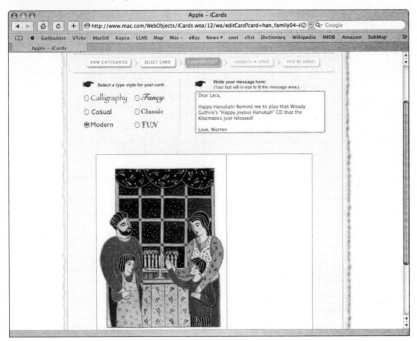

Web page courtesy of Apple, Inc.

You must be a .Mac member to use your own image on an iCard. You might want to do this to send a holiday photo of your family, share a favorite vacation photo, or show grandparents a scan of your kid's latest artistic scribblings. To place your image on an iCard, follow these steps:

1. **Save your image in either JPEG or GIF format.**

2. **Name the image following these guidelines:**

   ▪ End the file name with a .jpg or .gif extension.

   ▪ Use only uppercase letters (A–Z), lowercase letters (a–z), numbers (0–9) or the underscore (_) in the file name.

   ▪ Don't use spaces, accented letters, or special characters or symbols.

   ▪ Don't start a file name with a period (.)

3. **Copy the file into the Pictures folder on your iDisk or into a folder within the Pictures folder.** The folder name must also follow the naming guidelines in the previous step.

4. **On the iCards Main Categories page, click Create Your Own.**

5. **Enter your password if necessary and press Return.**

    On the Create Your Own page, you see the contents of your iDisk Pictures folder in the list on the left. If you need to add other images to the pictures folder of your iDisk, do so and then click Update Folder. Select a new folder from the pop-up menu, look inside a folder by selecting it and clicking Open, or select an image and click Preview to see a thumbnail on the right. When you find the image you want, click Select This Image.

6. **Send the iCard. (Refer to Steps 4 to 6 in the first list in this section.)**

If a recipient cannot view the iCard (which is a JPEG attachment to the e-mail message), his or her e-mail application may not display attached images automatically. Ask the recipient to open the JPEG file attached to the message to view it.

Summary

This chapter examined Mac OS X's optional .Mac services suite, available for $99.95 from Apple.

We took a detailed look at each of the .Mac services, as well as the included Mac OS X applications that work with .Mac, and programs you can download from .Mac after you are a member.

New features to Leopard include Back to My Mac, iChat theatre (built into iChat), and tighter integration of .Mac into the Leopard Finder. Groups have been added to the .Mac service menu to allow easier collaboration by multiple users. Increased storage for .Mac members has been added to meet users' growing space demands.

Chapter 15

Managing Fonts

There is no computer platform that handles typefaces in such a consistent and reliable way as a Macintosh. Many publishing companies and advertising agencies use Macs and Mac fonts to create magazines, books, and other outstanding printed pieces. The Mac single-handedly created the desktop publishing revolution and is still spearheading it with OS X Leopard. One of the most important aspects of that revolution is font management with consistency.

This chapter discusses what exactly a font is and what font technologies the Mac employs. It examines what features are incorporated into Mac OS X Leopard for working with fonts. The font standards supported by Mac OS X are listed and described, and where the fonts reside is demystified. The chapter also looks at managing fonts with font management software and how Font Book fits into the picture, and you can find information on font utilities and some useful tips for working with fonts.

Understanding Fonts

Before the arrival of the Mac and desktop publishing technology, fonts were cast in metal and sets of each character stored in drawers with many compartments. In order to generate the front cover of the *New York Times,* men with ink-stained hands would pick and choose the individual letters from these drawers and arrange them within a tray, tighten them up with little slivers of lead (thus the term "leading" which defines the amount of space between lines of text), and then roll ink over the metal letter and press the paper on top. A time-consuming process, to say the least. The fonts were provided by foundries and ordered as families. They were expensive, awkward to use, and there weren't thousands of fonts to choose from at any particular print shop.

The owners tended to choose a few key fonts that were common and typeset from the available collection. The metal font technology went as far as to cast entire pages of metal type in a typesetter foundry for the presses. To date, the companies that supply font families are still called *foundries*, although it is doubtful that Adobe still has any blacksmiths on staff.

A *font* is a collection of type characters in a particular style and size from a particular *typeface*. That's the quick and easy definition, but to understand how fonts fit into the worlds of typography and computers, it's helpful to know a couple of other terms.

The most common misunderstanding is to confuse *font* with *typeface*. The difference is that a font is a design for a complete collection of letters, punctuation marks, and special symbols with specific attributes such as height, weight, posture, and orientation (for example, Helvetica Bold Oblique 12 points). A typeface is the overarching design features that make up the visual characteristics of a font.

Typefaces are themselves a subset of *font families*. Such families are groups of typefaces and fonts that have similar design elements and features. For example, the Times New Roman font family has roman and italic styles in regular, semi-bold, and bold weights. In typography, each of the style and weight combinations is called a *typeface*, with each *point size* being an individual *font*. Confused yet? Let's try to make this a bit simpler. Look at this handy outline format below to see how the different elements interrelate.

> **Font Family: Times New Roman**
>
> Typeface: Times New Roman Italic
>
> *Font: Times New Roman Italic 10 Point*
>
> *Font: Times New Roman Italic 16 Point*
>
> Typeface: Times New Roman Bold
>
> *Font: Times New Roman Bold 12 Point*
>
> *Font: Times New Roman Bold 18 Point*

Sadly, the word *font* has come to be used in place of *typeface* and *family*, much to the frustration of typography purists. This is because today a single computer "font" file can contain many families of a single typeface. The digital representation of a font family/typeface/font is all stored in a so-called *font file*.

In general usage today, a font has come to mean a digital file that contains the information necessary for a computer to render characters of a unique, unified design on the screen and in print. The visual concept that represents a letter, punctuation mark, or symbol is called a *character*.

Behind the scenes, these individual characters are represented by numbers between 1 and 256, following an old standard called ASCII (for example: a = 97, A = 65, b = 98, B = 66, and so on). Each of those ASCII characters is stored in one memory chunk, called a *byte*. However, 256 proves to be a rather limited number, considering that there are many symbols not used in English but necessary in other languages. In the early 1990s, *Unicode* was developed as the answer to this problem. The Unicode standard uses 2 bytes to represent each character, expanding the range to 65,536 distinct characters per set (basically, they made the "serial number" of the letters longer, so they could gain the ability to have more letters). Currently, Unicode version 4.0.0 has a unique identifier for 96,382 glyphs in use by the world's principal languages as well as mathematical and other symbols.

One last piece of vocabulary: The shape of any given character within a font is called a *glyph*. As you may have noted above, the height of characters/glyphs in a font is measured in *points,* with each point measuring about 1/72 of an inch. When you elect to use a particular font, at a particular size, in a particular style, embedded in that so-called font file is the mathematical definition of the elements of the font family and the specifics of the typeface, and the various rules regarding specific point sizes, all allowing the computer to generate the font's *glyphs* to meet the user requirements. That's a lot of sub-sub-sub categories just to make "the quick brown fox jumped over the lazy dog."

Understanding Mac Font Formats

There are different *formats* or font *types* supported by OS X on the Mac. Each format has a different approach at describing the glyphs in a font to the computer. OS X supports the most common and important formats used by the printing and publishing industries. Following is a list of OS X's supported font formats:

- PostScript
- PostScript Multiple Master
- TrueType
- OpenType
- dFont

Bitmap fonts

Bitmap fonts (sometimes referred to as *bitmapped* or *fixed-size* fonts) are the original fonts used on the very first Macs in 1984. Mac OS X Leopard does not use bitmap fonts, but Mac OS 9 and earlier iterations of OS X used them (through Classic, which is no longer supported . . . officially). It is hoped that at this point most users have switched to more-advanced font types. Although bitmap fonts are fast becoming a historical curiosity, knowing something about them is helpful in understanding font technology.

In a bitmap font, every character is represented by an arrangement of dots. Figure 15.1 shows the dots in an enlarged view of two characters of a bitmapped font.

FIGURE 15.1

Bitmap fonts contain dot-for-dot pictures of characters(Times capital *A* and *G* at 12-, 14-, and 18-point sizes enlarged to show detail).

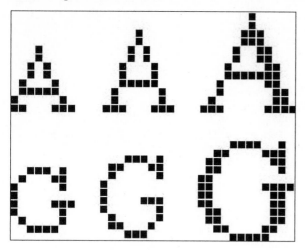

The name *bitmap* refers to each dot's value (filled in or not) being stored in one or more *bits* of data. For monochrome fonts (and images), one bit is sufficient to record each dot's value. For shades of gray or colors, each dot requires more than one bit of data.

The computer translates the bitmap into *pixels* (picture elements) to display it on a monitor, or into ink dots to print it. The way each font looks on the screen, or after printing, depends on how its point size relates to the *resolution,* that is, the density of dots displayed on the monitor or produced by the printer. In printers, resolution is measured in *dots per inch*; typical resolutions go from 300 to 800 dots per inch (dpi). For monitors, the pixel resolution is measured as the number of pixels that can be displayed, for example 1,280 wide x 1,024 tall. Another important value for monitors is called *pixel setting,* which in older Mac monitors was 72 dpi; newer monitors use a 96 dpi pixel setting.

Each bitmap font is designed for display in one size only, so bitmap fonts usually are installed in sets. A typical set includes 9-, 10-, 12-, 14-, 18-, and 24-point font sizes. If you need text in a size for which no bitmap font is installed, the Mac OS must scale a bitmap font's character bitmaps up or down to the size you want. The results are misshapen or blocky, as shown in Figure 15.2.

FIGURE 15.2

Bitmap fonts look best at installed sizes; in this scaling of the Times 24 font, note the blockiness of the 20- and 30-point font sizes (enlarged to show detail).

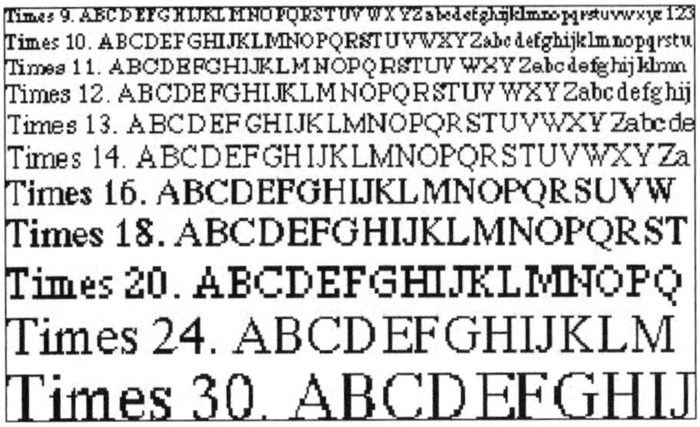

```
Times 9. ABCDEFGHIJKLMNOPQRSTUVWXYZabcdefghijklmnopqrstuvwxyz123
Times 10. ABCDEFGHIJKLMNOPQRSTUVWXYZabcdefghijklmnopqrstu
Times 11. ABCDEFGHIJKLMNOPQRSTUVWXYZabcdefghijklmn
Times 12. ABCDEFGHIJKLMNOPQRSTUVWXYZabcdefghij
Times 13. ABCDEFGHIJKLMNOPQRSTUVWXYZabcde
Times 14. ABCDEFGHIJKLMNOPQRSTUVWXYZa
Times 16. ABCDEFGHIJKLMNOPQRSUVW
Times 18. ABCDEFGHIJKLMNOPQRST
Times 20. ABCDEFGHIJKLMNOPQ
Times 24. ABCDEFGHIJKLM
Times 30. ABCDEFGHIJ
```

PostScript fonts

PostScript fonts were part of a series of innovations that started the professional desktop publishing revolution. Introduced by Adobe Systems in 1984, they were the first fonts to maintain a consistent appearance when resized. For this reason they are known as *scaleable* or *variable-size* fonts. Currently, PostScript fonts are an industry standard.

By using mathematical *descriptions* of the outline of the glyph that make up a character, the computer can redraw it at will without losing any details. PostScript fonts were the first of the many types of *outline fonts*. See Figure 15.3.

This outline is made out of connected lines, each a special kind of *vector graphic,* known as Bezier curves. Vector graphics are the bread and butter of professional applications like Adobe Illustrator. In fact, Illustrator can be used to create or alter PostScript fonts.

Type 1 PostScript fonts have two files that must be properly installed for the font to function when displayed and printed. Each PostScript font has a *screen font* file and its associated *printer font* file. The screen font file contains a bitmap representation of the font in at least one point size and the *font metrics* data, with information about *kerning pairs* (kerning, in loose terms, is the space between letters, with some pairs getting specific adjustments to maintain a clean look), leading (pronounced "lehd-ing," not "leed-ing," leading is the space between the lines), and other useful values; the printer font file contains the scalable outline font.

FIGURE 15.3

PostScript fonts are based on outlines. Here, a lowercase *a* in 18-point Bauhaus 93 regular is shown in Adobe Illustrator CS with an outline of the same character. Three Beziér handle points are activated.

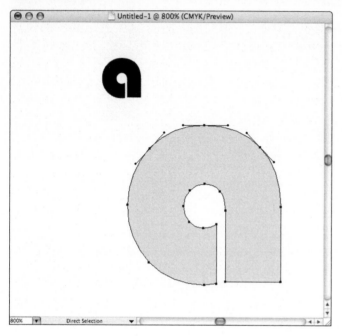

Although a PostScript screen font appears in font menus and displays accurately, without the associated printer font installed, this screen font does not print correctly. Conversely, a font does not appear in a font menu, nor does text previously formatted with that font show properly on-screen, without its associated screen font installed.

PostScript fonts are divided into two main categories: Type 1 and Type 3. Most PostScript fonts in use are Type 1. They yield great results at small font sizes and low resolutions. Although Type 1 fonts generally look better, Type 3 fonts are more elaborate. The characters in Type 3 fonts have variable stroke weights and are filled with something other than a solid color, such as shades of gray or blends that go from white to black. Type 3 fonts were popular in the late 1980s, and are still used for custom fonts and special effects.

Mac OS X Leopard includes built-in support for PostScript Type 1 fonts in three variations:

- Screen font files, optionally in a font suitcase, plus corresponding PostScript Type 1 outline fonts for printing (standard Type 1 fonts)
- QuickDraw GX-enabled font suitcases
- QuickDraw GX-enabled Multiple Master font suitcases

PostScript font metrics information included with the font screen file contains kerning pairs information and hints that help the font look better at different sizes. Additionally, PostScript offers more than just outline fonts: it's a *page description language* that precisely specifies the location and other characteristics of every text and graphic item on the page.

PostScript fonts are regularly used by professional graphic artists in print production and other disciplines. Many organizations have large collections of them. PostScript fonts will not be completely replaced with another format in the foreseeable future.

Multiple Master fonts

Multiple Master (MM) fonts are special versions of certain PostScript Type 1 fonts that allow variation of one or more font parameters, most often weight (bold or light), style (italic or plain), or width (condensed or extended). This enables the creation of an unlimited number of different styles, known as *instances,* from the same font file, a unique advantage.

However, the MM technology was not entirely a success. Not all applications support it, and the MM fonts can be difficult to output correctly. There are only about 50 MM fonts, and most are from Adobe. In late 1999, Adobe announced that it would no longer develop MM fonts.

 **Mac OS 10.2 and above can activate existing instances of this font type, but cannot create ate instances. (To *activate* a font means to make it available to applications for use.)**

TrueType fonts

TrueType fonts are outline fonts that contain both screen and printer font information in a single font file — an advance over PostScript fonts on the file management side.

TrueType fonts look good at all sizes. They work with all Mac OS applications and all types of printers, including PostScript printers. The Mac OS smoothly scales a TrueType font's character outlines to any size on a display screen and on printers of any resolution, all with equally good results. Figure 15.4 is an example of TrueType font scaling. TrueType differs from PostScript in how it mathematically specifies font outlines and adjusts the outlines for small font sizes and low resolutions.

TrueType was developed by Apple and licensed to Microsoft. Initially it was developed as a response to the closed nature of PostScript fonts and the exceedingly high license fees charged by Adobe to include a PostScript rendering engine in LaserWriter printers. TrueType was introduced in 1991 as an integral part of Mac System 7 and Microsoft Windows 3.1. Adobe responded to this assault on the turf it controlled by releasing Adobe Type Manager to improve the on-screen appearance of PostScript Type 1 fonts, and by disclosing the PostScript Type 1 definition, allowing competition in the marketplace for PostScript fonts.

FIGURE 15.4

TrueType fonts scale smoothly to all sizes and resolutions (enlarged to show detail).

```
Times 9. ABCDEFGHIJKLMNOPQRSTUVWXYZabcdefghijklmnopqrstuvwxyz123
Times 10. ABCDEFGHIJKLMNOPQRSTUVWXYZabcdefghijklmnopqrstu
Times 11. ABCDEFGHIJKLMNOPQRSTUVWXYZabcdefghijklmn
Times 12. ABCDEFGHIJKLMNOPQRSTUVWXYZabcdefghij
Times 13. ABCDEFGHIJKLMNOPQRSTUVWXYZabcde
Times 14. ABCDEFGHIJKLMNOPQRSTUVWXYZa
Times 16. ABCDEFGHIJKLMNOPQRSUVW
Times 18. ABCDEFGHIJKLMNOPQRST
Times 20. ABCDEFGHIJKLMNOPQ
Times 24. ABCDEFGHIJKLM
Times 30. ABCDEFGHIJ
```

TrueType was at the time only a limited success. Font foundries were reluctant to develop TrueType fonts, concentrating instead on PostScript Type 1. However, this has been changing rapidly and now foundries have TrueType versions of many PostScript fonts. One great aspect of TrueType fonts is that they look great on the screen as a result of techniques such as *hinting* and *anti-aliasing*. Even at small sizes they are readable. Another important improvement introduced by TrueType fonts is Unicode support, in which more than 65,000 glyphs can be stored and accessed in a single font file, allowing for multi-language support as well as a barrage of important symbols used by professional graphic artists.

Mac OS X Leopard can recognize traditional Mac TrueType files and font suitcases, which are folder-like containers of TrueType Mac font files. Because Mac font files have two forks (parts), called the *data fork* and the *resource fork*, these font files and font suitcases must be stored on disks or other volumes that have the Mac OS Extended format (also known as HFS Plus).

> **NOTE** Mac OS X Leopard also recognizes native Windows TrueType font files, which have the filename extension of .ttf or .ttc. Windows files do not use resource forks.

TrueType fonts are commonly used in home or office environments. They are infrequently used in graphic production; however, they are supported by most *RIP* systems by encapsulating the TrueType font information on PostScript Type 42 fonts. (A RIP is a Raster Image Processor, which is hardware or software that prepares digital files for printing.)

If you are a designer using TrueType fonts, be sure to *embed* them within your documents when making a PDF or PostScript file to avoid problems during the RIP process. Since the introduction of True Type fonts in 1991 with System 7, Apple has been improving them. Today, OS X Leopard is able to use the TrueType GX standard, which utilizes the features of QuickDraw GX and has some Apple-only extensions to the font format, such as a Line Layout Manager and Style Variations.

Currently, Apple and Microsoft are contributing to TrueType technology as well as Adobe. The new Microsoft/Adobe effort is called TrueType Open v.2.0 or *OpenType*, a format capable of containing PostScript and TrueType fonts as well as many typographical controls. More features of OpenType are discussed in the following paragraphs.

Raster Image Processor

Raster images are made up of bitmaps that precisely describe position, weight, and color. Whether the image is in black and white, grayscale, or color, each component will go through this *rasterizing* process. A raster image processor (RIP) is a machine that *rasterizes* into a *bitmap* image all the mathematical definitions of each character, graphic, or object that will be printed. The quality of the printouts is defined by the device resolution in dots per inch (dpi). (A typical laser printer RIP has a resolution of 600x600 dpi.) PostScript really shines in this process because it standardizes printing by equalizing output no matter what device you use. RIPs are everywhere, from the one that renders images in your computer screen, to your laser printer, all the way to the giant systems used by publishing companies such as Wiley & Sons. Many RIP machines output to film, which is developed to prepare printing plates. The most advanced RIPs generate their output directly to printing plates. Just remember that the quality of your RIP will have an impact in the quality of your printouts.

OpenType fonts

An extension of the TrueType Open format from Microsoft, the OpenType format supports both PostScript Type 1 and TrueType font data. OpenType can be considered a superset of PostScript Type 1 and TrueType fonts. The technology allows for the embedding of each of the font standards into a single, unified file structure, which in turn allows for backward application compatibility.

The promise of OpenType fonts is great; however, it is still too early to tell if OpenType will eventually replace PostScript Type 1 and/or TrueType fonts. Of course, Mac OS X Leopard supports the OpenType standard. Currently, Adobe InDesign and Adobe Photoshop support the full set of OpenType extensions and refinements introduced by Adobe, Apple, and Microsoft.

OpenType takes away the burden of managing different font standards and allows the user to access a broader set of glyphs and even *program* the font set for automatic glyph substitution. Even if your application has basic support for OpenType, you will be able to use the basic character set (the first 256 glyph locations); however, if your system has full Unicode support (unless your computer has vacuum tubes powering it, it supports Unicode), you can access more than 65,000 glyphs on the same font file. Cross-platform compatibility is another important aspect, meaning that, like current TrueType support on OS X Leopard, font files are interchangeable between a PC and a Mac. OpenType fonts and the operating system services that support them provide users with a simple way to install and use fonts, whether the fonts contain TrueType outlines or PostScript outlines.

The new OpenType standard tries to integrate the best features of PostScript and TrueType font description implementations and put it to good use within applications such as Adobe InDesign. Information from the manufacturers indicates that the goals they try to reach with this new standard include the following:

- Broader multiplatform support
- Better support for international character sets

- Better protection for font data

- Smaller file sizes to make font distribution more efficient

- Broader support for advanced typographic control

OpenType is a powerful standard able to meet the current and future demands of experienced users. Many important features missing in both PostScript Type 1 and TrueType fonts are implemented in OpenType. Many font designers may be delighted to find that they have the ability to add high-quality glyphs and glyph substitution technologies, as well as the ability to sign their creations or allow them to be used by a particular application or purpose.

OpenType also makes fonts easy to install because it is up to the operating system implementation to manage the display and print features of the fonts. Mac OS X Leopard has addressed all the features needed to put those fonts to good use. In the Mac you will find that those fonts may have a .TTF or .OTF extension. The extension .TTC identifies a TrueType font collection file, which is considered part of the OpenType standard, even when there are no OpenType layout tables inside the collection. Applications such as Adobe Illustrator correctly identify the fonts installed in the system by their particular icons, as shown in Figure 15.5.

FIGURE 15.5

Adobe Illustrator CS shows each font file format. This application fully supports Multiple Master fonts.

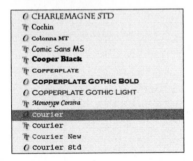

Mac OS X system dfonts

Mac OS X introduced the *dfont* format, which is a special Apple version of TrueType fonts that contain their information in the data fork instead of a separate resource fork as did previous Mac font files (see Figure 15.6). dfonts are compatible with Unix file systems, such as the Unified File System (UFS) that can be installed optionally with Mac OS X. The system software uses the dfonts internally, and they are located in the `System/Library/Fonts` folder.

Some of the dfonts are high-quality fonts with extensive glyph sets, so graphic designers may be interested in using them. If you are installing PostScript or TrueType fonts on your system, be aware that some of their names conflict with some of the dfont names. As described later in this chapter, you should remove the conflicting fonts you don't want.

Mac OS X Font Facts and Features

Mac OS X Leopard is full of font-related features and technologies. Here are some facts you should know:

- Mac OS X 10.5 provides native support for more font types than any other operating system. As a result, a better utilization of available resources is reached as well as an unprecedented level of cross-platform interaction.

- Mac OS X 10.5 does not impose a limit on the number of fonts you can have installed on the system. It is good practice to manage your fonts by grouping them by purpose or kind. There are many utilities that allow you to handle large numbers of fonts. Apple's own Font Book utility, included in OS X Leopard and described later in this chapter, gives you a great deal of control and flexibility when managing installed fonts.

- Mac OS X uses anti-aliasing edge smoothing (as part of its Quartz implementation) to increase the perceived resolution of fonts rendered on-screen; Apple calls this *font smoothing*. The readability of fonts that Mac OS X 10.5 displays can be controlled in the Appearance pane of System Preferences. In the Font Smoothing style pop-up menu, you may choose Standard (best for CRT displays), Light, Medium (best for flat-panel displays), or Strong. At small font sizes, the smoothed fonts can seem fuzzy, so you can set the font size below which the operating system turns off text smoothing in the pop-up menu at the bottom of the Appearance pane.

- Mac OS X provides multiple font locations, with different access privileges for each location. This gives you better control and more options to organize fonts for different users and uses. It can also be confusing and frustrating, but "with great power comes great responsibility."

- As a startup point, Mac OS X Leopard includes about 100 font families, including support for non-roman languages. Many fonts utilize the Unicode space to provide many useful glyphs.

- Mac OS X protects itself by checking the integrity of a font when it is displayed or printed. Apple calls this *font validation*. If the operating system detects a corrupt font, it will be automatically deactivated.

- Apple Advanced Typography (AAT) is a Mac OS X system-level feature that supports sophisticated typographic capabilities previously found only in typesetting applications such as QuarkXpress or Adobe InDesign. Included in these capabilities are kerning (customizing the spacing between certain pairs of letters), tracking (adjusting the spacing between groups of letters and entire blocks of text), ligatures (two or more letters combined into one character), and many other adjustable attributes, which are available to many included applications, as well as TextEdit.

- Mac OS X Leopard implementation has built-in routines designed to protect font file integrity. Unlike OS 9, font files are opened with read-only privileges that ward off misbehaving applications or glitches. There are many utilities that have the ability to fix damaged font files, which are described later in this chapter. Apple has resolved many of the issues related to font management and general usage; however, there are always third-party utilities to help with font management, which can be useful and permit the professional user to achieve an unprecedented degree of control over fonts.

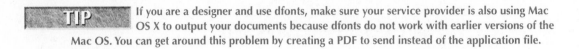

TIP   If you are a designer and use dfonts, make sure your service provider is also using Mac OS X to output your documents because dfonts do not work with earlier versions of the Mac OS. You can get around this problem by creating a PDF to send instead of the application file.

FIGURE 15.6

Mac OS X Leopard uses dfonts, which are located inside `/System/Library/Fonts`, to communicate with the user. Moving or deleting these files can have negative consequences. If you do so, make sure you can recover those files to their original location.

Mapping Mac OS X Font Locations

One of the many useful features of OS X is its ability to use font files stored in different locations. Enforcing its security and privacy aspects, OS X Leopard keeps the integrity of each user's font installations. Another important side of OS X is its capacity to share fonts among users, protecting the font's integrity, as well as use font files that have been presented by network resources (that is, servers and the like). The OS X system also keeps a special location for the fonts it uses to interact with the user. Although it seems complicated, this methodology actually helps to keep font files organized and undamaged. This is a feature that has been present on OS X since its introduction by Apple.

Mac OS X has a predefined priority sequence to search for fonts on five designated folders. Following you will find a description of those folders, their locations, and their general purpose. Notice that Mac OS X follows the sequence in the order described here:

- **Application folder:** Some applications install fonts in a location within their own folder. At font selection time, that location is the first one to be searched. Duplicate fonts uncovered in subsequent locations are ignored. This holds true only for that particular application.

- **User's home folder at** `/Users/username/Library/Fonts`: No one but the user can access these fonts. This is the most common location for fonts to be kept for most users.

- **General font folder at** `/Library/Fonts`: Fonts kept here are available to all users with accounts on the machine. Font Book and other applications allow the installation of fonts inside this location; however, you have to authenticate as system administrator to access the folder.

- **From a Network Server at** `/Network/Library/Fonts`: Access this folder via the Network icon, which is located below the iDisk icon in the Finder. The font files listed inside the folder are stored in another computer and are accessed via your network connections. Many organizations and professional service bureaus keep their fonts organized within the network folder to have a single management place for all the users in their network.

- **System fonts at** `/System/Library/Fonts`: The system uses this location to store the fonts used to manage the communications with the user and the overall look and feel of the computer. No fonts should be installed here. It is important to keep the consistency of the operating environment under which all the applications are executed. The system fonts are TrueType under the *dfont* format.

With this knowledge about the different locations for font files, it becomes important to decide where to place those files. One aspect that cannot be overlooked is that font management utilities can and do alter the search order just described. Mac OS X Leopard allows for many ways to manage your environment. Some suggestions for your font files are as follows:

- Always back up your original font files, preferably on CD or DVD, and store them in a safe location.

- Font Management applications, including the built-in application Font Book, can change the search order of your font files. This is an important aspect to consider. Font Book and other third-party font management applications are discussed later in this chapter.

- If you are the only user on your system, put your fonts in the general fonts folder at `/Library/Fonts`. In order to do that, it is recommended that you create a general user and an administrator account. Use the administrator account to install your fonts and the general user account to operate the machine. Creating the administrator account has many advantages. Always keep your administrator account information private. (See Chapter 18 for more on user accounts.)

- In a workgroup environment, it is better to load the fonts from a network resource. Any OS X Leopard system can be utilized as a server and supply font files to the network. Many corporate environments and professional service bureaus use this approach. No fonts are installed in individual computers; instead, they are loaded from `/Network/Library/Fonts`. This method enables the font administrator to manage the fonts from a single location in the environment, allowing any added font to be immediately available to all users. Many network administrators remove fonts from the `/Users/username/Library/Fonts` and the `/Library/Fonts` folders. They also remove fonts with name conflicts from the individual systems in order to avoid font duplication and resource name confusions. Individuals in the network use utilities such as Font Book to create libraries and activate or deactivate fonts at will, as the work requires. Those individual settings do not affect other systems.

- It is recommended that you organize your added fonts inside your computer's official Fonts folders using subfolders. The system looks into those to present the fonts to the applications that need them. This age-old technique is effective, simple, and a common Mac practice.

Removing fonts from individual systems is a tempting proposition for network administrators. Because network resources are fast and reliable, it is reasonable to put all the fonts in a network resource and manage them from there. However, it is important to leave the following fonts in their `/System/Library/Fonts` location because this will ensure normal operation of the computer:

- Courier.dfont
- *Geneva.dfont*
- *Keyboard.dfont*
- *LastResort.dfont*
- LucidaGrande.dfont
- Monaco.dfont

The fonts marked in bold italics are 100 percent necessary for the general operation of the computer. Removal of these fonts will make your computer unable to boot (because the "Welcome to Mac OS X" messages are all rendered using these fonts)!

Some applications, such as Microsoft Office, also install fonts that are essential for their normal operation. For example, removing Hiragino Kaku Gothic Pro may lead to problems with Microsoft PowerPoint (see Figure 15.7). This font is located in the `/System/Library/Fonts` folder.

FIGURE 15.7

Removing Hiragino Kaku Gothic Pro may stop Microsoft PowerPoint 2004 from starting.

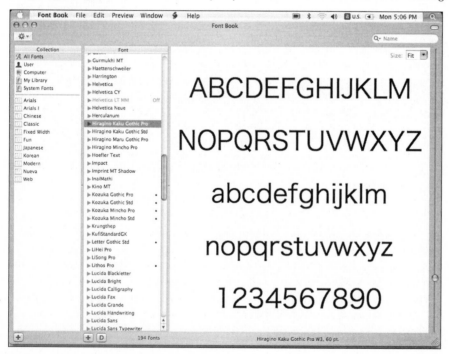

Managing Fonts in Mac OS X

There are many utilities in the Mac world designed to manage fonts, group them into collections, activate them, check them, and fix them. However, Mac OS X Leopard includes Font Book, a powerful utility designed to ease your way around the fonts provided with the system software. Leopard also includes the Font Panel utility and the Character Palette, which complement the power of Font Book. At installation time, there are approximately 100 fonts you can set up and place at your disposal. For many users, that amount is enough to cover every need. All the included fonts are of great quality and have been carefully selected by Apple to provide great satisfaction to you and produce impressive results on paper or the screen.

Font Book

Apple introduced Font Book with the release of Mac OS X Panther (version 10.3 for you version trackers). In the same manner as Mac OS X Leopard, the Font Book application has also evolved and matured. You will find Font Book inside the Applications folder. It can handle most of your needs when dealing with fonts.

Font Book is a nifty utility that empowers you to handle most font management tasks in its OS X Leopard incarnation. Font Book enables you to do the following:

- Install fonts in two major default locations, while also checking the font's integrity.
- Create font libraries, which can be located anywhere in your system, including the network, and then select which fonts should be activated at login time.
- Preview a font and its character set and appreciate the power of Unicode in combination with TrueType and OpenType Font schemes.
- Create font collections and be able to activate or deactivate entire groups of fonts, or select a particular font to turn on or off depending on your needs.
- Resolve duplicate font problems and validate font files. Font Book disables conflicting fonts, keeping your selection enabled. You can also select a font and perform a validation operation on it.
- Search your font files for a particular font in the different font locations, including libraries.

Installing fonts

Mac OS X Leopard provides a simple way to install fonts on your system. To install a font, follow these steps:

1. **Locate the font file with the Finder.**
2. **Double-click the font file you want to install, as shown in Figure 15.8.** (You can select more than one file by pressing ⌘ and clicking on each item and then selecting Open.)
3. **Font Book displays a preview of the font and enables you to install it on your system.**

587

FIGURE 15.8

Double-click a font file to check if it is installed. If the font is not installed, Font Book enables you to install it in the current library or collection by clicking the Install Font button.

You should be careful to note where your fonts will be installed. You can put them in the /Users/username/Library/Fonts folder, which is your home folder; or in /Library/Fonts, the general font folder. You can select your default location for installation in the Font Book Preferences pane. The home folder will be referred to as the *user location* and the general font folder as the *computer location*. (See Figure 15.9.) Be sure to have administrative privileges if you choose the computer location and that you have created an administrative account.

FIGURE 15.9

Notice the differences between the Computer and User library locations for font installation. You can enable or disable Font Validation at installation time in the Preferences pane.

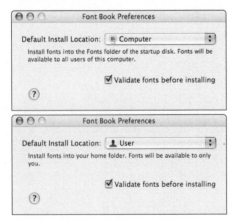

In the same Preferences pane, you can select to validate the font at installation time. Font Book has a powerful built-in font validation utility, which is discussed later in this chapter.

There are other ways to install fonts on your system and make them available to your applications. Font collections and the new font libraries enable you to locate your fonts anywhere in the system. The difference between a collection and a library is that the library can be selected to list the fonts that will be enabled at login time.

It is recommended that you remove font files with errors or duplicate font files from your Mac. Always remember that font resources are recognized *by name only*, so be careful because many foundries provide the same font (their version). Font files from different formats such as TrueType and Adobe Type 1 can have the same name but behave completely differently when formatting text. To preserve your sanity, take time to review your font resources. Keeping all of your fonts in a unique location and organizing them properly is good practice. Font Book provides all the necessary tools to locate your files, pinpoint duplicated and damaged fonts, and create archival copies for safekeeping.

You don't have to install a font to use it. If the file is available to you from your system, you can add the font to a collection or a library. This feature makes managing fonts from a network resource a snap. The same feature enables you to remove noncritical fonts from your system and keep them in a network resource without loss of functionality.

Creating font libraries

A library is a special collection of fonts located anywhere in your computer, including present network resources. This capability has been implemented in Font Book with the release of OS X Leopard. Unlike standard collections, the New Library feature makes it possible for you to load font resources initially from a location other than the standard user or general font folders. This is a feature commonly found on professional font management utilities. From a network administrator point of view, this is a great feature — the users create their startup libraries from the network font pool and the library selections apply only to the individual user. To create a font library, follow these steps:

1. **From the Font Book menu select File ➪ New Library.**

2. **The library creation pane appears, asking for a library name.** Assign a meaningful name to the library.

3. **Add Fonts to the New Library.** To add a font, Control+click it and select the Add Fonts option, or press the plus sign (+) on the font list pane, and then use the Finder to locate the fonts you want to add. You can select multiple font files, including folders containing complete font families. If there are fonts with errors, the Font Validation pane opens with a list of problems, as shown in Figure 15.10. Take notice and read carefully the error descriptions. Fixing your font problems is a very important task.

FIGURE 15.10

Font Book describes in detail errors found in installed fonts. At this point, Font Book does not have a font repair option.

Previewing fonts

By selecting a font, you can appreciate its look and feel in the preview pane. (See Figure 15.11.) There you can change the display size either by moving the slider on the right side of the preview pane or by selecting a predefined size from the drop-down box in the upper right corner (if you are in Sample mode). There are three predefined modes: Sample, Repertoire, and Custom.

The listed fonts are displayed as font families for a particular typeface. You can expand the included faces and preview each to decide which typeface suits your needs.

 A bullet next to the name of a typeface indicates that it is duplicated.

You can display a lot of information about a font by selecting Preview ➪ Show Font Info, as shown in Figure 15.12. Unlike previous versions of Font Book, in this version Apple displays much more information about a font, including its foundry, history, and copyright information, among other useful data. However, you will not see the font glyph set, just the font name, which will be portrayed in its typeface view. This is known as a WYSIWYG (pronounced *wiz-zee-wig*) font name, which means "What You See Is What You Get."

FIGURE 15.11

Select Repertoire view, move the slider all the way to the top, and browse through your fonts to see the great variety of glyphs presented by some font families.

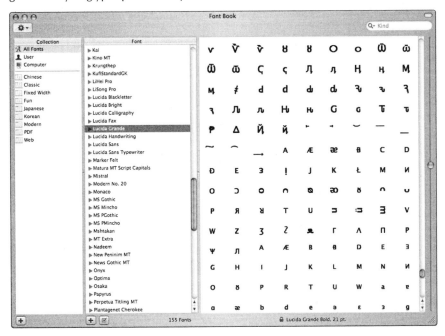

Many characters and symbols are included with font families that comply with the Unicode standard. Those characters can be viewed using the Repertoire preview selection from the menu. If you want to appreciate all of the symbols available to you, call up the Character Palette, which is a system facility that makes it easy for you to add special symbols to your text. The Character Palette, the Font Panel, and the Keyboard Viewer will be discussed later.

FIGURE 15.12

Select Preview ➪ Show Font Info to display the font file location and other useful and interesting information about each font.

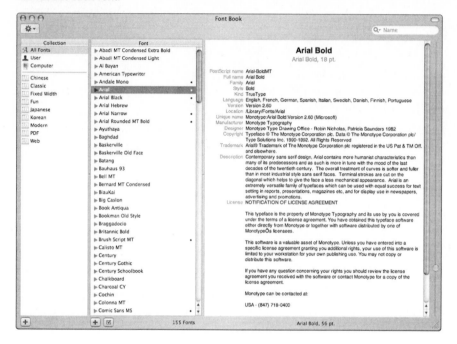

Creating font collections and turning fonts on or off

As expected with any font management system, you can enable or disable fonts at will without uninstalling them from the system. But the true power of font management comes with the ability to turn on or off whole sets of fonts called *collections*. A collection is a group of fonts that you have selected to perform a particular job. Creating a collection is easy. Follow these steps:

1. **Select File ➪ New Collection, or place the mouse pointer on the collection pane, Control+click, then select New Collection.**

2. **Give the collection a meaningful name.**

3. **After the collection has been added, you can attach fonts to it.** Click the collection you created.

4. **Click the plus sign (+) on the bottom of the font pane to add fonts.** The Finder window enables you to choose the fonts you want to add. Keep in mind that fonts are identified on OS X Leopard by name only. Make sure you select the correct font file to add to your collection.

Backing Up Your Fonts

It is important to keep a "hard copy" of your fonts, and Font Book provides a great utility for this purpose. In order to back up all of your fonts, select All Fonts from the Collection pane in Font Book and then select File ⇨ Export Collection. A copy of all of your fonts will be created in the location you selected. You can then burn the generated folder onto a CD or DVD.

In professional environments, jobs submitted to production companies (print shops or video production companies) must include the original font files used to create the piece as well as the image files and other important documents required to reproduce it.

Creating collections that comprise the fonts used to produce a job will make your job easier, not only when you are working on the job, but when you are ready to send it to the shop.

In the same manner as when adding fonts to a library, Font Book validates the fonts you add to the collection.

Turning fonts on or off in Font Book is very simple. To do so, follow these steps:

1. **Locate the font file or family on the font pane and click it.**

2. **If the font is enabled (on), click the button with a check mark (disable) at the bottom of the pane.** Disabled fonts have an *off* indicator and are *grayed out*. The button at the bottom of the pane changes also — the checkmark disappears — after you disable the font.

3. **If the font is enabled, a warning message appears, as shown in Figure 15.13, requesting confirmation to disable the font.**

FIGURE 15.13

Font Book warns you before disabling a font.

To turn collections or libraries on or off, follow these steps:

1. **Click the collection or library you want to enable or disable.**

2. **Control+click it and select Enable "<name>" or Disable "<name>".**

You can also use the Font Book menu to perform these tasks. To enable or disable fonts, libraries, or collections select Edit ➪ Disable "<collection name>" or Edit ➪ Disable "<font name>" depending on your choice.

After disabling a font or collection, it will be grayed out and the word *off* will appear next to it. Remember that disabling a font has consequences on the applications and files that may be using it. Be careful when disabling entire collections or libraries.

> **TIP** If you disable the All Fonts library, not all fonts will be disabled. The fonts Lucida Grande and Geneva remain active. The system needs to keep a couple of fonts active to continue to communicate with you. Try disabling the All Fonts library and then browse the All Fonts library to see which fonts remain active in your system.

Detecting and resolving duplicate fonts and validating font files

Font files are solely identified by name. For example, if you have a Helvetica dfont and a Helvetica PostScript Type 1 font, you have a duplicated font. Font Book marks a duplicated copy of an installed font by placing a bullet next to its name. To resolve duplicate fonts, select the font name or font family you want to resolve, and then choose Edit ➪ Resolve Duplicates, as shown in Figure 15.14. Only the selected font will be enabled; the others will be disabled.

FIGURE 15.14

Font Book has a built in feature to help resolve duplicate fonts. Using it is as easy as clicking a menu option!

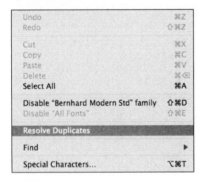

> **CAUTION** Caution is advised when resolving duplicate font names. Common sense dictates that you review the font information when selecting which font will be used to resolve the duplicate entries. Choosing the wrong font can cause text misalignments, text reflow, and glyph substitution errors that you want to avoid.

It is easy to install multiple versions of a font in your system if you do not follow a particular method to organize your fonts and analyze the font information provided with it. Many professional users assign a single location to store their fonts and organize their folder names identifying a particular typeface and its associated font file, which is a time-consuming but effective way to manage font files.

NOTE Removing system fonts from their installed location may cause some problems. If you want to remove fonts from the `/System/Library/Fonts` folder you will need an administrator account to proceed.

Earlier in this chapter we discussed that OS X Leopard validates font files at installation. However, you can verify the integrity of any installed font file, as outlined in these steps:

1. **Select the font you want to check.**
2. **Control+click the font and select Validate Font, or choose File ⇨ Validate Font.**
3. **Font Book displays the Font Validation pane with the results.** You can choose more than one font file or a family to validate.

You can also select fonts with errors to be removed from the system. To do so, select the fonts you want removed and then click the Remove Selected button to remove those fonts from the system. You will receive a warning message to verify your decision, as shown in Figure 15.15.

FIGURE 15.15

Removing invalid fonts may resolve problems with applications that behave erratically when loading documents with corrupt fonts.

Notice that the font validation does not fix the problems with the font file. The best route to fix a problematic font is to reinstall it from its original files. Some font management applications such as Font Agent Pro, from Insider Software, Inc., have built-in utilities to fix problematic font files.

Searching for installed fonts

Similar to the Finder search facility, Font Book provides you with an easy way to find font files. The options presented by the Search field are geared toward font characteristics and can help you in finding the correct font files. Following is a list of the different selection criteria you may use:

- Name
- PostScript Name
- Family
- Style

- Kind
  - TrueType
  - PostScript Type 1
  - OpenType PostScript
- Language
  - English, Japanese, French, German, Spanish, Italian, Dutch, Swedish, Norwegian, Danish, Finnish, Portuguese, and Korean
- Copyright

Font Book also searches your libraries for the fonts that match your selection criteria, so you can have fonts located in another system and access them across the network. Once you have selected a criterion in the Search field, the fonts that match are presented, as shown in Figure 15.16.

FIGURE 15.16

To choose the available options for a font search, just click the search field and browse through the predefined search criteria options.

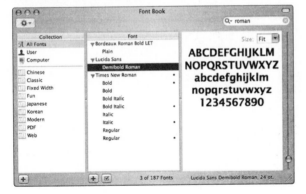

The Font panel

OS X Leopard makes several core services and technologies available to other applications, making working with fonts a pleasurable experience. Those services enhance productivity and permit the inexperienced user to perform complex tasks with minimal training.

By enabling simple applications, such as TextEdit, to access these services, their usability and productivity increases noticeably. Let's get down to business and explore some of those utilities.

The Font panel, shown in Figure 15.17, is embedded in many applications within OS X Leopard, including Safari, Stickies, TextEdit, and many others. As a system utility, it has access to the core Quartz resources and is able to manipulate many variables related to font display and print.

FIGURE 15.17

The Font panel complements the functions of the Font Book by providing font management services to simple applications. However, those services are quite sophisticated, going all the way to serious typographic management options.

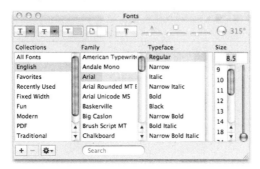

To access the Font panel, launch TextEdit and select Format ➪ Font ➪ Show Fonts. Expand the top pane to have a better look at the font rendering, move the slider, and watch how the font resizes inside TextEdit.

Any font selections performed by the Font Book are reflected in the Font panel and vice versa. However, the Font panel permits unprecedented access to font typography parameters, allowing for a great degree of control over the appearance and behavior of the text. For all fonts, you can control many parameters such as the background color and shadow (angle, color, opacity, blur, and offset), and you can also set the font size and other attributes such as underlining and strikethrough, all with color management.

Depending on the information stored in the font file, the Font panel allows you to change many typographic parameters. Such capability is found only in professional page layout packages such as Adobe InDesign or QuarkXpress. To access these options, click the Action button at the bottom of the Font panel window, then select Typography to see what has been enabled for your selected typeface. (See Figure 15.18.)

The Font panel enables you to create a special collection called *Favorites*. This collection is not accessible by Font Book. Another interesting feature is your ability to add sizes to your fonts. The Font panel keeps track of your added sizes. Just click the Action button and select Edit Sizes. You can add sizes that are important you, as shown in Figure 15.19. However, those sizes will not be reflected in other applications.

Keep in mind that changes made in the Font panel to the collections are reflected in Font Book. OS X Leopard has included many of the font management capabilities in TextEdit as an example of the degree of control you can achieve by using the System Core Services. It is recommended that you play with the font controls in TextEdit to become familiar with the language as well as the results of your choices.

FIGURE 15.18

Not all fonts are created equal. Some fonts allow more control than others.

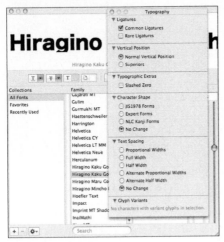

FIGURE 15.19

Adding necessary font sizes is a simple task in TextEdit, after you invoke the Font panel and click the Action button at the bottom of its pane.

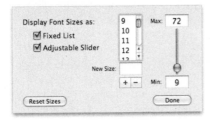

The Character Palette

Adding another level of capability and user support, OS X Leopard includes the Character Palette in its core services. It functions as a glyph directory by which you can locate variations or renditions of a particular character in the different fonts installed (and active) on the system. It is a great utility and you will find it available in most applications.

The Character Palette is not enabled by default. You can check its status through the System Preferences in the International pane. Select the Input Menu pane to see the status of the Character Palette. Notice that you can also enable the Keyboard Viewer in the same place. (See Figure 15.20.)

FIGURE 15.20

Once enabled, the Character Palette and the Keyboard Viewer appear as icons on the Apple menu bar. Select Show Input Menu on the Menu bar and notice where you can access those utilities.

Once activated, the Character Palette presents your glyphs in many different ways. Apple provides the following views:

- Roman
- Japanese
- Traditional Chinese
- Korean
- Simplified Chinese
- All characters
- PI fonts
- Glyph

Each of the previous options has been optimized to facilitate the location of particular symbols or characters. It is important to play with the different options available to each view. The most interesting aspect of the Character Palette is the Unicode standard. OS X Leopard is able to organize all of those glyphs by the order in which they have been defined in Unicode, including the original ASCII code. If you choose the Glyph option, you will access the whole set of characters for any installed font, as shown in Figure 15.21. By far, the Character Palette is probably the most useful native utility on OS X Leopard for font operations.

TIP You can drag and drop glyphs from the Character Palette, which is a handy feature when your font does not have all of the symbols you may need for a particular job.

TIP If you are looking for a character, you might find it by name. Just type the name in the search field at the bottom of the Character Palette pane. Remember to expand the Character Palette using the Character Info option. You can see the name of the selected glyph as well as its rendition in other fonts.

FIGURE 15.21

Double-clicking a glyph inserts it on the active application from which the Character Palette was called forth, a useful feature that will make your job easier when dealing with special characters or foreign languages.

The Keyboard Viewer

As an additional tool for your convenience, the Keyboard Viewer, shown in Figure 15.22, is also available, in the same manner you activated and displayed the Character Palette. Experiment with it to see where character mappings are for each font.

FIGURE 15.22

Select a font to check its mappings on the keyboard. Key combinations are important to appreciate all mappings (that is, ⌘+Shift or Option+Shift).

Third-party font management utilities

Historically, Apple has had a gang of excellent third-party application developers, which greatly enhance the functionality of the Mac. OS X Leopard is no exception and many companies have enthusiastically joined the developing efforts that have always made the Mac stand out. When it comes to font management, four systems are worth mentioning:

- FontAgent Pro from Insider Software, Inc. (see Figure 15.23)
- Extensis Suitcase Fusion (see Figure 15.24)
- FontExplorer X from Linotype (see Figure 15.25)

These applications make short work of general font management operations and are geared toward the professional environment; yet the novice user will greatly benefit from the powerful capabilities integrated in these programs. The developers have devoted substantial amounts of time analyzing the way print publishing companies and advertisement agencies work and have developed their products from those points of view.

The utilities mentioned here will empower you to do the following:

- Activate and deactivate individual fonts or entire libraries at will.
- Share fonts across a network environment and provide a management console from which to establish a font scheme for all users.
- Import and integrate new fonts in a comprehensive font database. The fonts selected for installation can be checked for errors. Errors can even be repaired!
- Print glyph samples from your font sets. (This is useful when planning a document layout.)
- Install fonts in a user-defined location in your system or the network.
- Automatically activate font sets when an application starts. (This is a convenient feature that streamlines workflow in professional environments.)
- Scan for duplicate fonts and remove the undesired ones.
- Compare several fonts, letting you analyze the difference in glyph design and style.

TIP Many users prefer a simple yet powerful font manager such as Insider Software FontAgent Pro, which suffices for a small workgroup environment and works wonders for the individual user. For professional environments and demanding, heavy-duty users, Extensis Suitcase Fusion will maximize font resources, in particular if all the fonts are located in the same network volume and there is a Font Administrator. FontExplorer X has a convenient tool built in to make acquisition of new fonts a snap. Always visit the Web sites of font manufacturers and review the claims of their products before committing to a particular solution.

FIGURE 15.23

Notice the available options for font installation, typical of professional font utilities. FontAgent Pro has a superior font verification and repair algorithm that can be activated at font installation time — just make sure to check the right options in FontAgent Pro's preferences.

FIGURE 15.24

Extensis Suitcase Fusion enables users to make multiple "font sets," which can be created and organized thematically, stylistically, or by purpose.

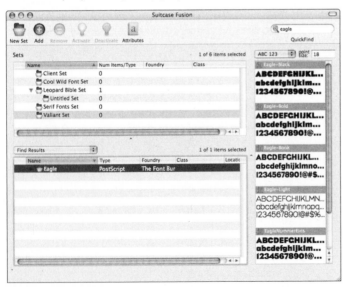

The Font Commandments

- Know your fonts. Because fonts are identified in OS X Leopard by name only, some programs may present a font with an incomplete name. Selecting that font may lead to problems if you do not verify that your selection is indeed the right font file.

- Test new fonts in isolation. If a font is provided to you, create a special collection or set to contain it because the font may have parameters that have been modified for a particular purpose. Using your version of that font may lead to changes in a document layout. Be careful when receiving fonts that are not coming directly from the foundry or font installation software. There are many utilities that can alter a font file and introduce subtle changes that may become a nightmare, especially in a professional setting. Make sure you have original fonts for professional work. If you install your fonts using the Finder, make sure to enable font-checking options in your font management utility. Font Book can help you identify problematic fonts.

- Prepare custom sets. Always prepare your font sets for a particular job and make sure to disable all other, nonessential fonts while working on it. This is a great practice that can save you many headaches.

- Keep your fonts organized. With time you may end up with thousands of fonts installed on your system. It is always preferable to have a Font Server to deploy your fonts and organize them there. You can choose to manage them by foundry, location, provider, and so on. Avoid organizing all of your fonts by name because it may lead to confusion down the road. Most font managers, including Font Book, list your fonts in alphabetical order and make it easy to locate them by name, but you should still keep your fonts organized in the Finder using folders and subfolders to identify them easily as you navigate around your Mac's hard drive.

- Sniff out the new fonts when added. Many applications install fonts as additional goodies or use them to operate properly within OS X Leopard. When you finish installing an application it is important to look for new fonts installed on your system. A common location for those fonts is /Library/Application Support/Adobe/Fonts, which is where Adobe applications install fonts. Another common location is /Applications/ Microsoft Office 2004/Office/Fonts. It is recommended that once you locate the fonts, you create a collection or set and then generate a backup of those fonts for safe-keeping. Also, after you have those fonts located, you can enable or disable them at will depending on your needs.

- Back up your fonts. Collect your fonts and store them outside your computer. Keeping font files intact can save you time. Make CD or DVD copies of your font collections and identify them with a meaningful name. If you need to reinstall your system, all of your fonts will be ready to be put back in the system already organized.

FIGURE 15.25

FontExplorer X from Linotype is a powerful tool. And best of all, its free!

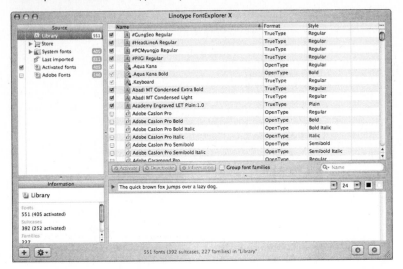

Summary

In this chapter we touched on the concept of fonts, typefaces, and font families, which are important terms to know when working with text on your Mac.

The concepts behind bitmap and outline fonts were explained as well as Adobe Type 1, TrueType, OpenType, and dfont formats. The importance of a device output resolution was also described, along with how the OpenType standard introduced by Microsoft encompasses Type 1 and TrueType font formats.

You learned how the Unicode standard has expanded the font character sets, allowing for true multilanguage support, and the five predefined locations for font installation under OS X Leopard were explained, as well as working concepts and recommendations on how to work under this environment.

The usage of Font Book, the Font panel, the Keyboard Viewer, and the awesome Character Palette were explained, and three important third-party utilities were mentioned. Although detailed characteristics were not mentioned (they are not part of the scope of this book), it was noted how much more functionality is packed on them and what are the most appropriate environments in which to use them.

Some common-sense tips on working with fonts were touched upon to give you a starting conceptual point to manage your fonts.

Part III

Beyond the Basics of Mac OS X

Chapter 16

Printing and Faxing

his chapter discusses how to print and fax in Mac OS X Leopard. Aside from the data that appears on-screen, printing is one of the most common forms of output in computing. Because Mac OS is a preferred platform in print and graphics industries, Apple did everything in its power to equal and often surpass the printing capabilities of its predecessors and its competition. Not only does Mac OS X deliver print connectivity options superior to any other OS, but it also provides built-in faxing and PDF capabilities.

Overview of Mac OS X Printing

Regardless of printing needs — from graphic artists, Apple Certified Technical Coordinators (ACTCs), and book or newsletter editors, to letters and birthday cards printed at home — understanding the underlying technology that the Mac OS X print architecture is composed of is helpful in its operation. Mac OS X's printing services are based on the Common UNIX Printing System, better known as CUPS. CUPS is a cross-platform open source printing architecture that supports both PostScript and raster printers.

Mac OS X supports a multitude of printer connectivity types: AppleTalk, Bluetooth, IP Printing, Bonjour, USB, FireWire, and Windows Printing.

In order to print, Mac OS X requires a driver. A *driver* is a piece of software that enables the operating system to control a hardware device. If during the initial installation of Mac OS X the additional print drivers were installed, the OS supplies by default a sizable collection of third-party printer drivers for popular printers, including printers from Brother, Canon, Epson, Hewlett-Packard, and Lexmark. All of these print drivers are located in the top

Library folder of your startup disk, grouped into folders by manufacturer. If, by chance, the required driver is not present for your printer, check the printer manufacturer's Web site for availability and the most recent iteration.

Overview of Printers

Parallel, serial, USB, Bluetooth, FireWire, network, PostScript, raster, inkjet, laser, LED, dye sublimation, thermal wax, dot matrix, and impact are all ways to categorize printers. There are overlaps between the categories. For example, just because many PostScript printers are networked and laser-based doesn't mean that a USB inkjet printer can't be networked or PostScript-enabled. Also, although Macintosh computers do not include the parallel ports required for many popular printers (for Windows), that doesn't rule out a Mac using a Windows printer. Several third-party manufacturers sell USB-to-parallel converter cables that enable Macs to print to a select number of supported printers.

A quick review of the printer technology scene is as follows: Networked printers are printers accessed via a network connection such as Ethernet or AirPort using either IP or AppleTalk networking protocols. USB printers are physically connected to your Mac or to a USB hub, which in turn is connected to your Mac. Printers that use serial connectivity are literally and figuratively dinosaurs in the sense that they are being replaced by USB and Bluetooth connectivity, and as such no recently manufactured Macintosh computers even include a serial port.

PostScript is a *page description language* (PDL) developed by Adobe Systems. PostScript is a mathematical language that has operators, variables, and commands that control precise shape and placement information for everything that gets drawn on a page, not just the fonts, although they are the most obvious example people see. A PostScript printer has a *raster image processor* (RIP), which translates the PostScript code into a *raster image* (set of discrete dots) that represents the data on the printed page at the current printer resolution. Thus, a one-inch line that is 1/6 of an inch thick is translated into 15,000 dots at 300 dpi, and into 240,000 dots at 1200 dpi. Because the RIP is an embedded computer requiring its own memory, PostScript printers are generally more expensive than non-PostScript printers. (And add the fee Adobe or another RIP vendor charges to the printer manufacturer for using their RIP.) Although more common on laser printers, you can also find PostScript-enabled inkjet printers and dye-sublimation printers.

An alternative to PostScript RIPs are raster RIPs. A raster image processor uses a combination of hardware and software that converts images described in the form of vector graphics statements into raster graphics images or bitmaps.

Inkjet printers produce their output by spraying streams of ink through tiny nozzles onto the paper, transparency, or other media. Laser printers use heat to affix tiny particles of toner to the output medium.

On the surface, the least expensive printer type, at least initially, is the inkjet. However, if you're going to be producing a lot of output you'll find that the cost of consumables (ink cartridges) is fairly high. A single cartridge typically lasts about 500 pages and costs approximately $20 (some less, some more). In contrast, a typical laser printer produces about 4,000 pages from one toner cartridge that costs approximately $100.

Mac OS X ships with the ability to use most new printers; to verify if your printer is compatible, visit www.apple.com/macosx/upgrade/printers.html.

NOTE   The Mac OS X Finder does not include a Print command in its File menu (or any other Finder menu for that matter). If you want to print a Finder window or the Desktop, you need to take a snapshot of the screen using the key commands ⌘+Shift+3, ⌘+Shift+4, or ⌘+Shift+4+Spacebar, or the Grab utility. You then need to print the Finder window or Desktop from the Preview application or Grab utility, respectively. Another way to deal with this feature deficiency is to use the third-party shareware utility Print Window.

Configuring Page Setup

Before a document can be printed, page parameters must be established. In Mac OS X, this is handled through the Page Setup dialog box located in an application's File menu. Although the options may vary slightly from application to application, generally speaking the Page Setup dialog box is where you specify the size paper to print on, whether you are going to print portrait (tall) or landscape (wide), the direction of the paper feed, and whether your document is going to be reduced or enlarged. All of these options are called *page attributes* and are document specific and managed through one screen, which is shown in Figure 16.1.

FIGURE 16.1

General document printing parameters are set in the Page Setup dialog box.

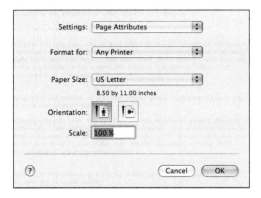

Depending on the application you are working in, the Page Setup pop-up menu may have two additional choices: Custom Paper Size and Summary. As the name implies, Custom Paper Size allows for the specification of custom paper sizes. The Summary choice is a consolidated report of the various choices made under Page Attributes. The Summary pane is handy when you have made a lot of changes in different panes and want to verify the settings without having to go through the panes one at a time.

Applications use the information from Page Setup to establish the parameters for margins and where page breaks occur.

When you pull down the Page Attributes pop-up menu in the Settings dialog box, the following option appears:

- **Save as Default:** Enables you to change the default setting for all documents created in that application. This is especially useful if you find yourself making the same format changes over and over again.

The Format pop-up menu provides the following options:

- **Any printer:** Formats the document for any printer
- **Current printer:** Allows you to format your document with setting specific to your printer
- **Print and Fax preferences:** Opens the Print and Fax preference pane

Pulling down the Paper Size pop-up menu presents the following options:

- **Paper Size:** Enables you to select from the various paper sizes. A generic printer supports only US Letter, US Legal, A4, and B5 paper sizes, but specific printers generally support a wider range, possibly including such things as #10 envelopes or 3-x-5-inch index cards. The physical dimensions of the paper size appear below the Paper Size pop-up menu.
- **Orientation:** Determines whether the top of the printed page is on the short edge of the paper (portrait), the bottom of the long edge (landscape), or the top of the long edge (also landscape).
- **Scale:** Reduces or enlarges the printed document according to the percentage you enter based on the document's original size. Full size is 100 percent. Because the page image is rendered in resolution-independent PDF, you don't have rigid minimum and maximum values imposed for scale. However, as a general rule, you should keep in mind the physical limitations of your printer and the resolutions it can print.

Printing and Faxing Options

After the page parameters have been established, you need to select Print from an application's File menu (⌘+P), which produces the Print dialog box, a GUI interface for configuring printing options. The Print dialog box lets you select printers and their configuration options as well as preview, print, fax, or create a PDF of a document.

Adding a printer

To print from Mac OS X for the first time, you need to add a printer. Adding a printer is the process that configures Mac OS X to utilize printing hardware regardless if it is connected locally or over a network. To add a printer, follow these steps:

1. **Select Add Printer from the Format for pop-up menu.** This opens the Print and Fax preference pane.

2. **Click the Add (+) button to display the available printers.** This in turn opens the default browser, shown in Figure 16.2, which displays all of the available printer connections.

FIGURE 16.2

Mac OS X Leopard's default printer browser has been completely overhauled.

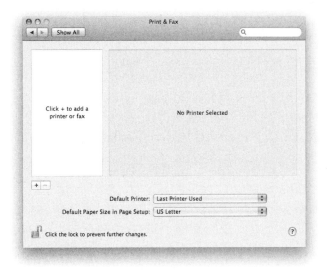

3. Select a connection method from the toolbar:

   ▪ Default if your Mac is directly connected to a USB printer.

   ▪ Fax to utilize your Mac's built-in fax modem.

   ▪ IP to connect to a printer via TCP/IP. Mac OS X supports IP printing via LPD/LPR, IPP, Socket, and Jet Direct. In order to configure IP printing you need to select the appropriate protocol, specify the IP address or the DNS name for the printer, and provide a designation for the printer queue.

   ▪ Windows Printing to utilize a Windows (SMB) printer on a network.

   ▪ Bluetooth if connecting to a printer via Bluetooth (wireless) connectivity.

   ▪ AppleTalk to connect to an AppleTalk-enabled printer over a network, as shown in Figure 16.3. In order to connect to an AppleTalk-based printer, the AppleTalk networking protocol must first be enabled within the Network pane of System Preferences. If it is not, Mac OS 10.5 automatically enables AppleTalk on your behalf. When you select a printer, the print Setup utility then attempts to determine the printer type and bind the corresponding printer description to your selection. You can also manually select the appropriate printer description or, if your network is configured for it, a different AppleTalk zone.

4. **Click the Add button to add the printer to your selection of available printers.**

FIGURE 16.3

The Add a Printer dialog box facilitates the selection of USB, Bonjour, IP, Windows, AppleTalk, and Bluetooth printers.

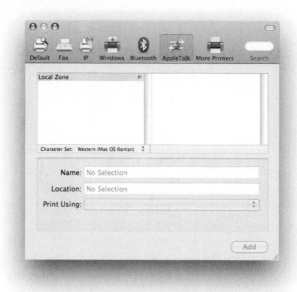

To remove a printer, just select the printer you want to delete in the Print & Fax Preference pane list and click the Delete icon in the toolbar.

Setting print options

After the printer has been configured, the next step in the printing process is selecting your printing options.

When you choose to print a file, the Print dialog box is collapsed by default, presenting the following choices. The choices presented in this window vary according to the application you are printing from:

- **Printer:** This drop-down menu allows you to choose the printer you would like to print to. You can also choose to add another printer to your list or open the Print & Fax Preference pane.

- **Presets:** This pop-up menu enables you to save and name groups of print options from the unlabeled menu in the Print dialog box. This permits the quick selection of a group of print options without individually selecting them. To save the current settings for the print job, click the Presets pop-up menu and choose Save As. You can use the Rename command on the Presets pop-up menu to rename a saved preset if you want to change its name. In future print sessions, that choice appears in the Presets pop-up menu at the top of the Print dialog box.

■ **Preview:** This button creates a temporary PDF file, which is then opened in the Preview application for perusal. If you like, you can save the file from within Preview as a BMP, JPEG-2000, JPEG, PDF, PICT, PNG, or TIFF, or you can simply print it. Previews do not display the effects of print options such as Front and Back printing or printing several pages per sheet. Within the Print dialog box window there is also an option to Show Quick Preview, which displays a miniaturized preview of the document to be printed. You can scroll through the various pages to be printed using the left and right arrow buttons located under the actual preview window. This preview is useful to get a feel of how the document is formatted within the specified page size.

■ **PDF:** This option allows you to save the document as a PDF file (.pdf) or a PostScript file (.ps), and to send a fax. If your computer has a modem, regardless of whether it is internal or external, the send a Fax option will utilize it in like manner to an analog fax machine. Faxing is covered in greater detail later in this chapter.

■ **PDF:** This option enables you choose from the following PDF options: Save as PDF, Save as Postscript file, Fax PDF, Mail PDF, Save as PDF-X, Save PDF to iPhoto, Save PDF to Web Receipts Folder, and Edit menu.

Clicking the disclosure triangle to the right of the printer name expands the window, revealing the following options:

■ **Copies:** This option allows you to specify the number of copies desired. You can also indicate whether to collate the printout and in what manner it should be output — one full copy followed by the next, or all of the copies of each page together.

■ **Pages:** Here you can also specify whether you want all pages of the document printed, just a specific range of pages, or to reverse the order of how a document should print. For example, you can specify the ending page in the From box and beginning page in the To box to print from the last page to the first page of a document.

■ **Paper Size:** This option allows you to select the paper that you would like to print on. Among the paper choices are US Letter, US Legal, Executive, and others. There are also various envelope sizes. If you don't find the paper or envelope size you need, you can choose Manage Custom Sizes.

■ **Orientation:** This option allows you to choose which way the document lies on the page: portrait or landscape.

Depending on the application you are working in, the following options also may be available:

■ **Layout:** This option allows you to determine the number of pages per sheet and the layout direction of output for tiled documents, define a border to encompass the document, and specify two-sided printing, which if available and selected uses both sides of the paper and lets you indicate the orientation for binding purposes.

- **Scheduler:** This option allows you to define a specific time for a print job, to print it on hold, and specify its priority for print queue handling.

- **ColorSync:** This option allows you to configure ColorSync output options without modifying the colors in a document.

- **Cover Page:** This option allows you to select a preconfigured print-job cover page, indicate whether to print it before or after the document, and indicate billing information.

- **Error Handling:** This option allows you to configure Mac OS X to print error reports, which may be useful in troubleshooting PostScript errors.

- **Printer Features:** This option allows you define the output resolution of a print job.

- **Paper Type/Quality:** This option allows you to tell the printer whether to print in color or black and white, what type of media (paper, film, or transparency) is being used, and whether to emphasize speed or quality.

- **Summary:** This option allows you to see a summarized report of your settings for all the printer options that are available.

Most LaserWriter drivers offer at least some of the following additional choices:

- **Paper Feed:** This option allows you to specify the location from which the paper feeds. Set the pages to come from the same source, or click the "First page from" radio button to choose a specific source for the first page, as well as a source for the remaining pages.

- **Error Handling:** This option enables you to indicate whether you want a detailed report of any PostScript errors. You can also specify whether to switch paper trays if one runs out of paper and the printer has more than one tray available.

Using proprietary software supplied by the printer's manufacturer, some printers support the ability to print PostScript files independently of any print command, which may be of use in some prepress environments. PostScript files can also be converted into PDFs using the Preview application. Applications often have at least one application-specific print option choice. For example, when printing from iTunes, the Print dialog box looks very different from the Print dialog box you may see in TextEdit. In the Print section, options include CD jewel case insert, Song listing, and Album listing. Theme options depend on the print layout you choose. For example, if you choose to print a CD jewel case, the following options appear under the Theme drop-down menu: Text only, Mosaic, White mosaic, Single cover, Text only (Black & White), Mosaic (Black & White), Single side (Black & White), and Large playlist (Black & White). A brief description of the Theme appears directly beneath your selection and a preview of the your CD cover appears to the right as shown in Figure 16.4. The mosaic layouts are generated based on the available album artwork from the selected playlist or library in iTunes.

FIGURE 16.4

The print options in iTunes make it quick and easy to print a CD cover.

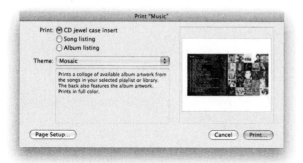

Using the Print & Fax preference pane

The Print & Fax preference pane has been streamlined for Mac OS 10.5. Although it certainly aids in the simplification of printer configuration, its design was motivated by the need to make the operating system more intuitive to the Windows user experience. To access the Print & Fax preference pane you can either open the System Preferences located in the Applications folder, or select Print & Fax Preferences from the Printer pop-up menu.

The Print and Fax preference pane, shown in Figure 16.5, performs the functionality formerly handled by the Printer Setup Utility. Here you can view available printers, view the print queue, printer options, supply levels, and view descriptions of the available printing devices. These descriptions consist of Name, Kind, Status, and Location. Clicking the Options & Supplies button opens a sheet that presents three columns: General, Driver, and Supplies. The General tab provides printer information including the printer's name, location, queue name, host name, driver version, and URL. The Driver tab gives you information on the driver associated with the printer, and the Supply tab shows you toner levels. The Printing panel also enables you to specify the default printer and define behavior within the Printer pop-up menu in the Print dialog box, such as whether the default printer or the last printer used appears first. Finally, you can specify the default paper size within the Page Setup window.

Sharing a printer in OS 10.5 is very simple. Simply select the printer you want to share from the printer list and click the Share this printer check box. You can now share your printer with other users.

FIGURE 16.5

Use the Print & Fax preference pane as a quick way to configure printing within Mac OS X.

Receiving a fax

The Print & Fax preference pane, shown in Figure 16.6, enables you to configure receiving faxes on your computer. To receive a fax, follow these steps:

1. **After adding the fax to your printer list, click the Receive Options button. Place a check mark in the box next to Receive faxes on this computer.**

2. **Specify the desired number of rings to answer and receive faxes on in the field adjacent to When a fax arrives: Answer after (entry field) rings.** Specify the location to save faxes to in the Save to pop-up menu.

    -   Place a check mark in the box next to the Print to drop-down menu and select the printer you want your faxes to print to.

    -   Place a check mark in the box to the left of the Email to drop-down menu and specify an e-mail address to which to forward received faxes.

3. **When you return to the main Print & Fax preference pane you can choose to:**

    -   View the status of a fax, the name of the job, the user assigned to the fax, when the fax was sent, and if the job was completed, by clicking the Open Fax Queue.

    -   Place a shortcut in the Finder's menu bar where you can enable and disable faxing, as well open the Print & Fax preference pane, by selecting Show fax status in menu bar.

    -   Share your fax with other users on your local area network by selecting Share this fax.

616

FIGURE 16.6

Configure your faxing options in the Receive Options menu in the Print & Fax preference pane.

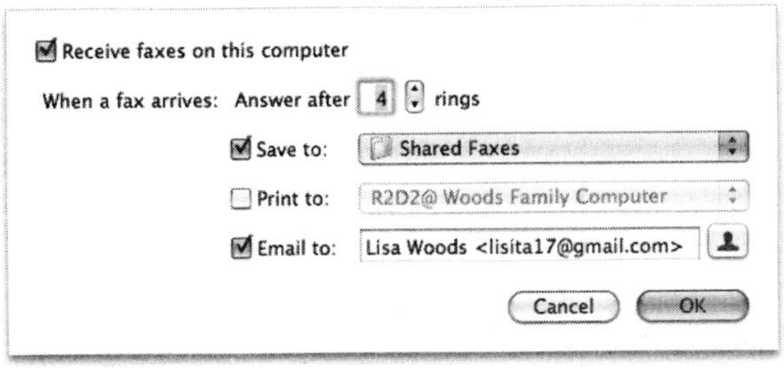

Sending a fax

Although the Microsoft Windows operating systems have had integrated faxing capability for years, the ability to send and receive faxes on your computer is a recent addition to the Mac OS. Traditionally, faxing on a Mac platform has always been handled by means of third-party software or services, such as FaxSTF, 4-Site Fax, or eFax. In fact, up until Panther, Apple included a copy of SmithMicro Software's FaxSTF as part of its software bundle with most shipping Macs. If you have used FaxSTF on Mac OS X in the past, you will undoubtedly find Panther's integrated faxing to be similar in operation. Although the usefulness of faxing has been somewhat nullified by e-mail, faxing can be handy in communicating with the computer-challenged and as a means of printing when on the road and no printer is available.

As mentioned earlier in this chapter, faxing allows you to utilize a local or shared analog modem, regardless if it is internal or external, in like fashion to a fax machine. To fax, select the Fax PDF option from the PDF button within the Print dialog box. This displays a Fax dialog box as shown in Figure 16.7.

The Fax dialog box operates in similar fashion to the Print dialog box with a few exceptions, the most obvious being the To and the Dialing Prefix fields, the use cover page check box, and subject and message text fields. The To field is where you specify the recipient of the fax. This can be done manually or using your Address Book. To the right of the To field is a button with a silhouette of a man. This button opens your Address Book application. The addresses in this window are derived from the contents of the Address Book application located in the Applications folder.

The Prefix field is where you specify a dialing prefix such as *70 to disable call waiting, and/or a country code such as 01144 for the United Kingdom.

Cover Page and Modem are two noteworthy selections that appear in the unlabeled Print dialog menu when faxing. In Cover Page, you can specify the inclusion of a cover page as well as input a subject and a message. In Modem, you can specify whether to dial using tone or pulse, whether the sound should be on or off, and whether to wait for a dial tone before faxing.

FIGURE 16.7

The operation of Mac OS X's built-in faxing is similar to that of FaxSTF.

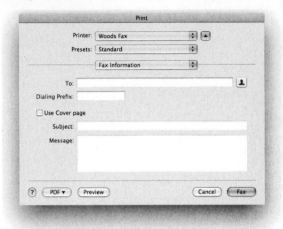

Administering Print and Modem Queues

In Mac OS 10.5, the Printer Setup Utility has been done away with, and the majority of printer configuration and administration is done via the Print and Fax preference pane, which is shown in Figure 16.8. There are two ways to access the Print and Fax preference pane. The first and most direct way is to open it from System Preferences. Another way to is to select Print and Fax preferences from the Printer pop-up menu that resides in all Print dialog boxes.

As previously stated, the Print and Fax preference pane is where you can add and remove printers, and show info about configured printers. In addition, the Print and Fax preference pane has the ability to display the status of all print and fax jobs pending. This information can be found in what is referred to as the printer's print queue or a fax's modem queue. Open the Print and Fax preference pane and either double-click a printer in the Printer List whose queue you want to manage, or click Open Print Queue as shown in Figure 16.8. Here you can delete a job, hold a job, resume a job, or pause the queue entirely as well as access the online Apple Store to replenish printing consumables.

> **TIP** If you are on the road and you want to print but your printer is unavailable, you can stop the print queue and then issue the print command. Even if you turn off the computer, print jobs are retained. When you can restart the print queue, the document will be printed automatically.

To view the modem queue, select View ⇨ Show Fax List in the Printer Setup utility and either double-click a modem in the Modem List whose queue you want to manage, or select the modem and choose Printers ⇨ Show Jobs (⌘+O) to open a window for that modem's queue, as shown in Figure 16.9.

FIGURE 16.8

The printer queue in Leopard provides more information to the user, including the status and name of the printer, the user the job is assigned to, and when the job was sent as well as if the job was completed.

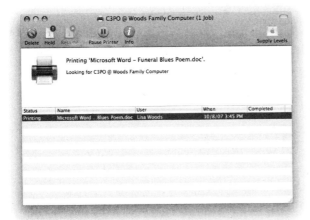

FIGURE 16.9

Except that it is managing modem queues, the administration of the Fax List is identical in operation to that of the Printer List.

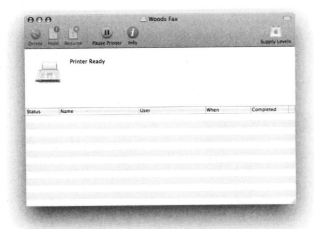

For those of us not satisfied with status quos, the toolbars in the Printer List and Fax List windows, as well as those on the print and modem queues, can all be customized in a similar fashion to a toolbar in a Finder window. From the top menubar choose Printer/Customize toolbar or hold the Option and ⌘ keys while clicking the tiny pill-shaped button in the upper right-hand corner of the Add a printer window, and a custom options sheet drops down, as shown in Figure 16.10.

FIGURE 16.10

Like the King of Burgers, you can have it your way.

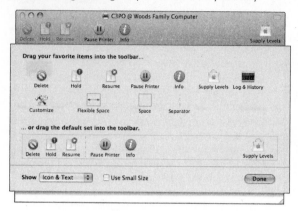

You can also customize the columns in the Printer List and Fax List to contain any of the following headings: Kind (inkjet, PostScript, and so on), Host (a computer sharing a printer), Status (Stopped, Printing, and so on), Location (location of printer), and Jobs (name of current job printing). To do so, open the desired Printer List or the Fax List window and make your selections under the Columns option in the View menu.

Other abilities of interest in the Print and Fax preference pane include the following:

- **Default Printer:** This option determines from a list of printers which one will be the default. To select a default printer, select the desired printer from the drop-down menu.

- **Default Paper Size in Page Setup:** This is where you specify the paper size that will be automatically selected when printing.

Maximizing OS X Printing

For many of us, printing is a part of our daily routine. Every day we print documents, e-mails, driving directions, shopping lists, and dinner recipes. OS X provides a number of ways to streamline the printing process.

Using printer shortcuts

Why take the long way, when you can take a shortcut? Mac OS X supports three types of shortcuts for printing: Desktop, Dock, and Finder printing. A Desktop Printer, shown in Figure 16.11, is an iconic representation of a print queue or a modem queue that can be accessed via the GUI. This icon can be saved anywhere the user account has access. By clicking the Desktop or Dock Printer you can directly administer the queue that you want to manage, circumventing the need to first open the Print & Fax preference pane and then selecting the queue you want to administer. To create a Desktop, Dock, or Finder Printer, go to the Print & Fax preference pane. Select the printer that you want to create a shortcut for and drag and drop the icon of the printer onto the desktop; once you've created a Desktop Printer, you can drag that icon into the Dock, or a Finder window. The queues that Desktop and Finder represents also temporarily manifest themselves in the Dock as print jobs are being processed. As with previous versions of the Mac OS Desktop printers, Mac OS 10.5 allows for drag and drop printing. You can also open the Desktop Printer and drag the desired document into the print queue, as well as drag jobs between print queues.

FIGURE 16.11

Desktop printers are basically printer aliases (shortcuts); they even share the small black arrow in the lower left-hand corner of the icon.

> **TIP** There may be times when your printer becomes unresponsive and it needs to be reset. To reset a printer in OS 10.5 open the Print and Fax System Preferences, Control+click on the printer that needs to be reset, and select Reset printing system.

Pooling printer

As with the previous version of OS X, Leopard includes the Pool Printers feature. Pool Printers enables you to create a collection of printers, called a printer *pool*. A printer pool helps avoid printing delays by channeling a print job away from a busy printer to one that is not. If all printers in a printer pool are busy, the print job prints to the first available printer. To make a printer pool, select two or more printers in the Printer List by clicking a desired printer and subsequently ⌘+clicking any additional printers. Click the Create Printer Pool button as seen in Figure 16.12. Enter a name for the printer pool in the Printer Pool Name field.

> **TIP** Another way you can administer the print services of Mac OS X is via the CUPS Web interface. As mentioned at the beginning of this chapter, CUPS (Common UNIX Printing System) is a cross-platform open source printing architecture that is the heart of Mac OS X's print services. The CUPS Web interface is accessed through a Web browser utilizing the internal host address of the system (127.0.0.1) on port 631. To access the CUPS Web interface, launch Safari and enter: `http://localhost:631` in the address field. Although not as intuitive as the Printer Setup Utility, the CUPS Web interface provides another GUI way to administer Mac OS X print services.

FIGURE 16.12

Setting up a Printer Pool in OS X is quick and easy.

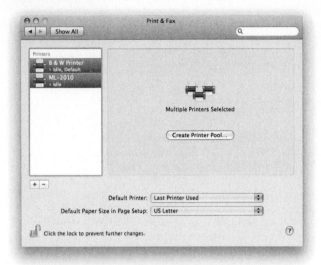

Summary

In this chapter, you've seen how to print, fax, and make PDFs, as well as configure printers and manage print and modem queues. Mac OS X is a modern OS, and its CUPS-based print services reflect that. With its built-in support for numerous print connectivity options, in addition to its built-in faxing and on-the-fly PDF capabilities, Mac OS X's print services are an evolutionary leap over its predecessors and its competition.

Chapter 17

Managing System Preferences

Modern computers are highly configurable. Numerous settings let you adjust most aspects of a computer's operation. You can adjust the interface and appearance, the hardware's performance, and network communication settings, as well as overall system operation preferences. Within Mac OS X, system software configuration and settings are managed by a central program known as the System Preferences application. Configuration of individual system settings within the System Preferences application are done through Quartz GUI elements, known as *panes*. When a specific system preference is selected, the corresponding preference pane is loaded within the System Preferences application. Preference panes redraw themselves within the confines of the initial System Preferences window. The System Preferences window has a fixed width, but it resizes vertically to accommodate the contents of the preference pane being viewed.

The contents of the System Preferences application are divided up into five preconfigured categories: Personal, Hardware, Internet & Network, System, and Other. The Personal section contains the preferences for Appearance, Desktop & Screen Saver, Dock, Exposé & Spaces, International, Security, and Spotlight. Through the Hardware section, Bluetooth, CDs & DVDs, Displays, Energy Saver, Ink, Keyboard & Mouse, Print & Fax, and Sound preferences can be configured. Within the Internet & Network section, .Mac, Network, QuickTime, and Sharing preferences can be configured. The System section contains the Accounts, Classic, Date & Time, Software Update, Speech, Startup Disk, and Universal Access preferences. The Other section appears only if there are preferences to set that fall outside of the previous four categories; these preference panes are typically of third-party origin.

In addition to these categories, you also find a Spotlight search field in the System Preferences toolbar, similar to the one found in a Finder window. Use this field to locate which preference panes contain what settings. There are also Forward, Back, and Show All buttons that are intended to facilitate navigation within the System Preferences application.

This chapter discusses details about many, but not all, System Preferences. Table 17.1 specifies where each System Preference pane is covered in the book.

TABLE 17.1

Coverage of System Preferences

System Preferences Pane	Covered In
Accounts	Chapter 18
Appearance	Chapter 2
Bluetooth	Chapter 11
CDs & DVDs	This chapter
Date & Time	This chapter
Desktop & Screen Saver	Chapter 2
Displays	This chapter
Dock	Chapter 2
Energy Saver	This chapter
Exposé & Spaces	Chapter 2
Ink	This chapter
International	This chapter
Keyboard & Mouse	This chapter
.Mac	Chapter 14
Network	Chapter 11
Parental Controls	This chapter
Print & Fax	Chapter 16
QuickTime	Chapter 7
Security	Chapter 24
Sharing	Chapter 12
Software Update	Chapter 21
Sound	This chapter
Speech	This chapter

System Preferences Pane	Covered In
Spotlight	Chapter 3
Startup Disk	This chapter
Time Machine	Chapter 21
Universal Access	This chapter

Using the System Preferences Application

This section describes the scope of preference settings: how to open System Preferences, display a pane whose settings you want to see or change, configure the System Preferences toolbar, and deal with locked settings in System Preferences.

Opening System Preferences

You can either click the System Preferences icon in the Dock, or you can choose System Preferences from the Apple menu to open System Preferences. When open, System Preferences displays a window that shows buttons for the different panes of settings. Figure 17.1 shows the contents of the System Preferences application.

FIGURE 17.1

When the System Preferences application opens, the window displays buttons for all available preference panes.

Each button in the System Preferences application corresponds to a pane of preference settings. To see a pane, click its button or choose the pane by name from the View menu. The System Preferences application changes to show the settings for the pane that was clicked, and the title of the window changes to the name of the corresponding pane. If you want to return to the display of buttons for all panes, click the Show All button in the upper left corner of the window or choose View ↪ Show All.

Harnessing Spotlight

As mentioned at the start of this chapter, System Preferences includes a Spotlight search field that can assist with finding which preference panes contain what settings. This feature supports both Windows and Macintosh terminology for system settings/preferences configuration. To harness the power of Spotlight within System Preferences, simply type what you are looking for in the search field, which is denoted by a magnifying glass symbol at the top right-hand side of the System Preferences application. As you type your very first letter, a drop-down list appears containing system preference terminology, as shown in Figure 17.2. As additional characters are input into the search field, Spotlight narrows the displayed result. From here select the desired preference.

FIGURE 17.2

Let Spotlight take the guesswork out of system preference administration.

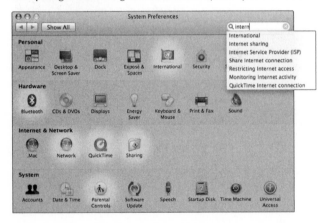

Unlocking preference settings

The settings in some of the System Preferences panes can be locked. You can tell whether settings are locked in two ways:

- The locked settings are dim (displayed in gray text rather than black text).
- The security button padlock icon near the bottom left corner of the window appears locked.

Table 17.2 lists the system settings that can be locked.

TABLE 17.2	

Preference Settings That Can Be Locked

System Preferences Pane	Settings That Can Be Locked
Accounts	All settings except Picture and Startup Items.
Date & Time	All settings except the menu bar clock settings.
Energy Saver	All settings.
Network	All settings except choosing a different location.
Parental Controls	All settings.
Print & Fax	Sharing.
Security	All settings except Set Master Password and Turn On FileVault. These two items require independent authentication and authorization.
Sharing	All settings.
Startup Disk	All settings.

To change locked settings, you must have access to the name and password of an administrator account. Chapter 1 noted that an admin account is created via the Setup Assistant during the installation of Mac OS X. You can find more information about the administrator account in Chapter 18. To unlock preference settings, follow these steps:

1. **Click the locked security button denoted by the icon of the padlock in the lower left corner of the preference pane.**

2. **In the dialog box that appears, enter the name and password of an administrator account.** By default, the current logged-in user's account name is pre-entered in this dialog box; so if the account you are logged into is that of an administrator, simply enter the corresponding password. If you are logged into an ordinary account, you have to enter the password and also change the name. Figure 17.3 shows the dialog box in which you enter the name and password to unlock preference settings.

3. **Click OK.**

FIGURE 17.3

Unlock protected preference settings by entering the name and password of an administrator account.

Configuring CDs & DVDs Preferences

The CDs & DVDs preference pane enables you to configure the behavior of Mac OS X when a CD or DVD is inserted into the computer's optical drive. The options that are available are configured in accordance to the type of optical media being inserted into the drive. There are three menus based upon optical media type: music CD, picture CD, and video DVD, as shown in Figure 17.4. Details on each of the five menus are listed as follows:

FIGURE 17.4

The CDs & DVDs preference pane determines the behavior of Mac OS X upon optical media insertion.

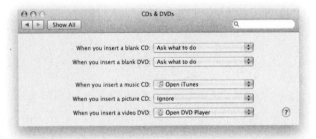

- The **"When you insert music CD"** pop-up menu provides the following choices: Open iTunes, Open other application, Run script, Ignore.

- The **"When you insert picture CD"** pop-up menu provides the following choices: Open iPhoto, Open other application, Run script, Ignore.

- The **"When you insert video DVD"** pop-up menu provides the following choices: Open DVD Player, Open other application, Run script, Ignore.

With respect to the three different media types, the options tell Mac OS how to behave when the media is inserted, as follows:

- **Open iTunes, Open iPhoto, and Open DVD Player:** These options tell Mac OS X to open one of those applications, respectively.

- **Open other application:** This option tells Mac OS X to open a predefined application, such as Roxio's Toast or the Mac OS X Disk Utility.

- **Run script:** This option tells Mac OS X to run a specified AppleScript that can execute a sequence of actions. Although no actual scripts are provided with Mac OS X, you could make your own script. An example of such a script is one that executes an automatic Finder backup of specified content to given optical media.

- **Ignore:** This option tells Mac OS X that upon insertion of given optical media, do nothing.

Configuring Date & Time Preferences

In addition to displaying a clock on your menu bar, your computer uses date and time information for a variety of operations. For example, your computer uses date and time information to provide files with creation and modification dates and to time-stamp sent e-mail messages. You can configure your computer's clock and calendar settings in the Date & Time preference pane.

The Date & Time preference pane is divided into three panels:

- Date & Time
- Time Zone
- Clock

Each panel is accessed by clicking the button with the corresponding name at the top of the Date & Time preference pane.

Date & Time panel

Click the Date & Time button to set the current date and time.

- **To set the date & time automatically:** Select the Set Date & Time automatically option. This enables OS X to automatically synchronize the computer's internal clock to a time server over a network or the Internet using Network Time Protocol (NTP). The "Set date

& time automatically" pop-up menu enables you to select an Apple time server that is based in the Americas, Asia, or Europe. It also allows for the manual input of an NTP server other than the ones that Apple provides.

- **To change the date:** Click the little arrows next to the month and year and click a day in the monthly calendar.

- **To change the time:** Drag the hands of the analog clock and click the AM/PM indicator next to this clock. Alternatively, click the digital hour, minute, or second and then either type a new value or click the little arrows next to the digital clock.

You must click Save to put the new time and date into effect. Figure 17.5 shows the clock and calendar settings in the Date & Time panel of the Date & Time preference pane.

 If the controls arrows for changing the date and time are absent, you need to deselect the option labeled "Set date & time automatically."

FIGURE 17.5

The Date & Time panel also contains an Open International button, which is a shortcut to the International preference pane.

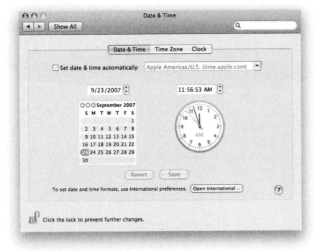

Time Zone panel

Click the Time Zone button to set your time zone in the Time Zone panel of the Date & Time preference pane. The pop-up menu lists regions that may have different time zones in the highlighted part of the world. You can click another part of the world to highlight it. If daylight saving time is in effect for the currently selected time zone, a sunburst graphic appears in the lower left corner of the map next to the time zone's abbreviation. After selecting your time zone, you can then select the closest city to your location in the pull-down menu.

Clock panel

Click the Clock button to open the Clock panel and configure the appearance of the clock in Mac OS X. By default, Mac OS X places a clock in the Finder's menu bar. You can see the date by clicking the clock in the menu bar. This action displays a menu with the date at the top of it. In addition, this menu has choices for viewing the clock in analog or digital format and for opening the Date & Time pane of System Preferences.

The menu bar clock initially appears at the right end of the menu bar. You can move it by pressing ⌘ and dragging it. You can remove the menu bar clock by ⌘+dragging it off the menu bar.

In addition to configuring the appearance of the clock in the Finder's menu bar, the Clock panel allows the clock to be viewed in a separate window. As with the menu bar clock, you can configure the window clock's display in either analog or digital format.

At the very bottom of the Clock panel, you can elect to have the clock announce the time on the hour, the half-hour, and the quarter-hour. You can also use the Customize Voice button to open the sheet that allows for the configuration of the voice in which the time will be announced, as shown in Figure 17.6.

FIGURE 17.6

The Customize Voice sheet has every possible option except *don't be annoying.*

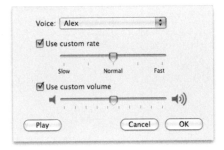

Configuring Display Preferences

If you stare at your display screen for hours on end, you want the view to be crisp and easy on the eyes. If you work with color, you want your screen to display colors as accurately and consistently as possible. If you work with more than one display screen on your computer, you want to have control over how the two work together. If your display is a CRT-type display, you should set up a screen saver to protect the display against image burn-in.

Toward these goals, you can adjust your display by using the Displays and Screen Saver panes of System Preferences. You can also make quick adjustments with the Displays menu icon.

Like the Date & Time preference pane, the Displays preference pane is divided into several panels accessed via buttons at the top of the Displays preference pane. Depending upon your hardware configuration, the Displays preference pane may provide some or all of the following panels:

- **Display:** This panel includes settings for screen resolution, number of colors, refresh rate, contrast, brightness, and Finder menu bar access.

- **Geometry:** This panel includes settings for adjusting the shape and position of the screen image (generally only available for Apple CRT displays).

- **Color:** This panel includes settings for selecting a color profile and calibrating your display.

- **Arrangement:** This panel includes settings for adjusting how multiple screens work together (present only if you have more than one display attached and your computer can work with them independently).

Display panel

Click the Display button to adjust the resolution, number of colors, refresh rate, contrast, or brightness of your display, as shown in Figure 17.7. You can also change a setting to show or hide the Displays icon in the menu bar. Some settings are not available with some types of displays. For example, no contrast setting for the LCDs (liquid crystal displays) is used in MacBooks, MacBook Pros, and flat-panel displays.

FIGURE 17.7

When using a MacBook or a MacBook Pro that is attached to an external monitor, use the Detect Displays button to have OS X recognize that display.

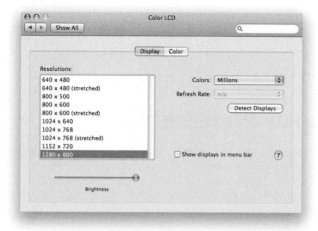

Resolution and colors

The two most basic display settings are resolution and number of colors. *Resolution* is the size of the rectangular screen image — the number of pixels (picture elements or dots) wide by the number of pixels high. The number of colors, often called *color depth*, is the number of different colors that can be displayed for each pixel of the screen image. Color depth is sometimes referred to as *bit depth*, which is a measure of the amount of memory it takes to store each pixel (more colors require more bits of memory per pixel).

The higher the number of colors, the more realistic the screen image can look. However, increasing the number of colors doesn't necessarily make the screen display better, because the picture appearing on-screen may not make use of all of the available colors. For example, a black-and-white photograph is still black, white, and shades of gray when it appears on a screen capable of displaying millions of colors per pixel.

Although you are provided with three choices, for all intents and purposes you have two practical choices of color depth in Mac OS X: thousands or millions of colors per pixel. Mac OS X can't accurately render its Aqua interface with a lower color depth.

The settings for resolution depend on the capabilities of the display and the computer's video card, but in general range from 800 x 600 pixels (the size of the original iBook display) up to 2560 x 1600 pixels (the size of a 30-inch Apple Cinema HD Display). Modern flat panel displays all have an optimal resolution, which is set by the manufacturer and will be noted in the documentation included with your display. Although LCDs *can* typically operate at different resolutions, the results may be a bit blurry or jagged-looking.

Resolution and number of colors are related because increasing either requires more video memory. If you increase the resolution, Mac OS X may have to automatically reduce the number of colors. Conversely, you may be able to set a higher number of colors by decreasing the resolution.

Refresh rate

The significance of the refresh rate setting gets into the mechanics of displaying an image on the screen. The video card sends the screen image to the display one thin line of pixels at a time. After the video card sends the last line, it starts over again with the first line. The refresh rate is a measure of how fast the video card sends lines of the screen image to the display. A higher refresh rate means the entire screen image gets redisplayed more often. The refresh rate is of concern on a CRT (cathode ray tube, or picture tube) display. If the refresh rate is below about 75 Hz, the CRT's glowing phosphors may fade perceptibly before they are refreshed. Your eyes perceive this as a flickering of the video image, and the flickering can lead to eye fatigue and headache. An LCD (liquid crystal display) doesn't flicker regardless of the refresh rate.

Each make and model of display has certain combinations of resolution and refresh rate that produce a clear, bright image with minimum flicker. If you set the refresh rate to a value that is not recommended for the display, the image probably will be distorted or dark.

Display settings in the menu bar

Besides using the Displays preference pane to adjust the resolution and colors of your display, you can also enable a Displays menu in the Finder's menu bar. Do this by placing a check mark in the box adjacent to "Show displays in menu bar." A pop-up menu enables you to select how many choices are presented in the Displays menu. The increments are 0, 3, 5, and 10. After you've enabled it, you can click the Displays icon in the Finder's menu bar to see a menu of available screen resolutions and numbers of colors. This menu lists all of your displays and has a command for turning mirroring on or off. The menu also has a command for opening the Displays pane of System Preferences. Figure 17.8 shows the contents of the Displays menu on a 13-inch MacBook.

FIGURE 17.8

Use the Displays menu to directly open the Displays preference pane without having to first open the System Preference application.

TIP   You can move the Displays icon by pressing the ⌘ key and dragging the icon. Drag the icon left or right to change its position relative to other icons on the right side of the menu bar. Drag the icon off the menu bar to make it vanish in a puff of smoke.

Geometry panel

With some displays, such as an Apple CRT display, the Displays preference pane has a Geometry panel that enables you to adjust the shape and position of the image seen on the screen. You can expand the display area so that less black border is visible. You can also change the pincushion (how concave the sides of the picture are) and the rotation of the display. Figure 17.9 shows the settings you see when you click the Geometry panel in the Displays preference pane on an eMac.

The graphic buttons on the right side of the panel reflect the various adjustments that you can make. These buttons change according to which setting you have selected to adjust. You can also make adjustments by dragging edges or the center of the small screen; the shape of the pointer tells you which way to drag. If you wreak havoc on your display by experimenting with the geometry settings, click the Factory Defaults button to return the settings to their factory presets.

FIGURE 17.9

If your screen image isn't centered, use the Geometry panel to adjust the shape and position of the image on the screen.

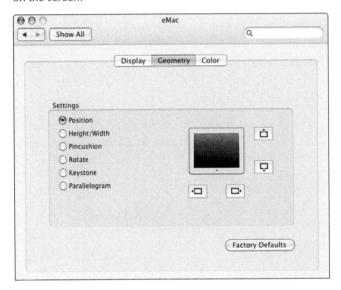

Color panel

The Color panel enables you to select a color profile for your display or to calibrate the display. After you calibrate the display, the Mac OS requires you to name and store the new settings as a color profile.

You can create a custom profile for your display by clicking the Calibrate button in the Color panel. A custom profile accounts for your display's age and individual manufacturing variations. What's more, you can configure custom profiles for different resolutions, white points, and gamma corrections. With most displays, clicking the Calibrate button opens the Display Calibrator assistant. The Calibrator walks you through the process that calibrates your display and creates a new ColorSync profile.

NOTE If you have an Apple ColorSync display, AppleVision display, or 21-inch Apple Studio Display, a Recalibrate button may appear in lieu of the Calibrate button. Clicking Recalibrate activates the self-calibrating hardware built into these displays.

Display Calibrator assistant

The Display Calibrator is actually a stand-alone application that acts as an assistant (those coming from the Windows world call it a wizard) that walks you through the process of creating a custom ColorSync profile for your display. If your ColorSync profile accurately reflects the behavior of your display, applications that take advantage of ColorSync can better display images in their intended colors. Similarly, if you have a proper profile for your printer, the colors match when printed — that's the *sync* in ColorSync.

You can use Display Calibrator to create a custom profile for your display and your viewing preferences. A custom profile accounts for your display's age and individual manufacturing variations. What's more, you can configure custom profiles for different resolutions, white points, and gamma corrections (more on all of these terms shortly). Display Calibrator walks you through the process that calibrates your display and creates a new ColorSync profile. Figure 17.10 shows the Display Calibrator's introduction.

FIGURE 17.10

Display Calibrator walks you through calibrating a display and creating a custom profile.

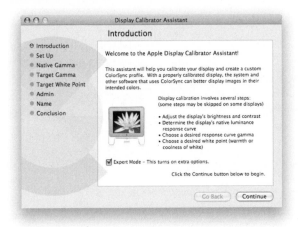

Depending upon the type of display being calibrated, the Display Calibrator assistant takes you through some or all of the following steps:

1. **Introduction:** Decide whether to use expert calibration settings instead of basic settings. There isn't much difference to the casual user, but graphics professionals who use ColorSync for color-correct output may find it useful to select Expert Mode before moving on to the next step. (Expert mode gives you more granular control over the settings in Display Calibrator, although for all intents and purposes it doesn't change the operation of the Display Calibrator dramatically.)

2. **Set Up:** Set your display to its highest contrast setting and then adjust the brightness. A test image helps you find the proper setting. This step is omitted on some displays.

3. **Native Gamma:** Provide information about the display's current gamma correction. *Gamma* refers to the relationship between the intensity of color and its luminance.

Gamma correction compensates for the loss of detail that the human eye perceives in dark areas. In regular mode, you make adjustments to a gray image; in Expert mode, you determine the current gamma by adjusting sliders until red, green, and blue test images look right. This step is omitted on some displays.

4. **Target Gamma:** Specify the gamma correction that you want the display to use:

   - 1.8 is the standard gamma for Mac displays.

   - 2.2 is the standard gamma for television displays, video editing equipment, and Windows computers.

   - Native is gamma that is determined between input voltage and display brightness. Typically this feature is not available with LCD displays due to the fact that the backlight runs at a constant level of illumination.

   A low gamma setting makes colors appear more washed out. A high gamma setting makes colors appear more brilliant and with higher contrast. In this step, the Expert mode allows you to use a slider to choose a very specific gamma setting.

5. **Target White Point:** Select your preferred *white point,* which determines whether colors look warm (reddish) or cool (bluish). You can also choose to make no white-point correction. In Expert mode, you can use a slider to choose a specific white point measured in degrees Kelvin, which is a temperature scale commonly used in science.

6. **Name:** Name and save the custom profile for future use.

7. **Conclusion:** Close the Display Calibrator assistant and select your newly created display profile under the Display Profile menu in the Color panel.

You can repeat the calibration process to create a number of profiles if you use your display at different resolutions or for different purposes.

Arrangement panel

If your computer has two displays or more, you may be able to arrange how they work together. In one arrangement, called *display mirroring* or *video mirroring,* the second display shows exactly the same image as the first display. The other arrangement treats each display as part of an extended Desktop — as you move the pointer across the Desktop, it goes from one display to the next. Some older Mac models can use two displays only for display mirroring, not for an extended Desktop. Multiple displays are configured using the Arrangement panel.

You can change the relative positions of the displays in an extended desktop by dragging the small screens in Displays preferences. You can also set which display has the menu bar by dragging the little menu bar to the appropriate small screen in Displays preferences. When you have two or more displays in an extended desktop, Displays preferences has a separate window on each display. Each window has a Display panel, Color panel, and Other panel for adjusting the display where the window is located. Only the primary display's preference pane contains an Arrangement panel.

Configuring Energy Saver Preferences

All Macs capable of using Mac OS X can save energy while they are inactive by taking advantage of sleep mode. During sleep mode, a typical desktop computer uses between 13 and 30 watts, and a display made after the middle of 1999 uses between 8 and 13 watts. These numbers reflect the requirements to comply with the U.S. Environmental Protection Agency's Energy Star program. Most Macs that can use Mac OS X comply with the Energy Star requirements, and all Apple displays made since the middle of July 1999 comply. Using the sleep mode is advantageous in two ways. The first benefit is that when waking from sleep the computer is usable sooner than from a cold start. Not only is the computer already powered on, but the sleep state keeps applications and documents open so that when you wake the computer, you can start work from where you left off. Second, the computer can still wake up via network or modem if configured to do so while in sleep mode.

Naturally, you can save even more energy by switching off your display when you leave your computer for a while. Although shutting down your computer would conserve even more energy, you would lose the quick-start advantage.

The Energy Saver preference pane is divided into two panels: Sleep and Options. Their controls and settings let you determine when your computer sleeps and wakes. If your computer is a MacBook or MacBook Pro, you can also set an option to show the battery status in the menu bar. The battery status option is not present on a desktop Mac.

Sleep panel

Use the Sleep panel to adjust how much energy your computer saves by setting how long it remains active before going to sleep. The panel's options will vary based on whether the system is a desktop or a portable.

When used with Mac Book and Mac Book Pro computers, Energy Saver provides a number of features intended to help road warriors improve the performance of their portable computers. The majority of these features are managed via a combination of two pop-up menus: Settings for and Optimization. The Settings for pop-up menu allows you to apply your settings based on whether you are running off the power adapter or the battery. The Optimization pop-up menu contains a number of predefined energy saver settings that are distinguished between system performance and energy savings; there is also the option to specify a custom configuration. In like manner to the Network preference pane's Locations, when combined, these two options provide the ability to configure the system appropriately to the environment in which it will be used.

The Sleep panel can display its contents as an overall/general configuration or in a granular detailed view. To view in detail, click the button labeled Show Details. As shown in Figure 17.11, you can set separate sleep timings for the whole system and the display, and choose whether to put the hard disk to sleep when possible.

FIGURE 17.11

The Screen Saver button is a shortcut that opens the Screen Saver panel from the Desktop & Screen Saver preference pane.

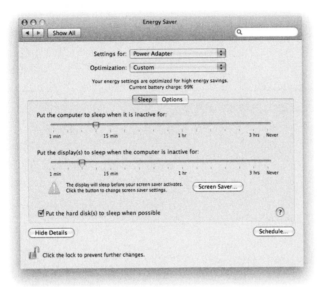

NOTE Some PCI cards may prevent a Power Mac from going to sleep according to the timing for system sleep as set in the Energy Saver preference pane. This behavior depends on the particular make and model of the PCI card. Some cards can be upgraded to eliminate this behavior. Even if the system can't sleep, you can still set separate timings for display sleep and hard disk sleep.

Options panel

The principal function of the Options panel is to allow the configuration of when your computer wakes from sleep; but you can also configure the power button to sleep the computer, to reduce display brightness, to restart the computer after a power failure or a freeze, and to show battery status in the menu bar.

You can use the battery icon in the Finder's menu bar to monitor the condition of your computer's battery. The appearance of the battery icon indicates whether the computer is using or recharging the battery, and how much battery capacity remains, as detailed in Table 17.3.

Besides indicating the battery condition graphically, the battery icon can report the battery condition in words. You can see this information by clicking the battery icon and looking at the top of the menu that appears. If the computer is using the battery, the first item in the Battery menu reports the hours and minutes of life remaining. If the computer is charging the battery, the menu reports the hours and minutes until the battery is fully charged. You can show the hours and minutes or an equivalent percentage in the menu bar by choosing from the Show submenu of the Battery menu.

> **TIP** You can move the battery icon by pressing the ⌘ key and dragging the icon. Drag the icon left or right to change its position relative to other icons on the right side of the menu bar. Drag the icon off the menu bar to make it vanish.

TABLE 17.3

Battery Icon Appearance

Battery Icon	Meaning
◀■▮	Battery fully charged and computer operating on AC power
⏦▮	Battery charging and computer operating on AC power
◼▮	Battery in use and partly depleted
✕▮	No battery; computer operating on AC power

Schedule sheet

The Schedule sheet, shown in Figure 17.12, is accessed by clicking the Schedule button at the bottom of the Energy Saver panel. The utility of the Schedule sheet provides the convenience and assurance that a given system is on at a specified time and/or off at a specified time. Selecting Start up or wake the computer enables you to select the frequency and what time the computer should start up. The frequency pop-up contains the following selections: Everyday, Weekdays, Weekends, and the days of the week. Placing a check mark to the right and selecting Shut Down or Sleep from the lower pop-up menu enables you to specify when the computer shuts down or sleeps. As with the Start up option, the frequency pop-up menu contains frequency settings.

FIGURE 17.12

Use the Schedule sheet to set your computer to start up/wake and shut down/sleep automatically.

Processor performance

When administrating the Energy Saver preference pane on portables, the Options panel contains a processor performance pop-up menu. As the name implies, this menu enables you to increase and reduce the overall performance of the processor in the computer. The benefits of reducing processor performance include extended battery life and a reduction of operating temperature.

Starting sleep manually

Although Mac OS X puts your computer to sleep after a period of inactivity, you gain additional energy savings by putting it to sleep manually if you know that you won't use it for a while. Some of the following methods may work on your computer:

- **Choose Sleep from the Apple menu.** (The Sleep command is dim on a Power Mac with a PCI card that prevents system sleep.)

- **Press the power button on a keyboard that has one.** On an Apple Pro keyboard, which does not have a power key, press the Control and Eject keys at the same time. (The Eject key is in the upper right corner of the numeric keypad.) After pressing the power button or Control+Eject, a dialog box appears asking whether you want to restart, sleep, cancel, or shut down. Click Sleep or press the S key.

- **Close the lid on a MacBook or MacBook Pro.**

- **Press the power button on the computer.**

- **Press the power button on the display on newer Apple displays.** (On the older CRT-type Apple displays, pressing the power button simply turns off the display.)

Waking up your computer

To make your Mac wake up, try the following methods:

- **Click the mouse button.**

- **Press any key on the keyboard.** (The Caps Lock and function keys may not work for this purpose.)

- **Open your Mac portable (formerly known as a "laptop" before a rising frequency of heat/groin related injuries became common knowledge).**

Configuring Ink Preferences

Culled from the now defunct Newton PDA, Inkwell is Mac OS X's stylus-based input technology. Inkwell facilitates the input of digital ink (drawings, signatures, and so on), the conversion of handwriting into text, and the execution of commands via the stylus. The latter differentiates itself from the use of the stylus as a mouse, by permitting the operator to input ⌘+key shortcuts without the use of the keyboard.

To utilize Inkwell, you need to use a third-party graphics tablet because Apple does not manufacture one of its own. Wacom Technology (www.wacom.com) provides the most popular options. After you acquire a tablet, make sure to download and install the latest drivers from the manufacturer's Web site.

Ink preference pane

The configuration of Inkwell is done from the Ink preference pane located in the Hardware section of the System Preferences application, as shown in Figure 17.13. The Ink preference pane is divided into three panels: Settings, Gestures, and Word List.

 The Ink preference pane presents itself in the System Preferences application only if a graphics tablet is attached to the Macintosh being administered.

FIGURE 17.13

Before Inkwell can be used, click the On button to the right of "Handwriting recognition is," at the top of the Ink preference pane.

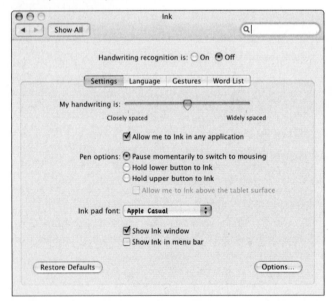

Settings panel

The principal functions of the Settings panel depicted in Figure 17.14 are to configure Inkwell to accommodate a user's writing style and to increase reliability for handwriting-to-text conversion. The panel contains adjustments for spacing of characters and words, the selection of language (English, French, German), and the selection of the font to be used to display recognized text in the Ink pad. Apple recommends using the Apple Casual font and emulating its style for handwriting input to increase reliability of character recognition.

In addition to the previously mentioned selections, other options are Allow me to write anywhere, Recognize Western European characters, Show Ink window, and Show Ink in menu bar.

- **Allow me to write anywhere:** Specifies whether your writing is to be used solely with the Ink pad, or in any application that supports handwriting input. The Inkpad is contained in the Ink window. Inkpad is a floating toolbar/palette available in any application and the principal interface for handwriting input.

- **Recognize Western European characters:** Specifies whether to recognize language-specific marks incorporated into various western European languages.

- **Show Ink window:** Specifies whether the Ink widow should be present while using Mac OS X.

- **Show Ink in menu bar:** Specifies whether the Finder's menu bar should contain an Ink menu, as shown in Figure 17.14.

FIGURE 17.14

The Ink menu provides the ability to enable or disable Write Anywhere, Show or Hide Ink Window, and open the Ink preference pane.

Using the Restore Defaults button reverts any changes made in the Settings panel back to factory defaults, and the Options button opens an additional sheet for greater granular control of handwriting recognition. These settings include speed controls for delay of handwriting recognition, distance of movement required for input, and delay before the stylus can be used as a mouse. The other selections available in this sheet include Recognize my handwriting when pen moves away from tablet, Hide pointer while writing, and Play sound while writing.

Gestures panel

The Gestures panel, shown in Figure 17.15, contains a predefined list of characters that can be enabled or disabled on an item-by-item basis and used in lieu of entering nonprintable characters such as spaces and tabs and performing actions such as undo, copy, and paste.

Word List panel

The Word List panel allows for the input of words that Inkwell has difficulty recognizing. This list is typically used for the input of names of people and places, foreign words incorporated into the specified language in the setting panel, and out-of-the ordinary lexicons.

FIGURE 17.15

Though not as complex as using Palm's Graffiti method of data input, you must avail yourself of Gestures in order to properly use Inkwell's handwriting recognition.

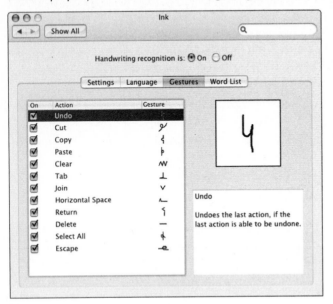

Ink window

As stated earlier in this chapter, the Ink window is a floating toolbar/palette that is available in any application and is the principal interface for handwriting input. A series of icons runs horizontally across the toolbar, aptly titled *Ink*. These clickable icons facilitate the switching between using the stylus for handwriting recognition or as a mouse, the selection of modifier keys such as ⌘, Shift, Option, and Control, and the opening and closing of the Ink pad. It also contains a pop-up menu that opens the Ink contents within Mac OS X's help system or the Ink preference pane.

The Ink pad is a predefined scratchpad where you can write text, enter gestures, and draw simple pictures. There are two buttons at the bottom left side of the Ink pad to change between writing and drawing input. There are also two buttons on the right side titled Clear and Send. The Clear button clears out any contents entered in the Ink pad, and the Send button enters the contents of the Ink pad in the document you are working on. Finally, if a word is not recognized properly, hold the Control key and click the word intended for correction. A pop-up list of words appears containing words from Inkwell's handwriting recognition dictionary and words that were entered in the Word List panel.

Configuring International Preferences

Mac OS X is a multilingual and multiregional operating system. It can display menus, dialog boxes, and other text in a variety of languages. These include not only languages that use the Roman alphabet, such as English, Spanish, French, and German, but also languages with much larger sets of characters, such as Japanese. Besides accommodating differences in language structure, writing direction, and alphabetical sorting, Mac OS X can also adjust for regional differences in formats for displaying dates, times, numbers, and currency. With Mac OS X, you're not limited to working in one language at a time. You can work in multiple languages and switch languages while you work. However, you may need to install special applications to create documents in different languages.

Language panel

Most but not all Mac OS X applications are able to display their menus, dialog boxes, and other text in a number of different languages. Applications with this ability include the Finder and the majority of the applications preinstalled in the Applications and Utilities folders. You can choose the language you want these Mac OS X applications to use.

The selection of language preference for menus and dialog boxes for Mac OS X's Finder and applications is done in the Language panel. The Language panel contains a Languages list of available languages. Each time you open an application, Mac OS X tells it to use the languages in the list specified in order of preference from top to bottom. If the application doesn't support menus in that language, Mac OS X tells it to use the next language in the list, and so on down the list. Not all languages are available with a default installation of Mac OS X; some languages may require you to install additional fonts before you can view the characters for those languages. Check the Mac OS X Install Disc for the availability of additional fonts.

Language Script Systems and Keyboard Layouts

The world's languages have many different alphabets and methods of writing (vertical or horizontal, left-to-right, or right-to-left). The software that defines a method of writing is called a *language script system,* or simply a *script.* Do not confuse this kind of script with the kind of script you create with AppleScript (as described in Chapter 22).

A language script system specifies which character in the specified language each keystroke produces as well as how the characters should behave—for example, the direction in which text flows. The script also specifies sort order, number and currency formats, and date and time formats.

Multiple languages can use one language script system. For example, the Roman script is used in most Western languages, such as English, French, Italian, Spanish, and German.

Associated with each language script system are one or more keyboard layouts. A keyboard layout defines the relationship between keys you press and characters entered. For example, the keyboard layout for U.S. English produces a # symbol when you press Shift+3, but the same keystroke produces a £ symbol with the British English keyboard layout.

You change the order of preference for the language that Mac OS X applications use by rearranging the order in the Languages list. Drag your first language choice to the top of the list. Drag your second language choice to the second spot on the list and continue in this manner so that the languages are in descending order of preference. Language changes take effect in the Finder the next time you log in.

You can add languages to the list and remove them from it. Click the Edit button to see a dialog box that lists all installed languages. In this sheet, select the check box of each language that you want to appear in the Languages list. You can change the sorting in the dialog box by clicking a column heading.

The somewhat trickier task is to apply and configure the language preferences for a specific application. This is done within the Show Info window of a selected application from within the Finder. Figure 17.16 illustrates the Languages portion of the Show Info window of the TextEdit application. Within the Languages section of the Show Info window, you also see a list of available system languages. The list of languages is alphabetized and cannot be reordered. Checking and unchecking the boxes adjacent to the languages can alter the application's language selection.

FIGURE 17.16

The Languages section of the Show Info window of an application allows you to specify your preferred language, as well as remove unwanted or add needed language selections.

For example, say that you want to open QuickTime in French, but only QuickTime. You would need to highlight the QuickTime player within the Finder, choose Show Info from the File menu, and select Languages from the pop-up menu. Next, you would uncheck all the languages except for French. This task can be executed regardless of whether the application is active, but in order for the language change to take effect for an active application, you need to quit and then relaunch the application. Upon restart, the application opens in the desired language, which in this example is French, as shown in Figure 17.17.

FIGURE 17.17

SACRÉ BLEU — QuickTime en Français!

In the event that more than one language is checked within the Language section of the Show Info window, the preferred language of the application is determined by the order of the languages within the Language panel of the International preference pane. For example, say that both Spanish and French are checked within the Show Info window of the TextEdit application (refer to Figure 17.16), and the order of languages within the Language panel of the International preference pane is as follows: English, Deutsch, Español, Français, Nederlands, Italiano, and Chinese. Upon launching, TextEdit's default language would be Spanish.

Customize Sorting sheet

As stated earlier in this chapter, the software that defines a method of writing is called a language script system, or simply a script. Languages may use the same script, yet have different rules for alphabetizing, capitalizing, and distinguishing words. In Mac OS X, this set of rules is called a *text behavior.* You choose a text behavior for Mac OS X applications by clicking the Customize Sorting button. In this sheet, select one of the installed language script systems from the list on the left and then choose one of the script's regional languages from the adjacent pop-up menu on the right. For example, the Roman script system in Mac OS X has different text behavior rules for Austrian, Brazilian, Canadian French, Catalan, Danish, Dutch, English, Finnish, French, German, Italian, Norwegian, Portuguese, Spanish, and Swedish.

Formats panel

You can set up standard formats for displaying dates, times, numbers, currency, and measurement units. The Finder uses these formats in list views, the Info window, and elsewhere. Other applications may use these formats, or they may have their own preference settings. The Region pop-up menu has preset geo-localities that can facilitate all configurations within this panel. If your region is not displayed in the menu, place a check mark in the box adjacent to Show all regions. Of course if you need to take a more customized approach, all the options within this panel can be individually configured.

You set date, time, and numbers formats for Mac OS X applications in the Formats panel, as shown in Figure 17.18. This is accomplished by selecting the region the computer will be used for, such as Botswana or Zimbabwe. You can also create a custom format by using the customize buttons. The aptly named Currency pop-up menu allows you to specify your desired monetary unit, whereas the Measurement Units pop-up menu allows for the selection of U.S. or Metric measurement units.

FIGURE 17.18

Use the Calendar pop-up menu to set your desired calendar selection. We Westerners mostly use the Gregorian calendar.

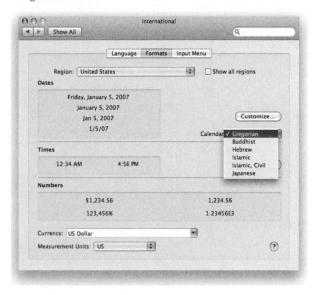

Input Menu panel

Each language has a different keyboard layout. For example, on the keyboard layout for Spanish, you can type the letter n with a tilde (ñ) by pressing one key instead of the three keys required for the same letter on a U.S. English keyboard layout. In addition, the question mark is in a different location, with an upside-down question mark next to it on the Spanish keyboard layout, and the keys for adding accents to vowels are more accessible. But even regions with the same language, such as Australia, Britain, Canada, and the U.S. still have different keyboard layouts. You can even find special keyboard layouts for alternate typing methods, such as the Dvorak layout for typing English.

You can switch to a different keyboard layout or input method to facilitate entering or editing text in another language. You switch keyboard layouts by using several different methods. If you regularly use multiple languages, you can set up the keyboard menu. You can also employ keyboard shortcuts for switching keyboard layouts, and you can have Mac OS X automatically switch the keyboard layout when you select text that uses a different script. For Mac OS X applications, you configure this using the Options sheet of the Input Menu panel.

NOTE Keep in mind that the key labels printed on your keyboard do not change when you switch keyboard layouts. If you change to a different layout, some keys no longer generate the characters printed on them.

If your computer has more than one language script system, switching keyboard layouts may also change script systems. Each keyboard layout implicitly designates a script system. For example, switching from the U.S. keyboard layout to the Japanese keyboard layout implicitly switches from the Roman script system to the Japanese script system.

You set up a keyboard menu and configure other keyboard options for Mac OS X applications by clicking the Input Menu sheet (within the International preference pane), which displays a list of available keyboard layouts. You can change the sorting in the list of keyboard layouts by clicking a column heading.

If you want to be able to rapidly switch between the last two used input sources, use the key combination ⌘+Option+Spacebar or have Mac OS X automatically switch layouts when you select text that uses a different script. You can always cycle through all of the language scripts available in Mac OS X by pressing ⌘+Spacebar or activate and use the Input Source selector from the Input menu from the Finder's menu bar.

NOTE The default keyboard shortcuts for the International input sources (⌘+Spacebar and Option+⌘+Spacebar) conflict with Spotlight. For some odd reason, Apple hasn't rectified this. When you activate multiple language support, you need to change the keyboard shortcut for Spotlight or for International in the Keyboard Shortcut sheet in the Keyboard and Mouse preference pane (explained later in this chapter).

The default behavior of Mac OS X is to allow a different input source for each document. If that is not to your liking you can specify to use one input source for all documents within the Input source options portion of the Input Menu panel.

By checking Show input in menu bar or by turning on more than one keyboard layout, a keyboard input menu appears in the Finder's menu bar, as shown in Figure 17.19. The keyboard input menu lists the keyboard layouts that are turned on in the Input Menu panel. You can change the active keyboard layouts by choosing a different one from the list in this menu.

FIGURE 17.19

Switch Mac OS X's keyboard layout by choosing another one from the Keyboard menu.

To view keyboard layouts place a check in the box next to keyboard viewer in the Input Menu panel and select Show Keyboard Viewer (located in the Input menu on the Finder's menu bar) shown in Figure 17.20.

FIGURE 17.20

Use the Keyboard Viewer to identify what key combinations generate which characters.

Character palettes

Depending upon the languages that are selected, the keyboard menu displays character palettes. Character palettes are floating windows that facilitate the use of difficult-to-remember or difficult-to-reproduce foreign language characters. The last item in the keyboard input menu is Open International, which is a shortcut for opening the International preference pane. Languages with large character sets augment the keyboard with other methods of inputting characters. For example, Japanese has input methods that involve a control palette, additional windows, and a menu, as shown in Figure 17.21.

FIGURE 17.21

Japanese and other languages with many characters offer additional input methods besides a keyboard.

Configuring Keyboard and Mouse Preferences

Although you may think of Mac OS X as something you look at, you also touch it by means of the keyboard, mouse, or trackpad. The behavior of the keyboard, mouse, or trackpad is adjustable to allow for differences among users. If you have trouble double-clicking or if you feel that the mouse pointer moves too slowly or too quickly, you can adjust the mouse or trackpad sensitivity. Likewise, if you end up typing characters repeatedly when you mean to type them only once, adjust the keyboard sensitivity. You adjust the sensitivity of the keyboard, mouse, or trackpad by using the Keyboard & Mouse preference pane.

Keyboard panel

When you press and hold almost any key on the keyboard, the computer types that character repeatedly as long as you keep the key pressed. (The ⌘, Option, Control, Caps Lock, and Esc keys don't repeat.) Use the Keyboard panel to change how quickly the characters repeat and how long you must hold down a key before the repeat feature kicks in. If you find repeating keys annoying rather than handy, disable the repeat by setting the Delay Until Repeat control to Off. The field that contains Type here to test settings allows for you to immediately test your settings without having to leave the Keyboard & Mouse preference pane.

By default, when using Mac OS X on portable computers the function keys have control over a number of hardware features, such as LCD brightness, volume, and, if applicable, keyboard illumination. Some applications have shortcuts that utilize function keys that conflict with Mac OS X's hardware controls. To override this behavior place a check mark in the box adjacent to Use the F1–F12 keys to control software features. From then on you will need to depress the Fn key in conjunction with a function key to utilize hardware controls.

If for some reason a modifier key is in conflict with its assignment, clicking the Modifier Keys button subsequently displays a sheet that can facilitate the reassignment of the Caps Lock, Control, Option, and ⌘ keys, as shown in Figure 17.22.

Click the Restore Defaults button to remedy any mayhem you might cause here.

Mouse and Trackpad panels

Depending on whether your computer is a desktop or a laptop, you can change the way Mac OS X responds to your manipulation of your computer's mouse or trackpad by setting options in the Mouse and/or Trackpad panels. Trackpad options are typically only available on a MacBook or MacBook Pro computer because they contain options specific to a trackpad.

The settings in common in the Mouse and Trackpad panels have the following effects:

- **Tracking Speed:** This option determines how fast the pointer moves as you glide the mouse or trackpad. You may want to adjust the tracking speed if you change the display resolution. For example, if you change the display resolution from 1024 x 768 to 800 x 600 pixels, you may want a slower tracking speed because the pointer has a shorter distance across the display screen.

- **Double-Click Speed:** This option determines how quickly you must double-click for Mac OS X to perceive your two clicks as one double-click rather than two separate, unrelated clicks.

Bluetooth panel

If your computer is equipped with Bluetooth capability, the Bluetooth panel is where you manage Bluetooth keyboards and mice. To mate a Bluetooth-enabled keyboard or mouse you need to click the Set Up New Device button, which opens the Bluetooth Setup Assistant that walks you through the process of adding a new Bluetooth peripheral. Once mated, and if the device supports it, the panel displays the battery level of your wireless keyboard or mouse. As with the Bluetooth preference pane, there is an option for showing Bluetooth status in the Finder's menu bar.

NOTE   Bluetooth devices are insecure and are also susceptible to broadcast interference because they share the 2.4 GHz spectrum with other wireless technology such as 802.11 networking and cordless phones.

Keyboard Shortcuts panel

Using the keyboard is often faster or more convenient than using the mouse, trackball, or trackpad. The Keyboard Shortcuts panel, as shown in Figure 17.23, contains a list of predefined keyboard shortcuts. You can add or delete items from this list as well as change key combinations for the predefined list. Some shortcuts are solely to be used with keyboard navigation and Universal Access, which is discussed later in this chapter.

FIGURE 17.23

Keyboard shortcuts can be of great benefit to those who have difficulties using a mouse.

Changing an existing keyboard shortcut

To change an existing keyboard shortcut, take the following steps:

1. **Double-click the shortcut you wish to change in the list.**

2. **Press the new key combination.**

Adding a keyboard shortcut

To add a keyboard shortcut, take the following steps:

1. **Click the Add (+) button.**

2. **From the newly drawn sheet, choose an application from the Applications pop-up menu.** To apply a keyboard shortcut to all applications, select All Applications from the pop-up menu. If your application is not listed, select Other to specify.

3. **Specify the menu command exactly as it appears in the applications menu in the Title field.**

4. **Enter the key combination to which you want to assign the menu command in the Shortcut menu.**

5. **Click the Add button.**

Removing a shortcut

Conversely, to delete a keyboard shortcut, highlight the shortcut in the list in the Keyboard Shortcuts panel and click the Delete (–) button.

Remember that no matter how badly you mess up here, you can always revert back to the default configuration by clicking the Restore Defaults button.

How Keyboard Shortcuts Work

If you've ever wondered why ⌘+N with the Caps Lock key down isn't equivalent to pressing ⌘+Shift+N or similar things, the reason is fairly straightforward, if a bit geeky.

Mac applications (including Mac OS X applications) respond to *events,* such as a window activating or pressing a key. One such event is the *keydown event.* Keys such as Shift, Option, Control, and Caps Lock do not generate an event—their state (up or down) is recorded in what is called the *modifier field* of the event record. Therefore, when you press the N key, the programmer writing the code needs to check the state of the various modifier keys to determine whether it is just text being typed or whether it is some sort of a command. Every key on the keyboard has a separate state entry in the modifier field.

This method is not peculiar to Macs. The same techniques are used in Windows programming.

Full keyboard access

For those who have difficulty using the mouse, Mac OS X provides the ability to use the keyboard for navigation. Full keyboard access enables you to use the keyboard to navigate to an item in a folder, operate menus in the Finder, and operate push buttons, check boxes, radio buttons, sliders, and other controls in some windows and dialog boxes. You can also specify the behavior for navigation within windows and dialog boxes to focus on text boxes and lists only or all controls. Some Mac OS X applications respond more completely to full keyboard access than others. To give yourself full keyboard access, type Control+F1. Under the Keyboard heading in the list of keyboard shortcuts, you can enable and disable as well as designate the key combinations that allow the keyboard to perform actions in lieu of the mouse. When full keyboard access is turned on, you press certain keys to navigate the menu bar, the Dock, the active window's toolbar, a palette, a window, or a dialog box. Table 17.4 lists the keystrokes that determine the actions using full keyboard access.

 After you turn on full keyboard access, you may need to quit a Mac OS X application and open it again before it responds to keyboard control.

TABLE 17.4

Changing the Focus of Full Keyboard Access

Action	Function Keys
Full keyboard access on or off	Control+F1
Highlight on menu bar	Control+F2
Highlight on Dock	Control+F3
Highlight on toolbar	Control+F5
Highlight on a palette (utility window) and then on each palette in turn	Control+F6
Focus on next window of the same application	Control+F7

You press other keys to navigate and highlight one of the items on which the keyboard is currently focused, such as a menu item, an icon in the Dock, a toolbar button, or a control setting in a dialog box. The highlighted item has a dark border. You press yet another key to select the highlighted item or take another action. Table 17.5 lists the key combinations that highlight items, select items, and take other actions.

TABLE 17.5

Highlighting and Taking Action with Full Keyboard Access

Action	Keystroke
Highlight the next icon, button, menu, or control	Tab
Highlight the previous icon, button, menu, or control	Shift+Tab
Highlight the next control when a text box is selected	Control+Tab
Highlight a control next to a text box	Control+arrow keys
Highlight the next menu item, tab, item in a list, or radio button	Arrow keys
Move slider	Arrow keys
Restrict highlighting in the current window to text boxes and lists, or allow highlighting of any control in the current window	Control+F7
Select the highlighted item, or deselect it if it is already selected	Spacebar
Click the default (pulsating) button or the default action in a dialog box	Return or Enter
Click the Cancel button in a dialog box	Esc
Close menu without selecting highlighted item	Esc
Cancel menu bar, Dock, or toolbar highlight	Esc

Configuring Parental Controls

In this modern era, the younger generations are getting more and more technically sophisticated and spend more and more time using their computers both for school and for fun. Of course, it's best to supervise the young, but when that's not possible, it's nice to know that the Mac can give parents a helping hand via the Parental Controls pane.

After creating an account for a younger user (as detailed in the Accounts section in Chapter 18), open the Parental Controls pane and select the username as shown in Figure 17.24.

There are five sections of the Parental Controls pane: System, Content, Email & Chat, Time Limits, and Logs. Each is important to review to ensure that you are closing enough virtual doors while not making the computer unusable.

Adjusting the System

The first and most severe option is the Use Simple Finder option. This setting is designed for the very young, and deactivates most features of the OS, eliminating the need for double-clicking and such. Truly this setting is designed for children that are only just getting their motor skills together. (May I suggest a drool-proof keyboard?)

FIGURE 17.24

Select the user you want to restrict, and select Turn on Parental Controls to reveal the bevy of options available.

Next is the Only allow checked applications setting. This setting allows parents the granular control of which programs their children can access. You can give children access to iPhoto so that they can learn to play with photographs, but eliminate Safari access so that they cannot get onto the Internet, for example. See Figure 17.25 for a look at the System-level controls.

The four check boxes at the bottom are system oriented-controls.

- **Can administer printers:** This setting allows the user to add, remove, and calibrate printers.

- **Can burn CDs and DVDs:** This setting allows the user to create CDs and DVDs, using the allowed applications (as per the Only allow checked applications list).

- **Can change password:** This allows users to add, remove, or change their password.

- **Can modify the Dock:** Allows users to add and remove items from the Dock, as well as turn on special features of the Dock, including magnification and hiding.

The entire Mac OS can be restricted to use the Simple Finder.

Restricting Content

In this section, administrators can restrict the content available to the children in the family. See Figure 17.26 for an overview.

- **Hide profanity in Dictionary:** This option eliminates the most obvious so-called dirty words from being explored and explained in the dictionary. The children will have to learn those words from their friends like we did.

- **Limit access to websites:** Activating this option allows users to have granular control of the Web content visible to the children, as per the lower panel.

- **Try to limit access to adult websites:** The OS X Internet Content filter is engaged when this option is selected. When active, this filter blocks the most obvious "bad" sites known on the Web. The Configure button opens a subpanel where an administrator can override the default settings and Always allow some sites, and Never allow some others. See Figure 17.27 for a peek.

- **Allow access to the following websites only:** This option is an absolute white-list, where only certain Web pages are allowed, and all other content is blocked.

FIGURE 17.26

The Content section of the Parental Controls pane is where specific information is blocked.

FIGURE 17.27

To override the OS X Internet Content filter, enter some Web sites here.

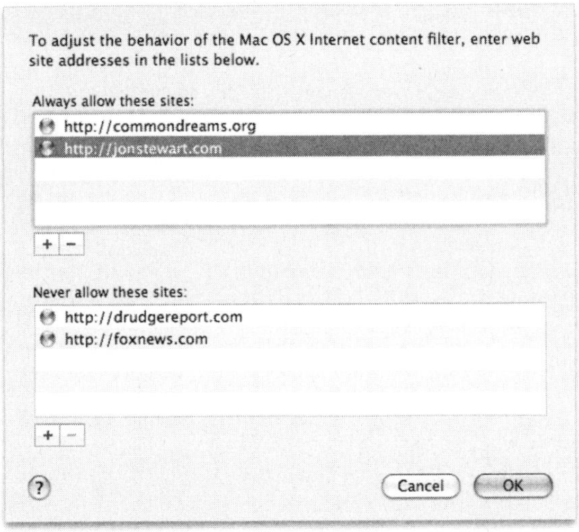

Limiting Email & Chat

In this third subpane of the Parental Control preference pane, parents can limit communication to certain chat names and e-mail addresses. This ensures that the only people interacting with younger users are approved and trusted sources. See Figure 17.28 for an overview.

Once the Limit email and instant messages options is checked, administrators add and remove valid e-mail addresses and chat names that can communicate with the restricted user. Enter an administrator's e-mail address in the Send permission emails to field, and when the child wants to add a new person to their communication list, they can request it via e-mail.

FIGURE 17.28

The Email & Chat subpane grants control over communication applications and the addresses allowed to communicate with younger users.

Managing Time Limits

In the fourth subpane administrators can limit the amount of time a user can access the computer and also set a computer bedtime rule, ensuring that the computer isn't used when a certain young so-and-so should be sleeping! See Figure 17.29 for an overview of this pane.

FIGURE 17.29

The Time Limits pane of the Parental Controls pane manages the amount of time users can access a computer, and even locks out during designated bedtimes.

The three subsections are rather straightforward, with a check box to engage the time limits option — during the week, on weekends and to activate the bedtime controls. The small arrows increase or decrease the amount of time allowed, and push back or forward bedtimes.

Checking Logs

The last pane is the most important for supervision purposes. It is one thing to use a computer's filters and preset defenses, but it's another thing to count on them blindly. A regular review of the activity logs goes a long way to ensuring that your security settings are being obeyed and are sufficient. See Figure 17.30 for a look at the Logs pane.

FIGURE 17.30

Reviewing the activity logs is a good way to keep in touch with a user's behavior.

There are four logs that are being collected: Websites Visited, Websites Blocked, Applications, and iChat.

- **Websites Visited:** Shows the sites visited, the number of times and when they were visited.

- **Websites Blocked:** Shows information on attempts to exceed your settings and when they occurred.

- **Applications:** Shows which applications were used and when.

- **iChat:** Shows information on the chats, including who was chatting and when.

Adding additional restricted users

One last area to cover is the global settings within the preference pane itself. The small gear icon in the lower left of the pane contains settings to either remove Parental Controls from a particular user or to copy that user's overall settings and then paste them onto another user. See Figure 17.31 for a look at that tool.

FIGURE 17.31

Parental Controls can be completely removed in one fell swoop, or copied to another user for easy duplication.

Configuring Sound Preferences

You can adjust the alert sound and other sound settings for Mac OS X applications in the Sound preference pane of System Preferences. The Sound preference pane consists of three panels to access its settings: Sound Effects, Output, and Input. No matter what panel you're in, you can adjust the main system volume or mute it altogether. You can also turn on an option to adjust the volume from a volume menu in the Finder's menu bar. After the volume slider in the menu bar has been enabled, click its menu bar icon and use it to raise and lower the overall system sound output volume, as shown in Figure 17.32.

TIP You can move the Sound icon by pressing the ⌘ key and dragging the icon. Drag the icon left or right to change its position relative to other icons on the right side of the menu bar. Drag the icon off the menu bar to make it vanish.

FIGURE 17.32

Use the Sound icon to adjust the main volume level.

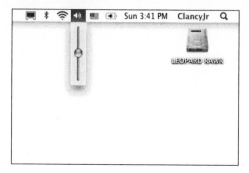

Sound Effects panel

Use the Sound Effects panel to select an alert sound and set its volume to be as loud as or quieter than other sounds. You can also enable and disable interface sound effects and audio feedback when the volume keys are pressed. If an additional sound output is available other than the one that shipped with your Macintosh, you will also be provided the option to select that audio output device to play alerts and sound effects through. Figure 17.33 shows the Sound Effects panel.

FIGURE 17.33

Adjust volume and balance controls and select an alert using the Sound Effects panel.

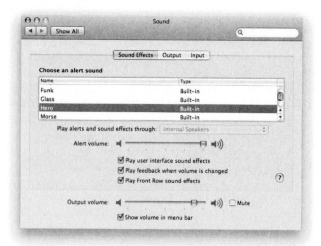

You can add more alert sounds by placing sound files of the AIFF format in the Sounds folder inside of your home folder's Library folder. If System Preferences is open when you add or remove sounds from your Sounds folder, you must quit System Preferences and open it again to see the effect of your changes.

Output panel

The Output panel controls audio out. Use this panel to select and control the audio hardware for sound output. Within this panel, you can also set the stereo channel balance if your output hardware supports it.

Input panel

Use the Input panel to select the audio device you want used for sound input and set the input volume for the device.

Configuring Speech Preferences

Many works of science fiction have depicted humans interfacing with computers by means of natural verbal communication. Macs have been capable of speaking text aloud since 1984, but it wasn't until 1993 that Apple introduced the ability for humans to speak to Macintoshes — although some would argue the Macs are still not listening. Seriously though, with the advent of Mac OS 10.5, speech recognition has become quite usable.

As shipped, Mac OS X's built-in English Speech Recognition is designed to understand a hundred spoken commands for controlling your computer. You can add to and remove some of the commands that the speech recognition system understands, but you can't turn it into a general dictation system. If voice dictation interests you, check out IBM's ViaVoice for Macintosh (`www.ibm.com/software/speech/mac/`) and MacSpeech's iListen (`www.macspeech.com`).

Getting a speech recognition microphone

Typically, speech recognition requires a special microphone. If you use a reasonably modern iMac, or any Mac Mini, MacBook, or MacBook Pro, the built-in microphone will work just fine for speech recognition. However, the microphone built into some older iMacs and iBooks/PowerBooks does not really work well enough for accurate speech recognition. Apple is characteristically vague about exactly which iMac and PowerBook microphones don't work properly, so you just have to try your own. If you don't have any luck with your Mac's built-in microphone, consider upgrading your input hardware; you'll probably get the best results with speech recognition if you use a headset that includes a noise-canceling microphone designed for voice recognition. Many brands and models are available.

Configuring speech recognition

Open the Speech preference pane as depicted in Figure 17.34, click the Speech Recognition button, and then click the On/Off button. Now you can turn speech recognition on and off and specify the kind of feedback you get when you speak commands. You can also click a button to see the contents of the Speakable Items folder, which is covered in more detail later in this chapter.

You can get your computer to listen to you, but it's not the best listener out there . . . and it gives terrible advice.

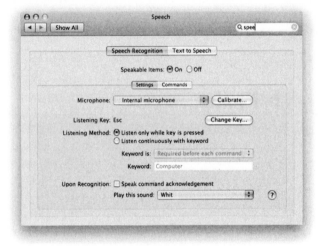

Turning on speech recognition

When you turn on speech recognition, a round feedback window appears. The first time you turn on speech recognition, it displays a welcome message that explains how speech recognition works. (You can read this message again by clicking the Helpful Tips button in Speech Preferences.) This setting, like all others in the Speech Recognition panel, is user account-specific and does not have an effect on other user accounts.

Setting feedback options

Below the On/Off controls in the Speech Recognition panel are settings that specify what feedback effect you get when a spoken command is recognized. You can turn the Speak confirmation option on or off using the Speak Confirmation check box to have Mac OS X speak an acknowledgement to your spoken commands.

Also, you can change the sound that indicates the computer has recognized a spoken command. Choose a sound from the pop-up menu or choose None if you don't want to hear a sound signifying recognition. This pop-up menu lists the sounds from System/Library/Sounds; the Sounds folder of the main Library folder; and two special sounds, Single Click and Whit, which are part of the speech recognition software. Any sounds you put in ~/Library/Sounds are not included in the speech feedback pop-up menu.

Using the feedback window

The speech feedback window appears when you turn on speech recognition and has several unusual attributes. First, the window is round. It floats above most other windows. What's more, this window has no close button, minimize button, or zoom button. Figure 17.35 shows the speech feedback window in several states.

FIGURE 17.35

A feedback window indicates when speech recognition is idle (left), listening for a command (middle), or hearing a command (right).

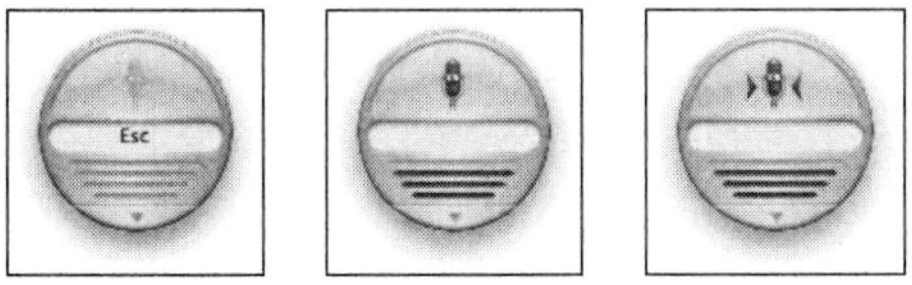

Interpreting feedback

The speech feedback window provides the following information about speech recognition:

- **Attention mode:** This section indicates whether the computer is listening for or recognizing spoken commands, as follows:
  - **Not listening for spoken commands:** The small microphone at the top of the feedback window looks dim.
  - **Listening for (but not hearing) a command:** The small microphone at the top of the feedback window looks dark/bold.
  - **Listening to a command you are currently speaking:** You see arrowheads move from the edges of the feedback window toward the microphone picture.

- **Listening method:** This section indicates how to make the computer listen for spoken commands. You may see the name of a key you must press or a word you must speak to let the computer know that you want it to interpret what you are saying as a command.

- **Loudness:** Colored bars on the bottom part of the window theoretically measure the loudness of your voice. In practice, there seems to be no relationship between the indicated loudness level and successful speech recognition. If you see no bars or one blue bar,

667

you're speaking relatively quietly; a blue bar and one or two green bars mean you're speaking louder; and these three bars plus a red bar mean that you're speaking very loudly. Apple recommends you speak loudly enough to keep green bars showing but rarely should the red bar appear.

■ **Recognition results:** When the computer recognizes a command that you have spoken, it displays the recognized command in a help tag above the speech feedback window. The displayed command may not exactly match what you said because speech recognition interprets what you say with some degree of flexibility. For example, if you say, "Close window," speech recognition probably displays the command it recognized as "Close this window." If speech recognition has a response to your command, it generally displays it in a help tag below the feedback window. Figure 17.36 shows how speech recognition displays the recognized command and its feedback in help tags.

FIGURE 17.36

Help tags above and below the speech feedback window display the command that the computer recognized and its response, if any.

Using feedback window controls

The only control in the speech feedback window is a pop-up menu, which you can see by clicking the small arrow at the bottom of the window. One menu command opens Speech Preferences, shown earlier in Figure 17.34. Another command in the pop-up menu opens a window that lists available speech commands.

You can move the feedback window by clicking it almost anywhere and dragging. You can't drag from the bottom of the window because clicking there makes the pop-up menu appear.

Minimizing the feedback window

Although the speech feedback window has no minimize button, you can minimize it by double-clicking on it, or with a spoken command, which is "Minimize speech feedback window." While minimized in the Dock, this window continues to provide most of the same feedback as it does when it is not minimized. While the feedback window is minimized, you don't see help tags containing the recognized command and response. In addition, the window's pop-up menu is not available in the Dock. Figure 17.37 shows the speech feedback window in the Dock.

After minimizing the speech feedback window, you can open the window by clicking it in the Dock. You can also open the window by speaking the command "Open speech feedback window."

FIGURE 17.37

While minimized in the Dock, the speech feedback window continues to indicate speech recognition status.

Looking at the Speech Commands window

Instead of seeing your spoken command and the computer's response to it displayed briefly in help tags, you can see a list of all of your recent spoken commands and the responses to them. The list of commands appears in the Speech Commands window, and also lists the commands you can speak in the current context. You can display this window by choosing Open Speech Commands Window from the pop-up menu at the bottom of the round speech feedback window. You can also open the Speech Commands window with the spoken command "Open Speech Commands window."

The commands you have spoken appear at the top of the speech commands window in bold, and any responses appear below each command in plain text. The bottom part of the window displays the commands you can speak in the current context. The list is organized in the following categories:

- **Name of current application:** This category appears only if the application you're currently using has its own speakable commands.

- **Address Book:** This category contains commands related to contacts in your address book, such as "Mail to" and "Chat with."

- **Speakable Items:** This category includes commands that are available no matter which application you're currently using.

- **Application Switching:** This category lists commands for quitting applications and switching to specific applications. (Switching to an application opens it if necessary.)

You can hide or show the commands for a category by clicking the disclosure triangle next to the category name. You can adjust the relative sizes of the top and bottom parts of the speech commands window by dragging the handle located on the bar between the two parts of the window. You find out how to add speakable commands later in this chapter.

Setting the listening method

The Listening panel of the Speech panel facilitates the configuration of when the computer should listen for spoken commands:

- **Push-to-talk method:** This is the most reliable method because the computer listens for commands only when you are pressing a key that you designate.

- **Keyword method:** The computer listens for its code name and tries to interpret the words that follow it as a command.

Setting the push-to-talk method

To set the push-to-talk method and the key that makes speech recognition listen for spoken commands, follow these steps:

1. **Click the Speech Recognition button.** The Speech Recognition panel is organized into two sub-panels titled Settings and Commands.

2. **Click the Settings button.** You see the options for setting the speech recognition listening method. Figure 17.38 shows the Listening panel set for the push-to-talk method with the Esc key, which is the initial setting.

3. **Set the Listening Method option to Listen only while key is pressed.** This setting means you can hold down the listening key to make speech recognition recognize your spoken commands.

4. **If you want to change the listening key, click the Change Key button.** A dialog box appears in which you can type the key or combination of keys that you want to use as the listening key. You can use the Esc key, Delete key, any key on the numeric keypad, one of the function keys F5 through F12, or most punctuation keys. You can combine one of these keys with any one or more of the Shift, Option, Control, or ⌘ keys. You can't use letter keys or number keys on the main part of the keyboard.

FIGURE 17.38

Speech recognition can be set for push-to-talk listening, but *be warned*: Prolonged use of Speech Recognition may also push your buttons.

Setting the keyword method

If you prefer to have the computer listen for a code name that you say before speaking a command, use these steps:

1. **Go to the Speech preference pane.** The Speech pane is organized into two sub-panes titled Settings and Commands.

2. **In the Settings sub-pane, set the Listening Method option to Listen continuously with keyword.** This setting changes the function of the listening key to an on and off toggle. Turning listening off puts speech recognition on standby, which at times may improve the performance of the computer.

3. **Specify a keyword.** Type a keyword for speech recognition in the text box; the default keyword is Computer. (The text box is not case-sensitive.) Use the pop-up menu above the keyword field to specify when you must speak the name.

   In the pop-up menu, the default selection requires the keyword before a command is executed. Another choice makes the keyword optional before commands, but this selection is not without risk: The computer might interpret something in general conversation as a voice command, so choose your keyword wisely.

   Other choices in the pop-up menu make the keyword optional if you spoke the last command less than 15 seconds ago or 30 seconds ago. The idea is that when you have the computer's attention, you shouldn't have to get its attention immediately following the previous command. You can tell whether you need to speak the code name by looking at the round speech feedback window. If you see the code name displayed in the middle of the feedback window, you have to speak the name before the next command.

Specifying what commands to listen for

Speech has commands organized by group. You choose which groups of commands Speech will listen for in the Commands panel. To choose commands by group, follow these steps:

1. **Click the Speech Recognition button.**

2. **Click the Commands button.**

3. **Click the check boxes to select and deselect groups of commands.** To activate the Front Windows commands group and the Menu Bar commands group, you must select Using Assistive Features in the Universal Access preference pane. As you add and remove groups of commands, the groups appear and disappear in the Speech Commands window.

4. **Select or clear the check box next to Require exact wording of Speakable Item command names.** Requiring the speaker to use the exact name of the command improves recognition accuracy and response time. If this is deselected, Mac OS X attempts to identify a command from more relaxed, casual speech.

Specifying which microphone to use

If your Mac has more than one microphone connected, such as a built-in microphone and an external microphone, you can specify which option you want speech recognition to use. Follow these steps:

1. **Click the Speech preference pane.**

2. **Choose an available microphone from the Microphone pop-up menu.** If your computer has a microphone jack, the pop-up menu includes it as a choice even if no microphone is plugged into the jack.

3. **Calibrate the microphone.** Click the Calibrate button, and adjust the slider left and right to ensure your speaking voice isn't overloading the microphone (by pushing the meter into the "red"), nor inaudible (not moving the meter at all). By doing so, you will vastly improve the quality of speech recognition.

Specifying the spoken user interface

Mac OS X speaking ability is not just a one-way conversation. Speech can be used to vocalize OS X's responses back to the user. This capability is configured in the Text to Speech panel—which is the other half of the Speech preference pane—as shown in Figure 17.39. Click the Text to Speech button within the Speech preference pane. Here you can specify what voice is to be used, and define when, what, and how things are spoken. You can set your alert options and choose from the list of built-in alert phrases or add your own phrases, too. You can define a different voice just for alert messages from that of the default voice, and you can specify the time delay before the alert is spoken. You can also choose to have selected text spoken as well as the date and time announced.

Choosing a voice for Mac OS X

The voices that the Speech preference pane employs are numerous. You set the default voice in the pop-up menu titled System Voice at the top of the Text to Speech panel, as shown in Figure 17.40. You can also modify the selected voice's rate of speaking from slow to fast.

To set a voice and a speaking rate for Mac OS X, follow these steps:

1. **Click the Text to Speech button.**

2. **Click the System Voice pop-up menu.**

3. **Select any voice from the list.** Once a section has been made, you can hear a sample of it by clicking the Play button.

4. **Optionally, change the speaking rate by adjusting the Rate slider.** Each voice has a preset speaking rate. You can hear a sample of the voice at the current rate by clicking the Play button.

FIGURE 17.39

Use the Open Universal Access Preferences button as a shortcut to the preference pane.

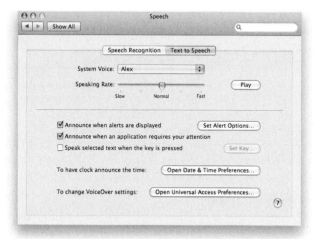

FIGURE 17.40

Although the options appear to be bountiful, try as you may, no combination of options here will get you close to having your computer sound as good as HAL from *2001*.

Reading documents aloud

If you are using an OS X application, Speech may be available as a Service. Services are available to OS X applications from the Application menu. (Refer to Chapter 9 for more on Services.)

Configuring Startup Disk Preferences

Selecting an alternate startup system for your computer is an easy process. The only real requirement for selecting an alternate system folder is that it is a *valid boot system* for startup. Depending on your Mac OS X install strategy, you may have alternate boot-capable Mac OS Systems on a single partition or on entirely different volumes. You can select any of the eligible Systems in the Startup Disk preference pane, or choose the Network Startup option to search for any available NetBoot Volumes to start up from, as shown in Figure 17.41.

FIGURE 17.41

Use the Target Disk Mode button to restart your computer in Target Disk Mode.

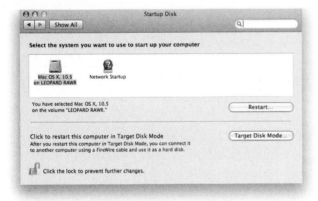

After selecting a valid System for startup, you can restart using the newly selected System right away by clicking the Restart button at the bottom of the preference pane. If you don't want to restart yet, you can close the Startup Disk preference pane, quit the System Preferences application, or switch to another application. Regardless if you click Restart or not, an alert appears asking you to confirm that you want to change the System Folder for the next startup.

Configuring Universal Access Preferences

In the Universal Access pane, you can adjust the display and behavior of OS X to accommodate for different needs of sight and sound, as well as to set up alternative methods of using the keyboard and mouse for individuals who have disabilities that preclude them from using the computer in standard configuration. Mouse Keys lets you use the numeric keypad portion of the keyboard to move the pointer on the screen and to click as if you were using the mouse button. Sticky Keys lets you type combination keystrokes such as ⌘+O one key at a time. The Universal Access pane was introduced with Mac OS X 10.1. All four panels of the Universal Access pane show the same check box at the bottom of the panel:

- **Enable access for assistive devices:** This option allows for third-party wares to harness the capabilities of Universal Access.

Seeing panel

With its large type the Seeing panel, as shown in Figure 17.42, provides options to assist people who have various vision-oriented limitations. You can enable speech recognition via VoiceOver, turn Zoom on and off, reverse the display to show white text on a black background instead of black on white, and set the display to grayscale.

FIGURE 17.42

For individuals with difficulty seeing, the Seeing panel of Universal Access provides vision-oriented display options.

Hearing panel

The Hearing panel offers a full-screen flash option as a substitute for alert sounds, provides a test of the flash screen substitute, and provides a button to open the Sound System Preferences to adjust the sound volume.

Keyboard panel

Use the Keyboard panel to set up the Sticky Keys feature for Mac OS X applications. If you turn on this feature, you can type a combination of modifier keys — ⌘, Shift, Option, or Control — one key at a time. For example, you can type ⌘+Shift+S (the standard keyboard shortcut for File ➪ Save As) by pressing ⌘, Shift, and S one key at a time.

Besides turning Sticky Keys on or off, you can set an option to hear a beep, not the system alert sound, when you press a modifier key. You can also set an option to see the symbols of modifier keys superimposed on the screen. If the option to use keyboard shortcuts is turned on at the top of Universal Access Preferences, you can turn Sticky Keys on or off by pressing Shift five times in succession.

When Sticky Keys is turned on, and the option to show modifier keys on-screen is also on, pressing a modifier key causes the key's symbol to be superimposed on the screen. Press another modifier key, and its symbol is superimposed as well. Press the same modifier key a second time, and its symbol is removed. Press any other key to have it combined with the modifier keys whose symbols are currently superimposed on the screen. Press Esc to cancel all the modifier keys whose symbols are currently superimposed on the screen.

Mouse & Trackpad panel

Use the Mouse panel to set up the Mouse Keys feature. If you turn on this feature, you can click, drag, and move the pointer with the numeric keypad instead of the mouse or trackpad. The Mouse panel includes the following settings:

- **On and Off:** If the option to use keyboard shortcuts is selected at the top of Universal Access Preferences, you can turn Mouse Keys on or off by pressing the Option key five times.

- **Initial Delay:** This option determines how long you must hold down a keypad key before the pointer starts responding. As long as you keep pressing keypad keys to control the pointer, the delay does not recur. The delay occurs only with the first press of a key after a period during which you have not used the keypad for pointer control.

- **Maximum Speed:** This option determines how fast the pointer gets going if you keep holding down a key. You have better control with a slow speed, but moving the pointer across the screen takes longer.

- **Cursor Size:** This option can enlarge the size of the pointer arrow within Mac OS X.

When Mouse Keys is on, the 5 key in the keypad acts like a mouse button. Press once to click; press twice to double-click. The eight keys around 5 move the pointer left, right, up, down, and diagonally. Pressing 0 locks the mouse button down until you press the period key in the keypad. You do not have to hold down 0 like you hold down the actual mouse button.

TIP If the pointer seems unresponsive, make the Initial Delay shorter and the Maximum Speed faster in Universal Access Preferences. Conversely, if you feel like you don't have enough control over the pointer, make the Initial Delay longer and the Maximum Speed slower.

Summary

In this chapter, you learned the following:

- The settings in the System Preferences application affect all Mac OS X applications.

- The CDs & DVDs pane determines behavior of Mac OS X upon optical media insertion.

- In the Date & Time preference pane, you can adjust the majority of your computer's clock and calendar settings.

- In the Displays preference pane, you set screen resolution, number of colors, refresh rate, contrast, and brightness. You also select a color profile and calibrate your display. If you have multiple displays, you may be able to adjust how they work together. With some displays, you can adjust the shape and position of the screen image.

- The Energy Saver preference pane sets timings for sleep mode and options for starting, sleeping, and turning off the computer automatically.

- The Ink preference pane contains the settings to configure Mac OS X's handwriting input/recognition capabilities.

- The International preference pane contains settings for language preference, text behavior, date and time formats, number formats, and keyboard layout in Mac OS X applications.

- The Keyboard & Mouse preference pane contains settings to configure the sensitivity of the keyboard and the mouse or trackpad. You can also set up full keyboard access to use the keyboard to control the mouse and type combination keystrokes one key at a time by setting up Mouse Keys and Sticky Keys in the Universal Access preference pane.

- The Parental Control preference pane enables parents to restrict the available avenues of exploration on the Macintosh for their children.

- The Sound preference pane contains settings to adjust the overall sound volume, the alert sound, and its volume for Mac OS X applications.

- The Speech preference pane allows for configuration of plain verbal communication between humans and Macintosh computers.

- The Startup Disk preference pane contains settings to specify which Mac OS System Folder is used the next time your computer starts up.

- Universal Access provides a set of adjustments for individuals with visual, hearing, and physical limitations.

Chapter 18

Managing User Accounts and Privileges

This chapter examines the types of user accounts in Mac OS X. You find out how to create, manage, and limit those user accounts, and how to assign privileges using Get Info.

Mac OS X and Privileges

As discussed in Chapter 1, Mac OS X is Apple's first true multiuser desktop operating system. Because of its Unix underpinnings, Mac OS X provides the ability to employ a Unix-style security model. In Mac OS X, each user is provided with his or her own user account. Each user account provides a separate customizable environment. An example of this is that each user account contains its own home folder in which to save its documents. Additionally, each user account can be customized with its own preference settings. For example, your Appearance preferences such as your desktop picture don't affect other users, and vice versa.

Central to Mac OS X's multiuser security model is the concept of *privileges*. Simply stated, privileges (which Unix folk refer to as *permissions*) provide the control mechanism for access to files, folders, and applications within Mac OS X. Because Mac OS X was designed for a single computer to be shared among many users, it requires a means to prevent one user's data from being accessed or deleted by another user, as well as preventing standard users from deleting files, folders, or applications they shouldn't be. This is where privileges/permissions come into play. In an OS X system, every file, folder, and application is assigned a set of privileges. In fact, even running processes have ownership.

IN THIS CHAPTER

Identifying types of user accounts

Configuring account preferences

Enabling Parental Controls

Administering privileges using Show Info

NOTE Some preference settings affect all users (a global effect) and are typically denoted by a lock in the bottom left-hand corner of their respective preference panes, and can be modified only by an account with administrative privileges.

Identifying Types of User Accounts

All user accounts are assigned a series of attributes. These attributes include a long name, short name, password, and User ID (UID). A UID is a behind-the-scenes mechanism that OS X employs to identify users by unique numeric designations. There are six types of user accounts within OS X: root, administrator (admin), managed with parental controls, sharing only, guest, and *normal* user.

Root

In Unix, the root account, which is sometimes referred to as the *system administrator* or the *superuser* account, has complete access to all settings and files within the operating system. When you're logged in via the root account, you are master of all that is within Mac OS X. The root account has complete control over all folders and files on your Mac, including the contents of the normally off-limits System folder. Mac OS X is carefully organized so that users shouldn't need to move, delete, rename, or otherwise change the system files and folders that are located in the System folder and in several hidden folders. All the parts of Mac OS X that users may need to change are located in the main Library folder, where an administrator can change them, or in the Library folder inside each user's home folder, where the user can change them. Additionally, the root account has unfettered access to all users' folders and files. Be extremely careful: The root account operates without the safety net of Mac OS X's security model and is generally used for the express purposes of system administration. Administration via the root account is something to grow into. As useful as the root account may be for administering an OS X system, for the less-skillful user there is an equal chance of really messing things up. Therefore, you're better off working with an administrator account if you're unsure of exactly what you're doing.

You don't need to create a root user account; all OS X systems have a preexisting root account, but it's disabled by default. Apple intentionally designed Mac OS X in this fashion to prevent less-adroit users from breaking the OS. In order to gain access to the root account, you must first enable it. You can enable the root account via the Directory utility.

Administrator (admin)

For day-to-day system administration, the administrator (admin) account is where it's at. The admin account has enough power to get the majority of the system administration tasks done without the potential liabilities associated with the root account. An admin account provides access to all of Mac OS X's system preferences and utilities, and it provides the ability to install applications and system-wide resources. An admin account also has the ability to create and manage other user accounts and enable the root account if needed within an OS X system. However, by default an administrator cannot view the contents of another user's home folder. Table 18.1 lists system preference settings that can be changed only with an administrator account's name and password.

TABLE 18.1	

Protected Settings That Only Administrators Can Change

System Preferences Pane	Protected Settings
Date & Time	All settings except the menu bar clock settings
Energy Saver	All settings
Login	All login window settings but not the list of login items
Network	All settings except choosing a different location
Sharing	All settings
Software Update	Actual installation of updates (changing of update schedule is not protected)
Startup Disk	System folder selected for startup
Accounts	All settings except current user's password
Print & Fax	Enable Printer Sharing
Parental Controls	All settings
Time Machine	All settings

As mentioned in Chapter 1, the Mac OS X Installation Setup Assistant walks you through the initial configuration of the first administrator account. Within Mac OS X, there can be multiple admin accounts per OS X system. This feature is useful in the event that one administrator forgets his or her password and requires a password reset, which can be accomplished only by another accessible admin account. You can also facilitate a password reset for any account by booting from the OS X installer disk and using the password reset utility. In fact, you are advised to do so when you click the Forgot Password button from the login window.

User

A normal user account does not allow system-wide administration of Mac OS X. As a result, if a user attempts to install software, a screen with a padlock appears with the message that any installation requires an administrator's authorization. In addition, a normal user account cannot modify system-wide preferences. These include Date & Time, Energy Saver, Login (Window), Network, Startup Disk, Parental Controls, Print & Fax, Time Machine, and Users. Normal users typically have the ability to modify any other preference that pertains only to their own account.

Groups

Within the Unix security model, groups are typically used to simplify the assignment of system access to a series of users. Generally these users are intended to share the same level of system access. In previous versions of Mac OS X, the system handled the assignment of groups. In some cases this still happens. The staff is the standard group all user accounts are assigned to. Admin users are also members of the admin and wheel groups. The admin and wheel groups have access to make system-wide changes. Just as users are assigned unique numerical user IDs, every group has a uniquely assigned Group ID (GID) as well.

Previously one would have to use NetInfo Manager or the command line to manage groups. In Leopard, Mac OS X provides an easy-to-use GUI for managing groups. Groups can be assigned to have or be denied access to folders and files on the computer. As a result all users in that group share at least the same access.

Configuring Account Preferences

As noted, during the installation of Mac OS X or when first starting a Mac with a factory preinstallation of Mac OS X, the Setup Assistant creates the first account, which is an administrator account. Subsequently, within Mac OS X's GUI, day-to-day user account administration is done through the Accounts preference pane depicted in Figure 18.1. The Accounts preference pane can create and delete user accounts and groups; it's also the location where you can select items to open automatically at startup, enable Parental Controls for a given user account, grant admin privileges, and specify system-login options. Depending on the type of account being administered and the current user account that is logged in, the Accounts preference pane can present up to two panels: Password and Login Items.

FIGURE 18.1

The Accounts preference pane

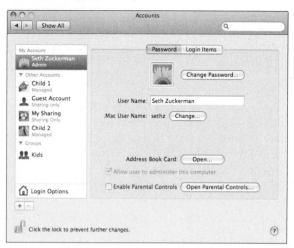

When opening the Accounts preference pane for the first time, you'll notice that the admin account generated by the Setup Assistant during the Mac OS X install process is present. By default, Mac OS X is configured to automatically login utilizing this admin account. After an additional user account is created, you're queried as to whether you want to turn off automatic login. If automatic login is disabled, on the next restart you'll be presented with a list of user accounts to choose from for logging in.

As previously stated, you can have more than one admin account on the same machine. Conversely, you can delete an admin account, but you'll be prevented from deleting all admin accounts. As a safety feature, every OS X system must have at least one admin account at all times.

When you create a new user account, you also simultaneously create a home directory folder for that user. However, when you delete a user account, you're provided three options, as shown in Figure 18.2: Save the home folder on a disk image, Do not change the home folder, and Delete home folder immediately.

Selecting the Delete home folder immediately button eliminates the account and its corresponding contents. It leaves no trace of that particular user.

A new feature in Leopard is the Do not change the home folder option, which keeps all files in their current location. This is a non-destructive deletion.

The last option is to save the home folder as a disk image. This choice eliminates the user account. The corresponding contents of that user's home folder will be archived into a single DMG file incorporating that user account's home folder and located in the Deleted Users folder in *hard drive*/Users. The DMG file will contain the user's short name.

As usual, there is always the option to click Cancel to negate the entire process.

FIGURE 18.2

The confirmation dialog sheet for deleting a user account is initiated by clicking the button with the - symbol (minus sign) in the lower left-hand corner of the Accounts preference pane.

CAUTION   You can accidentally delete the user's home folder and all of their data if you don't select the correct option. By default the Delete home folder option is selected. This deletes all of the user's data immediately.

Password panel

Each user account has a password associated with it. If you are a standard user or manager user, you have the rights to change your own password. If you are an administrator, you can change your password and reset the password of other users.

To change your password, select your name in the user list on the left column of the Accounts System Preference pane, and then click Change Password. You will be asked to enter your old password, and your new one twice. You can add a hint if you choose.

If you want to reset the password of another user on the system, log on as an administrator, select the user whose password you want to reset, and click Reset Password. You will be asked to enter the new password twice, and optionally enter a hint.

NOTE   When you reset the password of another user, their Keychain password remains the same. Unless that user remembers their old password, their passwords are lost forever.

Adding an account

You create standard user accounts, groups, administrator and sharing only accounts using the Accounts Panel and clicking the plus sign. See Figure 18.3. When creating a user account you assign two unique names, a "long" Name, and Short Name. Users logging in can use either their Name or Short Name. When assigning Names and Short Names, use any identification system that you like, but keep in mind these names are case-sensitive. When tabbing from the Name field to the Short Name field, the Short Name is automatically generated. But don't worry; at this point, it can still be changed. A Short Name has a maximum of eight lowercase characters and cannot contain any spaces or the following characters:

     < > * { } [ ] ( ) ^ ! \ # | & $? ~

At any time, the Name and password can be changed, but after the account is created, the Short Name is permanent. After you've chosen your Short Name, you'll need to provide a password. Finally, the last field allows you to provide yourself an optional password hint if desired.

NOTE   Some third-party utilities can change the short name once a user has been created, but these programs are not supported and not recommended.

CAUTION   Do not assign anyone the user name or short name "root." This name has a special meaning in all operating systems based on Unix, including Mac OS X. If you create a user named root, problems will result.

FIGURE 18.3

Adding a user account

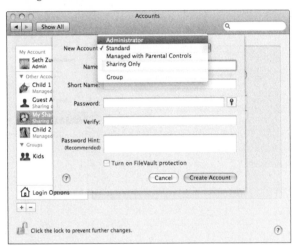

Besides the Name and Short Name, each account has a password. The password can be left blank, but in practice it should not be, regardless of the account type. Although a password can be greater than eight characters, passwords may contain uppercase and lowercase letters, blank spaces, and extended characters, but colons should be avoided; Mac OS X does not consistently recognize passwords that contain colons.

Creating a user account

You create a user account in the Accounts preference pane within the System Preferences application. You don't need to log in using an administrator account. If you log in as an ordinary user, you can unlock the settings in the Accounts pane of System Preferences with an administrator's name and password. To create a user account, follow these steps:

1. **Open System Preferences and choose View ➪ Accounts or click the Accounts button.**

2. **To unlock the user account settings if they're locked, click the Lock button.** In the dialog box that appears, enter an administrator's name and the correct password, and then click OK. If you entered a valid name and the correct password, you return to the Users window with all settings unlocked.

3. **Click the plus button located below the unlabeled column on the left side of the Accounts preference pane to add a new user account (refer to Figure 18.3).**

4. **Select the type of account:**

   - **Standard:** A standard account is an account that can log in but not administer the system.

   - **Administrator:** An administrator is an account that has administrative rights. It can change all system settings.

   - **Managed with Parental Controls:** This is a standard account that is managed with the Parental Control software.

   - **Sharing Only:** This account is only for connecting users remotely via file sharing. It cannot log in. Permissions are dictated by the Sharing System Preference.

   - **Group:** This is a group of the above users.

5. **Enter a Name and a Short Name.**

6. **Click in the New Password field and enter a password.** Optionally, you may click the button with the key icon to the right of the password field. This opens the Password Assistant as shown in Figure 18.4. This will help you select a more secure password. Once a password is selected, you may also enter a password hint.

   The password hint is displayed if the user enters the password incorrectly three times in a row during login, as long as show password hints is selected in Login Options. If you enter a hint, make it a hint — not the actual password! As you enter the password in the New User dialog box, you'll notice that Mac OS X keeps it secret by displaying dots (Lock Font) instead of what you actually type. Because you can't visually check what you've entered, you have to enter it twice consistently to verify it. If the two entries are not consistent, Mac OS X prompts you to reenter them.

FIGURE 18.4

For those who have difficulty making up passwords, OS X's Password Assistant offers five methods to automate the process: Memorable, Letters and Numbers, Numbers Only, Random, and FIPS-181 compliant.

Subsequently, after the account is created, users can login and change their passwords on their own.

To delete a user account, follow Steps 1 and 2, but instead of clicking the plus button in Step 3, select the account to be deleted from the unlabeled column on the left side of the Accounts preference pane and click the minus button to the right of the plus button. Before an account can be deleted, make sure it isn't encrypted with FileVault. Then chose the way you would like to delete the account. You can choose Save the home folder on a disk image, Do not change the home folder, or Delete home folder immediately.

On a final note, to grant a user administrator privileges place a check mark in the box adjacent to the label Allow user to administer this computer. By doing so you will grant the user account system-wide administrator privileges.

Changing your picture

Use the user's picture, shown in Figure 18.5, to select a graphic that will be a visual representation of a user account. By default, Mac OS X selects a random picture for each account. These pictures are used by Mac OS X's login window, as well as by Address Book and iChat applications. Login pictures can be manually chosen as well. By default, Mac OS X provides 30 selections to choose from. If these do not meet your aesthetic sensibility, click the Edit button to customize your own, as shown in Figure 18.6.

FIGURE 18.5

Apple provides supplied pictures in the Accounts pane.

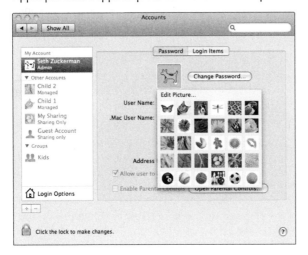

FIGURE 18.6

Create your own picture selections by taking a video snapshot or using a preexisting image.

Creating a sharing only account

Sharing Accounts are new to Leopard. You can share files on your computer with other users on a network by creating a sharing only account. A sharing only account allows users to connect with your computer just like a server. However, you cannot physically log into a computer using a sharing only account name like you can with most other accounts.

A user on the network will be able to use the account name and password to access files in each user's Public folder. You can manage the files and folders that sharing only accounts have in Sharing preferences. This is covered more in detail in Chapter 12.

Just as in creating a user account, follow Steps 1 and 2. In Step 3, instead of choosing a User Account, choose a Sharing Account. (See Figure 18.7.) Continue to follow through Step 5. A Sharing Account cannot be an administrator because it is designed for file access only and cannot log on to the computer.

Creating a group

New to the Mac OS X client GUI is the creation of a group. Groups are a type of account that consists of one or more other users, called members. When sharing files you can give access of files to a group, and all the accounts that are members of the group will have access to the files. Access to files is managed in the Finder, in the Sharing preference.

Just as in creating a user account, follow Steps 1 and 2. Click the plus button located below the unlabeled column on the left side of the Accounts preference pane to add a Group (see Figure 18.8).

FIGURE 18.7

Creating a Sharing Account called Secretaries

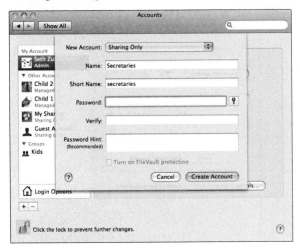

FIGURE 18.8

Creating a group

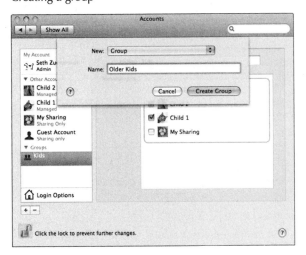

Once the Group is created, it is highlighted in the Accounts preference in the left column. Here is where you select the members of your group, as shown in Figure 18.9. You can select other groups as part of a group. This is called nested groups. Each nested group inherits the permissions of the groups it contains.

FIGURE 18.9

Selecting members of a group

For example: I create two groups. One is Kids, signifying the 5-13-year-olds in the house. The second is Older Kids for the teenagers 14 and older. Because the older kids sometimes need access to the younger kids' files for school help, they are members of the Kids group. This grants them access to the younger kids' files. However, the younger Kids group doesn't have access to the teenagers' files.

Enabling a guest account

Guest accounts are temporary. They do not require a password to log on. When a user logs out of the account, all the data goes with it. You have the option to use Parental Controls on a guest account to protect your computer. You also have the option of allowing or disallowing guests to connect to shared folders. Follow these steps:

1. **Open the Accounts System Preference pane.**

2. **Select Guest Account.**

3. **If you want to allow guests to connect to your computer's shared folders using file sharing check the box Allow guests to connect to shared folders.**

4. **To allow guest users to log into the computer, check Allow guest to log into this computer.**

5. **If you want to enable Parental Controls, selec**t Enable Parental Controls.

Having a guest account is a great idea on a computer in a public space. For example, if you are a doctor and your office has a computer for patients to surf the Web while waiting, a guest account is perfect. It allows the user to log in. At the end of they day when you log out, the mess the patients have made is deleted.

Login Items panel

The Login Items panel, shown in Figure 18.10, enables the selection of items that are to be started automatically when a user logs into the system. You can set up a list of documents and applications that you want to open automatically when you log in. You can also designate the order of those items and whether they should be hidden. Each user account has its own private list of login items.

FIGURE 18.10

Change the list of items opened during login by clicking the Login Items tab in the Login preference pane.

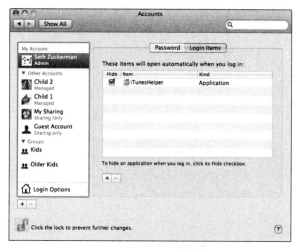

To have an item open automatically during login, follow these steps:

1. **Open the Accounts preference pane inside of the System Preferences application.**

2. **Select your user account.**

3. **Click the Login Items button.**

4. **Click the plus button located below the list of items that will open automatically when you log in.** You can also add items to the Login Items list by dragging their icons from Finder windows or the Desktop to the Login Items list.

5. **In the dialog box that appears, select one or more items and click Open.** Click once to select one item; Shift+click to select adjacent items; and ⌘+click to select nonadjacent items.

   - **To remove an item,** select it in the list and click Remove.

   - **To rearrange the order in which listed items open during login,** drag items up or down in the list.

■ **To hide an item automatically when it opens during login,** click the Hide check box next to the application name in the list. A hidden item stays open but doesn't take up any screen space.

NOTE If you set an application or a document as a login item and it requires a password to open, it doesn't open during login. Its icon appears in the Dock, and you must click the icon and enter the password to open the item. Examples of such items include e-mail applications and encrypted documents.

Login Options panel

Not to be confused with the Login Items panel, at the bottom of the list of accounts in the unlabeled column on the left side of the Accounts preference pane is a Login Options button, which is depicted with a home folder icon. Use this button to configure additional system login options, as shown in Figure 18.11.

FIGURE 18.11

Login Options offers additional customization of the login process.

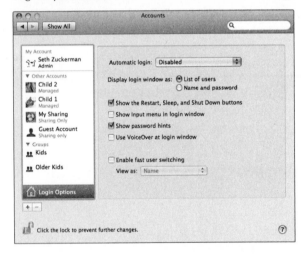

■ The **Automatically login as** option configures Mac OS X for automatic login with a specified user account that is selected within the pop-up menu to the right of this label. The pop-up menu shows the list of users on the system as well as the Disabled option. In order to automatically log in as a user other than yourself, you must know that user's password.

■ The **Display Login Window as** option changes the login window from a list of users, shown in Figure 18.12, to a name and password field, shown in Figure 18.13.

FIGURE 18.12

Login window as a list of users

FIGURE 18.13

Login window as name and password

- The **Show the Restart, Sleep, and Shut Down buttons** determine whether users can restart or shut down the computer by clicking buttons in the login window.

- **Show the Input Menu in the login window** allows for different character sets or input devices to be chosen at login. For example, if you have a password in Japanese, you can show the input menu and select a Japanese character set to type with.

- The **Enable VoiceOver at Login** option enables Mac OS X's spoken interface at login to assist those who might have limitations preventing them from reading the text on the screen. When the user is at the login screen the computer reads the text on the screen to the user.

- The **Show password hints** option allows the display of password hints that are assigned to user accounts at login in the event of a mistyped password after three attempts.

- The **Enable fast user switching** option permits more than one user to stay logged into a computer at the same time without having to quit applications or close documents.

  When fast user switching is enabled, the Name, Short Name, or icon (depending on which is chosen) of the user currently logged in appears in the upper-right corner of the Finder's menu bar, as shown in Figure 18.14. To switch between user accounts, click the menu and select the name of the user account you want to switch to. If the selected user account requires a password, you will be prompted to enter it as shown in Figure 18.15. If the account does not require a password, Mac OS X automatically makes the switch. When the transition of user accounts occurs on a Mac that fully supports Quartz Extreme, the effect appears as a rotation of a 3-D cube. Otherwise, the screen momentarily turns black before the new account can be used. In order to restart or shut down a computer that has multiple users logged in using fast user switching, all user accounts must be logged out. If not, you will be prompted with a dialog requesting admin authentication in order to do so. This results in the loss of unsaved changes in all user accounts that are currently logged in at the time of restart or shutdown.

FIGURE 18.14

Using fast user switching alleviates the need for a logged-in user to log out so that another user account can be utilized.

FIGURE 18.15

If you switch to a user account that requires a password, you'll be prompted with a dialog box similar in appearance to Mac OS X's initial login screen.

Advanced Options

In prior versions of Mac OS editing, advanced user account options were accessible through NetInfo Manager. In Leopard that application is gone. Most of those advanced features have been incorporated into the Advanced Options in the Accounts preference.

To access the Advanced Options, select the user you want to edit. Hold down the Control button, and then click that user. A menu pops up with that user's Advanced Options. Click it.

 If you are not an advanced user, *do not* edit this information. You can corrupt user accounts very quickly.

Here you can change the following:

- **User ID:** The unique number that identifies your user account. As you create user accounts Mac OS X client starts at 501 and counts up from there consecutively.
- **Group ID:** The unique number that identifies the group you are part of.
- **Short Name:** The name of your home directory and user ID.
- **Login Shell:** The script that is used when telnetting into the workstation.
- **Home directory:** The location of your home directory.
- **UUID:** Universally Unique IDentifier. That also references your account. It is a random sequence of letters and numbers.
- **Aliases:** The least volatile thing you can add is an alias. An alias is another reference to your user account. For example, if I want to log in as sethz, or szuckerman or sethzuckerman, I can add those aliases to my account so when I login I can use any of those names.

The advanced options are useful troubleshooting tools, especially in a client-server environment, but they are beyond the scope of this book.

Workgroup Manager

Another method of managing users, groups, and other NetInfo features that are not accessible via the Accounts pane is using Workgroup Manager. Workgroup Manager is part of the server administration tools for Mac OS X server. You can download these tools from `www.apple.com/downloads/macosx/apple/macosx_updates/serveradmintools105.html` free of charge.

1. Download the Server Admin Tools for 10.5 directly from Apple.

2. Install the server tools and then launch Workgroup Manager (/Applications ➪ Server ➪ Workgroup Manager).

3. When prompted, put in localhost (without the quotes) or 127.0.0.1 (the loopback address) for the address, and your admin user name and password in the appropriate fields and then click Connect. You can use the Server ➪ View Directories menu item to connect as well.

4. You'll get a warning about working in a local directory node; ignore that and press OK.

   The Accounts option should be highlighted in the toolbar on the left, and you should see the users you've created on your machine. See Figure 18.16.

FIGURE 18.16

Workgroup manager displaying the local users

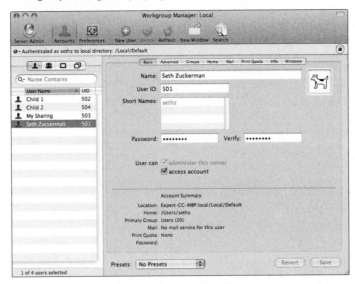

If you want to manage the built-in users and groups, click the View menu ⇨ Show System Users and Groups. This displays the hidden and built-in users and groups, as shown in Figure 18.17.

FIGURE 18.17

Workgroup manager displaying the system users

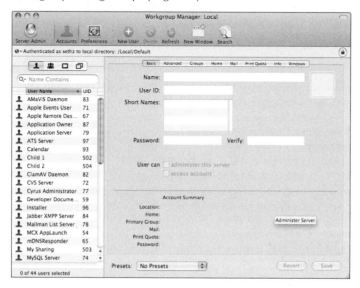

5. **You can now edit many of the options you could change in the old NetInfo Manager.** For example, you can be more granular in which groups each user is part of.

This is an easy method of making your workstation act more like a server. It doesn't have the granular services features that Mac OS X server has, but it is excellent for more deeply managing user accounts and groups.

Managing Accounts via Parental Controls

Parental Controls System Preference Pane is used to dictate what selected users have and don't have access to. These controls have been greatly improved in Leopard. Parental Controls can be set for any user account other than an administrator and can only be set from an administrator account. Use Parental Controls to enhance Mac OS X's security model. Five categories can be configured: System, Content, Mail & iChat, Time Limits, and Logs. Each category has many different options an administrator can control. In prior versions of Mac OS X parental control restrictions were located in the Accounts preference pane. They are now part of the System Preferences under Security.

Before employing the features of the Limitations panel, make sure that there are no incompatibilities with any installed third-party applications.

To limit a user's capabilities:

1. **Open System Preferences and choose Parental Controls.**

2. **Select an account to be administered from the unlabeled column on the left side of the preference pane.** This can only be a managed user with Parental Controls.

3. **Select the appropriate category for limitations.**

System

To manage the way the system operates, use the System panel. This allows the selection of a Simple Finder, and restricts access to specific applications. You can also restrict access to printers, CD and DVD burning, password changes, and dock modifications.

Simple Finder provides a limited version of the Finder. This is a simplified version of the Dock that can't be modified. It provides access to applications solely provided via a My Applications folder located in the Dock, as well as documents in the Documents folder on the Dock. There is also a Shared folder which is globally shared and accessible to all users on the computer. This is especially useful when introducing young children to the Mac OS. Simple Finder is mostly unbreakable. See Figure 18.18.

The System panel provides the following options:

- **Only allow selected applications:** In this pane, you have the option to specifically designate applications this user is allowed to have access to. Apple has done a good job of attempting to group applications by type. There is an iLife, Internet, Widgets, Utilities, and Other selection. For the Applications you wish to grant this user access to, just select them in the box.

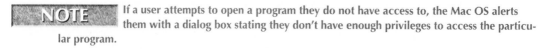

If a user attempts to open a program they do not have access to, the Mac OS alerts them with a dialog box stating they don't have enough privileges to access the particular program.

- **Can administer printers:** If checked, this allows the user to add and remove printers in the system.

- **Can change password:** If selected, this allows the user to change their password. For children, generally this is unselected so they don't accidentally change the password to something they don't remember.

- **Can burn CDs and DVDs:** If you would like to allow the user to burn CDs and DVDs, check this box.

- **Can modify the Dock:** If you want to prevent Dock modification, leave this off.

FIGURE 18.18

The Simple Finder for Child 1

Content filter

Leopard has added a much more robust content filter than in prior versions of Mac OS. Although not as robust as some third-party applications, it is a step in the right direction. Here you can block access to certain words in the Mac OS Dictionary, as well as specifically block or allow certain Web sites. To configure, select the user you wish to filter, then click Content at the top of the pane. See Figure 18.19. The top of the Content pane provides the following option:

- **Hide profanity in the Dictionary:** The Dictionary application provides comprehensive definitions of English words, including slang; some terms may not be appropriate for all users. You can use this parental control to filter out unsuitable words from the Mac OS X Dictionary. The Dictionary application does not filter terms used in the Internet dictionaries, which are viewable through the application.

FIGURE 18.19

The Content pane of Parental Controls

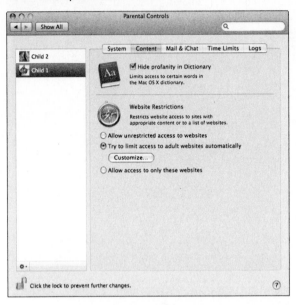

You can use parental controls to help prevent users from viewing inappropriate content on Internet Web sites. Parental controls can preview Web pages before they are displayed and attempt to block content that is not suitable for kids. The following Web site restrictions are available:

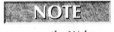 **Although Parental Controls attempts to block known adult Web sites and filter for inappropriate content, it is not always possible to identify the suitability of information on the Web.**

- **Allow unrestricted access to websites:** This is the default selection. No filtering is in place if this is selected.
- **Try to limit access to adult websites:** This is best-effort filtering. It blocks adult content as best as it can. If you want to specifically block or allow certain Web sites, click Customize. See Figure 18.20. The following settings are available:
  - **Always allow these sites:** These sites are always allowed access by the user. To add a site to this list, click the plus sign at the bottom left of the allow box and type the Web site that you want to allow. To remove a Web site, select the site and click the minus sign.

■ **Always block these sites:** These sites are always blocked. If the content filter is unable to block a particular Web site, you can place it here for specific blocking. The procedure for adding and removing sites is the same as for allowing sites.

FIGURE 18.20

Customize pane to specifically bock and allow certain Web sites

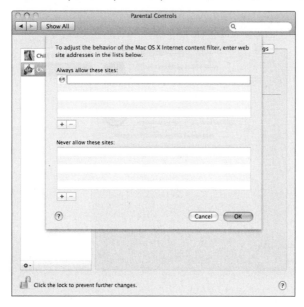

■ **Allow access to only these websites**: This is the most restrictive method of content filtering. Here you specifically allow sites to be viewed. All other sites are blocked. When a user encounters a restricted Web site they will get a warning displayed on their screen. See Figure 18.21. Some basic Web sites come pre-configured in the Parental Controls. You can add Web sites with the plus sign at the bottom left of the pane or remove sites with the minus sign.

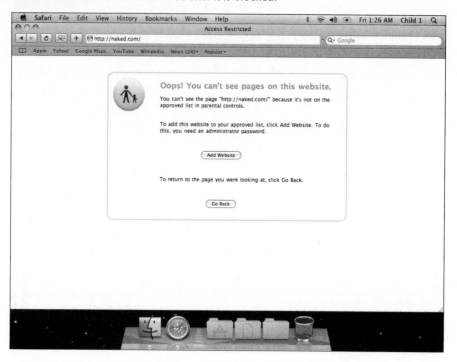

FIGURE 18.21

This user cannot see this adult Web site. It is blocked.

When you allow access to specific Web sites, they show up in Safari as bookmarks for easy access. You can create folders, or you can create groups to keep a few of the same type of Web site together. The bookmarking feature works only for Safari.

Mail and iChat

Here you can choose who your restricted account can instant message and e-mail. You also can allow your restricted user to request an addition to the permissible list. To limit instant messaging, check the Limit iChat button. To limit e-mail, check the Limit Mail button. Several options are available:

- To add an e-mail address, Jabber account, or AIM account, click the plus sign at the bottom left of the window. A pane pops up requesting you to add that person's first and last name, as well as the type of account you are allowing. By default it is an e-mail address. Click that pull-down menu and select the appropriate account type. See Figure 18.22. Once the information is complete, click the Add button at the bottom right of the pop-up.

You can add a person to your address book here by selecting the Add to Address Book button at the bottom of the pop-up.

FIGURE 18.22

Adding an allowed e-mail address janedoe@mac.com manually

- You can add someone from your address book. Click the arrow just to the right of the Last Name field. The pop-up expands to reveal your address book. Select the appropriate user(s) and click the Add button. See Figure 18.23.

- If you select **the Send permission requests to:** box and add your e-mail address, this sends an e-mail notifying the recipient (you) that the user is attempting to exchange e-mail with someone not on the list. This is an excellent monitoring tool as well as a way to add addresses as needed.

FIGURE 18.23

Adding an allowed e-mail or AIM address

Time Limits

New to Leopard is a Time Limit panel. In this panel you can specify weekday and/or weekend time limits. This restricts the number of hours the computer can be used during the day. You can also restrict a block of hours during the day, such as 8 p.m.–3 a.m. during the week or 9 p.m.–5 a.m. during the weekend. See Figure 18.24. The following options are available:

- **Weekday time limits:** If you select this box, the user has a maximum amount of time they can use the computer during any given weekday. If you set the limit to two hours, the user has two hours of computer time Monday through Friday.

- **Weekend time limits:** Weekends are generally a time for play, so Apple separated weekdays from weekends in Time Limits. Here you specify how much computer time this account can have during a typical weekend, Saturday and Sunday.

- **Bedtime:** If your child is not supposed to use the computer during his or her bedtime, you can restrict when the computer can be used on school nights (Sunday through Thursday) and on weekends (Friday and Saturday). By default the computer is set to not allow access from 11 p.m. to 9 a.m.

FIGURE 18.24

Time Limits Parental Control pane

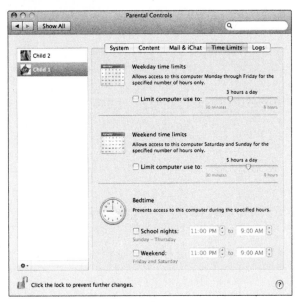

NOTE When a user is not allowed to log on, the login screen has a red dot next to that user's name and tells the user when they can log on again. If they attempt to log on, it flashes their desktop and then goes back to the login screen.

Logs

Perhaps the most important feature added to Parental Controls is the Log feature. Here you can view which Web sites were visited and/or blocked, which Applications were opened, and which iChat buddies were contacted and when. The system-blocking feature is effective only if its function can be observed and monitored. Here you can do that. See Figure 18.25. You can set the following options:

- **Show Activity**: Here you can select how much activity history you would like to see. The options are one week, one month, three months, six months, one year, and all.

- **Group by:** Here you can group by Web site/application/contact or by date. The type of group depends on which log collection you have selected.

FIGURE 18.25

Viewing the past activity for one week grouped by Web site

Easier parental management

Once you have set the parameters for one account, you can copy the settings to another account. This makes for much faster parental management. Another new feature in Leopard is Remote Management. If you have many computers in your home, you can manage each one of them from one central location. The following options are available:

- **Copying settings from one user to another:** This takes the settings from XXX user and copies them to YYY user. Follow these steps:

   1. Select the managed user.
   2. Click the cog at the bottom left of the window.
   3. Select Copy Settings for "XXX user."
   4. Select the user you want to copy the settings to.
   5. Click the cog again and select Paste Settings to "YYY user."

- **Enabling Remote Parental Management:** This allows you to manage many computer users from one location. Follow these steps:

   1. Go to the workstation you want to manage.
   2. Log on as an administrator and open the Parental Controls System Preference pane.

3. Select the user you wish to manage remotely.

4. Click the cog at the bottom left and then Allow Remote Setup.

■ **Managing Parental Controls Remotely:** This is how to activate the Parental Controls on the main computer to manage the other ones in the home. Follow these steps:

1. In the Finder, choose Go ➪ Connect To Server, and then click Browse.

2. Select the other computer from the list of computers on your network and enter the administrator name and password for the remote computer.

3. In the Finder, choose Apple menu ➪ System Preferences, and click Parental Controls.

4. If the preferences are locked, click the lock icon and type the administrator name and password for this computer.

5. In the Accounts list, in the Other Computers section, select the remote user account you want to change. See Figure 18.26.

FIGURE 18.26

Selecting the remote computer and entering the administrator name and password

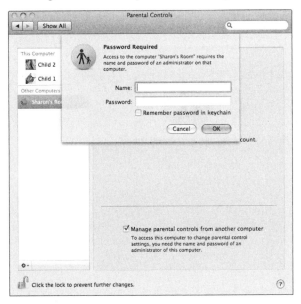

6. Enter the Administrator name and password.

7. The remote accounts display just below Other Computers. See Figure 18.27.

8. Manage these just as you would a local account.

FIGURE 18.27

Selecting the account that is to be managed on the remote computer

Administering Privileges Using Show Info

Within OS X's GUI, privileges are set via the Finder using the item's Get Info window. Select the item within the Finder, and choose the Get Info command under the File menu or press ⌘+I and turn down the chevron adjacent to the label Ownership and Permissions.

For years, standard POSIX (Portable Operating System Interface for uniX) permissions did a mediocre job of defining access to a system's files and folders. In all previous versions of Mac OS X, client POSIX permissions were standard. POSIX permissions let you control access to files and folders based on three categories of users: Owner, Group, and Everyone. Although these permissions give adequate control over who can access a file or a folder, they lack the flexibility and granularity that many organizations require to deal with elaborate user environments. This is why Apple, beginning with Mac OS 10.4 Server, started to apply Access Control Lists (ACLs) on top of POSIX permissions. This added the granularity and Windows compatibility the Mac OS desperately needed.

There are many examples of the deficiencies of POSIX permissions. Say that you have a family of four, two parents and two children. In this example assume the parents would like to share a folder that is private between themselves, and disallow access to their children. In prior versions of Mac OS X the computer administrator would have to go to the command line (or use the server Workgroup Manager), add a group, place the parents into the group, and then give that new group access to that particular folder. It was very complicated. With Access Control Lists you can add each individual to the control list and give him or her access as you want.

Another example of the deficiencies of POSIX permissions is most evident in a client-server environment. In order for permissions to propagate properly on a server, both the client and the server must be speaking the same permissions language. If the server was running Mac OS X Tiger with ACLs and the client had POSIX permissions, when one user moved his or her file from one place on the server to another, the effective permissions of that file did not change. This could mean that if someone else wanted to access the file they might be locked out due to the ownership and permissions not propagating properly to the relocated file.

As our needs have become more complex, operating systems have begun implementing ACLs to help handle more advanced permissions needs. Apple has recognized the deficiencies of POSIX permissions and has placed them first into Mac OS 10.4 Server, and now into Leopard. An ACL provides an extended set of permissions for a file or folder and allows for multiple users and groups to be set as owners, as well as allowing for a list of users and groups access to a particular file or folder. In addition, ACLs are compatible with Windows Server 2003 and Windows XP, giving you added flexibility in a multiplatform environment.

Editing folder permissions

OS X's GUI groups the assignment of permissions into four selections: Read Only, Write Only (Drop Box), Read & Write, and None. Although folders can be assigned any of these privileges, files can only be assigned Read Only, Read & Write, or None. When a folder is assigned Write Only, that folder becomes a shared *drop box* for users other than its owner. This means users can drop files into that folder but are unable to open that folder or view its contents. Table 18.2 explains the various privileges that can be assigned for an item.

TABLE 18.2

File and Folder Privileges

Privilege	Description	Where Applicable
Read Only	The specified user or group can read an item but not save over or modify it.	Files and folders
Write Only (Drop Box)	The specified user or group can save and copy documents in this designated folder, but not see the result once it is done. It is like a mailbox; once you put something in you can't get it out.	Folders only
Read and Write	The specified user or group has full access to read, write, modify, delete, save, or rename the designated item.	Files and folders
No access	The specified user or group has no access to the designated item. They cannot even open the item.	Files and folders

To modify a folder's permissions, select the folder, and hold down Command ⇨ I for the Get Info dialog box. See Figure 18.28. In this example, my Documents folder, I have Read & Write access and everyone else has no access. You can do the following:

FIGURE 18.28

My Documents folder's Get Info dialog box

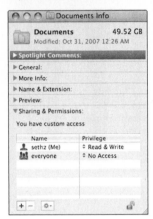

■ Change permissions of an existing user or group. Follow these steps:

1. If the Get Info dialog box is locked, unlock it by clicking the lock icon and entering an administrator name and password.

2. Select the user or group whose permission you want to change.

3. On the right side under privilege change the permissions to whatever you like. See Figure 18.29.

FIGURE 18.29

Changing the permissions of "Everyone" on my Documents folder

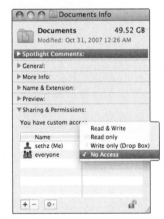

- Grant or deny an additional user or group access. Follow these steps:

  1. If the Get Info dialog box is locked, unlock it by clicking the lock icon and entering an administrator name and password.

  2. Click the plus sign at the bottom of the box. A window pops up with the Users & Groups and Address Book.

  3. Select the user or group whose access you want to grant or deny, and click Select. See Figure 18.30.

 If the user is not in your system you can add him or her from the address book. If you do this the system asks for an administrator name and password.

FIGURE 18.30

The dialog box for adding a user to my Documents folder

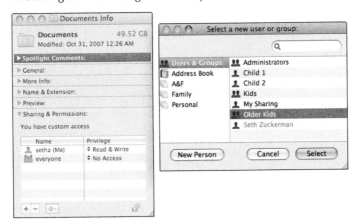

  4. The user or group shows up in the Get Info dialog box, where you can select the appropriate permission. See Figure 18.31.

- Remove a user or group from an item. Follow these steps:

  1. If the Get Info dialog box is locked, unlock it by clicking the lock icon and entering an administrator name and password.

  2. Select the user or group you want to remove.

  3. Click the minus sign at the bottom left of the box to remove them.

- Undo what was just done. If you mistakenly added or deleted someone, you can undo the last action. As long as you don't close the dialog box, this works. Follow these steps:

  1. Click the cog in the Get Info dialog box of the item in question.

  2. Click Revert Changes. This brings the item back to its original state before you started to edit it this time.

FIGURE 18.31

Delegating Child 2 Read & Write access to my Documents folder

■ Apply your changes to enclosed folders. You can take what you have just done to a folder and apply it to all encompassing items within that folder. After you have made your changes, click the cog at the bottom of the Get Info dialog box and click Apply to enclosed items. This takes the folder's permissions and applies them to all files and folders within it.

In the prior versions of Mac OS X you could not specify more than one user or group when changing the permissions of a file or folder. Your options were Owner, Group, and Everyone Else. Now you have this ability.

Be careful when planning who has access to what. Just because the power exists doesn't mean you shouldn't plan how to use it. It is very simple to accidentally give everyone access or to accidentally remove access to a folder. This is why Apple created the undo option for permissions.

Summary

Here's what you learned in this chapter:

■ If you use Mac OS X with an administrator account, you can change all system preference settings and install software in the Applications folder and main Library folder. An administrator can also create, edit, and delete other users' accounts and assign privileges.

■ If you use Mac OS X with a normal account, you can still administer locked system settings by authenticating with an admin user account's name and password.

- Groups and managed accounts now can be added via the Accounts System Preference Pane.

- You create, administer, and delete user accounts in the Accounts preference pane.

- People take turns using Mac OS X by logging in and out. Login can be automatic for one user account, but other user accounts will require manual logging in. Fast user switching allows the simultaneous login of more than one account.

- Each user can set up a list of documents and applications to be opened during login, which is configured in the Login Items panel of the Accounts preference pane.

- You can change the privilege settings of your folders and files by using the Finder's Show Info window. You can also set an option to have Mac OS X ignore privilege settings on volumes other than the boot volume.

- Apple has added more detailed parental controls to manage user accounts.

- You can manage Parental Controls for any computer that has them enabled.

- Permissions for files and folders have been drastically improved to give more granular control.

Chapter 19

Integrating in a Windows World

A re we really writing about the Windows OS in the Mac OS X Bible? Indeed! Like it or not, this is a Microsoft world, and the Macintosh represents a very small portion of the total computer market. There will be a time when the average Mac user needs to share files or network resources with their PC friends, and this chapter discusses how to do that. In addition, the latest generations of Apple Computers are now using Intel processors (instead of the IBM/Motorola-developed PowerPC chip), and can actually run Microsoft Windows and all Windows-native applications in addition to Mac OS X, giving Mac users an unprecedented amount of flexibility. There are a few different ways that Mac owners can use Windows, and this chapter talks about a few of the major methods of taking advantage of this breakthrough in unified computing.

Using Microsoft Windows on the Mac

There are many different ways to install and use alternative OSs on the Mac. From Apple's sanctioned Boot Camp application, to Parallels for Macintosh Desktop emulation suite, to VM Ware's Fusion emulation suite, Mac users have options. This section goes over a few of the most popular methods of using Windows on your Mac.

Boot Camp

Shortly after Apple released the first Intel-based Macs, the Mac community as a whole began exploring the possibility of "hacking" the Mac to run

Windows. In the spirit of "if you can't stop 'em, help 'em," Apple released Boot Camp — an official Apple-designed tool to help Mac users install a fully native version of Windows on their Macs. Mac users can now reboot their Mac straight into Windows, and take advantage of the incredible speed and performance of the new Mac hardware while using Microsoft Windows-based software that isn't available or is out-of-date on the Mac platform (programs like AutoCAD, Microsoft Access, Microsoft Visio, and Internet Explorer). To access your Microsoft Windows OS, you need to reboot your Mac into that operating system, either by using the Startup Disk control panel, or by rebooting and holding down the Option key and selecting the appropriate OS when prompted.

Your Mac OS will not be available until you reboot again, holding down the Option key and selecting the Mac OS. This process may seem cumbersome, but it is the most foolproof and best performing configuration of Windows available. There is no emulation and no Mac OS computing "overhead" to gobble up computer resources; it's pure Windows OS.

Installing and configuring Boot Camp

The details of the installation process are outlined very effectively in the instructions included with the Boot Camp application. This book avoids duplicating that information and simply overviews the process. You will need an Internet connection, a copy of Microsoft Windows (XP or Vista), a printer, and a blank CD to complete the Boot Camp install process.

The first and most important step is to run Software Update on your Mac to ensure that you are running the latest firmware and software.

Next print the enclosed 26-page PDF instructions. The instructions are very detailed, and absolutely necessary to have on-hand during the installation process. Next, run the Boot Camp Assistant application in your Applications/Utilities folder.

The Boot Camp Assistant process is roughly as follows:

1. **Burn a Mac/Windows Drivers CD.** During this step, you create a CD that is filled with the crucial hardware drivers that will tell Windows what kind of hardware your Mac has, ranging from video card to network interfaces to keyboard and mouse.

2. **Create a partition for Windows.** During this step, you block off a slice of your drive to be dedicated to the Windows operating system.

3. **Install Windows.** During this step, you install Windows XP or Vista and follow the on-screen instructions in the Microsoft installer, supplemented with your printed Boot Camp instructions.

4. **Install Mac/Windows Drivers.** During this last step, insert the CD burned in Step 1, and add the drivers as prompted to complete the process.

Considerations with Boot Camp

Windows is notoriously susceptible to computer viruses and computer threats. Installing Windows on your Mac doesn't make your Mac more susceptible, but your Windows OS is wide open and naked on the Internet if you don't take precautions. Windows has a built-in Windows Update application at the top of the Start Menu. After completing the Windows installation and adding all drivers in the final step, run Windows Update and install all of Microsoft's critical updates; if you don't, your Windows system is just not safe. In addition, it's of the utmost importance to install an antivirus suite on your Windows OS as soon as possible. There are dozens of options out there, some free, some with annual fees, some store-bought. Any of the following will suffice, and many not included in the below list are fine. Do your research, and choose the antivirus application that is right for you. Please keep in mind that there will always be viruses that get around antivirus software and cause problems. Back up your data often, and be prepared for the unknown!

- Norton Antivirus 2008 (`www.symantec.com/norton/products`)
- Trend Micro Antivirus plus Antispyware 2008 (`www.trendmicro.com`)
- Grisoft AVG Antivirus (`www.grisoft.com/`)

Virtualization

There is a new movement in the world of computing called *virtualization*. Computer hardware has gotten so powerful that it's possible to actually run multiple simultaneous software-based computers all at the same time on the same hardware. In the context of this chapter, the main advantage of virtualization technology is that users do not have to reboot their computers to use different operating systems. The disadvantage is that the virtualized operating system suffers some performance degradation as opposed to an operating system running natively (non-virtualized). The performance hit is less noticeable the better your computer and the better crafted the virtualization system is. We'll discuss a few of the great ones here.

Parallels

One of the major players in the Apple virtualization world is Parallels Inc. Their Parallels Desktop 3.0 for Mac products is a powerful, easy-to-use software package that allows you to use Windows (or Linux) on top of a running version Mac OS X. Parallels is $79, and is available for download at `www.parallels.com`.

Installing Parallels

One of the best features of the Parallels Desktop installer is the Windows Express assistant. With Windows Express, it's actually easier to install Windows on a Mac than it is on a native PC! The sole interaction that you have to have with Windows is post-install. After you enter your name, organization (that is, Company Name), and serial number, Parallels takes over and finishes the job. See Figure 19.1 for a screen shot of the Windows Express interface.

FIGURE 19.1

Parallels has a Windows Express installation mode that makes it easy to install Windows on your Mac. Easier than on a PC!

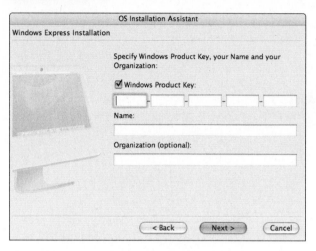

Considerations with Parallels

As we noted with Boot Camp, viruses can victimize Windows. The same rules apply with virtual Windows-based machines. Run your Microsoft updates, keep your system safe with antivirus software, and be prepared for the unknown. Backup often!

The most important consideration is the third-party hardware support. With each update and patch from Parallels, the list of supported hardware grows, but also shifts. Some devices that worked before suddenly will break. Because the software is emulating direct communication between the hardware and the Windows OS, there are often problems in the communication, unfortunately. At present, FireWire devices don't work very well, and Bluetooth support is limited. In addition, there are a number of mobile phones and such that do not communicate properly; from the BlackBerry to the Treo, there are unfortunate gaps in support. Parallels works feverishly to repair the broken drivers and to improve the list of supported hardware, but don't be too surprised if your new hot mobile phone just doesn't sync up with your Microsoft Outlook 2003 in Parallels.

Ways to use Windows in Parallels

Because Parallels is emulating Windows within your Mac OS, there are a number of ways to view and interact with Windows. You can simply have a window open and use it like any other application; you can run the OS in full-screen mode to effectively look and feel like you're running Windows natively; or you can use the paradigm-shifting Coherence-mode:

■ **OS Window Mode:** You can simply have Windows open and within a window itself, to avoid it taking over your screen. See Figure 19.2 for a look at Windows-in-a-window.

Windows in windowed mode. It's just one of three ways to look at Windows in Parallels.

■ **Full Screen Mode:** This mode is the most familiar to users because it's just Windows! Select Fullscreen from the View menu, and your Mac renders Windows full screen. See Figure 19.3 for an example of this most intuitive setup.

■ **Coherence Mode:** In an effort to suppress as much Microsoft Windows interface elements as possible and make the experience of using Parallels more natural-feeling, the Parallels group developed Coherence Mode. In this view, the Windows desktop background and icons are removed, and only the active applications and the Start Menu remain visible. It's a bit strange, but once experienced, is actually quite useful. See Figure 19.4 for a peek.

FIGURE 19.3

Windows in Full Screen Mode. The most intuitive way to use Windows because there's no other OS to clutter your view.

FIGURE 19.4

Coherence Mode. Yes, that is a Start Menu and the Dock living together in harmony!

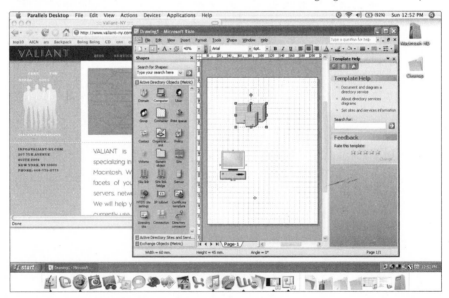

Sharing Files with Parallels

The best feature that helps push Parallels to the head of the emulation pack is the ease with which users can share files between their OSs. For example, what could be easier than just dragging a file into the Windows OS window, or out of that window back onto your Mac desktop? Just drag and drop and presto! Files are copied and available to the other OS. This option is only really feasible if you are using Parallels in Window mode though. For Full Screen and Coherence mode, it's worthwhile to set up a Shared Folder. Do this in the Configuration Editor (available before you launch your Parallels OS, or after you stop it, before quitting the Parallels application). The interface for adding these Shared Folders should be intuitive by now. Click the plus sign, and select the folder you want to share. After your Parallels OS is launched, the contents of the selected folder are available to both OSs. See Figure 19.5 for the Configuration Editor's Shared Folder interface.

FIGURE 19.5

Creating shared folders is easy in Parallels. Using the Configuration Editor, just select the folder you want to share and you're done!

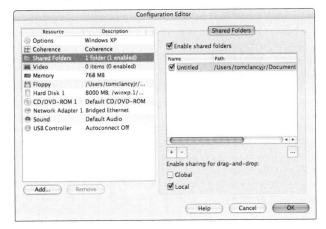

VMware Fusion

VMware Fusion is another virtualization tool. Although performance and stability of Parallels is impressive, Windows performance has lately been reviewed as being faster and more stable in Fusion. In the interest of maximum flexibility, VMware Fusion can run your Boot Camp partition without rebooting, so that you can access that single OS in both a virtual environment and then use Boot Camp to run the OS natively (with all the speed benefits of that mode). See Figure 19.6 for a look at a Vista Boot Camp partition running in Fusion.

FIGURE 19.6

With VMware Fusion, you can run your Boot Camp's Microsoft Windows Vista Business Ultra Platinum Garlic and Onion Flavored Edition as a virtual machine, avoiding inefficient reboots.

While Parallels' Windows installer is supremely easy to use, the VMware team has developed so-called Appliances, which are bundled OS and Application suites, all conveniently downloadable and easy to access. Once accessed, these Appliances are ready to go and perform their designated task (like running a Wiki-type collaboration tool, for example). The fully functional Appliances are all various flavors of Linux though: because Windows requires the purchase of a license key, the VMware team can't exactly give those away. There are Windows Appliances, but they require valid serial numbers to activate. Remember folks: Don't Steal Software.

Installing VMware

Installation of VMware Fusion is a snap. Follow these steps:

1. Purchase the software and download the installer from www.vmware.com.

2. Mount the disk image by double-clicking.

3. Run the Install VMware Fusion application (see Figure 19.7).

4. Select a destination disk for the application.

FIGURE 19.7
_____

The VMware application installs easily. Configuring the virtual machines is a bit more complex.

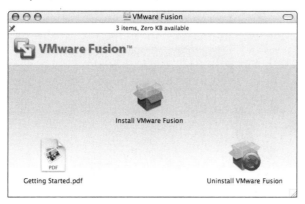

Now that the application is installed, it is time to create a virtual machine. There are three ways to create virtual machines for your use:

- **Download a premade virtual machine.** Select the Download button, which launches your Web browser and brings you to the VMware marketplace where numerous pre-made systems are ready to download.

- **Modify your Boot Camp partition for use in Fusion.** After you've created your Boot Camp partition, the VMware application automatically detects it and can utilize it after making a few modifications. Select the Boot Camp partition in the Virtual Machine Library window (see Figure 19.8).

- **Create a custom virtual machine.** A step-by-step process assists users in creating a virtual machine. The process includes choosing an OS type, specifying a location for the virtual machine, and specifying the size of the virtual machine's virtual hard disk. After those steps are complete, the application creates your virtual machine for future use. See Figure 19.9 for a look at one of the intermediate steps of the process.

FIGURE 19.8

To use your Boot Camp partition in VMware Fusion, select it from the Virtual Machine Library window, and Fusion does the rest of the work to prepare the OS for use.

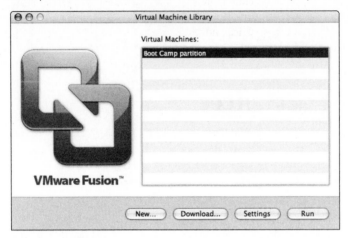

FIGURE 19.9

During the process of creating a custom virtual machine, users must select the OS type as well as the desired location and disk size.

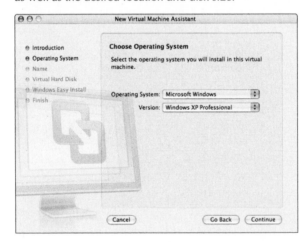

Considerations with VMware

Windows is still vulnerable to viruses, no matter the emulator. Keep your antivirus running and up-to-date and keep your Microsoft patches applied. As with Parallels, third-party device support is not guaranteed, although recently more mobile devices work in VMware Fusion than in Parallels. Both VMware Fusion and Parallels have demo versions available free of charge, so if peripheral support is mission-critical, download both, and try your gadgets with each, to see which environment works best for you.

Sharing Resources with PCs

In addition to actually running Windows yourself on your Mac, there will come a time when you need to share files with another user, and with over 90 percent of the computing market running Windows, you'll most likely need to know how to play nicely with Windows. This section outlines the basics of giving and taking files from Windows machines, and allowing Windows users to give and take from you.

Connecting to a PC's sharepoint from your Mac

The developers at Apple know that Windows is the dominant OS on the market (we'll not specu-late on if this is a deserved rank or not). As such, they've built in the tools for your Mac to play nicely with Windows as best as possible, because the developers at Microsoft have little inspiration to make Windows play nice with the Mac. With all of this in mind, it's often easier for a Mac user to get files *from* a Windows machine than it would be for a Windows user to get files from a Mac.

Configuring the PC

There are a few pieces of information that the users involved have to know and be prepared to share with each other before their computers can learn to share. Starting with the PC, you need to know

- **IP Address:** In Windows XP, go to the start menu, click Run, type **cmd**, and when con-fronted with the old-fashioned white-text-on-black interface, type **ipconfig**. This spouts a bunch of information, the most important of which is the IP Address. See Figure 19.10 for the resulting view from Windows XP.

- **Name and Password:** The valid Windows user must go to the User Accounts control panel on the Windows workstation, and either create a new temporary user account for the Mac user, or reveal the name and password of an already existing user.

FIGURE 19.10

Windows XP's command-line interface can reveal the PC's IP address.

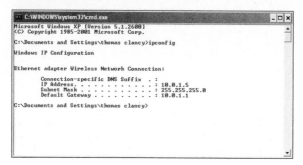

Creating a sharepoint

Remember, a sharepoint is just a folder that is being made publicly available. The PC owner/administrator must select a folder to share. Follow these steps:

1. Right-click on the folder and select Properties.

2. Go to the Sharing tab (see Figure 19.11).

3. Check the box next to Share this folder on the network.

4. Check the box next to Allow network users to change my files.

FIGURE 19.11

To share a folder, a Windows user must choose to share the folder and name the share.

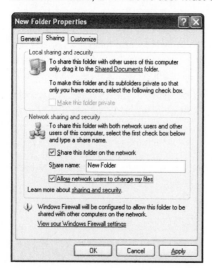

The PC is ready to accept incoming connections.

Connecting from the Mac

From the Finder on the Mac, press Apple+K or select Connect to Server from the Go menu. You'll be presented with a pop-up screen as shown in Figure 19.12. In the Server Address field, enter in the following command: **smb://xxx.xxx.xxx.xxx** (where the x's are the IP address of the PC), and click Connect. You are required to enter the username and password provided by the PC administrator.

FIGURE 19.12

The Connect to Server window. It's a bit nonintuitive, but enter the **smb://** and the IP address of your destination, and you should be good to go!

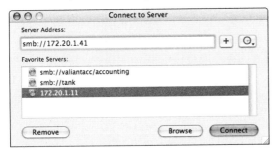

A Few Words about Protocol

A protocol is a set of rules governing the communication between computers. It falls somewhere between a language and an etiquette guide. The string of text in the Connect window that precedes the IP address of the Windows computer (smb://) is the protocol header, indicating to your machine which protocol to use. In this instance, the header tells your Mac that it should connect to that sharepoint using the SMB protocol, rather than its own native AFP (Apple File Protocol).

SMB is short for Server Message Block, and is the communication method that Microsoft's OS uses to share files. SMB is often called "Samba," but to be technically accurate, Samba is a reverse-engineered free version of SMB, which enables other computers to communicate with SMB-enabled computers. So, in the above example, your Mac is using Samba to connect to an SMB sharepoint on a Microsoft Windows computer. If you were to try to communicate to the Windows-based machine without the smb:// header, your Mac by default would be using the wrong protocol, "speaking" in AFP, and not getting very useful results from the SMB-based server system.

Connecting to a Mac sharepoint from a PC

Because you're reading this chapter so carefully, you're ready to be the IT guru that can just walk his or her unfortunate Windows-using friends through gaining access to a sharepoint on your Mac, right? Well, you've got to configure a few things on your Mac first.

Configuring the Mac

For more detailed instructions on how to set up Sharing, please refer to Chapter 12. As a brief review, the general steps are as follows:

1. **Create a user for sharing in the Accounts preference pane.**

2. **Activate Sharing in the Sharing preference pane.**

3. **Create a folder to share in the Sharing preference pane (and put stuff in it!).**

That being said, to enable sharing to grant Windows systems access, there are few extra steps to endure.

1. **Create an SMB-qualified user.** Even though Leopard has introduced "Sharing Only" users, to share with Windows-based systems, a "Sharing Only" user account won't cut the mustard. There are some security risks that are currently unacceptable to Apple, or perhaps some inherent limitation in the Leopard built-in sharing system that prevents Sharing Only users from accessing a Leopard share via SMB. Sadly, you need to create a full-on Standard user account and then enable that account to access via SMB. To do this, open your System Preferences and click the Accounts pane. Click the plus sign to create a new user, and set the user as Standard. In practice, creating this separate user account is wise, as this prevents you from having to give your own password away to allow SMB sharing. For example, create a Standard user called sharinguser with the password shareme, as in Figure 19.13.

FIGURE 19.13

Create a new user with the Standard privilege set (Sharing Only won't work!) to maintain a secure environment.

2. **Engage file sharing.** After the new user is created, go to the Sharing preference pane in System Preferences. Check the box to engage file sharing.

3. **Activate SMB Sharing.** Click the Options button in the lower right of the Sharing preference pane, and select Share Files and Folders using SMB. Turning this option on allows Windows users to access your files. Check the box next to each user you wish to grant SMB access. Notice that Shared Only users are *not* available to be granted SMB access. This "no-Sharing Only-user-via-SMB" limitation may be cured in future patches, but at release, this limitation is in place, and we have to work with it.

NOTE For each SMB user, you need to pre-enter the password in the Sharing preference pane. This method of storing the password is less secure than the way AFP sharing works. Such is the price you must pay to play with Windows users.

See Figure 19.14 for a look at the File Sharing Options pane.

FIGURE 19.14

In the options for File Sharing, you have the option to activate sharing via AFP, FTP, SMB. Each sharing system has its advantages and risks.

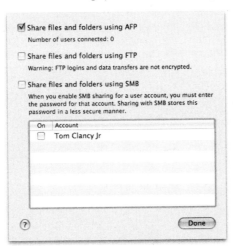

4. **Specify the folder to be shared.** By default each user's Public folder is shared as a read-only folder with a built-in drop box, but a new feature of Leopard is that administrators have the flexibility to create numerous unique shared folders each with their own level of security. As an example, create a new folder at the root of your hard drive called Shared. Then select that folder in the sharing interface. Remember, more detail on Sharing can be found in Chapter 12.

5. **Set the access privileges for each user.** The options here are set per-user and are somewhat flexible, because you can specify Read Only access (to share with guests, but to prevent modification of your files), Write Only access (to serve as a drop box for other users), or Read/Write Access. Click the plus signand select your sharing user. This adds the user to the list of users in the Sharing pane. Then specify privileges for your sharing user. Figure 19.15 shows that user list and privilege options.

FIGURE 19.15

Each user has their own particular level of access to each sharepoint.

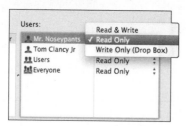

NOTE   The preference pane gives your computer's specific address information and thus your network sharepoint for remote users. This information makes clear the best way for remote users to find your machine with language like: "Other users can access your computer at afp://10.0.1.195/" In the case of Windows users, they would replace afp:// with smb:// (as noted earlier, that's the protocol header, telling the guest machine what protocol to use). Your computer's specific address and sharename will of course be different, to reflect your machine's address and your active file shares.

Figure 19.16 shows the Sharing preference pane.

Connecting

After the preceding has been configured, your Windows-using compatriots are ready to connect! From Windows, open the Start Menu, select Run and enter the information given in your Sharing preference pane as noted earlier (for example, **smb://10.0.1.195/Shared**). No quotes and no additional information are needed to initiate the contact. Once this information is entered, Windows users are prompted for a username and password (in the previous example, it would be **sharinguser** and **shareme**), and they now have access to the shared folder you created. Figure 19.17 shows an already populated Run dialog box and the open Home folder. This folder is revealed because the Run command is populated with the IP address and a user's shortname, which reveals their Home folder. Only the Public folder is readable, and in that, only the Drop Box is writeable.

In the Sharing preference pane, administrators set shared folders and access privileges.

The Windows Run command populated with the connection information and the revealed folder hierarchy.

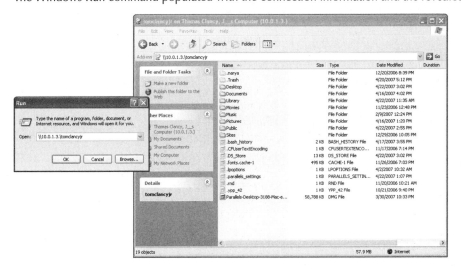

Optionally, to make finding your computer easier for Windows users, you can add your Mac to the Workgroup. Here are the steps:

1. **Discover the workgroup name.** In Windows XP, right-click My Computer and select Properties.

2. **Go to the Computer Name tab.** The name of the computer's workgroup appears there. This is commonly set to HOME or WORKGROUP but sometimes is something customized. Either way, your Mac needs to match for maximum ease of connection. See Figure 19.18 for an example of the Windows Computer Name pane.

FIGURE 19.18

The Computer Name screen in Windows XP shows the name of the machine and the name of the workgroup the machine is ready to communicate with.

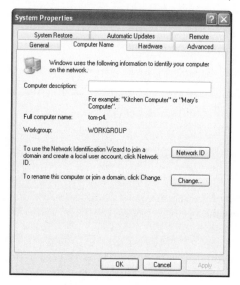

3. **Join the Mac to the workgroup.** On the Mac, open the Network preference pane. Select your primary network interface (Ethernet is recommended for speed and reliability over AirPort/Wireless). Select the WINS tab, and enter a matching workgroup name in the workgroup field. See Figure 19.19 for a peek.

FIGURE 19.19

In the newly designed Network preference pane, users set workgroup memberships for each network connection.

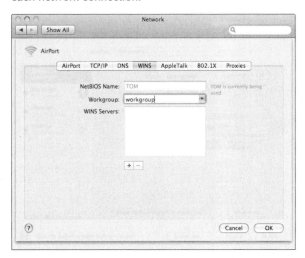

Limitations

Each custom shared folder has total flexibility as to security settings and access rights. A few limitations, however, are built into the Mac OS. Most notably there is a limit of ten simultaneous user connections to a Macintosh system. This limit is lifted with Mac OS X Server, but stands immutable for the standard Mac OS. Also, the preconfigured Public folder for each user has a few limits. Sharing users can only *read* the contents of the Public folder, which is set as a read-only folder. This means that they can copy the files from Public to their own computers to modify as they like. That being said, if sharing users want to give files back to you via the Public folder, they must use the Drop Box lodged within the Public folder. Shared users cannot read the content of the Drop Box; it is a write-only folder. This methodology keeps the items of one shared user away from the prying eyes of other sharing users. You share whatever you like in the Public folder, and other users dump files in the Drop Box — thus you maintain control!

Introducing Windows Domain Architecture

One of the biggest and most significant features of Microsoft Windows is network computing. We all know that Windows machines are more susceptible to viruses and other security breaches than Macs, but this is because the Windows PC is designed to work best in a network environment — a member of an armada, rather than a lonely fishing boat at sea. Of course, one new iteration of the MYDOOM.97 virus can transform that mighty armada into the Spanish Armada, sunk at the bottom of the Irish Sea, but I digress. Microsoft calls their network-computing world a *Domain*, with the user's credentials all stored in an *Active Directory*. This is quite different from Workgroups, the peer-to-peer networking described in the previous sections.

Network computing is an incredibly powerful model of technology usage. Each individual workstation is a mere cog in a mighty machine. User credentials, printer access, file server permissions, mail accounts, and more are all managed and maintained on central servers. The workstations themselves are completely replaceable and commoditized. After a computer joins the network, any user can simply log in and get to work with her own settings and files all preloaded. This type of computing requires a lot of initial work from the IT department and significant hardware investment from the organization, but the dividends paid are enormous later on.

For a Mac user in this world of Windows networks, there are some specific settings that must be configured to take advantage of this architecture.

Configuring the PC servers

The most important work to be done is at the Windows Servers themselves. For easiest access to fileshares, the sysadmin (fancy name for "IT Guy") can simply install Services For Macintosh, and create a Macintosh sharepoint matching each existing Windows-only sharepoint. The Install Services for Macintosh window is shown in Figure 19.20 After services for Macintosh are installed and Mac shares are created, any users with the privilege to access a particular sharepoint can easily do so from a Windows machine or from a Mac. Their credentials will work from either platform. No special users need to be created, just a normal Active Directory user account for each Mac user that will have access to the Domain's sharepoints.

FIGURE 19.20

Installing services for Macintosh is something many tech-staffers are loathe to do, but it is possible.

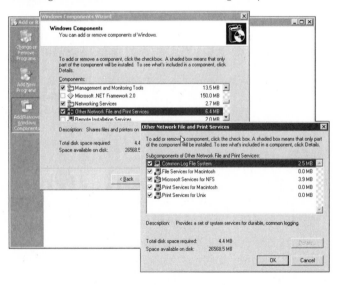

The Services for Macintosh package provided by Microsoft is functional, but it can be problematic, so many IT pros won't install it on their server except under extreme duress. Also, to grant Macs access to other network resources like shared printers, scanners, and the like, the administrator has a few larger concerns. Apple advises domain administrators make schema changes to their network security policy to allow the Macs to gain full access. A *schema* is an overall collection of policies that determine how the network behaves, and what is and isn't allowed. To make global changes to something so profound to let a minority of users play nicely is not only unfair, it's also unnecessary. Worse, it's also beyond the scope of this book.

Configuring the Mac

If the shares are set up to have Macintosh sharing enabled, no special configuration is necessary. Just select Connect from the Go menu, and put in the IP address of the server, authenticate with your username and password, and presto!

If the servers in question are part of a Windows Domain rather than a peer-to-peer workgroup, your Mac will need to be configured differently to access the *other* resources that are shared, like shared printers, network scanners, and roaming user profiles.

> **NOTE** Roaming profiles are perhaps the most advanced feature of network computing. With roaming profiles configured, each user's *entire* environment, their collection of documents, desktop items and so on, are all centrally stored, allowing any user to log onto any machine and get to work within their own familiar workspace.

To use any of the above noted advanced network computing features, your Mac will need to "join" the domain, and be validated both by an administrator and by your own credentials provided by the administrator. The steps involved in joining your Mac to the domain are described very clearly by Apple in the online support knowledge base in this article:

```
http://docs.info.apple.com/article.html?path=DirectoryAccess/1.8/
     en/c7od45.html
```

Introducing third-party apps that help

There are a number of nifty tools available that make life among the masses of Windows users more palatable. We'll briefly discuss a few of them, and point you in the right direction to get more information from the makers.

ADmitMac/Dave

As noted earlier, allowing Macs to use all of a Windows Domain's resources involves some heavy lifting for both the server administrator as well as the desktop system's administrator. Various schema changes are required and the Macs have to be shoehorned into the Active Directory. ADmitMac from Thursby software (www.thursby.com) makes this process easier. With ADmitMac installed on your Macs, no schema changes are needed, and the Windows administrators can manage the Mac users much more easily. The Macs really do become members of the larger community of Windows systems, as far as the administrators are concerned.

Dave, also from Thursby software, is a product installed on your Macintosh that effectively replaces the Mac's Samba protocol (remember that Samba is the built-in freeware version of Microsoft's SMB communication protocol) to ease the Mac's usage of SMB sharepoints.

ExtremeZ-IP

ExtremeZ-IP from Group Logic (www.grouplogic.com) is an application installed on the Windows servers that vastly improves the built-in Apple File Sharing tools that Microsoft provides. Some server administrators are skittish about installing anything on their servers, and rightly so; but this is a product to consider because it is simply a recompilation of the Apple File Services kernel, and improves speed and reliability of communication between Mac clients and Windows servers dramatically.

MacDrive

From Mediafour software (www.mediafour.com), MacDrive is actually an application installed on Windows desktop systems, enabling them to read Macintosh-formatted disks and volumes. In the odd case where there are a majority of Macs and a few Windows computers, this is an ideal application to ease the Windows user's communication.

Revealing Other Considerations

In addition to the nitty-gritty issues covered earlier in this chapter, there are some more wide-reaching behaviors to embrace and some to avoid as a Mac user in a Windows world. File naming and font problems are perhaps the most significant.

File naming problems

All operating systems have their own rules and regulations for filenames. For example, filenames can be only a certain length, and each system has certain forbidden characters. On the Mac, only the colon (:) is forbidden. Any attempt to name a file with a colon is met with a vague message as shown in Figure 19.21.

FIGURE 19.21

Sure would be nice if the Mac would just tell us the colon is a problem. Oh well. Now you know! No colons in filenames, ever!

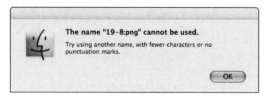

Windows users are also restricted from using certain characters, but because your Mac doesn't have the same restrictions, any attempt to share a badly named file with a Windows user will be met with frustration. It is left to sensitive Mac users to remember the special needs of their Windows brethren and thus avoid certain characters in filenames.

The forbidden characters are *. " / \ [ ] : ; | = ,

The most commonly encountered problem character is the slash (/) because it's just so convenient to put slashes in when naming a file based on calendar information (for example, pictureofmydog-03/17/07.png). That file will never work for a Windows user without some modification. In addition, if the files are saved on a Windows server, automated backup processes will fail to back them up. This is because Windows uses the / character to denote folders, so the Windows-based computer will look for a folder called pictureofmydog-03, a folder within that called 17, and finally a file named 07.png.

Bottom line: Just avoid the slash. Use dashes for your date separators.

Conversions Plus and MacLinkPlus

Files coming from different platforms may behave strangely when opened, even in compatible applications (for example, a Microsoft Word 2003 file from a PC going to a Microsoft Word 2004 application on a Mac). MacLinkPlus from DataViz (www.dataviz.com) eases the transition by converting the file independent of any application. To avoid errors and quirks, install the application on your Mac and drag your PC-originated files to it for quick conversion. The Windows-installed counterpart application is Conversions Plus, also from DataViz.

Font issues

Fonts have been the bane of many a sysadmin's life for years. Only with recent advancements in font technology has the possibility of truly uniform cross-platform fonts become a reality. To avoid lengthy, costly, and painful font troubleshooting, it is recommended that you replace troublesome fonts with new OpenType fonts. Adobe has led the charge in advancing this technology, and the results are impressive (www.adobe.com/type).

Summary

In this chapter, you learned the following:

- How to set up your Macintosh to run Windows in Boot Camp
- How to install and configure Parallels and VMware to use Windows within a virtual computer
- How to configure your Macintosh to share files with a PC
- How to connect the PC to the Mac sharepoint
- How to configure a PC to share files with a Mac
- How to connect the Mac to the PC sharepoint
- The basics of Windows Domain architecture
- The importance of forbidden characters in a filename

Part IV

Making the Most of Mac OS X

Chapter 20

Enhancing with Utilities

Every major operating system revision, including Mac OS 10.5, brings with it significant enhancements in performance and ease of use over previous versions. Nevertheless, Apple can't think of everything. Developers step in to create software that enhances Mac OS X in novel ways that can increase your productivity and computer experience. This chapter presents some of the tools and packages available to enhance your computing experience. You'll also discover some of the different licenses that developers use to release their software, and you'll find some useful places to begin your search for new software packages.

Finding Utility Software

The Internet has truly changed the way software is distributed. Because most software is distributed over the Internet in demo form, without dropping a dime or leaving your house you can easily find and test several products to find the one that suits your needs best. Web sites have sprung up whose sole purpose is to track software for different platforms and provide download links so that you don't have to go searching all over the Internet. In addition, most software developers, even noncommercial ones, have their own Web sites where you can find out about their products, download the latest versions, and even obtain demo copies.

The software mentioned in this chapter is just a small fraction of what you can find. The multifaceted environment that Mac OS X brings to the table has drawn thousands of developers, and you, too, can discover many interesting products while you're visiting a developer's Web site to obtain one of the utilities listed in this chapter.

There are some great places to find useful utilities, hacks, and software packages on the Internet if you know where to look. Here are some places to start:

- **Mac OS X Downloads pages:** Apple provides an extensive collection of current software that you can download for Mac OS X. This site has shareware, software updates, demo versions of commercial software, and free software in every category. The site is well organized, with a search function. You will find information on each piece of software offered for download but no reviews. Go to www.apple.com/downloads/macosx.

- **Apple's Mac OS X Applications page:** This Web page is also hosted by Apple and has a database that you can use to search for Mac OS X applications and hardware. Although a good resource, there are no downloads available; even so, it's a good place to find out about great software. Its main thrust is commercial software. Find it at http://guide.apple.com/macosx/.

- **VersionTracker online:** One of the best software resources available online, VersionTracker is a great Web site that keeps tabs on the latest versions of Macintosh software. You'll find Mac OS X, Mac OS 9, Windows, and Palm software in different tabs, and the database is updated throughout the day with the most recent updates appearing right on the front page. You can search for a particular software title or by using keywords that describe something about the type of software you're trying to find. There is also a pro version of the Web site (subscription fee required), which alerts you to updates of the software packages you specify, as well as provides more-advanced searching capabilities. It's at www.versiontracker.com.

- **CNET's software library:** This library offers extensive shareware, demo software, and freeware. Go to www.download.com. If you can't find what you're looking for at this site, you may find a shareware or freeware title at its sister site, Shareware.com (www.shareware.com).

- **Applelinks.com:** This is another, lesser-known, stockpile of shareware, freeware, and demo versions of retail software. Go to http://search.applelinks.com.

Trying Out Shareware and Freeware

Most of the software available for download from the sites listed in the preceding section cannot be found in retail stores or ordered from mail-order companies. This software is most often created by individuals who program in their free time, usually for fun, but mainly because they have an idea that they want to share with others. Such products are usually distributed as *shareware* or *freeware* and sometimes even as *postcardware* or *donationware*. Shareware titles are generally distributed on a trial basis. Aside from the cost of your Internet connection, you pay nothing to obtain and try out shareware; the authors generally only ask for payment if you find the product useful and decide to keep it. Authors of shareware encourage you to try their software and to share copies with your friends and co-workers. Some shareware authors accept payment directly. Many authors accept payment on the Internet through a clearinghouse, such as Kagi (www.kagi.com). Look for payment instructions in the Read Me file or other documentation files that come with the software.

In some cases, the shareware has a couple of key features removed, or it expires after some time. When you pay for the software, you get a registration code that you enter to remove the restrictions. Crippled, demonstration versions of shareware are becoming more commonplace as authors try to cope with the failings of the honor system.

Freeware, on the other hand, is completely free of these types of restrictions. The author is providing the world at large with the fruit of his or her labors and asks nothing in return. Usually, software released as freeware performs a specific task and doesn't have a very large scope. Other authors ask that you send them a note or a postcard to acknowledge the freeware; this type of freeware has been dubbed *postcardware*. *Donationware*, on the other hand, is free of charge, but the author asks for a donation of "whatever it's worth" to you. Should you not feel like paying, you don't have to, but if you enjoy the product and want to show your gratitude, send a donation. Regardless of the nature of the license, it is important to make sure that you read the license to ensure that you are properly abiding by the author's wishes.

A mounting current in the developer community is referred to as *open-source* software. It fits in with freeware, in the sense that all the software that is released under an open-source license doesn't cost money, but it does have some interesting twists. Open-source software is distributed with the *source code* to the program. The user can get at the inner programming of the software, see how the author designed it, make changes, and release the software himself with any changes he or she likes. Depending on the license that the original software was released under, the new author usually has to reference the original program and must distribute the new source code under a similar license (that is, with the same restrictions that the original license provided). Most open-source software is released under the GNU Public License (GPL). You can find more information about open-source software at `www.opensource.org`.

Understanding that free software and shareware do not become your property is important. Most freeware authors (and all shareware authors) retain the copyrights to their work. Their products are not in the public domain. You have a license to use the software, and you're generally encouraged to pass it around, but you can't sell it. For specific rules about distributing a particular product, read the license agreement that comes with the product.

Support Shareware Authors

Shareware depends on the honor and honesty of the people who use it. If you decide to keep shareware installed on your disk, the Honorable Society of Civilized People politely insists that you immediately send payment to the author. The fees that you pay for the shareware you use today (often between $5 and $50) help fund development of even greater shareware by giving the authors incentive to continue coding. For detailed information about the amount of payment requested for a particular shareware product and where to send payment, check each product's Read Me file, About menu command, on-screen Help menu, or Web site.

Using shareware and freeware

Although some of the software described in this chapter is shareware and free software, it does not include detailed operating instructions. This chapter is intended to be only a starting point because there is such a wealth of software to be found but not enough space to describe more than a few choice tools. Because such software can often only be downloaded from the Internet, it doesn't come with printed manuals. Instead, this software usually comes with a text document, frequently named the Read Me file. You can also check for on-screen help in the Help menu while the software is running.

Shareware and freeware programs aren't always as stable as commercial software. (Then again, commercial software isn't always as stable as shareware and freeware programs can be.) Be sure to follow the instructions and discussions provided by the authors in their Read Me or Help files before using any of these programs.

CAUTION   You use shareware and freeware at your own risk. Authors of any software package can make mistakes, and shareware and freeware authors are no different. Because the developers of shareware and freeware are usually individuals and not gigantic mega-corporations, they often cannot beta-test their packages as thoroughly as commercial software. Make certain that your system is supported by the requirements outlined in the Read Me file, and that you read the guidelines set forth by the author. This can often help you prevent data loss or the instability of your system.

Getting support for shareware and freeware

Shareware and freeware are typically developed by an individual rather than a whole company full of programmers and support staff. These individuals can afford neither the time nor the money required to provide technical support by telephone. Most developers do, however, provide support by e-mail.

Although the developers of shareware and free software may not be able to hold your hand, they tend to release new versions of their products frequently. Each new version may introduce minor improvements and fix a few bugs that users reported via e-mail.

If you're having trouble with shareware or free software, check the developer's Web site for a new version. Look for a description of what has changed since the version of the software you're using was released. You may find that the problem you're experiencing has been fixed in a newer version of the software. You may also find a list of frequently asked questions (FAQs) and other information that was not included with the software. You'll probably find an e-mail address where you can submit a bug report describing a problem you've discovered that doesn't appear to have been fixed in the latest version. If you do find a bug, the author will usually welcome your input because it will better the program for everyone.

List of Mac OS X Utilities

Apple, commercial developers, and shareware and freeware authors offer thousands of utility programs to the Macintosh community. Many new programs become available every day. The software listed in this chapter is not meant to be all-inclusive, but instead to be examples of the types of software that are available to enhance the performance of your computer, and your enjoyment of it.

The variation in computer models and configurations makes predicting accurately whether a particular shareware or free software product works on your system impossible. Authors of shareware and free software don't typically have the facilities to test their products with every type of software combination and computer model. Instead, they fix the problems reported by people who try out the software.

> **NOTE** Some Read Me files and documentation reference the minimum systems and software configurations required and whether there are any known conflicts, but others do not. If you decide to try some software, check the Read Me file or any included documentation for compatibility information. If the compatibility information doesn't assure you that the software you want to try is compatible with your computer model and Mac OS version, you should take the precaution of making a backup of your hard drive before trying the software. (Chapter 21 discusses backing up your hard drive.)

The software items described in this chapter are listed alphabetically, with a short description of each of their features. Software is updated often, and you may find that newer versions of programs have features not described here. This is by no means a complete list, and the sheer volume of cool software grows by the day.

You'll find that some of the features provided by the software listed in the following sections can be found in some form, somewhere in the Mac OS X operating system. The authors of these products have recognized that there are ways to make things better or give you more control; they may even just have wanted to provide you with a different way to go about your business. On the other hand, some of the software described does vastly different things than Apple ever intended.

Airfoil and Audio Hijack

Three cool applications by Rogue Amoeba software complement each other rather nicely. Audio Hijack is a sound hack that lets you record the sounds created by any of your running applications — in essence, hijacking the sound as it's coming out of the application and allowing you to record it without having to use a microphone in front of your speakers. Detour gives you ultimate control over the sound output ports on your computer. You can send the music from your iTunes out to your headphone jack, while routing your system sounds to the USB Speakers of your Mac. It will recognize any output that the system recognizes as a valid sound port — the more ports available, the more flexibility you have. Apple's AirTunes allows you to play your music from iTunes through remote speakers attached to an AirPort Express Base Station. However, Apple has not provided for sending sound from any other applications. That's where Airfoil comes in. You can use AirfoilFind demos online at www.rogueamoeba.com.

Back Up User Prefs

Backing up your software and documents is easy, but backing up your User Preferences folder isn't all that painless. You have to worry about permissions and invisible files. Back Up User Prefs takes care of everything for you and even has an Auto-Pilot feature that walks you through everything. Go to www.m-t-software.com.

BatChmod

An application with a silly name, BatChmod (see Figure 20.1) is a GUI front end for the chmod Unix command (though it uses a bit of chgrp as well). Although you can tweak permissions settings directly in the Finder using the Get Info command, the Apply to Enclosed Items button doesn't always succeed. BatChmod, on the other hand, excels at applying permissions recursively; it also lets you change specific privileges or ownerships without messing with any others. As an added benefit, it lets you force-empty the trash for those sticky situations where a file refuses to make it to the Dumpster. All in all, a good tool to have in your arsenal. Find it at `http://mac-champion.com/arbysoft`.

BatChmod is a great application that lets you change permissions on files and folders (recursively) using a drag-and-drop GUI. It even comes complete with a Matrix/Batman-esque icon for your viewing enjoyment.

Carbon Copy Cloner/SuperDuper!

Mac OS 10.4 provides the Restore command in the Disk utility, which allows you to make backup images of volumes, or even to just make a bootable clone of a Mac OS X volume. Prior to version 10.4, this feature wasn't available, and those of us who needed to copy Mac OS X volumes turned to Carbon Copy Cloner (see Figure 20.2). Carbon Copy Cloner does just what its name suggests: It clones a volume onto another disk, allowing you to have a bootable backup in the case of emergency. It's also wonderfully convenient when making disaster recovery disks or general-use build disks. In addition to all this, Carbon Copy Cloner allows you to synchronize disks as well as schedule clones (these features require you to install a command-line utility called pSync), something that Mac OS 10.4 doesn't provide. Carbon Copy Cloner will clone local disks only. SuperDuper! is somewhat more full featured, and user friendly, providing easy-to-understand descriptions of what will happen as you change options. For network disk installations, look at NetRestore, also by Bombich Software, in combination with Apple Software Restore. Find NetRestore and Carbon Copy Cloner at `www.bombich.com/software/index.html`. Super Duper! can be found at `www.shirt-pocket.com/SuperDuper`.

FIGURE 20.2

Carbon Copy Cloner has a very simple, easy-to-understand interface. Just choose the source disk, choose the target disk, and then click the Clone button. The Preferences button reveals advanced features, even providing an easy means to install pSync.

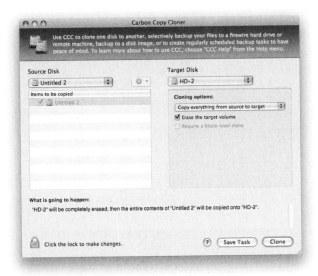

Cocktail

If ever there were a Swiss Army knife tool of utility software, it would be Cocktail. Written entirely in AppleScript Studio (see Chapter 22), Cocktail is a definite must-have piece of software. Cocktail gives you a very easy-to-use GUI look into the commands at the fingertips of Unix pros, and also some tools that let you play with the interface of Mac OS X. You can update prebinding, mess with Finder and Dock interface elements (even make the Dock appear at the top of the screen, under the menu bar), optimize your network configuration, and clear out cache files, among many other options. Find it online at www.macosxcocktail.com.

coconutBattery and coconutWiFi

CoconutBattery and coconutWiFi by Christoph Sinai of coconut-flavour.com are two great mini applications. CoconutBattery can show you how your laptop's battery is doing as compared to the original specifications so you can know even better how it's doing. It shows you the number of charge cycles, as well as the total charge the battery will take. CoconutWiFi is a menu bar item which shows you how many wireless networks you are in range of, as well as the total number of networks available. Visit www.coconut-flavour.com.

CronniX

CronniX is a GUI front end for the Unix command cron, a Unix system service that allows you to schedule the execution of scripts, programs, and applications from the command line. Well written and easy to use, CronniX brings scheduled operations to the normal Macintosh user. Find it online at `http://www.abstracture.de/projects-en/cronnix`.

DragThing

DragThing has been tidying up Mac desktops since 1995 and knows how to do it right. Use DragThing to create as many docks as you like, and populate each dock with your choice of applications, files, folders, disks, file servers, and Internet addresses. Click a docked application to open it or bring it to the front. You can customize the look of your docks with icons, folder tabs, or just text. DragThing provides some of the same features as Drop Drawers X and PocketDock. Be sure to look at all of them and see which works better for you. DragThing is $25 shareware from TLA Systems at `www.dragthing.com`.

Drop Drawers X

Drop Drawers X provides handy places to keep snippets of text, Web addresses, and other URLs, pictures, sounds, movies, and more. The drawers can hold aliases of applications, documents, and so on. You can also have a drawer that lists applications and processes that are currently running on your computer. The drawers pull out conveniently from the sides of your screen, so their contents are always at hand. You can configure each drawer to your liking, and you can even protect drawers with passwords. The Dock is nowhere near as versatile as Drop Drawers X. Drop Drawers X provides some of the same features as DragThing and PocketDock. Be sure to look at all of them and see which works better for you. Drop Drawers X is shareware from Sig Software and is available at `www.sigsoftware.com`.

GeekTool

A system preference pane for the geek in all of us, GeekTool puts a transparent (if you want it to be) console log viewer on your desktop. Very useful for servers and the criminally inquisitive, it can be a convenient means of keeping tabs on the goings on of your system. It can also show Unix Command output and images from the Net. Take a look at it at `http://projects.tynsoe.org/en/geektool`.

GraphicConverter X

One of the most highly touted, noncommercial image editors of all time, GraphicConverter X, seen in Figure 20.3, is an amazing image-editing bargain. The number of graphics formats that GraphicConverter can open and save to is unheard of — virtually every format found on Mac, Windows, Unix, Amiga, and Atari computers. GraphicConverter imports more than 100 file formats and exports more than 40 file formats — and these numbers keep growing. Even better, the program has tools and filters for editing pictures. Even professional photo editors buy this program for its image-conversion utility. Get this $30 graphical can opener by Thorsten Lemke at `www.lemkesoft.com`.

FIGURE 20.3

GraphicConverter can open so many formats they can't even all be shown in one screenshot. Note the up and down arrows on *both* ends of the pop-up.

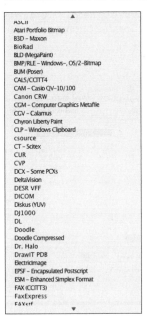

```
ASCII
Atari Portfolio Bitmap
B3D – Maxon
BioRad
BLD (MegaPaint)
BMP/RLE – Windows–, OS/2–Bitmap
BUM (Poser)
CALS/CCITT4
CAM – Casio QV–10/100
Canon CRW
CGM – Computer Graphics Metafile
CGV – Calamus
Chyron Liberty Paint
CLP – Windows Clipboard
csource
CT – Scitex
CUR
CVP
DCX – Some PCXs
DeltaVision
DESR VFF
DICOM
Diskus (YUV)
DJ1000
DL
Doodle
Doodle Compressed
Dr. Halo
DrawIT PDB
ElectricImage
EPSF – Encapsulated Postscript
ESM – Enhanced Simplex Format
FAX (CCITT3)
FaxExpress
FAXstf
```

Haxies

Mac OS X as it was released dropped a number of features that hardened old Macintosh users have gotten quite used to — windows that shuttered closed in place, or maybe an audio soundtrack. Unsanity has created a set of programs called *Haxies,* so named because, Unsanity contends, they are minihacks of the Mac OS. Window Shade X is a program that restores the minimize-in-place functionality of Mac OS 9. Fruit Menu grants you control over the Apple menu by allowing you to place your own items there. Xounds brings the soundtrack concept back to the Macintosh and even lets you use all of your old soundtrack files from Mac OS 9. Exercise extra care in the use of these applications because they have been known to interfere with some applications' ability to correctly run. Haxies require the Application Enhancer (APE) System Preference Pane to be installed. As of the release of 10.5, the APE has been known to cause some issues. APE and these haxies and more can be found at www.unsanity.com.

Logorrhea (and Chax)

iChat is a great way to connect with friends and family, but many people have overlooked its ability to log chats to your Documents folder. (Go to iChat preferences, and check the Automatically Save Transcripts box under the Messages tab.) You'll find it's quite nice to have a transcript of your conversations for later perusal. The problem with this is that actually finding something in a saved chat is very difficult. Well, Logorrhea to the rescue. It allows you to quickly flip through old chats by user and date, and previews them in a pane below (see Figure 20.4). Even more convenient is the Search tab when you can't even remember who said it. Check it out at `http://spiny.com/software/`. Chax is a great iChat add-on that adds a whole host of new little features to everyone's favorite chat program. In versions previous to iChat 4.0, Chax adds tabbed chat windows. One of the more useful features of Chax is the integrated chat log viewer. Find out more and download it at `www.ksuther.com/chax/`.

FIGURE 20.4

Logorrhea is perfect for those cases when you just have to prove how ridiculous-sounding your IM was.

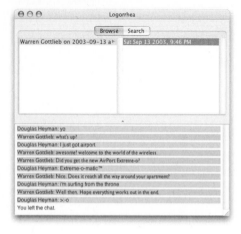

MacTracker

A handy tool for the collector and Macintosh aficionado in all of us, MacTracker is a database with information on all the Macintosh computers ever built. It's updated as new machines are released, has icon images for all of the models, and contains detailed information about original shipping configurations, maximum RAM and hard disk capacities, and much, much more. Find information on MacTracker at `www.mactracker.ca`.

MoRU and Spotless

Almost everyone agrees Spotlight is a phenomenal way to search, and has revolutionized the way we organize our computers — now that we don't have to. Kidding aside, there are some people who don't like Spotlight. It takes up space on your drive, it's constantly cataloging metadata (which can run your batteries down), and it could be a security issue in certain instances. Spotless is an easy-to-use program that lets you turn off and on the spotlight process, on a volume-by-volume basis. You can delete the metadata store, or even force a re-index. MoRU, on the other hand, is for those who don't like Spotlight for its *lack* of interface. They like the speedy and all-over search but miss the control over the file types and locations that the Find functions of older Mac OS system versions provided. MoRU uses Spotlight metadata, but gives you complete control over your searching (see Figure 20.5). Find MoRU at `www.windstormsoftware.com` and Spotless at `www.fixamacsoftware.com`.

FIGURE 20.5

MoRU is Spotlight your way, with infinitely more control over the way you search.

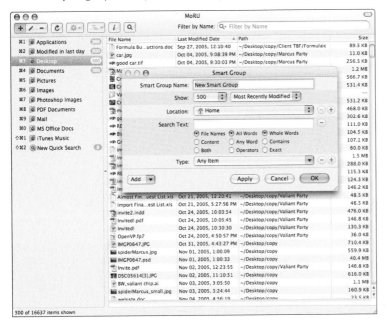

NetNewsWire and Vienna

NetNewsWire by Ranchero Software, shown in Figure 20.6, is a full-featured RSS newsfeed reader. If there are Web sites that you frequent and they get updated throughout the day, having to keep going back to check can be inconvenient. Many Web sites have implemented a technology called RDF Site Summary (RSS), which allows an online publisher to create a "feed" which a client can subscribe to. NetNewsWire polls the Web sites you subscribe to as often as every 30 minutes. It then updates its database with the latest headlines. Double-clicking a headline launches your default browser right to the headline page of the Web site. It contains presets for several other news sites, including the most-known front-page news outlets (the BBC, *Wired* magazine, and so on), tech havens (Slashdot, the Register, and CNET), lots of Macintosh news sites (MacNN, MacSlash, and MacCentral), and a whole host of personal blogs. Safari has incorporated this technology, but NetNewsWire can be a more powerful program, and the pro version allows you to update your blog as well. You can find more information about NetNewsWire at `www.newsgator.com/Individuals/NetNewsWire/`. Vienna is a Freeware RSS newsfeed reader but don't let the "free" fool you, it's a great application that does RSS well and CHEAP. Download it at `www.open-community.co.uk/vienna2.php`.

FIGURE 20.6

Ranchero Software's NetNewsWire is a great application for keeping up to date with the Web sites you visit regularly. It comes with preconfigured feeds you can subscribe to, as well as those you input on your own.

Neo Office/Open Office

One of the great pieces of software to come out of the open source movement is the office suite Open Office. Fully compatible with Microsoft Office documents, it's completely free, and cross platform. Unfortunately on the Macintosh, it runs in X11, which is the Unix windowing system. Thus, it's not quite as Mac-friendly as most of the applications Macintosh users interact with. Neo Office, on the other hand, is a fully native port of Open Office. It uses the Open Office source code to leverage all of the advantages, but wraps it in a fully Macintosh-integrated application suite. It's definitely worth checking out, if you need a word processor and want to save three hundred dollars or so. Open Office can be found at `www.openoffice.org`, and Neo Office can be found at `www.neooffice.com`.

Renicer

Mac OS 9 was based on *cooperative multitasking;* the front-most running process decided how much of the CPU power it wanted to give up. In preemptive multitasking, the OS has a hand, through the task scheduler, in the divvying up of the clock cycles, and can *preempt* another process if it decides the other process is more needy of the CPU. Generally, the OS does a good job of making sure every process has what it needs. Renicer shows you all the processes currently running and gives you the ability to modify their priority, using the Unix command renice. This is especially useful when you're rendering something that is CPU-intensive in the background, and you want to give it priority over checking your mail. Download Renicer at `www.northernsoftworks.com/renicer.html`.

Pseudo

Pseudo is an application that allows you to launch other applications as root. (See Chapters 21 and 23 for more information on the root user.)

This can be useful for mucking about where you're not supposed to because you'll have access to all the files and folders on the computer. On the flip side, care is of the essence when using this application, because modifying something that shouldn't have been modified, and completely confounding the operating system, is very easy to do. Pseudo was written by the same author as BrickHouse, Brian Hill, and you can find out more about this application at `http://personalpages.tds.net/~brian_hill`.

QuickImageCM

QuickImageCM (see Figure 20.7) is perhaps one of the coolest timesavers this side of Kraft Minute Rice. As its name suggests, QuickImage is a really quick way to preview images. Because it's a contextual menu, all you have to do is either Control+click or right-click an image and it opens in its own window. Because no application is launched, the preview is almost instantaneous—on snappy Macs at least. The little toolbar along the top of the window has some nice menu options. Although it breaks with Apple's interface guidelines, that's forgivable based on how dang convenient the program is. Download and find more information about QuickImage at `www.pixture.com/software/macosx.php`. (There you'll also find a number of other cool applications by the author.)

FIGURE 20.7

Seeing the image is a lot easier when it's not a tiny preview in the paned view of the Finder. Using QuickImageCM from the Finder is easy and fast.

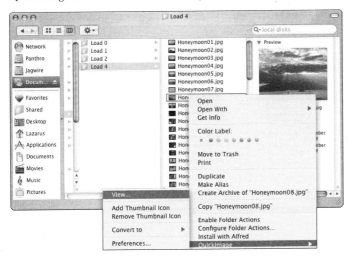

QuicKeys X2

A venerable program, QuicKeys has been around for ages, helping people bring macros into their daily lives. QuicKeys has evolved over the years into a very full-featured macro building/scripting package. You can time-delay, schedule, script, and assign just about any OS action to a button. In essence, it's a very powerful tool (much like AppleScript) that brings the world of automation to the consumer level. Using the intuitive interface, you can compress multistep tasks into shortcuts that comprise one keystroke. If you don't know anything about creating macros, QuicKeys X2 can record your actions and play them back. The Clips Shortcuts is useful for storing frequently used media for use later at the touch of a key. Use Typing Shortcuts to automate the entry of commonly used text. Menu Action Shortcuts let you select menu items via the keyboard that do not normally have key equivalents. Discover what QuicKeys has to offer at www.cesoft.com.

Salling Clicker

Salling Clicker is one of the coolest little preference panes in terms of sheer show-off factor. Clicker interfaces with a Bluetooth phone or Palm Pilot (currently only Sony Ericsson phones are supported) and allows you to control your Macintosh wirelessly. If you've got a keynote presentation to give, fire up Salling Clicker, and while you're walking around the room, you'll be able to control the slideshow without any other tools but your phone. It's extensible — you can set it to engage custom AppleScripts at the push of a button. Even more impressive is the ability to set iChat's status depending on whether your phone is in range. (If you walk away with the phone, iChat changes your status to away.) Find out more about Salling Clicker at www.salling.com. A competing freeware product is Romeo by Arboreal (http://irowan.com/arboreal).

SharePoints

One of the limitations of Mac OS X, as compared to both Mac OS 9 and Mac OS X Server, is that you don't have complete control over the sharepoints you want to make available to the rest of your network. The only folder you can share is the /Users/Public folder. SharePoints is a free preference pane that restores your ability to have complete control over what folders are shared across the network. Any folder on your hard drive can be shared via Apple Filing Protocol (for Macs) or SMB (for PCs). You're even able to create users and groups again. This program does not get around Mac OS X client's ability to have more than 10 concurrent Apple File Sharing users connected at the same time. (This limitation is lifted by purchasing the unlimited version of the server product.) SharePoints is created by HornWare and can be found at www.hornware.com.

SideTrack

Windows laptop users have had the wonderful ability to use certain areas of their trackpads to do more than just control the mouse. Apple used the same Synaptics trackpads for many years, but it had never enabled these extra abilities until recently. The last revision of the G4 PowerBooks and all MacBook and MacBook Pro's have a different, Apple-designed trackpad which has a hardware-enabled scrolling feature, but older PowerBooks were out of luck until SideTrack. SideTrack is an alternative trackpad driver that enables you to use parts of the trackpad to scroll both horizontally and vertically. In addition, you can map corner taps to different mouse buttons or virtual keystrokes. See www.ragingmenace.com for more information.

Snapz Pro X 2

Although you can use the built-in screenshot functionality of the Mac OS (⌘+Shift+3 for the whole screen, or ⌘+Shift+4 to select an area of the screen), Snapz Pro X 2 adds considerably to your ability to take a snapshot of your screen. Snapz Pro X 2 allows you to save your screenshots in many formats (rather than just the PDF of the Mac OS). It also allows you to take QuickTime Movie snapshots of a process. The new Fatbits feature allows you to zoom in on images as you create them. There is also a delayed-execution feature, so you can have the screenshot taken in the middle of an event that you normally wouldn't be able to capture. See more at www.ambrosiasw.com.

StuffIt (Standard/Deluxe)

StuffIt Expander ships with Mac OS X, but to actually create StuffIt archives, you need either StuffIt Standard or StuffIt Deluxe. StuffIt Standard is a full package that takes over where Expander leaves off. It provides droplet programs, which allow you to create ZIP, tar, and StuffIt archives by dropping anything you want onto them. Aladdin has created an even more powerful interface in StuffIt Deluxe. Among its more impressive features, StuffIt Deluxe integrates directly into the Finder, allowing you to append a .sit to the end of a document or folder name, and have that folder archived. This function works for all supported archive formats, and also in reverse. StuffIt Standard and Deluxe retail for $49.95 and $79.99, respectively. Find them online at www.aladdinsys.com.

SubEthaEdit

SubEthaEdit is one of the many applications that have sprung up around Apple's zero-config networking technology, Rendezvous. SubEthaEdit is a full-featured (but not bloated) text editor that lets users on a network collaborate on documents with almost no configuration of the software. You share a document, and then other people on your network who have SubEthaEdit installed can see the documents you're working on in SubEthaEdit with zero configurations using Bonjour.

You can even share documents over the Internet with other people using SubEthaEdit across the country. SubEthaEdit uses Safari's Web core engine to display HTML and is a great collaborative tool for programmers. For more information, go to www.codingmonkeys.de.

Timbuktu/Apple Remote Desktop/VNC

Netopia's Timbuktu is *the* remote control application for the Macintosh. It's been around for years and its refinement definitely shows. One of its greatest features is that it's cross-platform, so that you can control a Windows PC from a Mac and vice versa. It has a nice built-in user database where you can set up a number of different users with different privileges, and a very fast file transfer tool. Check it out at www.netopia.com.

Apple has its own remote control application called, of all things, Apple Remote Desktop (ARD). The ARD server is built into Mac OS 10.5 and is great for managing a computer lab or classroom because it has more administration features than Timbuktu. You can remotely launch applications and install packages (to multiple computers at once). The newest version of ARD is cross-platform—it can control PCs using the VNC protocol (see the following paragraph) or Windows machines running VNC. You know where to go: `www.apple.com`.

If you're interested in remote control on the cheap, look at AT&T's Virtual Network Computing (VNC). VNC is bare-bones, but it's completely free and has been ported to a number of different operating systems. Find it at `www.realvnc.com`. It's high on compatibility, but low on speed because it essentially transmits snapshots of the screen a few times a second. Because VNC is open-source software, you'll also find several implementations if you search on `www.version tracker.com` for VNC — "Chicken of the VNC" scores points for stupid name of the century.

TinkerTool/OnyX

With TinkerTool, you can activate hidden options of Mac OS X. You can control font smoothing, select default fonts used in Cocoa applications, activate transparent Terminal windows, display the Trash on the desktop, and more. None of these options requires typing Unix commands. Instead, you use familiar Aqua controls such as check boxes and pop-up menus, as you can see in Figure 20.8. TinkerTool is free software from Marcel Bresink Software-Systeme and can be downloaded from `www.bresink.com/osx/TinkerTool.html`. A competing program, OnyX, is also available freely at `www.titanium.free.fr/pgs2/english/onyx.html`.

FIGURE 20.8

TinkerTool provides settings for a host of hidden Mac OS X options.

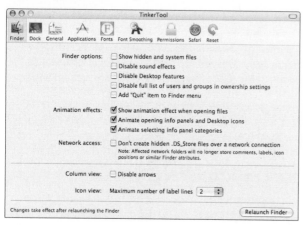

Toast Titanium 8/Burn

Mac OS X's Disk Burner and Disk Utility are great for the beginner in terms of ease of use, but for those who really want control over their CD/DVD burning, Roxio Toast is the way to go. With support for HFS+, Hybrid, ISO9660, VCD, and multisession discs, Toast lets you create discs easily and often supports more CD-RW features than the Mac OS. One of the new features of version 6 lets you burn a CD-R or DVD-R directly from a FireWire-enabled video camera. If you take a few extra minutes, Toast even provides you with the tools to throw some titles in right before you burn it. The coolest new feature has to be ToastAnywhere, which lets you burn to a CD-RW drive attached to a different computer on your network that is also running Toast (it uses Rendezvous). Titanium 8 is now shipping with a Macintosh version of TiVo to Go, so you can take your DVRed video with you. To find out how well it integrates with iMovie and your video on the go, visit `www.roxio.com/toast`.

A free alternative to Toast, without all the bells and whistles, is the open-source program aptly titled Burn. It allows you to burn every format that Toast does, for free. It's not as flashy, and it doesn't have any of the video conversion or DVD from video streams, but it's one of the most reliable media burners out there. Visit `http://burn-osx.sourceforge.net/`.

Transmit/Fetch/Cyberduck

Transmit, by Panic software, is a full-featured, clean FTP program. The first thing you'll notice about Transmit is that it has a familiar-looking interface, with some well-executed iconography. Transmit supports both the standard FTP protocol, and the more secure SFTP. The newest version of Transmit now supports resumable file transfers and is even easier to use. You can find Transmit at `www.panic.com`.

The venerable Fetch is showing its age in Mac OS X, but it's still a good, easy-to-use FTP client. Go to `www.fetchsoftworks.com`.

Cyberduck is a completely free, open-sourced FTP client. It's not the prettiest in the world, but it gets the job done and the price is right. See it at `http://cyberduck.ch/`.

USB Overdrive X

Have you ever seen a mouse, trackball, joystick, or gamepad you just *had* to have, but there were no Mac drivers for it? Enter USB Overdrive, a truly universal, Universal Serial Bus (USB) driver for Mac OS X. USB Overdrive can handle all sorts of wheels, switches, and extra buttons, and it'll even allow you to customize the function of each on an application-by-application basis. It supports scrolling (even if you don't have a wheel-mouse!), keyboard commands, and other more complicated functions with mere mouse clicks. You can find it at `www.usboverdrive.com`.

VideoLAN Client/MPlayer/Flip4Mac Player

VideoLAN Client (VLC) is a cross-platform, free media player that can handle most video formats, including QuickTime, MPEG (1, 2, and 4), DivX, and Windows Media files. The VideoLAN project as a whole is a multimedia package designed to support the streaming and playing of video along a network across multiple platforms. VLC is released under the GPL and is free software. You can find more information about the project at `www.videolan.org`. A competing product, MPlayer, is also open source. The differences seem mostly cosmetic, but some people swear by one over the other. MPlayer can be found here: `http://mplayerosx.sourceforge.net/`.

Now that Microsoft has stopped shipping Windows Media Player for the Macintosh, Flip4Mac has stepped in and provided an alternative. Essentially a plug-in for QuickTime Player that enables the decoding of WMV files, the basic version is free. There are some more expensive versions which allow you to manipulate the video if you need to convert file formats or do basic editing as well. Find it at www.flip4mac.com.

Webmin

A Web-based tool for configuration of Unix-based services, Webmin has been ported to many operating systems. Using the Web server built into Mac OS X, Webmin provides a graphical interface that helps you administer the Unix underpinnings of Mac OS X, giving you access to file sharing, DNS, user accounts, and more. Unlike a standard Mac OS X application, you access Webmin's interface by using a standard Web browser, and pointing it back toward your own machine. Webmin is freeware and is released under the open-source BSD license. More information and downloads can be found at www.webmin.com.

Summary

In this chapter, you've been introduced to a few of the shareware, freeware, and commercial programs available for Mac OS X. You've learned about some great resources for finding software that fills your needs. You should now know some of the differences among shareware, freeware, and commercial software. Although you're encouraged to distribute copies of most shareware and freeware (a sort of grassroots advertising campaign, if you will), authors generally retain copyrights to their software. Shareware authors ask that you send payment for products that you decide to keep, but freeware is free software.

Although most of the utilities we've looked at are small programs designed to fulfill specific tasks, there are quite a few well-polished pieces of software that you'd be hard-pressed to tell weren't commercial offerings — Cocktail, Cyberduck GraphicConverter, Transmit, VLC, to name just a few. As the Internet has managed to provide a perfect, I-need-it-now software delivery model, and as commercial software houses are beginning to offer electronic-only downloads, the line between commercial software and shareware is blurring.

Chapter 21

Maintaining Mac OS X

I n this chapter, you find out about the structure of the Mac OS X system architecture and some basic system maintenance, as well as discover the importance of a good backup.

Exploring the Mac OS X Library Folders

The core of Mac OS X hangs out in the System folder. You can look in the System folder hierarchy, but touching the files contained inside is generally unwise, a fact that is evidenced by taking a look at the permissions of the folders contained therein. This file hierarchy belongs to the system, and the only visible item is a Library folder. This folder is one of three Library folders you'll be introduced to, but also the one that we discuss the least because its contents are beyond the scope of this book. It hosts a number of important files and is where the code and resources required for core Mac OS X functionality reside. Make changes to this folder at your own risk.

The second Library folder, and perhaps the most easily located one, is found at the top level of your system disk. This folder is modifiable by those users with administrator access, and it's where such a user would place items in order to make their functionality accessible to all users. It holds the fonts, sounds, screen savers, and so on that are available to all of the accounts on your computer. Resources required by installed applications, as well as drivers for peripheral devices, such as printers, are usually found here.

Yet another Library folder can be found in each user's home folder. This one stores personal settings, fonts, sounds, and other configuration objects for each user and can only be accessed by the corresponding user or someone with "root" access. Application support files can be stored here as well as in the Library folder, but these items will be available only to the specific user whose Library folder it is.

Now that you have some idea of the Library folder, you should understand the concept of search paths. Simply stated, a *search path* is a hierarchically ordered acquisition of system resources. This hierarchy stems from Mac OS X's security model. In general, most search paths work their way from user-specific resources to system-wide resources. The system first checks the local user Library (~/Library) for a resource such as a Preference pane, then checks the main Library (/Library), and then checks the System Library (/System/Library).

Managing the main Library folder

The main Library folder (/Library) is the repository of all the files required to make your Mac OS X user experience work. This folder is the closest thing you can find to the System Folder of Mac OS 9 or the Windows directory on a PC. It contains all the files that support the applications installed in the Applications folder (/Applications) as well as any preference settings that apply to the Mac as a whole. The following is not a complete list of the folders found within the main Library folder, but rather of ones that you have the greatest chance of interacting with.

- **Address Book Plug-Ins:** This folder is not populated by default but can be used by a third party.

- **Application Support:** Contains shared libraries used by installed applications, such as Palm HotSync libraries, Adobe application support files, and Shockwave libraries. Applications sometimes store files here so that other applications can share capabilities.

- **Audio:** A repository for sounds used system-wide and sound-related plug-ins. If you want to make an alert sound available, save it as an AIFF sound and put it in the Alerts folder of the Sounds folder in this Audio folder (/Library/Audio/Sounds/Alerts).

- **Caches:** Holds temporary and permanent cache files used by applications.

- **CFM Support:** Carbon applications store some plug-ins and application-specific support files here.

- **ColorSync:** Holds the ColorSync profiles for a wide variety of devices and monitors in the Profiles subfolder and support AppleScripts in the Scripts subfolder. You can save some space by removing profiles for devices you don't have.

- **Contextual Menu Items:** Where you can place contextual menu items, such as QuickImageCM, that third parties have developed to extend the operating system.

- **Desktop Pictures:** A collection of the JPEG files available for use as a background picture for the desktop. Items placed in this folder are available to all users. Each user can set a desktop picture by using the Desktop pane of System Preferences.

- **Documentation:** Holds user manuals, help files, and copyright information for installed applications and services.

- **Fonts:** Contains the various font files that are not required by the System but that are available to all users of your Mac. As discussed in Chapter 12, Mac OS X supports a wide range of font formats. The Fonts folder (`/Library/Fonts`) is where you can install fonts you want all users to be able to access, and if there are fonts in here that you don't want to use, you can remove them. The best way to remove and add fonts, however, is to use Font Book.

- **Frameworks:** Frameworks are another kind of shared library that is *dynamic* (only loaded into memory when being used). Frameworks are similar to System Extensions in OS 9.

- **Image Capture:** Contains a Scripts folder in which the AppleScripts that perform the Image Capture application's hot-plug actions (see Chapter 22) reside.

- **Internet Plug-Ins:** Holds the plug-ins that add functionality to Web browsers and other Internet applications. Examples include the QuickTime plug-in, which allows you to watch QuickTime movies in your Web browser.

- **Java:** Contains, by default, an alias to the Java support files and libraries in the Library folder hierarchy of the System folder (`/System/Library`). It also contains Java libraries installed for use by various Java applications.

- **Keyboard Layouts:** Where keyboard layouts (analogous to keyboard scripts under OS 9) can be stored. Detailed information can be found in Apple Technical Note TN2056 (`http://developer.apple.com/technotes/tn2002/tn2056.html`).

- **Logs:** Holds the log histories for applications that send debug and status information to the system console.

- **Modem Scripts:** A collection of files describing the characteristics and capabilities of a wide variety of modems. You can feel free to remove the files for modems you don't have. If you acquire a new modem, you might have to reinstall its modem script into this folder.

- **Perl:** Where the scripting language Perl is installed by default on OS X.

- **Preference Panes:** Where third-party System Preference panes are stored so that all users can access them. This folder is not created by a default install; an installer or system administrator can create this folder to make extra functionality accessible.

- **Preferences:** Holds the .plist (property list) files describing preference and state settings for system-wide services. For example, `com.apple.loginwindow.plist` contains the user number (as maintained in NetInfo) for the last user to log into Mac OS X, whether or not that user is currently logged in; and `com.apple.PowerManagement.plist` contains the settings made for Energy Saver in System Preferences.

- **Printers:** Contains the printer drivers and PPD files used by Print Center in recognizing, configuring, and enabling your printers. (For more information on printers, see Chapter 16.)

- **QuickTime:** Where additional codecs and other QuickTime support files should be installed. For example, Roxio Toast includes a QuickTime codec to convert to VCD MPEG (VideoCD-ready MPEG-1) format, and that file is installed here.

- **Receipts:** Contains files left by the Installer application describing the changes to your Mac OS X installation after a package has been installed.

- **Screen Savers:** A folder you can fill with screen-saver modules to be available to all users of your Mac via the Screen Saver pane of Systems Preferences.

- **Scripts:** Contains folders of AppleScript scripts that are available to all users of your computer. The scripts in this folder appear in Script Runner's pop-up menu and in the menu of the Script Menu icon, as described in Chapter 22.

- **User Pictures:** Contains folders of small pictures suitable for assigning to user accounts. Each user account can have a picture that appears in the login window's list of user accounts. Pictures are assigned to user accounts in the Users pane of System Preferences.

- **WebServer:** Holds the Common Gateway Interface (CGI) scripts that enable add-on Web server functions, such as forms submittal, for Mac OS X Web Sharing. (Turn on Web Sharing in the Sharing pane of Systems Preferences.) The sub-folder titled Documents also contains the documentation for Apache, the software that turns your Mac into a Web server.

Exploring your personal Library folder

In your home folder, you see another folder titled Library. Many of the subfolders in this folder have the same names as those discussed earlier in this chapter (see "Managing the main Library folder"). When you encounter a folder with the same name, it has the same functionality, except that it contains items specific to *your* use of the Mac rather than items for all users. As an example, you install fonts for your personal use in the Fonts folder of the Library folder in your home folder (path ~/Library/Fonts) if you aren't making them available to other users of the Mac. Similarly, alert sounds or screen savers that aren't shared would go in a folder of your personal Library folder.

Some of the other folders you may see in your personal Library folder include:

- **Application Support:** Contains shared libraries used by applications you installed when not acting as an administrator. For example, the folder for information from your Address Book was located in the Library as Addresses, but in Mac 10.2, the Addresses folder has moved to inside the Application Support folder.

- **Assistants:** Contains files used by various Assistants. For example, if you were unable to connect during your initial setup to register Mac OS X, a file named SendRegistration.setup (a .plist file) is saved here with your registration information and preferences.

- **Audio:** Sounds and plug-ins you install when not acting as an administrator.

- **ColorPickers:** Where you find additional ColorPickers to augment the collection Apple provides.

- **Documentation:** Holds user manuals, help files, and copyright information for installed applications and services that you have installed. Like the other files associated with applications installed by you when not acting as an administrator, these are not accessible to other users on the system.

- **Favorites:** Where your Favorites are stored. This may have seemed like a great idea to Apple some time ago, but it's a pretty useless folder. Apple's idea was for you to throw some aliases in there and add it to your sidebar. But you could do that with any folder. At this point, it seems that its only point is to be a repository for your saved servers.

- **FontCollections:** Where your choices for font collections (see Chapter 15) are cached.

- **Frameworks:** Where the support frameworks (shared program libraries) for personal applications are stored.

- **Internet Search Sites:** Used to contain folders for each of your Sherlock channels, each containing the search-site plug-in files for that channel. See Chapter 6 for more about Sherlock and its channels. You might not see this folder until you've performed at least one Internet search in Sherlock. Sherlock doesn't exist in OSX as of 10.5, so you will see this folder only in previous versions of OS X.

- **Keyboard Layouts** Contains any custom keyboard layouts you've installed.

- **Keychains:** Holds your Keychain files (see Chapter 6 for more information about the Keychain).

- **Mail:** Your personal mail folder. The Mail application (see Chapter 6) keeps its databases and other files here.

- **Preferences:** Your personal preferences folder. Where applications store their preferences independently of other users, so that each user can customize the system and his or her applications as desired. Some system-type preferences are kept here, so that each individual user can have a customized experience. However, certain settings like network and startup disk attributes are kept globally.

- **Recent Servers:** Contains the URL files to the servers that you've recently used. These are the servers that show up under Recent Servers in the Connect to Server dialog box's pop-up menu.

- **Scripts:** The repository for your personal AppleScripts, if you have any.

- **Stickies Database:** Although not a folder, the Stickies database is found in your personal Library folder.

Depending upon what other applications you've installed or run, other folders may be found in your personal Library folder, such as OmniWeb, if you've installed that Web browser.

> **TIP** You may find at times that an application is not functioning normally. It may not open correctly, or it may just be acting strangely. One of the first actions to take is to go to the `~/Library/Preferences` folder, and move any items that look like they pertain to the misbehaving application to the desktop. The application will re-create a preference file according to its default preferences. All your changes to its settings (such as user names, save locations, or other customizations) will be lost, but the application may be restored to its normally functional state. If the application is still acting strangely, place the removed preferences back where you found them, and try some of the other suggestions found later in this chapter. Most applications follow Apple's preference-naming convention and look something like `com.author.applicationname.plist`, though some create their own folders or use the software maker's name instead of the application name. Try to look for the application name in the filename, and if you can't find it, look for the software company's name instead.

One User, Multiple Accounts

Always have at least two—yes, two—user accounts on any machine. Make sure that they are both administrators, especially if there are no other users on the machine.

An important troubleshooting step when things go strange with Mac OS X is to log in as a different user, and see if the problem still occurs. If it doesn't, you know that the problem lies only with the first user and is not a system-wide issue.

You may someday (we hope you never do) wake up to find that your user account will not let you log in. It tries to let you in, but you get a blue screen, or perhaps the spinning beach ball of death. If you have only one user, trying to clean up the mess won't be very fun, but if you have another user, you can log in and try cleaning out the broken user's Library (path ~/Library) folder to revive the user. (You can also try restarting from a second hard drive or a CD, but it's not always convenient to carry extra disks around with you.)

A second account can also be useful for separating processes out, using Multiple Users to log two accounts in at the same time and run different sets of programs at the same time. This allows you to minimize screen clutter and concentrate on what you're doing. Be aware that some programs only allow you to open up one instance at a time, such as iTunes. Also, iChat will change your status to offline, so that you cannot have multiple accounts logged into iChat at the same time.

Practicing Good Housekeeping

As with any disk-based operating system, debris accumulates and storage space becomes fragmented over time. A few basic maintenance operations, performed on a regular basis, provide improved performance and stability.

The most critical of these is to *back up your data*. We cannot stress enough how important a regular backup routine can be — the first time you accidentally delete or overwrite some file(s) you need, you'll be very glad to have a backup from which to restore them. Data recovery is one of the most expensive propositions a company or individual can face. In this case, an ounce of prevention is *definitely* worth a pound of cure.

Backups

A computer user who doesn't make backups is like a parachutist who doesn't check his equipment before jumping — he may be lucky for a while, but his luck runs out eventually, usually at a really inopportune time. It's not a matter of *if* you will encounter a problem with one of your files; it's merely a matter of *when*.

Software and media

At one time, personal computer users could back up all their files on diskettes — in fact, the first IBM PCs and the first Macs didn't even have hard disks, and everything was kept on floppies. Now that multiple gigabytes are required merely for the Mac OS X system, backing up to floppy (or even zip disk) is no longer practical or even possible. Even the use of CD and DVD discs is becoming impractical as a general backup medium when you take into consideration the files generated by programs like iMovie. Perhaps more astonishing, the use of tape drives is becoming less of a choice even for the enterprise. Hard Drives are quickly becoming both large and cheap enough to use in a backup strategy that makes sense. Long a leading purveyor of backup software, EMC Dantz (formerly Dantz Development, www.dantz.com) produces Mac OS X versions of its Retrospect backup for several markets, from the casual desktop user to the enterprise. Apple provides Backup software as part of its .Mac package. Backup (www.mac.com) allows you to automate backup to CD and DVD, as well as to your .Mac storage space. Roxio Toast 8 (www.roxio.com) has included Déjà Vu, a Preference pane that provides unattended backup to CDs and DVDs through Toast. Many purpose-built backup drives, such as the Maxtor One Touch line, as well as external drives from the major players ship with tools that let you script backup operations (www.lacie.com, www.seagate.com). There are a number of different backup programs, of which the previously mentioned ones are but a small selection. Explore the Web sites indicated in Chapter 20, and you can find a package that suits your needs.

Regardless of the hardware and software you choose, it can't be repeated enough that you should perform backups regularly and often. A month-old copy of your magnum opus won't be of much use if you've been updating it steadily over the past few weeks, all those changes and additions are lost, and the deadline is tomorrow.

Time Machine

All of the previous having been said, one of the most highly anticipated features of Mac OS 10.5 Leopard is named Time Machine. Apple has finally included an automated backup program with one of their operating systems. And what a backup system it is; designed by Apple to be user friendly as well as reliable, it succeeds in both the ease-of-use as well as the flashy-eye-candy departments. The main requirement of Time Machine is that you have at least a second hard drive available for it to store its data on. You can use a second partition, but you'll get scolded (and it's not a good idea anyway); you can use a network volume. Originally Apple had stated that you would have to use a volume that wasn't "bootable," but this doesn't appear to be the case. A folder named "Backups.backupdb" will be created on the volume that you choose to back up to. Perhaps the easiest way of ensuring you have a place to back up to is just to purchase an external drive that can be plugged in via USB or FireWire. Just be sure that your machine supports USB 2.0 if you are going to be using a USB-connected external drive, otherwise your backups will proceed at a snail's pace (USB 1.0 tops out at 12 Mbps, USB 2.0 is 480 Mbps, and FireWire comes in 400 Mbps and 800 Mbps flavors). If you have a tower model, you can also install an internal drive fairly easily. The advantage to an internal drive is that it will always be there and available, as well as being marginally faster; the disadvantage is that you cannot easily take it with you for offsite backups. If you are backing up to a network volume, you may want to ensure you have a gigabit switch, which also makes your backups proceed quickly. Also, if you are using a network share point, note that backups are going to be considerably slower if the network share point is not on your local network (that is, if you are mounting it over the Internet or through a VPN tunnel).

Time Machine keeps getting better and better. Since its announcement, it's gained some seriously useful features that put it ever above other utilities. Boasting an automatic stop and resume functionality, Time Machine will just stop the backup where it is, and then resume where it was as soon as the volume comes online again. Handy if you're backing up over the Internet, or have a laptop you need to take with you *right now*. Like most backup systems, you can back up everything, but you can also exclude items that aren't important, like the video e-card your mom sent you last Valentines day.

Sometimes your machine blows up so spectacularly, you hardly have a machine at all. No worries, just plug your Time Machine backup drive into another computer and you're browsing and restoring in seconds. Voila, you're back in business. Hand in hand with this is support for migration assistant. While you're browsing your blown up computer's backup, go ahead and click a button, and your entire user is back online, on a new computer, right where you were when your computer blew up on you.

Configuring Time Machine for backups

In accordance with its name, Time Machine aims to give you the ability to "turn back time" with regards to your documents and folders. Setup is simple. Plug in a blank disk, and Time Machine will ask if you want to use that drive as a backup. But if you said no, you can always go to the System Preferences application, go to the Time Machine preference pane and slide the slider to On (see Figure 21.1) In the upper right-hand side of the preference pane, click the Change Disk button; a dialog sheet will come down showing you a list of drives. Choose the volume you want to use as a storage device (see Figure 21.2). You will be able to choose what drives to backup or exclude. Other than that, it's pretty automatic. Time Machine keeps hourly backups for 24 hours, daily backups for the past month, and weekly backups until the disk is full.

FIGURE 21.1

The main window for Time Machine, located in System Preferences, where you can turn backup on, and configure what to backup, when and where

FIGURE 21.2

Click Choose in the main screen and a sheet appears, enabling you to choose the location of your backup.

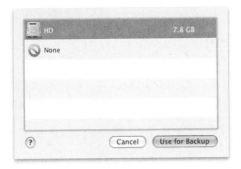

Using Time Machine to view your history

Launch the Time Machine application from within the Applications folder on your hard drive. Your screen shifts up and a starry night scene with a nebula appears in the background (see Figure 21.3). On the right you'll see a timeline. Note the dates that are positioned along the left side of the time-line. As you mouse over the date hatch marks, notice that some are transparent looking, and others are filled with light gray. The gray ones have backed-up data, and the transparent ones are empty. You can navigate to a specific date by using this timeline, or just go back in time using the arrows on the bottom left of the timeline. You will see a view of the Finder back through time as changes have been made and backed up. By clicking folders in the Finder window you can search for the particular files you need to recover. Select the file or folder you need by clicking it once, and then click the Restore button on the bottom right of the screen to get your files back. It's that easy. If you just want to see when a particular file was changed, select the file, and then on the bottom left side of the screen choose Only Show Changes. This restricts the view to the dates that only have changes for the file you've selected. To exit Time Machine, click Cancel in the lower left corner.

FIGURE 21.3

The main Time Machine viewer, where you view the results of your backup process

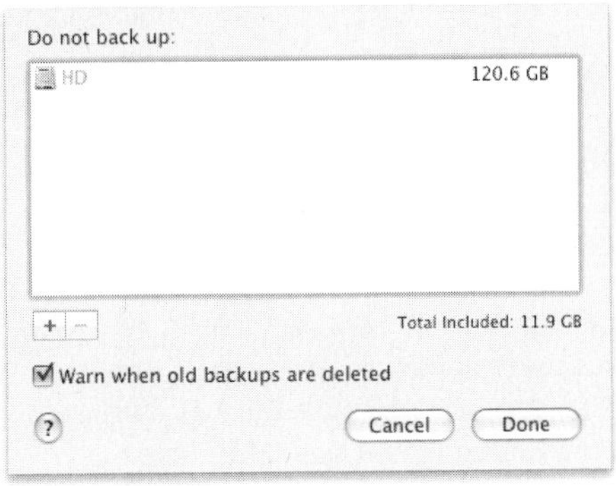

Do not back up:

HD	120.6 GB

Total Included: 11.9 GB

☑ Warn when old backups are deleted

Cancel   Done

Backup rotation

Any useful backup strategy includes regular rotation of your media and periodic archiving of your backups. Writing repeatedly to the same media can frequently be problematic — not only does media degrade under frequent use, but you could easily be overwriting a good copy of a file with a corrupted copy.

If you're backing up data that is of the utmost importance to you or your employer, you'll want to make your plan as fail-safe as possible. Because there is no such thing as a single completely fool-proof solution, having multiple solutions in place, where each has a minimal chance of failure, is best. It is far better to have many backups that you can't trust, than only one that you *think* you can trust. Having quite a few sets of backup media is only one facet of a good overall plan to secure your data. When the data is irreplaceable, there's no such thing as too many backups. Some facets of a good backup are shown in the following sections; use them as a starting guide.

Backing up important data daily is best. You can reuse media for a while, but it is recommended that you archive and replace your media every so often to ensure you've got a good copy. This is especially true when backing up to magnetic media (such as a hard drive, floppy, or tape). Backing up your data to a disk that doesn't actually work is a complete waste of time.

A good reason for using multiple tapes or disks is to be able to keep a copy of your data *somewhere else*. If you're a business owner, think about what would happen to your company if you walked in one morning and the building had fallen down or flooded. Would you be able to continue without any of your files? If you had a copy at home, even if it was a week old, you could turn around, and get things back up in a matter of hours or days, instead of declaring bankruptcy.

You can use incremental backups for daily backups, but creating a full backup to brand new media is best for archival purposes. Think about how far back you want your archive to reach. At a certain point, you can reuse some of your archival media because it doesn't get as much wear as daily media.

If you receive a virus or notice disk corruption at some point, you have a number of backups to choose from, including backups that are one day old, three days old, a week old, two weeks old, and so on. If you find corruption on Thursday, you have Wednesday's backup, Tuesday's backup, Monday's backup, and the previous Friday's archive on top of any previous weeks' archives you've kept. If your data is less mission-critical, you can scale things back to every other day, and possibly only once a week.

For personal backup, the scheme can be a little less arduous depending on the number of files you generate and work on daily. We still recommend that you back up once or twice a week, rotating between at least two different disks or tapes, and archiving your data every month or so, depending on the sensitivity of the data. Entering two weeks' worth of Quicken checkbook data is a time-consuming task that you probably didn't enjoy much the first time around.

Generally, you don't need to back up applications and system software because these items are easily reinstalled and replaceable. However, backing up your user's home folders is a good idea because these folders usually contain application preferences, e-mail storage, a Stickies database, Internet bookmarks, and user documents. A backup of the Classic Preferences folder is good to have in the event of a disk crash (`/System Folder/Preferences`). You should also know where your applications keep their data, so you can be sure that you're backing up what you think you're backing up. You may want an archive of application updates and software downloaded from the Internet, just so you can get to those patches and updates quickly if you need to reinstall. Archive data periodically and keep at least two different backup tapes or disks active at once for some measure of redundancy.

Maintaining the file system

Although Mac OS X can read and write a wide variety of disk formats, it (at least currently) can only start up from two different formats: Mac OS Extended (also known as HFS Plus or HFS+ for *hierarchical file system plus*) and UFS (Unix File System, sometimes called ffs for *fast file system*). Apple recommends the use of the Mac OS Extended format, and so do we. The Classic application environment will not operate from a UFS-formatted disk. This has become somewhat of a moot point because Apple's recent crop of machines are Intel based, don't support Classic, and 10.5 doesn't include it either. Most Carbon applications perform better in the Mac OS Extended format, because the file system doesn't have to translate the files to emulate the multiform files to which many Mac applications are accustomed. It is recommended that you use the HFS+(Journaled) format, which is the default scheme from 10.4 onward.

Mac OS X comes with a basic disk diagnostic and disk-directory repair tool, Disk Utility, which is covered in depth in Chapter 6. Other vendors of well-regarded disk utilities include Micromat with Drive 10 and TechTool Pro (www.micromat.com), Alsoft with DiskWarrior (www.alsoft.com), and Symantec with Norton Utilities and Norton SystemWorks (SystemWorks is a bundle of Utilities and AntiVirus; www.symantec.com). A relative newcomer to the field is Prosoft Engineering with Drive Genius (www.prosoftengineering.com). Unfortunately Norton Utilities and SystemWorks were both dropped by Symantec a few years ago, so if you have an older copy, do not use them past Mac OS X version 10.2. All of these tools have assorted functions they can deploy, with the exception of Alsoft's DiskWarrior. DiskWarrior is fairly purpose-built to repair directory damage, and it does its job very well. DiskWarrior is one of the most trusted disk repair tools in the industry. TechTool Pro repairs directory damage, but tries to provide a whole host of troubleshooting tools that attempt to help you diagnose problems ranging from faulty RAM to main board components. Drive Genius sits in the middle of the spectrum of these two applications, being less broad-ranging in its toolset because it relates only to disk utilities, but it provides much more in the way of utility than DiskWarrior by allowing you to resize partitions on the fly and defragment your drive as well (in addition to other tools in its belt).

Journaled File System

A Journaled file system is one that keeps a record (on a very low level) of the writes to disk as they happen. When a system crash occurs, the file system knows exactly where it was when the crash happened (because the journal will have stopped at the crash point), allowing for a much speedier verification and repair process. Journaling was first introduced in 10.2.2 Server, and then in 10.3 across both the client and server versions alike. More information on journaling as it relates to Mac OS X can be found in Apple's knowledge base article number 107249.

> **NOTE** If you restart in single-user mode (hold down ⌘+S during startup), you can run the Unix command-line tool `fsck` (File System Check), with the `-y` option, to repair many problems with the directory structures. If you choose this route, you should rerun it repeatedly until it comes back with no errors found.

The directory, sometimes referred to as the *catalog* of your hard drive, is like a library's card catalog; it's a list of items that provides information to the user regarding where everything in the library can be found. In ideal use, the directory would never have a problem, but with power outages, crashes, reboots, or brownouts, sometimes things in your disk's directory structure get out of order or even broken. Depending on the location of the damage, an incorrect directory structure can cause your computer to act up, lose files, or even refuse to boot to the desktop.

This is where the disk utility software comes in. Prosoft's Drive Genius, Alsoft DiskWarrior, and Micromat's tools read through the directory structure and compare it to what is actually found in the places they are told to look. If a miscompare occurs, it is noted, and you're prompted to repair it. Norton and Micromat's philosophy of disk repair is to patch the directory. If there is a problem area of the directory, they will remove the incorrect entries and replace just those errors with the correct data. Alsoft on the other hand believes that it is better to create a brand new directory structure from scratch, avoiding any problems that could be created by the patching process. DiskWarrior is generally regarded as the most reliable of the repair tools listed here, though TechTool pro and Drive Genius have more tools in their bags of tricks and allow you to do more than just repair directory damage. DriveGenius actually gives you the option to repair a directory or create a brand new one as well. You'll want to have a few tools at your disposal — sometimes even the most reliable tool will not be able to solve a problem you encounter, but a different utility with a different approach may get the job done.

> **NOTE** There is a third philosophy when it comes to disk damage: Hard drives are cheap these days, but your data is expensive to replace, and even a successful repair of the directory doesn't exclude the possibility of further damage. Two companies, Prosoft Engineering (www.prosoftengineering.com) and BinaryBiz (www.binarybiz.com) make disk tools that focus on the *recovery* of your data rather than the repair of your disk. Data Rescue II (Prosoft) and VirtualLab Data Recovery (BinaryBiz) will even scour a disk that is beyond recovery using the disk utilities listed earlier, and find your files for you, allowing you to copy them to a new drive and throw away or replace the damaged disk.

Invisible files and folders

Apple and the graphical user interface try very hard to conceal the sometimes cryptic Unix underpinnings of Mac OS X from you. For example, the standard command-line directories (folders) are hidden from you when you're in the Finder or using an Open or Save dialog box. These directories have such revealing names as /bin (binary executables), /dev (devices), /etc (et cetera, miscellaneous items), /sbin (more binary executables, mostly run at startup time), and /usr (user directory hierarchy).

Now, you may ask, if the Finder hides these from me, how do I ever find out where they are? You can use a few easy ways to find out: Use Unix commands in a Terminal window (as described in

Chapter 24) or use OS X's Find command to search for items whose visibility is off (as shown in Figure 21.4). You may need to choose "Other" from the search modifier list and then pick visibility, in order to obtain the visibility. You can also make use of utilities such as TinkerTool and Cocktail (see Chapter 20 for more information) to turn off the invisibility of all the files on your hard drive and browse them like any other files.

FIGURE 21.4

Mac OS X's Find command is powerful and allows you to set many constraints on your file search. You can use the Find command to search for invisible files by selecting the Visibility item from the "Other" selection.

Because these folders are invisible, Mac OS X's Find command won't let you double-click them to open them in the Finder. To see what they contain, you'll have to make them visible, or be constrained by the use of the Terminal and then enter Unix commands — `ls -F /bin`, for example, gives you a listing of all the files in the `/bin` directory and indicates whether they are directories (appending a /), executables (appending an *), or a link (appending an @).

There are several ways to see invisible files, but perhaps one of the easiest is to use a program like TinkerTool (see chapter 20 for more info on TinkerTool) to show all invisibles as visible.

Protecting against viruses

Although computer viruses are not nearly as prevalent on Macs as on Microsoft Windows PCs, Mac viruses do exist, and many of the so-called macro viruses developed on PCs (generally infecting Microsoft Office documents) can infect Macs. If you perform a search on one of the popular antivirus sites such as www.symantec.com, you'll find millions of viruses, but only a handful of viruses for the Macintosh, many of which don't even apply to Mac OS X. Security through obscurity is not a very strong defense, however, and taking steps to protect yourself is always recommended.

I Forgot My Password and I Can't Get Up!

If a user can't remember his or her password on your computer, you can log in as an administrator and reset the user's password. If there are no other accounts, or no one can remember the password of an administrator account on your computer, you can reset passwords of ordinary user and administrator accounts by using the Mac OS X installation Disk.

To reset a password when no administrator account passwords are at hand, follow these steps:

1. **Restart the computer with the Mac OS X installation Disk.** Insert the Disk and choose Apple ⇨ Restart.

2. **When you hear the computer's startup chime, press and hold the C key until the computer begins starting up from the Disk.** You can release the C key when you hear the sounds of activity coming from the Disk. After a minute or two, the Installer application opens.

3. **In the Installer, choose Installer ⇨ Reset Password.** The Password Reset application opens.

4. **At the top of the Password Reset window, select the Mac OS X disk that has the user account whose password needs resetting.**

5. **For each user account whose password needs resetting, do the following:**

   1. **Click the pop-up menu and choose the user account whose password you want to reset.**

   2. **Type a new password in both text boxes and click Save.** If the two entries are not identical, you are asked to reenter them.

   3. **In the dialog box that appears, click OK.** The dialog box informs you that the password you entered was saved.

   4. **When you finish resetting passwords, choose Password Reset ⇨ Quit Password Reset.** You return to the Installer.

   5. **In the Installer, choose Installer ⇨ Quit Installer.**

   6. **In the dialog box that appears, click Restart.** The computer restarts.

Viruses invade your computer through documents or applications that you've downloaded from the Internet, through electronic mail attachments, through any type of removable disk (including floppy disks), or network volumes you may use with your computer. Although some viruses may be relatively innocuous, doing little more than taking up space on disk and slowing down your computer a bit, others can be highly destructive, causing crashes and erasing files. The Unix system of file permissions underlying Mac OS X make infection from viruses even less likely to cause extensive damage — at least as long as you don't log in with the root account.

The best way to protect your Mac from computer viruses (aside from completely shutting your computer off from the outside world) is to install an antivirus utility on your computer. Antivirus software warns you if a virus attempts to infect your system, scans your disks for viruses that may be lurking (or may already have caused some damage), and eradicates almost any virus that it finds. Symantec's Norton Antivirus, MacAfee's Virex X, and Sophos Anti-Virus, and Intego Virus Barrier, among others, are available for Mac OS X. A reasonably new addition to the mix is the completely free Open Source-based ClamXav. A recent test by Macworld magazine showed that Intego's Virus Barrier was the fastest scanner, and ClamXav was the slowest. A downside of ClamXav is that it can't repair files, only detect them (Sophos AV tends to make it difficult to repair files as well).

Whichever antivirus software package you choose, make sure that you keep it up to date; each time a new virus appears, the antivirus packages must generally be updated to recognize it. Most of the time, you receive updates by downloading them from the software publisher's Web site or accessing them in public download Web sites or FTP sites. Usually, you have a limited subscription to updates to the virus software itself. With Virex, you can pay an additional fee to have updates e-mailed directly to you. Norton AntiVirus includes a LiveUpdate feature that automatically down-loads and applies the latest virus definitions for you. A full year of virus definition updates is nor-mally included in the price of your software package; after the year is up, you must pay a subscription fee to continue to receive updates. If a newer version of the antivirus software has been released in the past year, purchasing the newer version is sometimes a better deal than sub-scribing to the update plan. Virex and Norton AntiVirus are targeted at home and small-business users, and Sophos Anti-Virus is aimed at the larger networked and cross-platform market. Sophos Anti-Virus generally runs on a server, and can be set to scan files on access rather than at a set time. Intego, MacAfee, Symantec, and Sophos post new virus definitions to their Web sites monthly (normally in the first week of every month), possibly more frequently if a particularly destructive virus is discovered. If you're either a Virex or Norton AntiVirus customer, you should consider marking your calendar to check on the first of the month and to bookmark the company's virus definitions page for easy access. An even easier way is just to set your AV client to check for new updates automatically at a set interval.

Mac OS X is mostly free of virus infection; however, viruses in the PC world can affect Mac users. The widespread worms that have been hopping around the Internet, being propagated by insecure Microsoft Windows machines have caused other problems on the Mac. Although not an infection, these worms spread themselves by e-mailing hundreds, sometimes thousands of people in the address books of those computers that are infected. Mac users have been inundated with these virus-containing messages, and although they pose no direct threat of corruption or data loss because they can't infect the Macintosh that receives them, getting 30 or more spurious messages a day is quite a pain. Even worse is the fact that some viruses spoof the originator, and Mac users can be incorrectly pegged as virus propagators. Take heart that you haven't been infected, and keep on top of what viruses are rampant in the wild so that you can determine the actual threat to your data.

Computer Viruses, Worms, and Trojan Horses

A *computer virus* is a piece of software designed to spread by illicitly attaching copies of itself to legitimate software. Although not all viruses perform malicious actions (such as erasing your hard disk), any virus can interfere with the normal functioning of your computer.

A *macro virus* is a virus written in the *macro language* of an application (a programming language that enables you to automate multiple-step operations in an application). By far, most macro viruses infect Microsoft Word (Version 6.0 and later) and Excel (Version 5.0 and later) documents. Like other viruses, macro viruses can be very destructive.

Viruses, alas, are not the only potentially destructive software that you may encounter. *Worms* are similar to viruses in that they replicate, but they do not attach themselves to files. A worm replaces a legitimate program or file on your system and performs its mischief whenever that legitimate program is run.

A *Trojan horse* is an intentionally destructive program masquerading as something useful, such as a utility, software updater, or game. Although worms and Trojan horses are not viruses, most commercial antivirus programs can detect and remove them.

Keeping software up-to-date

Unfortunately, no software of any consequential size and complexity is completely free of bugs (bugs being improperly programmed instructions). Some bugs may be features that don't function as planned or more serious errors, causing crashes or data corruption. Many bugs are so obscure, requiring an unusual confluence of events, that you're likely never to encounter them. But a few bugs may appear to take a nip at you. As one of the largest bodies of code on your Mac, Mac OS X also is not completely bug free.

Customarily, after software publishers become aware of a problem with their product, they take action to correct the anomaly by doing one of the following:

- Documenting a workaround while they work on a new version that fixes the problem
- Providing an *updater* that updates the application to a new version with the problem fixed

Registering your software (either by sending in the postcard that came with it or via the Internet, as you did when you performed your Mac OS X setup) and checking the publisher's Web site regularly are two good ways to keep informed of workarounds and updaters. Many software publishers, such as Aladdin Systems, include in their applications the ability to automatically check the publisher for updates just as Apple does with Mac OS X and QuickTime.

Mac OS X, like Mac OS 9 before it, provides a live Software Update capability. The Software Update pane of System Preferences is easily accessible from the System Preference application. Keeping your operating system software up-to-date with the latest enhancements and bug fixes from Apple should be part of your maintenance regimen.

To install software updates:

1. **Launch the System Preferences application.** It can be accessed from the Dock or from the Apple menu by choosing System Preferences.

2. **In the System section of the System Preferences application, click the Software update icon.** You can also select Software Update under the Apple menu (skip Step 3 if you use this route).

3. **Click the Check Now button.** Your computer must be connected to the Internet, and you'll see a progress bar in the bottom of the window. If there are any updates to be installed, the Software Update application launches (see Figure 21.5).

FIGURE 21.5

The Software Update Preference pane can be configured to automatically check for updates on a daily, weekly, or monthly basis.

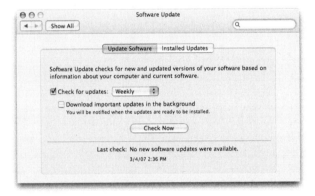

4. **Click an update in the list of available updates to see more information about the update in the lower pane of the window.** Make sure that the updates you want to install are checked, and click the Install button in the lower right corner of the window. Some updates require the computer to restart, and they will have an icon next to them that indicates this.

After you've chosen to install the selected updates, the Software Update application connects to Apple's servers and automatically downloads and installs the updates you've chosen. Some updates can be rather large; if you're on a dial-up account, you should pay attention to the size of the update so you can plan accordingly.

Here are some excellent sources to check for software from Apple (and others):

-   Apple's Mac OS X Web site (www.apple.com/macosx/)
-   Apple's Software Updates library (www.apple.com/swupdates)
-   VersionTracker (www.versiontracker.com/macosx)

Despite testing by Apple and various software publishers, some older software products are incompatible with the Classic environment. Assuming that you've already verified that they work with Mac OS 9, you should keep them separate and run them only when you start up with Mac OS 9 until a Mac OS X-compatible version becomes available.

Maintenance measures

As discussed in other chapters, Mac OS X brought with it the concept of permissions. To a certain extent, this security model has grown from the Unix multiuser environment and is designed to keep users out of places they shouldn't have access to, such as each other's home folders. The system and all the documents, applications, and folders contained on your hard drive each have their own permissions, which tell the operating system who and what is allowed access to each item. These permissions can get messed up over time and can cause applications to cease functioning in the way they're supposed to. Fortunately, Apple has provided a means of repairing the permissions on your computer to their proper settings.

Repairing system permissions

The included Disk Utility application provides a method to repair the permissions of the system and the installed applications. If the permissions of your Disk Utility application are incorrect, it may in some very obscure instances be unable to properly function. In this case, you can boot your computer from a Mac OS X installation CD and repair the permissions using the Disk Utility command under the Utilities menu. Alternatively, boot from an external or separate drive that has Mac OS X installed and repair permissions from the Disk Utility on that volume. Permissions can only be repaired on drives that have Mac OS X installed; drives that only contain data or are Mac OS 9 boot volumes are not supported. Disk Utility uses the receipts that are left behind after an application or software update is installed. Each boot disk will have its own unique permissions based on the applications that have been installed. Therefore, it is better to repair permissions from the disk you're booted from than to reboot from another drive to repair permissions. You will, however, encounter situations in which you'll have to use another drive to repair permissions in an emergency. If this solves your problem, it would be a good idea to reboot and use the disk's own permissions set to repair permissions again afterwards.

Disk fragmentation

When the files on a disk become fragmented, disk performance suffers considerably. In addition, files themselves (including applications) can become fragmented on a disk. A single file may be split into several pieces spread around in different locations physically on a disk. Fragmentation degrades disk performance because the drive must take extra time to move from one piece of a file to the next.

A fragmented file is analogous to a single track on an audio CD being split into multiple segments, so that the beginning of the track may be at the beginning of the CD, the middle at the end, and the end of the track someplace in the middle with other unrelated files interspersed between. If audio CDs were mastered in that fashion (which, fortunately, they are not), you would likely notice a delay as the CD player's laser moves to play the next segment.

In a disk with no fragmentation, each file physically resides in a single contiguous block. As a disk begins to fill up and new files are created and deleted with increasing frequency, files and the free space start to become fragmented. A heavily fragmented disk is more likely to experience a variety of problems, including corrupted directory structures and damaged files.

Beginning with Mac OS X 10.3, Apple designed the operating system to perform on-the-fly defragmentation. Commonly used applications and data are defragmented automatically on the fly, as they are accessed. In practice, this has not been a complete solution. Only files that are less than 20MB are defragmented on the fly.

Without any special software, you can eliminate fragmentation by copying the entire contents of a disk to another disk, erasing the disk, and copying everything back. An easier solution is to use a commercial disk defragmentation utility, such as the SpeedDisk component of the Norton Utilities from Symantec (www.symantec.com), PlusOptimizer from Alsoft (www.alsoft.com), Drive 10 from Micromat (www.micromat.com), or Drive Genius from Prosoft Engineering (www.prosoftengineering.com). Note, however, that older disk optimization utilities are not compatible with the Unix File System (UFS) and you should check for compatibility before attempting to run a disk optimizer on a UFS volume.

NOTE Do not use Speed disk on a drive that has been running any version of the operating system after 10.2. It will cause problems which will likely result in you having to reinstall the operating system.

Before optimizing any disk, take the time to make a full backup because virtually every byte on the disk can be erased and moved to a different location. If an error occurs during this process you stand the chance of losing some or all of your data.

Scheduling Maintenance

Taken together, all the maintenance tasks discussed in the preceding sections — backing up, virus checking, securing your system, repairing permissions, defragmenting your drive, and periodic cleaning up — can help ensure that your Mac experience is relatively error and hassle free. This section briefly outlines a schedule of maintenance for you to use as a guideline in keeping your computer running smoothly.

■ **Daily:** You should turn on and shut down your Mac only once a day (at the beginning and end of your workday or Mac session), if you elect to do so at all. You can put your Mac to sleep, spin down the hard disk, and make other energy-saving settings in the Energy Saver pane of System Preferences (see Chapter 14). The most wear and tear on your computer's components occurs during startup and shutdown due to the power draw that those processes require. Leaving your computer on overnight once in a while is a good idea because Mac OS X runs maintenance scripts late at night to tidy up after itself.

You should also check your disk space levels — open the Macintosh HD icon and look at the status section of the window at the top (you may have to choose View ➪ Show Status

Bar to make it visible) to make sure that you have disk space available. In a business setting, you may also want to back up on a daily basis or every other day.

- **Weekly:** Scan your computer with virus software, if it's not already designed to run in the background. If your machine is for personal use, you may want to back up on a weekly basis, according to the media rotation schedule you've devised.

- **Monthly:** Update your virus definitions if your virus software doesn't do this for you automatically. Check for updates to Mac OS X at least once a month. If the Software Update pane of System Preferences isn't set to update automatically, go to this pane at least once a month and click the Check Now button to initiate an update manually. In addition, every few months you should defragment your hard disk. If you put yourself on a schedule to defragment your disk regularly, it will take less time per session. Repair the permissions of your drive monthly, especially after an update to the Mac OS system has been applied.

- **Every three to six months:** Run a session from one of the Disk Utility packages mentioned earlier in this chapter. Clean house — remove applications, preference files, and other software that you no longer need. If you're a light computer user, defragment your hard disk.

Maximizing System Performance

Some Mac problems manifest themselves in slow performance rather than in crashes or system errors. If your Mac has been performing more slowly than usual, the following sections discuss a few possible causes and solutions.

Memory problems

If you open memory-consumptive applications or documents, Mac OS X employs *virtual memory* (treating part of your hard disk as memory, also called the *swap space*) to continue to work. If your software has to continually access the disk to retrieve data because of this, you experience significant performance degradation. Other than dealing with smaller documents or using applications with lesser appetites, the solution here is to purchase and install more RAM. Although Apple specifies a minimum of 256MB of RAM for PPC and 512 of RAM for Intel-based systems in order to run Mac OS X.5, a realistic minimum is 1GB to 2GB. Even more generally speeds up your computer drastically, especially if you work with large files. The authors of this book wouldn't care to use a computer with less than 2GB, and we generally strive to install as much as possible.

Insufficient drive space

Running low on hard-drive space can affect performance in various ways. You should archive and delete files that you don't need everyday access to, and remove any applications you no longer need. If you don't regularly leave your computer on overnight, use a utility such as Cocktail to manually run the Mac OS X maintenance scripts that delete overlong log files, and clean out cache space that piles up over time. An application such as the Omni Group's OmniDiskSweeper (`www.omnigroup.com`) can help you figure out which directories are taking up the most space, saving you time in the cleanup process.

If you've purged as much as you can stand but you're still low on space, you may need to add additional storage space to your computer. Apple's tower models support four internal hard drives in capacities up to 1TB each (at the time of this writing, though hard-drive manufacturers are constantly creating more voluminous drives). Check your computer's manual or Apple's support page to determine what type and size drives your computer supports. For computers that don't support multiple internal drives, you can, with varying degrees of difficulty depending on the model, replace the internal drive with a bigger model. A third alternative for the faint of heart is to invest in an external drive — FireWire enclosures are becoming increasingly popular due to their extreme ease of use and portability. You can purchase external FireWire drives in capacities ranging from 0GB (just an enclosure — you add your own drive, such as the one you just removed from your computer to make way for a bigger one) to several Terabytes or more using multiple disks. Hard drives come in different physical sizes, ranging from the very portable $2\frac{1}{2}$-inch laptop-sized drives to the standard $3\frac{1}{2}$-inch desktop-sized drives. The $2\frac{1}{2}$-inch drives make for very portable data storage when coupled with a FireWire enclosure, and they can be found at many retailers online and off.

Summary

In this chapter, you learned where different system, application, and personal support and preferences files are stored in Mac OS X. You also learned how to perform preventive and basic maintenance on your hard disk(s). You should now recognize the importance of a good backup system, and you should know how to devise a backup strategy to maintain your data and recover in the event of a disk or system problem. Preventative maintenance is a worthy cause to invest in and should not be dismissed lightly. Often, users do not recognize the importance of a good maintenance and backup regimen until it's too late and their data is lost to them. Visit `www.drivesavers.com` and find out the cost of data recovery if your files were ever lost. In addition to the expense of recovery, you'll be happy with the downtime you've saved yourself by thinking ahead.

Chapter 22

Automating and AppleScript

Although computers have been touted for years as the ultimate tool to perform redundant tasks, you may feel as though computers have generated new monotonous tasks. In previous chapters, you learned about technologies in Mac OS X that help you launch documents, edit text, manipulate multimedia, print, and perform hundreds of other tasks. And though you may be impressed by components in all of those technologies, the individual components don't do much by themselves — they tend to require user input. Scripting has long been a way to coordinate the different components of a task by allowing you to compose a script that plays back a set of commands in order.

The AppleScript scripting language is a simplified programming language that enables you to control your applications and perform tasks automatically. Scripts range from the simplest to the highly complex, depending on your skill at scripting, your knowledge of AppleScript's nuances, and the requirements of your task. This chapter contains enough information about AppleScript that even a scripting novice can get scripts up and running.

You begin by learning the underlying technologies that make AppleScript possible — messages and events. After you understand messages and events, it's on to an introduction of AppleScript and a look at the tools that enable you to run, modify, and create scripts of your own. Finally, you run through a few basic scripts, gaining an understanding of the AppleScript language as you go.

Understanding Messages and Events

Macintosh applications perform tasks in response to events. Users originate events with the keyboard and mouse, and applications respond to the events by performing tasks. Similarly, an application can make other applications perform tasks by sending messages about events.

The events that applications send to each other in messages are called *Apple events*. AppleScript makes applications perform tasks by sending them Apple events.

When an application receives a message about an Apple event, the application takes a particular action based on the specific event. This action can be anything from performing a menu command to taking some data, manipulating it, and returning the result to the source of the Apple event message.

For example, when you choose Shut Down or Restart from the Apple menu, Mac OS X sends an Apple event message to every open application saying a Quit event occurred. For this reason, applications quit automatically when you choose Shut Down or Restart.

When you drop document icons on an application icon, the Finder sends a message to Mac OS X saying this event happened, and the system sends the application an Apple event message that says an Open Documents event occurred. The Open Documents message includes a list of all the documents whose icons you dragged and dropped. When you double-click an application icon, the Finder sends the system a message that says this event happened, and the system sends the application an Open Application message. When you double-click a document, the application that created the document gets an Open Documents message with the name of the document you double-clicked.

Virtually all Mac applications respond to at least three Apple events: Open Application, Open Documents, and Quit Application. Applications that print also respond to the Apple event Print Documents. Only very old, very specialized, or poorly engineered Mac applications don't respond to these basic Apple events.

Applications that go beyond the three basic Apple events understand another two-dozen core Apple events. These Apple events encompass actions and objects that almost all applications have in common, such as the Close, Save, Undo, Redo, Cut, Copy, and Paste commands. Applications with related capabilities recognize still more sets of Apple events. For example, word processing applications understand Apple events about text manipulation, and drawing applications understand Apple events about graphics manipulation. Application developers can even define private Apple events that only their applications know.

Mac OS X provides the means of communicating Apple event messages between applications. The applications can be on the same computer or on different computers connected to the same network. To understand how Apple event messages work, think of them as a telephone system. Mac OS X furnishes a telephone for each application as well as the wires that connect them. Applications call each other with messages about Apple events.

Apple events offer many intriguing possibilities for the world of personal computing. No longer does one application need to handle every possible function; instead, it can send Apple event messages to helper applications.

Some Classic Programs Cannot Receive Apple Event Messages

In the Classic compatibility environment, only application programs can send and receive Apple event messages; true control panels and desk accessories cannot, although these items are now uncommon. Control panels that are actually applications (listed in the Classic environment's Applications menu when open) are not subject to this limitation. And a desk accessory can work around this limitation by sending and receiving through a small surrogate application that is always open in the background. This background application does not have to appear in the Classic environment's Application menu, and the computer user does not have to know that the application is open.

Introducing AppleScript

Apple event messages aren't just for professional software engineers. Macintosh enthusiasts with little technical training can use Apple event messages to control applications by writing statements in the AppleScript language. For example, suppose that you want to quit all open applications. Mac OS X doesn't have a Quit All command, but you can create one with AppleScript. You can use AppleScript commands to automate simple tasks as well as to automate a more complicated series of tasks, as the rest of this chapter demonstrates.

AppleScript language

With AppleScript you tell applications what to do using natural language. This means simply that AppleScript is a programming language designed especially to make it easy for computer users, not computer engineers, to build their own solutions. (Actually, engineers use it, too.)

You tell applications what to do by writing statements in the AppleScript language. Although AppleScript is an artificial language, its statements are similar to sentences in a natural language, such as English. You can look at many AppleScript statements and easily figure out what they're supposed to do.

The words and phrases in AppleScript statements resemble English, but they are terms that have special meanings in the context of AppleScript. Some terms are commands, and some terms are objects that the commands act on. Other terms control how AppleScript performs the statements.

A single AppleScript statement can perform a simple task, but most tasks require a series of statements that are performed one after the other. A set of AppleScript statements that accomplishes a task (or several tasks) is called a *script*. The term *script* is used because the computer follows the statements you put in order, much like an actor follows the script of a movie. A script can rename a batch of files, change an application's preference settings, copy data from a database to another application, or automate a sequence of tasks that you previously performed one at a time by hand. You can develop your own script tools to accomplish exactly what you need.

As an added boon, AppleScript can actually watch you as you work with an application and write a script for you behind the scenes. This process is called *script recording*.

Although AppleScript is designed to be a simple-to-understand language, it offers all the capabilities of a traditional programming language and won't frustrate programmers and advanced users. You can store information in variables for later use; write `if...then` statements to perform commands selectively according to a condition that you specify; or repeat a set of commands as many times as you want. AppleScript also offers error checking and object-oriented programming.

Scripting additions

AppleScript has an expandable lexicon of terms. It knows meanings of basic terms, and it augments this knowledge with terms from other sources. Many additional AppleScript terms come from the very applications that AppleScript controls. We explore this source of AppleScript terms in greater detail later in this chapter.

Additional AppleScript terms also come from special files called *scripting additions*. AppleScript looks for scripting addition files in the following folders:

- **ScriptingAdditions:** Located in the Library folder of the System folder (path `/System/Library/ScriptingAdditions/`) — contains standard scripting additions from Apple that are available to all users of your computer. (This folder may also contain other files that are not scripting additions.)

- **Scripts:** Located in the main Library folder (path `/Library/Scripts/`) — contains more scripting additions that are available to all users of your computer.

For older versions of OS you'll find some additional folders:

- **Scripting Additions:** Located in the folder named System Folder (path `/System Folder/ Scripting Additions/` unless you have moved or renamed System Folder) — contains more scripting additions that are available in the Classic environment to all users of your computer.

- **Scripting Additions and Scripts:** Located in the Extensions folder of the folder named System Folder (path `/System Folder/Extensions/Scripting Additions/` and path `/System Folder/Extensions/Scripts/` unless you have moved or renamed System Folder) — contains more scripting additions that are available in the Classic environment to all users of your computer. (This Scripting Additions folder usually exists only on computers that previously used Mac OS 8.)

You need separate scripting additions for Mac OS X and the Classic environment. Scripting additions made for Mac OS X do not work in the Classic environment. Conversely, scripting additions made for Mac OS 9 and earlier work only in the Classic environment. If you get more scripting additions made for Mac OS X, put them in one of the ScriptingAdditions folders inside a Library folder. If you get more scripting additions made for Mac OS 9, put them in one of the Scripting Additions folders inside the System Folder used for the Classic environment.

> **TIP** If the ScriptingAdditions folder doesn't exist in a Library folder where you want to put a scripting addition file, create a new folder and name it ScriptingAdditions (put no spaces in the name). Put your scripting addition file in this new folder.

Introducing Script Editor

For creating and editing AppleScript scripts, you can use the Script Editor application included with Mac OS X. Script Editor can also run scripts, and it can make scripts into self-contained applications that run when you double-click them in the Finder. Script Editor is normally located in the AppleScript folder in the Applications folder.

> **TIP** If you end up doing a lot of scripting, you may want to replace Script Editor with a more capable script development application, such as Script Debugger from Late Night Software (www.latenightsw.com). Make sure you get a version made for Mac OS X.

Scriptable applications and environments

The scripts you create with Script Editor can control any *scriptable application*. A prime example of a scriptable application is the Finder. Other scriptable applications included with Mac OS X include Apple System Profiler, ColorSync Scripting, Internet Connect, iCal, iChat, iPhoto, iSync, iTunes, Safari, Mail, Print Center, QuickTime Player, Sherlock, StuffIt Expander, Terminal, TextEdit, and URL Access Scripting. Interestingly enough, even the Script Editor is scriptable. In addition, many Mac OS X applications not made by Apple are scriptable.

Plenty of Classic applications are also scriptable. Although a Classic version of Script Editor is included with Mac OS 9, you can use the Mac OS X version of Script Editor to make scripts for the Classic environment as well as for Mac OS X.

Looking at a script window

When you open Script Editor, an empty script window appears. Each script window can contain one script. The top part of the script window is the script editing area, where you type and edit the text of the script just as you type and edit in any text editing application. The bottom part of the window is the script description area. You use this area to type a description of what the script does. Figure 22.1 shows an empty script window.

> **TIP** You can change the default size of a new script window. First, make the script window the size you want and then choose Save as Default from the Window menu in Script Editor.

FIGURE 22.1

A new script window appears when Script Editor opens.

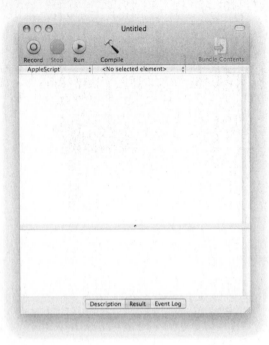

The tool bar of a script window has four buttons. You find out more about each of them in later sections, but the following list summarizes their functions:

- **Record:** AppleScript goes into recording mode and creates script statements corresponding to your actions in applications that support script recording. You can also press ⌘+D to start recording. You cannot record scripts for every scriptable application, because software developers must do more work to make an application recordable than to make it scriptable. You can find out whether an application is recordable by trying to record some actions in it.

- **Stop:** Takes AppleScript out of recording mode or stops a script that is running, depending on which action is relevant at the time. Pressing ⌘+. (period) on the keyboard is the same as clicking Stop.

- **Run:** Starts running the script that is displayed in the script-editing area. You also can press ⌘+R to run the script. Before running the script, Script Editor scans the script to see if you changed any part of it since you last ran it or checked its syntax (as described next). If the script has changed, Script Editor checks the script's syntax.

- **Compile:** Checks for errors in the script, such as incorrect punctuation or missing parts of commands. If any errors turn up, Script Editor highlights the error and displays a dialog box explaining the problem. Script Editor also formats the text to make keywords stand out and the structure of the script more apparent. Script Editor may even change the text, but the changes do not affect the meaning of the script.

  If the script's syntax is correct, Script Editor tells AppleScript to *compile* the script, which means it converts the text of the script into codes. These codes are what Apple event messages actually contain and what applications understand. You don't usually see these codes in Script Editor because AppleScript translates them into words for the enlightenment of human beings.

- **Bundle Contents:** We'll talk more about bundles later in the chapter. However, if you are editing a script that is saved as a bundle, this button will show you the contents.

Creating a Simple Script

An easy way to see how a script looks and works is to type a simple script into a new script window. If Script Editor is not already the active application, open it or switch to it. If you need to create a new script window, choose File ➪ New Script. In the script-editing area at the bottom of the new script window, type the following statements:

```
tell application "Finder"
activate
set the bounds of the first Finder window to {128, 74, 671, 479}
set the current view of the first Finder window to icon view
set the icon size of the icon view options of the first Finder
    window to 32
select the first item of the first Finder window
end tell
```

Check your script for typographical errors by clicking the Compile button in the script window. If Script Editor reports an error, carefully compare the statement you typed in the script window to the same statement in the book. Pay particular attention to spelling, punctuation, omitted words, and omitted spaces.

When you click Compile, Script Editor formats your script, changing the text formatting as it compiles the script using different type styles to show different kinds of terms. The statements that you typed probably changed from Courier font to Verdana font after you clicked Compile. Script Editor normally formats text that hasn't been compiled as 10-point Courier. Most other words, including commands from scripting additions and application dictionaries, are normally formatted in plain 10-point Verdana. Verdana 10-point Bold normally indicates native words in the AppleScript language. Figure 22.2 shows how Script Editor formats the script that you typed.

Before running this script, return to the Finder and make sure that a Finder window is displayed. If you really want to see the script in action, set the front Finder window to list view and resize the window so that it is very small.

FIGURE 22.2

Check your script for errors and format it for readability by clicking the Compile button.

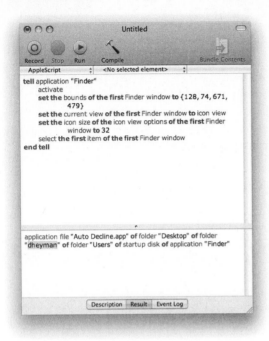

After setting the stage for the script, switch back to Script Editor and click Run in your script's window. AppleScript executes each script statement in turn. When the script finishes running, the Finder window should be a standard size and set to icon view. The item that comes first alphabetically in the window should be selected.

Switch to Script Editor again and examine the script. You find that the script is fairly understandable. It may not be fluent English, but many of the commands should make sense as you read them.

Analyzing a Script

Having looked through the script that you wrote in the previous example, you may be surprised to learn that AppleScript doesn't know anything about the Finder's operations. Although your recorded script contains commands that set the position, size, and view of a Finder window and selects an item in it, AppleScript doesn't know anything about these or other Finder operations. In fact, AppleScript knows how to perform only the six following commands:

- Copy
- Count
- Error
- Get
- Run
- Set

AppleScript learns about moving and resizing Finder windows from the Finder. More generally, AppleScript learns about commands in a script from the application that the script controls. The application has a dictionary of AppleScript commands that work with the application. The dictionary defines the syntax of each command. AppleScript learns about more commands from scripting addition files on your computer. Each scripting addition file contains a dictionary of supplemental AppleScript commands.

Learning application commands and objects

Look at the sample script you created. The first statement says:

```
tell application "Finder"
```

To AppleScript, this statement means "start working with the application named Finder." When AppleScript sees a `tell application` statement, it looks at the dictionary for the specified application and figures out what commands the application understands. For example, by looking at the Finder's dictionary, AppleScript learns that the Finder understands the `select` command. The dictionary also tells AppleScript what objects the application knows how to work with, such as files and windows. In addition, an application's dictionary tells AppleScript how to compile the words and phrases that you write in scripts into Apple event codes that the application understands.

After learning from the `tell application` statement which application it will send event messages to, AppleScript compiles the remaining statements to determine what Apple event messages to send. One by one, AppleScript translates every statement it encounters in your script into an Apple event message based on the application's dictionary. When the script runs, the Apple event messages are sent to the application named in the `tell` statement. The application receives the messages and takes the appropriate action in response to the Apple events.

AppleScript stops using the application dictionary when it encounters the `end tell` statement at the end of your script.

A complex script may have several `tell application` statements that name different scriptable applications. In each case, AppleScript starts using the dictionary of the application named by the `tell application` statement, compiles subsequent statements using this dictionary, and stops using this dictionary when it encounters the next `end tell` statement. Because AppleScript gets all the information about an application's commands and objects from the application itself, you never have to worry about controlling a new application. As long as the application has a dictionary, AppleScript can work with it.

Inspecting a dictionary

Just as AppleScript can get information about an application's commands and objects from its dictionary, so can you. Using Script Editor, you can display the AppleScript dictionary of an application to see what commands the application understands and what objects the commands work with. You can also look at the dictionaries of scripting addition files.

Displaying a dictionary window

In Script Editor, choose Open Dictionary from the File menu. A dialog box appears, listing scriptable applications and scripting additions. Select an application or scripting addition file in the list and click Open. Script Editor displays a dictionary window for the application or scripting addition you selected, as shown in Figure 22.3.

FIGURE 22.3

An AppleScript dictionary defines suites of commands and objects for a scriptable application or a scripting addition file.

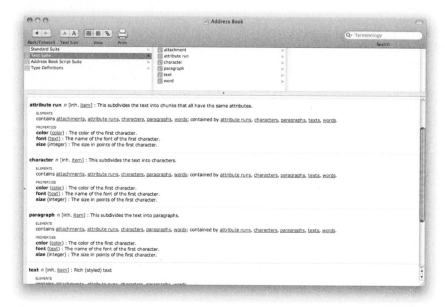

TIP
In the Open Dictionary dialog box, you can select several applications and scripting additions whose dictionaries you want to display (each in a separate window). To select adjacent items in the list, drag across or Shift+click the items. To select nonadjacent items, ⌘+click each item that you want to select.

Looking at a dictionary window

The top of the window shows hierarchically the commands that are available to you. In the left-most pane is a list of groups of related commands called *suites*. They appear with a box with an S in it next to them. When you click a suite, you see its constituent commands displayed in the middle pane. Commands are depicted with a square with the letter *c* inside. Clicking a command displays its constituent elements and properties (depicted with an *e* and a *p*, respectively). Verbs are shown with a blue square, and nouns have a purple square; elements have orange squares, and properties have purple. Below the triple-paned view, you will see the full explanation of the commands. The commands appear in bold, and objects appear in italics. Script Editor groups related commands and objects into suites and displays the names of suites in bold. You don't have to worry about suites when you're scripting.

The description of a command briefly explains what the command does and defines its syntax. In the syntax definition, bold words are command words that you must type exactly as written. Words in plain text represent information that you provide, such as a value or an object for the command to work on. Any parts of a syntax definition enclosed in brackets are optional.

The description of an object very briefly describes the object and may list the following:

- **Plural Form:** States how to refer to multiple objects collectively. For example, you can refer to a specific window or to all windows.

- **Elements:** Enumerates items that can belong to the object. In a script, you would refer to `item of object`. For example, you could refer to a file named `index.html` in the folder named Sites as `file "index.html" of folder "Sites"`.

- **Properties:** Lists attributes of an object. Each property has a name, which is displayed in bold, and a value, which is described in plain text. Scripts can get and set property values, except that properties designated [r/o] (means read only) can't be changed.

Saving a Script

In Script Editor, you save a script by choosing Save or Save As. When you choose one of these commands, Script Editor displays a Save sheet. (The sheet does not appear when you choose Save for a script that has previously been saved.) In the dialog box, you can choose any of several different file formats for the saved script. The five options are Script, Application, Script Bundle, Application Bundle, and Text.

Looking at Script File Formats

Script Editor can save a script in three basic file formats. When you save a new script or a copy of a script, you specify a file format by choosing the format from the Format pop-up menu in the Save dialog box. Script Editor can save in the following file formats:

- **Script/Script Bundle:** Saves the script as Apple event codes rather than plain text. You can open it with Script Editor and then run or change it. In versions of OS X prior to 10.4 you run compiled scripts by using the Script Runner application and applications that have a script menu, such as AppleWorks. In 10.4 and above, the OS manages the running of the scripts. You can save scripts as Run Only so they cannot be edited, only run.

- **Application/Application Bundle:** Saves the script as an application, complete with an icon. Opening the icon (by double-clicking it, for example) runs the script. When you choose the application format, the following two options appear at the bottom of the Save dialog box:

  - **Run Only:** Script application cannot be edited, only run.

  - **Stay Open:** Causes the application to stay open after its script finishes running. If this option is turned off, the application quits automatically after running its script.

  - **Show Startup Screen:** Displays an identifying window that appears when the application is opened. The Startup screen confirms that the user wants to run the script.

- **Text:** Saves the script as a plain text document. You can open it in Script Editor, in a word processing application, and in many other applications. Although a more portable file, this format is not as efficient as the others because the script must be compiled in Script Editor before it can be run.

Beginning with AppleScript 1.9.2, the version that shipped with Mac OS 10.4, is the ability to save scripts as Mac OS X bundles. Cocoa applications are bundles (another name for packages) which, though they appear as a single item or application, are actually a collection of the files and resources that the application needs to run. If you Control+click a Cocoa application, you can see inside of an application's bundle by choosing *Show Package Contents*. You'll see all of the necessary files and folders that make up an application's contents. It is the concept of an application bundle that allows developers to make their applications installable via drag-and-drop, instead of using an installer that places files all over your computer. When you save a script as either a Script Bundle or an Application Bundle, it creates a similar package from your script, and you can Control+click your saved document and see the package contents just like any Cocoa application. The differences between a bundle and a standard script or application are beyond the scope of this chapter and are mainly geared toward developers of applications. See the AppleScript documentation for developers online at `http://developer.apple.com/documentation/AppleScript/` if you are interested in more information about bundles and how they can be used. Access to this documentation requires registration with the Apple Developer Connection; you can find information about ADC and sign up at `http://developer.apple.com/index.html`.

Creating a More Complex Script

You now know how to use Script Editor to create a simple AppleScript script. This type of script, however, has limited value. A simple script that doesn't take advantage of the full AppleScript language is not very intelligent.

More frequently, you'll use AppleScript to create more complex scripts. This section explains how to create a full-blown script quickly and use the resulting custom utility to augment an application's capabilities.

Making a Finder utility

Your Mac OS X disk is full of special folders, but when someone sends you a file, it's up to you to figure out where the file belongs. For example, you have to sort TIFF and JPEG files into your Pictures folder, QuickTime files into your Movies folder, and MP3 files into your Music folder. You also have to classify and put away fonts, sounds, and so on. The Finder doesn't help you sort out any of this.

You can, however, write a simple script that recognizes certain types of files and uses the Finder to move files to the folders where you want the files to go. The destination folders can be any folders that you have permission to change. These include all the folders in your home folder. If you log in as a user with administrator privileges, the destination folders can also include folders in the main Library folder.

Beginning the script

To begin writing a new script in Script Editor, choose File ➪ New Script, and then type the following statement in the script editing area of the new script window:

```
choose file
```

This command gives the script user a way to specify the file to be moved. The choose file command displays a dialog box for choosing a file. This command is part of a scripting addition that is preinstalled in Mac OS X. The name of this scripting addition is Standard Additions.

Seeing the script's results

The script isn't finished, but you can run it now to see the results of the one statement you have entered thus far. Click Run to run the script in its current condition. When AppleScript performs the choose file statement, it displays a dialog box for choosing a file. Go ahead and select any file and click Choose. Because there aren't any more script statements, AppleScript stops the script.

Changing AppleScript Formatting

You can change the way Script Editor formats text by choosing Script Editor ➪ Preferences and clicking the Formatting icon in the toolbar. A dialog box appears listing various components of AppleScript commands and the text format of each component. You can change the format of any component by selecting it in the dialog box and then choosing different formatting from the Font and Style menus.

AppleScript shows you the result of the last script action in the result window. If this window isn't open, choose Show Result from the Script Editor Controls menu. The result window contains the word *alias* and the path through your folders to the file you selected. This wording does not mean that the file is an alias file. In the context of a script, *alias* means the same thing as *file path*. Figure 22.4 shows an example of the result window.

FIGURE 22.4

Script Editor's result pane shows the result of running a script.

Using variables

The result of the `choose file` statement is called a file specification, or *file spec*. A file spec tells Mac OS X exactly where to find a file or folder. You need the file spec later in the script, so you must put it in a *variable,* which is a container for information. You can place data in a variable and then retrieve it whenever you want to before the script finishes running. The data in a variable is called the variable's *value*. You can change a variable's value by placing new data in it during the course of the script.

On the next line of the script, type the following statement:

```
copy the result to thisFile
```

This statement places the result of the `choose file` statement in a variable named `thisFile`. You can include the `thisFile` variable in any subsequent script statements that need to know the file spec of the chosen file. When AppleScript sees a variable name, it uses the current value of the variable. In this case, the value of variable `thisFile` is the file spec you got from the first statement.

When you run the script, you see that the `copy` command doesn't change the result of the script (as displayed in the result window). Because the result is just being copied to a variable, the result doesn't change.

Capitalizing script statements

You may notice the capital *F* in the `thisFile` variable and wonder whether capitalization is important when entering AppleScript statements. In general, you can capitalize any way that makes statements easier to read. Many AppleScript authors adopt the convention of capitalizing each word in a variable name except the first word, hence `thisFile`. This practice helps you distinguish variables from other terms in statements, which are generally all lowercase.

Getting file information

Ultimately, the script you are creating decides where to move a selected file based on the type of file it is. In Mac OS X, a file's type may be indicated by an extension (suffix) at the end of the file's name or by a hidden four-letter code known as the *file type*. Therefore, the script needs to determine the name and the file type of the selected file. You can use another command from the Standard Additions scripting addition to get this information. (Standard Additions is preinstalled in Mac OS X.) Enter the following statements beginning on the third line of the script:

```
copy the info for thisFile to fileInfo
copy the name extension of the fileInfo to nameExtension
copy the file type of the fileInfo to fileType
```

The first of these statements uses the `info for` command to get an information record about the selected file that is now identified by the variable `thisFile`. The first statement also copies the entire information record into a variable named `fileInfo`.

A record in AppleScript is a structured collection of data. Each data item in a record has a name and a value. AppleScript statements can refer to a particular item of a record by name, using a phrase similar to `item of record`. This is the phrasing used in the second two statements listed earlier.

Each of the second two statements gets an item of a record and copies it into a variable. The item names in these statements, `name extension` and `file type`, are taken from the AppleScript dictionary definition of the record. In this script, the record was obtained by the `info for` command in a previous statement.

To test the script so far, run it, choose a file, and look at the result. The result window contains the four-letter file type of the file you chose, displayed as a piece of text. Figure 22.5 shows the whole example script so far.

FIGURE 22.5

The StandardAdditions dictionary description of the `info for` command shows what the command returns.

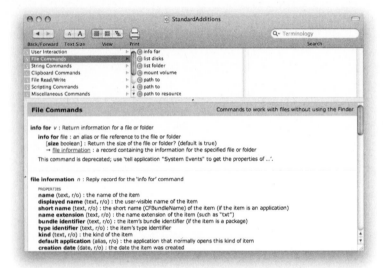

Using parentheses

You may notice that when AppleScript compiles the example script, which happens when you run the script or check its syntax, AppleScript adds parentheses around `info for thisFile` but does not add parentheses in other statements. AppleScript adds parentheses around a command that returns a value, which any `info for` command does. However, AppleScript does not add parentheses around a command at the end of a statement, such as the `choose file` command in the first statement of the example script. Nor does AppleScript add parentheses around elements that refer to a property, such as the `name extension of the fileInfo` in the example script.

Parentheses group elements of a command together. You can type your own parentheses around elements that you want to group in a statement. Parentheses make a complex AppleScript statement easier to read. Parentheses may also affect the result of a statement because AppleScript evaluates elements within parentheses before evaluating other elements of a statement.

Working with an application

For the next part of the script, you need to add statements that move the chosen file to the folder where it belongs. The script can use an application — the Finder — to move the file. Add the following statement to have AppleScript start using the Finder:

```
tell application "Finder"
```

After AppleScript encounters this statement, it knows all the commands and objects from the Finder's AppleScript dictionary. This means that subsequent statements use commands and objects that the Finder understands. AppleScript sends these commands and objects to the Finder in Apple event messages. The script doesn't yet include any statements for the Finder, but we add some next. Later we add an `end tell` statement to have AppleScript stop using the Finder.

Performing script statements conditionally

When creating complex scripts you may want to give your script the ability to decide what to do based on the factors you specify. AppleScript, like all programming languages, lets you include a series of conditional statements, or *conditionals* for short. Each conditional begins with an `if` statement, which defines the condition to be evaluated. The `if` statement is followed by one or more other statements to be performed only if the condition is true. The conditional ends with an `end if` statement. In AppleScript, a simple conditional looks like this:

```
if the fileType is "MooV" or the nameExtension is "mov" then
move thisFile to folder "Movies" of home
end if
```

In this example, the `if` statement contains a two-part condition. The first part of the condition determines whether the current value of the `fileType` variable is `MooV`, which is the four-letter file type of QuickTime movie files. The second part of the condition determines whether the file name ends with `mov`, which is the file name extension of a QuickTime movie file. If either part of the condition is true, AppleScript performs the included `move` statement. If both parts are false, AppleScript skips the included `move` statement and goes on to the statement that follows the `end if` statement. Remember that AppleScript sends the `move` command to the Finder because of the `tell application` statement earlier in the script.

 AppleScript considers the dot, or period, between the file name and the extension to be a separator. The dot is not part of the extension or the file name as far as AppleScript is concerned.

Finding a Folder Path

If you don't know the full path of a folder, you can use a script to get this information. Open a new window in Script Editor and type the following script in the script editing area:

```
choose folder
```

Run the script and select a folder. The result is a file spec for the folder you selected. You can copy the text from the result window and paste it in any script.

You may notice that the file spec has a colon after each folder name. AppleScript uses colons in file specs to maintain compatibility with Mac OS 9 and earlier. Outside of AppleScript, Mac OS X generally follows the UNIX and Internet convention of putting a slash after each folder name.

Finding a File's Type

You may not know the file type of the files that you want to move. For example, you may know that you want to put font files in your Fonts folder, but you may not know that the four-letter file type of a font file is FFIL. To make a script that reports the file type, copy the following three-line script to a new Script Editor window:

```
choose file
copy the result to thisFile
copy the file type of the info for thisFile to fileType
```

Run this three-line script and select a file whose four-character file type you need to learn. If the result window is not visible, choose Show Result from the Controls menu. The result of the script is the file type of the selected file. You can copy and paste the result from the result window into a conditional statement in any script window.

If you choose a file that has no file type, one of two things happens: The result window displays an empty value (indicated by quotation marks with nothing between them) or AppleScript reports an error, saying that it can't get the file type.

Include as many conditionals in the example script as you want. In each conditional, use the four-character file type and corresponding file name extension for a different type of file, and specify the path of the folder to which you want AppleScript to move files of that type. A quick way to enter several conditionals is to select one conditional (from the `if` statement through the `end if` statement), copy it, paste it at the end of the script, and change the relevant pieces of information. You can repeat this for each conditional you want to include.

You can make the above script a bit more interesting by using the choose folder in place of a hard coded folder path:

```
move thisFile to choose folder
```

This will ask the user where to place the file after it is moved.

Breaking long statements

When you type a long statement, Script Editor never breaks it automatically (as a word processor does). Long sentences wrap to the width of your window. Remember that each *line* is a statement and a *return* delimits a line, whereas a *break* only *visually* ends the line and doesn't change the *statement*. You can break a long statement manually, for better readability, by pressing Option+Return. (Do not break a statement in the middle of a quoted text string, however.) AppleScript displays a special symbol (¬) to indicate a manual break. Here's an example:

```
if the fileType is "JPEG" or ¬
the nameExtension is "jpg" or ¬
the nameExtension is "jpeg" then
move thisFile to folder "Pictures" of home
end if
```

In this example, the first statement, which goes from `if` through `then`, takes three lines because it has two manual line breaks.

Ending the use of an application

After the last statement that is directed at the Finder, the script needs a statement that makes AppleScript stop using the application. Type the following statement at the end of the script:

```
end tell
```

This statement doesn't include the name of the application to stop using because AppleScript automatically pairs an `end tell` statement with the most recent `tell` statement. Subsequent statements in the script can't use the commands and objects of that application.

Now is a good time to recheck the script's syntax. If you tried to compile recently, you got an error message about a missing `end tell` statement. Click Compile now, and after AppleScript compiles the script you see Script Editor neatly indent statements to make the structure of the script more apparent. If AppleScript encounters any errors while compiling your script, Script Editor advises you of them one by one.

Trying out your script

After creating a new script, you must run it and test it thoroughly. To test the script that moves files according to their type, follow these steps:

1. **Run your script.**

2. **When the dialog box appears, select a file that is of a type your script should recognize but that is not in the destination folder, and then click Choose.**

3. **Switch to the Finder, and make sure that the file you selected actually moved from the source folder to the destination folder.**

4. **Repeat the test, selecting a different file type that your script should recognize.**

Figure 22.6 shows an example of a script with four conditional statements that move a selected file depending on its file type or file name extension.

FIGURE 22.6

This script uses conditional statements to determine where to put a file.

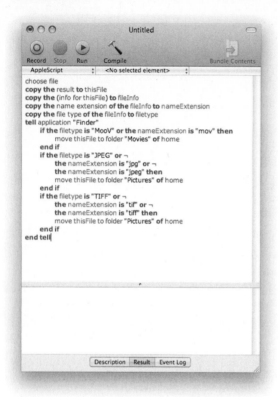

```
choose file
copy the result to thisFile
copy the (info for thisFile) to fileInfo
copy the name extension of the fileInfo to nameExtension
copy the file type of the fileInfo to filetype
tell application "Finder"
    if the filetype is "MooV" or the nameExtension is "mov" then
        move thisFile to folder "Movies" of home
    end if
    if the filetype is "JPEG" or ¬
        the nameExtension is "jpg" or ¬
        the nameExtension is "jpeg" then
        move thisFile to folder "Pictures" of home
    end if
    if the filetype is "TIFF" or ¬
        the nameExtension is "tif" or ¬
        the nameExtension is "tiff" then
        move thisFile to folder "Pictures" of home
    end if
end tell
```

Creating a Drag-and-Drop Script Application

Although the sample script you created is useful, it would be more useful as an application with an icon on your desktop. Then you could drag files that you wanted to sort into folders and drop them on the application's icon. This would cause the application to run and move the files to their appropriate folders. You wouldn't have to open Script Editor every time you wanted to sort files into folders, and you could sort more than one file at a time. Applications respond to this type of drag-and-drop Apple event, and so can Apple Scripts.

You already know that AppleScript can save a script as an application. With a little extra work, you can make an application with drag-and-drop capability so that you can simply drag files to it to choose them.

Retrieving dropped files

Remember that when you drop a set of icons on an application in a Finder window, the Finder sends that application an Open Documents message that includes a list of the files you dropped on the icon. This message is sent to all applications, even to applications that you create yourself with AppleScript.

You need to tell your script to intercept that event message and retrieve the list of items that were dropped onto the application icon. Place the following statement at the beginning of your script:

```
on open itemList
```

Now enter the following statement at the end of your script:

```
end open
```

This on open statement enables the script to intercept an Open Documents event message and puts the message's list of files in a variable named `itemList`. The end open statement helps AppleScript know which statements to perform when the open message is received. Any statements between the on open and end open statements are performed when the script receives an Open Documents event message.

Save this script by choosing the Save As command from the File menu. From the Format pop-up menu in the Save As dialog box, choose the Application option. (You may want to save the script on the desktop, at least for experimental purposes.) If you switch to the Finder and look at the icon of the application you just created, you can see that the icon includes an arrow, which indicates that the icon represents a drag-and-drop application. The application has this kind of icon because its script includes an on open statement.

Processing dropped files

The script won't be fully operational until you make a few more changes. As the script stands, it places the list of files in a variable, but it doesn't do anything with that information. If you dropped several files on the application now, the script would still display a dialog box asking you to pick a file and then quit, having accomplished nothing.

First, you need to eliminate the script statements that obtain the file to be processed from a dialog box. Delete what now are the second and third lines of the script (the ones beginning with the words choose and copy) and replace them with the following:

```
repeat with x from 1 to the number of items in the itemList
copy item x of the itemList to thisFile
```

Between the end tell and end open statements, which are the last two lines of the script, enter the following statement:

```
end repeat
```

Figure 22.7 shows the complete sample script modified for drag-and-drop operation.

FIGURE 22.7

This script application processes items dropped on its icon.

Save the script so that your changes take effect and then switch back to the Finder. You now have a drag-and-drop application that you can use to move certain types of files to specific folders.

Using a repeat loop

In the modified script, AppleScript repeatedly performs the statements between the repeat and end repeat statements for the number of times specified in the repeat statement. This arrangement is called a *repeat loop*. The first time AppleScript performs the repeat statement, it sets variable x to 1, as specified by from 1. Then AppleScript performs statements sequentially until it encounters the end repeat statement.

In the first statement of the repeat loop, variable x determines which file spec to copy from variable itemList to variable thisFile. The rest of the statements in the repeat loop are carried over from the previous version of the script.

When AppleScript encounters the end repeat statement, it loops back to the repeat statement, adds 1 to variable x, and compares the new value of x with the number of items that were dragged to the icon (as specified by the phrase the number of items in the itemList). If the two values are not equal, AppleScript performs the statements in the repeat loop again. If the two values are equal, these statements are performed one last time, and AppleScript goes to the statement immediately following end repeat. This is the end open statement, which ends the script.

Extending the script

Anytime you want the application to handle another type of file, open the script application in Script Editor, add a conditional that covers that type of file, and save the script.

The script in its drag-and-drop form now no longer functions if you double-click it. You can modify the script to restore this functionality by placing a copy of the original script at the end of the end open statement.

TIP You can't open a script application to edit it by double-clicking it because doing so causes the application to run. To open a script application in Script Editor, choose File ⇨ Open in Script Editor or drop the script application on the Script Editor icon in the Finder.

Borrowing Scripts

An easy way to make a script is to modify an existing script that does something close to what you want. You simply duplicate the script file in the Finder, open the duplicate copy, and make changes. You can do this with scripts that have been saved as applications, compiled scripts, or text files. (You can't open a script that has been saved as a run-only script.)

Apple has developed a number of scripts that you can use as starting points or models for your own scripts. You can find some scripts in the Example Scripts folder, which is in the AppleScript folder in the Applications folder. Another place to look is the Scripts folder, which is in the Library folder. The official AppleScript site has some (www.apple.com/applescript/). Check out the Learn and Explore areas of this site. You'll find snippets of code, links to third-party resources, and even some scripts to download directly.

If you have upgraded to Mac OS X from a previous version of the Mac OS, look for Mac OS 9 scripts in the Automated Tasks folder of the Apple Menu Items folder, which is located in the System Folder. You may find more Mac OS 9 scripts in the AppleScript folder of the Apple Extras folder, which is normally in the folder named Applications (Mac OS 9). Additional Mac OS 9 scripts are located in the AppleScript Extras folder of the CD Extras folder on the Mac OS 9 CD-ROM.

Running Scripts from the Menu Bar in OS 9

For a script menu in the Classic environment, you need the OSA Menu software. OSA Menu allows you to quickly run Mac OS 9 scripts while any Classic application is the active application. The scripts are listed in a permanent menu near the right end of the Classic menu bar. You can also use the Script menu to start recording a script or open the Classic version of Script Editor. OSA Menu is a system extension for Mac OS 9. It's on the Mac OS 9 CD in the AppleScript Extras folder, which is in the CD Extras folder.

Running Scripts

After you've built up a collection of scripts that you run frequently, you're not going to want to switch to Script Editor every time you want to run one. This reason is precisely why Mac OS X has included the Script Menu since version 10.2, which replaces the Script Runner application in 10.1 and earlier. The Script Menu sits in the OS toolbar at the top of the screen. You can run any of the listed scripts by choosing the script from the pop-up menu. To activate the Script Menu, run the AppleScript Utility application from the `/Applications/AppleScript` folder. You can use the AppleScript Utility to work with folder actions, as well as enable GUI scripting. You can even change the default script editor, should you find a third-party editor you prefer.

Linking Programs

You have seen how AppleScript can automate tasks on your own computer. Beginning with Mac OS X 10.1, AppleScript can also send Apple events messages to open applications on other Macs in a network. As a result, you can use AppleScript to control applications on other people's computers. Of course, the reverse is also true: Other people can use AppleScript to control applications on your computer. To send and receive Apple events over a network your Mac must be running with Mac OS X 10.1, 10.2, or Mac OS 9.

Sharing programs by sending and receiving Apple events messages across a network is called *program linking*. For security reasons, program linking is normally disabled. Computers that you want to control with AppleScript must be set to allow remote Apple events. Likewise you must set your computer to allow remote Apple events.

Mac OS X 10.1 and up use the TCP/IP protocol to send and receive Apple events messages over a network. Therefore, Mac OS X 10.1–10.3 can send and receive Apple events messages over the Internet as well as a local network. Mac OS X 10.1–10.3 can't use the AppleTalk protocol to send or receive Apple events over a remote network as can Mac OS 9 and earlier. Mac OS X 10.0–10.0.4 can't send or receive remote Apple events at all.

Allowing remote Apple events

If you want a Mac OS X computer to receive Apple events from remote computers, you must set it to allow remote Apple events. First, open System Preferences and then choose View ⇨ Sharing (or click the Sharing button). In Sharing Preferences, check On for the Remote Apple Events service. New in 10.4 was the ability to restrict the execution of Apple events to specific users. If you want the computer to receive Apple events from remote Mac OS 9 computers, click the options button to the right of the preference pane, then turn on the option labeled Allow Mac OS 9 computer to use remote Apple events. From the drop down sheet you must enter a password that Mac OS 9 users will have to use when sending Apple events messages to the computer. Figure 22.8 shows remote Apple events turned on in Sharing Preferences.

FIGURE 22.8

Set Mac OS X to receive remote Apple events by using the Sharing pane of System Preferences.

Scripting across a network

Using AppleScript to run a program across the network doesn't take much more work than writing a script to use a program on the same computer. For example, the following script sends commands to the Finder on the computer at IP address 192.168.1.203:

```
set remoteMachine to machine "eppc://192.168.203"
tell application "Finder" of remoteMachine
  using terms from application "Finder"
        activate
        open the trash
  end using terms from
end tell
```

Turning On Program Linking in Mac OS 9

If you want a computer that's using Mac OS 9 to receive remote Apple events messages from your computer, the Mac OS 9 computer must have program linking turned on. To do this, open the Mac OS 9 computer's File Sharing control panel and click the Start button in the control panel's Program Linking section. In addition, turn on the option labeled Enable Program Linking clients to connect over TCP/IP. The Mac OS 9 computer is ready for program linking when the button's label changes to Stop and the File Sharing control panel reports "Program Linking on."

Mac OS 9 can be configured to receive remote Apple events only from specific users. These access restrictions are set up with the Users & Groups tab in the File Sharing control panel. In addition, each application on a Mac OS 9 computer can be set to not receive any remote Apple events. This restriction is set in each application's Info window in the Finder.

The example script begins by setting the value of variable `remoteMachine` to the URL of a remote computer. A URL for remote Apple events begins with `eppc://` and is followed by the remote computer's IP address or DNS name. (The prefix `eppc` stands for event program-to-program communication.) Starting with Panther, machines can also be called by their Bonjour name in scripts (no URL required).

The second statement of the example script names the application, in this case Finder, and uses the variable `remoteMachine` to identify the remote computer.

Inside the `tell application...end tell` block is another block that is bracketed by the statements `using terms from` and `end using terms from`. When AppleScript encounters the statement `using terms from`, it compiles subsequent statements using the named application's scripting dictionary but does not send the resulting Apple events to this application. The Apple events from a `using terms from` block are sent to the application named in the enclosing `tell application` block. In the example script, AppleScript compiles the `activate` and `open the trash` statements using terms from the Finder's scripting dictionary on the local computer (your computer) but sends the resulting Apple events to the Finder on the remote computer.

When you run a script that sends remote Apple events, AppleScript has to connect to the remote application. Before doing this, AppleScript displays a dialog box in which you must enter a name and password of a user account on the remote computer. If you connect successfully, the script continues. At this point the example script should cause the remote computer's Finder to become the active application and open the Trash in a Finder window.

If you run the script again, you don't have to go through the authentication process. After AppleScript is connected to an application on a particular remote computer, you don't have to go through the authentication dialog box each time you want to send an Apple event.

AppleScript Studio

You have seen that AppleScript is a very powerful scripting language, and you should now have some ideas as to how you can make your own life more automated. Although AppleScript is billed as a scripting language, it is, for all intents and purposes, a programming language as well. Apple knows this, and has built into the developer's tools a means to easily create an application-quality front end to your AppleScripts. Using AppleScript Studio in concert with Script Editor you can build full-fledged applications with icons, menus, and all of the interface elements associated with a complete application. AppleScript Studio has been incorporated into Xcode and Interface Builder and is included free with Mac OS X.3 on the Developer Tools CD. Cocktail and Carbon Copy Cloner, utility applications mentioned in Chapter 20, are two good examples of applications that were written in AppleScript and given a proper Mac OS X interface using AppleScript Studio.

Automating with Automator

You have seen that using AppleScript is an extremely powerful tool to create your own applications and make your life easier by scripting repetitive tasks simply and cleanly. In Tiger, Apple introduced an even easier tool to Automate your life — Automator. Automator is kind of a visual analog to the AppleScript language. Instead of building scripts using natural language pseudo-sentences, you can drag and drop commands into a Workflow to tell programs what to do.

Automator has a very basic windowed interface, as shown in Figure 22.9. It has three basic sections: a paned section similar to a Finder window where you can choose from a list of applications, a description pane on the right, and the workflow pane on the bottom. The top-left frame contains three panes, one that groups actions by application or name, one that holds your application "library," and one that holds the "actions" available for each application. To the right of these three panes is a frame that provides descriptions for actively selected actions. The pane on the bottom is your workspace — you drag actions from the left to build your workflow here.

Your Library contains available actions and workflows that you can drag to the right frame in order to create new workflows to automate your life. Let's begin by making a QuickTime Slideshow from a folder of images. If you'll remember from Chapter 7, the process was not difficult, but we promised that there would be an easier way. Let's begin by having Automator help us to choose our files.

Click the Files and Folders library in the Library pane to show the available actions for the Finder. Click and drag the list — Find Finder Items — action to the workspace pane. You can use this action to predefine a specific search in the same way that you would use the find function in the Finder. Type **.png** in the name field. Note that you can leave the text boxes blank, click the Options button in the upper bottom portion of the action, and select Show this action when the workflow runs, and when you run your workflow you will be prompted to specify the parameters for the search. Alternatively, you can use one of the other file-choosing actions in the Finder library to get files, such as Get Selected Items From Finder, which allows you to select whichever files you want manually and then run your workflow.

FIGURE 22.9

The Automator interface has a paned application selector, a description pane, and a workspace on the bottom.

Next, drag the Open Files action to the workspace. You'll see the action pop into place right below the action you already placed: Find Finder Items. Notice that there is a little white triangle at the bottom of the Find Files In Finder action, which is dovetailed with the gray portion of the action just below it, Open Files. This is a graphical representation of the idea that the output of the previous action is passed to the action just below it, which in this case is a string of found files. The workflow you have just created searches your computer for PNG files and once found, opens them in the default application for JPEGs on your system, usually Preview. This is not particularly useful for our purposes, so let's remove the Open Files action from our workflow.

You can remove an action from your workflow in several ways that should be familiar to you by now. First, you can click the gray x in the upper right of each action; alternatively, you can click and drag an action out of the workspace. You can also select an action and press Delete on your keyboard. Because you probably don't want to create a QuickTime Slideshow out of PNG files that have the word *John* in them, you should use one of these methods to clear your workspace of actions and we'll begin again.

Begin by dragging the Ask for Finder Items action from the Finder Library, and then select Start at: desktop and Type Folders. If you want to select multiple folders at a time, make sure that you specify that multiple selections can be made using the check box labeled Allow Multiple Selections, as shown in Figure 22.10; otherwise, you will only be able to select one folder in the dialog box during runtime.

Next, you can make things interesting by using CoreImage to do some image processing. From the Photo actions, drag Apply Quartz Composition Filter to Images. Apple has made it as easy as possible to prevent accidents from happening. Because the Quartz Composition Filter makes changes to the original files, the act of dragging the action over to the workflow triggers Automator to ask you if you'd like to add an action, which makes a copy of your files before applying the filter action. Figure 22.11 shows the resulting dialog box.

FIGURE 22.10

Get ready to make a slideshow by telling Automator to choose files during runtime.

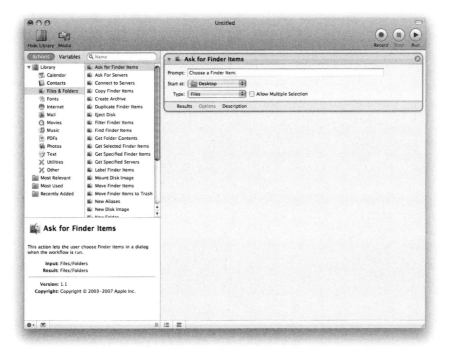

FIGURE 22.11

Automator is smart; it asks if you want to add an action to copy your files.

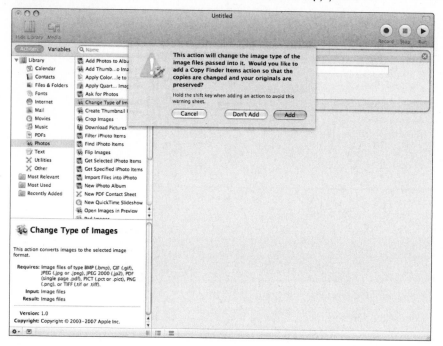

Choose to add the copy action, and specify in the resulting action that you would like to choose where to put the duplicated files during the running of the Workflow. In Figure 22.12, you can see the runtime option is checked for the copy action, but not for the filter. Choose Sepia from the pop-up menu in the Apply Profile Filter to Image to make an old-style movie slideshow.

FIGURE 22.12

You can use CoreImage new Quartz Composition filter action to make your pictures look like old-time photos.

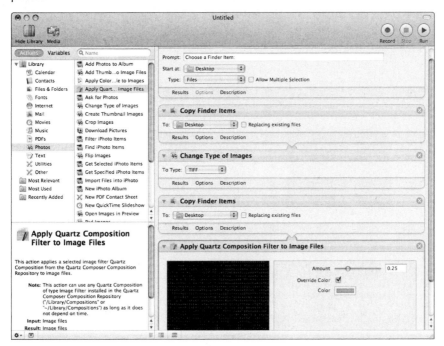

Still in the Photo actions library, choose New QuickTime Slideshow and drag it into your Workflow after the Filter action. As shown in Figure 22.13, you can change the length of time each image stays on-screen, make a self-contained movie or slideshow, and choose where to save the resultant movie. As always you can choose to be prompted to configure these settings during the playback of the Workflow by checking the Ask When Run check box near the bottom of the action. Choose the standard four seconds per image, Movie, Self Contained, and Save in source images folder from the options. If you choose Slideshow instead, you will be able to manually advance through the slideshow, while Movie automatically plays all the pictures in sequence. A self-contained movie or slideshow has the source images inside of itself and doesn't need to have the original pictures around as a reference. A self-contained movie wastes more space but is more portable; you don't need to remember to carry the pictures in the slideshow around with you to show off your children's pictures.

FIGURE 22.13

All the pictures fit to show, made sepia and ready for your enjoyment. Isn't this much easier than the other way?

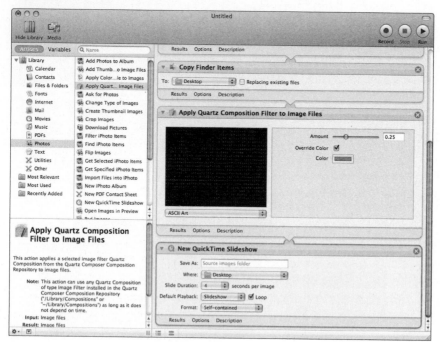

You have just created a slideshow-making workflow that you can use over and over again. Wasn't that easier than in Chapter 17? In order to reuse the workflow, however, you need to save the workspace. Similar to AppleScript scripts, there are two forms in which you can save a workspace: as an Application or as a Workflow document. Like AppleScript applications, Automator Applications can't be edited without directly opening them from within Automator, and Workflows can't be run outside of Automator.

Another neat way to use Automator workflows is to create a plug-in for other programs out of your workflow. By choosing File ⇨ Save As Plug-in you can add the workflow as a contextual menu item in supported applications such as the Finder.

Recording actions

New to Leopard is the ability to record your actions to build workflows and create Automator Actions. This addition makes Automator even easier to use and automate your life. Be aware that it is recording mouse movements and keystrokes, and will play them back in sequence, so it is not as elegant a solution as using an application's built-in workflow actions. However, if an application developer has not provided the interface that you need to build a workflow, or you want to do something more complex, this can be an easy way to accomplish your goal. In order to begin recording and using this feature, you have to have Assistive Devices enabled in the Universal Access System Preference pane. If you do not have Assistive Devices enabled and attempt to record an action, Automator prompts you to enable it. To begin recording an action, click the Record button in the main Automator window. Begin the procedure you want to record. When you are done recording the set of keystrokes, return to Automator and click the stop button. Your recorded keystrokes and mouse movements will be grouped together in a single new workflow action that you can see and edit.

Summary

Here's what you learned in this chapter:

- AppleScript makes applications perform tasks by sending applications Apple event messages.

- AppleScript is a programming language designed with everyday users in mind, but with enough power for advanced users and programmers.

- Many AppleScript terms come from the applications the script is controlling. AppleScript terms also come from files called scripting additions.

- Use the Script Editor application to create, edit, and run AppleScript scripts. Script Editor can also make scripts into applications.

- Script Editor can display the AppleScript dictionary of an application to see what commands an application or scripting addition understands and what objects the commands work with.

- You can save a script in any of three formats: text, compiled script, or Application.

- You type AppleScript statements into a new Script Editor window, check the syntax for errors using the Compile button, and run the script to test it. Your script can use a `copy` statement to set the value of a variable. To start controlling an application, you use a `tell application` statement. A matching `end tell` statement stops controlling the application. With `if` statements, you can have AppleScript perform some operations only when specified conditions are met. Repeat loops execute a group of statements over and over. To make a drag-and-drop script application, you include an `on open` statement and a matching `end open` statement.

- Apple has developed a number of scripts that you can use as starting points or models for your own scripts.

- You can use the Script Menu to run compiled scripts no matter what application is currently active.

- AppleScript can control applications over a network or the Internet on computers that are set to allow remote Apple events.

- Automator is a graphical interface to AppleScript that is not as powerful but is much easier to use for the average person.

- You can save Automator documents as plug-ins to extend the usefulness of other programs that support Automator, or as stand-alone applications you can provide for other people to use.

Chapter 23

Commanding Unix

Mac OS X is built upon a Unix foundation. This foundation is more than a mere graft of Apple's graphical user interface (GUI) over an already existing Unix operating system. Instead, Apple integrated and developed various technologies, to create Darwin — essentially a combination of the Mach microkernel and BSD (Berkley Systems Distribution) Unix. In Darwin, Apple has made their core operating system rock solid, as well as available under the open source model. Being open source means that anybody can download the Darwin OS for free, learn from it, and/or submit bug fixes and modifications to Apple. Although Darwin is free, Mac OS X, in its entirety, is not. The fully fledged commercial version (the one you have to pay for, or that comes pre-installed on your Mac) layers the Darwin core with Apple's Aqua user interface (part of the "User Experience" layer) along with other custom-made Apple technologies like QuickTime and Bonjour (part of the "Application Services" layer) as well as the Quartz engine and Core Image graphics (part of the "Graphics and Multimedia" layer). The result is a marriage of an open source core with Apple-developed interface and technology, analogous to the two ways you can interface with Mac OS X: pointing and clicking in Apple's GUI with the mouse, or using the keyboard to type commands into the Unix command-line interface (CLI).

This first section of this chapter presents a brief history of Unix and shows you how to begin harnessing its power. Unix is a mature operating system with literally hundreds of commands. Apple designed Mac OS X such that you should never have to access the Unix command line if you do not want to; however, if your curiosity gets the better of you, this chapter will help you start exploring Unix.

In this second section, we move on past the basics of using Unix and start to explore some of the advantages of having a Unix-based system. Now that

Apple is the world's leading provider of Unix systems, Macintosh users can get in on the power and flexibility that in the past was available only to users of high-end workstations.

Introduction to Unix

Unix was developed at Bell Laboratories in 1969. It was designed to be a multiuser operating system, meaning that more than one person can use a single computer at a time. Before Unix, the prevalent computers of the time were called mainframe systems. On these systems, only a single user at a time could use the computing resources made available, by creating programs on punch cards and feeding them to the system, then awaiting the output of the program on a nearby paper-and-ink printer. This system tended to isolate programmers and users from each other and provided no facility to save data for reuse. Because the computers of the day were rare and expensive, computing time was at a premium. Unix was designed from the ground up to overcome these and other obstacles. In addition to providing access to more than one program or person at a time, Unix was designed to be interactive, providing output via an electronic Terminal or console display, rather than from a paper-and-ink printer. Unix went through many revisions in the 1970s and 1980s. AT&T was prohibited by law from selling computers or software at that time; instead, it granted licenses to many universities, where deployment and development rapidly took place. Even Apple produced a Unix-based system for its Macintosh line, A/UX (Apple Unix), in the late 1980s and early 1990s. Additionally, the NeXT operating system, acquired by Apple with the purchase of NeXT, is a Unix-based operating system. Much of the original NeXTStep or OpenStep operating system concepts are present in Mac OS X.

A standard Unix implementation includes a large variety of commands that enable users to perform a multitude of operations, from editing text and creating multimedia, to providing and utilizing network services. Most software you would expect to see on a modern desktop computer is available in Unix, including a word processor, e-mail client, Web browser, games, and more. Because Unix was initially developed by and for programmers, you'll find that a large variety of programming languages and tools are pre-installed in standard Unix installations.

CLI in a GUI world

History, or at least folklore, tells us that Apple's graphical user interface (GUI) development arose from a visit to Xerox PARC (Palo Alto Research Center). Apple executives, including Steve Jobs, were impressed with the fledgling foray into a new user experience — the graphical user interface that was implemented on Xerox's Star and Alto workstations. At the time, the newly developed personal computer industry was dominated by machines that used the command-line interface (CLI). Pointing devices, such as mice, were virtually unheard of; the only method of controlling one's computer was to type in commands using the keyboard.

Apple's Lisa, revolutionary at the time, was the first consumer machine to be introduced with a GUI, but at $10,000 each, little software available, and limited (and proprietary) development tools, the Lisa was soon eclipsed by another Apple product, introduced a year later—the Macintosh. From the beginning, traditionalists decried the Mac and its GUI as a toy and opined that "real computer users use the command line." Thus began a religious argument that still occasionally flares today, concerning the advantages and disadvantages of the two approaches. The evolution of Microsoft's operating system from DOS to Windows, along with the advent of windowing systems for Unix seems to demonstrate that the computing tasks in which most of today's users engage are best suited to a GUI. Browsing a Web site containing images and sounds, or even viewing a picture from your digital camera would be difficult, if not impossible on a computer with only a command-line interface. However, there are also many tasks that are easier to perform using a CLI, and some that are impossible to do without one. In Mac OS X, for example, there are certain file permissions that can be viewed and set only from the command line, and in all Unix-based systems, sophisticated text and file searches can be performed in the CLI with little snippets of code that GUI users can only dream of using.

The traditional Unix interface is command line only, although all modern Unix distributions provide graphical interfaces as well. These GUIs include an assortment of window managers running under the X Window System (X Windows, for short). X Windows is a windowing environment for Unix that allows the command line to be eschewed for the graphical interface comprised of the familiar desktop, folders, menus, and of course, windows.

NOTE Apple bundles Xfree86, a freely redistributable open source implementation of the X Windows System with Leopard. Installing this allows you to run almost any of the prodigious number of standard Unix programs right on your Mac! X Windows, or X11 as Apple refers to the software, is an optional installation, covered later in this chapter.

The Terminal

You can access the Unix command line in Mac OS X by using the Terminal application (found within the Utilities folder, inside of the Applications folder). The only thing you really need to do in order to use the Terminal is to type into it! The initial Terminal window is shown in Figure 23.1. The Terminal window presents a few clues about your Unix environment, if you know how to read them:

- **The prompt:** The $ character at the end of the line is called the *command prompt*. It indicates that you are logged in as a standard user (and not as the System Administrator, or root user) as well as, with the cursor directly after it, where your commands will appear when you type them. The prompt also identifies which shell (shells are discussed later in this chapter) you are in. In Mac OS X 10.5 Leopard, the default shell is called the bash, or "Bourne-Again Shell," which is what the $ indicates. The Bourne shell (sh) also uses the $. Other shells, the csh (c-shell) and tcsh (t-shell) are indicated by the % sign.

- **The user ID, or short name:** Indicates the currently logged-in user, which in this case is warren. If you are using your own computer, the short name should be yours!

- **Your working directory:** The directory (the Unix term for *folder*) that you are currently in appears directly to the left of the user ID. In Figure 23.1, the tilde (~) followed by the username (warren) indicates that the user warren is inside of his home folder.

- **The computer:** The leftmost item in the line indicates the name of the physical machine that is in use. In Figure 23.1, the computer is named Ironsides.

FIGURE 23.1

FIGURE 23.1

The Terminal window gives you many clues, if you know how to decipher them.

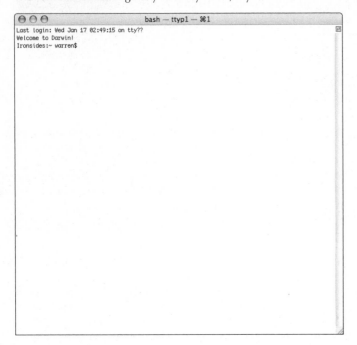

The command-line interpreter in Unix is called a *shell*. The next section delves a little deeper into the default shell and the other shell choices available to you. Apple has had a shell, called MPW, available as part of a package for Macintosh programmers (and other users) since 1986 (and as a free download for almost a decade). The MPW shell differs from the shells available in the Terminal mostly in the following ways:

- The command names are different.

- The wildcards used are different.

- The MPW shell is also a full-featured text-editing environment.

- A Unix shell can spawn processes and has more control due to Unix's multitasking model.

TIP Sometimes applications have options available from the command line that aren't necessarily available through the GUI. For an example, open a Terminal window, type the word **screencapture** and press Return. Read the options for use of the screencapture command carefully — they're much more extensive than the options that the ⌘+Shift+3 and ⌘+Shift+4 keyboard shortcuts allow you to use.

The Shell

The shell is an application that reads user input and reports system or program output. The shell is the primary way a user communicates with a Unix system, and is the primary way the system communicates with a user. Although the kernel does most of the work, the shell is the part that is visible to the user. Various shells are available, such as sh (standard Unix Bourne shell), csh (Berkeley Unix c-shell), and ksh (Korn shell). The Bourne shell, sh, is generally useful in shell scripting, which is discussed later in this chapter. For interactive work, or in Unix parlance, for login sessions, a more maturely featured shell is generally desired. In versions previous to Panther (Mac OS X 10.3), the default login shell was tcsh, which is a significantly enhanced version of csh. Beginning in Tiger (10.4) and now in Leopard (10.5), the default login shell is bash. Bash is the GNU Project's Bourne Again Shell, which has the same syntax as sh but with features similar to tcsh and zsh, such as command-line editing, job control, brace expansion, and a command history similar to csh. More important, bash is the default shell in most Linux distributions. Having the same shell on Mac OS X machines is a great boon for both Linux and Macintosh users. Often, there will be more than one machine on a network, and by becoming familiar with shell usage on the Macintosh, via the Terminal application, you'll know your way around a Linux or other Unix system when you encounter it.

TIP For more information on bash, the project's homepage (`www.gnu.org/software/bash/bash.html`) has all the information.

A Mac OS X installation provides five shells in the standard distribution: sh, csh, tcsh, bash, and zsh. Shells fall into two general camps: sh derivatives and csh derivatives. These camps don't differ by much superficially, but they do some things differently. For example, csh derivatives use setenv to set environment variables, and sh derivatives use a combination of set and export to set these variables.

As mentioned previously, sh is generally used for shell scripts. The same goes for csh, although the beginning shell scripter should be warned against using csh for shell scripting. For further information on that topic, read "Csh Programming Considered Harmful" by Tom Christiansen, available at `www.faqs.org/faqs/unix-faq/shell/csh-whynot/`. Of interest is that, although both sh and csh are available on a Mac OS X system, in fact the man page for sh is a copy of the bash page, and the csh man page is a copy of tcsh page. Both bash and tcsh behave slightly differently when called by their other names (sh or csh). As an aside, the various shells are pronounced differently when speaking: sh is generally referred to as *s-h,* csh is frequently called *c-shell*, tcsh is called *t-shell*, and bash is always pronounced *bash*, which rhymes with cash (never b-a-s-h or b-shell).

In many respects, you can think of the different shells as different dialects of the same language. After you learn one shell, you can pretty much communicate in any of the shells; however, you will occasionally encounter differences in syntax, making the command of a new shell's full range of enhancements difficult. For example, if you're fully proficient in every aspect of csh, all of that knowledge is usable in bash. But to get the full power of bash, you can take advantage of its command history, command substitution, and other enhancements. Command history lets you recall previous commands using various keyboard shortcuts; command substitution lets you reuse previous commands in new instances. Moving to zsh, you would learn different techniques for some of these enhancements.

Some common special characters

Unix originated in an era of extremely limited memory and disk space. Conservation of resources was critical; therefore, command names became abbreviated. Commands and filenames became case-sensitive, which provided more diversity in short names and eliminated the need to provide code-parsing commands into a consistent case for comparisons.

In addition, a number of special and punctuation characters were employed as shortcuts or abbreviations. Some are shown in the following list:

- ~   home directory
- .   current directory
- .. parent directory to the current directory
- /   topmost or root directory

Scripting the shell

All provided shells support *shell scripting*. A shell script is simply a text file containing a list of commands that the shell executes in order. A shell script supports many programmatic constructs such as variables, conditionals, and loops, as well as supports a number of control and redirection operators.

Perhaps you left out the .doc extension on a folder of Microsoft Word files that you want to share with a Windows-using colleague. You can write a very simple shell script to rename all the files in a directory. Your script contains a list of instructions to the shell, using all the constructs listed here. It holds the text string `.doc` in a variable, and uses a loop to first create a list of all files in the directory, then append the variable to each item in the list. Then it writes a log file using output *redirection*. That is, instead of putting output on the screen, as a command is likely to do, output is redirected to a file. The shell provides a control function that enables you to run this program in the background while you do other things, rather than wait for the program to complete before resuming your own operations.

You can find entire books devoted to Unix shell scripting. Here, we give you the basics to get you started, and pointers to where you can find more information. Read on; later in the chapter, we return to this topic, but first we need to cover a bit more background. (The man pages for sh, csh, bash, and tcsh are a good place to begin if you're curious.)

Basic Unix Commands

Unix has hundreds of standard commands. A basic design philosophy of Unix is to have small commands that do exactly one thing right. For example, a Macintosh application may be called Super File Friend. Our imaginary application can do all types of things with files: it can show the contents of a file, duplicate a file, rename a file, delete a file, and even read a file! In Unix, all these functions are possible via the use of separate programs: cp, mv, rm, and cat. All of these small commands can be combined to accomplish any desired result because the small, specialized programs provide an incredible degree of flexibility.

Unix command syntax

The basic form of a Unix command is

```
command-name options arguments
```

The *command-name* is the Unix name of the command, such as ls or mv. *Options* (also called *switches*, or *flags*) are the options you can specify to modify the default behavior of the command and are usually preceded by a minus sign (-). *Arguments* are strings (frequently, but not always, file-names) that provide the command's input and may also specify the output destination. The command to delete the directory called "myfolder," for example, would read

```
rm -R myfolder
```

where "rm" is the file deletion *command*, "-R" is the *option* that specifies recursion (the traversal, and in the case of the rm command, removal of the file and directory hierarchy within the directory specified), and "myfolder" is the *argument*, and in this case, also the file's name.

Unix commands are the CLI equivalent of Mac OS X applications and menu selections. Although Unix command files can be placed anywhere in the file system that you have permission to access, traditionally, they are located in one of several predictable directories such as /bin, /usr/bin, /sbin, or /usr/sbin. Other directories are specified by the PATH environment variable. (Type **echo $PATH** in the Terminal to see what directories, separated by colons, are automatically searched-for commands.) If the command is not located in one of these directories, its location must be fully specified for the shell to execute the command. You can browse these directories in the Terminal by using the ls command. Try typing **ls /bin** to display the command files listed in the /bin directory. In this command, the "ls" (list directory contents) is the command. There are no options this time, and the "/bin" is the argument, again representing the name of a file (in this case, a directory). Your Terminal display should look like Figure 23.2.

A traditional Unix file system is case-sensitive in the naming of files and directories — that is, the file called INSTALL is different from the file Install, which is also different from the file install. Mac OS X modifies this behavior so that filenames are not case-sensitive in the GUI, but case-sensitivity is still the rule when you're working in the shell.

FIGURE 23.2

Using the `ls` command to view the contents of the `/bin` directory

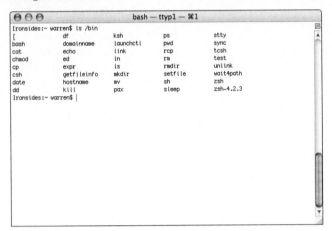

```
Ironsides:~ warren$ ls /bin
[                df              ksh             ps              stty
bash            domainname      launchctl       pwd             sync
cat             echo            link            rcp             tcsh
chmod           ed              ln              rm              test
cp              expr            ls              rmdir           unlink
csh             getfileinfo     mkdir           setfile         wait4path
date            hostname        mv              sh              zsh
dd              kill            pax             sleep           zsh-4.2.3
Ironsides:~ warren$
```

NOTE Although in Mac OS X filenames are case-insensitive, there are still Unix commands and options that retain their case sensitivity. Notably, when Apple adds their own custom Unix commands, they will always be found in camelcase, such as the **CpMac** or **SetFile** commands. (Both are available only after installing Apple's Developer's tools, covered later in this chapter.) Make sure to enter such commands in the proper case.

The man pages

One of the best things about most flavors of Unix is that they come with full documentation, built right into the system. Mac OS X is a prime example of this. Unix documentation comes in the form of manual pages, better known as man pages. Every Unix program has a corresponding man page. If you ever need to learn more about a Unix command's functionality and/or its syntax, you can find all of that in the program's corresponding man page. In Mac OS X, you can load a program's man page by simply using the syntax:

```
man nameofcommand
```

For example, if you want to read more about the chmod command, type the following into the Terminal window:

```
man chmod
```

Mac OS X displays its man pages using the less program, (covered a bit later in the chapter) a simple text display program. When you press Return after typing your man request, the Terminal screen displays text corresponding to the command in question. As the text is in the less program, use the spacebar to advance the text and type a **q** to quit the display program. If you have followed the example and brought up the man page for **chmod**, you can see that there are pages of information, many advanced options, and even examples of things that you can do.

Specifying Filenames

The Macintosh file system is hierarchical in that you can use unlimited levels of folders to contain files and other folders, which all lead back to a single parent directory. You can consider each volume (other hard drives, CDs) to be a separate hierarchical entity. Your hard disk (usually called Macintosh HD) is the top, or root level of your file system's hierarchy. Viewed as an upside-down tree, the top of the Unix hierarchy is called by a single-character name, /, which represents the *root* of the tree. When speaking a file's path name aloud, the / character is referred to as "slash." Under some Unix systems, other volumes are represented as directories within the file system hierarchy of the hard drive. Under the Mac OS X GUI, there is a separate "Computer" level, outside of the file system of your Macintosh HD, which appears to contain any other volumes that are present. In the Mac OS X command line, you can see that these volumes are actually mounted in a /Volumes folder, which is a directory residing on the root level of the Macintosh HD.

The slash character is also used to separate levels in the *path* from root (or any other reference point) to a given file. For example, the full path to a file named ToDo.rtf in the Documents folder of a user named Warren would be:

```
/Users/warren/Documents/ToDo.rtf
```

If you omit the leading slash, you're assumed to be specifying a path *relative* to your current directory rather than an *absolute* path specification.

Deciphering the Unix man pages can be a little daunting. They can be succinct to the point of being nonsensical, and appear complicated to the point of uselessness. Don't worry—the important thing to realize is that all the man pages are based on the very simple Unix command syntax that we have just discussed. Keeping the command-name options arguments syntax in mind enables you to utilize commands solely by reading about them in their man pages. The good news is that the more man pages you read and understand, the easier new ones become to decipher. With enough practice, they begin to make sense on first read!

If you do not know the exact command name, but know what you are trying to do, you can do a search for man pages by using keywords. If you want to try mounting an afp volumee and are not aware of the **mount_afp** program, you can try typing **man –k afp** to initiate a keyword search of the man pages for the term "afp." Sure enough, the last result is the **mount_afp** entry. Some people prefer to use the separate **apropos** command in place of **man –k**, but both accomplish the same goal.

Logging in and logging out

Remember, Unix is a multiuser system. Even if you're the only person who uses the computer, you're still in a multiuser world. As the Activity Monitor application shows you, even when you are the one using the computer, there a number of different users who execute system-level processes. Try running the top command in the Terminal (shown in Figure 23.3) to see the command-line equivalent of the Activity Monitor. Type Control+c (^c) to return to the command prompt.

FIGURE 23.3

The `top` command is analogous to the GUI-based Activity Monitor.

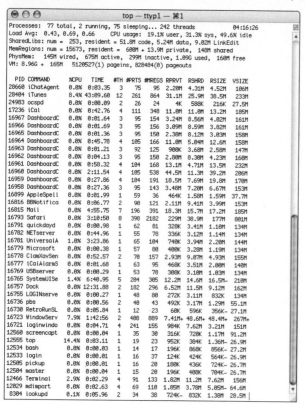

When you first installed Mac OS X, you created an administrator account and assigned it a password. Partially masking OS X's multiuser nature, this account logs in automatically when you start your computer; however, you can turn off automatic login in the Accounts pane of System Preferences (refer to Chapter 17) if your computer is going to have multiple users; you might not want the system to automatically grant access to your account (and thus all of your files) every time your Mac is rebooted.

Just as you're always logged in as a specific user when using the Mac OS X GUI, you're also logged in as a specific user when you use the Terminal application — the CLI. One difference is that you can use Unix commands to change which user identity is in effect for part of your Terminal session. The command used to change users is called `su` (for substitute user). Until you create other accounts or enable root login, no other identities are available to you.

> **TIP** You can execute a single command as root, even if you haven't enabled the root login by using the `sudo` command followed by the desired command as an argument to `sudo`. For example, the command `sudo chown root myfile` executes the `chown` (change owner) command, causing the file `myfile` to belong to root. As a caution, you'll be prompted for your own password when using a command through `sudo`. Access to `sudo` is configured by a text file etc/sudoers. This file is edited via a program called visudo. Visudo is a wrapper application, which opens the /etc/sudoers file for editing, but in addition it locks the file so the file can't be changed by the system while being edited. For more information on `sudo` and visudo, including configuring `sudo` for multiple users, consult man sudo, man visudo, and man sudoers.

The most visible effect of each user having a distinct identity is that, when each user creates files, the files are marked as belonging to that user. You can see this in the Finder by choosing File ⇨ Get Info and then choosing the Details disclosure triangle under the Ownership & Permissions pane in the info window. In Terminal, type **ls -l** *filename* (assuming *filename* is the file's name).

As shown in Figure 23.1, the default command-line display includes your user name. If you've changed your prompt or you're unsure, or just curious, typing the whoami command displays the currently active user's name.

If you use the `su` command to switch the user to the root user, two things change in the Terminal. The user, instead of your username, is listed as root. The second difference is that the prompt changes. Instead of the $ appearing at the end of the line, you will see a #. The # makes it easy to see, even with a quick glance, that you are logged in as the root user. Because the root user has full permissions for the entire file system, (including the ability to delete crucial system files) it is important to be aware of your root login.

One advantage of using the Terminal to execute commands as another user is that you don't have to switch out of your own user environment and into another user's to run commands as said other user, as you would have to do even under Leopard's GUI-based Fast User Switching. In the CLI, you can just `su` to that user, as shown in Figure 23.4, execute the commands, and terminate their shell session with `exit` or `control-d` (^d). This is often faster and more convenient than changing users in the GUI.

Managing files and directories

Just as you always have an active window in the Finder or a current folder in which an application opens or saves files, you have a *current directory* (also known as *working directory*) when using the Terminal application. As you can see in the previous figures, the default shell prompt provides your current directory and user account name. However, you can customize the shell prompt, (possibly to make it shorter) and still find your working directory by entering the pwd (print working directory) command.

As noted earlier in this chapter, some shortcut symbols are used with the shell. In particular, shortcut symbols for directories are ~ (user's home directory), . (current directory), and .. (parent directory to the current directory).

FIGURE 23.4

Use the `su` command to temporarily change your identity.

```
Last login: Wed Jan 17 04:17:35 on ttyp1
Welcome to Darwin!
Ironsides:~ warren$ whoami
warren
Ironsides:~ warren$ su flywheel
Password:
Ironsides:/Users/warren flywheel$ exit
exit
Ironsides:~ warren$ su root
Password:
Ironsides:/Users/warren root# exit
exit
Ironsides:~ warren$ logout
[Process completed]
```

To change your current directory, you use the `cd` (change directory) command. For example, `cd ~` takes you back to your home directory, and `cd /` takes you to the root of the file system.

Obtaining a list of the files in a directory is as simple as entering the `ls` command. This command has a number of switches available that you can use to modify its behavior; the more useful and common ones are described in Table 23.1:

TABLE 23.1

`ls` Options

Option	Description
-a	Show all files, even invisible (those whose names start with a .) ones.
-F	Append a character to the names of executables (*), directories (/), and links or aliases (@). Characters for sockets are =, for whiteouts are %, and for queues are |, which we do not cover in this book.
-f	Don't sort the output (the default list is sorted alphabetically).

Option	Description
-L	If the file is a link, resolve the link and list that file.
-l	Long listing, including owner, group, size, permissions.
-n	Use the user and group ID numbers rather than names in a long listing.
-R	Recursively list all subdirectories.
-r	Reverse the sorting order.
-S	Sort by size, largest first.
-s	List the number of 512-byte blocks actually used by each file.
-t	Sort by time modified, most recent first.
-x	Sort multicolumn output across page rather than in columns.
-1	Force output to one item per line (the screen output defaults to multicolumn).

Another useful command when dealing with files and directories is the `file` command. If you type **file /Users**, the `file` command attempts to tell you what kind of file /Users is — in this case, a directory. The `file` command also recognizes other file types, such as TIFF, RTF, text, and so on.

Using Unix to delete stubborn files

Sometimes, the Finder is unable to move or delete files that are in the trash. The error message "The operation cannot be completed because you do not have sufficient privileges for some of the items" often appears. In this event, there are two options in the command line that you can use to permanently remove the files. The first way is to use `rm`. Use the following steps to try both options:

First, try simply removing the file, using `sudo` to have root privileges used for the operation.

1. **Type** sudo rm –f *filename* (**or** sudo rm -rf *foldername* **if it's a folder**). `sudo` then prompts you for your password.
2. **Type the password, and the prompt should return.** If there is no error, the file has been removed.

If that fails, it's because of a special file flag, which has been set on the file and marks it to the system as locked or protected.

First, you remove the flag, and then you remove the file.

1. **Type** sudo chflags -R nouchg filename. After taking your password, the prompt returns.
2. **Now type** sudo rm filename **to remove the file.** If you simply want to place the file in the trash and delete it later, you can now use the Finder to put the file in the trash.

Autocompletion of filenames

One of the really nice features of bash and tcsh is that you don't always have to type long file-names. Just as Safari attempts to complete URLs as you type, these shells attempt to complete the name for you, if you press the Tab key while typing a filename. Upon a single press of the Tab key, if you have only one choice that completes what you've typed thus far, the shell completes the name; however, if multiple possibilities exist, the Terminal bell beeps, indicating that there is no exact match for your prefix. Upon pressing the tab key a second time, a list prints (as shown in Figure 23.5) and displays the items that share the common prefix you began to type. After the list is another command prompt with the characters you have typed in, giving you further opportunity to be more specific. This process continues until your typing prior to pressing the Tab uniquely identifies a file or, using wildcards as described shortly, a group of files.

FIGURE 23.5

Desktop and Documents are offered as possible completions for the letter *D* as entered. To complete either choice, continue typing either word, then press Tab as soon as it becomes unique.

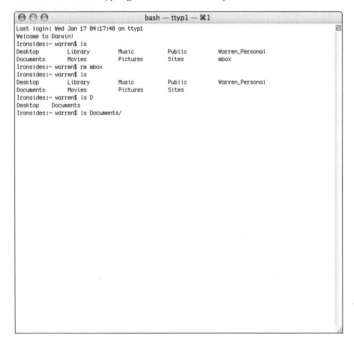

Unix wildcards and regular expressions

You're probably getting the idea by now that one of Unix's characteristics is to express the most amount of information in the tersest manner. Using *regular expressions,* a shorthand notation for arbitrary strings of characters, the shell buttresses this impression. If you've used BBEdit

(BareBones Software, `www.barebones.com`) or any of a number of other applications, you've encountered *grep* (global regular expression parser), and the power that this shorthand provides in matching patterns and strings.

Regular expressions can be used on the command line within a command's arguments, or within applications (particularly text editors) to perform searches or find and replace operations (also called substitutions).

In its simplest form, an *expression* is a string of characters, such as document name. Two special wildcards are used in regular expressions:

- **Asterisk (*)**, which stands for any sequence of characters
- **Question mark (?)**, which stands for any single character

You can also tell the shell to match any character from a list by enclosing the list in square brackets, which makes what is called a *character set*; for example, `[aeiou]` would indicate that any lowercase vowel would be a matching character. You can even tell the shell to match any character that is *not* in the list by preceding the list with a caret (^) placed inside of the square brackets. For example, the regular expression `[^aeiou]` would match any character that is not a vowel. You can also use special characters called *anchors* if you want your query to match a string of characters at either the beginning or the end of the line. A caret (^) placed outside of the square brackets (really, at the beginning of any pattern to be matched), for example, `^[aeiou]`, would match any line beginning with a vowel. A dollar sign ($) placed at the end of the pattern to be matched, for example, `[aeiou]$`, would match lines ending in a vowel. Finally, a pattern enclosed by the anchors, for example, `^[aeiou]$`, will match lines containing only that pattern and nothing else.

NOTE Yes, the caret is used for both negation and to denote beginning-of-line. Here, you need to be aware of the context. If the caret is the first character within square brackets (a set of characters), it means "anything except the characters enumerated." But if the caret is outside the brackets and is the first character of the expression, it means "beginning of line."

Giving you even more to remember (but less to type), you can specify ranges of characters, for example `[a-z]`, to specify any lowercase alphabetic character. Now, the obvious question arises, "But what if I want to match a hyphen?" The so-called *escape character* (\\) comes into play here; any character following the escape character is to be taken literally. In other words, a \\ is used to escape any special character and to hide its meaning from the shell. In the case that you want to use a \\ literally, you'll escape it as well by using the \\ character, as in \\\\.

TIP Certain escape characters have special meaning in regular expressions. To denote a line break, you use \\n; to specify a tab character, use \\t; and to match a page break, use \\f.

You can use *metacharacters* to specify how many times a pattern may repeat. The pattern may be a literal character, a wildcard character, a character class, or a special character. The asterisk (*) denotes zero or more occurrences of the pattern — therefore, the pattern is always true. Similarly, the question mark (?) signifies zero or one occurrence of the pattern. Finally, the plus sign (+) tells the shell to find one or more occurrences of the pattern.

> **NOTE** There is actually another repetition indicator. You can enter a {*n*}, where *n* is a digit, to indicate matching exactly *n* occurrences of the pattern. Entering {*n*,} specifies matching *n* or more occurrences of the pattern, and entering {*n,m*} indicates matching at least *n* but no more than *m* occurrences of the pattern.

Just as you can combine patterns to form more-complex patterns, you're provided with an *alternate* character (an or operator), enabling you to match any of a collection of patterns. This character is the vertical bar (|).

Table 23.2 illustrates some of the ways you can use wildcards and regular expressions to find matches.

TABLE 23.2

Use of Wildcards and Regular Expressions to Find Matches

Pattern	Meaning
[Ff]ile[0-9]	Match anything spelled file, whether or not the f is capitalized and followed by a single digit
*.pdf$	Match any string ending in .pdf
^From*Warren$	Find any line starting with From and ending with Warren
^[^a-z]	Find the first character of any line that does not start with a lowercase letter
1[01]:##[\t][Pp]\.[Mm]\.	Find any time entry starting at 10 p.m. but before midnight
sam|tom|doug	Find any sam, tom, or doug (but not on the command line; only in grep, Unix's global regular expression parser command)

You can even create remembered patterns by enclosing the pattern within parentheses. These remembered patterns are often referred to as *tagged regular expressions*. Within the same command, you can specify the remembered patterns by specifying \1 for the first, \2 for the second, and so on in a subsequent argument. Such references are referred to as *back references*. Back references can take considerable time to evaluate; however, they are of particular advantage when doing search-and-replace operations in an editor.

> **NOTE** Operators function in precedence (order) in regular expressions. Repetition operators are evaluated before concatenation operators, and concatenation takes precedence over alternation.

Grep

Unix wildcards and regular expressions can be used simply to specify file names on the command line. For example, if your working directory is your home folder, and you want to view the contents of all of the folders inside of your home folder that begin with the letter *D*, you can type the command `ls D*`. The asterisk indicates a match of any number of characters coming after the letter *D*.

Wildcards and regular expressions are infinitely more powerful, however, when paired with grep, the global regular expression parser. For our purposes, grep is essentially an extremely powerful text searching tool. A common way to use grep is to redirect the standard output of a command, and instead of displaying the results on-screen, use the grep filter to further narrow down the output. This is known as piping, and is represented by the vertical bar (|) character. For example, the command `ls | grep motorcycle` will first list the contents of the working directory, and pipe that output to a grep of the word *motorcycle*. The command will return on screen only those files that have the word *motorcycle* in their names. See more on piping and output redirection later in this chapter.

Creating and deleting directories and files

Analogous to the Finder's New Folder command, the shell offers the `mkdir` command to create a new directory. You can even create a new (empty) file by using the `touch` command and specifying a file name that does not already exist. Running the `touch` command on an existing file changes the file's modification date and time to the current date and time.

Unix doesn't really need a `rename` command because it has something just as good; the `mv` (move) command. If you move a file with a new name rather than copy it into the directory in which it already resides, you have renamed it. Moving a file deletes the original. Of course, you use a `cp` (copy) command when you don't want to delete the original. Both commands have similar syntax and typically have two arguments: the source filename(s) and destination filename. Moving a picture file called motorcycle.jpg from the working directory to the documents folder would read:

```
mv motorcycle.jpg ~/Documents
```

Both `cp` and `mv` have a number of options available, which you can read about by typing **man cp** or **man mv** at the Terminal command prompt.

You delete files with the `rm` (remove) command. Unix shows a different mindset from that typical of the Mac OS or Windows; the effects of `rm` are immediate and irrevocable. If you want to provide a little bit of safety while possibly increasing the annoyance factor, you can use the `-i` option, which interrogates you regarding each file that you have specified to delete, as shown in Figure 23.6. Entering **y** when prompted indicates an affirmative response. Anything else is taken as a negative. One option of note is the –R flag, which tells the shell to recursively copy or move the contents when a source argument is a directory.

To remove an empty directory (one with no files inside of it), you use the `rmdir` command. If the directory isn't empty, you receive an error message to that effect, and the directory will not be deleted. You can, however, use the `rm` command with either the `-R` or `-r` switch to recursively delete a directory and its contents. Again, adding the `-i` switch causes the shell to interrogate you for each file and directory before deleting it.

FIGURE 23.6

FIGURE 23.6

Using the -i option with the rm command

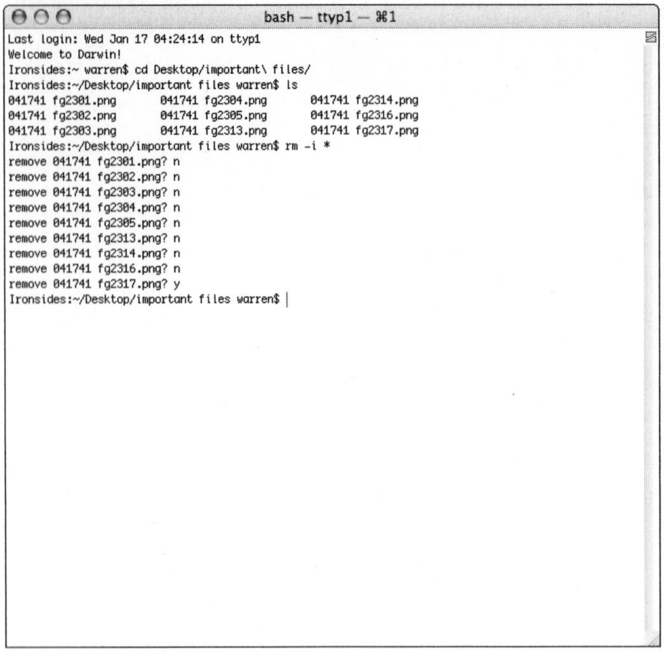

```
000                    bash — ttyp1 — ⌘1
Last login: Wed Jan 17 04:24:14 on ttyp1
Welcome to Darwin!
Ironsides:~ warren$ cd Desktop/important\ files/
Ironsides:~/Desktop/important files warren$ ls
041741 fg2301.png      041741 fg2304.png      041741 fg2314.png
041741 fg2302.png      041741 fg2305.png      041741 fg2316.png
041741 fg2303.png      041741 fg2313.png      041741 fg2317.png
Ironsides:~/Desktop/important files warren$ rm -i *
remove 041741 fg2301.png? n
remove 041741 fg2302.png? n
remove 041741 fg2303.png? n
remove 041741 fg2304.png? n
remove 041741 fg2305.png? n
remove 041741 fg2313.png? n
remove 041741 fg2314.png? n
remove 041741 fg2316.png? n
remove 041741 fg2317.png? y
Ironsides:~/Desktop/important files warren$ |
```

Disk and file system statistics

Two commands, du (disk utilization) and df (display free space), allow you to find out how much space you're using for your files and directories and how much space is available.

Displaying free space

By default, the df command gives you a report such as the one shown in Figure 23.7. It gives you a list of all the file systems you have mounted, where they are mounted, how many 512-byte blocks are on the file system, how many are used, how many are still available, and the percentage of capacity utilized. Divide the number of blocks by 2 to get the number of kilobytes, or use the -k option to specify that you want the results in kilobytes.

FIGURE 23.7

df tells you how much space each file system has and how much is being used.

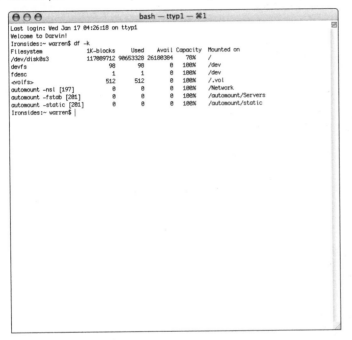

You can give a single file as an argument to df to get statistics for just the file system on which the specified file resides. Notice that the file system names are not normally the names of the volume (such as Macintosh HD) but rather the cryptic Unix device names. You can make more sense of these names by using the diskutil command, the command-line equivalent of Apple's Disk Utility. Type **man diskutil** for more information.

Disk utilization

The du command breaks the information down into finer increments, giving you statistics for files and directories, as shown in Figure 23.8. With no argument(s), du reports on utilization by all files and directories, recursively, from the current directory. With a file for an argument, you get the number of 512-byte blocks used by that file. With a directory as an argument, du gives you the information for that directory and recourses, or continues, through any directories contained within the directory. Employing the −s option tells du to summarize (not enumerate), also shown in Figure 23.8.

FIGURE 23.8

To get an itemized breakdown of disk space used, use du with no options — the -s option gives a summary. The output here shows the first, cancelled list of individual items, and the second, one-line summary from the -s flag.

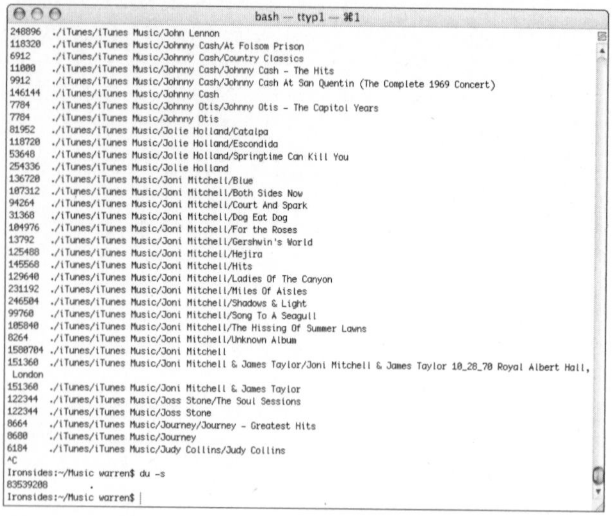

```
000                    bash — ttyp1 — #1
248896   ./iTunes/iTunes Music/John Lennon
118320   ./iTunes/iTunes Music/Johnny Cash/At Folsom Prison
6912     ./iTunes/iTunes Music/Johnny Cash/Country Classics
11808    ./iTunes/iTunes Music/Johnny Cash/Johnny Cash - The Hits
9912     ./iTunes/iTunes Music/Johnny Cash/Johnny Cash At San Quentin (The Complete 1969 Concert)
146144   ./iTunes/iTunes Music/Johnny Cash
7784     ./iTunes/iTunes Music/Johnny Otis/Johnny Otis - The Capitol Years
7784     ./iTunes/iTunes Music/Johnny Otis
81952    ./iTunes/iTunes Music/Jolie Holland/Catalpa
118720   ./iTunes/iTunes Music/Jolie Holland/Escondida
53648    ./iTunes/iTunes Music/Jolie Holland/Springtime Can Kill You
254336   ./iTunes/iTunes Music/Jolie Holland
136720   ./iTunes/iTunes Music/Joni Mitchell/Blue
187312   ./iTunes/iTunes Music/Joni Mitchell/Both Sides Now
94264    ./iTunes/iTunes Music/Joni Mitchell/Court And Spark
31368    ./iTunes/iTunes Music/Joni Mitchell/Dog Eat Dog
104976   ./iTunes/iTunes Music/Joni Mitchell/For the Roses
13792    ./iTunes/iTunes Music/Joni Mitchell/Gershwin's World
125488   ./iTunes/iTunes Music/Joni Mitchell/Hejira
145568   ./iTunes/iTunes Music/Joni Mitchell/Hits
129640   ./iTunes/iTunes Music/Joni Mitchell/Ladies Of The Canyon
231192   ./iTunes/iTunes Music/Joni Mitchell/Miles Of Aisles
246504   ./iTunes/iTunes Music/Joni Mitchell/Shadows & Light
99768    ./iTunes/iTunes Music/Joni Mitchell/Song To A Seagull
105040   ./iTunes/iTunes Music/Joni Mitchell/The Hissing Of Summer Lawns
8264     ./iTunes/iTunes Music/Joni Mitchell/Unknown Album
1588704  ./iTunes/iTunes Music/Joni Mitchell
151360   ./iTunes/iTunes Music/Joni Mitchell & James Taylor/Joni Mitchell & James Taylor 10_28_70 Royal Albert Hall,
London
151360   ./iTunes/iTunes Music/Joni Mitchell & James Taylor
122344   ./iTunes/iTunes Music/Joss Stone/The Soul Sessions
122344   ./iTunes/iTunes Music/Joss Stone
8664     ./iTunes/iTunes Music/Journey/Journey - Greatest Hits
8608     ./iTunes/iTunes Music/Journey
6184     ./iTunes/iTunes Music/Judy Collins/Judy Collins
^C
Ironsides:~/Music warren$ du -s
83539200      .
Ironsides:~/Music warren$
```

Viewing and Editing Files

Unix's command-line environment brings with it a number of tools for dealing specifically with editing information, not only within the files, but about the files themselves. You have tools to display a file's contents, and many kinds of editors, from ones that execute commands a line at a time, through screen editors, to stream editors that process commands against entire files.

Standard input, standard output, and pipes

To the shell (and to Unix in general), any place it obtains or places data is a file. The keyboard data stream is a file, the window in which output appears is a file, and files on your disk are files. The input stream from your keyboard is the default for a special file called standard input (stdin). The default file for output, your Terminal window, is called standard output (stdout). You can redirect standard input to come from some other file by preceding the filename with a less-than sign (<). Similarly, you can redirect standard output by using a greater-than sign (>). If, for example, you wanted to create a file containing a directory listing of your Documents folder, you could type **ls Documents >docdir.txt**, as shown in Figure 23.9. A number of commands display the contents of files. Among these commands are cat, less, pr, head, and tail. The meaning for each command is provided in Table 23.3.

FIGURE 23.9

Output from the list directory (`ls`) command is redirected into a text file docdir.txt. The concatenate (`cat`) command is used to view the file.

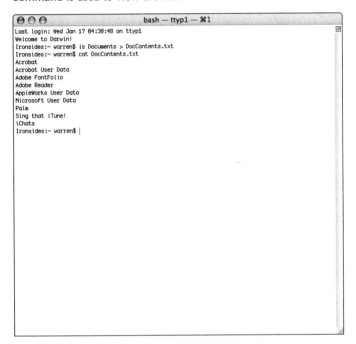

TABLE 23.3

Commands that Display Contents of Files

Command	Meaning
cat	Concatenate the files given as arguments and display on standard output.
less	Display the arguments on standard output a page (window full) at a time. You type a space to get to the next screen; type **b** to go back a screen. Typing a return advances one line, and typing **q** terminates the command.
pr	Similar to `more`, but it includes page headers and footers at would-be page breaks if the output were directed to a printer.
head n	Display the first n (10 if n is omitted) lines of a file on standard output.
tail n	Display the last n (10 if n is omitted) lines of a file on standard output.

Paths and Variables

With few exceptions, such as cd, almost every command you enter at the Unix prompt is a program stored on your disk. The shell is a programming environment, complete with loops, conditionals, and variables. Shell programs are usually called *scripts*. Shell programs are *interpreted* rather than *compiled*. Therefore, when a shell script or command executes, the shell parses the command, evaluates the variables, and then executes instead of having the instructions reduced to binary machine instructions.

You create shell variables by using the set command. For example, set myPath = "~/MyApps" would create a variable named myPath that had the value /Users/warren/MyApps (assuming that your user name is warren). You can determine the current value of any shell variable by issuing the echo command, with the variable name, preceded by a dollar sign ($), as an argument. One very important shell variable is PATH. PATH is the variable the shell evaluates to determine where it should look for commands you issue. The following figure shows the initial value of PATH for the user warren.

```
⬤ ⬤ ⬤                    bash — ttyp1 — ⌘1
Last login: Wed Jan 17 04:28:21 on ttyp1
Welcome to Darwin!
Ironsides:~ warren$ echo $PATH
/sw/bin:/sw/sbin:/usr/local/bin:/bin:/sbin:/usr/bin:/usr/sbin:/usr/X11R6/bin
Ironsides:~ warren$
```

As you can see, PATH is a series of directory specifications separated by colons. Every time you issue a command, such as ls or cp, the shell starts checking each directory in PATH until it finds the command and executes it. If the command cannot be found in any directory in PATH, you receive an error message to that effect. If the program is not in one of the PATH directories, you need to specify a directory path to it. To execute a command in your current directory, you precede it with ./. If you're curious as to which directory holds the command you want to execute, you can use the which command (a built-in shell command). The which command can come in handy if, for example, you're attempting to execute a newly installed command, and the wrong command executes because a command with the same name was located in an earlier PATH directory.

> **TIP**
>
> You can append output to an existing file by using two successive greater-than signs. For example, `ls Movies >>docdir.txt` would append the directory listing for your Movies folder to the file docdir.txt.

You can chain commands together with the pipe symbol, a vertical bar (|), so that the output from the first command is the input to the next. For example, `ls –R | more` would display a recursive directory listing one screen at a time.

Most commands default to taking their input from standard input. For example, if you omit the file argument from the cat command, cat patiently waits for you to enter it from the keyboard. When you enter data from the keyboard, you need to indicate that you're finished by entering the Unix end-of-input character, accomplished by pressing the Control key and typing the letter **d** (Control+d).

Learning permissions

In addition to read and write permissions, you find that all Unix files have execute permissions at the file level. Because Unix commands aren't applications with an APPL file type (or a bundle with an .app extension), the shell needs some way to indicate that a particular file is executable. Unix has used this method of file-based permissions for over three decades now.

The execute permission is a great example of something that you can access from the command line, and not from the graphical interface. In Figure 23.10, a Finder Get Info window, you can see full read and write configuration options for the owner, group, and user of the file, but nary an execution option in site. In Figure 23.11 you can see the ls –l command and the permissions for each file consisting of r, w, x and – characters. The first group indicates owner permissions, the second, group permissions, and the third, permissions for everyone. The x character is the execution permission, glaringly absent from the GUI.

FIGURE 23.10

File permissions in the Finder, with no execution options

FIGURE 23.11

File permissions in the Terminal, with r, w, and x all present and accounted for

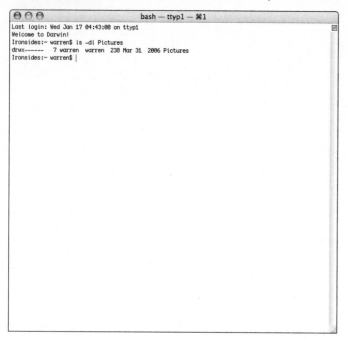

```
● ● ●                    bash — ttyp1 — ⌘1
Last login: Wed Jan 17 04:43:00 on ttyp1
Welcome to Darwin!
Ironsides:~ warren$ ls -dl Pictures
drwx------   7 warren  warren  238 Mar 31  2006 Pictures
Ironsides:~ warren$ |
```

> **NOTE** Each file has three sets of r, w, and x, representing owner, group, and everyone; yet, if you look carefully, there are ten characters at the beginning of each line. This is because the first character represents the file type. In the case of Figure 23.11, a dash indicates a regular file, and a d represents a directory. Special files, such as links or device drivers, have different indicators.

Permissions on directories have a slightly different but analogous meaning compared to files, as shown in Table 23.4.

TABLE 23.4

Unix Permissions and Meanings

Permission	Meaning for a File	Meaning for a Directory
r read	Ability to view contents of a file	Ability to view contents
w write	Ability to edit the contents of a file	Ability to create, rename, or delete files within directory
x execute	Ability to run a command, script, or application program (called executables)	Directories need the execute permission set in order to behave properly

Permission	Meaning for a File	Meaning for a Directory
- hyphen	Indicates no permission	The hyphen means that the permission in question has not been set
t sticky bit	Doesn't effect executable files	Special directory permission that doesn't allow deletion of files by users who didn't create them

Commands, programs, and shell scripts are examples of files for which execute permission should be enabled. As with any other file, these files have three levels of permission: owner, group, and everybody.

NOTE Unix users typically refer to permissions as three (octal) digit numbers. Read permission is worth four points, write permission is worth two, and execute permission is worth one. Therefore, when you hear that a file has 740 permission, the first digit being 7 means that the owner can read, write, and execute the file (4 + 2 + 1 = 7); the second digit being 4 means members of the group can read the file (4 + 0 + 0 = 4); and the third digit being 0 means everyone else has no permissions with respect to the file (0 + 0 + 0 = 0).

Changing permissions

The chmod command enables the owner or root user to change the permissions on a file. The simplest form of this command is to follow chmod with the new permissions and then the file or list of files to receive those permissions. For example, chmod 777 myscript.sh would give read, write, and execute permission to everyone for the file myscript.sh.

If you do not want to do the math, you need to remember only letters: u for user (called owner in the Finder), g for group, o for others (called Everyone in the Finder), a for all, r for read, w for write, and x for execute. You also need to remember three symbols: + to add a permission, - to subtract a permission, and = to set permissions. For example, chmod g+w dirdoc.txt would add write permission for members of the group to the file dirdoc.txt without affecting any other permissions.

Changing owner and groups

Only the owner of a file and root user (system administrator) have the authority to change a file's owner. Assuming that you either own the file, or have logged in as root or are running from an administrator account and using the sudo command, the syntax to change a file's owner is chown newownername filelist. The newownername is either the new owner's login name or the numeric user ID, (retrievable through the id command) and filelist is the file or files whose ownership is to be changed.

If you're a member of the group to which you want to change group ownership, and have write and execute permissions to the files and directories in question, you can change the group ownership of a file with the chgrp command, whose syntax is the same as the chown command except that you use a group name or number rather than a user name or number.

> **TIP** To determine to which groups you belong, you can enter the `groups` command. You can also determine to which groups another user belongs by typing groups with the user name as an argument.

Advanced Unix Topics

Unix is a highly configurable environment with a wealth of tools. This section introduces some tools and commands available to you when interacting with a shell in Terminal.

Environment and shell variables

Every time you log in, open a new Terminal window, or switch shells, the shell checks its initialization files to establish your environment and your shell variables. Each shell handles its initialization files and environment settings somewhat differently. The default shell (bash) is covered in this section.

First, bash reads files referred to as *shell initialization files*. These files set specific behaviors for the shell. There is usually a system-wide shell initialization file located at `/etc/profile`; this file will be read and used by all users on the system. Generally, a user would like to set personal options for his or her shell. For this reason, the home directory is scanned for the following invisible files: ~/.bash_profile, ~/.bash_login, or ~/.profile. (Remember that by using a period as the first part of a filename, the file will be invisible to an `ls` command, unless the `-a` switch is provided.) For introductory purposes, the three files are functionally equivalent. If none of these files are in your home directory and you want to experiment with changing local variables such as your shell prompt, default editor, and so on, you should create a ~/.bash_profile file and make changes in that file.

> **NOTE** By convention, environment variables are all uppercase, and shell variables are all lowercase. Thus, the environment variable `PATH` and the shell variable `path` can (and usually do) have different values.

Enter the `env` command to see a list of your current environment variables and the `set` command to see a list of your current shell variables. Examples of both are shown in Figure 23.12.

Changing environment variables

You can change environment variable settings or declare new environment variables for the current session by entering a command of the form: export VARIABLENAME=new_value where VARIABLENAME is the environment variable you want to change or declare and new_value is the value you want to give it. This value persists until you log out or exit the shell in which you're working.

FIGURE 23.12

The env and set commands display environment and shell variables, respectively.

If you want to make the change apply to future sessions, you need to edit the ~/.bash_profile file (or the ~/.bash_login or ~/.profile file). You can do this with a shell editor, such as vi, emacs, or pico. You can also do so with a Mac OS X text editor, such as TextEdit or SimpleText (SimpleText still survives as part of the Developer Tools installation!). But you first have to make an unhidden copy in the shell (the Open dialog boxes won't display hidden files), edit that copy, and make sure to save the result as plain text, and then replace the hidden file with the edited copy. Proceed as follows:

1. **If it's a new variable, add the export command to the .bash_profile file.** If it's a change to an existing variable, find the line where that variable is declared and change the line.

2. **Save the file and exit the editor.**

3. **Enter the command source** .bash_profile **if you want the change to take effect.**

 The default location of .bash_profile is your home directory.

The source command feeds the contents of the file arguments to the shell as input.

Changing shell variables

To define a temporary value to a shell variable, use the following command:

```
variable_name=value
```

The value of this variable remains set until you exit from this shell. The value of this variable is not exported to other shells when they're invoked.

To give a lasting value to a shell variable, follow these steps:

1. **Use an editor to open your ~/.bash_profile file and add the following line:**

   ```
   variable_name=value
   ```

2. **Save the file and leave the editor.**

3. **Enter the command:**

   ```
   source ~/.bash_profile
   ```

   The value of the shell variable is added to your shell's present environment. When subsequent shells are invoked, they also have this variable set.

Creating aliases

No, these aren't the same aliases available under Mac OS X. Unix aliases are shortcuts for other Unix commands. To create an alias for use with the bash shell, add the command alias alias-name=what-it-stands-for to the ~/.bash_profile file and enter the source .bash_profile command, making the obvious substitutions.

One example of an alias is the following:

```
alias whatamirunning='ps –aux | grep $USER | more'
```

This command sequence pipes (sends) the output of the process status command as input to grep, which searches that input for the processes you're running and then displays the results a screen at a time.

You can even chain multiple commands together in an alias by separating them with semicolons. For example, alias `tree ='cd; ls –R'` would display a complete directory hierarchy of a user's home directory when the command `tree` was entered.

Manipulating text file contents

Just as Unix provides the cat, pr, head, tail, and less commands (mentioned earlier in this chapter) to display files or parts of files, it provides a variety of editors and other tools with which to create, edit, and summarize text file contents. In addition to the ancient command-line editor, ed, you also have vi, pico, and emacs, all of which are screen editors. Screen editors offer functionality similar to line editors where you enter commands describing the editing action you want to take, and the windowing editors where you directly manipulate text, generally making selections with a mouse, such as TextEdit. In a screen editor, file contents are displayed on a Terminal screen, and you move the cursor around via the keyboard and shift modes between overstrike and insert, with the option of still using the commands of the old-line editors. Although multiple editors are available in Mac OS X, among the screen editors, only vi is guaranteed to be included with every Unix distribution, so a knowledge of vi, whether or not it is your editor of choice, is recommended.

Each editor is well documented in its man pages, and full books are written about their use. Which is the best for you is a decision only you can make after trying them out. Each has a devoted, almost religious, following.

Some other tools you can use to work with file contents are listed in Table 23.5.

TABLE 23.5

Text File Tools

Command	Description
Compress	Reduces the size of files by encoding, similar to StuffIt or WinZip, but only compresses individual files. Use uncompress to restore the file to its original state. Convention has it that the .z extension indicates a compressed file. To create compressed archives, use tar to create the archive and then compress to reduce its size.
Cut	Selects portions of each line of a file.
Diff	Compares two files.
Fmt	Reformats the files given to have consistent line lengths — default is 65, maximum is 75 characters. This tool originated primarily for the manipulation of line breaks in e-mail messages.
Grep	The (in)famous regular expression parser is used to find all instances of patterns within a file or list of files.
Sed	A stream editor, it reads the file(s) specified, modifying the input based upon the command(s) listed and passing the result to standard output. The editing commands may be stored in a file, one per line.
Sort	Reorders the lines of a file into a user-defined order. Sort order can be alphabetical, reverse alphabetical, or other combinations.
Split	Divides a file into multiple parts, each (except possibly the last part) of the same size. Use cat to recombine the files.
Tar	Creates (uncompressed) archives of the files given as arguments. Short for *tape archiver*, it's used to package files together.
Uniq	Removes duplicate adjacent lines. Pipe the output of sort to uniq if you want to remove all duplicates.
Wc	Reports the number of characters, words, and lines in a file.

Writing shell scripts

You can do more with the shell than just execute commands. The shell is a programming language that you can use to write your own text programs or commands. These programs are called *shell scripts*. The main strength of shell scripts is that you can use them to invoke a possibly long and complex sequence of instructions, with logical branches, as though the sequence were a simple command.

Writing a shell script is similar to entering the commands manually in a Terminal window, with a few significant differences:

- You may want your command to accept arguments. The shell automatically assigns any strings following your script's name on the command line to a set of parameters: shell variables named $1 through $9. You don't have to do anything special to obtain arguments from the command line; they're already available in the parameter variables when your script begins its execution. If you need more than nine arguments, you can use the shift operator in your script to access later variables.

- You may want your new command to support options. The shell passes options to your script the same as any other arguments: Each command-line string is set into the $n variables (also accessible in the special shell array variable argv[n]).

- Usually, you enter keyboard commands with all information explicitly stated; however, commands inside shell scripts are often parameterized and can be executed conditionally. You parameterize a command by providing variable references and filename substitutions as the command's arguments instead of literal text. You need to use the shell's if, switch, while, and foreach commands to handle alternative paths of executions. You rarely use these commands at the keyboard, but they occur often in shell scripts.

Regardless of the use to which you're going to put a shell script, almost all shell scripts are developed using the following general plan:

1. **Develop a text file containing the required commands.**
2. **Mark the text file executable,** using the chmod command chmod +x filename to make it executable for all users.
3. **Test the shell script.**
4. **Install the script in its permanent location.**
5. **Use it.**

If the script is for your personal use, create a ~/bin directory and add it to your search path, as described earlier in this chapter (see the "Changing shell variables" section). After you create a new script, you can just mark the script executable and drop it in your personal bin directory, and it will be available for use.

When testing a script, you may want to see which commands are being executed so that you can track an unexpected behavior. To do so, invoke your script with the command bash -x scriptname or embed a set echo command in your script.

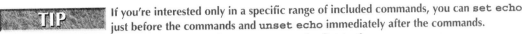

TIP If you're interested only in a specific range of included commands, you can set echo just before the commands and unset echo immediately after the commands. Remember to remove these set and unset commands after testing.

As with most any other programming language, internal documentation in the form of *comments*— lines that are not executed but are meant to explain what is going on—is considered very good form. Lines beginning with a *splat* (MIT jargon for the sharp or number sign character, #) are taken as comments by the shell. In fact, the shell ignores anything starting with a splat to the end of that line as a comment unless the splat is escaped with the backslash character (\).

Making Use of Unix

Apple provides a wealth of applications with a default installation of Mac OS X. However, a plethora of additional software is available for Unix to meet all your needs and wants. From more flexible network utilities and Internet clients to graphic applications and office suites, they're all available and easily installed. In this section, we provide an overview of major free software available for Mac OS X and cover the installation of Unix-based software on Mac OS X.

What Can I Do with Unix?

The preceding section provides a rough survival guide for Unix. Now that you're familiar with the underpinnings of the system, it's time to roll up your sleeves and see what you can do with this new operating system.

The programs of the most interest as you explore the Unix side of Mac OS X are Terminal, which you have already been introduced to, and X11. Terminal and X11 are found in the Utilities folder inside the Applications folder. X11 may require a separate installation, depending on how Mac OS X was installed on your computer. (We discuss this later in the chapter.)

The reason for all the excitement regarding these perhaps unfamiliar applications is that prior to OS X, they were never part of Apple's operating system. Of course, Telnet and other Terminal emulation applications have been available for ages, since around 1988 when Apple developed MacTCP and licensed it to universities and developers. However, these programs were used to connect your Macintosh to the command-line interface of other computers, usually large hosts that were shared by many users. X-Windows servers were also available for pre-Mac OS X systems; however, these too were used to connect to clients on other computers. Terminal and X11 on Mac OS X focus internally. That is to say, they connect to your own computer. If you've had access to a Unix machine located elsewhere (for example, at your ISP or in a computer lab), having a full-fledged Unix machine on your own desk can be an exciting prospect.

NOTE In the world of X-Windows, traditional concepts of client-server are turned upside down. The program that you use to connect to an application either on your own computer or on a host computer is called a *server*. The program that runs on a host computer listening for connections and allowing access to authenticated visitors is called a *client.*

With access to a Unix system, you can do all kinds of fun and useful things, from working on systems at work or in other locations to providing services to other users. Programs are available on Unix systems that are unavailable for other systems. If you manage other Unix systems, either at work or elsewhere, a home Unix system is indispensable. Most of the Internet is based on Unix systems in some shape or fashion. Having the same system at home opens a lot of doors for exploration and enables you to do a lot of things that you could never do before, either because you wouldn't have administrative access to the system, or just because you never had it so close at hand.

Network services are transparent using Unix. Most popular Internet services were developed on Unix systems. The protocol TCP/IP, which is used for almost all Internet traffic, was developed on Unix systems. TCP/IP is the native communications protocol for Unix systems. Therefore, communicating with other systems is a simple matter. It's easy to connect to other computers, for Web surfing, file transfer, or anything else you may want to accomplish. Files can be copied and even edited in place with very simple commands. Where older operating systems required networking to be explicitly enabled, or the installation of additional software, networking is part of the core of Unix.

More programming languages are compatible with Unix than with any other mainstream operating system. That makes Unix a great asset for anyone who is interested in learning how to program a computer. Programming languages other than AppleScript are out of the scope of this book, but you're using the right operating system, should you decide to pursue any type of programming.

Installing Additional Software

Apple has included a good selection of software with Mac OS X. However, sooner or later you'll find yourself wanting to do more with your computer than work with the included applications. You may also want to avail yourself of the wealth of software available for Unix. To install traditional Unix software on your Macintosh, you'll first need to ensure that you have the right tools.

Installing Apple software for Unix

Apple provides several software tools that allow further access to the Unix system than do the applications that come shrink-wrapped with Mac OS X. In order to install additional Unix software, Apple Developer Tools must be installed. Read on for an explanation of the developer tools and why you'll need to have them installed.

When software developers write software, they write it using a computer language. In the past, for the Macintosh, traditionally this was Pascal. On Mac OS X, however, there are many more choices for the developer. Popular choices are C, C++, Objective-C (developed by NeXT Computer, and now called Cocoa by Apple), Java, and many others. After source code is written, it is run through a piece of software called a *compiler*. The compiler takes the human-readable code that the programmer or programming team wrote, and transforms it to machine code that the computer can execute. When code is compiled, the result is a binary file, which is no longer human readable. If programmers want to make a change to a compiled program, they would need to make changes to their source code and then recompile the code, producing a new binary program. Generally, when you purchase software for your computer, you're given only the binary application, not the source code. In other words, when you purchase software for your computer, no assembly is generally required.

Working with Unix software is an entirely different experience. Unix has its roots in academic research and its initial user base was mostly programmers. The operating system was designed by programmers and for programmers. The standard way of distributing software for Unix is by distributing the source code. This is considered useful because the user is now empowered. Don't like the way something works? Change it yourself. Find a bug, fix it, and e-mail the developer with what you did. This active participation means that the user never has to wait for a vendor fix. Of course, most users are busy doing other tasks and don't generally feel compelled to fix bugs in their software. However, knowing that you can fix a bug is a comfort for many.

A user is expected to have the tools installed on his or her own system to compile or build the software locally, after making changes to the source code. The advantage to this is that the software can be written in one place but can run on a variety of systems. This is immediately visible when you consider that much software has been written to run on Linux, but it can be compiled on a Mac OS X system and run as if it were designed for a Mac. We cover installing some popular free software utilities later in this chapter. For now, you have to install some tools that will allow you to install software later.

 If you haven't already done so, you'll have to install the Apple Developer Tools software. The Developer Tools software is part of the new Xcode software for software developers.

In order to install Developer Tools, you need to insert the Mac OS X Leopard install DVD into your computer. Navigate to the Xcode Tools folder, launch the Install Xcode Tools package (XcodeTools.mpkg), and click through the first few screens. When you get to the installation type, choose Custom, and then select at least Developer Tools Software and the Mac OS X SDK as shown in Figure 23.13. Other packages are optional. When the installation has completed, you can see the software by navigating to the /Developer folder.

With Xcode tools, Apple has included, with every Mac OS X installation, a fully fledged programming and development environment. The main feature is the Xcode application itself, which supports a plethora of programming languages, from C, C++, and Objective C to Java, and can be used for building full graphically interfaced applications as well as command-line-only utilities. Also included are a number of sample and demonstration applications, performance and debugging software, extensive documentation, and a folder of Apple-created Unix commands. These commands have been created to help bridge the gap between Unix and Mac OS X's proprietary attributes. The `SetFile` command, for example (mentioned earlier in this chapter) is needed to set file attributes such as visibility or whether or not to hide the file extension, that are unique to Apple's Finder and do not exist in the Unix world. Notice that while Unix commands are traditionally lowercase, Apple differentiates their homegrown ones by using mixed, or camelcase.

FIGURE 23.13

Use the Xcode Tools installer to install Apple's Developer Tools software.

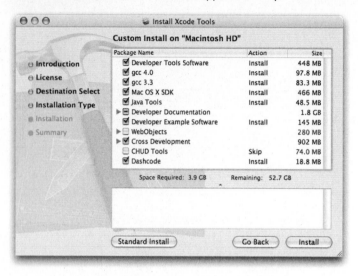

Installing X11 for Mac OS X

Because OS X is based on Unix, it would make sense to be able to run the large number of programs that already exist for Unix. Apple has provided a way to do just that with a fully featured X-Windows implementation in their X11 software. X11 encompasses an entire graphic environment for a computer. Everything that Aqua does for Mac OS X, X-Windows does for a Unix system. Apple has done a great job of hiding this complexity. X-Windows systems provide what is called a *window manager*. The window manger does exactly what it sounds like it does: It manages windows, including where windows are located on-screen, whether windows are minimized, window dimensions, and so on. In short, all the things that you see on-screen are, in fact, managed.

X11 for Mac OS X also contains a window manager. This one is different from what you would see on a traditional Unix or Linux system. The one that Apple provides is invisible. The elements that it draws are functionally and visually equivalent to their Aqua counterparts. Hence, a window's title bar looks the same whether it is being presented by Aqua or X11. This is a significant achievement, although it looks like nothing. This allows you to seamlessly switch between applications, regardless of which system they were originally designed for. As discussed in the Appendix, when using Classic, application title bars and menus also appear differently from the way they do in Mac OS X-native applications.

If X11 was installed on your computer at the factory or when you installed or upgraded to Leopard, it will be available in your Utilities folder. If X11 has not been installed, you will need to use the Leopard installation media and install it manually. Open the Optional Installs package and choose X11 from the list of software under the customization panel, and let the installer complete its task.

Using Third-Party Installation Tools

Now that you have ensured that both Apple Developer Tools and X11 are installed, you're ready to leap into the deep end of software installation. There are two ways to go about installing software on your system: the surefire, longer way; and the very easy way, which may sometimes not work quite the way you would like, requiring you to go back to the long way. In this section, you'll set up the system to run third-party software designed to aid you in the task of installing additional software. The little bit of effort in installing this software will more than pay off in ease of use for installing software in the future. And it will keep your installed software up to date. This is an important benefit because most open-source software projects are constantly improving; the only way to benefit from these software improvements and security updates is to be running the latest versions.

The day the first public beta of Mac OS X became available, there were thousands of software programs already available for the new OS in the form of source-code downloads. Early adopters rushed to build their favorite software on Mac OS X, and they found that with simple tweaks to the makefiles and other install files (both of which are mostly of use only to programmers and compilers), the software would build and run. Over time, many developers integrated these changes that were made by individual users into their own software distributions, making their programs easier to install on the Mac. However, each program has to be dealt with individually; some have been adapted for Mac OS X, and others have not.

Fink — Gateway to Unix Software

Tracking which software will build out of the box, and which requires little tweaks can be a real chore. If you're simply looking to use a program that may be useful to you, you probably don't want to spend a lot of time trying to get it to work on your computer. This is where Fink comes in. The developers of Fink have tracked hundreds of software packages and integrated the changes that let this software build and run under Mac OS X, patching the source code where necessary and doing other busy work so that you don't have to.

The Fink Project

Fink is a project that grew out of the excitement of Mac OS X being based on Unix. Early adopters to Mac OS X realized the power of the new operating system and were eager to mine the wealth of free Unix software available at sites like `http://freshmeat.net/`, `http://sourceforge.net/`, and other such repositories. Although building each individual software package was not entirely difficult, each package offered its own unique challenges. The Fink developers, initially Christoph Pfisterer and others, started to make notes of what had to be done to each package, and then developed a tool to automate making these changes. Also, most Linux systems have software that automates not only the installation process, but also the upgrade process. After a piece of software is installed on your system, you should be able to upgrade it simply. Often, upgrading Unix software can be a chore. The goal was to ease this operation, and make the entire procedure more Mac-like in the process. To learn more about Fink and their project goals, visit their Web site at `http://fink.sourceforge.net`.

Over time, the Fink project has collected many Unix applications and has made installing these applications on your Macintosh extremely simple. Fink was initially built to be run from the command line. However, you can also use Fink in conjunction with another piece of software called FinkCommander. FinkCommander provides a graphical user interface (GUI) to the Fink software. This provides all the utility of the command-line program with the familiar ease of use of a Macintosh application. First, you install Fink, and then you install FinkCommander.

Fink can be downloaded from the project homepage at `http://fink.sourceforge.net`. Follow the download link and click to download the binary installer. The current version is 0.8.1; however, the software is continually updated, so make sure to get the latest version. The binary installer is available as a disk image (.dmg) file. After downloading and expanding the disk image file, you'll have a disk image with several items. The main feature is the Fink Installer.pkg file. Double-click the package file to launch the Fink installer to install Fink on your system, as shown in Figure 23.14.

FIGURE 23.14

Run the Fink installer from the binary installer disk image.

After the installation is complete, a shell script opens in a new Terminal window. The script asks for permission, before changing your shell configuration files to execute the script `/sw/bin/init.sh` at login. Fink creates a directory at the root of your hard drive called `sw`. The script `/sw/bin/init.sh` adds `sw` to your search path as well as enables any http or ftp proxies that may be set in the Fink configuration file. Figure 23.15 shows the `pathsetup` script launched in a Terminal window.

When the Fink install is completed, a script named `pathsetup` is launched in a Terminal window. Enter **Y** to continue.

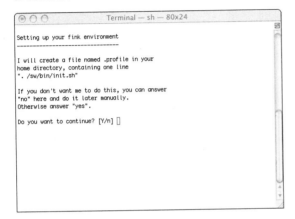

```
● ○ ○              Terminal — sh — 80x24

Setting up your fink environment
--------------------------------

I will create a file named .profile in your
home directory, containing one line
". /sw/bin/init.sh"

If you don't want me to do this, you can answer
"no" here and do it later manually.
Otherwise answer "yes".

Do you want to continue? [Y/n] ▯
```

Using Fink to Install Software

You can use Fink in several different ways to browse through available software and install and upgrade software packages on your Mac OS X system. For complete information and instructions, please refer to the Fink documentation provided at the project's documentation home page, `http://fink.sourceforge.net/doc/users-guide/`, or follow the links in the included Documentation.html file in the Fink installer disk. A brief listing of the available ways to use Fink follows:

- **Fink:** This is the catch-all command. It works to download and compile source code on your computer. This no-frills command will generally work when other invocations pose problems. You use the fink command to install software in the following section. In order to use the fink command you'll need to have the developer tools installed. To use the fink command, simply type **fink** in a Terminal window.

- **dselect:** Dselect is a curses-based application that runs in Terminal. Curses is a Unix library which controls screen display in a Terminal window, providing menus and inverse video, and allows a program to run in full-screen mode (full Terminal window mode, that is), rather than as line-based output. Like other curses-based applications, dselect takes over the entire terminal window, allows you to use the arrow keys for navigation, and is very friendly to use, as far as command-line-based software goes. Dselect has extensive built-in help pages and is very simple. You can use dselect to browse the Fink software collection. A useful feature of dselect is that it will show you the version of the software that you have installed, and will show you the latest version available from Fink. This is helpful in order to ensure that the software you're running is the most up to date. If there is a newer version available, upgrading is as simple as selecting the package for installation. Figure 23.16 shows the dselect program running in a Terminal window.

FIGURE 23.16

Browsing available packages with dselect

- ■ **Apt-get:** Apt-get is the engine that does the heavy lifting for dselect. Apt-get is invoked at the Terminal, as are the other utilities. We will not be discussing the use of apt-get. If you are curious, however, typing **apt-get -h** in a Terminal window will get you started.

- ■ **FinkCommander:** FinkCommander is a GUI for Fink. Its functionality is identical to dselect, except that it's a traditional Mac OS X GUI application. FinkCommander is included in the Fink installer disk. Simply drag the application folder from the mounted installer disk to your hard drive, preferably in your Applications folder. To launch the software, double-click the icon in your Applications folder. Using FinkCommander to browse available software is shown in Figure 23.17.

NOTE   It is important to realize that there are two main types of Fink installation packages: binary, and source. Binary packages are ideal — they require merely to be downloaded and installed, and are ready to use shortly. This is because they are applications that have already been complied for use on Apple hardware under Mac OS X. Less ideal are the source code packages. Although still quite useable, the source packages need to be compiled after they are downloaded, which can take many hours per package.

FIGURE 23.17

Browsing available packages with FinkCommander

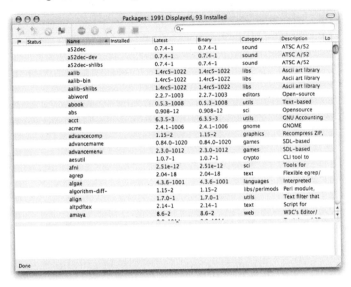

Now that Fink is installed on your system and you're comfortable using it to locate, install, and update software, you need to explore this treasure trove of software.

Adding Useful Software

In this section, we give a brief overview of additional software that can be installed on your Mac OS X system, to make your computer a bit more usable, flexible, and fun. All the software discussed in this section can be installed in several ways. Because the software mentioned is all open source, full source code can be downloaded from the respective projects' home pages. In the spirit of Unix, we installed the following packages with Fink from the command line. FinkCommander can be used to install the software as well.

Lynx

Lynx is a text-based Web browser, meaning that it runs in a Terminal window. Lynx has no GUI. It doesn't display graphic images as pictures; instead, it displays their addresses. This sounds useless but it can prove indispensable in troubleshooting Web pages, because most search engines "see"

Web sites in text form only. It's great to see what's going on with a remote site that is proving slow to load. Also, it can be invaluable in tracking down Web bugs either in Web pages or e-mail. Web bugs are generally invisible and cannot be viewed with a traditional Web browser. Figure 23.18 shows the Lynx browser in action.

FIGURE 23.18

Text-based Web browsing with Lynx

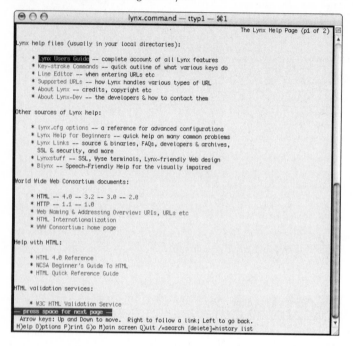

To install Lynx using Fink, simply type **fink install lynx**, as shown in Figure 23.19. For more information on Lynx, visit the project home page at http://lynx.isc.org/.

FIGURE 23.19

Installing Lynx with Fink

```
                          bash — ttyp1 — ⌘1
Last login: Wed Jan 17 05:08:33 on ttyp1
Welcome to Darwin!
Ironsides:~ warren$ fink install lynx
Password:
Information about 4721 packages read in 5 seconds.
The following package will be installed or updated:
  lynx
curl -f -L -O http://distfiles.master.finkmirrors.net/lynx2.8.4.tar.bz2
  % Total    % Received % Xferd  Average Speed   Time    Time     Time  Current
                                 Dload  Upload   Total   Spent    Left  Speed
100 1895k  100 1895k    0     0   206k      0  0:00:09  0:00:09 --:--:--  225k
dpkg-deb -b /sw/src/fink.build/root-fink-buildlock-lynx-2.8.4-25 /sw/src/fink.build
dpkg-deb: building package `fink-buildlock-lynx-2.8.4-25' in `/sw/src/fink.build/fink-buildlock-lynx
-2.8.4-25_2007.01.17-05.13.10_darwin-powerpc.deb'.
Setting build lock...
/sw/bin/dpkg-lockwait -i /sw/src/fink.build/fink-buildlock-lynx-2.8.4-25_2007.01.17-05.13.10_darwin-
powerpc.deb
Selecting previously deselected package fink-buildlock-lynx-2.8.4-25.
(Reading database ... 15839 files and directories currently installed.)
Unpacking fink-buildlock-lynx-2.8.4-25 (from .../fink-buildlock-lynx-2.8.4-25_2007.01.17-05.13.10_da
rwin-powerpc.deb) ...
Setting up fink-buildlock-lynx-2.8.4-25 (2007.01.17-05.13.10) ...
bzip2 -dc /sw/src/lynx2.8.4.tar.bz2 | /sw/bin/tar -xvf - --no-same-owner --no-same-permissions
lynx2-8-4/
lynx2-8-4/ABOUT-NLS
lynx2-8-4/CHANGES
lynx2-8-4/COPYHEADER
lynx2-8-4/COPYING
lynx2-8-4/INSTALLATION
lynx2-8-4/LYHelp.hin
lynx2-8-4/LYMessages_en.h
lynx2-8-4/PROBLEMS
lynx2-8-4/README
lynx2-8-4/VMSPrint.com
lynx2-8-4/WWW/
lynx2-8-4/WWW/Library/
lynx2-8-4/WWW/Library/vms/
lynx2-8-4/WWW/Library/vms/COPYING.LIB
lynx2-8-4/WWW/Library/vms/libmake.com
lynx2-8-4/WWW/Library/vms/descrip.mms
```

NcFTP

NcFTP is a command-line FTP client. It's a full-featured FTP client, with many modern features, and it's free! It has a wealth of features that make using FTP from the command line a pleasure. Some features of NcFTP are progress meters, command-line editing, filename completion, auto-resume downloads, bookmarks, host redialing, downloading of whole directories, and more. NcFTP is very much like a Web browser for FTP servers. Figure 23.20 shows the NcFTP help text.

FIGURE 23.20

NcFTP—full featured FTP from the command line

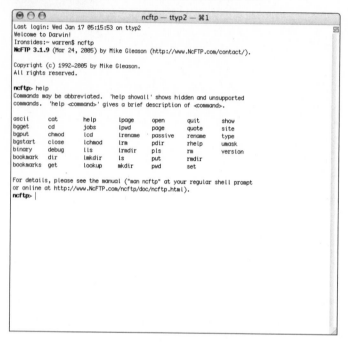

NcFTP also comes with the utility programs ncftpget and ncftpput. These programs are provided as conveniences for shell scripting. These programs can be used in shell scripts to automate FTP actions, such as downloading logs from a Web server or uploading data to a server on a nightly basis.

For more information on NcFTP, visit the NcFTP client home page at www.ncftpd.com/ncftp.

To install NcFTP, simply type **fink install ncftp**, as shown in Figure 23.21.

Wget

GNU Wget is designed for downloading Web content from the command line. Where Lynx is a full-featured Web browser, Wget is specifically designed for when you're trying to download the files comprising a Web site. Additionally, Wget can download from FTP servers using the FTP protocol. Wget is useful for when a server is very busy. You can copy the address from your Web browser into your Clipboard and let Wget download the file for you.

Wget is easily scripted, making it a perfect tool to use in automated scripts that you run at night via cron. You could run scripts to download nightly builds of Mozilla or other actively developed software projects.

FIGURE 23.21

Installing NcFTP with Fink

Wget is very useful when you want to download an entire Web tree — perhaps a documentation section of a Web site, or a site you're working on and want to archive a local copy of the site. For example, you can download the documentation for Wget from www.gnu.org. Enter the following command:

```
wget -r --level=1 -p -k
    http://www.gnu.org/software/wget/manual/wget-
    1.8.1/html_node/wget_toc.html
```

-r turns on recursive retrieval.

--level=1 sets the depth of recursion to one. This downloads only files in the same directory as the target document. Setting the level to 0 gets the entire site. In practice, setting the level to a low number to conserve bandwidth and disk space is generally most efficient.

-p downloads all page requisites, images, and files needed to display the page.

-k converts the links in the document to relative links that will work correctly from your hard drive, allowing you to view the site offline.

This form of usage is very handy if you want a local mirror of a Web site, or if you want to back up a remote site. Such a command can also be used in a shell script and called by cron nightly.

For additional information on Wget, visit `www.gnu.org/software/wget/wget.html`.

To install Wget, simply type **fink install wget**, as shown in Figure 23.22.

FIGURE 23.22

Installing GNU Wget with Fink

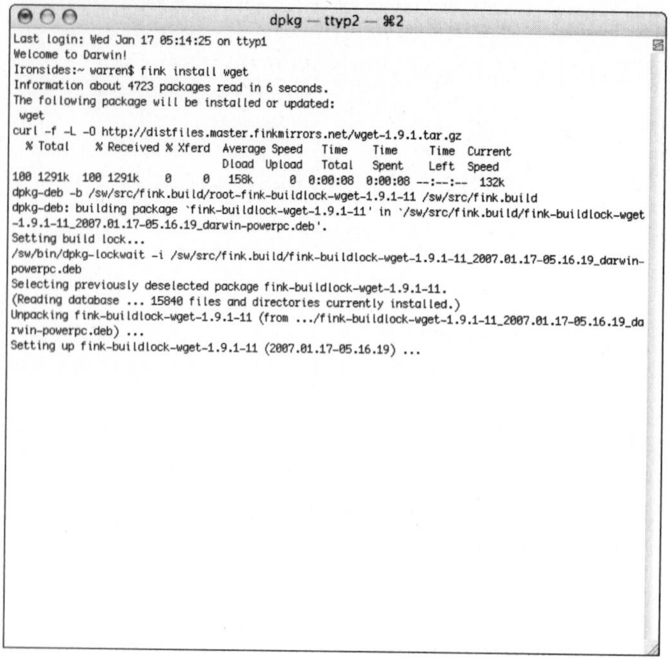

```
dpkg — ttyp2 — ⌘2
Last login: Wed Jan 17 05:14:25 on ttyp1
Welcome to Darwin!
Ironsides:~ warren$ fink install wget
Information about 4723 packages read in 6 seconds.
The following package will be installed or updated:
  wget
curl -f -L -O http://distfiles.master.finkmirrors.net/wget-1.9.1.tar.gz
  % Total    % Received % Xferd  Average Speed   Time    Time     Time  Current
                                 Dload  Upload   Total   Spent    Left  Speed
100 1291k  100 1291k    0     0   158k      0  0:00:08  0:00:08 --:--:--  132k
dpkg-deb -b /sw/src/fink.build/root-fink-buildlock-wget-1.9.1-11 /sw/src/fink.build
dpkg-deb: building package 'fink-buildlock-wget-1.9.1-11' in '/sw/src/fink.build/fink-buildlock-wget
-1.9.1-11_2007.01.17-05.16.19_darwin-powerpc.deb'.
Setting build lock...
/sw/bin/dpkg-lockwait -i /sw/src/fink.build/fink-buildlock-wget-1.9.1-11_2007.01.17-05.16.19_darwin-
powerpc.deb
Selecting previously deselected package fink-buildlock-wget-1.9.1-11.
(Reading database ... 15840 files and directories currently installed.)
Unpacking fink-buildlock-wget-1.9.1-11 (from .../fink-buildlock-wget-1.9.1-11_2007.01.17-05.16.19_da
rwin-powerpc.deb) ...
Setting up fink-buildlock-wget-1.9.1-11 (2007.01.17-05.16.19) ...
```

GIMP

GIMP stands for the *GNU Image Manipulation Program*. GIMP is free software distributed by GNU. GIMP is basically a free implementation of Adobe Photoshop. Although GIMP is not as complete as Photoshop, it's quite capable. It has most of what you want from a graphics program — it does considerably more than simply converting graphics between file formats. It is a handy piece of software to have installed, for those times that something comes in via e-mail or otherwise, and you want to make changes to it. Figure 23.23 shows the GIMP at work. The project home page is located at `www.gimp.org`.

FIGURE 23.23

The GIMP in action

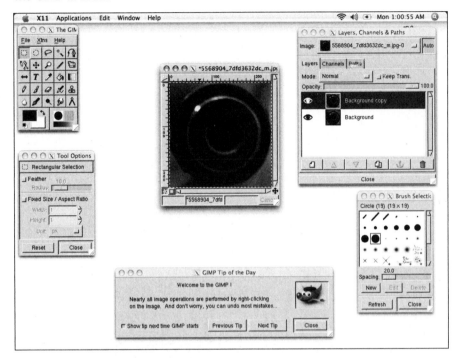

If you do not have a copy of Adobe Photoshop or Macromedia Fireworks installed on your system, the GIMP is invaluable software. Even if you do already have a full-featured image editor installed on your system, GIMP is worth installing—it's interesting to see just how good free software can be.

Installing the GIMP can be very complicated because there are many separate pieces of software that need to be built. Thankfully, Fink has GIMP in its library, so although installing GIMP is initially as simple as typing **fink install gimp**, there are more stages to this install than others we have seen thus far. The GIMP install process takes quite a while because there are a lot of software packages that require download; thankfully, Fink automates almost the entire process. Because the GIMP relies on many different software packages, you'll have to answer some questions before continuing. Run the (now) familiar `fink install gimp` command.

Fink needs to know the answers to several questions. The first question regards how to handle GIF images. There are two available libraries, one with LZW and the other without. The two packages offer the same functionality; the distinction is due to politics and copyright issues. Either choice will result in a working GIMP. The second question is for Fink to know where and how X-Windows is installed on your system. Before Apple made X11 available for Mac OS X, installing X-Windows was generally a task that Fink would have been used for. In our case, we have installed our own copy, one that Fink has nothing to do with, so we choose Option 1, which is a place-holder packing for xfree86. This simply tells Fink not to concern itself with the specifics of X-Windows, and to just assume that it is correctly installed. This is illustrated in Figure 23.24.

FIGURE 23.24

Fink must have a few questions answered before installing the GIMP.

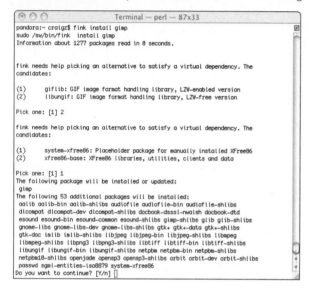

```
                    Terminal — perl — 87x33
pandora:~ craigz$ fink install gimp
sudo /sw/bin/fink  install gimp
Information about 1277 packages read in 0 seconds.


fink needs help picking an alternative to satisfy a virtual dependency. The
candidates:

(1)     giflib: GIF image format handling library, LZW-enabled version
(2)     libungif: GIF image format handling library, LZW-free version

Pick one: [1] 2

fink needs help picking an alternative to satisfy a virtual dependency. The
candidates:

(1)     system-xfree86: Placeholder package for manually installed XFree86
(2)     xfree86-base: XFree86 libraries, utilities, clients and data

Pick one: [1] 1
The following package will be installed or updated:
 gimp
The following 53 additional packages will be installed:
 aalib aalib-bin aalib-shlibs audiofile audiofile-bin audiofile-shlibs
 dlcompat dlcompat-dev dlcompat-shlibs docbook-dsssl-nwalsh docbook-dtd
 esound esound-bin esound-common esound-shlibs gimp-shlibs glib glib-shlibs
 gnome-libs gnome-libs-dev gnome-libs-shlibs gtk+ gtk+-data gtk+-shlibs
 gtk-doc imlib imlib-shlibs libjpeg libjpeg-bin libjpeg-shlibs libmpeg
 libmpeg-shlibs libpng3 libpng3-shlibs libtiff libtiff-bin libtiff-shlibs
 libungif libungif-bin libungif-shlibs netpbm netpbm-bin netpbm-shlibs
 netpbm10-shlibs openjade opensp3 opensp3-shlibs orbit orbit-dev orbit-shlibs
 passwd sgml-entities-iso8879 system-xfree86
Do you want to continue? [Y/n] []
```

The GIMP is an X-Windows-based application. Therefore, to run the software, you first have to launch X11. X11 should be installed on your system. If X11 is not already installed, refer to the "Installing X11 for Mac OS X" section earlier in this chapter. X11 is located in your Utilities folder. Launching it automatically launches an application named xterm. Xterm provides a window that looks almost exactly like a Terminal window. In the xterm window, a command prompt appears. Type **gimp** at the prompt, as shown in Figure 23.25.

Fink and X-Windows

Fink can work with an existing X-Windows installation, or it can install X-Windows for you. It is recommend that you work with Apple's provided X11 and use the Apple-provided installer to provide you with the necessary files, because this ensures compatibility with future Apple software updates. For information on configuring Fink to work with the Apple X11 installation, read the documentation posted on the Fink Project's Web site. As of this writing the URL is http://fink.sourceforge.net/doc/x11/index.php.

FIGURE 23.25

Launching the GIMP from an xterm

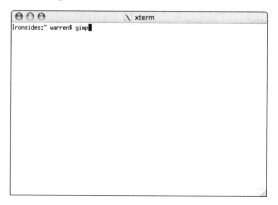

When the GIMP is launched for the first time, a folder must be created in the user's home directory, and additional configuration must be completed. The GIMP presents the following series of user installation dialog boxes (Figures 23.26 through 23.29) that you'll need to okay. Click Continue in each box to confirm your settings and installation.

FIGURE 23.26

The GIMP user installation splash screen

FIGURE 23.27

Creating your personal GIMP directory

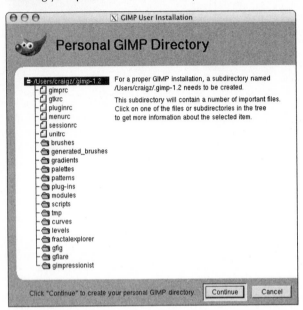

FIGURE 23.28

Setting GIMP performance tuning options

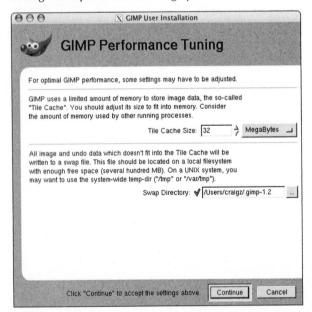

FIGURE 23.29

Setting monitor resolution information for the GIMP

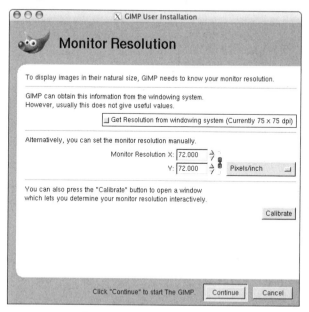

When you're finished working with the GIMP, you can press Control+Q or choose Quit from the File menu in the main tool palette, as shown in Figure 23.30.

FIGURE 23.30

Choosing the Quit command from the GIMP's main menu

Fink Software Trees

The Fink developers have organized available software into separate trees. Most of the software available is in the Stable tree. This is software that has been tested on a wide variety of systems and by a large group of users, who report no major issues.

There is another tree called Unstable. The latest software available is in this tree. Sometimes newer versions of software will be in Unstable, with an older version available in the Stable tree. This software has not been tested as rigorously, nor by as many users. Most of the software in Unstable is quite usable; however, a bit more work may be necessary to get the exact results you want. Don't let that scare you — a lot of the fun stuff can be found in Unstable.

By default, the Fink software will not search the Unstable tree for available software. In order to configure the software to search that tree, you'll have to edit the file /sw/etc/fink.conf and add `unstable/main` and optionally `unstable/crypto` to the line that begins with `Trees:`, as shown in the following figure.

For more information on the Unstable software tree, refer to the Fink Web site: `http://fink .sourceforge.net/faq/usage-fink.php?phpLang=en#unstable`.

CinePaint (filmGimp)

CinePaint is a special version of GIMP, created by and for motion picture professionals. It's designed to work with 35mm film and other high-resolution images. CinePaint displays images in a 32-bit-per-channel color range. This means no resolution is lost from scanning the film and digitizing the footage. CinePaint can work with all standard image formats, and it supports industry-specific formats such as Industrial Light & Magic's OpenEXR (www.openexr.com) and Kodak's Cineon (www.cineon.com). CinePaint is in use at many major effects studios, on feature films such as *Harry Potter; 2 Fast, 2 Furious; Stuart Little II; Cats & Dogs*; and many more. A feature list is available at the projects home page at http://cinepaint.sourceforge.net.

CinePaint used to be known as filmGimp, and Fink has both listed in its package list. The older filmGimp is in the stable distribution list, while the newer CinePaint is still listed in unstable. In order to install CinePaint, you'll need to configure Fink to use its unstable distribution list (see the "Fink Software Trees" sidebar).

After ensuring that Fink is searching the unstable list, simply type **fink install cinepaint** to install it.

Where to Find More Information

Unix is a complete operating system, and we can only touch on the surface of it in this book. Fortunately, as mentioned previously, Unix comes with a lot of internal documentation in the form of man pages. Enter **man** followed by the name of the command, and you receive chapter and verse about that command. You can even read the man pages on the man command itself by typing in **man man** and pressing Return.

> **TIP** If you find yourself in an unthinkable situation, namely, not on a Unix system, take heart in knowing that man pages are Google-able! Instead of typing **man** and the desired page into the Terminal, try typing it into the Google search engine. Plenty of versions are available online.

You can find a number of excellent books on Unix. If you want a gentle introduction, we recommend *Unix For Dummies*, 5th Edition, by John R. Levine and Margaret Levine Young (published by Wiley), or *Learning Unix for Mac OS X Leopard*, by Dave Taylor (published by O'Reilly).

As always, the Internet provides a wealth of references. For Unix introductions, some Web sites we particularly recommend include:

- A Unix Guide at www.ed.com/unixguide.
- Unix is a Four-Letter Word at http://unix.t-a-y-l-o-r.com/. You can find hundreds of others. Use Safari's Google field to do an Internet search for Unix, and you'll be amazed at the number of sites that have Unix as a keyword.

Summary

In this chapter, you discovered a little bit about how to use the Mac OS X Unix underpinnings, known as Darwin, as well as a little history about Unix in general. You saw how to use the Terminal application, modify your Unix shell environment, edit file permissions and ownership, enter commands in the shell, and write basic shell scripts. You also learned how to install Apple's Developer Tools and X11 software, bridging the gap between the Mac and Unix. Fink was introduced as a way to install and maintain Unix native software packages. You also saw that we barely touched the surface of Unix's complexity, and we've given you some pointers to learn more if you're interested.

Chapter 24

Securing Mac OS X

This chapter provides an overview of Mac OX security, common types of threats and vulnerabilities, and the tools built into Mac OS X and third-party software to help safeguard your data.

Introduction to Unix Security

When considering computer security, it's most important to understand that there is a trade-off between ease of use and flexibility versus safety and security. The more secure a system is, the more complex it becomes. Think of system security in the context of an automobile. You could leave the doors unlocked and keep the key in the ignition. Then you wouldn't ever need to search for the keys to open the doors, and with the keys handily stored in the ignition, you wouldn't ever have to fumble to insert them. As far as ease of use, it couldn't get simpler. However, under those conditions in the great metropolis known as the Internet you'd be lucky to find your car where you left it; eventually someone else would just open the door, turn the key, and carjack — or in this case, Macjack — your vehicle. The same thing goes for a computer. If you are the only user, it's easy to assume that nobody would want anything you've got and just leave the "doors" wide open.

The main issue at hand is what you've got to protect, and how much you're willing to put into securing it. The more valuable the asset, the more effort needs to be put into protecting it.

What Is a Vulnerability?

In the field of computer security, a vulnerability is a broad term used to describe a weakness or other type of opening in a system. A vulnerability generally allows an attacker undesired and, frequently, unexpected access to a system. Vulnerabilities are often the result of bugs in software installed on the system, although they can also be the result of a misconfiguration of software.

Classifications of vulnerabilities

There are multiple types of vulnerabilities. Generally two factors categorize the range in severity of a vulnerability: the method of access and the level of privilege granted by the vulnerability. Regarding access, the range in severity is from those that require local accounts on your system in order to exploit, to those that are remotely exploitable. If vulnerability exists that is remotely exploitable, one need not have access to your machine, nor a local account in order to take advantage of the situation.

The second factor is the privilege granted by the successful exploitation of the vulnerability. The types of events that can occur include the reading or writing of files on the system, including files that are used for configuration of access to the system, unauthorized execution of programs on the system, and the installation and execution of arbitrary programs on the system.

There are several efforts underway to catalog known vulnerabilities; one of the most developed is the Common Vulnerabilities and Exposures list, commonly referred to by its initials, CVE. The CVE list assigns tags to vulnerabilities as they are discovered and reported. Due to the fact that any number of researchers may work on the same bug at the same time, this effort helps greatly in coordinating research by allowing for a common ground in reference. For more information about the CVE list check the CVE Web page at www.cve.mitre.org/about/.

Keeping aware of vulnerabilities

An entire community of researchers spends a great deal of time investigating computer software vulnerabilities. You may find that people with many different motivations meet in the center when it comes to computer security research. One common classification of these researchers, although flawed in its simplistic nature, regards the color of a particular researcher's hat, or motivation. There are two predominant hat colors available to security researchers: black and white. The black hat is said to be the hacker-type character who is looking for unfound faults in the system that he or she can utilize to gain unauthorized access. The nemesis of the black hat is the white hat, someone who represents corporate and other interests in the role of cop. These white hats also look for insecurities in software, but their stated goal is to get the bugs fixed before they are taken advantage of by the black hats. (I think the lines are bit more blurred, and one is much more likely to find gray hats everywhere they look. However, the hat metaphor is quite nice in its simplicity.)

That said, there are several public mailing lists that offer quite an insight into the world of security research, where software vulnerabilities are discussed in detail. The most radical in the community prefer a method called *full disclosure*, where details and frequently working code are provided to exploit found vulnerabilities. More temperate members describe the vulnerability in detail, but do not provide working proof of concept code.

> **TIP** Exercise caution if you decide to try any code you find posted to a public list. Run such software on a non-production machine that ideally is not connected to a production network, because any such software code should be treated as suspect, especially if you do not understand exactly how it is written and what it is attempting to accomplish.

The Web site SecurityFocus (`www.securityfocus.com`) is home to the mailing list Bugtraq, one of the oldest full-disclosure mailing lists in existence. The Symantec Corporation acquired SecurityFocus in 2002. The Bugtraq mailing list is an excellent place to start reading, and from there you may find other less broad information to your liking. Current mailing list postings are available at the SecurityFocus archive located at `www.securityfocus.com/bid`.

For more information on the various mailing lists available, and for general computer security news, visit the main SecurityFocus Web site at `www.securityfocus.com`.

Thinking Securely

Historically, Macintosh users have not had to worry much about matters of system security. Previous versions of the Mac OS prior to Mac OS X were quite difficult to harm from the outside. The one major issue that has affected legacy Macintosh operating systems is in fact related to mis-configured third-party software.

Here is the best example of this: On legacy Mac OS systems that did not benefit from preemptive multitasking and that served Web or other Internet services, the appearance of a modal dialog box would divert resources from server programs, thus slowing them down. A shareware program called Okie Dokie was developed that would simply select the default button in a modal dialog after a user-definable period. This helped servers to do their work with optimal resource allocation rather than wait for user input.

Another somewhat popular third-party application is Timbuktu Pro. Timbuktu allows for remote screen control along with other features. A feature of the program is to allow guests to ask permission to use the machine. However, with Okie Dokie installed, when a guest asked for permission, a modal dialog box was presented, with a default of "allow." Okie Dokie would automatically click the allow button and the interloper would be allowed access to the system. This unfortunate mis-configuration was quickly identified and rectified by system administrators in short time. As a result of the nature of the software involved, this problem affected only a very small population of Macintosh users: those who were operating their Macintosh computers as Internet servers. Server configurations aside, there have never been any major attacks on Macintosh computers running the legacy Macintosh OS.

Today, things are much different. Because Mac OS X is a Unix-based operating system, it employs a Unix-style security model that is best evidenced by its true multi-user. However, the trade-off for this great flexibility is that we now have concerns and issues that were never of any consequence to

Macintosh users before. Using Mac OS X, your personal computer has much more in common with industrial strength servers in use in server rooms, such as database servers and Web and file servers, than it does with a Macintosh running Mac OS 9.

The additional power and flexibility of Unix comes at a price. That price is your consideration of security issues regarding your computer. At a minimum, this comes down to ensuring that your OS is kept up to date. Apple frequently issues software updates that are designed to replace various bits of the system that contain bugs that can allow unauthorized users access to your system. Simply allowing the Software Update mechanism built into Mac OS X to run at regular intervals keeps your software current, and ensures your machine's basic security.

When considering security, two angles need to be covered: physical and local security, and network security. Physical security refers to the actual computer and hardware. Local security is like the inside view of your computer, from logging in to the computer, to what users can do on the computer once they are logged in. Network security refers to the outside view of your computer: how is it connected to the network or the Internet and what folks on other computers can see of your computer. Although most serious security concerns focus on network security (that is, hardening your computer to the outside and allowing only authorized and necessary access to your computer from the network), there are several things that need to be taken care of locally. That is how we will start examining the situation.

Physical Security

Physical security means *you* are the security of your actual computer. For some time now, Macintosh desktop computers have been designed to be easy to open, and the internal parts are readily accessible. This ease of use is great for when you need to go into the machine and swap parts, add components, and so on. It also makes it extremely easy for anyone to walk up to your machine and take parts out. Although a user may not know the name and password information required to log in to your computer, if he or she can simply open the machine and walk away with your hard disk, the information contained on your computer is as good as theirs. Most desktop Macintosh computers now come with slots for locks. Adding a lock to your computer if it's in a public place is a very good idea. Laptop computers, of course, are easy targets for theft. It's critical to ensure that your machine stays where you expect it to be and isn't simply walked away with.

The other major issue with regard to physical security is that the computer stays turned on. If you are providing any services to other users on your computer, and it is inadvertently turned off, those services will be unavailable. For these reasons, server computers are traditionally kept in a locked room. By locking the room, only those authorized to access the computer are granted physical access to the power button, keyboard, and mouse. Clearly, you wouldn't want to keep your personal computer under lock and key, but it is helpful to be aware of the potential issues.

Setting an Open Firmware password

Open Firmware is the processor- and system-independent boot firmware used in Apple Macintosh products. More information on Open Firmware and Apple's implementation of the technology is available at www.openfirmware.org/1275/home.html.

Apple provides a utility to set password security in Open Firmware. This utility disables any key presses at startup that modify how the computer boots. With security set, the computer, for example, will not boot from a CD when the C key is pressed. In order to use special key sequences at boot, the application must be run again to disable security. To boot off a disk that is not selected in the Startup Disk preference pane you can hold the Option key on startup to access the Startup Manager. From the Startup Manager, you may select an alternate disk or CD, but you will be prompted for the Open Firmware password that you have established.

Follow these steps to establish an Open Firmware password:

1. **Download the utility from** http://www.apple.com/support/downloads/ openfirmwarepassword.html.

2. **Mount the resulting .dmg image.**

3. **Launch the Open Firmware Password Application.** Figure 24.1 shows the program window.

4. **Click the Change button and enter your administrator password when prompted.**

5. **Select the Require password to change Open Firmware settings check box.**

6. **Enter and verify your password.**

FIGURE 24.1

Setting an Open Firmware password

Using the Security preference pane

The Security preference pane has several options that can be selected to increase the security of your computer. The first option you can select is to require a password to resume use of the computer from either the screen saver or sleep. Check this option to enable this feature, as shown in Figure 24.2.

FIGURE 24.2
_____

Check require password and log out time

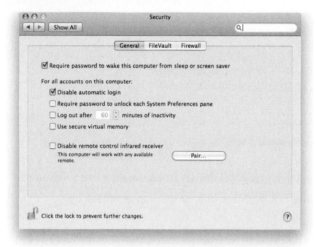

There is another option for logging out based on inactivity. Select this option and set the time interval. These settings are useful for when you leave your computer, because they prevent users from helping themselves to your system and perhaps stealing your data or changing system settings to their benefit.

Enabling FileVault protection

FileVault is a feature in Leopard that can keep all of the files in your home directory encrypted. FileVault uses AES-128-bit encryption to encrypt your home directory. The initial encryption process can take up to 20 minutes; however, when it is finished, all newly created files are encrypted, and you do not have to wait for the process to complete. As you open files, they are unencrypted invisibly.

This ability offers a great degree of protection especially if you are using a laptop computer or if you share your computer with other users. Only people who know your password can read or copy your files.

This security means that you must keep track of your password. If you lose your password you will be unable to access your documents in a clear text form. For this reason, Apple has implemented the Master Password. To set the Master Password, open the FileVault panel within the Security preference pane, and click the Set the Master Password button, as shown in Figure 24.3. Make sure to choose a significant and memorable password for the master password because this is your safety net. If you choose to use FileVault and you forget your password, or for that matter if any local user account on a system requires a password reset, you can enter the master password to reset the password. If both passwords are forgotten, there is no way to recover the data, so do take care when choosing this password.

FIGURE 24.3

FileVault can be enabled only from within the desired user account.

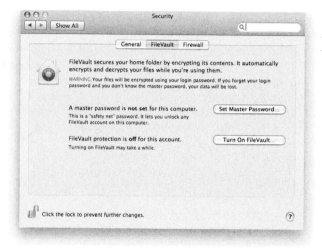

Using Secure Empty Trash

A feature in Leopard is Secure Empty Trash. Traditionally, when you place a file in the trash and choose Empty Trash, the file is not physically deleted. A disk usage file is updated to reflect that the space on the disk occupied by the file that you've "trashed" is now available as free space. Anyone who's run Norton Utilities or other Macintosh disk utilities is aware that frequently you can recover deleted files. This can be quite useful. However, sometimes you want to throw something away and ensure that it will never be recovered. There have been third-party utilities available to fill this task by actually writing zeros or other data over the place in the disk where the file existed. After data is written to the disk, your data no longer exists. The Department of Defense has developed guidelines regarding the secure deletion of files, and Apple now includes this feature built into Leopard. Simply select Secure Empty Trash from the Finder menu to erase all traces of that offending file, as shown in Figure 24.4.

FIGURE 24.4

Secure Empty Trash

Viruses

A common security concern of almost all computer users in all walks of life is viruses. Because most of our machines are connected to the Internet for various uses, and most of us are avid e-mail users, viruses are a concern. The most common vector of infection for viruses is via e-mail. The easiest step to increasing the security of your system is to install antivirus software. More important than simply installing the software, however, is to keep your virus definitions up to date, because new viruses appear on a daily basis. The good news is that, as determined as virus authors can appear, there is an equally vigilant antivirus community. Your job is simply to ensure that the software you run is kept up to date and that you enable any automatic update mechanism the software vendor makes available to you, to ensure that you are getting the most recent virus definitions installed.

Understanding the difference between carrier and infected

It is quite tempting as a Mac OS X user to not pay much attention to talk of computer viruses, because the overwhelming majority of these malicious programs are directed at users of operating systems and applications created by Microsoft. However, there is still plenty of reason to take care of protecting your own system. Two of the most prominent reasons are

- Many viruses use the macro language present in the Microsoft Office applications as their vector of infection. Although these viruses pose no direct threat to Mac OS X computers, we do nothing to inoculate the document and pass the virus along to our Windows-using colleagues, family, and friends.

- As more and more users install and make use of virus protection software on their Macs, they will be unable to open documents created on your system if your documents carry viruses, even if those viruses cause no direct harm to your system.

Further Information

A great source of background information regarding viruses on the Macintosh can be found in the Usenet FAQ: Viruses and the Macintosh, which can be found at `www.faqs.org/faqs/computer-virus/macintosh-faq`.

In both of these situations, the infected Macintosh does not present any abnormal behavior, so it is quite easy to overlook the infection. In the first situation, frequently there is a change made to the file that Microsoft Word uses as a template for all new documents, Normal.doc. That change causes all documents created using Word on your system to contain an embedded version of the virus. When that virus is opened by a user on a Windows system, the payload does whatever it was programmed to do. It doesn't matter how many Macintosh systems the file has been passed through, because the macro remains embedded in the document and passes along unmolested until it encounters a system with antivirus software installed, which can strip the macro from the file, leaving the document content intact.

The second situation is becoming more and more common in corporate environments, where network-installed antivirus software recognizes the document to be carrying a malicious payload and simply quarantines the document, not allowing the user to open the file. This can cause quite a bit of trouble because it delays the intended audience from working with your file. It is clearly best to avoid either situation.

Antivirus software

As mentioned earlier in this chapter, the best solution to the security problem posed by computer viruses is to install antivirus software on your computer. There are several solutions for antivirus software on the Mac: Symantec's Norton AntiVirus (`www.symantec.com/nav/nav_mac/index.html`) and Intego's VirusBarrier (`www.intego.com/virusbarrier/`) are popular antivirus programs. There is even a Macintosh port of the very popular open source antivirus engine ClamAV. The software is aptly named ClamXav and can be downloaded from `http://www.clamxav.com`.

Network Security

When your computer is connected to a network, either a local network at home or at the office, or to the Internet via a dial-up connection or dedicated broadband connection (DSL or cable), it becomes visible to anyone else on either your local network or on the Internet. Refer to Chapter 11 for a more detailed explanation of computer networking. A brief networking primer follows.

Understanding TCP/IP

When you connect your computer to the Internet, your machine becomes part of a large network. You mostly think of the Internet connection as providing connectivity to other machines, generally Web servers. You'll use a client application on your computer, usually a Web browser to connect to other machines, as you browse the Web. Your Web browser hides the underlying complexity of the network as you enter Web site addresses; it simply presents you text, images, and multimedia objects as delivered by the Web servers you connect to.

The Internet is composed of several layers through which data passes before delivery to your client application. A detailed discussion of the communications protocols involved is out of the scope of this chapter; however, a brief explanation follows. There are many layers of network protocols that are used in combination with each other to provide Internet connectivity. These layers are commonly described as the Internet protocol suite. The sections that follow sketch out the basic operation of these communication protocols.

There are two separate acronyms in use when looking at TCP/IP communications. Both ends of a connection use both TCP and IP to send and receive data.

TCP stands for Transmission Control Protocol. TCP is responsible for breaking up large sources of data into individual packets on the sending side, and on the receiving side reconnecting the individual packets into a solid chunk of data. Additionally TCP on the receiving side ensures that all segments have been received. In a data network, it is extremely likely that parts will arrive in a different order than that in which they were transmitted. TCP is responsible for reordering data as it arrives, and ensuring that all parts are intact.

IP stands for Internet Protocol. IP is the layer responsible for moving the individual data packets between machines. It helps to think of IP as transport. Whereas TCP is responsible for ensuring that packets all arrive as they should and in their entirety, IP simply moves the data. The IP protocol has no sense of what it is moving, or if it's arrived as it should; it just moves the packets.

Understanding network security threats

To protect your computer against network security threats, you must have a basic understanding of the type of threats out there. Although many different types of security vulnerabilities exist, the types of attacks can be distilled into three basic types: denial of service attacks, theft of data attacks, and unauthorized use of computing and network resources. For a more detailed overview and an extensive list of additional resources, download the document located at www.cert.org/ archive/pdf/attack_trends.pdf.

Denial of service attacks

Denial of service attacks are probably the hardest to protect against, due to the nature of sharing resources. If your system allows access from outside, perhaps by serving Web pages, how do you determine the difference between legitimate requests for data and illegitimate requests, which are designed to simply tie up your resources? Denial of service attacks are extremely easy to implement, requiring little to no technical competence on the part of the attacker.

A denial of service attack is a situation where a specific resource is the target of excessive or malformed traffic. Example services are a Web server, ftp server, mail server, and so on. Usually many compromised machines are used in a denial of service attack. The end result is that if you a are victim of such an attack, you are unable to engage in the communications you expect to because you will be tied up responding to excessive fake clients.

Denial of service attacks can also cause real headaches when they are directed at a resource that you require in order to do day-to-day tasks. For example, a service that is required for most productive work on the Internet is DNS. DNS stands for *domain name system*. A DNS server translates friendly name-based addresses such as www.apple.com to numerical IP addresses such as 17.112.152.32. DNS translates numerical IP addresses such as 17.112.152.32 to a friendlier, familiar name-based address such as www.apple.com. If we didn't have access to a DNS server, and had to use numbered IP addresses for all communications, such as Web surfing, sending e-mail, and so on, the Internet would be much less useful to us. DNS is a distributed database of numbers to names and is based on a system built of Root Servers. There are currently 13 Root Servers worldwide. These 13 servers are the authoritative servers for global DNS services. These 13 servers point at local DNS servers worldwide. The Root Servers serve information for what are called Top Level Domains, such as .com, .net, .org, and .edu. A successful denial of service attack against these 13 servers would render much of the Internet inaccessible to most users.

Data theft

Theft-of-data attacks occur when somebody from the outside manages to obtain access to your computer and takes files from your machine. These types of attacks are the most discussed in the media and elsewhere, as they often involve real financial loss. The data stolen can be personal information, such as credit card numbers and bank account information, or it can be intellectual property. This kind of attack is much like a bank robbery where your personal property is stolen from you. Unlike in the physical world, you may retain copies of the files, because just copying them does not ensure destruction. Although many times data is destroyed in the process, it is not necessarily the case. In fact much of the time that data has been stolen, the victim may be completely unaware that the theft has occurred. That is, until a later time, when unauthorized financial activity occurs or similar events take place.

Unauthorized use of computing and network resources

Unauthorized use pertains to a situation where your computer or network resources are utilized by unauthorized users. Viruses are frequently responsible for such situations. The recent Mydoom, Netsky, and Bagle viruses are examples of unauthorized use violations. The virus, once installed in your computer, then uses your computer to scan the network for other vulnerable hosts, and to attack those computers. In addition, many viruses of these types have as their goal bringing your computer into an ad-hoc network of infected computers. Once your computer is tagged in to the network, it will await further instructions. Frequently the goal is to use your computing and network resources along with those of other such compromised machines to launch denial of service attacks against large high-profile Internet hosts. Microsoft is frequently a target of such attacks.

Not all types of unauthorized use are virus related. Suppose someone on the Internet finds a way to connect to your computer, and is able to log in via a software bug (called a vulnerability) or a misconfiguration of some network component; the hacker then may be able to configure network services on your machine that you are unaware of. A common situation today is where an unauthorized user creates a directory on your machine and configures FTP access to that directory. You could then be the unwilling host of a treasure trove of pirated music, software, and movies. Many times such access can go unnoticed, because today's hard disks are large enough to contain such additional data without running out of space, and broadband connections provide adequate bandwidth to support these supplementary connections alongside legitimate Internet access.

Services

Chapters 12 and 13 discussed various services that could be enabled on your Mac OS X computer. Simply turning on the services enables various daemons (processes) on your computer. This section takes a look at what's really going on with your computer when these services are enabled.

Port usage

The Internet is composed of clients and servers. You, as the client, want some information from the Internet, and it is located on a server. A client uses an application to browse the Internet. All computers that are connected to the Internet have an IP address. The IP address serves as the main address for the machine. Each service on the system has a unique identifier called a *port*. A port is a unique number between 0 and 65535. A list of ports is available on each Mac OS X system, in the file /etc/services. The ports between 0 and 1023 are referred to as "well-known ports." A small program that runs on the computer, called a *daemon*, handles each service that is available on a computer. The daemon launches and binds to a specific port, then waits and listens for connections to come in to that port. When a connection is opened to that port, the daemon wakes up and sends a reply to the client.

Arguably, port 80 is the most well-known port. It is the port most often used for HTTP, which is Web traffic. When you type the address www.apple.com into your Web browser, the browser first performs a DNS lookup, and then sends a request to the server's IP address, at port 80. However, sometimes your Web browser is redirected to another port. Most common is https on port 443 (secure HTTP), which is used for online purchases, banking, and so on. Other popular ports are 25, used for Simple Mail Transfer Protocol (SMTP), which handles the sending of e-mail; 110 POP (Post Office Protocol), which is used for checking e-mail; 143 IMAP (Interactive Mail Access Protocol), which is an alternative to POP for checking e-mail; 21, used for FTP; and 22, used for ssh (secure shell).

TCP/IP does not dictate what ports are used for which applications. You can operate a Web server on any port you want. Port 8080 is popular as a default port for the Apache Web server. The well-known ports system is offered as a convenience. Much as DNS is useful to assist in translating hard-to-remember numeric addresses to easily remembered text-based hostnames, the well-known ports serve as a basis for standardization. Instead of having to ask which port to connect to for each individual Web site, we can simply agree to use port 80 for Web servers and get about the business of browsing rather than searching.

Principle of least privilege

A long-standing guideline in computer security is the principle of least privilege. This states that users be given only the privileges that they need to perform their jobs or tasks. Rather than leave everything unlocked and provide all users all privileges available, which makes administrative tasks simple in the short term because you never have to unlock anything, simply to allow administrative access, you take a longer-term approach and provide each user with exactly the level of access they require for day-to-day work. In a special situation, you can elevate specific user-access rights to provide granular rights to privileges without leaving everything unlocked. A practical example is this: You want to share your printer with other users in your office. There is no reason to allow those users to log in to your computer and change file-sharing preferences.

The same guiding principle applies when it comes to offering network services from your computer. The ideal situation regarding services is to first ensure that your machine is offering no services whatsoever. If you do not intend to share any resources with neighboring users, there should be nothing enabled on your computer. Often there are services enabled by default, or the installation of third-party software may open ports or add services to your computer's configuration. If you plan to share any resources from your computer, best practices are to start with a clean slate. Turn off all services, and ensure all ports are closed. Then determine which services you want to offer, turning the services on one by one. As you enable services, check your system and see which ports have been opened, and ensure that only those you require are active. Doing this adds very little additional time to your configuration process, and ensures that you are not exposing more than you expect to the Internet. The next section describes how to check which ports are open on your computer.

Monitoring open ports

Run a check on your system each time you install or upgrade any kind of services to ensure that you are opening only ports that you want to have open. The way to do this is to run port-scanning software. Port scanners are a major tool in the hacker's arsenal. By running a port scan, they can see what your computer is offering and then use those openings to penetrate your system. By running a port scan against your own computer, you'll know what the hackers know, and can close off any unintended openings.

To check which ports are open on your system, you'll want to run third-party software because the Apple-supplied Network Utility is not entirely thorough. Like most things regarding interacting with Unix in Mac OS X, you have the choice between using a graphical interface or a command-line interface.

If you are curious, Apple provides an application in the Utilities folder, inside the Applications folder, called Network Utility, which does provide a rudimentary port scan. To access the port scan, launch the application and click the Port Scan tab in the bar on top. Figure 24.5 shows Apple's Network Utility.

FIGURE 24.5

The Apple Network Utility Port Scan

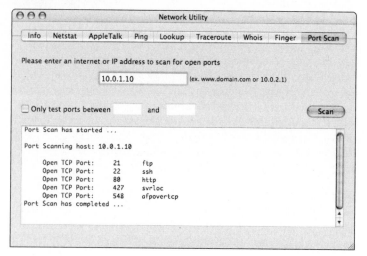

For a quick fix, you can utilize an online service that port scans your computer from the outside. The following URL links to a port-scanning service provided by Gibson Research Corporation, a maker of security software for Windows systems. The service can be reached by following the ShieldsUP! link from `www.grc.com`. Run the two tests called Test My Shields and Probe My Ports. As always, your results may vary. It's best to install your own software to do this task, but if you're in a hurry, the Web-based check is quite thorough.

Using a graphical interface to check open ports

Several third-party programs are available that can show you what daemons are running and what ports they are listening on. A description of several popular tools follows:

- AysMon (Are You Serving Monitor) is written in Java and is available at `www.pepsan.com/aysmon/index.html`. It is distributed as a disk image file. To mount the image, simply double-click the .dmg file and then drag the AysMon folder to your Applications folder. AysMon comes with a list of services, checks your computer for each one, and shows you the results. AysMon is shareware and costs $5.

- whatPorts v 1.1 is a freeware port scanner available at `www.davtri.com/index.py/freeware`.

Built-in Firewall

A computer firewall is either software or hardware intended to protect your computer from outside threats, while allowing you to use the Internet and to share specific resources. Firewalls are often installed on corporate computer networks in order to protect inside computers from outside attacks. However, having a firewall on your local computer is of great benefit. With a firewall enabled, you can browse the Internet unhindered, but connections to your machine will be denied, if they are not explicitly allowed. For example, if you are providing Web services, you can configure the firewall to allow access only to the Web server and to no other ports on your computer.

Apple shipped a software firewall as part of a standard Mac OS X installation since Version 10.0. This is just one way that Mac OS X users have benefited from Mac OS X's Unix heritage. The included software is called ipfw for IP Firewall. ipfw is actually a front end to two individual programs called dummynet and ipfirewall.

Inspecting firewall rulesets using Terminal

If you are interested in directly interacting with the firewall, you can do so by opening the Terminal application and using the ipfw command. To learn more about the ipfw command and how to use it, open the Terminal application and type the command **man ipfw**. To see what rulesets are in place, type the command **sudo ipfw list**. If you've not implemented any rules, the only rule listed is the catchall rule, 65535 allow IP from any to any, which lets any IP traffic from any port on any host to any port on your computer. Although further discussion of manual ipfw configuration is out of the scope of this chapter, as you set up various firewall rules using methods discussed later in this section, you can always check the rules that have been created by issuing the command **sudo ipfw list** in a Terminal widow.

Implementing firewall rulesets using Sharing preferences

Apple includes a simple GUI for configuring ipfw rules with Mac OS X. To access this, open the Firewall panel of the Sharing preference pane. From here you can enable the firewall and select what type of traffic to allow to your computer. Example services are Personal File Sharing, FTP Access, Printer Sharing, and Personal Web Sharing. There are several more to choose from. Figure 24.6 shows the Firewall preferences. You can see that services you have selected to share in the Services panel of the Sharing preference pane are already selected for you. Any additional ports you want to open may be checked here as well.

FIGURE 24.6

Leopard by default has its firewall configured to Allow all incoming connections.

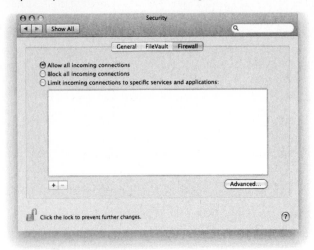

Protecting Yourself from System Bugs

One of the best things you can do to protect yourself from attackers abusing vulnerabilities present in software on your system is to keep your software up to date. At the time the software you are running ships, it is free from known bugs, or at least it sure should be! However, the second it leaves the developer, whether downloaded from the Web via the file transfer protocol (FTP) or via the pressing of CD/DVDs, and enters the public, it is a waiting game to see if bugs are discovered. The more recent you keep your installed software, the less likely you are prone to fall victim to exploitation.

Apple Software Update

Apple Software Update is the mechanism by which Apple periodically issues and installs updates to your system. As described in Chapter 1, Software Update is included in Leopard.

By running Software Update on a regular basis and installing the updates as they become available, you are protecting your system against the majority of attacks. Apple does a good job of keeping up to date with the various security issues out there, and its record of providing timely updates is so far quite good. Of course the update does not help you until it is installed, so do yourself a favor and take the time once a week or so to ensure that you are up to date. Although the software comes pre-installed, you need to configure it to check for updates weekly, and be sure to install updates when the system notifies you.

Third-party software updates

As time progresses, most of the major software vendors are providing their own automated update mechanisms. At the time of this writing, Microsoft provided Microsoft AutoUpdate with Microsoft Office 2004, which runs as a background process that periodically checks for new versions of Microsoft software and which alerts you to newly available patches, updaters, and the like.

Adobe Systems and Macromedia both have mechanisms that run at the launch of some of their applications that check to see if you are running the latest release of their program, and that alert you if a new version of the application is available. Many shareware and freeware programs have implemented similar features, whereby they connect to a server on launch and inform you via a dialog box if there is a newer version of their software available for download.

Whether your software implements such features or not, you should take a moment when you are installing software to familiarize yourself with the versioning of that software and find out how the vendor communicates software updates, and then ensure that you are keeping up to date with these updates. Several Web sites exist simply to keep track of Mac OS software updates, such as MacUpdate (www.macupdate.com) and VersionTracker (www.versiontracker.com). In addition, the major software updates are usually given mention on the various Mac OS news Web sites, of which undoubtedly you will have a favorite.

System Logs

Out of the box, a Mac OS X computer logs much of the activity that happens on the system. The system logs most events that involve sharing in any way over the network, such as Web or FTP server, and most events that involve changes happening on the system. Logs are often overlooked and are consulted only in the event of a system failure, security breach, or other catastrophic event. Familiarize yourself with the types of items your system logs and the content of those logs when things are normal.

If you have a good idea of what goes on under normal circumstances, you will know when things are happening that are out of the ordinary. The log files are simply text files, and there are a variety of ways of interacting with these log files. This section explains how the system decides what to log and where, and discusses making some changes to the defaults to highlight important security-related events. We'll discuss both traditional Unix tools to view and parse the logs, as well as the included Console Application and some third-party GUI tools for reading log files.

Introducing Syslog

Syslog is the System Event Logger originally written by Eric Allman. Syslog is a standard component of Unix and other Unix systems. Instead of making each application author worry about where, how, and when to log, and burdening users with the concern about finding each individual program's log files, syslog offers developers simple logging routines to access from their programs in the form of openlog and other libraries. Syslogd is the logging daemon which is launched at system startup by the startup item `/System/Library/StartupItems/SystemLog`. The file `/etc/syslog.conf` is read by the syslog daemon as it starts up, and configures how the daemon processes incoming messages. There is also a user command called `logger` that can be used interactively or by shell scripts to create entries in the system log.

Programs that take advantage of syslog for logging, and this includes the Mach Kernel, write their messages to a special file, which only the syslog daemon reads. Syslog parses the incoming messages according to its configuration file and takes one or more of these four actions:

- Forwards the message to a syslog daemon running on a different host
- Appends the message to a specified file
- Outputs the message to `/dev/console`
- Outputs the message to the screen of defined users if they are logged in

The `syslog.conf` file defines how messages are handled based on two specific criteria called levels and facilities. The levels refer to the severity of an event, and the facility refers to the specific program running. Both the levels and facilities supported by Mac OS X are described in the man page for `syslogd.conf`.

Configuring Syslog to separate interesting messages

The directory `/var/log` is where most log files are kept on a Mac OS X system. Syslog is configured by default to log most messages to the file `/var/log/system.log`. Separate log files are created by default for authorization actions (generally logins), lpr printer messages, mail, ftp, and netinfo errors. This is a reasonable set of defaults. However, in the interest of securing your system, and by way of example, you'll make modifications to the configuration to isolate messages from both sudo and ssh.

All lines in the `/etc/syslog.conf` take the form of `selector <Tab> action`. It is critical that in the examples that follow and in any changes you make to the file that you use a Tab between items on a line, or unpredictable results may occur. Before making any changes to the `syslog.conf` file, make a backup of the original file, just in case. To backup the file, open the Terminal application and enter the following command: **sudo cp /etc/syslog.conf /etc/syslog.orig.conf**.

Separating sudo messages

Sudo is configured to log messages to a facility called local2. It just so happens that sudo is the only program installed in a default system that uses the facility local2. This makes it a trivial matter to isolate messages generated by sudo. Open `/etc/syslog.conf` in your favorite editor and make the following addition to the file:

```
local2.*          /var/log/sudo.log
```

In this example, we've told syslog to select all messages from the facility local2 at all severity levels and write those messages to the file `/var/log/sudo.log`.

Syslog does not create a file by itself, so you'll have to create the log file. In addition, you'll set the proper permissions on the file, and finally restart syslog to force it to reread its configuration file. Open the Terminal application and type the following commands:

```
sudo touch /var/log/sudo.log
sudo chmod 640 /var/log/sudo.log
sudo kill -HUP `/bin/cat /var/run/syslog.pid`
```

Separating ssh messages

If you are allowing connections to your system via ssh, you'll want to log those connections so you can monitor them. In order to do this you'll need to modify both the sshd configuration file and the syslog configuration file.

First open the ssh server configuration file located at `/etc/sshd_config` with sudo and your favorite editor and change the value of `SyslogFacility` from AUTH to LOCAL7. Ensure that you've removed the # character from the beginning of the line. Then remove the # character from the `LogLevel` line immediately below. Save the file and close it.

Next, open `/etc/syslog.conf` in your favorite editor and make the following addition to the file:

```
local7.*            /var/log/sshd.log
```

In this example, you've told syslog to select all messages from the facility local7 at all severity levels and write those messages to the file `/var/log/sshd.log`.

Again, syslog cannot create files in the `/var/log` directory for you, so you'll create the log file with proper permissions, and then restart syslog to force it to reread the configuration file. Open the Terminal application and type the following commands:

```
sudo touch /var/log/sshd.log
sudo chmod 640 /var/log/sshd.log
sudo kill -HUP `/bin/cat /var/run/syslog.pid`
```

Viewing system logs

Now that you're familiar with syslog and the configuration of system messages written to log files, you need to examine these files to see what kind of events are occurring on your computer and ensure that everything is going the way you expect. Here you have several options. You can browse the log files in the Terminal application or use the Console application to view log messages. For debugging new services, and other system occurrences, looking at the log file in real time can be extremely helpful. A feature in Leopard is that Apple System Profiler also includes a log file viewer, as shown in Figure 24.7. This is useful if you need to provide copies of log files for technical support types.

FIGURE 24.7

Use Apple System Profiler to view system log files.

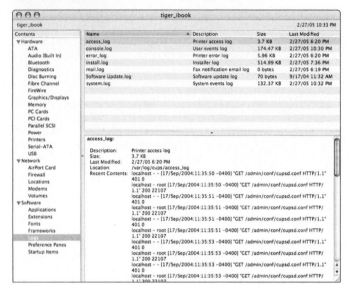

Using Terminal to view log files

The `tail`, `less`, `cat`, and `grep` commands are all very useful when it comes to viewing and searching log files.

Use the `tail` command to view the end of a log file by typing **tail /var/log/system.log**. Tail can be used to continuously monitor a file by using the `-f` switch. When `tail` is invoked with the `-f` switch, it does not stop when the EOF (end of file) marker is reached, but waits for additional input. To open and watch a log file type the command **tail -f /var/log/system.log**. Replace `/var/log/system.log` with the log file you are watching.

Use the `less` command to scroll through a log file page by page. You can search within the file you are reading by typing the / character followed by your search string (for example, `/craigz`). The first occurrence of your search term will be highlighted. You can jump to the next occurrence by typing the N key on your keyboard and continue typing N to move through found items. You can also move line by line down the file by using either the Return key or the down arrow. The up arrow can also be used to scroll upwards line by line. To move through the document page by page, use the Spacebar.

If you want to check on a specific text string in your log file, you can use the `cat` command in conjunction with `grep`. For example, to search for the string `craigz` in the system log file, type the following command: **cat /var/log/system.log | grep craigz**.

Using the Console application to view log files

The Console application is located in the Utilities folder inside the Applications folder. The left side of the application displays two stand-alone files, `console.log` and `system.log`, as well as three folders where logs are located, `/Library/Logs`, `~Library/Logs`, and `/var/log`. Each of these folders has disclosure triangles next them that can be expanded to show individual log files within. This window is shown in Figure 24.8.

Once a file is selected on the left, its contents populate the right side of the window. The search box on the top right is labeled Filter. You can type text in that window, and only lines containing that text string are left in the content window. Clicking the Clear icon clears the window. Using the Reload button refreshes the window content, and the Mark button inserts a line with a timestamp. The Mark button is quite useful if you are watching a file for a specific event because you can insert timestamps to mark your place, and note between similar-looking lines.

FIGURE 24.8

Use the Console application to view system log files.

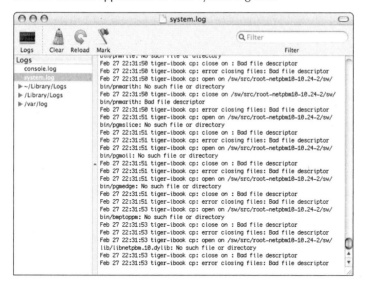

Summary

This chapter introduced the major concepts involved in computer security in general, and specifically how they relate to Mac OS X. We looked at both the physical security and the network security of your computer and its files, and how other computers can connect to your computer. We learned what kinds of threats exist on the Internet and developed an understanding of the issues that can affect us. We learned how to manage computer viruses on the Internet, and how to ensure that we are not virus carriers. We also examined Mac OS X's built-in firewall and learned how to monitor system logs.

This chapter covered a lot of ground but has barely scratched the surface. Entire books are written on the subject of security. Hopefully this introduction has given you a sense of the issues surrounding security and will help you think about security and how it relates to using your computer and safely sharing resources with others.

As was stated in the beginning of the chapter, computer security is a fast-moving target. You'd do well to read up on current events in the security world. The Web site `www.securityfocus.com` is a tremendous resource, with many mailing lists dedicated to the issue of computer security.

The best way to secure your system is to keep all software you are running current. Do this through Apple Software Update, and by maintaining current versions of all third-party software you install.

Glossary

absolute pathname A pathname that specifies the exact location of a single directory. An absolute pathname begins at the root directory, a slash (/), and traverses through the Unix file system, ending at the desired directory or file, and naming each directory that is passed through. Each directory that is passed through is named and separated by a slash. `/Users/warren/Documents` is the absolute pathname of my Documents folder. This contrasts to the relative pathname.

active application The application visible in the foreground. If iTunes is the active application, its name is visible in bold in the menu bar, directly to the right of the Apple menu.

admin See *administrator account*.

administrator account Admin is one type of Mac OS X user account in which the user has access to system-wide resources, including abilities to modify the System Preferences, create and edit other user accounts, and install applications. When OS X is initially set up, the first user created is an admin.

adopted ownership When a Mac OS X user account is deleted, its contents can be transferred to an existing admin account. The admin user is said to be adopting ownership of the previous user's files.

Advanced Memory Management Automatically and dynamically assigns and handles the allocation of both physical RAM and virtual memory to applications and processes as needed.

AirPort Apple's name for its implementation of the IEEE 802.11 standard for wireless networking.

This includes AirPort (802.11b) at speeds of 11 Mbps, AirPort Extreme (802.11g) at speeds up to 54 Mbps, and with the same name, 802.11n at speeds up to 248 Mbps.

AirPort Base Station An Apple hardware device that provides a wireless signal to 802.11-equipped computers, Macintosh or otherwise. A base station can be connected to the Internet and transmit a wireless net connection, and some older models can dial up directly through their own internal modems. Extreme and Express versions can wirelessly share USB printers. Some older Extreme models can be connected to an external antenna.

alias Also known as a shortcut, an alias is a representative file that can dynamically locate its target file or folder. The pathway is not lost if either the original or the alias is moved to a different location on the same volume. Under the Mac file system, each file has a unique identifier, which can be traced even if the file has moved.

anti-aliasing A technique that causes text and graphics to appear smoother and easier to read when displayed using the relatively low resolution of a computer screen. Shading and blending of otherwise jagged lines are used to fool the eye into seeing a cleaner image.

Apache An open source Web server provided within every copy of Mac OS X and Mac OS X Server. Apache is the most widely used Web server (over 60 percent of Web sites) on the Internet and runs on a variety of platforms, including Unix-based operating systems and Windows servers.

API See *Application Programming Interface*.

AppleCare Knowledge Base Located at www.apple.com/support, the Knowledge Base is Apple's official Web-based library of articles and information pertaining to the usage and support of their products.

Apple Menu Located at the top leftmost corner of the screen, it is a menu in the shape of an Apple logo, either gray or blue depending on the configuration. The Apple Menu contains commands that affect the machine on a user- or system-wide level, including changing the settings of the Dock, or shutting down the machine.

AppleScript A programming language used for automating tasks and customizing application features, as well as creating stand-alone applets. The language is heavily English-based, more so than most, making it easy to learn and decipher. AppleScript is included with every copy of OS X; a third-party application able to be affected by an AppleScript is said to be "scriptable."

applet A mini application program that is usually Java- or AppleScript-based. Java applets are often embedded within Web pages (like an Internet search engine), and AppleScripts are often integrated within a larger application to perform a certain function; within Apple's DVD Player application, for example, one can pull down the scripts menu and access a specific time within a movie.

AppleTalk A networking protocol created by Apple that dates back to the early Macintosh days in the mid-eighties. It was (is) popular due to its ease of use and the fact that network devices easily make themselves known on a network. It was the primary method of networking Macs and peripherals for many years and only now is being phased out in favor of less "chatty" protocols, such as TCP/IP networking and *Bonjour*, Apple's new "zero-config" networking protocol.

application A complete and self-contained program that, when launched (for example, by double-clicking), performs certain functions. The Finder, iTunes, and TextEdit are all examples of applications.

Application Programming Interface (API) The method by which an operating system can make certain requests of an application, or by which an application can make certain requests of an operating system in order to call upon and perform specific tasks. For example, the QuickTime API would be called upon to add movie and sound features to an application.

Applications folder The default location for all of the user accessible programs. For example, if one installs FileMaker Pro for the first time, it is automatically placed inside the Applications folder. Applications do not have to be placed here, but it is a good idea to keep them here for organizational purposes.

Aqua Apple's name for the look and feel of the graphical user interface that makes up OS X. The pulsating OK buttons, the huge photorealistic icons, and the fancy "genie" animation that occurs when a window is minimized to the Dock are all examples of Aqua.

archive A single compressed file containing files and folders, ready for e-mailing or backing up.

argument A piece of information that is passed to a Unix command on the command line. Arguments are usually file names or directory names. For example:

```
% chown warren:staff /Users/warren/
Documents
```

In this command, the argument is the Documents folder's file path.

ASCII (American Standard Code for Information Interchange) The most basic character set used by almost all modern computers. US-ASCII uses 0–127 to represent upper- and lowercase letters, punctuation, space, and numbers. More advanced ASCII sets, like Unicode, use more characters and can represent accented letters and more complicated punctuation.

authentication The process of verifying that someone is, in actuality, who he or she claims to be. Under Mac OS X, when one types in a correct password into the login screen, that person is being authenticated to log in to the system.

authoritative DNS server An authoritative DNS server is a computer that holds the definitive DNS records for a given domain name. A DNS server is a server that can hold and resolve the DNS entries for IP-aware entities connected to the Internet.

autoscrolling When scrolling is accomplished by dragging an item to the edge of a window (which causes the window's contents to scroll in that direction) and not by manually clicking the scrollbar or arrows.

background program A program that, while running, is usually not visible to the user of the system. Launch the Process Viewer to see examples of this. The iChat Agent is one such example. This process runs in the background and can sign the user onto AOL's Instant Messenger service even if the iChat application is not open yet.

backup A backup is created to guard against data loss, which occurs due to hardware failure, corruption, viruses, natural disasters, theft, and human error. Essentially a backup is a copy of existing information, so that if the original is lost, a copy exists. A backup can be a burned CD of some digital pictures, or a system in which an entire office of computers is automatically backed up via network to a central server every night, using programs like Retrospect or Time Machine.

binary The number system that computers use, which is base two, unlike the number system humans use, which is base ten. In binary, there are two number choices, a one or a zero. A single binary digit is called a *bit*. A group of eight bits is called a *byte*. For the sake of convenience a kilobyte is considered to be 1000 bytes, but more accurately, because it is within a base two system and is 10^2, a single kilobyte is 1024 bytes. Thus a gigabyte of RAM is really 1024 megabytes.

binary file A type of compressed and encoded file, usually containing the .bin suffix. MacBinary files are encoded so that the data contained in them can be stored on other operating systems (like Microsoft Windows) and transferred back and forth without issue. StuffIt Expander can decode these files.

BinHex A method of encoding and compressing binary files for download and transfer. BinHex files have a .hqx suffix and are the most common format in which to receive Macintosh software downloads. StuffIt Expander can decompress these files.

bit Stands for *binary digit*. A bit is the smallest unit of storage, a one or a zero, a yes or a no, an on or an off, a true or a false.

bit depth See *color depth* and *pixel depth*.

bitmap font Same as *fixed-size font*.

blessed Under Mac OS 9.x, or Classic, the term Blessed refers to a system folder that is active and recognized by the operating system as a valid and bootable OS. It is possible for a good system folder to become unblessed, causing a Mac not to recognize the folder as bootable. Running a utility such as DiskWarrior re-blesses an unblessed system folder.

Bonjour A networking technology requiring zero configuration. Turn on the device, and your computer can see it and use it. Because it is a new technology, older devices typically will not support Bonjour.

bookmark Refers to a saved URL (Uniform Resource Locator) within a Web browser. For example, if, when using Safari, you want to save MacAddict's Web site (`www.macaddict.com`) for future viewing, you can go to the Bookmarks menu and choose Add Bookmark to save the location for easy future access.

boot The act of powering on a machine and having the operating system loaded and started.

bridge A piece of hardware used to move traffic between two different types of networks or networking hardware. An AirPort Base Station is a bridge when it routes information from a wired Ethernet network to its wireless one.

BSD (Berkeley Software Distribution) There are many different versions or "flavors" of Unix, including distributions called Linux, Solaris, and AIX. BSD is an umbrella term for the Unix flavor that has been released by UC Berkeley. Mac OS X is based upon this version.

BSD subsystem Together with the Mach Kernel, the BSD subsystem makes up Apple's own flavor of Unix, called Darwin. On top of Darwin, Apple placed its proprietary frameworks like Carbon, Cocoa, and QuickTime, and its Aqua user interface, resulting in Mac OS X.

bug An error within a piece of software (like a program) or hardware (like a printer) that causes an unwanted behavior, usually resulting in a malfunction. A well-known bug was the Y2K bug, which left many computers (Macs excluded) vulnerable to reverting back to the year 1900 instead of the year 2000, due to the two-digit year limitation encoded in most software. Updates, or "bug fixes," are usually released to repair bugs.

built-in memory Apple's terminology for the RAM (Random Access Memory) that is physically installed in the machine.

bundle Another term for *package*.

burn When information is recorded onto a CD (compact disc), the disc is said to be burned. The term stems from the way a CD is recorded, which involves using a laser beam to heat a layer of photosensitive dye.

burn-in A condition affecting CRT monitors in which a vestige of an unchanging screen image remains visible after the image changes, and even after the computer has powered off. Today's computer screens are no longer susceptible to burn-in. Flat-panel LCD's (Liquid Crystal Displays) such as those found on Apple's PowerBooks are not affected by this condition.

byte One byte is comprised of 8 bits. A byte is the smallest unit of storage that the Mac OS recognizes. Bytes are commonly measured by many thousands (kilobytes, or K), millions, (megabytes, or MB), billions, (gigabytes, or GB), and trillions (terabytes, or TB) at a time.

case-sensitive Case-sensitive means that it matters whether or not letters are capitalized. Passwords in Mac OS X are case-sensitive. In some instances, such as in the screen saver password window, the dialog box tells you if the Caps Lock key is pressed, alleviating the frustration of being sure you typed the correct password but having it entered unknowingly in all caps.

character A written representation of a letter, digit, or symbol. A single character could be the letter *W* or an exclamation point (!).

check box Gives you the option of activating or deactivating a setting presented by the operating system or by a program. A check box is literally a box, which has three different states: blank, checked, or dashed. A check indicates a setting is chosen; a blank means a setting has not been chosen; and, in the case where a check box has a disclosure triangle and sub-check boxes, a dash is shown if some sub-check boxes are checked and others are not. In the realm of mathematical logic, a series of check boxes function as an "AND," that is, out of five boxes, you can select one and two and three. Contrast this to the *radio button.*

clean installation A type of Mac OS X installation in which a new, fresh copy of the system is installed, and the original system folder is left unaltered and moved into a Previous Systems folder at the root level of the hard drive. An option for preserving the user folders is available.

CLI See *command-line interface.*

click-through The ability to interact directly with an item in an inactive window. For example, you can operate the Close, Minimize, and Zoom buttons in most inactive Aqua windows.

client A program (or a computer running a program) that requests and receives information or services from a *server.*

clipping file A file created by the Finder to hold material that has been dragged from a document to the Desktop or a Finder window.

closed network An AirPort network that requires you to type its name (not simply pick the name from a list) to connect to it.

Cocoa Applications that are specifically developed for Mac OS X. Cocoa applications are incompatible with older Macintosh operating systems. Cocoa applications take advantage of all of Mac OS X's modern OS features, such as advanced memory, preemptive multitasking, symmetric multiprocessing, and the Aqua interface.

codec (compressor-decompressor) Something that compresses data so that it takes less space to store and decompresses compressed data back to its original form for playing or other use. A compressor may consist of software, hardware, or both.

collated Multiple printed copies of a document with each copy having all of its pages in the correct order.

color depth The number of bits of information that are required to represent the number of colors available on the screen. For example, a screen that can display thousands of colors is set at a color depth of 16 bits. Compare to *pixel depth.*

color picker The panel in which you specify a custom color either by clicking a color wheel, clicking a color sample, or entering color values.

command-line interface A non-GUI method of interacting with the operating system. A means of interacting with and controlling a computer by typing commands into the Terminal, one line at a time.

comment An AppleScript line that begins with a hyphen, or a Unix command line that begins with a number sign character (#), which in either case means that the line is descriptive and not a command to be performed.

compile To convert the human-readable text of a compiled programming language (such as C or any of its derivatives) into command codes that a Mac can execute. In AppleScript, compiling checks the script for nonconformance with AppleScript grammar, such as a missing parenthesis.

compression algorithm A method for compressing data so that it fits in less space and can be transferred more quickly. Each compression algorithm generally works best with one type of data, such as sound, photographs, video or motion pictures, and computer-generated animation. Three characteristics of a compression algorithm determine how effectively it compresses: *compression ratio*, fidelity to the original data, and speed.

compression ratio Indicates the amount of compression and is calculated by dividing the size of the original source data by the size of the compressed data. Larger compression ratios mean greater compression and generally (although not always) a loss of quality in the compressed data.

conditional A programming command that evaluates a condition (stated as part of the conditional) to determine whether another command or set of commands should be performed. (Also referred to as a *conditional statement*.)

contextual menu A contextual menu lists commands relevant to an item that you Control+click.

Control Panel A small Classic application that you use to set the way some part of the Classic environment looks and behaves. Similar to OS X Preference panes.

cooperative multitasking A scheme of *multitasking* used by Classic applications whereby multiple applications are open in the Classic environment and voluntarily taking turns using the Classic environment's processing time. While each Classic application is idle, cooperative multitasking allows other Classic applications to use the processor. Compare *preemptive multitasking*.

crack A means of circumventing a program's serialization and security.

crop markers Small triangles that indicate the beginning and end of a selected part of a movie in iMovie HD.

crossover cable A cable whose wires are reversed inside the plug at one end of the cable.

custom installation The process by which you can selectively install Mac OS X packages.

daisy chaining The process of connecting one peripheral or network device to another device, linking them so that they can share data. This is often done with Ethernet networking hubs to extend the size of an Ethernet network. It's also how multiple FireWire and SCSI devices are connected to a single Macintosh computer so that they can all be accessed by that computer.

Darwin A joint project between the Open Source community and Apple. The primary objective of the Darwin project is to build an industrial-strength UNIX-based operating system core that provides greater stability and performance compared to the existing iterations of the Mac OS to date.

dead keys The keys that generate accented characters when typed in combination with the Option key and in proper sequence. For example, typing Option+E followed by O generates ó on a U.S. keyboard. The Key Caps program highlights the dead keys when you press Option.

default browser The Web browser application that opens when you click a link to a Web page from a non-Web-browsing application.

default button The one button that pulsates in an Aqua dialog or alert box; in a Classic dialog or alert box, the default button has a heavy border. In either case it represents the action you'll most often want to take. If the most common action is dangerous, a button representing a safer action may be the default button. Pressing Return or Enter has the same effect as clicking the default button.

Desktop database Invisible files used by the Finder to associate Classic applications and their documents. Mac OS X keeps the Desktop database hidden because you don't use it directly. You can use the Classic pane of System Preferences to rebuild the Desktop database.

device A piece of hardware attached to a computer, either internally or externally. Some examples include keyboards, scanners, and drives.

device driver Software that controls a device, such as a printer or scanner. The driver contains data that the OS requires to fully utilize the device.

DHCP (Dynamic Host Configuration Protocol) A networking service in which a host device dynamically assigns network information (such as

TCP/IP addresses) to client computers to grant them access to other network services.

dialog box A window that displays options you can set or select. A dialog box typically has a button for accepting the changes and another button for canceling the changes. Both buttons close the dialog box.

digital signature Functions as a handwritten signature, identifying the person who vouches for the accuracy and authenticity of the signed document.

DIMM A DIMM (dual in-line memory module) is a small circuit board containing memory chips.

directory Another name for *folder*.

Directory Services Directory Services provide a consolidated user list that can be shared via multiple network services or servers for authentication. Directory Services do not provide the user list data itself but rather describe how they are set up and enable the communication of the data.

disclosure triangle A displayed control that regulates how much detail you see in a window. When the window is displaying minimal detail, clicking a disclosure triangle reveals additional detail and may automatically enlarge the window to accommodate it. Clicking the same triangle again hides detail and may automatically shrink the window to fit.

disk cache Improves system performance by storing recently used information from disk in a dedicated part of memory. Accessing information in memory is much faster than accessing information on disk.

disk image A file that, when mounted using Disk Copy or a similar utility, appears on the Desktop as if it were a removable disk.

display mirroring See *video mirroring*.

DNS (Domain Name System) A service that resolves domain names to IP addresses, and vice versa.

dogcow Also known as Clarus, dogcow is the official mascot of Mac enthusiasts. It looks vaguely like a dog (or a cow, thus the name) and is pictured in the Page Setup Options dialog box of Classic applications.

domain name The part of a *URL* that identifies the owner of an Internet location. A domain name has the form `companyname.com`, `organizationname.net`, `schoolname.edu`, `militaryunitname.mil`, `government agencyname.gov`, and so on.

double-click speed The rate at which you have to click so that Mac OS X perceives two clicks in a row as a single event.

download The process of receiving software or other computer files from another computer, over the Internet or a local network.

dpi (dots per inch) A measure of how fine or coarse the dots are that make up a printed image. More dots per inch means smaller dots, and smaller dots mean finer (less coarse) printing.

drag To move the mouse while holding down the mouse button.

drag-and-drop editing To copy or move selected text, graphics, and other material by dragging it to another place in the same window, a different window, or the desktop. Some applications do not support drag-and-drop editing.

drag-and-drop open To drag a document to a compatible application in the Finder, thereby highlighting the application, and then releasing the mouse button, causing the application to open the document.

drop box A shared folder located inside a user's Public folder in which other users may place items (when peer-to-peer file sharing is enabled), but only the folder's owner can see them.

DSL (Digital Subscriber Line) An add-on for standard telephone service that enables you to maintain a constant, high-speed Internet connection over a standard telephone line.

duplex A method of printing on both sides of the page that does not need a person there to flip the pages.

dynamic IP address See *DHCP*.

dynamic RAM allocation An operating system technology that allows the operating system to respond to an application's request for more or less memory, as needed.

Easter egg An undocumented "feature" usually hidden inside an application by a programmer without the publisher's knowledge. An Easter egg might be a hidden message or credits reel. You reveal it by performing secret combinations of keystrokes and mouse clicks.

edition A file that contains a live copy of the material in the *publisher* portion of a document belonging to a Classic application. When the publisher changes, the edition is updated. *Subscribers* contain copies of editions.

enclosing folder A file's enclosing folder is the folder in which the file exists.

encryption The process of making messages or files unrecognizable, for example to keep someone from reading a sensitive document.

escape character In UNIX, a backslash (\). An escape character can be other characters, based on which language you are using. Escape characters are used to indicate that the next character is to be used literally, not interpreted as a *wildcard* or other special character.

Ethernet A high-speed standard for connecting computers and other devices in a network. Ethernet ports are built into all Macs that can use Mac OS X and in many network printers. Ethernet networks can be wireless, as exemplified by AirPort wireless networks.

event message A means of *interprocess communication*. Applications can send event messages to one another. When an application receives an event message, it takes an action according to the content of the message. This action can be anything from executing a particular command to taking some data, working with it, and then returning a result to the program that sent the message.

Exposé Apple's window management function. Designed to afford users easy access to all open applications, windows, or the desktop.

extension The last part of a file's name, typically three or four letters, following a period. The extension helps to designate an item's file type. Also referred to as a file name suffix.

fair use Defines the criteria that must be considered before using another person's copyrighted work (printed or recorded materials).

file ID number The number that Mac OS X uses internally to identify the original item to which an alias is attached even if you have renamed or moved that original item.

file mapping The technique Mac OS X uses of treating a program file as part of *virtual memory* so that fragments of a program are loaded into memory only as needed.

file name extension See *extension*.

file server A computer running a program that makes files centrally available for other computers on a network.

file sharing Enables you to share files in your Public folder with people whose computers are connected to yours in a network.

file spec (specification) Tells Mac OS X exactly where to find a file or folder.

file system A method of organizing data on a volume. Macintosh OS X uses either HFS+ or the UFS file system.

file type A four-letter code that identifies the general characteristics of a file's contents, such as plain text, formatted text, picture, or sound.

FileVault A secure file storage method added to OS 10.4.

filter A technology that applies special effects to an image, such as a visual effect to a QuickTime movie.

Finder The core system application that allows users to graphically interact with the operating system.

firewall A device or software that prevents Internet users from getting access to computers on a local network. A firewall may also stop local network users from sending sensitive information out.

firmware Low-level programming that tells the hardware of a computer (or device) how to behave.

fixed-size font Contains exact pictures of every letter, digit, and symbol for one size of a font. Fixed-size fonts are called *bitmap fonts* because each picture precisely maps the dots, or *bits*, to be displayed or printed for one character.

folder-action script An AppleScript script attached to a folder so that it can watch and respond to user interaction with that folder in the Finder.

font A set of *characters* that have a common and consistent design.

font family A collection of differently styled variations (such as bold, italic, and plain) of a single *font*. Many *fixed-size, TrueType,* and *PostScript* fonts come in the four basic styles: plain, bold, italic, and bold italic. Some PostScript font families include 20 or more styled versions.

fonts folder Located in the System folder used for the Classic environment, this folder includes all *fixed-size, PostScript,* and *TrueType* fonts available in the Classic environment.

font suitcase A folder-like container specifically for *fixed-size* and *TrueType* fonts in the Classic environment.

fork Part of a Mac OS file. Many Mac OS files include a data fork and a resource fork where different types of information are stored. Although Mac OS X still supports them, they are being phased out and no longer exist in any Apple software.

fps (frames per second) Measures how smoothly a motion picture plays. More frames per second means smoother playback. This measurement is used when discussing the *frame rate* of time-based media.

frame One still image that is part of a series of still images, which, when shown in sequence, produce the illusion of movement.

frame rate The number of frames displayed in one second. The TV frame rate is 30 fps in the United States and other countries that use the NTSC broadcasting standard, and 25 fps in countries that use the PAL or SEACAM standard. The standard movie frame rate is 24 fps. See also *fps*.

frameworks Mac OS X frameworks contain dynamically loading code that is shared between applications. Frameworks alleviate the need for applications that utilize identical code to load multiple iterations of the same code simultaneously.

freeware Free software primarily distributed over the Internet and from person to person. Most freeware is still copyrighted by the person who created it. You can use it and give it to other people, but you can't sell it. See also *shareware*.

FTP (File Transfer Protocol) A data communications *protocol* that the Internet and other TCP/IP networks use to transfer files between computers.

FTP site A collection of files on an FTP server available for downloading.

full motion Video displayed at frame rates of 24 to 30 fps. The human eye perceives fairly smooth motion at frame rates of 12 to 18 fps. See also *fps* and *frame rate*.

gamma The relationship between the intensity of color and its luminance. Also the type of radiation wave that converted Dr. Banner into the Hulk.

gamma correction A method of compensating for the loss of detail that the human eye perceives in dark areas.

glyph A distinct visual representation of one character (such as a lowercase *z*), multiple characters treated as one (such as the ligature æ), or a nonprinting character (such as a space).

grid fitting The process of modifying characters at small point sizes so that they fit the grid of dots on the relatively coarse display screen. The font designer provides a set of instructions (also known as *hints*) for a *TrueType* or *PostScript* font that tells Mac OS X how to modify character outlines to fit the grid.

group Used to simplify the assignment of system privileges for clusters of users that have identical levels of access.

guest A network user who is not identified by a name and password.

GUI (Graphical User Interface) A means of interacting with and controlling a computer by manipulating graphical objects shown on the display, such as windows, menus, and icons. The opposite of CLI.

hack A programming effort that accomplishes something resourceful or unconventional. Often used as a disparaging term for a quick fix, or for a poorly skilled technician.

hacker A person who likes to tinker with computers and especially with computer software code. Some hackers create new software, but many hackers use programs such as ResEdit to make unauthorized changes to existing software. Hacker can also refer to one who maliciously breaks into secure systems over the Internet.

handler A named set of *AppleScript* commands that you can execute by naming the handler elsewhere in the same script. Instead of repeating a set of commands several times in different parts of a script, you can make the set of commands a handler and invoke the handler each place you would have repeated the set of commands. This is also sometimes called a subroutine.

helper application A program that handles a particular kind of media or other data encountered on the Internet.

help tag A short description of the object under the mouse pointer in a Mac OS X application. The description appears in a small yellow box near the object. Many objects do not have help tags. The equivalent in Classic applications is Balloon Help.

HFS+ (Hierarchical File System Plus) An extended file format designed for high-capacity hard drives.

Home folder The folder in which users store all of their personal files. The Mac OS X system also preserves settings for the user in the user's Home Folder Library.

Home page This term refers to the main page of a Web site, and it is also the page that appears when a Web browser first opens.

hot spots An area in a public place that has wireless Internet access (Wi-Fi). In QuickTime VR, hot spots are places in a panorama that you can click to go to another scene in the panorama or to a QuickTime VR object.

hub On an Ethernet network, a device that passes signals from any device connected to one of the hub's RJ-45 ports to all other devices connected to the hub. Hub can also refer to a device that splits USB or FireWire ports.

hyperlink Underlined text or an image on a *Web page* that takes you to another page on the same or a different Web site when clicked.

icon A small picture that represents an entity such as a program, document, folder, or disk.

iDisk A service within the .Mac service that provides remote storage accessible via the Internet.

inbound port mapping A scheme for directing all requests coming into a local network from the Internet for a particular service, such as a Web server, to a particular computer on the local network.

inherited permissions Privileges that propagate from a parent folder to child folders and all files within.

initialization A process that creates a blank disk directory. The effect is the same as erasing the disk. Initialization actually wipes out the means of accessing the existing files on the disk without actually touching the content of files.

insertion point A blinking vertical bar that indicates where text is inserted when you start typing.

installation The process of putting a new or updated version of software on your disk.

Internet A worldwide network that provides e-mail, Web pages, news, file storage and retrieval, and other services and information.

Internet gateway A device or software that enables all the computers on a local network to connect to the Internet, optionally sharing a single public IP address on the Internet.

Internet Service Provider (ISP) A company that gives you access to the Internet via your modem.

interpreted The technique used by Unix shells and other scripting languages such as Perl to perform each command as it is encountered instead of converting all commands to machine instructions in advance.

interprocess communication The technology that enables programs to send each other messages requesting action and receive the results of requested actions. Mac OS X has several forms of interprocess communication, one of which is *Apple events,* which is the basis of *AppleScript.*

IP address In IPv4, a 32-bit binary number, such as 192.168.0.1, that uniquely identifies a computer or other device on a network. IPv6 is the 128-bit successor.

ISDN (Integrated Services Digital Technology) A special telephone technology that allows for medium-speed network transmissions over long distances.

Java A programming language developed by Sun Microsystems. Java is platform independent, allowing its applications to function within any platform as long as the Java Virtual Machine software is available and installed.

kernel The kernel is the core of Mac OS X. The kernel provides services for all other elements of the operating system. See also *Mach 3.0 Microkernel*.

kerning Adjusting the space between pairs of letters so that the spacing within the word looks consistent.

keychain Technology that enables you to store passwords and passphrases for network connections, file servers, some types of secure Web sites, and encrypted files.

label A means of color-coding files, folders, and disks. Each of the eight label types has its own color and title.

LAN (Local Area Network) See *local network*.

landscape A printed page that is wider than it is tall.

language script system Software that enables the Mac OS to use an additional natural language, such as Japanese. Multiple languages can use one language script system (for example, the Roman script is used for English, French, Italian, Spanish, and German).

launch The act of getting an application started.

LDAP (Lightweight Directory Access Protocol) A software protocol that enables the location of individuals, groups, and other resources such as files or devices on a network.

Library folder Contains resources and preferences for Mac OS X. Library folders located within a user's Home folder are user-customizable.

ligature A glyph composed of two merged characters. For example, *f* and *l* can be merged to form *fl*.

link See *hyperlink*.

little arrows Displayed controls that let you raise or lower a value incrementally. Clicking an arrow changes the value one increment at a time. Pressing an arrow on the keyboard continuously changes the value until it reaches the end of its range.

localhost The standard generic name of a machine linked to an IP address. The equivalent of 127.0.0.1, or the Ethernet loopback address.

localization The development of software whose dialog boxes, screens, menus, and other screen elements use the language spoken in the region in which the software is sold.

local network A system of computers that are interconnected for sharing information and services and that are located in close proximity, such as in an office, home, school, or campus. Compare to *WAN*.

LocalTalk An Apple proprietary networking topology. Effectively obsolete.

location file A file that, when opened, takes you to a location on the Internet or a local network.

log in The process of entering a username and password to begin a session with Mac OS X or another secured resource such as a network connection.

log out A command to quit current user settings and return the OS X system back to the login screen.

loop To repeat a command, movie, song, or an entire *playlist*.

lossless A type of compression algorithm that regenerates exactly the same data as the uncompressed original.

LPR (Line Print Remote) printer A printer that contains a protocol that allows it to print via TCP/IP.

MacBinary A scheme for encoding the special information in a Macintosh file's data and resource forks into a file format appropriate for transmission over the Internet.

Mach 3.0 Microkernel Developed at Carnegie-Mellon University, the Mach 3.0 Microkernel has a closely tied history to BSD (Berkeley Software Distribution) Unix. Mach gives OS X the features of protected memory architecture, preemptive multi-tasking, and symmetric multi-processing.

man pages Documentation for some of the Mac OS X Unix commands (which are actually Unix programs) and other Unix components.

memory protection An operating system technology that makes it impossible for one active application to read and write data from another active application's space in memory. Memory protection helps applications run with fewer crashes.

MIDI The acronym for Musical Instrument Digital Interface. Developed in 1983 by several of the music industry's electronics manufacturers, MIDI is a data transmission protocol that permits devices to work together in a performance context. MIDI doesn't transfer music; it transfers information about the notes and their characteristics in a format another MIDI device can reconstruct the music from.

modem A device that connects a computer to telephone lines. It converts digital information from the computer into sounds for transmission over phone lines and converts sounds from phone lines to digital information for the computer. (The term *modem* is a shortened form of *modulator/demodulator*.) This term is also used informally for devices that connect computers by using digital technologies — for example, TV cable, DSL, and ISDN connections.

modem script Software consisting of the modem commands necessary to start and stop a remote access connection for a particular type of modem.

mount To mount means to connect to and access the contents of a disk or other volume. After mounting, the stored items in the mounted volume are then available to the local computer. In the case of internal hard drives, mounting is automatic and occurs every time you start up the computer.

movie Any time-related data, such as video, sound, animation, and graphs, that change over time; Apple's format for organizing, storing, and exchanging time-related data.

multimedia A presentation combining text or graphics with video, animation, or sound, and presented on a computer.

multitasking The capability to have multiple programs open and executing concurrently.

multithreading An operating system technology that allows tasks in an application to share processor time.

navigate To open disks and folders until you have opened the one that contains the item you need; to go from one *Web page* to another.

NetInfo The native directory service for Mac OS X. A NetInfo database/directory is referred to as a domain. The NetInfo database is hierarchical and contains both information on local and network users in addition to group authentication information.

network A collection of interconnected, individually controlled computers, printers, and other devices together with the hardware, software, and protocols used to connect them. A network lets connected devices exchange messages and information.

network administrator Someone who sets up and maintains a centralized file server and/or other network services.

networking protocol See *protocol*.

network interface card (NIC) An internal adapter card that provides a network port.

network location A specific arrangement of all the various Network Preferences settings that can be put into effect all at once (for example, by choosing from the Location submenu of the Apple Menu).

network time servers Computers on a network or the Internet that provide the current time of day.

newsgroup A subject on the Internet's *Usenet*. It is a collection of people and messages pertaining to that particular subject.

NFS (Network File System) The Unix equivalent of personal file sharing. NFS allows users to view and store files on a remote computer.

nonblocking alert An alert from a background Classic application that appears in a floating window so that the current application's activities are not halted.

object A kind of information, such as words, paragraphs, and characters, that an application knows how to work with. An application's *AppleScript* dictionary lists the kinds of objects it can work with under script control.

Open GL (Open Graphics Library) An industry standard for three-dimensional graphics rendering. It provides a standard graphics API by which software and hardware manufacturers can build 3-D applications and hardware across multiple platforms on a common standard.

open source Typically refers to software developed as a public collaboration and made freely available.

operating system Software that controls the basic activities of a computer system. Also known as *system software*.

original item A file, folder, or disk to which an *alias* points, and which opens when you open its alias.

orphaned alias An *alias* that has lost its link with its original item (and, therefore, Mac OS X cannot find it).

outline font A font whose *glyphs* are outlined by curves and straight lines that can be smoothly enlarged or reduced to any size and then filled with dots.

owner The user who can assign access *privileges* to a file or folder.

package A folder that the Finder displays as if it were a single application file. The Finder normally hides the files inside a package so users can't change them. A package is also a logical grouping of files that are related, such as all of the items that make up fax software or all of the parts of QuickTime. Sometimes referred to as a *bundle*.

palette An auxiliary window that contains controls or tools or that displays information for an application. A palette usually floats above regular windows of the same application.

pane An Aqua GUI element comprised of separate screens within a single window, typically accessed via a pull-down menu or tab. Panes and their subpanes when selected redraw within a single window, displaying alternate information and controls.

partition An identifiable logical division of a hard disk. Sometimes referred to as a volume. Also, to divide a hard drive into several smaller volumes, each of which the computer treats as a separate disk.

passphrase Like a password, but generally consisting of more than one word. (The larger a password or passphrase, the more difficult it is to guess or otherwise discover.)

password A combination of letters, digits, and symbols that must be typed accurately to gain access to information or services on the Internet or a *local network*.

path A way of writing the location of a file or folder by specifying each folder that must be opened to get at the file. The outermost folder name is written first, and each folder name is followed by a slash (/). See also *absolute pathname* and *relative path*.

PCMCIA (Personal Computer Memory Card International Association) Also known as Cardbus, PCMCIA is a hardware interface typically found in laptops. Small credit-card-sized devices are easily installed and removed from the laptop to expand functionality.

PDF (Portable Document Format) A platform-independent file format developed by Adobe. PDF files are often used in lieu of printed documents, as electronic transmission methods get more and more commonly accepted.

peer-to-peer file sharing A technology for allowing other client computers to access folders located on your client computer rather than a central file server. Less powerful than server-client file sharing, it is cheaper and easier to configure.

peripheral See *device*.

permissions See *privileges*.

ping A support tool that can be used to verify and validate the connectivity status of IP-aware network devices.

pipe A means of directing the output of one Unix command to the input of the next Unix command. Expressed in a Unix command line with a vertical bar symbol (|).

pixel Short for picture element, a pixel is the smallest dot that the computer and a display can show.

pixel depth The number of memory bits used to store each pixel of an image. The number of bits determines the number of different colors that could be in the image. For example, thousands of colors require 16 bits per pixel. Compare to *color depth*.

playhead A marker that tracks movie frames as they are shown, always indicating the location of the current frame in relationship to the beginning and end of the movie.

playlist A collection of songs arranged for playing in a particular sequence.

plug-ins Software that works with an application to extend its capabilities. For example, plug-ins for the Sherlock application enable it to search additional Internet sites.

POP (point of presence) A telephone number that gains access to the Internet through an Internet service provider. An entry point to the Internet.

POP (post office protocol) A client/server store-and-forward protocol for the receipt of e-mail.

pop-up menu A menu not in the menu bar but marked with an arrowhead that pops open when you click it.

port As referred to within the Network preference pane, a port is some form of physical connection to a data network.

portrait A printed page that is taller than it is wide. For example, a normal letter-sized page in portrait mode is 8.5 inches wide x 11 inches high.

PostScript font An outline font that conforms to the specifications of the PostScript page description language. PostScript fonts can be smoothly scaled to any size, rotated, and laid out along a curved path. Compare *TrueType*.

PostScript printers Printers that interpret Adobe-developed PostScript language to create printable images. Commonly used in environments where precise and accurate printing is a must.

PPD (PostScript Printer Description) A file that contains the optional features of a PostScript printer, such as its resolution and paper tray configuration.

PPP (Point-to-Point Protocol) An industry standard for the communication between computing devices over dial-up connections.

PPPoE (Point-to-Point Protocol over Ethernet) An implementation of PPP over Ethernet, used by ISPs that want to regulate access or meter usage of its subscribers, like DSL (Digital Subscriber Line) connections.

PRAM (parameter RAM) A small amount of battery-powered memory that stores system settings, such as time and date.

preemptive multitasking Prioritizes processor tasks by order of importance. Preemptive multitasking allows the computer to handle multiple tasks simultaneously. This method of managing processor tasks more efficiently allows the computer to remain responsive, even during the most processor-intensive tasks.

Preferences folder Holds files that contain the settings you make in System Preferences and with the Preferences commands of application programs.

primary script The *language script system* used by system dialog boxes and menus. If you are working on a computer that is set up for English, Roman is your primary script; your secondary script can be any other installed language script, such as Japanese.

printer driver Software that prepares pages for and communicates with a particular type of printer.

print job A file of page descriptions that is sent to a particular type of printer. Also called a *print request* or *spool file*.

print request See *print job*.

print server A device or software that manages one or more shared printers on a network.

private IP address An *IP address* for use on a local network. Compare *public IP address*.

privileges Privileges provide the control mechanism for regulating user access to files, folders, and applications within Mac OS X.

process Programs or threads (tasks) within a program that are currently running on the computer.

program A set of coded instructions that direct a computer in performing a specific task.

program linking The process of sharing programs by sending and receiving *event messages* across a network.

protected memory Isolates applications in their individual memory workspaces. In the event of an application crash, the program can be terminated without having a negative effect on other running applications or requiring a restart of the computer.

protocol A set of rules for the exchange of data between computer systems.

proxy icon A little icon next to the title of a Finder window. It represents the folder whose contents currently appear in the window. You can drag the proxy icon to any folder, volume, or the Trash.

proxy server A device that acts as an intermediary between a user's workstation and the Internet. When a request is made for Internet content, the request is passed along to the proxy server. The proxy server acts on behalf of the client and forwards the request on to the Internet. It then relays the retrieved response to the user.

public IP address An *IP address* for use on the Internet. Compare *private IP address*.

publisher A section of a document that is saved as an *edition*, which can appear as a *subscriber* in other documents. The documents all belong to Classic applications.

push button A displayed control that when clicked causes an action to take place. A label on the button indicates the action that the button performs. The label may be text or graphic. Push buttons with text labels are generally rectangular with rounded ends. Buttons with graphic labels may be any shape.

Quartz A powerful two-dimensional graphics rendering system. Quartz has built-in support for PDF, on-the-fly rendering, compositing, and anti-aliasing. It supports multiple font formats, including TrueType, Postscript Type 1, and OpenType. Quartz supports Apple's ColorSync color-management technology, allowing for consistent and accurate color in the print/graphics environment.

QuickTime Apple's proprietary, cross-platform multimedia authoring and distribution engine. QuickTime is both a file format and a suite of applications.

radio buttons A group of displayed controls that let you select one setting from a group. They work like the station presets on a car radio. Just as you can select only one radio station at a time, you can select only one radio button from a group.

RAM (random access memory) Physical dynamic memory built into the computer in the form of electronic chips or small circuit boards called DIMMs or SODIMMs.

RAM disk Memory set aside to be used as if it were a very fast hard drive.

raster image An image made of lines of discrete dots for the display screen or the printer. Compare to *vector image*.

record A structured collection of data in AppleScript (and in other programming languages), in which each data item has a name and a value.

regular expression A shorthand method of expressing a string of characters or various permutations of a string of characters. Used in Unix command lines.

relative path A *path* that does not begin with a slash character (/) and is therefore assumed to start in the current directory.

Rendezvous See *Bonjour*.

repeat loop An arrangement of *AppleScript* commands that begins with a Repeat command and ends with an End Repeat command. AppleScript executes the commands between the Repeat and End Repeat commands for the number of times specified in the Repeat command.

resolution The horizontal and vertical dimensions of a display, measured in pixels. Also refers to the perceived smoothness of a displayed or printed image. Printed resolution is measured in dots per inch (*dpi*). A high-resolution image has more dots per inch than a low-resolution image.

resolve an alias What Mac OS X does to find the original item represented by an *alias*.

resources Information such as text, menus, icons, pictures, or patterns used by Mac OS X, an application, or other software. Also refers to a computer's processing power, memory, and disk space.

rip To convert tracks from audio CDs typically into MP3 or AAC format. The first step to really irritating the RIAA.

RIP (Raster Image Processor) Software that translates PostScript code into an image made of lines of dots.

ROM (read-only memory) Non-editable information, typically located within a hardware device, with specifications as to the device's behavior. Compare to *RAM*.

root The name of the user account that has control over all folders and files on a computer, including the contents of the normally off-limits System folder. Root is also used as a term for the top-level directory of a file system.

root level The main level of a disk, which is what you see when you open the disk icon.

router See *Internet gateway*.

screen saver Software that protects against *burn-in* by showing a constantly changing image on the display while the computer is idle.

script A collection of *AppleScript* commands that perform a specific task. Also, short for *language script system*, which is software that defines a method of writing (vertical or horizontal, left to right, or right to left). A language script also provides rules for text sorting, word breaking, and the formatting of dates, times, and numbers.

scriptable application An application that can be controlled by *AppleScript* commands.

script applet *AppleScript* scripts saved as applets or small applications.

scripting additions Files that add commands to the *AppleScript* language, such as plug-ins that add features to applications.

script recording A process in which *AppleScript* watches as you work with an application and automatically writes a corresponding *script*.

scrolling list Displays a list of values in a box with an adjacent scroll bar. Clicking a listed item selects it. You may be able to select multiple items by pressing Shift or ⌘ while clicking.

scrub To move quickly forward or backward through a movie by dragging the *playhead*.

search path An ordered search for resources within a Mac OS X System.

selection rectangle A dotted-line box that you drag around items to select them all.

server Software or a device that provides information or services to *clients* on demand.

shared folder The place where local user accounts can share files among themselves locally on the system.

shareware Software distributed over the Internet and from person to person on a trial basis. You pay for it if you decide to keep using it. See also *freeware*.

sheet A *dialog box* that applies to and is attached to another window, ensuring you won't lose track of which window the dialog box applies to.

shell Part of the Unix operating system that interprets command lines.

sidebar A feature introduced in Panther, the Sidebar is located at the left side of all Finder windows and contains shortcuts to mounted volumes and commonly used folders.

single-user mode Entered during the system startup by pressing and holding ⌘+S during the boot process (just after the startup chime). Single-user mode goes straight to the command line, eliminating the GUI until a reboot occurs. This mode is typically used for troubleshooting.

slider A displayed control consisting of a track that displays a range of values or magnitudes and the slider itself, also known as the thumb, which indicates the current setting. You can change the setting by dragging the slider.

smoothing See *anti-aliasing*.

SMTP (Simple Mail Transfer Protocol) A protocol typically used in sending e-mail.

software One or more programs that consist of coded instructions that direct a computer in performing tasks.

soundtrack The audible part of a movie.

splat Unix jargon for the number sign symbol (#).

spool file See *print job*.

spooling A printer-driver operation in which the driver saves page descriptions in a file (called a *spool file*) for later printing.

SSH (Secure SHell) A protocol for securely accessing a remote computer.

standard input The source of Unix commands, which is the keyboard by default.

standard output The destination for the result of Unix commands, which is the Terminal window by default.

startup disk A disk that contains the software needed for the computer to begin operation.

static IP address An *IP address* that doesn't change when you begin an Internet session or when your computer starts up.

stationery pad A template document that contains preset formatting and contents.

status bar A strip in the top part of a Finder window that shows how much free space is available on the volume that contains the currently displayed folder.

streaming media Movies designed to be played over the Internet as they are downloaded.

stuffed file A file (or group of files) that has been compressed in the StuffIt file format from Aladdin Systems.

submenu A secondary menu that pops out from the side of another menu. A submenu appears when you click a menu item that has an arrowhead at the right side of the menu. Submenus are sometimes referred to as hierarchical menus.

subnet mask A 32-bit binary number used to identify a segment of a network.

subscriber A copy of an *edition* that has been placed in a document belonging to a Classic application. A subscriber can be updated automatically when the edition is updated by its *publisher*.

suite In *AppleScript,* a group of related commands and other items.

superuser See *root*.

switch A central device on an Ethernet network that passes signals from any device connected to one of its RJ-45 ports to one of the other devices connected to it. Also refers to options you can specify as part of a Unix command.

907

symbolic link A representative file that contains exact information as to where a file or folder resides.

symmetric multiprocessing The technology that allows the operating system to take advantage of two processors by assigning applications to a specific processor or by splitting an application's tasks among multiple processors simultaneously.

system administrator A person who has the knowledge and authority to make changes to settings that affect the fundamental operation of a computer's operating system.

system extension A software module loads when the Classic environment starts up. It adds features or capabilities to Mac OS 9 for the Classic environment.

system file Contains sounds, keyboard layouts, and language script systems, as well as the basic Mac OS 9 software for the Classic environment.

System folder Stores the Mac OS 9 software used by the Classic environment.

system software Software that controls the basic activities of a computer system. Also known as the *operating system*.

tabs Controls that look like the tabs on dividers used in card files. They divide the contents of a window into discrete pages called panes, with each tab connected to one pane of window content.

TCP/IP (Transmission Control Protocol/Internet Protocol) The basic communication language of the Internet.

Telnet An application that allows remote users to interact with Mac OS X's command line over TCP/IP, assuming they can gain authorization.

Terminal An application that allows local users to interact with Mac OS X's command line.

text behavior The set of rules used in a particular language for alphabetizing, capitalizing, and distinguishing words.

theme A group of all the settings in the Classic environment's Appearance control panel.

thread A string of messages about the same subject in a newsgroup. Also refers to a single task being executed within an application that may have multiple threads.

thumb The movable part of a *slider* control that indicates the current setting.

topology A description of a physical arrangement or layout of networking hardware.

track One channel of a QuickTime movie, containing video, sound, closed-captioned text, MIDI data, time codes, or other time-related data.

tracking The overall spacing between letters in an entire document or text selection. Text with loose tracking has extra space between the characters in words. Text with tight tracking has characters squeezed close together.

tracking speed The rate at which the pointer moves as you drag the mouse.

Translator A program that translates your documents from one file format to another file format, such as a PICT graphic to a GIF graphic.

Tristimulus A three-dimensional color space expressed in terms of X, Y, and Z coordinates.

Trojan horse Destructive software that masquerades as something useful, such as a utility program or game. Compare to *virus* and *worm*.

TrueType The outline font technology built into the Mac OS (and Microsoft Windows). TrueType fonts can be smoothly scaled to any size on-screen or to any type of printer.

Type 1 font A PostScript font that includes instructions for grid fitting so that the font can be scaled to small sizes and low printer resolutions with good results.

UFS (Unix File System) An alternative to the HFS+ file system format for Mac OS X.

UNIX (UNiplexed Information and Computing System, originally UNICS) A complex and powerful operating system whose TCP/IP networking protocol is the basis of the Internet.

unmount To remove a disk's icon from the Desktop and make the disk's contents unavailable.

unshielded twisted-pair (UTP) The type of cable used in a 10Base-T, 100Base-T, or Gigabit Ethernet network.

upload The process of sending files from your computer to another computer.

URL (uniform resource locator) An *Internet* address. This can be the address of a *Web page,* a file on an *FTP* site, or anything else that you can access on the Internet.

Usenet A worldwide *Internet* bulletin board system that enables people to post messages and join discussions about subjects that interest them.

user Someone who can log into your computer with a unique name and a password. A non-techie whose continued existence is tied to the economic survival of geeks everywhere.

user group An organization that provides information and assistance to people who use computers. For the names and phone numbers of user groups near you, check Apple's Web page (`www.apple.com/usergroups/find.html`).

username A name that can be used to log into a Mac OS X system.

user preferences Unique settings where users configure the behavior and appearance of applications and system software.

variable A container for information in a *script.* You can place data in a variable and then use it elsewhere in the script.

vector image A form of computer artwork comprised of lines and shapes, each defined by mathematical formulas. Unlike *raster images,* vector art can be resized to any dimension with no loss of quality, because it is not comprised of a finite amount of dots, but rather geometric lines and shapes.

verbose mode Displays all system activity in text format during the boot process. Useful for troubleshooting.

video mirroring The duplication of one screen image on two displays connected to a computer.

virtual memory Additional memory made available by Mac OS X treating part of a hard drive as if it were built-in memory.

virus Software designed to spread itself by illicitly attaching copies of itself to legitimate software. Some viruses perform malicious actions, such as erasing your hard drive. Even seemingly innocuous viruses can interfere with the normal functioning of your computer. Compare to *Trojan horse* and *worm.*

volume A disk or a part of a disk that the computer treats as a separate storage device. Each volume can have an icon on the Desktop. See also *partition.*

WAN (wide area network) Typically, a network composed of two or more *LANs,* a WAN is a network that is not compressed into one geographic location, but rather is spread out over a larger area.

Web browser A program that displays *Web pages* from the Internet.

Web page A basic unit that the Web uses to display information (including text, pictures, animation, audio, and video clips). A Web page can also contain *hyperlinks* to the same page or to other Web pages (on the same or a different Web server).

Web server A computer or a program running on a computer that provides information to a Web browser program.

white point A setting that determines whether colors look warm (reddish) or cool (bluish). Measured in degrees Kelvin, with warm white points having lower temperatures than cool white points.

white space Any combination of blank spaces, tab characters, or line returns.

wildcard A character that represents a range of characters in a *regular expression*. For example, an asterisk stands for any individual character.

worm Software that replicates like a virus but without attaching itself to other software. It may be benign or malicious. Compare to *Trojan horse* and *virus*.

write-protect The process of locking a disk so that it cannot be erased, have its name changed, have files copied to it or duplicated from it, or have files or folders it contains moved to the Desktop or trash.

.ZIP file A file (or group of files) that has been compressed by using Mac OS X's *Archive* command. Windows and Unix systems create .zip files as well, using WinZip or gzip, respectively.

Index

Numerics

L

labels
 defined, 900
 overview, 87–88
 position, 83
LAN (Local Area Network), 900
landscape, 900
Language panel (International preference pane), 647–649
language script system, 645, 649, 900
language used by AppleScript, 783–784
Last 12 Months screen saver, 34
Last Import screen saver, 34
launch, 900
layered networks, 364–371
LCD (liquid crystal displays), 32
LDAP (Lightweight Directory Access Protocol), 900
LDAPv3, 226
Learning Unix for Mac OS X Leopard (Taylor), 865
Lemke, Thorsten (developer), 748
Levine, John R. (*Unix For Dummies*), 865
Library folders
 defined, 900
 hard drive, 101
 main Library folder
  Address Book Plug-Ins folder, 760
  Application Support folder, 760
  Audio folder, 760
  Caches folder, 760
  CFM Support folder, 760
  ColorSync folder, 760
  Contextual Menu Items folder, 760
  Desktop Pictures folder, 760
  Documentation folder, 760
  Fonts folder, 761
  Frameworks folder, 761
  Image Capture folder, 761
  Internet Plug-Ins folder, 761
  Java folder, 761
  Keyboard Layouts folder, 761
  Logs folder, 761
  Modem Scripts folder, 761
  overview, 760
  Perl folder, 761
  Preference Panes folder, 761
  Preferences folder, 761
  Printers folder, 761

 QuickTime folder, 761
 Receipts folder, 762
 Screen Savers folder, 762
 Scripts folder, 762
 User Pictures folder, 762
 WebServer folder, 762
 overview, 759–760
 personal Library folder
  Application Support folder, 762
  Assistants folder, 762
  Audio folder, 762
  ColorPickers folder, 762
  Documentation folder, 762–763
  Favorites folder, 763
  FontCollections folder, 763
  Frameworks folder, 763
  Internet Search Sites folder, 763
  Keyboard Layouts folder, 763
  Keychains folder, 763
  Mail folder, 763
  overview, 762
  Preferences folder, 763–764
  Recent Servers folder, 763
  Scripts folder, 763
  Stickies Database folder, 763
Library (iTunes)
 removing songs from, 271–272
 searching in, 271
 shared libraries, 272
License screen (Mac OS X Installer application), 12
ligature, 900
link. *See* hyperlink
link lights, 371
liquid crystal displays (LCD), 32
List command, 66
list view
 columns, rearranging and resizing, 72–73
 disclosure triangles used to navigate, 73–74
 iTunes Music Store, 274
 options for, setting, 84–85
 overview, 72
 selecting from multiple folders in, 53
 sort order, changing, 72
listening method for speech recognition, 672–675
little arrows, 900
Local Area Network (LAN), 900
local connection, 227

Index